THE TEMPLE OF NINGIRSU

VOLUME 2

The Temple of Ningirsu

The Culture of the Sacred in Mesopotamia

PUBLISHED BY
EISENBRAUNS AND THE BRITISH MUSEUM

University Park, PA & London

SÉBASTIEN REY

*With contributions from
Angelo Di Michele, Elisa Girotto,
Holger Gzella, Fatma Husain,
Ashley Pooley, Jon Taylor and
Paul Williamson.*

Library of Congress Cataloging-in-Publication Data

Names: Rey, Sébastien, 1981– author.

Title: The temple of Ningirsu : the culture of the sacred in Mesopotamia / Sébastien Rey ; with contributions from Angelo di Michele, Elisa Girotto, Holger Gzella, Fatma Husain, Ashley Pooley, Jon Taylor and Paul Williamson.

Other titles: Culture of the sacred in Mesopotamia

Description: University Park, PA : Eisenbrauns ; London : The British Museum, [2024] | Includes bibliographical references and index.

Summary: "A comprehensive re-examination of the history of the temple site in the sacred Sumerian city of Girsu through modern excavations and the re-evaluation of earlier archaeological discoveries. Examines the role of rescue and preventative excavations as a way to stabilise and preserve exposed but inadequately recorded archaeological sites"—Provided by publisher.

Identifiers: LCCN 2023040167 | ISBN 9781646022649 (v. 1 ; hardback) | ISBN 9781646022649 (v. 2 ; hardback)

Subjects: LCSH: Excavations (Archaeology)—Iraq—Girsu (Extinct city) | Sumerians—Religion. | Temples—Iraq—Girsu (Extinct city) | Girsu (Extinct city) | Iraq—Antiquities.

Classification: LCC DS70.5.G57 R494 2024 | DDC 935—dc23/eng/20231208

LC record available at https://lccn.loc.gov/2023040167

Copyright © 2024 The British Museum and Sébastien Rey
All rights reserved
Printed in China
Published by The Pennsylvania State University Press, University Park, PA 16802-1003

Eisenbrauns is an imprint of The Pennsylvania State University Press.

The Pennsylvania State University Press is a member of the Association of University Presses.

It is the policy of The Pennsylvania State University Press to use acid-free paper. Publications on uncoated stock satisfy the minimum requirements of American National Standard for Information Sciences—Permanence of Paper for Printed Library Material, ANSI Z39.48–1992.

Cover illustrations: (*slip case*) reconstruction of the Ur-Bau plaza (digital model by Sandra Grabowski © The Girsu Project and artefacts-berlin.de); (*vol. 1 front*) the Thunderbird Mace Head, British Museum 23287 (photo by Dani Tagen © The Girsu Project); (*vol. 1 back*) reconstruction of the Early Dynastic Temple of Ningirsu (digital model by Sandra Grabowski © The Girsu Project and artefacts-berlin.de); (*vol. 2 front*) copper foundation peg from Gudea's New Eninnu, British Museum 96566 (photo by Dani Tagen © The Girsu Project); (*vol. 2 back*) reconstruction of the Ur-Bau plaza (digital model by Sandra Grabowski © The Girsu Project and artefacts-berlin.de).

CONTENTS

List of Illustrations | ix
List of Abbreviations | xvii

Part 1: General Introduction

CHAPTER 1   The Temple of Ningirsu from Its Origins to the Present Day | 3

CHAPTER 2   The Rediscovery of Ancient Girsu | 28

CHAPTER 3   A Contextualised Chronology of Ancient Girsu | 42

Part 2: The Mound of the House of the Fruits

CHAPTER 4   Introduction to the French Excavations on Tell K | 53

CHAPTER 5   The French Excavations on Tell K: Sarzec and Heuzey in Detail | 56

CHAPTER 6   After Sarzec: Cros in Detail | 71

CHAPTER 7   The Great Rift of Girsu: Genouillac and Parrot | 80

CHAPTER 8   Tell K: Plans and Sections | 91

CHAPTER 9   Photographs of Tell K, 1888–1931 | 107

CHAPTER 10   Tell K: A New History of the Temple of Ningirsu | 135

CHAPTER 11   The Origins and Early Historical Significance of the Temple of Ningirsu | 145

CHAPTER 12   The Lower Construction | 157

CHAPTER 13   The Objects from the Lower Construction | 174

CHAPTER 14   The Tessellated Earth | 193

CHAPTER 15   The Outer Block (P′Q′R′S′) and Associated Finds | 203

CHAPTER 16   The New Sanctuary: The Ur-Nanshe Building | 212

CHAPTER 17   The Eanatum Extension Phase | 237

vi   *Contents*

CHAPTER 18   The Stele of the Vultures | 243

CHAPTER 19   The Enmetena Restoration | 259

CHAPTER 20   From Enmetena to the Destruction of the Early Dynastic Complex | 290

CHAPTER 21   Darkness and Renaissance: Tell K in the Akkad, Lagash II and Ur III Eras | 307

Part 3: The Mound of the Palace

CHAPTER 22   An Overview of the French Excavations on Tell A | 325

CHAPTER 23   The French Pioneers on Tell A: An In-Depth Account of Their Findings | 328

CHAPTER 24   Plans of the French Excavations and a Plaster Maquette | 344

CHAPTER 25   Photographs of the Early French Excavations | 356

CHAPTER 26   The French Legacy: Challenges and Preserved Treasures | 380

CHAPTER 27   The Mound of the Palace Today: A Landscape of Trenches and Spoils | 385

CHAPTER 28   First Excavation Results: The French Historical Phase (1877–1930) | 394

CHAPTER 29   The Effects of Modern Looting | 408

CHAPTER 30   Coda: Objects from the Spolia of Tell A | 412

CHAPTER 31   Before the Big Move: The Early Dynastic and Akkad Temple Complex | 416

CHAPTER 32   The Early Dynastic Sanctuary of the Goddess Bau | 444

CHAPTER 33   The Ur-Bau Complex: The Relocated Ningirsu Temple and the Restored Temple to Bau | 458

CHAPTER 34   The Gudea Sanctuary of Ningirsu: The New Eninnu | 467

CHAPTER 35   The Historical Significance of the New Eninnu from Lagash II Times to the Old Babylonian Period | 502

CHAPTER 36   The New Eninnu from Lagash II Times to the Old Babylonian Period | 519

CHAPTER 37   The Statues of Gudea from the New Eninnu | 547

CHAPTER 38   Gudea's Temple Plan and the Physical Remains | 570

CHAPTER 39   The Metrology of Statue B | 581

CHAPTER 40   The Gates of the New Eninnu and the Monuments to the Slain Heroes | 591

CHAPTER 41   The Steles of Gudea | 608

CHAPTER 42   The Bricks of the New Eninnu | 630

CHAPTER 43   The Inscribed Clay Nails of the New Eninnu | 643

CHAPTER 44   The Foundation Deposits of the New Eninnu | 658

Part 4: The Ningirsu Temple in the Hellenistic Era

CHAPTER 45 The Renaissance of the Eninnu | 673

CHAPTER 46 The Stratigraphy of the Hellenistic Shrine | 687

CHAPTER 47 The Meaning and Purpose of the Hellenistic Eninnu | 724

CHAPTER 48 The End of the Hellenistic Eninnu | 744

Acknowledgements | 753
Table of Correspondences | 755
References | 759
Illustration Credits | 765
Index | 769

ILLUSTRATIONS

1. Statue of Gudea. British Museum 122910   4
2. City-states of Sumer in the third millennium BCE   7
3. The Thunderbird Mace Head. British Museum 23287   8
4. Reconstruction of the Early Dynastic Temple of Ningirsu   9
5. Artist's impression of a Sumerian temple   11
6. The Feathered Figure. Musée du Louvre AO221   12
7. The Mace of Mesilim. Musée du Louvre AO2349   13
8. Tablet containing the Hymn to the Reeds. Musée du Louvre AO3866   15
9. The Cylinders of Gudea. Musée du Louvre MNB1512 and MNB1511   17
10. Gudea as the Architect with a Plan (Statue B). Musée du Louvre AO2   18
11. Reconstruction of Gudea's New Eninnu   19
12. South-facing view of the sacred precinct of Girsu (the Urukug) in 2017   20
13. A copper foundation peg from Gudea's New Eninnu. British Museum 96566   21
14. The Temple of Ningirsu on Tell A: a view of the British Museum team's excavations in 2017   22
15. Plan of the British Museum team's excavation trenches on Tell A   24
16. Plan of the sacred precinct of Girsu (the Urukug), showing the reconstructed Lagash II and Early Dynastic shrines on Tells A and K, respectively   26
17. Ernest de Sarzec (front row, centre) with his escort in Tello   29
18. General Plan of the Mounds of Tello (Plan B), Sarzec and Heuzey 1912   30
19. Seated statue of Gudea: the Colossus (Statue D). Musée du Louvre AO1   31

20. Pencil sketches, made in 1850 by H. A. Churchill, of a statue of Gudea from Tell Hamman. British Museum 92988 / ME Ar. 184.9   32
21. British Museum keeper R. D. Barnett refitting the hands of the Gudea Colossus to the other preserved parts of the statue at a ceremony in the Louvre in 1958   33
22. Ur-Nanshe Plaque A. Musée du Louvre AO2344   36
23. The Silver Vase of Enmetena. Musée du Louvre AO2674   37
24. Gaston Cros with a group of tribespeople   38
25. Henri de Genouillac's excavations on Tell K, c.1930   40
26. The Early Dynastic inscribed stone Plaque of Enanatum. British Museum 130828   47
27. Objects associated with the Ur-Nanshe Building   59
28. Objects associated with the Lower Construction   62
29. Early Dynastic relief of a nude man carrying fish. Musée du Louvre AO4110   78
30. Pottery from Tell K I   83
31. Pottery from Tell K II   84
32. Pottery from Tell K III   85
33. Sarzec and Heuzey 1912, Plan C (1): The Ur-Nanshe Building. Plan C (2): Plan and Elevation of the Lower Construction, and a Cross-Section of the Central Area of Tell K   93
34. Sarzec and Heuzey 1912, Plan D: General Plan of Tell K   97
35. Cros 1910, Plan A: The Principal Excavation Area of Tello   100
36. Cros 1910, Plan B: Excavations in the Vicinity of the House of the Fruits   102
37. Cros 1910, SW and NE Sections of Tell K   103

ix

x   *Illustrations*

38. Cros 1910, Plan C: Stairways and Water Supply Network   105
39. Sarzec and Heuzey 1912, Pl. 54 (1): The SE Façade of the Ur-Nanshe Building   108
40. Sarzec and Heuzey 1912, Pl. 54 (2): The S Corner of the Ur-Nanshe Building   109
41. Sarzec and Heuzey 1912, Pl. 55 (1): The Enmetena Block   110
42. Sarzec and Heuzey 1912, Pl. 55 (2): The Oval Reservoir   112
43. Sarzec and Heuzey 1912, Pl. 56 (1): The Lower Construction   113
44. Sarzec and Heuzey 1912, Pl. 56 (2): The Stele of the Captives   114
45. Sarzec and Heuzey 1912, Pl. 57 (1): The Ring Post from pavement F   115
46. Sarzec and Heuzey 1912, Pl. 57 (2): The Well of Eanatum   116
47. Sarzec and Heuzey 1912, Pl. 57 bis (2): Stack of planoconvex bricks   118
48. Sarzec and Heuzey 1912, Pl. 58 (1): View from the top of the Large Stairway   119
49. Sarzec and Heuzey 1912, Pl. 58 (2): View from the bottom of the Large Stairway   120
50. Sarzec and Heuzey 1912, Pl. 58 bis (2): The curved channel on the edge of Tell K   122
51. Sarzec and Heuzey 1912, Pl. 52 (1): First view of the Pillar of Gudea   124
52. Sarzec and Heuzey 1912, Pl. 52 (2): Second view of the Pillar of Gudea   125
53. Diagram showing the construction of the Pillar of Gudea   126
54. Sarzec and Heuzey 1912, Pl. 53 (2): The Pillar of Gudea completely exposed   128
55. Cros 1910, View No. 1: Stairways and Water Supply Network   130
56. Cros 1910, View No. 2: Stairways and Water Supply Network   131
57. Genouillac 1934, Pl. 1 (2): Excavations on Tell K   132
58. Genouillac 1934, Pl. 46 (1): The Well of Eanatum   133
59. Comprehensive plan of Tell K   138
60. The Stratigraphy of Tell K from Early Dynastic times to the reigns of Gudea and Shulgi   140

61. Plan showing the principal constructions and notable objects excavated on Tell K, dating from Early Dynastic times to the reigns of Gudea and Shulgi   142
62. The Circular Bas-Relief. Musée du Louvre AO2350   149
63. Ur-Nanshe Plaque B. Musée du Louvre AO2345   152
64. An Ur-Nanshe copper foundation peg with a copper collar. British Museum 96565   153
65. Early Dynastic lapis lazuli cylinder seal, with motifs probably relating to Ningirsu's cosmic battle with the Slain Heroes. British Museum 22962   155
66. Reconstruction of the layout of the subterranean rooms and corridors of the Lower Construction   158
67. Reconstruction of the Lower Construction, showing its subterranean areas and above-ground walls   159
68. A foundation peg from the Lower Construction. British Museum 108980   160
69. Detail of a foundation peg from the Lower Construction. British Museum 108980   161
70. Reconstruction of the antecella in the Lower Construction   163
71. Late Uruk cylinder seal   167
72. Reconstruction of the Lower Construction's antecella and cella   170
73. The Thunderbird Mace Head. British Museum 23287   176
74. Presargonic shell plaque, showing Ningirsu with a horned crown fighting a seven-headed monster   180
75. Reconstruction of the Girsu Land Stele   182
76. Reconstruction of the Stele of the Captives   184
77. Reconstruction of the Circular Bas-Relief   186
78. Akkad cylinder seal from Nippur that shows a sandal attached to the shaft of a standard featuring a ceremonial mace head   188
79. A courtier at the court of Narmer of Egypt holding a pair of sandals belonging to the king. From the Palette of Narmer, *c.*3200 BCE   189
80. The Standard of Ur (detail of the war panel). British Museum 121201   190
81. Diagrams showing the way in which Sumerian temples were laid out with respect to the cardinal points   194
82. Evolution of the sign é, meaning 'house' or 'temple'   200

83. Three Sumerian signs: é ('house'); kid ('reed mat'); gan₂ ('field')   201
84. Reconstruction of the Ur-Nanshe Building on the summit of Tell K   213
85. Close-up of the massive platforms of Tell K   214
86. A two-part copper foundation deposit from the reign of Ur-Nanshe. British Museum 96565   216
87. An inscribed door socket of Ur-Nanshe. Musée du Louvre AO252   218
88. Four reconstructed views of the Ur-Nanshe Building   224
89. The Genealogical Plaques of Ur-Nanshe (Plaques A, B, C and D)   231
90. The Ur-Nanshe Building in the reign of Eanatum   241
91. The Thunderbird Mace Head. British Museum 23287   242
92. Reconstruction of the Stele of the Vultures   244
93. Two possible views of Ningirsu's divine chariot   247
94. Reconstruction of the obverse and reverse of the Stele of the Vultures   252
95. Reconstruction of Tell K in the reign of Enmetena   260
96. A view of the hanging gardens planted on Tell K by Enmetena   266
97. An Enmetena foundation deposit. Musée du Louvre AO2353   268
98. Reconstruction of the brewhouse   270
99. A cutaway view of the reconstructed brewhouse   271
100. A view of the interior of the brewhouse   272
101. Reconstruction of a bull lyre from Girsu   280
102. Detail of a lyre player and a singer on the peace panel of the Standard of Ur. British Museum 121201   282
103. The Plaque of Dudu. Musée du Louvre AO2354   294
104. Tablet containing the Lament over the Destruction of Lagash. Musée du Louvre AO4162   300
105. Fragment of a vase dedicated to Ningirsu by the Akkad king Rimush (TG3545)   309
106. Fragment of the Akkad Stele from Girsu. Musée du Louvre AO2678   311
107. Reconstruction of the Akkad Stele   312
108. Carved limestone basin inscribed in the name of Gudea   330
109. Objects from Tell A dating from the reign of Gudea   332
110. A selection of the fragments of the Gudea Steles recovered by Cros   336
111. Sarzec and Heuzey 1912, Plan A: Ground plan of the so-called Palace, with underlying Sumerian remains   345
112. Plaster Maquette of Sarzec's excavations on Tell A. Musée du Louvre AOmg246   348
113. Cros 1910, Plan H: The shrine and stone stairway on the NE side of Tell A   349
114. Sarzec and Heuzey 1912, Ground plan of the Hellenistic walls and underlying Sumerian remains (Heuzey's New Plan)   351
115. Genouillac 1936, Elevation and plan of the excavations on the Mound of the Palace   353
116. Sarzec and Heuzey 1912, Pl. 49 (1): The NE façade of the so-called Palace   357
117. Sarzec and Heuzey 1912, Pl. 49 (2): Close-up of the NE façade   358
118. Sarzec and Heuzey 1912, Pl. 50 (1): The Gate of Gudea (1888)   359
119. Sarzec and Heuzey 1912, Pl. 50 (2): A second view of the Gate of Gudea (1888)   361
120. Sarzec and Heuzey 1912, Pl. 51 (1): The external face of the Ur-Bau wall   362
121. Sarzec and Heuzey 1912, Pl. 51 (2): The inside face of the Ur-Bau wall   364
122. Sarzec and Heuzey 1912, Pl. 53 (1): The Gate of Gudea (1889)   365
123. Sarzec and Heuzey 1912, Pl. 53 bis (1): The Gate of Gudea completely exposed (1895)   366
124. Sarzec and Heuzey 1912, Pl. 53 bis (2): The continuation of the Hellenistic NW façade (OP)   367
125. Sarzec and Heuzey 1912, Pl. 61 (top): The exedra   368
126. Sarzec and Heuzey 1912, Pl. 61 (bottom): The cistern block   369
127. Sarzec and Heuzey 1912, Pl. 61 bis (top): The cistern block and the base of the Ur-Bau wall   370
128. Sarzec and Heuzey 1912, Pl. 61 bis (bottom): A second view of the cistern block and the base of the Ur-Bau wall   371
129. Cros, unpublished photo of the Gate of Gudea   372

xii   *Illustrations*

130. Cros, unpublished photo of the trench at the base of the Gate of Gudea   373
131. Cros 1910, View No. 11: The area of the Gudea Steles between Tells A and B   374
132. Cros 1910, View No. 12: Drainage channel close to the area of the Gudea Steles between Tells A and B   375
133. Genouillac 1936, Pl. 72 (2): The Gate of Gudea, seen from inside Court A   376
134. Genouillac 1936, Pl. 72 (1): Close-up of the foundation deposit uncovered on the SE side of the Gate of Gudea   377
135. Genouillac 1936, Pl. 73 (1): The well inside Court C   378
136. Heuzey's New Plan and Genouillac's plan of Tell A superimposed   383
137. Aerial view of Tell A   386
138. Plan of the Spoil Heaps of Tell A   367
139. Plan of the British Museum team's excavation trenches on Tell A   392
140. Aerial view of the central area of Tell A, showing the British Museum team's excavations and the surrounding French spoil heaps   395
141. Mount Sarzec (SH1)   396
142. Impressions of cylinder seals found on Tell A by the British Museum team   397
143. Aerial view of the French excavations on Tell A   401
144. Fragment of a Lagash II stone statue, showing two hands clasped in prayer (TG3067)   406
145. An oval looting pit cutting through the mud-brick walls of the New Eninnu   409
146. Objects discarded by looters   410
147. Plan showing the distribution of Lagash II and Ur III inscribed clay nails in the British Museum team's trenches   414
148. The sequence of mud-brick platforms excavated by the British Museum team on Tell A   418
149. The principal sections recorded by the British Museum team in Area B1   420
150. The two-step red platform and white platform, excavated by the British Museum team on Tell A   421
151. Detail of the stepped red platform in Area B1   421
152. The white platform in Area B1, showing the truncation caused by French excavation trenches   423

153. Early Dynastic ceremonial vessels from Tell A   425
154. Pottery from the Temple Platforms I   430
155. Pottery from the Temple Platforms II   431
156. Pottery from the Temple Platforms III   432
157. Pottery from the Temple Platforms IV   433
158. Pottery from the Temple Platforms V   434
159. Pottery from the Temple Building I   438
160. Pottery from the Temple Building II   439
161. Pottery from the Temple Building III   440
162. Pottery from the Temple Building IV   441
163. Pottery from the Temple Building V   442
164. Pottery from the Temple Building VI   443
165. Fragment of an Early Dynastic relief excavated by Sarzec between Tells J and K. Musée du Louvre AO48   445
166. Reattached fragments of an inscribed bowl dedicated to the goddess Bau. British Museum 90902   446
167. Plan of the Early Dynastic Urukug, showing the reconstructed shrines on Tells A and K   450
168. Statue of Ur-Bau from Tell A. Musée du Louvre AO9   459
169. Inscribed copper foundation peg and inscribed stone tablet from the reign of Ur-Bau, together with the clay pot in which the objects were supposedly found by Sarzec. Musée du Louvre AO311, AO261 and AO451   462
170. A cutaway reconstruction of Gudea's New Eninnu   472
171. Close-up of the reconstruction of the Ur-Bau plaza   475
172. The NE façade of the Ningirsu temple on the SE side of Gudea's New Eninnu   479
173. The inscribed stone door socket found by the British Museum team inside the main entrance in the NE façade of the Ningirsu temple   481
174. Section of the SE façade of the Ningirsu temple (wall 2139), showing the brickwork and the positions of the *in situ* clay nails   482
175. Section of the SW façade of the Ningirsu temple (wall 2159), with two *in situ* clay nails   483
176. The inscribed stone door socket and copper pivot found by the British Museum team inside the entrance to the cella of the Ningirsu temple   484
177. Artist's impression of the cella in the Temple of Ningirsu at the heart of Gudea's New Eninnu   487

178. Artist's impression of the antecella in Gudea's Temple of Ningirsu   488
179. The remains of the well (M) in the antecella of Gudea's Ningirsu temple   489
180. The podium, presumably for the Gudea Statues, on the SE wall of the antecella inside the Ningirsu temple   490
181. The internal walkway on the SW side of the Ningirsu temple   491
182. Section of the NE façade of the inner envelope wall (3049 and 2032) on the SW side of the Ningirsu temple, showing the positions of the *in situ* clay nails   493
183. Section of the continuation of the façade of the inner envelope wall (2031), showing a single *in situ* clay nail   494
184. Reconstruction of the central courtyard inside Gudea's New Eninnu, looking towards the south-east   495
185. Reconstruction of the central courtyard inside Gudea's New Eninnu, looking towards the north-west   496
186. Artist's impression of a gate in the external façade of the New Eninnu   497
187. Section of the NE wall (2059) inside the SW gateway passage in the temenos wall of the New Eninnu, showing four *in situ* clay nails   498
188. One of the oversized fired bricks that formed the cover of the foundation box (2092) installed in the E corner of the tower on the SE side of the SW gateway that gave access to Gudea's New Eninnu   500
189. The stone foundation tablet (TG1501) seen *in situ* inside the rectangular foundation box (2092)   500
190. Reconstruction of a cylinder seal belonging to Gudea. Musée du Louvre AO3541   503
191. Reconstruction of a cylinder seal belonging to Ur-Sharura, a servant of the deified Gudea   508
192. Reconstruction of a cylinder seal belonging to Lu-Dumuzi, a cupbearer to the deified Gudea   508
193. Inscribed fragments from Girsu unearthed by the British Museum team   510
194. The Stratigraphy of Tell A from Early Dynastic times to the Hellenistic era   520
195. Section of the SW ambulatory of the Ningirsu temple, showing a sequence of fills deposited from the Lagash II period through to Old Babylonian times   525
196. Section of the SE ambulatory of the Ningirsu temple, showing the early sequence of fills capped with Hellenistic foundation fill 2136   525
197. Repairs and fills inside the New Eninnu's SW gate   528
198. Impression of a Lagash II cylinder seal found inside the layer of burnt materials that were ritually deposited in the stairwell chamber of the Ningirsu temple   533
199. Pottery from the New Eninnu I   538
200. Pottery from the New Eninnu II   539
201. Pottery from the New Eninnu III   540
202. Pottery from the New Eninnu IV   541
203. Pottery from the New Eninnu V   542
204. Pottery from the New Eninnu VI   543
205. Pottery from the New Eninnu VII   544
206. Pottery from the New Eninnu VIII   545
207. The diorite statues of Tell A, including Statues A–F of Gudea and the portrait of Ur-Bau. Musée du Louvre, AO8 (A), AO2 (B), AO5 (C), AO1 (D), AO6 (E), AO3 (F) and AO9 (Ur-Bau)   549
208. Statues of the Akkad rulers Manishtusu (standing and seated) and Naram-Sin. Musée du Louvre, SB48, SB49 and SB53   550
209. Areas of damage on the diorite statues of Tell A   560
210. Areas of damage on the diorite statues of Tell A   561
211. Statue B. Musée du Louvre AO2   571
212. Close-up of the tablet on Statue B. Musée du Louvre AO2   573
213. The ground plan from Statue B superimposed on the plan of the British Museum team's excavations and Heuzey's New Plan   575
214. Old Babylonian tablet demonstrating a method for working out the square root of two. Yale University YBC7289   582
215. The standard unit on Gudea's measuring rod expressed as fractions of sixty and as a table of reciprocals   584
216. The ground plan from Statue B correlated with the standard units on the adjacent measuring rod   586
217. A two-stage geometrical method for constructing the ground plan on Statue B   589
218. The Ur-Nanshe Building on Tell K, showing its position with respect to the cardinal points and the path taken by the sun as it passes over Tello in the course of a year   593

xiv *Illustrations*

219. The New Eninnu of Gudea on Tell A, showing its position with respect to the cardinal points and the annual path of the sun   596
220. Reconstruction of the Gudea Stele devoted to Enki   617
221. Reconstruction of the Gudea Stele to Ningirsu and Bau   619
222. Reconstruction of the Gudea Stele with the seven-headed mace   621
223. Reconstruction of the Gudea Stele devoted to Bau and Gatumdug   622
224. Reconstruction of the Gudea Stele referred to as the sunrise relief   624
225. Reconstruction of the Gudea Stele referred to as the relief of abundance   625
226. Reconstruction of a two-sided Gudea Stele   627
227. Reconstruction of the Gudea Stele referred to as the music stele   628
228. The rectangular Thunderbird bricks found by the British Museum team   632
229. Models of structures built with square bricks (red) and rectangular half-bricks (pink)   638
230. A clay nail inscribed in the name of Gudea, seen *in situ* in the inner envelope wall (2031)   644
231. Diagrams showing the placement of Gudea's Standard Inscription on a clay nail   649
232. Close-up views of the Standard Inscription on the stem of a single clay nail   652
233. A typology of the clay nails found on Tell A   653
234. The inscribed stone tablet (TG1501) found *in situ* in its foundation box (2092) by the British Museum team   659
235. Inscribed stone tablet from the reign of Gudea. British Museum 91008   660
236. Four views of a copper foundation peg inscribed in the name of Gudea. British Museum 96566   661
237. Three copper foundation pegs from Girsu   666
238. A Hellenistic brick stamped in the name of Adadnadinakhe, found *in situ* by the British Museum team on Tell A   674
239. Sherd of a Hellenistic glazed tile found by the British Museum team on Tell A   675
240. Reconstruction of the Hellenistic shrine on Tell A, after it was enlarged around 250 BCE, showing the N corner and the articulated NE façade   680

241. Close-up of the reconstruction of the Hellenistic shrine's NE façade   681
242. Plan of the British Museum team's Area B12   684
243. Excavated section of the SW façade of the original Hellenistic shrine, constructed shortly after 331 BCE   688
244. Section of the NW façade of the enlarged Hellenistic shrine, showing the underlying mud-brick temenos of Adadnadinakhe   694
245. The W section of the British Museum team's Area B10   695
246. The E section of Area B10   696
247. Sumerian stone demon amulets   697
248. Pottery from the Hellenistic shrine I   706
249. Pottery from the Hellenistic shrine II   707
250. Pottery from the Hellenistic shrine III   708
251. Pottery from the Hellenistic shrine IV   709
252. Pottery from the Hellenistic shrine V   710
253. Pottery from the Hellenistic shrine VI   711
254. Hellenistic storage jar with a vertical neck and a band rim, dating from the late fourth century or early third century BCE   712
255. Aramaic inscriptions excavated by the British Museum team   713
256. Sumerian terracotta figurines found by the British Museum team   716
257. Terracotta figurines of riders on horseback from the Hellenistic shrine   717
258. Nude female terracotta figurines from the Hellenistic shrine   718
259. Terracotta heads of deities and presumed royal figures from the Hellenistic shrine   719
260. Terracotta plaque showing a goddess wearing a mural crown   721
261. Close-up of the point of impact on a Hellenistic-era terracotta fertility goddess (TG4293) that was possibly broken intentionally   722
262. Second close-up of the lower edge of the break on the same terracotta fertility goddess (TG4293)   723
263. Terracotta of a figure wearing a diadem (TG4436), showing possible intentional damage or decapitation   723
264. Reconstruction of Court A inside the Hellenistic shrine   725
265. Close-up of the reconstruction of Court A   726

266. Reconstruction of a niche inside the Hellenistic shrine, containing Statue A, a standing portrait of Gudea   727
267. Artist's impression of the bronze statue of Heracles (AO2890) found on Tell A by Sarzec   728
268. Sherd of a ceramic vessel decorated with a portrait of Alexander the Great   729
269. A silver coin struck in Babylon shortly after the arrival of Alexander the Great in 331 BCE   730
270. Sumerian terracotta figurine of a horned nude goddess (TG3842), retrieved by the British Museum team from the Hellenistic strata of Tell A   731
271. Corner of a limestone basin with a lion's head (part of a Thunderbird motif), inscribed in the name of Gudea. Musée du Louvre AO73   732
272. A selection of the Hellenistic spindle whorls unearthed by the British Museum team on Tell A   736
273. Some of the Hellenistic loom weights unearthed by the British Museum team on Tell A   737
274. Partly reconstructed drawings of the Alexander coin found on Tell A by the British Museum team   740
275. Terracotta showing a crowned head (TG2123)   742
276. Partly reconstructed drawings of the coin from the reign of Antiochus III found on Tell A by the British Museum team   746

ABBREVIATIONS

AO	*Antiquités Orientales* (Musée du Louvre)
Ashm	Ashmolean Museum, Oxford
BM	British Museum, London
CAD	The Assyrian Dictionary of the University of Chicago
CT	Cuneiform Texts from Babylonian Tablets in the British Museum
CUSAS	Cornell University Studies in Assyriology and Sumerology
DP	Documents présargoniques
DUROM	Durham Oriental Museum
EŞEM	Eski Şark Eserleri Müzesi, Istanbul
ETCSL	The Electronic Text Corpus of Sumerian Literature
FAOS	Freiburger Altorientalische Studien
HMA	Hearst Museum of Anthropology
IM	Iraq Museum, Bagdhad
NAMN	National Archaeological Museum of Naples
RIME	The Royal Inscriptions of Mesopotamia, Early Periods
ROM	Royal Ontario Museum
RTC	Recueil de tablettes chaldéennes
SB	*Suse Bis* (Musée du Louvre)
TG	Tello/Girsu
U	Ur
UET	Ur Excavations. Texts
VA	Vorderasiatisches Museum, Berlin
YBC	Yale Babylonian Collection

PART 3   The Mound of the Palace

CHAPTER 22

An Overview of the French Excavations on Tell A

A Brief Chronology

As is discussed in detail in the introduction to this book, Sarzec's first trip to Tello (Season 1) lasted from 5 March to 11 June 1877, shortly after his arrival in Basra, where he held the post of French vice consul. His interest in Tello was piqued when he heard of some ancient statues that had been found on the site, and his focus at the outset was on Tell A. Of momentous significance was the upper part of the Gudea Colossus (Statue D) that he uncovered on his 'first tour on horseback' (as he recalled) at the foot of Tell A, either at ground level or just below the surface. He returned to Tello for Season 2 in 1878, which ran from 18 February to 9 June, when his most important discoveries relating to Tell A were the Cylinders of Gudea (reportedly found on Tell I′) that chronicle and commemorate Gudea's construction of the New Eninnu. During his first two seasons Sarzec did not have the requisite formal permission from the Ottoman authorities to carry out excavations on the site, but he nevertheless sent a cache of finds to Paris in July 1878.

By January 1880 (Season 3), when authorisation had been obtained from the Ottoman Sublime Porte, Sarzec went back to Tello to carry out extensive excavations on Tell A, where he exposed walls belonging to the splendid building that he referred to as the Palace, along with Hellenistic inscribed bricks and smaller finds, as well as Lagash II statuary and other Sumerian remains. In the winter of 1880 he again travelled to Tello, working on Tell A from 12 November 1880 to 15 March 1881 (Season 4). As he dug rapidly and deeply in and around the complex he began to realise that the so-called

Palace architecture that he had first uncovered and attributed to the reign of Gudea was in fact part of a much later Hellenistic building that had been constructed under the authority of Adadnadinakhe, largely with reused Sumerian materials.

Between 1881 and 1888 Sarzec was unable to return to Tello due to the political situation and ongoing local unrest, but he worked closely with Heuzey during this time on the first instalment of *Discoveries in Chaldea* (1884), the published report of the initial findings. When he went back to Tello in 1888 (Season 5) he carried out further work on the central and northern parts of the Mound of the Palace (as it was known), attempting to distinguish between Hellenistic and Sumerian ruins, but his attention turned principally to Tell K, as is detailed in Part 2. Importantly, he was now accompanied by the surveyor and photographer Henri de Sevelinges, and the first photos of Tell A date from this year.

Five years passed, during which the excavations were interrupted for three years, and when Sarzec was able to return to Tello, he was mainly concerned with other areas of the site, above all Tell K. Eventually, in 1893, he decided to carry out further investigations on the Mound of the Palace, and these lasted for three seasons between 1893 and 1895 (Seasons 7–9). First, he explored the underlying levels of the south-east sector of the Hellenistic complex, exposing Sumerian architecture left by Gudea's Lagash II predecessor, Ur-Bau. Secondly, in 1895, he completely exposed the Gate of Gudea (as it became known) and uncovered more Hellenistic remains. His last excavations on Tell A were carried out during his final visit to Tello from February to May 1900 (Season 11). Although he was still mainly interested in other parts of the site (Tell K and Tell V, referred to as Tablet Hill), he re-excavated some of the deep trenches that he had previously opened at the heart of the Palace complex, apparently hoping to find more of the spectacular statues that had first drawn him to the mound. He returned to France in 1900 and died the following year.

When Cros, who was closely advised by Heuzey, subsequently took charge of the site, he began by opening soundings in several areas (notably on Tell K, as recounted above), but he also dug a deep trench on Tell A, in the area of the Gate of Gudea. This work was carried out between January and May 1903 (Season 12). As has been noted repeatedly, Cros had a much greater understanding of the pivotal importance of unbaked mud-bricks than his predecessor, and this allowed him to identify structures that Sarzec would surely have overlooked. Returning to Tello in 1904 (Season 13), however, Cros built a dig house among the archaeological remains, and although it was not erected on Tell A, it was constructed with inscribed bricks from the Mound of the Palace that had been discarded on various spoil heaps. He seemingly did not excavate further on Tell A in 1904, but he did undertake a thorough topographical survey of the entire site. In 1905 (Season 14), working on several areas at the same time, Cros investigated the area between Tell A and the rise referred to as the Mound of the Large Bricks (Tell B), where he exposed parts of the decorated fired-brick façades that were installed on the front of the massive mud-brick platform that supported Gudea's New Eninnu. Also uncovered were a stone stairway and the shrine that was previously thought to house the Gudea Steles (see Chapters 23 and 41 below). Cros's last trip to Tello took place in 1909 (Season 15), when he found more fragments of the Gudea Steles in the same area between Tells A and B.

It was twenty years before the French returned to Tello. Between January and April 1929 (Season 16), Genouillac opened a series of deep trenches across the site, beginning with the Mound of the Palace, where he focused on levels below the northern part of the Hellenistic structure and discovered some Lagash II foundation boxes that contained statuettes and inscribed tablets. Contributing greatly to the site's deterioration, he also used inscribed bricks from Tell A to build a new dig house amidst the remains, though not directly on the Mound of the Palace. The last systematic French investigations on Tell A were carried out by Genouillac between November and February 1930 (Season 17), when

he found more Lagash II sculptural debris and remnants of Sumerian paved floors and water installations. Three further seasons of work were undertaken between 1931 and 1933 (Seasons 18–20), led by Genouillac and Parrot (1931) and subsequently by Parrot alone, but no further excavations were conducted on Tell A.

Introducing the Published French Results

The results of the French digs that were carried out on Tell A before the Second World War were recorded in a series of formal reports published between 1884 and 1948. As with the presentation of the French findings from Tell K in the second part of this book, it is important to lay out the contents of these reports, together with the associated plans and photos (and in this instance a plaster Maquette showing the work in progress) in chronological order of publication. This helps to provide an understanding of how the fieldwork progressed, and how the excavators' discussions and interpretations of the recorded archaeological features evolved. Adopting the same method as is used in the synopsis of the French findings on Tell K, the early data relating to Tell A is first presented descriptively before being critically reassessed in the context of a general reinterpretation of the archaeology of the mound.

The first detailed account of the large-scale work on the Mound of the Palace, published in 1884 and covering Seasons 1–4, was contained in the first instalment of *Discoveries in Chaldea*, written and annotated by Heuzey in close cooperation with Sarzec, and based on Sarzec's notes, plans and sketches, supplemented by the information that he communicated to his colleague at the Louvre in meetings and interviews. In 1910 Cros included the preliminary results of his limited exploration of Tell A (Season 12) and the area of the Gudea Steles between Tells A and B (Season 14) in *New Excavations at Tello*. This was followed in 1912, more than a decade after Sarzec's death, by Heuzey's publication of the final instalment of *Discoveries in Chaldea*, which incorporated Sarzec's unpublished field notes from his last digs on Tell A (Seasons 5–9 and 11), as well as information recorded in the field by Cros, to create a revised, extended account of the work that had by then been carried out on the mound. In 1936 Genouillac summed up his own results from Tell A (Seasons 16 and 17) in the second volume of his *Excavations at Telloh: The Ur III Dynasty and Larsa*. Finally, in 1948, Parrot attempted in his *Tello: Twenty Seasons of Excavations* to produce an overview of all the findings and arguments relating to the Mound of the Palace, while offering his own interpretation of the remains.

Soon after his first encounters with the archaeology of Tell A, Sarzec reached the initial view that the mound was formed of a massive platform built of small square mud-bricks with sides of 0.2 m and a thickness of 0.1 m, from which monumental ramps, between 40 m and 50 m in length, ascended to the elevated building that was situated some 12 m above the surrounding alluvial plains. Though the building was referred to by Sarzec as a Palace (the source of the mound's familiar name), and his nomenclature is generally retained in this presentation of the French accounts of the mound, it is by no means the most accurate description of Tell A's upper layer of Babylonian–Hellenistic architecture (established in the late fourth century BCE and rebuilt during the time of the Seleucids) that Sarzec first uncovered. As was stressed by Heuzey, later excavations clearly revealed that the Mound of the Palace was made of superimposed archaeological layers—a fact that undermined Sarzec's early attempts to interpret the remains as a single entity. It is also ironic that the very earliest descriptions that were published in the first instalment of Sarzec and Heuzey's magnus opus relate to structures made of sun-dried mud-bricks because, in the eleven seasons of excavations that followed, Sarzec paid no attention whatsoever to any other traces of architecture built with unbaked bricks. More broadly, the excavation results contained in the first fascicle of *Discoveries in Chaldea* deal almost exclusively with the fired-brick structures that the excavators encountered. These derived from the Hellenistic building that was uncovered and described in detail.

The underlying superimposed layers to which Heuzey drew attention were subsequently excavated by Sarzec (followed by Cros and Genouillac) in deep soundings conducted at the bases of significant fired-brick structural remains. To reach these lower levels, the excavators demolished and removed the Hellenistic walls and their associated foundation fills, leaving Tell A in ruins when the sequence of campaigns targeting the mound came to an end in 1930.

While the French investigations were being carried out, it became increasingly clear that significant digging, levelling and backfilling had taken place previously, in the preparatory phase of the construction of the Hellenistic complex, more than two millennia before Sarzec and his successors destructively reshaped Tell A. These stratigraphic complications were not the determining factor in the way the French work was presented in their reports, however. Instead, the focus was mainly on the chronological sequence of the excavations, and (as with Tell K) the published accounts are first and foremost a chronicle of the work undertaken on the mound rather than a systematic interpretation of the excavated remains. Nonetheless, Sarzec and Heuzey do present a comprehensive plan of the Hellenistic Palace (as they conceive of it), supplemented by detailed descriptions of focal points in the building, including the construction platforms and the monumental entranceway known as the Gate of Gudea. The report produced by Cros (again under Heuzey's close supervision) and the much later record published by Genouillac discuss the results of their own soundings and some newly discovered features, and both make limited attempts to evaluate what their findings reveal about the stratigraphy of Tell A, while also laying out some evolving interpretations of particular structural elements.

CHAPTER 23

The French Pioneers on Tell A: An In-Depth Account of Their Findings

Sarzec and Heuzey, *Discoveries in Chaldea* (1884): Seasons 1–4

With respect to Tell A, Sarzec and Heuzey were aware of some significant problems of interpretation that, from the outset, they considered to be irresolvable. Nevertheless, after only four initial seasons on the site, they had formed the view that the architectural complex unearthed on the Mound of the Palace dated not from the time of Gudea in the late third millennium BCE but to the Seleucid period, two thousand years later, and that it had been built by a Babylonian–Greek named Adadnadinakhe. They envisaged it as a proteiform construction, completely atypical in its general layout and structural features, that is described in *Discoveries in Chaldea* as a huge Babylonian *barillet*—a barrel-shaped building (Sarzec and Heuzey 1912, p. 15). As strange as it sounds, they seem to have pictured it as an enlarged cylinder, shaped like the inscribed cylinder of Antiochus I Soter that was found in the Temple of Ezida in Borsippa. Subrectangular in plan and measuring 53 m × 31 m, the building as documented by Sarzec (see Sarzec's Plan A; Fig. 111 below) was oriented north-west–south-east, and its corners were aligned with the cardinal points. Its walls were made of reddish-green square and rectangular fired bricks that were laid in regular courses, with overlapping joints bonded with bitumen and (in places) mud mortar. The walls ranged in thickness between about 0.8 m and 1.8 m, and some were preserved to a height of about 3 m.

The detailed record of the excavations contained in the first part of *Discoveries in Chaldea*, which is written in the first person, is presumably a lightly edited version of the notes that Sarzec made while he was working on the site. Heuzey's comments on the report are included as footnotes. According to Sarzec's account, the NE perimeter wall seemed to be made up of three distinct parts or segments. In the middle was a wide rectangular buttress with dimensions of 5.5 m (w) × 1 m (deep) that was decorated with two sets of articulated pilaster strips (or three-step recesses), one on each side. The recessed pilasters, which were regularly spaced, measured 0.6 m (w) × 0.25 m (deep), and Sarzec found that the sections of wall on the two sides of the central portion were each decorated with an uninterrupted series of vertical tori or convex mouldings, with semi-circular cross-sections (0.5 m in diameter), forming half-columns that were built with bricks dating from the time of Gudea. The bricks, which were triangular with rounded edges, originated from the so-called Lagash II column bases or Gudea pilasters. Outside the NE wall, the ground was paved along the entire length of the façade, where the paving was 5 m wide in front of the central section and 4 m wide in front of the NE and SE flanking sections. The paving was made of square Lagash II fired bricks (possibly with standard-length sides of 0.32 m, though that is not explicitly stated) that were regularly laid on a bed of bitumen. The bricks were marked with what is here referred to as the Gudea Standard Inscription commemorating the rebuilding of the Eninnu for Ningirsu (RIME 3.1.7.37), and the text was placed face down.

In front of the large central buttress of the façade wall, flanking the gateway (M on Sarzec's Plan A), a stepped pedestal made of two substantial stacked slabs of different sizes held a monumental carved basin with dimensions of 2.5 m × 0.6 m × 0.7 m (h) that was inscribed in the name of Gudea (AO67A, AO67B and EŞEM5555). Carved from a single block of hard yellowish limestone, its two exterior lengths featured figurative reliefs that are described in the text as standing high priestesses, or possibly deities. With their arms outstretched and hands joined, each group holds a vase from which flows a double stream of water that lands bubbling on the ground, where it forms a rivulet (Fig. 108). Two cuneiform dedications to Ningirsu (RIME 3.1.7.58) were found inscribed on the shorter (respectively, flat and round) sides of the ritual container. The fragmentary text on the flat side reads: 'He transported . . . from . . . and fashioned a lofty basin from it for him'. The one on the round side reads: 'For Ningirsu, the powerful warrior of Enlil, his master, Gudea, ruler of Lagash, dedicated this (basin) for his well-being'.

According to Sarzec, the NW perimeter wall, like its NE counterpart, was also made up of three separate parts, though in this case the decorations were reversed, such that the half-columns ornamented the narrower buttressed section in the middle of the wall, while the recessed pilasters were placed on the two longer flanking segments. Unlike the NE tower buttress, the NW buttress, which measured 5.5 m × 0.7 m, included a decorative panel made of seven large vertical tori (each 0.5 m in diameter, exactly like the ones in the NE façade) that were framed with two flat columns or pilasters. Despite their differing decorative features, the segment walls on the two façades were, in Sarzec's view, methodically bonded and therefore all built at the same time (Sarzec and Heuzey 1912, pp. 13–54). Since external paving was found only outside the NE wall, Sarzec assumed that this was the building's main façade and that its principal entrance was gate M.

In total, the Palace's outer walls were pierced by five main entrances: gates M and L in the NE façade, gate G in the NW façade, gate K in the SW wall, and gate S in the SE wall. Gate M, which Sarzec says was subsequently closed off, featured two stone door sockets that he believed were functional (though this was mistaken, as is discussed further below). Otherwise, none of the entranceway passages showed any traces of door sockets or other closing fixtures. Sarzec notes that bricks of the same size as the Gudea bricks that were used to block off gate M were inscribed with the name of Adadnadinakhe (Sarzec and Heuzey 1912, pp. 17–18), and he recalls finding similar bricks in other parts of the building,

described as 'additions to internal constructions at the Palace' that were executed at later epochs. When he made this comment, Sarzec believed that the Palace had been built by Gudea, so the more recent period to which he refers is the Hellenistic era associated with Adadnadinakhe.

Whereas Gate M, which led to the central Court A (as marked on Sarzec's Plan A), was 1.2 m wide, two of the subsidiary entrances (L and G) were less than 1 m in width. In the exterior of the NE façade, gate M was flanked on its S side by a deep niche or alcove (marked N on the plan), which measured 1.5 m (w) × 5.5 m (deep), and at the end of which, facing north-east, lay the lower part of the seated Gudea Colossus (Statue D; AO1), with a dedicatory inscription to Ningirsu (RIME 3.1.1.7.StD).

The interior Palace walls, ranging in width from 0.8 m to 1.8 m, were found below a topsoil layer of earth and sand that was approximately 0.4 m thick. Their elevations ranged from 0.6 m to 2.4 m, with the central walls generally better preserved than the peripheral ones. Only the S corner of the building and its surrounding area presented major architectural lacunae. The internal walls, like the exterior façades, were made of square fired bricks, with sides measuring approximately 0.3 m (perhaps 0.32 m if they were salvaged standard Gudea bricks), and they were bonded with either bitumen or clay mortar.

The Palace was made up of thirty-six rooms, all rectangular or square in plan, and ranging in size from 3 m × 3 m to a maximum length of 4 m, that were arranged around three interior courtyards: Court A (17 m × 21 m), Court B (8.25 m × 9.25 m) and Court C (5.65 m × 6 m). The rooms, courtyards and interior passageways were all fitted with pavement floors that were tiled with uninscribed square fired bricks with sides of about 0.3 m, some of which showed signs of fire damage—calcination that led Sarzec and Heuzey (1912, p. 53) to believe that the building had burnt down. The pavements were laid on a thick layer of homogeneous backfill that was deposited on top of beds of mud-bricks that completely filled and sealed off spaces associated with underlying constructions. The foundations of the Palace's internal walls and façades were established directly on top of this extensive subterranean mud-brick filling, which formed the planned substructure of the Hellenistic edifice.

The N corner of the Palace was organised around Court C, which was identified by Sarzec as a harem (Sarzec and Heuzey 1912, p. 22). Not directly connected to the central area

330   The Mound of the Palace

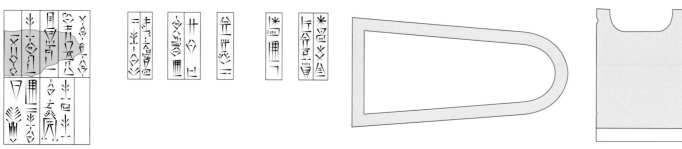

FIGURE 108. Carved limestone basin inscribed in the name of Gudea.

represented by Court A, it was accessed through gate L in the NE façade. Among the large cache of objects found in this part of the complex were: a well-constructed hearth or brazier in room 11; a wealth of Sumerian ex-votos in room 30, including a fragmentary inscription, with a dedication to Ningirsu in the name of Gudea, that originated from one of the Gudea Statues (Statue W: AO20; RIME 3.1.1.7.StW); the torso of a diorite statuette of a bearded man holding a vase against his chest in room 8; and three scattered fragments of another diorite statuette that were found in rooms 30, 32 and Court C, respectively. Outside the NE façade on this side of the complex, in the vicinity of gate L, was found a substantial, badly mutilated fragment of a standing statue made of green diorite (Statue K: AO10; RIME 3.1.1.7.StK). Inscribed on the back, almost certainly with a dedication to Ningirsu, its head and shoulders, as well as part of the feet and socle were broken off, and the losses were not recovered.

The W corner of the building, which was planned around Court B, included two wells and another brazier or fireplace in room 35. This W area also yielded important relics of Sumerian art, notably a headless standing statue of Ur-Bau at prayer, with his hands interlocked, that was inscribed with a text commemorating his building activities in Girsu (AO9; RIME 3.1.1.6.4). The artefact was uncovered, probably close to its original location in the so-called Palace, in the passage leading to an enclosed internal space (16 on Plan A), which also contained a large sacred vase made of bronze or copper.

At the heart of the complex, entrance corridor F, which was subsequently considered to be part of the Gate of Gudea (EFHI), yielded a fragment of an inscribed white limestone basin that was decorated with a protruding lion's head and dedicated to Ningirsu in the name of Gudea (AO73; RIME 3.1.7.59; Fig. 109). On the SE side of corridor F was a very substantial structure made with Gudea-inscribed fired bricks that were bonded with bitumen and laid with their cuneiform texts face up. Separating Courts A and B, this significant block comprised three terraces that together formed what Sarzec and Heuzey describe as a *Massif à étages*—a stepped or multi-storey platform (H, H′ and H″) that was ornamented with articulated pilasters. A solid construction made entirely with fired bricks, the meticulous attention to detail that was displayed in its planning and construction led Sarzec and Heuzey (1912, pp. 26–30) to suppose that its design was intended to satisfy special aesthetic as well as religious criteria.

The upper storey (H), which was the highest and best-preserved of the three platforms, was square in shape, with sides measuring about 8 m. Preserved to a height of 2.3 m, its NW face featured a decorated design of pilaster strips or niched recesses. The middle storey (H′) is described in the text as a lateral intermediate terrace that was bonded to the W corner of platform H (above), such that the top surface of H′ and the bottom of the upper storey (H), were separated by a distance of 1.1 m. The bottommost storey (H″), which was found beneath the floor of Court B, about 0.5 m below the paved surface, extended out 4 m in front of the intermediate level above it (H′). The NW face of H″ was decorated, and its upper surface, which was found 2.8 m below the top of the entire structure, was paved. Excavations to a depth of 1.3 m did not reach the base of the block (which was uncovered later), but a subrectangular pit measuring 1 m × 0.3 m that was filled with ash and charcoal was observed in its centre.

The SE side of the entire construction, which was organised around Court A and covered an area greater than 350 m^2, was the focal point of the edifice. It included a staircase (I), flanked by a chamber (36), that was set into the restored wall of the higher terrace (H) of the stepped archaic platform. It was also fitted with a deep, narrow niche (33) that measured 5 m × 1 m. Later additions to the central courtyard included a vestibule or antechamber incorporating the architectural feature O, O′ and O″, which was poorly built from the reused debris of original construction materials, among which were bricks stamped in the name of Gudea as well as bricks stamped in the name of Adadnadinakhe, all laid directly on top of the pavement floor. As is well known, Court A yielded many treasures. In addition to a significant fragment of an Early Dynastic statue (AO11) and the head of a sizeable Lagash II statue (AO12), seven seated and standing statues of Gudea were found there, all of which unfortunately lacked their heads. Made of diorite or a similar kind of imported dark stone, they were dedicated to the principal gods of the Lagash pantheon: Ningirsu, Bau, Inanna, Gatumdug and Ninhursag (Statues A–H, discussed in Chapter 37 below).

The area to the north and north-east of Court A included a staircase (R) and a series of small storerooms (as Sarzec describes them), rooms 4, 5 and 6, of which rooms 4 and 6 featured vaulted or arched low passageways. These spaces contained various votive and other symbolic artefacts, in particular an inscribed mace head and a fragment of a

332　The Mound of the Palace

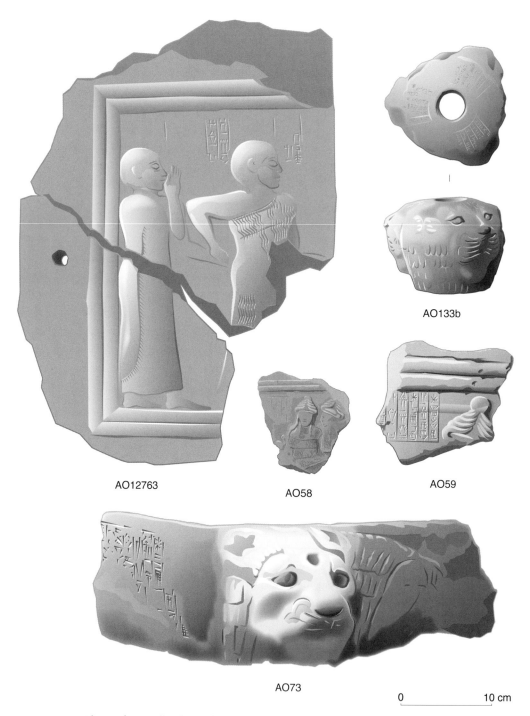

FIGURE 109. Objects from Tell A dating from the reign of Gudea: relief fragment showing the god Ningishzida (right) escorting Gudea, who is behind him (AO12763); stone mace head with lion motifs (AO133b); relief fragment, probably showing Bau and Ningirsu (AO58); fragment of a stele with a horned deity (AO59); fragment of an inscribed limestone basin dedicated to Ningirsu and decorated with a Thunderbird (AO73).

Gudea-inscribed relief plaque (AO59; RIME 3.1.7.60) made of grey, yellow and light red limestone on which part of a horned crown was preserved. As previously mentioned, gate M had been deliberately closed off with miscellaneous building materials and pieces of broken archaic ex-votos. Among the fragments were bricks marked in the name of Adadnadinakhe, a Presargonic relief featuring a lion-headed eagle mastering a lion, together with Fragment B of the Stele of the Vultures. The gate itself, which was 1.2 m wide, was fitted with the colossal stone door sockets mentioned above. Carved from diorite, and with diameters measuring between 0.5 m and 0.6 m, one of them was inscribed in the name of Gudea, and the other possibly in the name of Ur-Bau, as suggested by Heuzey (Sarzec and Heuzey 1912, p. 36). The dedicatory texts on both fittings commemorated the construction of Ningirsu's Eninnu. The passage or corridor (MM′) yielded a fragment of a limestone stele dated to the reign of Gudea that depicted a ritual procession on an upper register and a musician playing a bull lyre below; it was found with the iconographic scene face down (AO52).

The area to the east or south-east of Court A boasted the edifice's biggest room (27), which measured 12.5 m × 4 m. Room 27 was accessible from Court A via a monumental opening (P) that featured a threshold formed from a limestone slab measuring 2 m × 1.2 m × 0.3 m (t) that was inscribed in Gudea's name on its top and sides. Buried 1 m below the E corner of the Palace (the area containing rooms, 26, 27 and 28), underneath the bases of the Palace walls at a depth of 0.5 m, were the monumental remains of the W corner and the NW and SW walls of a structure built by Ur-Bau (later labelled ABC). Covered with earth and foundation deposits associated with the Hellenistic building, the Ur-Bau walls were made of large square fired bricks, some of which were inscribed in Ur-Bau's name (RIME 3.1.1.6.4). The bricks, which were bonded with bitumen, measured 0.47 m × 0.47 m in plan (Sarzec and Heuzey 1912, p. 401). No details are given of their thickness, but two examples in the Louvre (AO357 and AO358) are respectively 8 cm and 7.5 cm thick, which can be regarded as representative measurements, though with some caution because the dimensions of Ur-Bau's bricks are subject to slight variations. The walls included internal buttress-like features that, according to Sarzec (Sarzec and Heuzey 1912, p. 50), were preserved to a height of 1.1 m, though this is surely incorrect, as can be confirmed by looking at the façade in the first of Sarzec's two photos (Pl. 51 (1); Fig. 120),

where between twenty-two and perhaps twenty-four courses of bricks can be made out. If 7 cm is taken as an indicative value for the thickness of the bricks, that suggests a maximum height for the built structure, including mortar, of around 2 m (counting twenty-three courses and adding 17 mm for the thickness of the mortar between courses, as explained in Chapter 39). The upper parts and possibly the tops of the Ur-Bau walls (though it is not clear whether Sarzec is referring only to the SW façade) are described as sloping slightly from the south-west to the north-east. This might reduce the height of the buttresses slightly, but not by enough to account for the discrepancy between the presumably incorrect figure of 1.1 m and the recalculated height of about 2 m (Sarzec says the height differential between the wall's outer and inner faces was 12 cm). The walls seemed to Sarzec to have been laid on top of a bed of mud-bricks that could also have formed a systematically conceived construction, and the lowermost parts of the walls were hidden by an encasement base. The core of the structure enclosed by the fired-brick Ur-Bau walls was built of mud-bricks, while the S corner of the SW façade was bonded to a square-shaped reinforcing pilaster or buttress measuring 1.4 m (h) × 1.5 m (w) that was crowned with a three-stepped pyramidion. Deep soundings opened below the façade walls revealed a thick foundation deposit of soil, but no objects or other remains were found there. Conversely, in a trench that was opened along the SW face of Ur-Bau's SW façade wall, Sarzec found a huge number of exceptionally big clay cones, some of which were marked with inscriptions in Ur-Bau's name (Sarzec and Heuzey 1912, pp. 53–4).

As mentioned above, although the whole area to the south-west of Court A was badly eroded, rooms 19 and 20 (towards the Palace's S corner) were well preserved. Room 19, which was perhaps an enlarged vestibule, was accessed from Court A via the widest internal or external entranceway in the entire edifice (K′), which was approximately 2 m across and contained two large alabaster slabs, each measuring 2.5 m × 1.5 m × 0.6 m (t), that were stacked one on top of the other. The upper slab showed signs of severe fire damage, and the lower slab was placed on a hard layer of crushed bricks, mortar and bitumen with a thickness of 0.3 m. Below this sealing layer was a further band of sand and earth that was found to contain a considerable cache of archaic cylinder seals, amulets and cachets. Facing entrance K′ on the outer SW wall of the Palace was gate K, which featured a badly burnt and broken threshold, approximately 1.5 m wide, that concealed a favissa pit in which were found seals dating from the third millennium BCE. The SW façade wall included a second niche (T), with similar dimensions (5 m × 1 m) to niche N in the NE façade (mentioned above), at the innermost end of which was a plastered square pedestal with a height of 1.1 m. On the pedestal was a stone basin or water container that was connected to an open conduit built of fired bricks that stood on the pavement of Court A. Room 18, which was situated to the north-west of room 19, was covered with a layer of ash (0.3 m thick) and other calcined debris. It was equipped with a very unusual fireplace made of baked bricks, among which, secreted in the mortar courses, were numerous Sumerian cylinder seals, seemingly indicating that the room was used for ritual purposes.

Assessing the results of the first excavation campaigns detailed in Sarzec's reports, Heuzey realised that the archaeological record unearthed on Tell A was more complicated than it had first appeared. It was clear to him, of course, that the underlying Ur-Bau walls were much earlier than the so-called Palace constructions found above them, and he took this as the starting point for a proposed chronology. At this stage of his knowledge, he regarded the Ur-Bau walls not as the upright faces of an older building, but as a sacred enclosure, or peribolus—perhaps an open-air sanctuary dedicated to Ningirsu—and he conjectured that it stood on top of a broad mud-brick platform that was about 10 m high (Sarzec and Heuzey 1912, pp. 52–3). Heuzey goes on to suggest that two subsequent construction phases were carried out in the reign of Gudea. First, in his view, Gudea built the stepped tower (H, H′ and H″) to the north-west of the Ur-Bau walls. Secondly, taking the stepped tower as a central point, he constructed the rest of the Palace around it, above the walls of his predecessor (Ur-Bau), which were now buried. Leaping ahead in time, Heuzey then surmises that, after the conquest of Alexander the Great in the late fourth century BCE, the Palace that he attributes to Gudea was renovated by Adad-nadinakhe. Incredibly, therefore, Heuzey supposes that the Sumerian building was still standing and capable of being refurbished approximately 2,000 years after Gudea planned and executed it (Sarzec and Heuzey 1912, p. 53). Traces of the renovations that Heuzey says were carried out by Adadnadinakhe include the O, O′ and O″ structures, the new pavements, the blocking of gate M and several other features. Finally, Heuzey suggests, the refurbished building was destroyed by fire.

Cros, *New Excavations at Tello* (1910): Seasons 12 and 14

In Season 12, which ran from 1 January to 31 May 1903, Cros concentrated his efforts on Tell A in the area around the structures that together became known as the Gate of Gudea (corridor F and H, H′ and H″ on Sarzec's Plan A), where a deep opening revealed fragments of sacred platforms that have since been dated to Early Dynastic times. It is important to note that, from the outset, Cros's focus was on producing detailed descriptions of his actual findings rather than generalised interpretations of the results. Eschewing exegesis, therefore, the published account of his work is extremely factual, but this does not prevent it from yielding important insights, particularly into the very early architecture and the structures from the reigns of Ur-Bau and Gudea that lay buried underneath the Hellenistic remains. Two trenches, each 4 m deep, were dug along the SE and NW faces of the Gate of Gudea (Cros less precisely calls them the E and W façades). Extraordinarily, in the SE trench (presumably inside Court A) he found nothing whatsoever. Conversely, in the NW trench, which must have been dug in the gateway passage that led to Court B, he found a structure directly below its NW face that he believed to be a wall. It lay in front of the gate's threshold, at a depth of 3.4 m, and was placed on exactly the same orientation as the brickwork associated with the gateway (Cros 1910, p. 18). Discovered beneath a layer of sand and ash, its recorded dimensions were 0.9 m (h) × 0.5 m (t), and as Cros describes it the assemblage was built in a very particular way, using irregular blocks of clay that reminded Cros of the material used for the manufacture of clay tablets. It was found resting on a layer of sand. With the benefit of hindsight, it is now apparent that he was describing one of the Early Dynastic platforms that were re-excavated by the British Museum team.

While unearthing this supposed wall, Cros's workers encountered a small structure that was made of bricks (presumably fired bricks, though Cros does not actually say so) that were inscribed in the name of Gudea on their undersides. Located 0.78 m in front of, and 3.57 m below, the nearest pilaster to the gate's opening on the Gudea wall, it was found to be a box with interior dimensions of 0.6 m × 0.95 m × 0.85 m (h). Inside it were four square recesses with recorded side measurements of 0.3 m, but the only objects it contained were two small glazed green pots that Cros thought must have been lamps. The structure was lodged in the middle of a layer of sand, under which (after the box and the sand had been removed) was a deposit of mud-bricks. In the midst of the mud-bricks, placed precisely below the box, and with sides of the same dimensions, was a rectangular well that was filled with sand, ash and charcoal. It should be noted that, when Cros describes the uncovering of the mud-bricks in his text, he specifically refers to them as 'the' mud-bricks, as though it should be clear which structure they belong to, but he does not explicitly say that they were part of the underlying platform that is now known to be from Early Dynastic times.

Excavating the well shaft all the way down to the water table, Cros made some remarkable finds. At a depth of 6.6 m (measuring from the base of the corner block associated with the Gate of Gudea) he found a terracotta stamp of the kind used to mark bricks with the name of Adadnadinakhe (Cros 1910, p. 18); at a depth of 8 m he found numerous fragments of glazed green pottery; and at 10.2 m the workers discovered two statuettes, each showing a naked female figure holding her breasts, along with two bone or ivory knives and a fragment of a terracotta seal that was marked with perpendicular lines. Water flowed into the well shaft at a depth of 11 m, making it impossible to investigate further. Describing the enforced conclusion of this targeted excavation, Cros remarks (1910, pp. 18–19): 'It is nonetheless very instructive to see how the builders of relatively recent times drilled down through these old mud-brick foundations, trying to reach virgin soil in order to bury their votive objects. This shows how cautious one must be when drawing conclusions about the depth at which such objects are discovered.' It is a fascinating observation that reveals Cros's (and presumably also Heuzey's) advanced understanding of some of the problems that beset stratigraphic analysis—a discipline that was very much in its infancy when these words were written.

At the W corner of the gate's corner block Cros found nothing of any significance, though he did ascertain that the gate block rested on a layer of 'raw' mud-brick (2.5 m thick) that was laid on a bed of sand with a thickness of about 1.1 m, and that this, in turn, was placed on another mud-brick base. Finally, he observed (1910, p. 19) that the threshold and door jambs of the Gate of Gudea showed no traces whatsoever of fittings that might have been associated with functioning doors: there were no hanging devices, and nothing with which to open and close doors, or to lock them in place. Nor did he find remnants of materials that might have been used to reinforce the leaves of any doors.

Cros also reopened excavations in the area around the Ur-Bau construction, where he found the remains of another wall that was built with large fired bricks that he describes as lying 26.6 m from the W corner of the construction and 2.5 m from its S edge. It was exposed over a length of 5.4 m, along which its two edges were clearly defined, with its W edge forming a slope, as Cros says (1910, p. 17). Two other features that are described as markers (bornes) were found in the vicinity. Also made of fired bricks, and separated by a distance of 1.47 m, they are recorded as having been found 1.3 m to the west of the wall. Though Cros's language seems precise at this point, it is nevertheless extremely difficult to work out what he had in mind.

In 1905 (Season 14), Cros opened a broad trench in the NE sector of the site between the Mound of the Palace (Tell A) and the low rise known as the Mound of the Large Bricks (Tell B), where he exposed the ruins of the massive lower platform of Gudea's sacred complex, the New Eninnu. The excavations revealed a stone stairway in front of which stood a shrine that was fitted with pedestals on which (according to Cros) commemorative steles had been displayed, almost certainly to celebrate the renewal of the extended religious precinct. Fragments of the carvings were found on the ground in front of the building (Fig. 110), and it is now recognised that the structural and other remains were exceptionally important because they provided crucial insights into the extent of the area occupied by Gudea's newly built sanctuary and its overall stepped arrangement. Extraordinarily, little or no attention was paid to this extremely interesting data in the later interpretations of Gudea's New Eninnu that were produced by Heuzey, Genouillac and Parrot.

Located about 100 m north-east of the preserved corner of the Ur-Bau walls on Tell A, the trench revealed a flight of nine steps that were 3 m wide and carved, according to Cros, from either white limestone or tuff (a volcanic rock). On the front surface of the riser on the second step down from the top was an inscription in the name of Gudea to commemorate the construction of the new complex and its giguna (RIME 3.1.1.7.45): 'For Ningirsu, Enlil's mighty warrior, his master, Gudea, ruler of Lagash, made things function as they should and he built for him his Eninnu, the White Thunderbird. Therein he installed for him his beloved giguna, in the scent of cedar.' Cros (1910, p. 280) presumes that the text must have been repeated on some of the other slabs, but no evidence of this was recorded. As discussed in

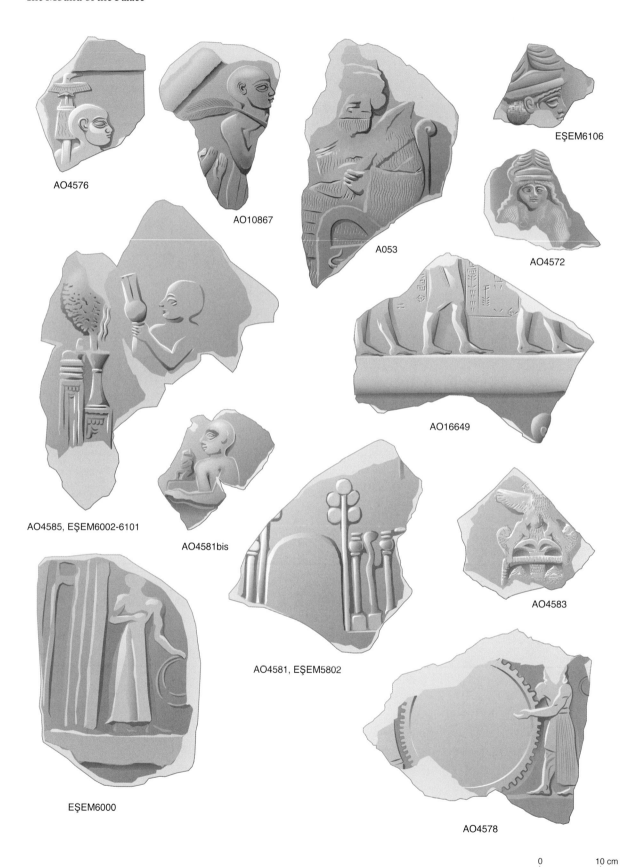

FIGURE 110. A selection of the fragments of the Gudea Steles recovered by Cros.

the introduction to this book, the meaning of the important word giguna, which appears in this inscription, is problematic. Etymologically connoting a reed structure, it is commonly treated as a metonym that refers to a temple built on a raised terrace—a meaning that it probably conveyed in the Presargonic period. By Lagash II times, however, the meaning of the word had evolved, such that it could be applied to a particular structure or annexe within the confines of Gudea's New Eninnu complex—as is seemingly confirmed by the way it is used in the inscription found by Cros. The precise nature of the giguna that was built or established by Gudea is not known. It is thought to have been a grove or garden of some kind, but since it also clearly had a brickwork component, it was perhaps a sacred plantation surrounded by walls. Contemporary texts, including the one just quoted, state that the giguna smells like cedar, and this again has several possible meanings: it might refer to the roof beams of a built structure, or the fragrance emanating from cedar trees that were planted inside an orchard that was surrounded by walls, or it might indicate the regular use of cedarwood oil as an incense at one or more locations in the sanctuary. Alternatively, the precise find location of the *in situ* inscription on the stone stairway that gave access to the upper levels of the temple complex might suggest that the word giguna still retained its earlier meaning, thereby designating a temple terrace. The further difficulty that should be highlighted in this regard is that commemorative inscriptions were not by any means always placed on or within the constructions to which they refer. For example, commemorative texts honouring the Tell A sanctuary were found on bricks from Tells K and I (see Chapter 21).

Set in the mud-brick fabric of the sanctuary's substantial lower platform, the stairway uncovered by Cros was flanked on each of its two sides by a foundation box containing a tablet and a figurative foundation peg in the form of the kneeling horned deity that was elsewhere used by Gudea to mark his construction of the New Eninnu. In the same alignment, about 40 m towards the south-east, the excavations brought to light a buttress that was shaped like a sizeable, gently sloping fired-brick pilaster with a water channel running through its middle. It was also built into the face of the massive mud-brick terrace, and Cros notes that the channel was probably designed to facilitate drainage, thereby protecting the mud-brick embankment from erosion. It seems that the platform's huge façade might also have originally been fitted with a facing of fired bricks that were probably laid in stepped recess

patterns, similar to those found around the Gate of Gudea inside the complex, for example on platform H″ (on Sarzec's Plan A, but subsequently labelled D′ on Heuzey's New Plan, as it is referred to here; Fig. 114). The fired bricks were probably stolen in antiquity, with Cros's plan and two photos (described below) confirming that only the damaged mud-brick side of the terrace survived.

The landing at the top of the flight of steps was situated around 3 m below the foundations of the Gudea Gate inside the sacred precinct. With the advantage of hindsight, it now seems clear that the Tell A complex was built on at least two superimposed and rather shallow platform terraces: the bottom one that was exposed by Cros and an intermediary platform of about the same height (1.5 m or 2 m). Cros (1910, p. 282) interprets the finds as proof of the fact that Gudea installed shallow ascending platforms, perhaps adorned with sacred gardens like the hanging gardens of the Old Serail in what was then Constantinople (as he says), and that the general arrangement was much simpler than the ziggurats or 'artificial mountains' built elsewhere in ancient Sumer, for example in Ur and Nippur.

In front of the stairway, at a distance of about 10 m from its base, Cros exhumed the foundations of a small rectangular construction that measured 8 m × 4.7 m. It seemed to have been divided into two similarly sized parts: a NW room (marked F on Cros's Plan H; Fig. 113) with outer walls made of fired bricks, and on the SE side a mud-brick floor (E on Cros's plan) that was fitted with a revetment and an external convex skirting that Cros describes as a 'heel' (*talon*). The skirting was plastered with a layer of greyish cement (about 0.05 m thick) that also covered the surrounding ground and was used to form the revetment. Under the floor of room F was a foundation box made of bricks that contained a Gudea foundation tablet and a copper statuette (EŞEM6506) of a rare type that depicts a man carrying a basket on his head (it is usually taken to represent Gudea on his way to mould or lay the first brick, but this is reconsidered below). The external SW face of the building that faced the stairway was fitted with three carefully bituminated brick pedestals (C, C′ and D on Plan H), the middle one of which, being 3 m wide and projecting out by 1.85 m from the SW side of the construction, was more substantial than the other two. Cros speculates that the tripartite arrangement was the support for a particularly significant ex-voto—a prediction that he says was soon confirmed by the discovery of fragments of sculpted reliefs in front of the building. Finally, about halfway between the pedestals and the stairway, was another small square block (labelled B on Plan H) that was also made of bitumen-coated bricks and identified by Cros as the base for a round column that had left its imprint in the top surface of the plinth's bitumen coating.

Heuzey, *Discoveries in Chaldea* (1912): Seasons 5–9 and 11

Following the publication of Sarzec's first findings (1884) and the report compiled by Cros (1910), the last instalment of *Discoveries in Chaldea*, which appeared in 1912, presents Heuzey's update on the work that had by then been carried out on Tell A, together with his interpretation of the findings. His account is based on the results of Sarzec's later excavations (Seasons 5–9 and 11), but it also incorporates the evidence uncovered by Cros in 1903 and 1905 (Seasons 12 and 14) that was laid out in Cros's book of 1910 (described in the previous section). In addition, Heuzey draws on other materials, notably the various plans that had been produced, the photos that were taken by Sevelinges and Sarzec, and the objects that were in the Louvre (though he left the museum in 1908). The most important thing to stress about the 1912 text is that by this date Heuzey's interpretation of the building and the chronology of the structural remains more generally had changed dramatically. He notes that, from the outset, Sarzec believed that the Adadnadinakhe construction that was discovered in the uppermost parts of the mound could have been a 'temple or a palace or perhaps both at the same time' (Sarzec and Heuzey 1912, p. 396). For the first four seasons (1877–81) Sarzec believed that the building had been constructed by Gudea, but analyses of the excavated bricks and objects that were carried out in the long interval between Seasons 4 and 5 (1881–8) showed that the upper layer of architecture was Hellenistic and that the Temple of Ningirsu lay beneath it. Heuzey writes that he was always sceptical about the attribution of the Palace to Gudea because of the contrast between its irregularly aligned façade walls and the exceptionally well-built and splendidly decorated platforms associated with the Gate of Gudea at the heart of the complex, and that is why he convinced Sarzec to excavate below the Adadnadinakhe walls to search for Sumerian remains and to clarify the site's chronology (Sarzec and Heuzey 1912, p. 396).

Accordingly, the excavations that were carried out when Sarzec returned to Tello, after the publication of the first results from Tell A in 1884 (outlined above), were focused on defined key areas: the Gate of Gudea and its related platforms, and the complicated series of walls to the north-east of the gate. The investigations turned up a number of new structures. More particularly, the insights derived from the renewed works that were carried out after 1888 around the Gate of Gudea convinced Heuzey that the NW sector of the Palace was a later addition and that the block on the SW side of the gate included several phases of rebuilding, though its core dated back to the time of Gudea. He notes the slight inclination of the façade on the SW side of the gate and mentions in passing that the pilasters and the overall width of the structures around the portal remind him of fortifications (Sarzec and Heuzey 1912, pp. 395–406). Heuzey illustrates his interpretation with a revised plan of the principal structures, referred to as Heuzey's New Plan (Fig. 114; see Chapter 24). Based on Sarzec's Plan A, it incorporates the later findings, especially the work done by Cros, and it relabels the various parts of the Gate of Gudea (H, H″ and corridor F on Plan A) so that its several constituent parts are carefully differentiated. Additionally, on Heuzey's New Plan the Ur-Bau walls are labelled ABC, with B marking the corner, and AB and BC marking the NW and SW façades, respectively.

Sarzec's removal of passage F (as marked on his Plan A) revealed the gate's two sides (EF and HI, as they are labelled on Heuzey's New Plan), with the result that the entire structure was now considered to be much more monumental than previously supposed and was furthermore thought to have been built in several phases. The new interpretation, as expounded by Heuzey, is that EFHI, representing the gate's entranceway in its entirety, was at one stage blocked off by wall EF, after which, in a later construction phase, EF was pierced by a new and very narrow passage F (as it appears on Plan A). This phase was thought to have coincided with the building of the Palace's NW wing. After removing all the later additions, Sarzec believed he had revealed what he referred to as the original Gate of Gudea, and the continued excavations around the gate also changed Heuzey's interpretation of the low-lying platform H″ (D′ on Heuzey's New Plan), which he incorrectly suggested was a front wall (*avant-mur*) because of its shallow foundations. Until then, with the shape of ziggurats in mind, he had regarded H and H″ as parts of a stepped tower.

A second objective of the 1888 campaign was to disentangle the intricate series of walls to the east of the Gate of Gudea, but these were not exposed until 1895, when it became clear that a broad wall had been blocked off by later walls during the construction of the NW wing. This substantial structure, which yielded numerous bricks marked in the name of Adadnadinakhe, was included on Heuzey's New Plan as wall OP. It was 15 m long and stretched from the Gate of Gudea almost to the NE façade wall, though the two were not bonded. The size and bulk of the Adadnadinakhe wall (OP on Heuzey's New Plan) again reminded Heuzey of a defensive structure, this time a castle (*chateau fort*), and he closes this section of his account by summing up his interpretation of the chronological sequence of this part of the complex. It began, he says, with the Gudea temple, followed by Adadnadinakhe's construction of a fortified building centred on Court A, with the OP wall forming its NW façade. After that came the NW extension (Sarzec and Heuzey 1912, pp. 403–6).

In 1893 and 1894 further work was carried out around the Ur-Bau construction (ABC on Heuzey's New Plan), which was now identified by Heuzey as a temple platform (Sarzec and Heuzey 1912, pp. 400–1). After removing the overlying Hellenistic walls of the Palace, Sarzec completely cleared the right-angled Ur-Bau walls (ABC, with their corner at B), and he noted that their bases were found at the same topographical height as the threshold of the Gate of Gudea. When describing ABC, Heuzey speaks of 'sloping, facing walls', by which he probably means their general inclination, but it is conceivable that he confuses the overall inclinations of the structures with the sloping top (*tête*) of the SW façade wall. As previously mentioned, the interior faces (AB and BC) of ABC were found to be fitted with buttresses, which Heuzey now says were 'constructed to resist the inclination of the external faces, as appropriate for the retaining walls of a platform or terrace' (Sarzec and Heuzey 1912, p. 400). Also as noted above, the deep soundings that were carried out by Sarzec beneath the Ur-Bau walls revealed hard, pure compacted clay, which was found to contain no fragments of any other material, and this led Heuzey to assume that the clay on which the Ur-Bau walls were founded had been ritually purified by sifting (Sarzec and Heuzey 1912, p. 401). As also previously mentioned, walls ABC were found to be constructed of square bricks with sides of 0.47 m, some of which were inscribed in the name of Ur-Bau and dedicated to Ningirsu.

Beneath the corner (B) of the platform was a foundation deposit that was believed by Sarzec and Heuzey, and thereafter by all subsequent commentators, to have been made up of a terracotta jar (AO451) that contained an inscribed stone tablet (AO261; RIME 3.1.1.6.6) and a copper deity (AO311). As is detailed below, however, the idea that the tablet and figurine were placed inside the jar was a clear error.

In addition to the work carried out at these particular points of interest, Sarzec excavated other areas of the complex in his post-1888 seasons. Close to the E corner of the Palace, 1 m below the bottom of the SW wall of room 27 (on Plan A), he found a long, narrow construction (K on Heuzey's New Plan). Measuring 3.5 m × 1 m × 0.65 m (h), it was built of square Gudea bricks bonded with bitumen, and its faces were also plastered with bitumen. An extension to K was found to the south-south-west of it, in the form of a water container or cistern (*bassin*), marked L on Heuzey's New Plan, with dimensions of 1.57 m × 4.69 m, that was divided by a partition into two differently sized compartments. A pavement floor was found on the E side of this double structure, abutting onto container L, though it is not entirely clear from the description whether the pavement actually extended under the cistern. Next to the pavement was a well (M on Heuzey's New Plan), with external and internal diameters of 1.5 m and 0.7 m, respectively. The well and pavement were quite roughly built with reused bricks. The cistern block was built of uninscribed rectangular Ur-Bau bricks (or half-bricks) with measurements of 0.47 m × 0.22 m. The pavement was made of square bricks with sides of 0.4 m, again without inscriptions, and the well was made of broken bricks that were enclosed within bitumen facings. Heuzey notes that the bases of these structures were found at the same level as the threshold in the Gate of Gudea and the bottom of the walls of the Ur-Bau platform (Sarzec and Heuzey 1912, p. 402). He proposes that structure K was built by Gudea, with extension L being earlier or later (it is not clear which), while the pavement is attributed to Ur-Bau.

Heuzey then goes on to describe an unusual rectangular structure (N on Heuzey's New Plan) that was uncovered approximately 1 m outside the S corner of the building. Made of bricks inscribed in the name of Gudea, it was embedded (whether partially or completely, Heuzey does not say) in the side of the mound, with its base at the same level as the cistern block and well (KLM). The external faces of the three-sided construction, which was open on its SW side (the side that faced the residential districts of ancient Girsu), were roughly made, while its interior walls, where the bricks were bonded with bitumen, were carefully finished. On the inside back wall, made of the same bitumen-bonded bricks, was a bench. Measuring 0.42 m (h) × 1.42 m (w) × 0.35 m (deep), it was judged to be broad enough to allow two people to sit comfortably side by side (Sarzec and Heuzey 1912, p. 402). The function of structure N was unclear, but Heuzey suggests it might have been a throne room or an exedra, and that its careful orientation might mean it was used for divinatory or celestial observations.

Finally, additional excavations were carried out in the four corners and beneath the floor of Court A, where new soundings were dug that descended 2.5 m lower than the 'level of Gudea', as defined by the threshold of the Gate of Gudea. Heuzey does not state what Sarzec found in the new openings, mentioning only that he recovered levelling deposits (Sarzec and Heuzey 1912, p. 403).

After presenting Sarzec's later results and considering them in combination with the findings made by Cros after Sarzec's death, Heuzey presents a new set of conclusions regarding the chronology and planned construction phases of the Tell A complex. First, in his view, the main temple of Girsu, the Eninnu of Ningirsu, was built by Ur-Bau on top of an artificial hill that was 6 m higher than the surrounding plain (Sarzec and Heuzey 1912, p. 403). The building took the form of a two-storey tower, of which all that remained was the corner of one of its levels (ABC on Heuzey's New Plan), and Heuzey suggests that it must have been rectangular in shape. He mentions that Cros traced the BC stretch of wall to a length of at least 27 m, and suggests that the additional, associated wall that Cros found (with defined edges and markers, as mentioned above in the summary of Cros's results) was probably a SE extension of the Ur-Bau platform. Heuzey reminds the reader that the AB stretch of wall was preserved to a length of more than 10 m and that its NE edge was curtailed by the slope of the tell (perhaps as a result of natural erosion, though Heuzey does not say that). Of particular interest is Heuzey's suggestion that the Ur-Bau construction, along with all the structures in the vicinity (on the E side of Tell A), were truncated in the Hellenistic period by Adadnadinakhe.

Secondly, according to Heuzey, the artificial mound was extended by Gudea to accommodate his new temple, of which all that remained were parts of a monumental gate:

the corner block (DEGH on Heuzey's New Plan) and the adjacent FIJ (Sarzec and Heuzey 1912, p. 403). Heuzey supposes that DEGH and FIJ had been cut down or truncated in Hellenistic times, and that they would also originally have extended further to the south-west and north-east, respectively (though he marvels at the fact that no trace of the extensions were found). Accordingly, the missing sections must have been carefully removed such that the central part of the monumental Gudea architecture could be incorporated into the newly built walls of the Hellenistic Palace. Importantly, Heuzey observes that the orientation of Gudea's DEGH was aligned with that of Ur-Bau's ABC walls, suggesting that the two structures might have coexisted. As can clearly be seen on Heuzey's New Plan, however, the alignment was not quite exact, and Heuzey therefore qualifies his conclusion with the following remark (Sarzec and Heuzey 1912, p. 404), in which Cros's measurements are given metrically in gradians (or grades):

It must be said that, according to our own plans, the parallelism of the two angles is not geometrically exact. Commander Cros, who checked the orientations at my request, measured a north-east direction of 354.7 *grades* for Gudea's DEF façade and 350 *grades* for the BA wall of Ur-Bau, which narrows the divergence and would make it imperceptible to the eye on the ground.

In Heuzey's opinion, therefore, Gudea simply expanded the Ningirsu temple complex that had been built by Ur-Bau, making it into a more significant building without changing its sacred character. He proposes that the space between DEGH and ABC, encompassing the NW corner of Court A, where Sarzec had found a well, was a spacious ceremonial courtyard or public walkway that was equipped with a well and associated amenities (Sarzec and Heuzey 1912, p. 405).

Thirdly and finally, in Heuzey's view, many centuries later Adadnadinakhe excavated Tell A, where he found the Sumerian temple and statuary, and used the Gate of Gudea (DEGH and FIJ on Heuzey's New Plan) as the nucleus of a fortified Palace, retaining the gate for symbolic reasons, 'in memory of the ancient sanctuary'. As Heuzey writes (Sarzec and Heuzey 1912, p. 405): 'the statues of the old *patesis*, particularly those of Gudea, which M. de Sarzec found lying in groups on the pavements of the new building, clearly indicate that this restoration was not carried out without a particular appreciation of the past and the time-honoured memories of the land'. Heuzey dates this renovation project to the mid-second century BCE, when (according to him) the NW façade of the Palace was defined by Adadnadinakhe's OP wall, and he suggests that the NW wing of the building, including Courts B and C, were added 200 or 300 years later, a theory based on the discovery of a jar filled with coins, some of which were from the first century CE (Sarzec and Heuzey 1912, p. 405).

Genouillac, *Excavations at Telloh*, vol. 2: *The Ur III Dynasty and Larsa* (1936): Seasons 16 and 17

Genouillac carried out excavations in Tello from 18 January to 15 April 1929 (Season 16). Following in Cros's footsteps, he reopened a series of trenches across the site, starting with the Mound of the Palace, where he targeted the NW side of the Hellenistic complex, laying out deep trenches and exposing Lagash II foundation boxes that contained ritual tablets and copper statuettes from the reign of Gudea. In his subsequent campaign, lasting from 27 November 1929 to 27 February 1930 (Season 17), he completed his fieldwork on Tell A, further exposing Lagash II sculptural debris, along with relics of paved floors and drains and wells dating back to Sumerian times. This operation, which was conducted in January 1930, represented the last regular digging on the Mound of the Palace in the period prior to the Second World War.

Genouillac (1936, p. 9) opens his account by reminding his readers that Sarzec initially mistakenly believed that Adadnadinakhe's architecture was built by Gudea. Corroborating the later revised interpretation laid out by Heuzey, he notes the difference in elevation between the Hellenistic and Sumerian remains: Gudea's building was found 1.25 m below the base of the Adadnadinakhe walls (1936, p. 9). He then briefly presents his own new discoveries and interpretations. When Genouillac started work on Tell A in 1929, the Hellenistic building had already been almost completely dismantled. In particular, the SE sector had been removed in its entirety, and only a small section of the NE façade was still standing, while a few adjoining pieces of walls belonging to rooms in the N corner had survived. The NW façade wall, which had been protected by spoil heaps, was better preserved, but nothing remained of the Ur-Bau platform. The

only visible survivals from the reign of Gudea were the Gate of Gudea (DEGH) and its pavement threshold (EFHI).

Among the devastation that had resulted from the preceding excavation campaigns, as well as from general collapse, Genouillac made several new finds, including three foundation boxes that were excavated close to the SE side of the Gate of Gudea. They are considered in Chapter 44, but apart from suggesting that they dated from the time of Gudea, Genouillac gives little further information about them (1936, p. 10). Three wells that he discovered are described in more detail. Well I, which is marked on Genouillac's plan (Pl. XV, top right, in front of *Chambre* I, where it is labelled *Puits* I; see Fig. 115) and shown in two photos (Pl. 73 (1 and 4); see Fig. 135), was an unusual construction that was made of alternating layers of bricks laid sideways, together with bricks (or fragments of bricks) laid flat, and the opening was protected by a partially preserved vaulted dome, the top of which was found just 0.6 m below the first brick of the Adadnadinakhe wall. Small animal figurines and clay tablets, apparently dating to the Ur III period, were found in the well, and Genouillac suggests that they must certainly have been discarded during the 'Aramean epoch' (his term for the Hellenistic period of Adadnadinakhe) because they were found in a layer that contained significant traces of iron oxide (1936, p. 10). He doubts whether the structure had been used to supply water because the brickwork did not descend deep into the shaft, and he suggests instead that it recalled the commonly found drains, or abzu(s) that were a feature of Sumerian temples.

Well II, as presented on Genouillac's plan and in his photo (Pl. 73 (2)), was discovered almost in the centre of the Hellenistic Palace, in the NW corner of Court A. It was covered by a formation that is described as a semi-cylindrical niche that Genouillac believes might have been produced during a clumsy attempt at restoration, when the builders failed to align the new brickwork correctly with the original well shaft. Well II was exposed to a depth of 4.5 m, but the brickwork was found to have been discontinued at a depth of 2 m. Genouillac records that the excavator came across a pocket of loose earth, which, when removed, opened up a narrow horizontal gallery stretching out towards the west, where a deposit of terracotta and mud balls was found. It was assumed to have been a cellar (1936, p. 11). Well III, which was found in Court B in the NW sector of the Palace, is described by Genouillac as a genuine well that was used to supply water (1936, p. 11). It was excavated to a depth of 8.5 m, at which point water began to flow into the shaft. Genouillac reports that, when the local workman who was digging in the well heard the sound of the spring, he declared that it was a jinn or spirit and refused to dig further. In the lowest layers of earth the workmen found a bitumen mace head, some copper nails, some fragments of statues, a large mace made of stone from the time of Gudea, as well as a few other objects that are not itemised in the text.

Between Wells II and III was found a pit that Genouillac describes as a sump (*puisard*), which was protected by a chimney that was shaped like a truncated shell and furnished with ventilation holes (see Genouillac's Pl. XXII). As can be seen in Genouillac's photo (Pl. 79 (3)), it was crowned with a cylindrical pipe, and as is clarified in his diagram (Pl. XXII), it rested on a base made of brick fragments. He tentatively associates this modest construction with the Sumerian temple, speculating that it might have been connected with an abzu, or perhaps a ki.a.nag, which he takes to mean a royal mortuary chapel (1936, p. 11), though this is reconsidered below.

Finally, Genouillac returned to the Gate of Gudea, where he uncovered nothing of note to add to the foundation boxes found close to its SE side in Season 16 (mentioned above). He theorises (1936, p. 10) that the corner block DEGH might have been part of a stepped construction or ziggurat that could potentially be identified as the enigmatic building referred to as the EPA in some of the inscriptions in Gudea's name (the meaning of the word EPA is considered in Chapter 38 below). He also shares his thoughts on the undefined structure N (Heuzey's exedra), which he suggests might have been a horned altar. Lastly, he proposes that the double water container L (part of the cistern block and well, KLM) was another ki.a.nag installation, linked with the cult of ancestors, and that the worshipping statues of Gudea that were found on Tell A would have been placed beside the well (M).

Parrot, *Tello: Twenty Seasons of Excavations* (1948)

More than a decade after Genouillac's departure, Parrot summarised the findings and interpretations of his predecessors, and offered his own elucidation of the site's archaeological remains. It must be stressed that Parrot never actually excavated on Tell A so his exposition is based entirely on the

reports detailed above. Consequently, after reiterating the various chronologies laid out in the principal publications, Parrot reviews the updated timeline presented by Heuzey in 1912, which he sets out as follows (referring to Heuzey's New Plan): the first phase of construction is represented by the Ur-Bau walls, ABC; next came the Gate of Gudea, DEGH and EFHI, and D′, which is interpreted as a front wall. These structures, along with the cistern block and well (KLM), and the exedra (N), were built by Gudea. Much later, Adadnadinakhe launched a two-stage reconstruction programme. In stage one he built EF in order to block off the Gate of Gudea (EFHI), but this was subsequently pierced with a narrow passage to connect the new NW wing with the older SE part of the complex (stage two). The OP wall, which Adadnadinakhe is said to have built during the first stage of his project, was subsequently refaced in stage two. Parrot's summarised chronology does not clearly state whether the decorated NW and NE façade walls were part of the first or second stage of Adadnadinakhe's reconstruction.

Next, Parrot offers his own interpretation of the Tell A complex. First, he suggests that the parts of the NE and NW façades that were articulated with sets of recessed niches were built during the reign of Gudea. Secondly, he sees D′ not as a front wall but as a lower platform, thereby reinstating Heuzey's initial idea that the corner block, DEGH, was a stepped tower (referred to as a ziggurat or EPA, as also envisaged by Genouillac), incorporating the various platforms associated with the Gudea walls. Contradicting his predecessors, Parrot does not believe that EF contained an open gate or passageway, but proposes instead that this was a pseudo-passage, closed off by the back wall of the gate. Countering all previous (and subsequent) theories, he interprets the entire feature that is known as the Gate of Gudea as a huge niche that was built to house a cult statue (1948, p. 155). Parrot then goes on to propose that ABC was part of the temple platform built by Ur-Bau. Gudea subsequently built a new temple, including a ziggurat or EPA (DEGH, D′ and EFHI), which was not pierced to make a gateway, but rather recessed to create a huge niche, as just described. He attributes the decorated sections of the NE and NW façade walls to the Gudea phase, together with the cistern block and well (KLM), which he locates inside the sanctuary. Well M he thinks was rebuilt after the time of Gudea. Structure N (Heuzey's exedra), which he does not explicitly link to any of the defined construction phases, remains an unsolved problem for Parrot. Lastly, in Parrot's view, in the second century BCE Adadnadinakhe built his Hellenistic Palace among the ruins of Gudea's temple. The significant number of statues dating from the time of Gudea that were found inside the new building prompt Parrot to suggest that Adadnadinakhe conceived of it as a museum.

Parrot ends his account with a poetic and colourful comment on what he considered to be the irresolvable enigmas presented by Tell A, and the fact that the many seasons of excavations carried out by the French had left behind nothing but a barren landscape (1948, p. 156): 'these uncertainties are decisive, because the monuments have now disappeared, and nothing is found in the excavation pits except the jackals that come every evening from their dens to moan on the desolate tell'. With the benefit of hindsight, this turns out to have been an unnecessarily pessimistic view. More than eighty years after Parrot wrote these words, the British Museum team's salvage excavations showed that the mysteries of Tell A were not to be forever shrouded in darkness. In this respect, Heuzey's concluding sentences (Sarzec and Heuzey 1912, p. 406),

written at his desk in the Louvre three decades before Parrot's lament, were remarkably prescient, despite the somewhat melancholy tone of his summing up:

Undoubtedly, the lower layers of Tell A might still conceal interesting structures that will shed light on the history of the ancient Chaldean city and its principal sanctuary. It is also possible that the clearing of the entire surrounding area might lay bare some new landmarks that will indicate the actual arrangement of the sacred buildings and their subsidiary structures with greater precision. In the absence of any connecting thread to link the poor remains of the Ur-Bau foundations and the Gudea block, however, and presuming that most of the missing enclosures and terraces were made of mud-brick, it has to be admitted that these works would require a great deal of time and effort to obtain very uncertain results, perhaps of secondary interest, and they would be subject to the mastery of chance.

CHAPTER 24

Plans of the French Excavations and a Plaster Maquette

Sarzec and Heuzey 1912, Plan A (1888)

Plan A (Fig. 111), the first plan of the uppermost layers of so-called Palace architecture found on Tell A, was drawn in 1888 by Paul Murcier, under Sarzec's supervision. It was produced several years after Sarzec had exposed numerous fired-brick walls and pavement floors (1877–81), some of which had already collapsed or been demolished. As this suggests, Plan A, which Sarzec himself considered to be little more than a rough sketch, is by no means an entirely accurate representation of the remains, and it should be treated with caution. After the first four campaigns, during which the structures shown on the plan were extremely rapidly exposed and dismantled, Sarzec returned to Tell A many times in later seasons, when he worked closely with Heuzey to try to make sense of the problems that had been created on the ground and to re-examine the stratigraphy.

Plan A, entitled 'Sketch of a Plan of the Palace of Tello' (*Le Palais de Tello, Essai d'un plan*) includes indications of scale and a north-pointing arrow in the lower right-hand corner. The Palace itself is placed on, and surrounded by, an amorphous mound of unbaked bricks that is labelled *Massif de briques crues*. Lightly watercoloured in shades of grey, the undifferentiated mud-brick mass frames the general area occupied by the building. The Palace walls, which are coloured with extremely dark (almost black) ink, are distinguished from a number of unshaded structures, most notably: platform H″ in Court B; the L-shaped wall and pyramidion (both Ur-Bau structures) in the E wing that were found below

the other Palace walls; and the complex installation made up of a two-part cistern block and a water channel (*Bassin and Conduit d'eau*) that was found inside the Palace walls towards the S corner. Areas of brick pavement are represented by hashed lines, as can be seen in the internal courtyards, as well as in some of the rooms and outside the NE façade, where the floor is labelled as a three-part fired-brick pavement: *Plateforme* (*briques cuites*). No legend is supplied to explain the different kinds of shading used on the plan, but the position of the unshaded Ur-Bau structure in the bottom left corner, below the very dark walls of the main Palace ground plan, indicates that the absence of shading is used to pick out earlier features. Wide borders of grey wash are applied to some of the unshaded outlines to suggest their stratigraphic depth, especially along the NW, NE and SE walls of Court A, around the item labelled as a vase in room 27, and in the S corner of Court B. Again, the grey shading shows that the excavations at these points were carried out below the levels of the much darker walls that form the main structure, and also below the brick pavements. This indicates that the vase in room 27, the statue fragments in the E wing and the well in the N corner of Court A all belong to earlier construction phases. A note of caution is required, however, because the vase and the pieces of sculpture could have been buried under the floors at a later date. It is also possible that the statue fragments were actually found on the pavement (like other sculptural remains that were discovered nearby) and shown on the plan as though they are floating (so to speak) above the deep trenches that were opened below them.

344

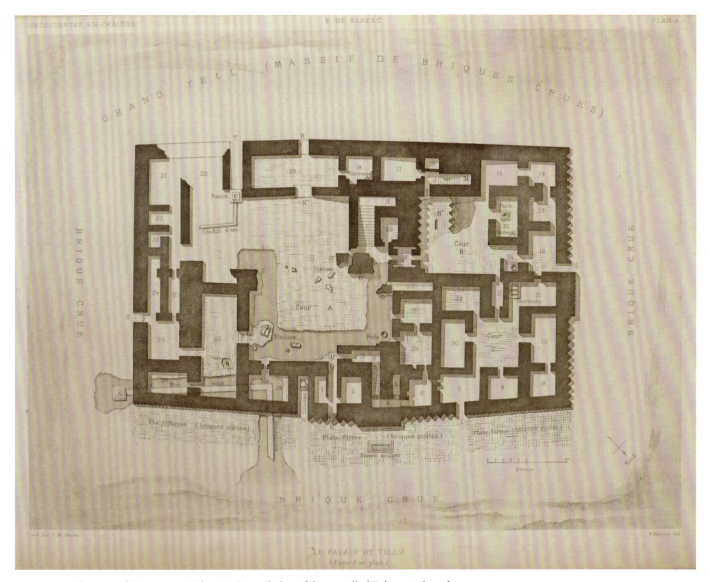

FIGURE 111. Sarzec and Heuzey 1912, Plan A: Ground plan of the so-called Palace, with underlying Sumerian remains.

Additional information that is marked on the plan includes the find locations of other fragments of statues, the carved basin (*Bassin sculpté*) in front of the NE façade, some ramps and steps, three wells (*Puits*) and three furnaces (*Fourneaux*). Also shown are the three-step recesses on the walls flanking the central part of the NE external wall and along most of the NW wall, and the uninterrupted series of shallow semicircular brick constructions on either side of the central parts of the NE and NW walls. With the exception of a missing wall in the S corner of the building, which is represented as an unshaded, roughly rectangular area defined by lines of dashes, the ground plan is remarkably complete. To create a greater sense of volume and to give it an almost three-dimensional quality, the entire plan is shaded as though the mound were illuminated by light coming approximately from the south. Accordingly, lines of shadows are inserted on the NE and NW sides of the walls.

Numerous assumptions about the design and layout of the depicted structures and installations are incorporated into the plan. The Palace is shown to be subrectangular, and its corners are aligned with the cardinal points. The two long NE and SW façade walls are not straight but slightly angled, or convex. According to the scale printed on the plan, the Palace measures 56 m × 30 m (1,680 m²), and it is made up of thirty-six defined internal spaces of various shapes and sizes that are numbered on the diagram in a spiral that starts in the middle of the NE façade and then runs anticlockwise around the outside and inwards towards the centre. Letters are used to indicate other architectural details, including niches, vestibules, doors and platforms, while the rooms are organised around three courtyards that are marked A, B and C. External decorations are restricted to the NW and NE walls. The floor in front of the NE wall is paved with fired bricks, and in front of its central façade there is the carved basin (mentioned earlier) that stands on a two-step pedestal.

The interior of the Palace is accessed via five doors that are marked on the plan. Gate M, which leads into Court A, is situated towards the E end of the decorated central section of the NE façade; a tiny detail noted on the plan shows that gate M was partially occluded by a three-step recess. Situated to the west of the NE wall's decorated central section, gate L leads into Court C. From that point, anticlockwise around the building, gate G, which allows entry to Court B, stands in the middle of the NW façade. In the SW wall is gate K (with an unshaded threshold), which provides access to Court A via a vestibule (19). Finally, on the SE external wall, gate S, which is also shown with a threshold, provides entry to a suite of rooms.

When the measurements obtained from the plan are compared with those given in the reports, it confirms that the plan, though detailed, contains several inaccuracies. Court A, to give one important example, measures approximately 18 m × 17 m on the plan, but is noted as being 21 m × 17 m in Sarzec's report. Surrounded by rooms on all sides, Court A has in its W corner the remnants of a construction that are labelled O, O′ and O″. Behind O is a narrow niche (33) that is 5 m in length. In the corner behind O′ and O″ there is an internal staircase, depicted with unshaded outlines, that leads to platform H. In the N corner of Court A, in front of the entrance to room 29, there is a well. The plan shows three (or possibly five) fragments of statues in the centre of Court A: two in the area of grey shading in front of the court's NE wall, and two in front of entrance P (shown with a threshold), which opens into room 27, where the find

location of a vase is marked. In its S corner Court A gives access to room 20, and it is possible that parts of the internal Palace structure are missing here, though no losses are indicated by lines of dashes in the same way as they are for the nearby missing section of external wall (also the S wall of room 20). It is conceivable (though Heuzey does not say this) that the open area between Court A and room 20 was the location of a wooden colonnade that was not recorded, either because it was completely obliterated by the fire that, according to Sarzec and Heuzey, finally destroyed the building, or because any surviving traces of it were not identified by Sarzec. The sizeable alcove or divan-type space on the opposite side of Court A might have contained a second colonnade, and this might explain the irregular layout of the courtyard, which could in fact have been a rectangular open-air space with two colonnaded porticoes on its NW and SE sides. The cistern block and connecting L-shaped water channel are also marked in the S corner, close to door K′ in the SW interior wall of Court A (leading to vestibule 19) and to gate K in the SW external wall. Both of the entrances (K′ and K) are shown to have thresholds. To the west of 19, connected to it by a small doorway, is the enclosed room 18, which has a furnace in its N corner.

On the other side of the building, in the hallway that connects gate M in the external NE wall with its internal counterpart, M′ (opening onto Court A), a detached slab-like fragment is illustrated. To the west of M′ is a narrow passage that leads to room 3 and stairway R, which is connected to room 4. Some details shown in this area, including the shaded walls between stairway R and room 4, and between rooms 4 and 5, are difficult to interpret from the plan alone, but in combination with the report it can be concluded that they must represent vaulted passageways.

Court A is connected with Court B to the north-west by an elaborate internal gateway, F (in the area that became known as the Gate of Gudea). Court B measures 9.5 m × 9 m on the plan, but 9.25 m × 8.25 m according to the report. In the S corner of Court B the plan shows an unshaded low-lying platform (H″) the façade of which is articulated with three-step recesses. Centrally on platform H″ can be seen a rectangular pit running parallel to the SW side of passageway F. The three-step recesses are echoed in the SE wall of Court B, from whose S corner a narrow passage leads to J (perhaps a lobby), from where platform H′ can be accessed via steps or a ramp.

The passage leading to J contains a find that is illustrated on the plan. From the W corner of Court B a passage leads to room 15, which opens into room 14 and (turning the corner) into room 13. Room 35, the door of which opens directly into Court B, contains a well and a furnace, while room 34 in the N corner of Court B might be described as a niched passageway with a well in a recess in its N wall. Court B connects with Court C via a small passageway or vestibule that is labelled D. Court C, which measures 5.5 m × 5.5 m on the plan (but 6 m × 5.65 m in the report), is surrounded by seven small rooms, six of which have openings that give access to it; the other room (9) is only accessible via room 10. Room 11 in the W corner of Court C contains a furnace. Unlike the other two furnaces, which are placed in corners and are therefore triangular, the one in room 11 is rectangular, with three compartments that are illustrated on the plan.

Several construction phases can be identified from the plan. The unshaded lower-lying structures are considered to be earlier than the very dark walls above them. The cistern block and L-shaped water channel, also shown unshaded, are similarly identified as predating the main Palace complex. Though this part of the plan does not unambiguously clarify the stratigraphic relationships between the unshaded and very dark structures, the location of the cistern block, which is placed in front of niche T, might suggest that it was not built at the same time as the Palace. It is possible that the finds and features shown in the grey shaded areas, for example the items seen along the walls inside Court A and the vase shown in room 27, also predate the pavement. Alternatively (as noted above), the remains might have been interred beneath the floor at a later date, or (as for the statue fragments) the intention might be to show their locations with respect to trenches that were dug beneath them, and this might be why they appear to be disconnected from the sketched context. The location of the well in the N corner of Court A, directly in front of the passage that leads to room 29, might suggest that the well was not built in the same phase as the structures presented in black. Similarly, the position of O, O′ and O″—on top of the pavement, but in front of, and almost entirely barring the way to, the staircase that leads to platform H and also to the entrance to niche 33—might mean that O, O′ and O″ postdate the heavily shaded walls. The same might be said of the structure that blocks gate M in the NE façade.

Sarzec, Plaster Maquette of the Excavations on the Mound of the Palace at Tello (late 1880s)

Towards the end of the 1880s Sarzec was also involved with the production of a plaster Maquette showing the excavations he had carried out on Tell A. Alongside some of the spectacular finds that he had unearthed on the mound, it was shown at the *Exposition Universelle* in Paris in 1889 (and perhaps again in 1900), among the exhibits dedicated to the history of labour, where Gudea was represented as an architect-ruler. In the centre of the pavilion that chronicled the role of labour in the progress of civilisation was a polychrome plaster effigy of Gudea that was exhibited close to a plaster cast of Statue B (the 'architect with a plan') on which it was modelled. It is therefore very likely that the Maquette of the Palace, which at that date was still thought to have been mostly built by Gudea, was commissioned to complete the tableau. The status of the Maquette as a historical record of the work that was actually carried out on the mound is intriguing. It must be presumed that Sarzec supervised its manufacture, and this suggests that it must have been largely or entirely completed before he returned to Tello in 1888, following his long absence. Since the first photos of the excavations were also taken in 1888, this means that the Maquette was probably based on Sarzec's sketches, recorded data and advice given orally. It is possible that further corrections were overseen by Heuzey after the first photos were taken, but only if some or all of the photographic plates were shipped back to Paris to be processed and printed almost immediately after they were taken, because it seems unlikely that Sarzec would have been able to develop the plates on site before sending them. Since Plan A (discussed in the previous section) was also completed in 1888, it may be that Sarzec worked on the plan and the Maquette in tandem, but they represent the archaeological remains in very different ways, and are indeed partially contradictory. One thing that should be noted is that the Maquette contains some salient details that are not shown anywhere else, notably the location of Sarzec's tent on the mound. Though the tent does appear in one of the photos (Pl. 61 (bottom); Fig. 126), it is in a different spot on Tell A. After 1900 the Maquette was kept in storage in the Louvre until it was shown at an exhibition in Louvre-Lens (the museum's Lens branch) in 2017.

348 The Mound of the Palace

FIGURE 112. Plaster Maquette of Sarzec's excavations on Tell A. Musée du Louvre AOmg246.

A photo of the Maquette (Fig. 112), taken looking southwards, shows it with its N corner in the foreground. The model reproduces the standing walls of the Palace, the deep excavations around the Ur-Bau walls and pilaster in the E wing (drawn without shading on the plan) that were found below the foundations of other Palace walls, and Sarzec's excavation tent. Unlike the plans, the Maquette indicates the state of preservation of the Palace, presumably as Sarzec had left it in 1881, and if that is the case then it provides an important link between the stylised plans and the facts on the ground as recorded in the photos that were taken after 1888. Indeed, it seems likely that, apart from any unpublished sketches that might conceivably be preserved in any archives left behind by Heuzey or Sarzec, the plaster model is the only physical record of the appearance of Tell A after the first four seasons of excavations. The Maquette, which measures 1.3 m × 1 m × 0.17 m (t), does not indicate the location of any finds, but the three-dimensional representation shows clear stratigraphic relationships and architectural details. A small part of the NE wall, next to the central façade, includes a few columns or stepped recesses, but the most striking decoration is modelled along DEGH and D' (as labelled on Heuzey's New Plan): the side of the Gate of Gudea that faced Court B and the low-lying platform in front of it (H" on Sarzec's Plan A), both of which are stepped.

As represented on the Maquette, the NW façade is less well preserved than it appears to be on Plan A, and the Maquette shows a round pit (perhaps an excavation pit) where the N corner of the NW façade would have been. The NE façade, with the carved basin in front of its midpoint, is also less complete on the Maquette than on Sarzec's Plan A. This may be because the plan was excessively rationalised, in which case the Maquette probably provides evidence of just how rapidly Sarzec dismantled the Palace walls, and it perhaps also gives some indication of the extent to which Plan A was a reconstruction rather than an accurate record of excavated structures. It seems that the Maquette's principal purpose was not to act as a model of the architecture, but rather to document the excavation works themselves, as was doubtless specially appropriate in the context of the exhibition for which it was made. Since it would have been impossible to create an overview sketch of the site from above, it must be supposed that the Maquette was built up from a series of drawings of details, along with a sketched bird's-eye view. The fact that it differs significantly from Plan A indicates that it was not based on the published plan. Instead, the Maquette and Plan A probably represent two different interpretations of drawings that were made *in situ*. The Maquette also helps to identify the exact spots from which some of the photos were taken, and it seemingly makes an important and interesting contribution to an overall understanding of the building and the excavation sequence.

Cros 1910, Plan H and the Schematic Cross-Section of the Convex Skirting

Plan H (Fig. 113), entitled 'Excavations to the North-East of the Palace: the Tell of the Large Bricks' (*Fouilles au N-E. du Palais (Tell-des-Grandes-Briques)*), features a north-pointing arrow (pointing down towards the bottom of the page) and a scale bar in the upper middle part of the plate on the left. It presents the built structures that were discovered to the north-east of the main Tell A complex. In addition to the architectural remains (including the foundation boxes), the plan shows some other details that were observed at this location. Most notably, at the top of the plan, the damaged mass of mud-bricks (*Massif de briques crues*) is drawn with undulating spindly lines on both sides of the stone stairway (*Escalier en pierre*). Centrally on the plan, the shaded irregular shapes record the find locations of fragments of the Gudea Steles (*Fragments sculptés*) that were unearthed in front of the pedestals. The built structures are generally left unshaded, except for the two pillars or benches that are shown on either side of the foot of the stairs. A sense of the height of the constructions is provided by the shadows that are added on their right (W or SW) sides, with the light

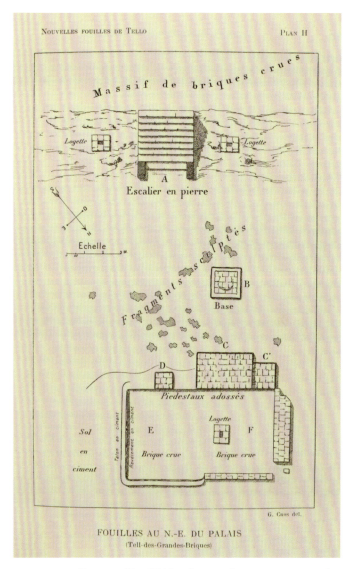

FIGURE 113. Cros 1910, Plan H: The shrine and stone stairway on the NE side of Tell A (the area of the Gudea Steles).

supposed to be coming from the E or SE side on the left of the page. Bricks, masonry and other details of the buildings, boxes and stairs are illustrated with shading. It is noteworthy that the structures and installations shown on the plan are all oriented so that their corners face the cardinal points.

The top third of the plan (approximately) is devoted to the stone stairway (*Escalier en pierre*), labelled A, which is built into the NE face of the mud-brick platform. The flight is made up of nine steps, with short, distinct lines providing indications of the masonry on the treads, while darker hatching is seemingly used to suggest the heights of the risers. The stairway is approximately 3 m wide, though the bottom step is reduced to about 2.4 m to allow for the flanking benches or low protrusions, one on either side, that both measure 0.75 m × 0.3 m. Two foundation boxes were found built into the mud-brick platform, one on each side of the flight of steps. Both were placed at a distance of 1.5 m from the sides of the stairway, and they both measured 1.05 m × 0.75 m. The plan shows that the foundation boxes were made of eight square bricks and half-bricks that formed a rectangle around the central cavity. Overall, the dimensions of the outer sides of the box appear to be three bricks by two and a half bricks, which makes sense, though the way the bricks are drawn on the topmost course is probably only indicative.

A square structure made of bricks (labelled B) is shown about 4.5 m from the foot of the stairs towards the north. As seen on the plan, the bricks, which are also square, have sides of 0.3 m and they are laid in rows of four (with very rough indications of the half-bricks needed at the corners, as discussed in Chapter 42), meaning the brickwork as sketched measures approximately 1.2 m × 1.2 m. The broken shaded circumference of a circle in the middle of the top-most course suggests a circular depression with a diameter of 0.75 m that describes the imprint of the presumed column that is mentioned in Cros's text. A thickish line placed at a distance of 0.15 m all around the bricks illustrates perhaps a skirting or a protruding shallow base plinth; short shadows have been applied on the NE and NW sides of this border to show that it was preserved to a certain height.

Below structure B on the plan, 2.7 m to the north-east, is brick block C, flanked by C′ to its north-west and by block D on the other side, about 1.2 m to the south-east. Structures C, C′ and D all abut onto the SW face of the mud-brick remains of the shrine that is located 10.8 m north-east of the bottom of the flight of stairs. The projecting features are described on the plan and in the text (Cros 1910, p. 282) as pedestals that stood with their backs against the SW wall (*Piédestaux adossés*), and this seems to imply that they were not bonded to the wall, though it is difficult to be sure. According to the plan, pedestal D, which measures 0.97 m × 0.97 m, is constructed of nine bricks laid in rows of three; C, which is the biggest of the three, measuring 3 m × 1.8 m, is constructed of six rows of bricks with ten bricks in each row; finally, next to C and abutting onto it is C′, which measures 1.2 m × 1.2 m and is made of sixteen bricks laid in rows of four. In each case rough indications of the half-bricks needed to create the bonding patterns are applied. Shadows added

on the right (NW) side of C suggest that it is somewhat taller than its neighbour (C′), which has a similar amount of shadow on its own NW side; markedly less shadow has been added to the NW side of pedestal D.

The rectangular mud-brick structure (with two internal spaces marked E and F) measures 8.7 m × 4.65 m, with the NW and NE faces constructed of mud-bricks, and the SW and SE sides outlined by a revetment and skirting of cement that are labelled *Talon en ciment* and *Revêtement en ciment* (the cross-section of those details is described below). The NW wall at the end of the rectangle that is marked F on the plan, which is described in the text (Cros 1910, p. 282) as being made of fired bricks, is three bricks deep and thirteen bricks in length, with the square bricks having sides of 0.3 m. This indicates a total length of about 3.9 m for the preserved section of this wall. To the north-east of the same wall's NE end can be seen a single brick a short distance away, but as there is no indication that the NW and NE walls met to form a corner, this might suggest that the N corner of the shrine was perhaps left unwalled, or alternatively that it was not preserved, or that it was made of unbaked mud-bricks and was not identified. That being the case, the single brick might conceivably be a stray that had become detached from the adjacent wall. The NE fired-brick wall (also at the F end of the building) is one brick wide and twelve bricks long, meaning it was 3.6 m (l) × 0.3 m (t). At the other end of the shrine (around the part marked E), the outer line of the cement skirting measures 4.2 m along the NE face and 4.65 m along the SE face. The SW side of the shrine, where neither a wall nor a revetment are illustrated, even though they can be seen on Cros's photo (View No. 11; Fig. 131), is the location of the three pedestals (D, C and C′, looking from left to right). The two approximately equal spaces inside the shrine on the SE and NW sides are labelled E and F, respectively. In the NW area (F), though not in the centre of that space, is a foundation box that measures 0.9 m × 0.75 m (three bricks long by two and a half bricks wide, like the ones by the stone stairway). Outside the shrine, towards the south-east, is a cement floor (*Sol en ciment*), the edge of which seems to be indicated with a wavy line that extends across the building's SW side in front of pedestal D.

Finally, Cros also provides a small cross-section (not reproduced here) to illustrate the cement skirting and revetment that ran around the end of the shrine that is labelled E. The drawing shows a floor of mud-bricks that is three courses thick, on top of which are seven courses of bricks that form one of the building's mud-brick walls. The ground (labelled *Sol en briques crues*) is coated with a thick layer of cement that has also been applied to the lower courses of the upright mud-brick wall. The angle where the mud-brick floor meets the mud-brick wall is shaped into a convex curve that has been coated with cement to form a skirting.

This small building was probably a roofed shrine made of fired bricks and mostly undetected mud-bricks that formed a single room that was subdivided into two separate spaces (E and F on the plan). The walls were probably coated with a revetment of white lime (Cros's *ciment*) that survived around the base and partly up the sides of some of the mud-brick walls. The pedestals that were built against the outer SW façade were designed to support monuments. It has often been thought that they held the Gudea Steles that give the area its familiar name, but this was probably not the case, as is detailed in Chapter 41. It is quite possible that more votives were housed inside the shrine.

Sarzec and Heuzey 1912, The Palace of Tello and the Remains of the Temple of Ningirsu (1912)

Fig. 114 shows the second architectural plan of the Hellenistic Palace and Sumerian ruins that was included in the last instalment of *Discoveries in Chaldea* (1912). Referred to in the present text as Heuzey's New Plan, it was drawn by the architect Édouard Autant, working with Heuzey and doubtless using the fieldwork reports produced by Cros. In so far as it was based on actual field observations—compiled with close reference to the notes and topographical sketches made by Cros, who was a trained surveyor—it can be regarded as

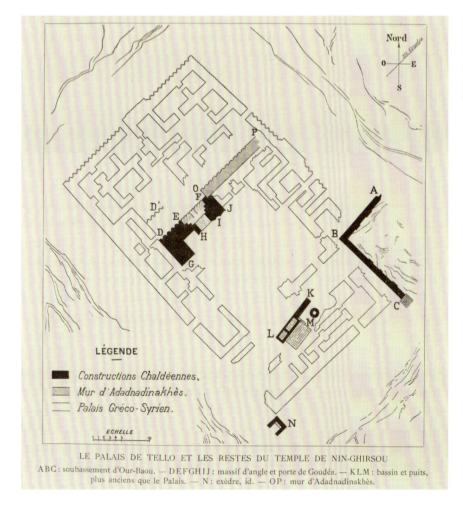

FIGURE 114. Sarzec and Heuzey 1912, Ground plan of the Hellenistic walls and underlying Sumerian remains (Heuzey's New Plan).

considerably more reliable than Plan A, and it also documents excavations that were carried out after 1888, when Sarzec resumed his work on the site. Entitled *Le Palais de Tello et le Restes du Temple de Nin-Ghirsou*, Heuzey's New Plan features a north-pointing arrow in the upper right-hand corner and a scale bar on the lower left, above which is a legend clarifying the degrees of shading used to differentiate structures from different periods: black for Sumerian constructions (referred to as Chaldean); grey for notable walls built by Adadnadinakhe; and no shading at all for the rest of what is referred to as the *Gréco-Syrian* Palace. Thin lines indicate topographical features in the Palace environs, and it is interesting to note that these correspond closely to the shading around the Palace on Sarzec's Plan A, especially in front of the NE wall. Whereas the shading and lines on Plan A explicitly represent the mud-brick mound, the unlabelled contours on Heuzey's New Plan might also indicate the outlines of the spoil heaps that must have surrounded the Palace after several seasons of excavations. Heuzey's New Plan shows no details of the find locations of artefacts or any of the ramps, steps, wells and furnaces that are marked on Plan A. Decorative architectural details are indicated on the NE and NW external walls, as also on the wall labelled OP (glossed as the 'wall of Adadnadinakhe') and on the Sumerian constructions labelled DEGH, FIJ and D′. The drawing of the Ur-Bau wall to the east (ABC), which is coloured black and therefore defined as Sumerian, shows its buttress-like features, which can be seen protruding very slightly from the inner faces of AB and BC.

When Heuzey's New Plan is compared with Sarzec's earlier Plan A (Fig. 111), it can be seen that sections of wall that are shown on Plan A are missing from the later overview of the remains. As marked on Plan A, the missing structures include: the external walls in the E corner of the Palace; part of the thick wall between room 27 and V (a narrow vestibule); the NE walls of rooms 26–8; the walls on either side of the staircase leading to H; structures O, O′ and O″ in Court A; passageway F in the area associated with the Gate of Gudea; niche 33; and the walls delimiting rooms 29–32 and rooms 6 and 7. The reason for their absence appears to be that these walls were dismantled after Plan A was compiled in 1888 (with the aid of the notes made by Sarzec between 1877 and 1881). Heuzey's New Plan almost certainly therefore records the deeper excavations that Sarzec carried out after his return to the site in 1888, in which case the preserved constructions noted by Cros and marked on Heuzey's New Plan

at these points must lie lower than, and therefore predate, the architecture referred to as *Gréco-Syrian*. Among them are: the Adadnadinakhe wall (OP), which is drawn where Plan A shows walls belonging to rooms 29–32 and rooms 6 and 7; the Sumerian constructions marked in black that are adjacent to wall OP; and structure N, outside the SE corner of the complex (referred to by Heuzey as the exedra). Also, below the SW wall of room 27 (on Plan A), Heuzey's New Plan shows the cistern block and well (KLM), which are captioned in the legend that was probably compiled with the help of Cros's notes: 'basin and well, older than the Palace' (*Bassin et puits, plus anciens que le Palais*). Heuzey's New Plan also describes some topography inside ABC—the Ur-Bau wall to the east, which was illustrated on Sarzec's Plan A, but in a slightly different location, with its corner in the middle of room 28. On the later plan the corner of ABC (at B) is placed beneath the SE wall of room 28.

In the centre of the complex, Adadnadinakhe's OP wall lies below the Palace walls, and its S corner is placed above the N corner of the underlying Sumerian constructions, which cannot be seen on the plan. This would situate OP chronologically between the Sumerian and the *Gréco-Syrian* constructions, presumably as a first phase of the work undertaken in the Hellenistic period. The discoveries that Cros made beneath the internal gateway F (as it is labelled on Plan A) are difficult to interpret on the basis of Heuzey's New Plan alone, where DEGH and FIJ are identified as 'corner block and Gate of Gudea' (*Massif d'angle et porte de Goudéa*). It is worth mentioning that, in the legend, they are listed as DEFGHIJ, thereby prioritising the entire NW and SE façades (DEF and GHIJ, respectively) rather than the two blocks (DEGH and FIJ). According to the New Plan, the gateway walls (marked in black) are 3 m thick and decorated with stepped recesses along their NW side. Between DE and F is an enlarged entranceway that is 5 m wide, but which narrows stepwise to form a more restricted entrance area (2 m wide) on its SE side that might be fitted with a threshold (suggested by the unshaded strip between the wider and narrower areas of hatching). The line of DE on the NW side of the composite structure is extended across the opening (EF), where its depth is indicated by series of diagonal lines that are not the same as the hatching used on wall OP, and they are also different from the lines that are used to shade the narrower side of the entrance (HI) on the south-east. The hatching on the NW side of the construction

(EF) breaks off in the middle to leave an unshaded strip that surely signifies a narrow gateway passage that runs from the north-west to the south-east between the walls on either side. It is extremely difficult to determine the construction phase to which this structure is assigned on the plan. Similarly, facing the gateway to the north-west on Heuzey's New Plan is a stepped wall marked D′, which represents platform H″ on Sarzec's Plan A. Since the space between D′ and DE (where Sarzec located platform H′) is not shaded, it is not clear what was intended at this point, but it seems highly unlikely that this area was considered to be part of the Hellenistic remains.

Genouillac 1936, Excavations at Telloh (Seasons 1929–31). The Palace Mound: Elevation and Plan

A third plan of Tell A (Fig. 115) was prepared by Genouillac after his excavations in 1929 and 1930. He focused on the central area of the collapsed Palace and produced a solitary composite diagram that was poorly executed. Entitled *Fouilles de Telloh* (*campagnes 1929–30–31*), it does not have a north-pointing arrow, scale bar or legend, but it does include an elevation (*Coupe*) at the top of the page; it also shows the location of trenches and gives their names, but no measured dimensions or depths are recorded. The elevation shows the towering spoil heaps in the background, which were breached on the lower left-hand side by the small-gauge railway tracks for the mine-cars that Genouillac used to remove spoil. In front of the spoil heaps are horizontal grey lines that are used to indicate the height of the surviving remnants of the NW façade. In front of that, an attempt is made to show the standing walls between *Chambres* II and III and between *Chambres* I and II, using two diagonally shaded patches placed at right angles. There appears to be another standing wall in *Chambre* II, as is indicated by the prominent vertical rectangle. It is not clear which wall this corresponds to on the plan on the bottom half of the page, but it might be the standing wall behind Adadnadinakhe's OP wall on Heuzey's New Plan (discussed in the preceding section). The elevation also gives comparative indications of the depths of the Trench of the Well and the East Trench (*Tranchée du Puits* and *Tranchée Est*), and the depth of *Puits* II (well II). Heights are not marked on Genouillac's plan but his report mentions that well II was excavated to a depth of 8 m, which would suggest

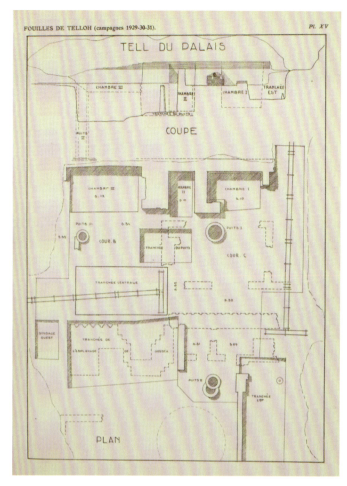

FIGURE 115. Genouillac 1936, Elevation and plan of the excavations on the Mound of the Palace.

that the Trench of the Well and the East Trench were about 3.4 and 1.4 m deep, respectively.

The plan itself shows unshaded walls, together with structures outlined with lines of dashes, as well as rectangular trenches. Shadows produced by an imagined light source in the top left corner have been added to the walls and trenches to create a sense of volume that contrasts with the flatness of the structures marked with lines of dashes. This suggests that the shadowed walls (drawn only as outlines) had been preserved, while the features drawn with dashes had been excavated and removed (whether they had accidently collapsed, been eroded by exposure to the elements, or deliberately demolished is unknown). It is unclear what the curtailed circle of dashes at the bottom of the page in the N corner of Court A is meant to depict. Thin broken lines around the Palace complex represent some of the topographical features seen on Plan A and Heuzey's New Plan, including the locations of spoil heaps. Genouillac marked the paths of the small-gauge railway tracks laid to evacuate spoils on his plan, and when these are compared with the elevation, it is clear that the tracks broke through earlier spoil heaps. These breaches are still visible on Tell A today.

The apparent neatness of Genouillac's plan was not reflected in his excavations, which were chaotic. Indeed, when his actual plan of the Palace is superimposed on Plan A and Heuzey's New Plan, it can be seen that Genouillac's is inaccurate in several places—a fact that makes comparisons more complicated. Nonetheless, it can be deduced that Genouillac's *Chambres* I, II and III correspond with rooms 10, 11 and 12, respectively, on Sarzec's Plan A. Genouillac shows the N part of the NW façade wall (at the top of his plan) without decorations, but with a thin wavy line, particularly on the right-hand side, perhaps suggesting either that the wall had collapsed or that the spoil heaps encroached on the standing structure.

Genouillac dug five trenches: the deep Trench of the Well (*Tranchée du Puits*) in front of *Chambre* II; the Central Trench (*Tranchée Centrale*) below the railway track to the south-west (about a third up from the bottom of the page on the left); the Trench of the Gate of Gudea (*Tranchée de l'Esplanade de Goudéa*) on the bottom left; the West Trench (*Sondage Ouest*), also on the bottom left, below room 17 (as labelled on Sarzec's Plan A); and the East Trench below room 5, staircase R and corridor MM' (again as labelled on Plan A), which extends out to the south-east beyond the confines of Genouillac's plan at the bottom of the page. No information is given to clarify what Genouillac found in these trenches. The only new details that were not documented on preceding plans relate to the four wells marked by Genouillac, two of which, in Court A (at the bottom of the page), are shown overlapping, perhaps to suggest successive construction phases. Sarzec's Plan A depicts a single well in the N corner of Court A, in front of room 29. The relative accuracy of the respective plans notwithstanding, it may be that Genouillac's two superimposed wells represent a feature that was maintained at roughly the same location during different construction phases, but which had shifted somewhat over time. The well in Court B on Genouillac's plan possibly relates in a similar way to the well drawn in room 35 by Sarzec. Only the large well in Court C on Genouillac's plan has no counterpart on Sarzec's Plan A.

Parrot 1948, Reproductions of Plan A and Heuzey's New Plan

Although he refrained from excavating the Mound of the Palace, Parrot reinterpreted the general stratigraphy of the tell, and he reproduced schematic versions of Plan A and Heuzey's New Plan in 1948 in *Tello: Twenty Seasons of Excavations* (p. 153). The two redrawn plans (a and b), are presented together on one page, with a north-pointing arrow, a scale bar and different shadings for distinct construction phases, following the method adopted by Autant in Heuzey's New Plan, though Parrot does not include a legend to explain the differences. Parrot's versions are basically neatly drawn diagrammatic reproductions of Sarzec's Plan A and Heuzey's New Plan (a nd b, respectively).

The Stratigraphy of the Three Palace Plans

Analysis of the three Palace plans that were drawn between 1888 and sometime between 1930 and 1936 helps to reconstruct an overview of the chronology of the construction phases on Tell A, as uncovered by the French pioneers. The phases align with the series of excavations carried out on the site, though of course the earlier plans (charting the upper archaeological levels) show more recent construction phases, while the later excavation results (from deeper inside the mound) detail increasingly ancient material. The building presented by Sarzec with extremely dark shading on Plan A is the Hellenistic Palace. Some features marked on his plan postdate the main Hellenistic phase, notably the structure in the opening of gate M and the three-part O, O′ and O″ ensemble in Court A. Conversely, the cistern block and water channel in the S corner of Court A predate the main Hellenistic phase. Wall OP, as noted on Heuzey's New Plan, predates the main Hellenistic architecture, while the decorations on the NW face of OP suggest that this was once an external wall. Structure OP is superimposed on the underlying Gate of Gudea, which is therefore older than OP. The cistern block and water channel (KLM on Heuzey's New Plan), along with the three-sided structure (N) on the same plan, were probably built around the same time as the Gate of Gudea. Wall ABC, identified on Heuzey's New Plan as the Ur-Bau foundation (*Soubassement d'Our-Baou*), is from an even earlier phase of construction. As mentioned above,

Genouillac's plan gives no details of what he found in his trenches.

Looking at the three Palace plans side by side, it can be concluded that they are pretty much in agreement, especially Sarzec's Plan A and Heuzey's New Plan. These two plans are also manifestly drawn to scale, meaning their measurements can be checked, and they are generally in accord with the dimensions given in the respective reports (though Plan A is a little less accurate). One caveat is that Plan A and Heuzey's New Plan both include features that were inferred rather than confirmed by observation, and both include some overzealous interpretations. Although Genouillac's plan, which lacks a north-pointing arrow and a scale bar, is more rudimentary than the other two, it nevertheless includes several details that provide valuable informative for the reconstruction of the history of the French excavations that was carried out in advance of the British Museum team's work on Tell A.

CHAPTER 25

Photographs of the Early French Excavations

THE FIRST FRENCH EXCAVATIONS ON TELL A WERE documented in a total of twenty-one published photos. As is the case for Tell K, it may be that other prints or photographic plates survive in personal or public archives, but they have not so far come to light, with the important exception of the recently discovered album compiled by Cros (see Chapter 2 above). Henri de Sevelinges, who joined Sarzec in Tello in 1888, took six photos of Tell A (in addition to photos that he took elsewhere on the site), which include the NE façade, the Gate of Gudea and associated platforms at two stages of the excavations, and the Ur-Bau wall from two angles. Sarzec himself took seven photos of Tell A during the campaigns of 1889 and 1900: two showing the Gate of Gudea and its platforms at two different stages of excavation; one showing the uncovered Hellenistic wall of Adadnadinakhe; one showing the unexplained construction (N) that Heuzey called the exedra; and finally there are three photos that capture different angles and stages of excavation of the cistern block and well that were found under the SE wing of the Palace. In the discussions of all the photos taken on Tell A, structures associated with the Gate of Gudea (DEFGHIJ and D') , the Ur-Bau construction (ABC) and the Adadnadinakhe wall (OP) are generally referred to as they are labelled on Heuzey's New Plan, but references to the internal courtyards and rooms (which are not explicitly identified on the New Plan) are to Sarzec's Plan A.

Between 1903 and 1909, Cros shot fourteen published photos in Tello, two of which show the area of the Gudea Steles between Tells A and B. His book contains no photos of

Tell A specifically, but some pictures that were taken on the mound were found in his personal album that resurfaced in 2019 in circumstances that are detailed in the introduction to this book. Two of these, both showing the Gate of Gudea, are described below. Six photos were taken on Tell A in 1929 and 1930 during the campaigns led by Genouillac. Two of them record details of one of the newly unearthed foundation boxes, and one captures Genouillac's excavations around the Gate of Gudea. The others are of freshly uncovered wells or well-like structures.

These rare pictorial documents are extremely useful for the wealth of information that they provide about the complicated stratigraphic relationships between the superimposed Hellenistic building and the underlying Lagash II to Ur III and Isin-Larsa archaeological deposits. They are also invaluable for what they contribute to the reconstruction of the early French digging sequence and the associated formation of spoil heaps. The surviving photos are described in detail in this section in order to clarify where they were taken and to give a detailed account of the information that they contain.

Sevelinges, The Great NE Façade (1888). Sarzec and Heuzey 1912, Pl. 49 (1)

This photo (Fig. 116) shows the NE façade wall of the so-called Palace, which is the structure that runs at a slight diagonal from centre left to bottom right. Leaning against another

Photographs of the Early French Excavations   357

| 1 Spoil heap | 2 Subfloor | 3 NE façade Wall | 4 Room 1/2 | 5 SE wall of Court A | 6 Court A |

FIGURE 116. Sarzec and Heuzey 1912, Pl. 49 (1): The NE façade of the so-called Palace.

part of the structure on the left is Sarzec, who is dressed in white, wearing a hat and carrying a stick. The most informative feature of this photo is the portion on the right that shows the remains of six of the half-columns that decorated sections of the building's façades. The niche-like structures with protruding walls that lie between Sarzec and the half-columns form the central part of the NE façade wall. This does not correspond with Sarzec's Plan A, however, which indicates a flat wall, and this further confirms that Sarzec's Plan A, which shows a heavily reconstructed and partly inaccurate interpretation of the remains, should be treated with caution.

By contrast, if the photo is compared with Sarzec's plaster Maquette (Fig. 112), which was probably based on sketches made prior to 1881 (as argued above), it is clear that the walls of the model are formed as they are seen in the photo, and this helps to verify that the section of the building recorded in Pl. 49 (1) is indeed the central part of the NE façade, in front of rooms 2 and 4. The view is taken looking towards the south, with Sarzec leaning back against the side wall of niche N (not to be confused with the so-called exedra (also N), by the S corner on Heuzey's New Plan), while behind him to the left is the S section of the NE façade wall. Also slightly behind Sarzec, stretching out to the left edge of the photo, can be seen the opening of a deep excavation around the Ur-Bau walls (ABC on Heuzey's New Plan). Accordingly, the brickwork directly in front of Sarzec (on which his outstretched legs are resting) is the SE part of gate M, while the remnant of wall that is parallel to the one on which Sarzec's feet are propped (a little closer to the camera) is the other side of the opening of gate M.

Behind Sarzec, on the left of the photo, is a rather high preserved wall that is the W corner of room 27; on the opposite side, in the upper right corner, is a group of spoil heaps; and in the foreground can be seen a shallow excavated depression that opens out towards the photo's lower right corner. A brick pavement, which had already been removed when the photo was taken, is recorded at this location on Plan A and in the associated reports. The placement of the pavement is also confirmed by the presence of the socle, made up of two rows of bricks, that lay under the six half-columns (described in the text as rising from the foundations next to the pavement). Remnants of the brick paving can be seen in the flat area to the left of the picture, adjacent to Sarzec's stick hand.

It is noteworthy that the half-columns are also reproduced on Sarzec's Maquette, where they are the only decorated part of the façade wall, and this suggests that the decoration on the central façade did not consist of three-step recesses, as is indicated on Sarzec's Plan A, but of half-columns. It is, of course, possible that the half-columns were found at a lower level, below the three-step recesses, or that portions of the recesses were preserved to a very limited extent at certain places on the façade, and that Sarzec took these scant remains as evidence of a feature that had once been extensively incorporated into the entire wall, as is shown on Plan A. Whereas the evidence provided by the photo is incontrovertible, and the Maquette seems designed to provide a faithful record of the work in progress, therefore, Plan A probably reflects a heavily edited interpretation of the archaeological remains that were actually observed.

Sevelinges, The Great NE Façade: Details of the Construction (1888). Sarzec and Heuzey 1912, Pl. 49 (2)

Looking towards the west or south-west, this photo (Fig. 117) shows a detail of the half-columns decorating the NE façade of the Palace. They are built on two courses of bricks, and the top of the wall is badly eroded. Behind the half-columned wall can be seen a mass of bricks and two walls that apparently meet at an angle towards the centre of the picture. Comparing the photo with Sarzec's Maquette, it seems reasonable to conclude that the structures seen immediately behind the section of façade shown in the photo belong to room 6.

FIGURE 117. Sarzec and Heuzey 1912, Pl. 49 (2): Close-up of the NE façade.

Sevelinges, The Gate of Gudea and its Corner Block: Excavations at the Palace of Tello (1888). Sarzec and Heuzey 1912, Pl. 50 (1)

This photo records part of the large structure inside the building, on the NW side of Court A, that was identified as the Gate of Gudea (Fig. 118). Taken looking towards the south-east, it records an early stage of the excavations that were carried out at this location. Running from the centre to the right of the picture, the main wall, decorated with three-step recesses, is wall DE (on Heuzey's New Plan). The fifth buttress from the right is noticeably wider than the others, while the one-step recessed buttresses to the left of that (as we look) are narrower and lower, reaching only to the height of the floor, which is visible as the flat expanse on the left of the photo, just below the horizon line. A partly eroded wall, on which can be seen a cloth sheet or perhaps a workman's jacket, is superimposed on these smaller buttresses. The block of bricks on the upper left-hand side of the picture, above and behind the flat floor, is part of structure FIJ. Fronting this is another wall, constructed on wall EF, that forms one of the sides of the opening, where it is used to narrow the actual entranceway.

Close analysis shows that this photo was heavily reworked to create a composite image that is made up of at least two photos that were combined into one and then further retouched and edited during the printing process. For example, the image splits diagonally into two almost perfect halves, from the bottom left corner up to the top right. In particular, the section that appears on the right-hand side of the passageway on the left of the picture, just above the notional dividing line that runs horizontally across the middle, does

FIGURE 118. Sarzec and Heuzey 1912, Pl. 50 (1): The Gate of Gudea (1888).

| 1 Platform D' (H") | 2 Platform DEGH (H) | 3 Platform FIJ (H) |
| 4 Wall EF | 5 Gate door jamb | 6 Back wall | 7 Court B |

not align properly with the low wall to the left, in front of the passageway. Additionally, below the two cloth-like shapes on top of the walls (a lighter one to the left and a darker one higher up to the right of it), the area that contains the three short pillars at the left end of the wall of stepped pilasters does not correspond with the architectural features observable in the other photo of the same features that is discussed below (Pl. 50 (2); Fig. 119). Furthermore, the darker of the two supposed textiles (the right-hand one of the two) seems to have been significantly adjusted during the printing process to try to make sense of an unwanted or unreadable form. The dark shape perhaps originally belonged to a background feature that could only be partly seen and therefore injected confusion into the image without adding any information. It could in fact be the top of one of the distant structures (or heaps of bricks) that are visible through the passageway in Pl. 50 (2) that happened to encroach awkwardly on the top of the wall on account of the viewpoint from which Pl. 50 (1) was taken. The inconvenient form was therefore probably reshaped and darkened to make it look like a second piece of cloth, forming a companion to the lighter piece that was seemingly left there before the photo was shot. The latter might have been left there accidentally, but it should also be noted that items such as the light-coloured textile were sometimes deliberately inserted into photos to give a sense of scale. It is also important to stress that the degree to which Pl. 50 (1) was manipulated cannot be defined with certainty, though it unquestionably draws attention to the fact that the photos taken on site were often subject to considerable editing during the processing and pre-printing stages prior to publication. The ongoing use of heliogravures, especially in the published reports of Sarzec and Cros, meant that it was relatively straightforward to make alterations to the original photos because the negatives were photochemically etched onto copper plates to produce an intaglio surface that could then be further worked by hand.

In terms of recorded details, thirty-two courses of the buttressed wall are visible behind the lower platform at the very front of the picture (D′ on Heuzey's New Plan). Since each course measures approximately 0.07 m in height, that indicates a maximum elevation of at least 2.24 m. The one-step recessed wall in the doorway (the bottom section of wall EF) is made up of thirteen visible courses, making a height of 0.91 m. Incorporating twenty-two courses, the structure on top of that reaches a height of 1.54 m. The visible part of the

three-step recessed lower platform D′ shows eight courses of bricks, each measuring 0.07 m in height, indicating a total elevation of at least 0.56 m. The sounding excavated between platform D′ and wall DE behind shows that the base of DE is deeper than the top of D′. The level to the left of D′ is the floor (or possibly part of the subfloor) of Court B. Below this surface, in the subfloor of Court B, at a depth of perhaps two or three courses, there appears to be a preserved course of bricks. The floor of Court B is at roughly the same height as the top of wall EF in the doorway.

This photo is highly informative because it is the only published view of the low-lying platform D′, but also because the recorded stratigraphy of the many walls suggests a chronology of construction phases. Structures DEGH and FIJ, which are found at a lower level than all the other brickwork, must have been erected first. Wall EF (in between FIJ and DEGH), which is situated stratigraphically below the floor of Court B and below the top of platform D′, must predate these other constructions. Platform D′ lies below Court B and must therefore predate the courtyard. The floor (and subfloor) of Court B possibly consists of two phases: an earlier phase represented by the course of bricks visible in its section, and the later phase evidenced by the paved floor of Court B that was discovered by Sarzec, but removed before this photo was taken. The fact that D′ is higher than the base of DE suggests that platform D′ was raised at least once at some point after the construction of DE. Furthermore, the buttresses that narrow the opening of the gate are built on top of EF and must therefore postdate it, while the interior parts of the walls used to narrow the gate (only one of which is visible on the left side of the opening) might also be of a later date.

At the right edge of the sounding between DE and D′, in the third recess to the right of the gate's opening, a brick seems to have been preserved on the floor of the recessed aperture. This brick is not visible in photos taken of later stages of the excavation, and must therefore have been removed. Its purpose is not clear, though it may perhaps be a remnant of D′ at the point where that lower platform met DE. Wall DE is damaged along three horizontal lines seen at different heights, and these horizontal lines might represent interment levels, where damage has been caused by differential erosion above and below ground, with intensified erosion at ground level. Alternatively, the horizontal damage lines might represent levels at which the wall was rebuilt, and this in turn might imply that DE was erected in distinct phases.

Sevelinges, The Gate of Gudea and its Corner Block: Excavations at the Palace of Tello (1888). Sarzec and Heuzey 1912, Pl. 50 (2)

This is another photo of the Gate of Gudea, taken from a higher vantage point and at a later stage of the excavations, and looking south-south-east, with Court A in the background (Fig. 119). On the right it shows four buttresses of wall DE (on Heuzey's New Plan), with the leftmost one, towards the centre of the image, being slightly wider than the others, as is also observed in Pl. 50 (1). The higher viewpoint clearly shows that this wider buttress forms a corner. Behind DE can be seen the outline of room 36, to the right of which is the SE wall of room 17. To the left of wall DE is the Gate of Gudea itself, with broad three-step recesses on both sides of the opening. In the previous photo (Pl. 50 (1)) there is a wall adjacent to DE on the left, on top of which was a piece of cloth or garment; this wall has now been removed. Thirteen courses of the equivalent wall on the left of the gate are still standing on top of the low wall (EF) that spans the underside of the gate's alcove. Seven small buttresses on the front of EF are now clearly visible, and although it runs across the entire gateway, EF's limited height and lack of an upper section indicate that it was not a closing wall, but was rather used to raise the floor leading into the passageway.

Behind EF, towards the horizon, the ground has been more deeply excavated, and towards the backs of the walls that form the sides of the opening can be seen two preserved structures, one on each side of the passage. Through the aperture the subfloor of Court A is visible, and behind that, on the far side of Court A (as we look), are the walls and W corner of room 27. Immediately to the right of this (again as we look), behind the interior part of DEGH that forms the block on the right side of the gate's opening, a row of bricks can be made out, and this is possibly the preserved remnant of a pavement floor. To the right of that is a low section of

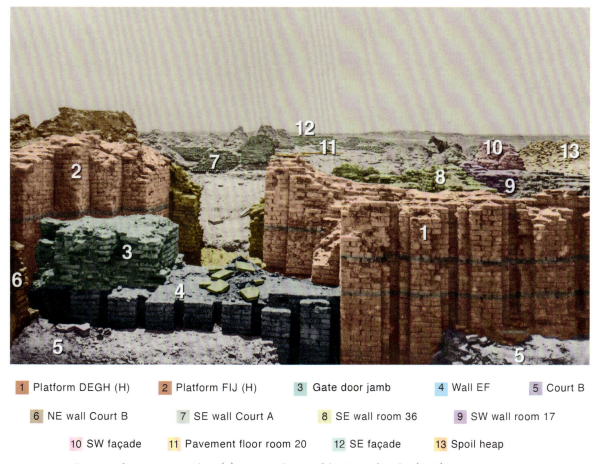

1	Platform DEGH (H)	2	Platform FIJ (H)	3	Gate door jamb	4	Wall EF	5	Court B
6	NE wall Court B	7	SE wall Court A	8	SE wall room 36	9	SW wall room 17
10	SW façade	11	Pavement floor room 20	12	SE façade	13	Spoil heap

FIGURE 119. Sarzec and Heuzey 1912, Pl. 50 (2): A second view of the Gate of Gudea (1888).

brickwork that is most likely a fragment of wall from room 20. To the right of the horse, behind room 17, the fairly prominent piece of wall is a preserved section of the SW façade, and to the right of that, on the extreme edge of the photo, is a spoil heap. The subfloor of Court B is visible in the foreground of the photo, where it appears truncated in front of the right corner of the gateway (the part of DEGH that is closest to the front of the photo). To the left of the subfloor of Court B, at the very front of the photo, the preserved section of wall perpendicular to block FIJ is the wall that forms the W side of Court B. In the background, behind FIJ, is a large heap of deposits.

The two images that make up Pl. 50 (1 and 2), which both show the Gate of Gudea, give an indication of the excavation sequence, but also of the construction phases of the architecture. They are especially informative when viewed in conjunction with the first two photos taken by Sarzec, Pl. 53 (1) and Pl. 53 bis (1) (Figs. 122 and 123 below).

FIGURE 120. Sarzec and Heuzey 1912, Pl. 51 (1): The external face of the Ur-Bau wall.

1 Spoil heap

2 Wall SE room 28

3 Wall SW room 26

4 Wall BC

5 Hellenistic backfill

Sevelinges, Subterranean Wall of Ur-Bau: Exterior (1888). Sarzec and Heuzey 1912, Pl. 51 (1)

This photo, taken looking north-west, shows the exterior of the Ur-Bau wall (ABC on Heuzey's New Plan), which extends below a perpendicular wall that faces the viewer in the background, with a higher wall on the left (Fig. 120). Since the internal part of the Ur-Bau wall was fitted with three buttresses, which are visible on Heuzey's New Plan and Sarzec's Maquette, it can be deduced that this photo was taken from the S corner of room 26, looking north-west. The wall on the left is therefore the SW wall of room 26, and the wall facing the camera a couple of metres into the distance is the N corner of room 27. As is also seen on the Maquette, the Ur-Bau wall is interrupted just after the third buttress, presumably where it had been previously damaged, certainly before 1881 and possibly in antiquity. Towards the right of the Ur-Bau wall must be the NE façade wall, which also marked the outer limit of the excavations. Next to the Ur-Bau wall in the background is a spoil heap.

The photo clearly shows the superimposition of room 27 on top of the Ur-Bau wall, while a comparison of the Ur-Bau construction with the wall on the left in the foreground provides an insight into the different kinds of bricks that were used at different phases of the construction. Sarzec mentions that the fired Ur-Bau bricks were 0.47 m × 0.47 m and therefore considerably larger than the Gudea (or reclaimed Gudea) fired bricks with indicative measurements of 0.32 m × 0.32 m that were used in the wall on the left, but this is not obvious in the photo, probably because of the angle from which it was taken. The way the Ur-Bau wall inclines steeply down from left to right clearly contrasts with the wall to the left, which appears flat on top, but the slope of the Ur-Bau wall could be the result of post-construction deformation. The exterior of the Ur-Bau wall is smooth and well worked, and this fits well with the idea that this is the external face of the Ur-Bau platform. As mentioned in Chapter 23, Sarzec's stated height of 1.1 m for the buttresses is presumably incorrect. It is extremely difficult to distinguish between some of the courses of bricks, especially towards the bottom of the photo, but there would appear to be between twenty-two and twenty-four, giving an approximate height of 2 m for the wall's external face (as calculated above).

Sevelinges, Subterranean Wall of Ur-Bau: Interior (1888). Sarzec and Heuzey 1912, Pl. 51 (2)

The second photo of the Ur-Bau wall (Fig. 121), which was taken looking west-north-west, shows the interior of the wall with its three buttresses. Contrasting with the smooth outer face, this side of the wall is rough and poorly finished, as are the buttresses. In all likelihood, this further confirms the theory that the buttresses served a structural rather than a decorative purpose. The entire structure, which formed the façade of the underlying Ur-Bau platform, was filled with compacted mud-bricks, and it is highly probable that the buttresses provided reinforcements to help contain the softer material within the fired-brick external walls. The roughness of the brickwork again makes it tricky to calculate the number of courses that make up the buttresses, but there would appear to be about twenty-three or twenty-four, approximately the same number as on the external face shown in the previous photo. Contrary to Sarzec's recorded figure of 1.1 m, this would indicate height of about 2 m for the buttresses (as also noted above), or perhaps a little less if the slope of the wall is taken into account.

Sarzec, Excavations of 1889: The Corner Block of the Gate of Gudea (Palace of Tello). Sarzec and Heuzey 1912, Pl. 53 (1)

This photo of the Gate of Gudea was taken looking east (Fig. 122). The wall in the centre of the photo that is decorated with three-step recesses is part of DEGH (on Heuzey's New Plan). Behind and above DEGH (in the shadows to the right of centre) are two men who are standing in room 36. To the left of DEGH, lower down and spanning the floor of the gateway, is wall EF, while above and behind that, a little further into the background, can be seen block FIJ, which forms the step-recessed NE corner of the Gate of Gudea.

On top of EF can be seen the remnants of the gate's NE buttress wall, and a substantial wall structure can be made out in the shadows to the left of wall FIJ. Though its features are obscured by the lack of light in this part of the photo, this wall, which is situated in front of and adjoining FIJ, must be the wide wall between rooms 30 and 32 on one side, and between rooms 29 and 31 on the other side, adjacent

FIGURE 121. Sarzec and Heuzey 1912, Pl. 51 (2): The inside face of the Ur-Bau wall.

to Court A (on the right as we look). Contained inside this broad structure must be the Adadnadinakhe wall that is labelled OP on Heuzey's New Plan. Perpendicular to it and extending out towards the left edge of the photo is the NE wall of Court B, with the courtyard on one side and rooms 32 and 33 on the other. Behind this, in the distance, can be seen the remains of walls that must have belonged to the rooms around Court C. In front of the NE wall of Court B, in the middle foreground and on the left as we look, there is a pile of seeming debris that has apparently been dumped in an area that must be the interior of Court B. It is possible that spoil was left there, perhaps temporarily. In the immediate foreground of the photo, on the right, is the NE wall of room 17, which abuts onto or perhaps partially encloses DEGH, the main block forming the SW side of the Gate of Gudea. The opening in the centre of the foreground, to the left of the NE wall of room 17, is entrance J (as marked on Sarzec's Plan A), and to the left of that, in the bottom left corner of the photo, is the SW wall of Court B.

The photo shows that the NE wall of room 17 met DEGH, and this provides further insight into the construction history of this part of the building, indicating that DEGH must have been built first, and that the lower wall, EF (spanning the entrance to the gateway), was erected before the buttress walls

Photographs of the Early French Excavations 365

FIGURE 122. Sarzec and Heuzey 1912, Pl. 53 (1): The Gate of Gudea (1889).

on top of it that were used to narrow the gateway passage. The next phase was the building of the NE wall of room 17 (abutting onto DEGH in the foreground), along with platform D', and these two structures formed entrance J (as marked on Plan A). It cannot be seen in the photo, but wall OP (on Heuzey's New Plan) was constructed next, after which Court B was built, together with its surrounding rooms (of which the SW wall of rooms 32 and 33 can be seen in this picture). The photo also shows the vertical face of wall DEGH, which leans backwards from the bottom to the top and the left to the right as we look, and the same is true of the block as a whole. This raises the interesting question of whether the inclination was an intentional feature of the architecture, or whether it resulted from the later erosion or compacting of the supporting mud-brick fill behind the wall.

Sarzec, Excavations at the Palace (1895): The Gate of Gudea Completely Cleared; the Wall of Adadnadinakhe. Sarzec and Heuzey 1912, Pl. 53 bis (1)

Taken looking towards the south-east, this photo (Fig. 123) shows Sarzec's completed excavation of the Gate of Gudea, with the buttressed wall DEGH on the right, the narrow opening with its stepped recesses in the centre and FIJ (the NE side of the gate) to the left of that. Still further to the left, and abutting onto FIJ, is the buttressed Adadnadinakhe wall (OP on Heuzey's New Plan). At the base of the structure, spanning the floor of the alcove that leads into the gateway passage, is a plinth that extends left and right below FIJ and DEGH, and disappears from sight to the left. At this stage of

366 The Mound of the Palace

| 1 | Platform DEGH (H) | 2 | Platform FIJ (H) | 3 | Blocking wall | 4 | Wall OP |
| 5 | Hellenistic backfill | 6 | Hellenistic backfill | 7 | SE wall Court A |

FIGURE 123. Sarzec and Heuzey 1912, Pl. 53 bis (1): The Gate of Gudea completely exposed (1895).

the excavations, the one-step recessed wall (EF) had been removed. At the back of the opening is a low blocking wall that is preserved to a height of twenty-three courses in its left corner and to a height of eight courses (about 0.5 m) in its centre. Some discolouration on the left wall of the gate's entrance area (part of FIJ) can be seen up to about the same height of eight courses or 0.5 m. Behind the opening, Hellenistic backfill in Court A is visible. In the distance, to the left of the two men who are standing behind the centre of the opening, is the NW wall of room 27.

By the time this picture was taken, the low-lying platform D′, which is seen in the foreground of previous photos, had been removed, so that deposits below wall OP are now visible on the left. Judged by comparison with the adjacent courses of brickwork on FIJ, these deposits are about 1 m deep. No traces of wall can be seen in the deposits below OP, and this suggests that any such lower walls were removed to make way for its construction. Wall OP has different buttresses from those that articulate DEGH on the opposite side of the gate. The left side of the gate (FIJ) and the buttressed wall OP (to its left) lean in different directions and are not bonded. An exception to this is in the centre of the corner formed by the meeting of OP and FIJ, about eleven courses down from the top of the meeting point, where at least two bonding bricks have been laid across the corner.

This photo again demonstrates the variety of construction activities that were carried out around the Gate of Gudea at different epochs. Considered as parts of the same structure, the lower bases of DEGH and FIJ predated wall OP. The lower wall (EF), which was removed by the time the picture was taken, reached up to the bottom of OP and must also therefore have predated OP. The construction of the lower blocking wall towards the back of the opening is more problematic. Its stratigraphic position, ascending from the level of the original plinth that spanned the gateway, suggests that this blocking wall was part of the first phase of construction. The fact that no clear separation between this wall and FIJ can be made out raises some questions: was this wall built up to the height of the opening, or did it form a step in the middle of the opening, with the buttressed walls on either side being used to narrow the gateway passage? Platform D′, which has been removed from the foreground of the picture, formerly rose to a higher level than the base of EF and therefore postdated the latter. It is remarkable that wall EF (seen in previous photos, but removed by the time this one was shot) was decorated with one-step recessed buttresses because it suggests that at least part of it was originally visible. Wall EF was about 1 m high, as can be estimated by comparison with the adjacent brickwork, and some faint discolouring can be seen up to about the same height as the discolouration on the gateway walls. This might suggest that EF was used at some point in the construction phases to raise the floor of the gateway passage, but since 1 m is a considerable increase, this interpretation alone may not fully explain EF's purpose.

Sarzec, Excavations at the Palace (1895): The Continuation of the Wall of Adadnadinakhe. Sarzec and Heuzey 1912, Pl. 53 bis (2)

This photo (Fig. 124), taken looking in a SW direction, records the continuation of the wall built by Adadnadinakhe, which is the buttressed wall on the left (OP on Heuzey's New Plan). Below the buttresses, the image shows a foundation made of varying courses of bricks, with four courses forming the foundation that is seen in the immediate foreground on the left. Centrally, the wall is somewhat damaged, particularly towards the bottom, where the upper course of the foundation seems

FIGURE 124. Sarzec and Heuzey 1912, Pl. 53 bis (2): The continuation of the Hellenistic NW façade (OP).

also to be missing. At this point the foundation steps up one course, while foundation fill is clear below the wall along its whole extent. A different type of deposit can be seen heaped up just behind the damaged central area of the wall, where a more compact deposit (lighter in colour and with a finer texture) is discernible. At the end of OP can be seen the buttresses of block DEGH (visible in previous photos on the right side of the Gate of Gudea). In this photo and from this angle, the marked slant of DEGH is particularly clear when contrasted with the upright verticals of OP. The wall on the right, with its end directly facing the camera, is the NW wall of room 30.

Sarzec, The Exedra Uncovered beneath the SE Wing of the Palace (1900). Sarzec and Heuzey 1912, Pl. 61 (top)

Looking southwards, this photo shows the exedra, as it was called by Heuzey—the apparently self-standing structure that was uncovered below the S corner of the Palace (Fig. 125). Labelled N on Heuzey's New Plan, it is made up of three walls. Its NE wall, topped with at least four courses of bricks, was built with some overhang, which suggests the structure was originally set into the mound. The edge of the pit that has been dug in order to reveal it is visible on the left of the photo, scarred with vertical pick marks. Towards the right is the start of a series of spoil heaps.

Sarzec, The Cistern Uncovered beneath the SE Wing of the Palace (1900). Sarzec and Heuzey 1912, Pl. 61 (bottom)

In this photo, taken looking north, can be seen the cistern block that was uncovered below the SE wing of the Palace (Fig. 126). It is in the large depression in the centre and on the left, where the workmen are standing. The walls of the exedra (N on Heuzey's New Plan, and the subject of Pl. 61 (top)) are visible in the immediate foreground. On the exedra's NE wall

FIGURE 125. Sarzec and Heuzey 1912, Pl. 61 (top): The exedra.

Photographs of the Early French Excavations   369

| 1 Structure N | 2 Cistern block KL | 3 Hellenistic backfill | 4 SE façade wall |
| 5 SW wall room 27 | 6 NE façade wall | 7 Court A | |

FIGURE 126. Sarzec and Heuzey 1912, Pl. 61 (bottom): The cistern block.

can be seen a ledge projecting inwards that is referred to in the text as a 'bench'—hence the name exedra, which implies a meeting room equipped with seats. Behind structure N can be seen the edge of the excavation pit in which it was found buried. The prominent wall to the left of structure N, in the middle distance and below the tent, is what is left of the Palace's SE façade. The tent, incidentally, has been moved from its earlier position, as recorded on the Maquette. To the left of the SE façade is the broad pit that contains the cistern block, labelled KL on Heuzey's New Plan. Stratigraphically higher, the wall directly behind KL is the SW wall of room 27. To the left of this, further in the background and towards the upper left part of the photo, are remnants of the NE wall of Court A, or the NE façade wall shown in Pl. 49 (1 and 2) above.

Sarzec, The Cistern under the Palace with a View of the Foundations of the Ur-Bau Wall, looking South-West (1900). Sarzec and Heuzey 1912, Pl. 61 bis (top)

This photo (Fig. 127), which was probably taken looking south-south-west, shows the cistern block under the SE wing of the Palace and the Ur-Bau wall (ABC on Heuzey's New Plan), which is visible in the lower left corner of the foreground. The AB part of the wall heads out of the picture towards the viewer on the left; the BC stretch, visible a little way to the left of AB, exits the picture perpendicular to AB. The high wall on the photo's extreme left edge is the Palace's SE façade (also forming the NW wall of rooms

370 The Mound of the Palace

| 1 Spoil heap | 2 Narrow Sarzec trench | 3 Wall AB | 4 Wall BC | 5 Platform core |
| 6 Cistern block KL | 7 SE façade wall | 8 NE wall Court A | 9 Hellenistic backfill |

FIGURE 127. Sarzec and Heuzey 1912, Pl. 61 bis (top): The cistern block and the base of the Ur-Bau wall.

23 and 24), behind which can be seen some heaps of spoil. Towards the centre of the photo, to the right of the group of workers, is the two-part cistern, KL (as marked on Heuzey's New Plan), with L on the far side, at a lower level than K. In front of KL (as we look) are some low structures made of bricks; most notably, between wall AB and KL there is a box next to a square construction made of bricks. These smaller structures are stratigraphically below the level of the SE façade wall to the left, but on more or less the same level as KL. The square structure has two steps, each of which is three courses of bricks high, while the NE facing wall of the highest step (facing the camera) has a shallow recess in its centre. The top of the square (with sides approximately three bricks in length) appears to form a platform that measures about 0.9 m × 0.9 m.

The prominent right-angled wall in the centre and on the right of the image is the NE wall of Court A. There is a large spoil heap in the photo's top right corner, and in the foreground are the lower edges of more such heaps. The wall of room 27 that is visible in Pl. 61 (bottom), on the far side of the cistern block, has here been removed. The area around KL, extending into the foreground between the right-angled NE wall of Court A and the spoil on the front edge of the picture, has been excavated laterally. In the foreground, in front of Court A's NE wall, can be seen a shallow cut, behind which are undisturbed deposits from Court A. This contrasts with the background, where long, narrow trenches can be seen cutting into the tell from the south-south-west. Between the group of two spoil heaps in the middle ground on the right side of the picture and the third heap that lies to the left of them is a deep, narrow trench that extends towards the viewer before bending to the right. To the left of the third heap just mentioned is another rather short, deep cut that runs diagonally into the mound.

Sarzec, The Cistern under the Palace with a View of the Foundations of the Ur-Bau wall, looking North-East (1900). Sarzec and Heuzey 1912, Pl. 61 bis (bottom)

This photo (Fig. 128), which was taken looking north-north-east, diametrically opposite to the viewpoint in the previous picture (Pl. 61 bis (top)), shows the other end of the cistern block. Structure L is closest to the viewer in the foreground, while the adjoining platform K is behind it, and M (the well) is to the right of K (all as marked on Heuzey's New Plan). Behind the well is a standing figure, and behind him is a square construction made of fired bricks, with sides that are three bricks long. This is the structure with two steps that is shown in Pl. 61 bis (top). To the left of it, on the other side of KL and wall AB, and behind the standing figures on the left side of KL, is another square structure made of fired bricks. It is difficult to see clearly, but this block is at least six courses of bricks high, while two superimposed stretches of brickwork that are laid out to form a step can be seen jutting out to the right (as we look).

In the middle distance, behind the cistern block, is the AB section of the Ur-Bau wall, with the BC section next to it, facing the camera on the right; the two parts of the wall

| 1 Spoil heap | 2 Sarzec cut | 3 Façade wall | 4 Hellenistic backfill | 5 Wall AB |
| 6 Wall BC | 7 Platform core | 8 Cistern block KL | 9 Well M | 10 Unexcavated area |

FIGURE 128. Sarzec and Heuzey 1912, Pl. 61 bis (bottom): A second view of the cistern block and the base of the Ur-Bau wall.

are not connected to form what would have been the W corner of the Ur-Bau platform, so that intersection must have been dismantled in the course of the excavations. The low mound behind BC (enclosed by AB and BC) appears to be the preserved remains of the internal mud-brick core of the Ur-Bau platform, in which a ramped trench has been cut that runs diagonally down from the top of the low mound on the right towards the centre of the tell in the middle of the photo. Steep excavation cuts are visible to the left of AB and also behind it, extending out to the left of the photo on the far side of the NE wall of Court A, which runs parallel to the front of the picture. In front of this NW wall is a trench, and in front of that, on the extreme left of the photo, is a mass of deep deposits. Forming a compact and homogeneous section, they make up the unexcavated ground in the centre of Court A. On the extreme right of the photo, behind the line of standing labourers, is the SE façade wall of the complex, which also forms the NW wall of room 23 and perhaps also of room 24. The sediments that can be seen below this wall must be Hellenistic backfill and Sumerian collapse material, and in front of it, where the labourers are standing, are the irregular excavation pits. At the back of the scene, behind all the excavations and spanning most of the width of the photo, are some high heaps of spoil.

Cros, The Gate of Gudea (1903). Unpublished

Taken looking south-east, this photo (Fig. 129) shows the DEGH block straight ahead, with the second block, FIJ, to the left, on the other side of the gate. The narrow gateway passage can be seen below (and to the left of) the standing figure; the buttresses of DEGH are visible below and in front of him on the right. At this stage of the excavations there is not much left of DEGH, while the low-lying platform D', seen in Pl. 50 (1) and Pl. 53 bis (1), has been completely dismantled. Unexcavated layers of Court A are discernible through the gate's opening, while the low wall across its base (with a height of 0.5 m) is also just about visible.

FIGURE 129. Cros, unpublished photo of the Gate of Gudea.

Cros, Excavations at the Foot of the Gudea Construction (1903). Unpublished

Taken looking south-west, this photo (Fig. 130) shows a group of workers in a deep sounding that has been sunk into the ground (possibly to a depth of around 2 m) below the base of structure DEGH that forms one side of the Gate of Gudea. There are two prominent standing men, with three seated figures behind them, and perhaps two more who are cut off at the right edge of the picture. It is interesting to note the bonding patterns of the buttresses. For example, the front face of the one closest to the viewer, which is two bricks wide, appears to be made with courses of half-bricks laid as stretchers, alternating with a central full brick that has half-bricks on either side of it to make up the corners.

The arrangement is comparable to that seen in the third buttress from the left in the reconstruction in Chapter 42 below (Fig. 229.7). The bottom two courses (again closest to the viewer) show some marked discolouration, presumably because they were beneath an original floor level. Thirty-two or thirty-three courses are visible in the buttress closest to the viewer, indicating a height of around 2.9 m (including mortar bondings of 17 mm, as discussed in Chapter 39) for this part of the structure, which is cut off at the top of the photo. At the other end of the wall, in the more faded part of the image, about thirty-seven or thirty-eight courses can be made out (including a course that is probably below ground level), representing a height of about 3.3 m. A line of damaged bricks can be seen running laterally across the entire façade, approximately six courses down from the recorded top of the

FIGURE 130. Cros, unpublished photo of the trench at the base of the Gate of Gudea.

front face of the buttress that is closest to the camera. This might have been caused by some rebuilding or raising of the structure, or it might have resulted from the different states of preservation of the upper and lower parts of the wall, particularly as the lower part of the wall was buried.

Cros, The Area to the North of the Palace: The Construction with Three Pedestals and the Stone Stairway. Cros 1910, Topographic View No. 11

This photo (Fig. 131), taken looking southwards in the area of the Gudea Steles between Tells A and B, has the French title: *Région au Nord du Palais: La construction aux trois piédestaux et l'escalier en pierre*. In the foreground it shows the structure of fired bricks and mud-bricks, here identified as a shrine, with the three brick pedestals abutting onto its SW wall; towards the top right corner can be seen the stone stairway set into the massive platform of mud-bricks. From the bottom right corner, running diagonally up across the photo towards the top left, can be seen the SW side of the building and the three pedestals: C', C and D (from right to left as we look). Seven courses of bricks can be seen in the NW face of C'; next to it on the left (to the south-east) pedestal C is two courses taller. Again on the left, further towards the south-east, is pedestal D, on which four courses of bricks can be made out in its upper section (the top course being partly made up of detached bricks). Below that, about half of the visible height of D seems to be plastered with the coating that Cros describes as *ciment*. The photo records that C', C and D all stand a couple of courses taller than the preserved parts of the mud-brick walls in the foreground.

At the base of the pedestals, along their NE face, stands a low section of mud-brick wall (not marked on the plan) that might be a plinth or the remains of the inner wall of the mud-brick shrine. To the left of D is the building's S corner, where the cement, which is in fact lime plaster, can be seen rising up the sides of the partly damaged mud-bricks. Towards the bottom left corner of the photo are the remains of part

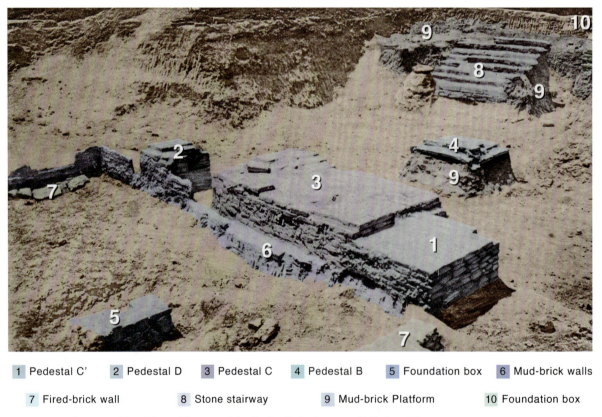

| 1 Pedestal C' | 2 Pedestal D | 3 Pedestal C | 4 Pedestal B | 5 Foundation box | 6 Mud-brick walls |
| 7 Fired-brick wall | | 8 Stone stairway | | 9 Mud-brick Platform | 10 Foundation box |

FIGURE 131. Cros 1910, View No. 11: The area of the Gudea Steles between Tells A and B.

of the foundation box in room F, and it must be presumed that the original floor of the shrine was slightly above the level of the top of the box.

To the right of C (to the south-west), and separated from it by a short distance, is the square pedestal that is labelled B on Cros's Plan H. The photo records a low rim or plinth that extends out from under the remains of a shallow square of bricks that is apparently made up of two surviving courses, the upper one of which is only partly preserved. Beneath the protruding plinth, which is just one brick high, the structure stands on a mass of soft deposits (not fired bricks) that appears to be either a soft foundation layer or a bed of mud-bricks. In the distance, behind column base B, towards the photo's top right corner, is the stone stairway, which is set into the edge of the mud-brick platform. By the time the photo was taken the two pillars or benches to the right and left of the flight's lowest step must have been removed, as was the foundation box to the left of the stairway (as we look). On the extreme right of the photo, near its top right corner, a few fired bricks are visible, and these must be part of the other foundation box. The mud-brick terrace has been removed from around the flight of steps, but it can be clearly discerned in the background—behind, beneath and on both sides of the stairway.

Cros, The Area to the North of the Palace: Buttress with Drainage Channel. Cros 1910, Topographic View No. 12

Entitled *Région au Nord du Palais: Contrefort avec caniveau*, this photo (Fig. 132) presents the fired-brick buttress, fitted with a central drainage channel, that was found in the area to the north of the main Tell A complex, in the vicinity of the shrine associated with the Gudea Steles and the stone stairway that are the subject of the previous photo (No. 11). It was probably taken looking towards the south-east, though that is not certain. The vertical fired-brick walls that form the drain can be seen along the right-hand side of the photo, where the installation abuts onto the mud-brick platform. Water cascaded down from the right onto the lower horizontal gutter, formed of two thick walls, that dominates the area directly in front of the viewer. The photo records that the vertical walls of the gutter on the right of the image were slightly inclined

FIGURE 132. Cros 1910, View No. 12: Drainage channel close to the area of the Gudea Steles between Tells A and B.

towards the mud-brick terrace behind them, and twenty-five courses of bricks survived on both sides. In the bottom right-hand corner of the photo is a low, narrow step or buttress that flanked the bottom of the gutter's vertical wall, at least on the side nearest to the camera (there may be slight traces of a similar low protrusion on the opposite side, but it might be a false impression caused by broken brickwork).

The thick brick walls that form the horizontal sides of the drain are the same width as the vertical wall, including the width of the low, narrow step or buttress. The cavity in the middle of the horizontal brick mass descends to a depth of about eight courses of bricks. The wall of the drain in the foreground of the photo is three bricks wide, while the top course is formed of two square bricks, with a half-brick on each side. The horizontal walls surrounding the water channel extend out onto the lower platform to a length of nine bricks, which suggests they are about 2.88 m long, assuming that these bricks also have indicative standard Gudea side lengths of 0.32 m.

Genouillac, Two Untitled Photos (1929–31). Genouillac 1936, Pls. 72 (1 and 2)

Though it is initially difficult to ascertain the exact location of these two untitled photos, taken by Genouillac sometime between 1929 and 1931, more information is contained in the second (Pl. 72 (2); Fig. 133), which provides a more panoramic view. Centrally, extending towards the photo's top right corner, can be seen two thick walls, probably parallel to each other, with the one behind slightly more distant from the viewer.

1 NE wall of niche 33   2 NW wall of room 31   3 NW façade wall
4 Platform DEGH (H)   5 Platform FIJ   6 Foundation box

FIGURE 133. Genouillac 1936, Pl. 72 (2): The Gate of Gudea (largely dismantled), seen from inside Court A.

Projecting forwards from the left end of the front wall are the remnants of an associated perpendicular wall that forms a corner. Presumably, the parallel wall at the back extends behind the front wall, which mostly obscures it. The right end of the rear wall is irregular, and this suggests that it might have had a perpendicular extension at this point, thereby forming a corner and projecting out towards the viewer. The two figures who are seated in the middle of the photo, just in front of the parallel walls, are resting on the remains of a lower wall that also runs parallel to the two just mentioned. This lower wall seems to be about five courses of bricks higher on the left, while on the right, at the same level as the seated men, are some remains that look like part of a corner block that extends into the picture away from the viewer.

To the right of the man with a cap (referred to by Genouillac as his *secrétaire* or clerk) is a foundation box on which can be seen a tablet and a copper figurine. The objects are not in their original locations inside the brickwork cavity and must therefore have been specially placed and arranged before being photographed. The truncated walls are probably all that is left of the Gate of Gudea following decades of destructive excavations. That being the case, the very low wall to the left of the man with the cap (behind him, at about the level of his waist) must be the SW block DEGH on Heuzey's New Plan, while the wall to the right, on which the two men are sitting, must be FIJ on the gate's NE side. The photo therefore shows the gateway passage from inside Court A, facing north-east. The higher parallel walls behind, which are part of the later Hellenistic construction, could be the NE wall of room 33, with the NE wall of room 31 behind it. To the left of these parallel walls, rising from the middle towards the top of the picture, is a pile of bricks, and behind or on top of that are about ten courses of a thick wall that runs perpendicular to the two main walls on the right. This could be part of the NW walls of rooms 30 and 32, or possibly the NW wall of Court C, depending on whether the surviving brickwork is a little further away from the camera than first appears. The other untitled photo in this group (Pl. 72 (1); Fig. 134), which is discussed further in Chapter 44, shows a close-up of the foundation box, with the tablet possibly still *in situ* and the copper figurine next to it, closer to the camera, in the middle of the image. If the tablet was photographed in its find location then this picture must have been taken before its more panoramic counterpart (Pl. 72 (2)).

FIGURE 134. Genouillac 1936, Pl. 72 (1): Close-up of the foundation deposit uncovered on the SE side of the Gate of Gudea.

Genouillac, Untitled (1929–31). Genouillac 1936, Pl. 73 (1)

This photo (Fig. 135) records a circular structure in front of a wall that has a corner at its right end (in the upper centre of the picture). The circular construction is built of a course of square bricks that are laid upright on their short, thick sides to form the outer surface of the cylindrical base. Superimposed on these uprights are two courses of bricks laid horizontally that appear to be rectangular (or half-bricks)—their short sides being visible on the outside face of the construction. On top of them comes another course of bricks laid vertically, above which the top of the structure is formed of bricks laid horizontally to create a dome that narrows or closes the cylindrical shape. These details help to locate the construction, which is marked on Genouillac's plan (Fig. 115), where this exact brickwork is indicated as the circular structure in front of the SE wall of Genouillac's *Chambre* I (Sarzec's room 10), captioned *Puits* I (well I). It is situated in Court C, in front of the wall that separates *Chambres* I and II (Sarzec's rooms 10 and 11). The wall behind the well in the photo is therefore the SE wall of *Chambre* I (Sarzec's room 10), meaning the picture was taken looking north. Note that, on the left of the photo, above the top of the well, about six courses of the SE wall can be seen. To the right of it is the N corner of *Chambre* I, and to the right of that, in the shadowy

FIGURE 135. Genouillac 1936, Pl. 73 (1): The well inside Court C.

background, would have been one of Genouillac's small-gauge railway tracks that he laid for the removal of spoil. The photo documents the position of the well below the level of the Palace walls.

Genouillac, Three Untitled Photos (1929–31). Genouillac 1936, Pl. 73 (2–4)

Three more photos that were taken by Genouillac are not reproduced here. Pl. 73 (2) shows a figure who appears to be an adult man sitting on a circular structure, the interior of which has been excavated. The horizontal brickwork descends below ground level to a depth of at least seven courses. Behind and to the left of the seated figure, next to the underground construction, are eleven courses of a half-preserved circular wall, which is a section of the superimposed well structures found in the N corner of Court A, as illustrated on Genouillac's plan. Comparing the brickwork seen in the photo with the plan, it seems that the photo was taken looking south, and that the mounds in the background are spoil heaps rising above the unexcavated floor of Court A. Pl. 73 (3) shows a young boy sitting on the rim of a partly collapsed circular construction, of which at least twenty courses are visible. The walls in the side of the structure facing the camera are about three bricks wide. In the background are some high spoil heaps, and just behind the brickwork is the edge of a trench. The details indicate that the photo shows the well (*Puits* III) in Court B on Genouillac's plan, and that the picture was taken looking west. Finally, Pl. 73 (4) records the well that was also the subject of Genouillac's Pl. 73 (1), but which is seen in this image from the opposite direction, looking west. The photo clearly illustrates how the well was built of bricks laid vertically and horizontally, and gives a good view of the narrowing dome-like structure that formed its top. The wall in the photo's top right corner is the S corner of *Chambre* I on Genouillac's plan (Sarzec's room 10 on Plan A). Behind it, and to the left, is the SW wall of *Chambre* II (Sarzec's room 11).

CHAPTER 26

The French Legacy: Challenges and Preserved Treasures

BASED ON THE PHOTOS, PLANS AND REPORTS THAT were produced by the French explorers, it is possible to identify the different excavation techniques and strategies that were employed on Tell A in the late nineteenth century and the early part of the twentieth century. When he undertook his first excavations on the mound, Sarzec began by opening long, narrow exploratory trenches that followed N–S and E–W orientations. In addition, he dug broad ramped trenches, working inwards from the edges of the tell to create wide cuts that sloped down towards its centre. In the centre itself, he levelled the remains horizontally by shaving off wide archaeological horizons. At targeted locations he also opened deep, narrow rectangular soundings, for example in Court A (on Sarzec's Plan A; Fig. 111), and these were always made at the bases of the fired-brick walls, following the lines of the walls' foundations.

With most of the tell and the upper levels of architecture having been previously revealed by Sarzec, Cros embarked on lower-lying excavations in the central area of the mound. In particular, he opened a deep rectangular sounding at the base of the Gate of Gudea. The photos and reports confirm that he dug down far enough to reach remains from the Presargonic period, and that this was done via a systematically excavated, well-designed trench. In addition, Cros targeted hitherto undisturbed remains that lay on the perimeter of the mound, notably in the area of the Gudea Steles between Tells A and B, where he uncovered the edge of Tell A's lowermost platform terrace. Embedded in the mud-brick mass he found the stone stairway that was constructed in Gudea's reign to give access to the upper levels of the complex, and opposite the stairway he uncovered the small shrine in front of which were found fragments of the Gudea Steles. He also discovered the superbly made drainage facility that is the subject of his View No. 12 (Fig. 132).

Following in Cros's footsteps, Genouillac opened a series of rectangular and square trenches in the N part of the collection of structures that were still known as the Palace. On the plan that he made (Fig. 115) these trenches seem to show well-defined excavations, but the photos reveal that they were in fact rather untidy. His plan and the accompanying section, which together show the exact locations of his soundings, indicate that by the time he collated his records, *Chambres* I, II and III (as labelled on Genouillac's plan) had been excavated to a depth of perhaps 2 m, though it is difficult to be precise as no scale bar is provided. A number of additional deep soundings were opened, namely: the Trench of the Well (*Tranchée du Puits*) in front of *Chambre* II; the Central Trench (*Tranchée Centrale*) in front of the Gate of Gudea and by platform D' (as marked on Heuzey's New Plan); the Trench of the Gate of Gudea (*Tranchée de l'Esplanade de Gudea*); the West Trench (*Sondage Ouest*) south-west of the Trench of the Gate of Gudea; and a broad East Trench (*Tranchée Est*) to the north-east of the Trench of the Gate of Gudea.

The combination of wide ramped trenches, in conjunction with horizontal levelling and deep soundings, eventually created a rectangular depression in the centre of Tell A, with the area where the deepest excavations had been initiated located to the north-west. At first, the spoil discarded by the French was deposited in the immediate vicinity of the trenches, covering the edges of the tell. The result of this was that the excavators eventually dug themselves into a central area that was surrounded by great masses of dumped materials—a haphazard arrangement that impeded their work. To counter these self-made obstacles, the first row of spoil heaps was breached in places to allow later discards to be evacuated between and behind the first generation of heaps. In consequence, when the excavation history is considered systematically, it becomes clear that the French works that were carried out over several decades had the unintended effect of inverting the topography of Tell A. When Sarzec arrived at the site, the central area of Tell A was the highest point of the mound, and its sides sloped down to the surrounding lower ground. This was, of course, mainly a reflection of the way the mound had been constructed by its original Sumerian planners and builders. Conversely, by the time the French had completed their work in the early 1930s, Tell A had been reshaped as a roughly rectangular central depression that was surrounded by generations of high spoil heaps, arranged in rows that radiated outwards from the sides of the crater towards the tell's circumference.

The basic achievements of the French excavations were to reveal the presence of the Hellenistic complex on Tell A and to confirm the existence of deeper and therefore older archaeological deposits beneath it. In their successive reports, plans and photos they described the Hellenistic building and noted its position in relation to antecedent structures. Using the French findings as a starting point, it is therefore possible to outline a chronology for the entire excavated construction, breaking it down into two main phases (plus definable subphases) that can be corroborated with respect to recovered material remains. The Hellenistic phase, which was initiated by Adadnadinakhe, was undertaken in three subphases. The first works were centred around Court A, when the OP wall (on Heuzey's New Plan; Fig. 114) was built as the principal NW façade, incorporating the earlier Gate of Gudea and platform H′ (which is labelled on Sarzec's Plan A, but not on Heuzey's New Plan). The second subphase included the extension of the building to the north-west, with the addition of a new sector around Courts B and C. This was undertaken in conjunction with the construction of substantial new NW and NE façade walls that were decorated with half-columns and possibly also stepped recesses. Next came a renovation phase, in which gate M was blocked and structures O, O′ and O″ (on Sarzec's Plan A) were added. This Hellenistic building was eventually destroyed by fire.

The Lagash II phase, which happened around 2,000 years before the time of Adadnadinakhe, can be broken down into two broad subphases. First, the Ur-Bau platform was built, as represented by walls ABC on Heuzey's New Plan. Secondly, the Ur-Bau construction was incorporated into an enlarged complex that was built during the reign of Gudea. In addition, the evidence provided by the remains of the Gate of Gudea, together with KL (the cistern block) and M (the well) on the opposite side of Court A (all as marked on Heuzey's New Plan), indicates that several rebuilding phases were carried out after the time of Gudea. The blocking wall that was found in the back part of the Gate of Gudea was probably built before the construction of wall EF, which was contemporaneous with the raising of both platform D′ and the SW block DEGH. The cistern block and well (KL and M) in the SE part of the complex were possibly built with reused bricks.

Importantly, the French accounts of the bondings used to connect some of the walls, and the French interpretations of the building sequence, clearly suggest that later structures incorporated elements of the earlier architecture. An in-depth assessment of the French excavation results highlights that, throughout the tell's long architectural history, floors and superimposed structures were repeatedly raised. This is exemplified in the multiple rebuilding phases around the Gate of Gudea, as well as in the rebuilding phases evident in the wells, and the stratigraphic anomalies arising from the fact that the passageway (presumably a stairway) leading to H (on Sarzec's Plan A) was found below the foundations of later walls. The repeated raising of the floor levels, it should be noted, was carried out in conjunction with the rebuilding or extension of existing walls and the erection of new walls during successive construction phases. The overall topography of the tell, which, in antiquity and still today, slopes down from the south-east to the north-west, further complicates the situation. The slope is manifested in the photos and in the measurements of the preserved courses of some of the walls. For example, the floor beneath Court C, which is associated with Adadnadinakhe's OP wall and was constructed before the extension of the Hellenistic NW wing, was actually found at a lower level than the floor of Court A, behind the gate of Gudea. This meant that the building of the later NW extension of the Hellenistic Palace involved the raising of an extended area in front of the old façade (OP).

The incorporation of the remains of the Gate of Gudea into the base of wall OP, which was the principal façade of Adadnadinakhe's new building, demonstrates that the Sumerian gateway façade served as the structural anchor for the Hellenistic building. In addition, as is also revealed in the archaeological record, it shows that significant digging, levelling and backfilling were undertaken in preparation for the construction of the Adadnadinakhe complex. These building activities, the last of which were carried out some 2,000 years before Sarzec started excavating the site, had already reshaped Tell A to a considerable extent before the French arrived there.

The most severe alterations were inflicted on the site during the century and a half that followed Sarzec's arrival, above all as a consequence of the destructive methods of the French excavators. From 1888 to 1895 Sarzec excavated and demolished the Gate of Gudea down to what he believed to be its original levels. He removed the intricate series of walls in front of wall OP, and in 1900, while searching for constructions from the time of Ur-Bau that predated the Hellenistic complex, he removed many walls from the upper SE part of the Palace. More destruction then occurred: first, because the excavations left the ancient walls exposed to the elements; and secondly, because the uncovered remains were used as a source of building materials both by local people and most devastatingly by the excavators themselves. In 1904 Cros built his dig house with collapsed inscribed bricks from Tell A, and Genouillac repeated the process in 1929, when he built his own shelter. Indeed, as is illustrated in the photographs taken during Genouillac's campaign, by the time his excavations came to an end there was very little left of the Hellenistic structure.

Especially problematic is the fact that some structures were not recorded before they were removed. For example, the final photographs taken by Sarzec in the SE part of the Palace (Pl. 61 bis; Figs. 127 and 128) show fired-brick structures at the same level as the three-part installation (KLM) and the Ur-Bau walls, but these are not logged in any of Sarzec's notes and reports, and they are not marked on Heuzey's New Plan. Moreover, Sarzec's repeatedly mentioned failure to recognise the importance of mud-bricks as a building material led to an exclusive focus on fired-brick remains, and this resulted in the extensive cutting, truncation, removal and destruction of softer earlier deposits. To exacerbate the terrible damage inflicted by the excavators, from the first French excavations until after the Gulf Wars of the late twentieth and early twenty-first centuries, the site was repeatedly left vulnerable to looters.

As all of this makes abundantly clear, prior to the work carried out by the British Museum team, the chances that new investigations might reveal undisturbed archaeological deposits on Tell A seemed vanishingly small. Nonetheless, the French reports, plans and photos indicated portions of the site where good archaeological deposits might have survived. These were judged to be at a number of key locations: below the spoil heaps at the edges of the main excavation area; in the central parts of presumed open areas, including Court A; and in the few places where structures, mainly wells, had been sunk deep into the ground. The French excavations also presented opportunities, especially where their large-scale digging, including the removal of structures associated with later building phases, made earlier deposits accessible. In particular, the French dug down to Early Dynastic levels that could be reaccessed by removing French backfill, along with wash and sediments that had accumulated since the 1930s.

In order to use the information made available by the French pioneers, thus turning challenges into opportunities by targeting areas with preservation potential and identifying openings that might lead to earlier levels, it was vital to analyse and plot the locations of the previous trenches that were opened on Tell A (Fig. 136). The plans, particularly the first two (Sarzec's Plan A and Heuzey's New Plan), which include indications of scale and north-pointing arrows, could be aligned with the present-day topography of Tell A. This exercise, together with ground-truthing, clarified the whereabouts of the striking topographical scars that had been left by the French works. More specifically, the narrow-gauge railway tracks laid by Genouillac to evacuate excavation spoil were fortunately included on his plan and could therefore be plotted and used to determine the orientation and scale of his drawings. The selection of new excavation areas was guided by the topography of the tell, which not only assisted the design of an excavation strategy, but also highlighted the way information gleaned from the tell's micro-topography could be used to analyse and understand the French works. Combined with observations made on the ground, the study of the French documents resulted in the following hypotheses: 1) as a consequence of the French excavations, the topography of Tell A had become inverted to form a central depression surrounded by high spoil heaps; 2) undisturbed archaeological deposits might have been preserved at the edges of the excavation area beneath the spoil heaps;

The French Legacy: Challenges and Preserved Treasures 383

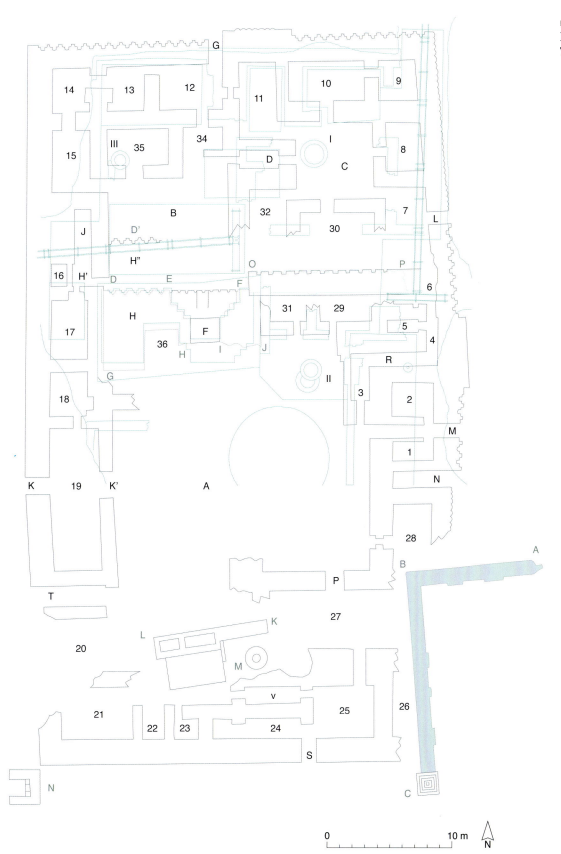

FIGURE 136. Heuzey's New Plan and Genouillac's plan of Tell A superimposed.

3) the French did not carry out deep excavations in Court A, which therefore might also conceal preserved archaeological deposits; 4) the NW area of the complex, which had been most deeply excavated, offered the best opportunity to reach earlier archaeological layers below the French excavations.

The following chapters present a detailed analysis of the topography of Tell A, including its central depression and encircling spoil heaps. The excavation of the spoil heaps and French cuts, together with wash deposits and modern gullies, helped the British Museum team to plot the locations and sequencing of the French excavations and also to assess the impact of their efforts on the site. This vital diagnostic work led to a new understanding of the mound and aided the discovery of invaluable archaeological deposits from a range of periods dating back to Sumerian times that have—almost miraculously—been preserved.

CHAPTER 27

The Mound of the Palace Today: A Landscape of Trenches and Spoils

WHEN THE BRITISH MUSEUM TEAM ARRIVED AT Tell A in 2016 the mound bore the visible scars of the twenty seasons of excavations that were carried out between 1877 and 1933, followed by eighty-three years of abandonment and erosion (Fig. 137). In appearance it was probably not unlike the no man's lands left behind in Verdun or the Somme after World War I. The excavation trenches from the first twenty seasons, and the way in which the early excavators managed the spoil heaps, had particularly profound impacts on the state of the site. Fortunately, the story of how the tell was excavated in the early days is told in the plans, reports and photos that have been described and analysed in great detail in preceding chapters. This information helped the team to understand the topography of the site as it was encountered in 2016 and to reconstruct what it must have looked like before the French excavations.

There were some other positives too. The destructive effects of the digs carried out by Sarzec and his successors were clear, but the tell also exhibited traces of work undertaken during the French campaigns that actually helped the British Museum team very precisely to plot the locations and ground plans of the principal structures on the mound. This facilitated the correlation of the French reports, plans and photos with the present-day physical reality of the site, enabling the team both to identify target areas for new research and to salvage whatever could be rescued from the scene of devastation. It also became possible to predict where the specific trenches and soundings excavated by the French predecessors were likely to be found, and that in turn allowed the team to identify the areas that were most likely to contain

undisturbed archaeological remains, notably under the many spoil heaps and in the vicinity of Court A (as marked on Sarzec's Plan A) at the heart of the sacred complex. In addition, a thorough understanding of the French records helped the team specifically to target deeper French trenches from which more recent archaeological layers had been removed, thus clearing the way for new soundings that aimed to uncover earlier archaeological deposits.

Tell A Prior to the British Museum Team's Excavations

The Central Depression and Microtopography

Perhaps the most important feature of Tell A as it presents itself to observers today is the central depression in the middle of the mound's summit and the associated microtopography of this broad, but relatively shallow crater (Fig. 138). The rectangular depression, which is visible both in the field and on images taken from overhead, runs through the centre of Tell A on a NW–SE alignment. Measuring approximately 45 m × 27 m, it is surrounded by sloping sides that are between 1.5 m and 2 m tall, starting at an overall height of about 15 m above sea level (the reference point for topographical heights in the discussion of Tell A) and rising to approximately 17 m. The base of the NW part of the rectangular depression, which is generally lower than the rest of the cavity, lies at a height of around 15 m. On the SE side the base level rises to 15.6 m, and it should be noted that the break of

FIGURE 137. Aerial view of Tell A, looking south, showing the walled sacred precinct and Tell K in the distance.

the slope generally follows a line that runs down diagonally from north to south through the rectangle. Also important is the fact that, in the S corner, some spoil has possibly slumped in from the tallest neighbouring spoil heap, known as Mount Sarzec (SH1), which towers up to a maximum topographical height of 20.5 m. The NW side of the principal rectangular depression seems also to contain a smaller, squarish hollow, measuring about 25 m × 30 m, of which the N and W corners are particularly well defined.

Archaeological Mounds and Spoil Heaps

The second extremely significant characteristic of Tell A that should be noted at the outset is the succession of smaller archaeological mounds and spoil heaps that encircle the tell. Before the British Museum team's excavations began, it was observed that Tell A is surrounded by a series of small rounded mounds, measuring between 6 m and 12 m in diameter, that seemingly demarcate an outlying concentric space, also generally rectangular in shape, that might once have enclosed an area of approximately 2 ha or 2.5 ha. In the site's current state of preservation only a few of these mounds are visible, particularly to the south of Tell A, where they appear to form two alignments that meet more or less at right angles, oriented north-east–south-west and north-west–south-east, respectively. The team compared these mounds with hillocks on the site displaying similar characteristics and orientations that were less disturbed by Sarzec, especially the ones that made up the area of the Gudea Steles between Tells A and B, to the north-east of Tell A, that were excavated by Cros. This suggested that some of the smaller mounds (or *monticules*, as Sarzec calls them) that are dotted around Tell A in quite large numbers might represent unexcavated archaeological traces of the contour of the sanctuary's lowest monumental platform, including the section of its NE façade that was identified by Cros precisely in the area of the Gudea Steles between Tells A and B.

Additionally, this series of smaller mounds or monticules can be expanded to include some of the other low-rising hillocks around Tell A that were excavated by Sarzec in his first

The Mound of the Palace Today: A Landscape of Trenches and Spoils 387

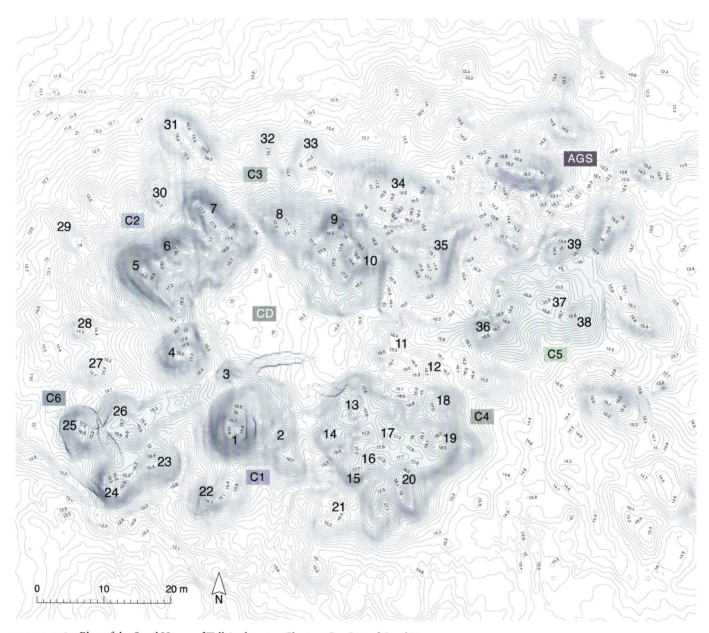

FIGURE 138. Plan of the Spoil Heaps of Tell A, showing Clusters C1–C6 and Spoil Heaps 1–39, together with the central depression (CD) and the area of the Gudea Steles between Tells A and B (AGS).

two seasons (1877 and 1878), notably the ones labelled R and T on Sarzec's general plan of the whole site (Plan B; Fig. 18), and the one to the south-east of Tell A that he refers to in the reports as S, but which is unfortunately not marked on any of the plans (see Sarzec and Heuzey 1912, pp. 71–3). Mound R, to the south-west of Tell A, yielded a set of four Lagash II foundation boxes inscribed in the name of Gudea. One of them was empty, but the other three all contained dedicatory copper pegs in the form of kneeling gods, together with inscribed stone tablets dedicated to Ningirsu's divine sons Igalim and Shulshaga to commemorate the construction of their shrines, Emehushgalanki and Ekitushakkilli, respectively. Whereas the low mounds between Tells A and B in the vicinity of the rather small building that was associated with fragments of the Steles of Gudea were well excavated by Cros, however, the contexts and precise locations of the deposits found in Sarzec's monticules R, S and T were not clearly recorded and cannot now be established with certainty. For example, it is not known whether the foundation boxes from monticules R and S were installed to commemorate the building of the expanded mud-brick platform that was established as the base for the Gudea's New Eninnu, or whether they instead related to supplementary shrines that were constructed in front of the massive platform, maybe close to the stairways that gave access to the tell's upper levels, as was the case with the set of installations discovered by Cros between Tells A and B. Alternatively, mound R might have housed a twin temple that included the two shrines of Igalim and Shulshaga that were closely connected to the New Eninnu, as noted in a number of ancient inscriptions, but this cannot be confirmed. One thing that does seem certain is that an identifiable series of lower humps or monticules around Tell A formed a more or less coherent rectangle that extended out equally on all sides of the main mound.

Clearly distinguished from these archaeological knolls are the spoil heaps that surround the central rectangular depression on Tell A. The highest heap, Mount Sarzec (SH1), which rises to a topographical height of 20.5 m and is located along the SW edge of the depression, is flanked by two smaller ones to the south-east (SH2) and to the north-north-west (SH3). These three together form a group that is referred to as Cluster 1. To the north-west of Cluster 1 is a rather large, isolated spoil heap (SH4) that rises to a topographical height of 18.9 m. The second highest spoil heap in the vicinity of Tell A (SH5), with an overall height of 19.9 m, is situated along the NW edge of the rectangular depression, where it is flanked by SH6 and SH7 to the north-east—the three together making up Cluster 2. Along the NE edge of the depression is Cluster 3, another group of three heaps (SH8–SH10), of which the tallest (SH9) reaches a topographical height of 19 m. Along the SE edge is Cluster 4, made up of a dispersed group of eight heaps (SH13–SH20), the tallest of which (SH19) rises to an overall height of 18.5 m.

Further away from the main buildings on Tell A than the series of clusters and heaps just described is a second concentric band of twenty spoil heaps (SH21–SH40), mainly grouped in the south-west and the east-north-east. The topography shows that this outer ring of spoil heaps was mainly deposited after the first set of heaps and clusters had been breached, and that they are made up of materials and spolia deriving from later Tell A excavations. The exceptions

are SH34 and SH35, which lie behind Cluster 3. In these cases, the fact that Cluster 3 appears to encroach upon SH34 and SH35 to the north-east suggests that they were laid down first. In all other instances, heaped remains in the outer band undoubtedly resulted from breaches made through the inner ring. This is particularly clear along the SW edge of the rectangular depression, where a track that cuts through the inner heaps leads to a group of dumps (Cluster 5), which is made up of four heaps (SH23–SH26), the tallest being SH26, which rises to a topographical height of 16 m. A similar state of affairs can be observed just to the north-west of Cluster 5, where a small fissure between SH4 and SH5 seems to lead to dumps SH27 and SH28 (with overall heights of 15 m and 14.7 m, respectively). In the N corner of the rectangular depression, on a SE–NW alignment, a pathway between Clusters 2 and 3 leads to two elongated spoil heaps, SH31 and SH32 (rising to heights of 15.1 m and 14.7 m, respectively). A little to the south-west of SH31 is SH30 (with a height of 14.7 m), which seems to have been created after a relatively minor path was cut between SH6 and SH7 in Cluster 2.

A marked opening that extends through the E corner of the rectangular depression leads to a scattered array of heaps (Cluster 6) that are made of spoil that was dumped further away from the central depression. This cluster consists of five heaps (SH36–SH40), with the tallest (SH36) reaching a topographical height of 16.9 m. The inner ring of spoil heaps was also breached in the S corner of the central depression, where a track leads to SH21, which has an overall height of 16.4 m. Behind Mount Sarzec (SH1) is SH22, which rises to a height of 16.7 m and does not seem to be related to Cluster 5, so it could have been approached via the opening that leads to SH21. The deposition histories of SH29 and SH33 are also more difficult to reconstruct as they are not clearly associated with tracks cut through the inner ring of spoil heaps, and they may therefore be connected with minor paths that branched out from the principal breaches, or with routes that possibly led over the heaps that make up the inner ring. Finally, to the north-east of Tell A, in the vicinity of Cluster 6, is another set of large spoil heaps that radiate out from around the remains of the elongated rectangular trench between Tells A and B that was opened by Cros in 1905.

Even before the British Museum team's excavations began, this data proved to be highly informative because it allowed the team to identify several phases of spoil heap formation that could be correlated with the long history of

French archaeological campaigns. In this regard, it should also be noted that, although Tell A was regularly excavated at least ten or eleven times between 1877 and 1930, the greater part of the mound in the central area that contained the so-called Palace was shaved off only in two seasons, namely Sarzec's campaigns of 1880 and 1881 (Seasons 3 and 4). The by-products of these expansive digs formed the first generation of enormous spoil heaps on the edge of the mound, around the main buildings (Clusters 1, 2 and 4; SH3, SH4, SH34 and SH35). More by accident than by design, these discarded residues sealed off the archaeological deposits that lay beneath them, protecting them from further investigation. Furthermore, the sequence of digging on Tell A was closely connected with the formation of successive spoil heaps because the extensive excavations generated the heaps. The relationships between the two can therefore be reconstructed by tentatively assuming a correlation between the locations of clusters and single heaps, on the one hand, and the locations and dates of the successive excavations that were carried out on the site between 1877 and 1930 on the other.

In consequence, as previously noted, the fact that Cluster 3 encroaches on SH34 and SH35 suggests that it was formed of second-generation discards, with SH34 and SH35 probably resulting from Sarzec's Seasons 3 and 4, when his focus was on exposing the NE frontage of the Hellenistic incarnation of the Tell A complex. This work was undertaken after a trench had been excavated on a NE–SW alignment, perpendicular to the NE frontage and extending down the sloping side of the mound. Chronologically, therefore, SH34 and SH35 must have been established between the time of the opening of the perpendicular NE–SW trench just mentioned and the later formation of Cluster 3, which must in turn have resulted from Sarzec's subsequent clearance of the interior of the so-called Palace that was built in Hellenistic times. It should also be recalled that Sarzec was unable to excavate in Tello between 1881 and 1888, when political circumstances made it inadvisable for him to travel to the region, but Cluster 3 is visible on a photo (Pl. 51 (1); Fig. 120) that was taken in 1888, when Sarzec returned to the site after his seven-year hiatus. It is therefore highly likely that Cluster 3 was created in that year.

Two more points of interest should be mentioned. On the one hand, Sarzec's later dumping of spoil in new locations outside the ring of first-generation of heaps is recorded on a photo (Pl. 61 (top); Fig. 125), taken in 1900, in which SH21 and SH22 are visible in the background, and this means that they must have been formed between 1888 and 1900; on the other hand, however, the fact that he also continued to add spoil from later digs to the inner ring of first-generation heaps is evidenced on other photos, notably Pl. 61 bis (bottom) (Fig. 128).

Nearly three decades later, in Seasons 16 and 17 (1929–30), Genouillac had no choice but to cut openings through the surrounding series of high dumps in order to evacuate his new spoils from the central area in which he concentrated his energies. The waste materials were removed on wheeled containers (essentially overground mine-cars) that ran on narrow-gauge railway tracks that extended out from key points in the middle of the mound, and the tracks are marked on the plan that he published in 1936, allowing their locations and routes to be traced. Genouillac's excavations resulted in breaches to the north between Clusters 2 and 3, and to the west between Cluster 1 and SH4. A fan-like third generation of heaps was thus created, radiating out from the main rectangular depression, and including Cluster 5, SH27, SH28, SH31 and SH32, and possibly also SH29, SH30 and SH33.

Though the chronology of Cluster 6 is less clear, an order of events for this rather dispersed set of heaps can be reconstructed. Three heaps (SH37–SH39) seem to have been deposited first, while SH36 and SH40, which are similar in shape and alignment, appear to have been dumped along the two sides of a path. It is worth mentioning, albeit tentatively, that a possible route across the surface of the platform that could have led to SH36 and SH40 might be visible in the photo taken in 1900 (Pl. 61 bis (bottom)), referred to just above. Finally, SH11 and SH12, which are apparently in the inner ring, in fact block the way to these outer spoil heaps and probably therefore represent the final phase of dumping in the direction of Cluster 6. It is therefore conceivable that they resulted from the final excavations carried out by Genouillac. The possible correlations (some of which are necessarily more speculative than others) between the sequence of digs and the associated formation of spoil heaps is laid out in Table 5.

New Excavation Areas Established by the British Museum Team (2016–22)

As well as providing concrete evidence of the extensive works that were carried out on Tell A by the early French explorers, the British Museum team's thorough examination of the

390   The Mound of the Palace

TABLE 5. The Chronology of Early Spoil Heap Formation on Tell A.

Date	Excavator	Season	Principal Archaeological Activities on Tell A	Associated Spoil Heaps
1877	Sarzec	Season 1	Limited trench opened in the E part of the tell.	First spoils possibly deposited to form SH34 and SH35.
1878	Sarzec	Season 2	Small-scale digging in the E and central areas.	Spoils possibly dispersed around the E side of the tell.
1879	Rassam	n/a	Limited soundings in the E part of the tell.	Spoils possibly added to SH35.
1880	Sarzec	Season 3	Large-scale digging in the central area.	First generation of spoil heaps (Phase I): Clusters 1, 2 and 4; SH3, SH4, SH34 and SH35.
1880–1	Sarzec	Season 4	Large-scale digging in the central area.	First generation of spoil heaps (Phase II): Clusters 1, 2 and 4; SH3, SH4, SH34 and SH35.
1888	Sarzec and Sevelinges	Season 5	Deep soundings in the N and W areas of the tell; excavations around the Ur-Bau platform; excavations around the Gate of Gudea; first photos of the Hellenistic Palace and Sumerian structures; first topographical plan of Tello (Plan B); first architectural plan of the main architectural ensemble on Tell A (Plan A).	Second generation of spoil heaps (Phase I): Cluster 3 (see Pl. 49 (1), which shows small heaps of Cluster 1; spoil heaps at the foot of Cluster 3 are also visible in Pl. 51 (1)); more possible first-generation dumping associated with the Gate of Gudea excavations, for example around SH4.
1889	Sarzec	Season 6	Excavations in the NW area of the tell.	Second generation of spoil heaps (Phase II): Cluster 3 (based on proximity); maybe also further dumping around Cluster 2.
1893	Sarzec	Season 7	Deep trench in the SE area of the tell; the Sumerian platform including the Ur-Bau wall.	Second generation of spoil heaps (Phase III): Cluster 6 to the east; possible additions to SH35.
1894	Sarzec	Season 8	Excavations below the SE part of the Hellenistic Palace; the Ur-Bau platform.	Second generation of spoil heaps (Phase IV): Cluster 6 to the east; possible additions to SH35.
1895	Sarzec	Season 9	Trenching in the central area focused on the Hellenistic Palace, the Gate of Gudea and the Adadnadinakhe wall (OP).	Second generation of spoil heaps (Phase V): possible further additions to SH4 and perhaps elsewhere.
1899	Sarzec	Season 10	No regular digging recorded.	
1900	Sarzec	Season 11	Deep soundings in the central area focused on the Hellenistic Palace and Court A.	Second generation of spoil heaps (Phase VI): Cluster 4, SH21 and SH22 existed by this date; additions to Cluster 3 and SH35 (see Pl. 61 (bottom) and Pl. 61 bis (bottom); the latter also shows a possible path across the Ur-Bau platform leading to SH36 and SH40, suggesting that Sarzec might have been responsible for part of Cluster 6).
1903	Cros	Season 12	Deep trench in the central area, but limited in extent.	Spoils possibly generally dispersed around the tell.
1904	Cros	Season 13	No regular digging recorded.	
1905	Cros	Season 14	No regular digging recorded; excavations around the small shrine and stone stairway between Tells A and B.	Spoil heaps to the north-east of Tell A.
1909	Cros	Season 15	No regular digging recorded; new fragments of the Steles of Gudea discovered in the vicinity of the shrine and stone stairway in the area between Tells A and B.	
1929	Genouillac	Season 16	Excavations in the N and W parts of the tell focused on the Hellenistic Palace, Sumerian ruins and Gudea foundation deposits.	Third generation of spoil heaps (Phase I): Cluster 5, SH27 and SH28; possibly SH31 and SH32; tentatively, perhaps also SH29, SH30 and SH33.
1929–30	Genouillac	Season 17	Soundings in the NW area of the main architectural ensemble.	Third generation of spoil heaps (Phase II): Cluster 5, SH27 and SH28; possibly SH31 and SH32; tentatively, perhaps also SH29, SH30 and SH33.
1930–1	Genouillac and Parrot	Season 18	No regular digging recorded.	
1931–2	Parrot	Season 19	No regular digging recorded.	
1932–3	Parrot	Season 20	No regular digging recorded.	

topography also confirmed the ways in which the French plans of the layout of the tell related to the actual ground surface. This understanding was aided in particular by the identification of the routes taken by the narrow-gauge railway tracks that were laid by Genouillac to facilitate the removal of his spoils (Fig. 136). In an attempt to place the correlation between the earlier French plans and modern survey plans on the firmest possible footing, a sounding was opened in the central area of the main rectangular depression to try to locate one of the most significant landmarks on Tell A—the sacred well of Gudea (M on Heuzey's New Plan; Fig. 114) that was situated in the central area of the mound, towards the SE end of the building detailed on Sarzec's Plan A (Fig. 111). The circular structure of fired bricks that was unearthed is shown in the photo taken by Sarzec (Pl. 61 bis (bottom)) that is also mentioned just above. It was assumed that, if this could be located, the French plans could be still more accurately correlated with the modern ones that were compiled during the course of the new fieldwork. In the hope that at least some of the fired-brick remains might have survived under the deposits with which the French trenching was filled, the team therefore estimated the position of the well and cut a small square trench measuring 3 m × 3 m in that exact spot, which lay within a massive French trench that was aligned north–south. Happily, the well was found just 0.1 m below the point where the earlier excavations had left off, and is marked as context 2143 on the British Museum team's plan of Tell A (Fig. 139).

Once the French plans of the tell were confidently correlated with the team's new plans, the relationship between the microtopography of the site and the history of the early sequence of excavations outlined above could also be confirmed. The main rectangular depression on top of the tell, which was the general excavation area opened up by the French pioneers, coincided with the site of the Hellenistic complex. The lowest part of the depression to the north-west was where the previous excavators (chiefly Cros and Genouillac) had opened their deep soundings. Cros focused especially on the area in the vicinity of the Gate of Gudea, where he excavated soundings that descended down far enough to reveal Presargonic deposits. Subsequently, Genouillac opened a further series of rectangular and square trenches in order to carry out further work around the Gate of Gudea and to re-excavate some previous cuts. In total, he carried out six more soundings in the NW part of the Palace complex.

With the plans of the Palace that were drawn by the French accurately plotted in the field, the team was also able to establish the position of the relatively unexcavated Court A on the generally higher SE side of the central depression.

Having completed this preliminary work, and following a thorough analysis of the French digs, the team decided upon the first new excavation areas. These were opened in 2016, when the N and W corners of Court A (Areas B2 and B3 on Fig. 139) were the first target. In addition, Area B1 in the NW part of the depression (north of the Gate of Gudea), where deep soundings had previously been opened, was established, with the aim of accessing earlier deposits that were presumed to lie below the Hellenistic and Lagash II structures. During the following seasons it became increasingly clear that the assumption that the French spoil heaps had protected underlying unexcavated deposits was correct. As a consequence, Areas B2 and B3 around Court A were enlarged and developed to incorporate extensive excavations below the adjacent spoil heaps.

During the first excavations that were carried out in 2016, Area B1 was set out as a square trench measuring 10 m × 10 m (with a surface area of 100 m^2); B2 measured 10 m × 15 m (150 m^2); and B3 was opened to extend B2 by 11 m to the west and 4 m to the south. In the spring of 2017 Area B1 was enlarged by 4 m towards the south over a width of 7 m, thereby adding 28 m^2 to its initial area. In the same year Area B4, measuring 15 m × 8 m (an area of 120 m^2), was laid out to the south of B3; also opened was B5, which extended 7 m from the NE corner of B2, covering 30 m of ground to the south of B2. Trench B5 was therefore aligned with the S edge of B4, adding 490 m^2 to the excavation area and extending across all the terrain between B4 and B2. Area B6 was laid out to the north of these central trenches and to the north-east of B1. Measuring 14 m × 6 m (80 m^2), B6 targeted the ground below the spoil heaps of Cluster 3.

In the autumn of 2017 work continued in trenches B1, B3, B5 and B6. Additionally, to the west of B3 and B4, a small trench (B7) with dimensions of 9 m × 9 m (81 m^2) was opened to give access to the layers beneath SH3. Lastly, in 2017 B8 was established along the S edge of B4 and B5, extending the central excavation zone further south by 5 m over a length of 33 m. In 2018 further work was carried out in B6 and B8, and the excavations were extended with the addition of B9 to the north-east of B1 and to the north-west of B6, allowing deeper excavations below the spoil heaps

392 The Mound of the Palace

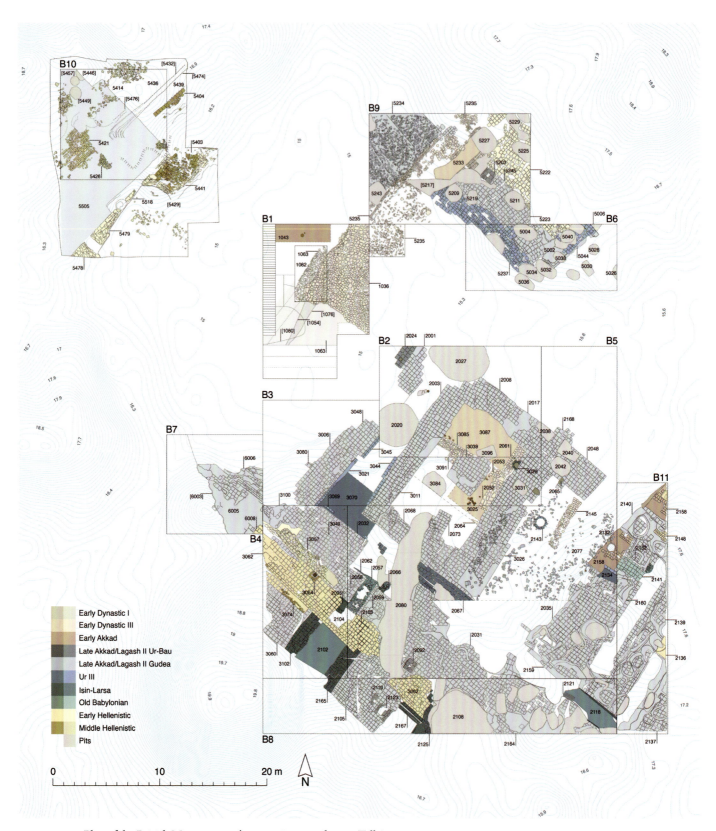

FIGURE 139. Plan of the British Museum team's excavation trenches on Tell A.

of Cluster 3. An extension was added to B1 (the first trench that was opened when the works began in 2016) to enlarge it on its S side. Initially measuring 10 m × 10 m, Area B1 was enlarged to take in a further 4 m × 7 m of ground, increasing the length of its W side to 14 m. Subsequently, in 2019 the excavations were developed in B5 and B9, and a new area (B10) was opened on the NW edge of the central depression to access layers below the spoil heaps of Cluster 2. Measuring 17.6 m × 12 m, B10 also included an E extension of 3 m along the S part of its E edge that increased its total area to 240 m². A further 175 m² was added to the excavations when B11 was extended by 5 m to the east of B5 and by 35 m to the south, along the entire E edges of B5 and B8. In 2021 the work focused only on B10 and did not go beyond the existing limits of the trench, so that, by the end of the 2021 season, the total excavated area on Tell A amounted to 1,955 m². Lastly, in the spring of 2022 Area B12 was set out to the north-west of B11, beyond the spoil heaps that encircle the central part of Tell A (Fig. 242). It began as a square cut (10 m × 10 m), which was aligned north-west to south-east, but it was subsequently extended until it eventually measured 13 m (north-west to south-east) × 23.5 m (north-east to south-west), adding 235 m² to the total excavated area, which amounted to 2,190 m².

CHAPTER 28

First Excavation Results: The French Historical Phase (1877–1930)

The Spoil Heaps

As outlined above, before the British Museum team's excavations, the central crater on Tell A was surrounded by an inner ring of spoil heaps that mostly resulted from the expansive digging carried out by Sarzec in 1880 and 1881 (Fig. 140). Hypothesising that the spoil heaps probably protected underlying archaeological deposits that had been left untouched by subsequent French digs, the team was aware that the new excavations should include the removal of parts of the old heaps in order to investigate what lay beneath them and to salvage any discarded objects that they might contain. Preliminary excavations at the bases of the clusters around the rectangular depression confirmed that unexcavated deposits were indeed preserved below. The descriptions that follow refer to Fig. 139, which shows the locations of the contexts (the numbered units of archaeological interest). It should also be noted that the cuneiform text referred to in the lists of finds as Gudea's Standard Inscription for the New Eninnu refers to RIME 3.1.7.37, while the usual variant of the standard text indicates RIME 3.1.1.7.41. The significance of the wording of the texts and the small differences between them are discussed in more detail in Chapter 42 below.

The heaps that form Cluster 1 (Fig. 138), which are situated along the SW edge of the French excavation area, cover an area of approximately 625 m^2, of which about 335 m^2 were newly excavated in sectors B4, B5, B7 and B8, including a small portion of the base of the spoils that were excavated in B3. These trenches were established at the bottom of the N part of Cluster 1, in the E half of the cluster. It was discovered that the spoil covered the entire area of B4, the SW corner of B5, the W corner of B8 and the S part of B7. The tallest parts of the cluster were found in B4 and B8, where the spoils rise to a topographical height of 20.35 m in the SW corner of B4 and the NW corner of B8. The spoil heaps slope down to 16.17 m in the NE corner of B4 (the sloping sector measuring 15 m × 8 m), and down to 16.25 m in the central part of B8, where the sloping part was found to occupy an area of approximately 17.2 m × 5 m. To the north, in B3, the spoil merges with the top layer of ground (context 3020) at overall heights ranging between 15 m and 16.6 m. In B5 (context 2029) the spoil slopes down from 17.27 m in the SW corner to 15.9 m in the centre of the trench (covering an area of about 11 m × 15 m). Spoils are also found on the surface of the ground, and merging with the surface at context 2000.

Undisturbed archaeology was found at various heights below the spoil heaps at 17.59 m (3057 and 3062) and running diagonally north-west to south-east through Area B4. The topmost level of untouched archaeological deposits sloped down on both sides of the contexts: to the north-east towards the centre of the excavation area, and towards the south-west, next to the edge of the tell, along a line indicating that oblique cuts had been made that crossed the principal NW–SE axis followed by the French excavators. This impacted the orientations of the spoil deposits to the south-west and also the erosion and deposition of wash towards the north-east. The French spoil deposits in B4 (3053, 3054, 3055, 3056, 3058, 3072, 3075 and 3076) and B8 (2074, 2075 and 2079) were disposed of along the edge of the tell. Accordingly, the deposits were found to be thickest in the SW corner of B8, where they

394

FIGURE 140. Aerial view of the central area of Tell A, showing the British Museum team's excavations and the surrounding French spoil heaps.

extended along the edge of the slope and piled up to contribute to the formation of SH1. It was therefore necessary to excavate 4.7 m of spoil before undisturbed archaeological deposits (3061) could be reached at topographical heights ranging between 17.06 m and 15.07 m (Fig. 141).

The spoils, which contained dumped materials from the French excavations, were made up of a very loose and unstable top layer (contexts 3053, 2029 and 2074) beneath which lay more French excavation debris (3054, 3055, 3056, 3058, 3072, 3075, 3076 and 2079) and overburden deposits (2075). It should be noted that the latter were probably indicative of the general topographical level of the site (between 16 m and 17.2 m) before Sarzec started his excavations and also therefore before any spoils were dumped. This overburden, which was found below the spoils that form Cluster 1 (2074) and Cluster 4 (2078), contained degraded mud-brick remains and demolished brickwork resulting from robberies, all mixed with wind-blown silts.

A total of 409 finds were retrieved from Cluster 1, most notably 236 Lagash II cones and three Ur III cones (and fragments of cones). Twelve Lagash II cones were inscribed in the name of Ur-Bau to commemorate the Eninnu of Ningirsu; 107 Gudea cones included the Standard Inscription dedicating the New Eninnu to Ningirsu, while sixteen Gudea cones were marked with the usual Gudea variant text; eighteen cones celebrated Gudea's building of the EPA. A number of Gudea cones were dedicated to other deities, including Bau (six cones), Gatumdug (four cones), Shulshaga (three cones), Igalim, Ninshubur and Nindara (two cones each), and Dumuziabzu (one cone). The dedications on sixty-two of the Lagash II cones were unclear. Finally, the three Ur III cones, which were all inscribed in the name of Shulgi, celebrated his rebuilding of the Esheshsheshegara for Nanshe.

Among the other most significant artefacts were: five cylinder seals, including one from the Early Dynastic IIIa period (TG743; Fig. 142), one possibly Lagash II or Ur III seal (TG1817; Fig. 142), two Ur III seals (TG851, TG1645; Fig. 142), and one from Isin-Larsa times (TG1739; Fig. 142); a Jemdet Nasr stamp seal (TG836); a fragment of a Gudea-inscribed statue (TG777; Fig. 193); a brick with a previously

FIGURE 141. Mount Sarzec (SH1) in the background, towering above the archaeological remains on Tell A.

unknown text in the name of Nammahni (TG2266); three votive mace heads (TG1647, TG1843 and TG1848); twelve fragments of stone vessels; an Isin-Larsa clay tablet (TG1639); a potsherd with an Aramaic inscription (TG740); a Hellenistic coin (TG606); and eighteen Sumerian and Hellenistic fragments of figurative terracottas (TG521, TG699, TG839, TG1735, TG1737, TG1746, TG1781, TG1800, TG1816, TG1826, TG1862, TG1987, TG2020, TG2021, TG2023, TG2058, TG2059 and TG2127).

SH3, which demarcates the N edge of Cluster 1, was excavated as part of Area B7. The excavations that were carried out on Cluster 1 covered a total area of 335 m², of which 47 m² lay in B7, where two spoil heap deposits (6002 and 6007) were found below the topsoil (6000). Deposit 6002 accounted for the two thirds of B7 that lay on the S side of the trench. Measuring 5.8 m × 2.89 m × 0.75 m (deep), it filled French cut 6003, which truncated the whole W section of B7, slicing through and disturbing archaeological deposits 6001, 6005 and 6006. French cut 6003 was recorded at topographical heights ranging between 14.88 m and 16.77 m. Spoil 6007 covered the NE corner of B7, where it occupied a volume of 9 m × 3 m × 0.3 m (deep), and filled another French cut (6119). Spoil deposits 6002 and 6007 were both made up of heavily mixed loose sandy silt.

The spoil (6002) that filled cut 6003 yielded ninety-nine artefacts, among which were seventy-seven Lagash II and three Ur III cones (and fragments of cones). Two of the cones were inscribed in the name of Ur-Bau in honour of Ningirsu and Bau, respectively. Of the many cones in the name of Gudea, twenty-nine contained the Gudea Standard Inscription, while three were inscribed with the usual variant and ten celebrated the construction of the EPA. Gudea cones with texts mentioning other gods and their shrines included seven for Gatumdug, six for Bau, four for the Emehushgalanki of Igalim, two for the Ekitushakkilini of Shulshaga and one cone for the god Nin-DUB. The dedications on thirteen Lagash II cones were unclear. The three Ur III cones were inscribed in the name of Shulgi: one to commemorate the renovation of the Eninnu for Ningirsu, and the other two to record the construction of the Esheshsheshegara of the goddess Nanshe. Other noteworthy finds were a complete beaded bracelet with a fish pendant carved in stone (TG1251), four fragments of stone vessels and five Sumerian and Hellenistic terracotta figurines (TG1252, TG1299, TG1305, TG1591 and TG1624).

TG743

TG2072

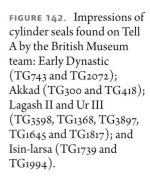

FIGURE 142. Impressions of cylinder seals found on Tell A by the British Museum team: Early Dynastic (TG743 and TG2072); Akkad (TG300 and TG418); Lagash II and Ur III (TG3598, TG1368, TG3897, TG1645 and TG1817); and Isin-larsa (TG1739 and TG1994).

TG300

TG418

TG3598

TG1368

TG3897

TG1645

TG1817

TG1739

TG1994

0   5 cm

Spoil deposit 6007 contained one fragment of an inscribed cone with a cuneiform dedication to Bau (TG1326).

The spoils that form Cluster 2 are situated along the NW edge of the French excavation area (Fig. 138). The cluster, which is generally rectangular in outline, is aligned with the edge of Tell A's central depression, where it covers a total area of approximately 884 m². Around 157 m² of this were excavated in Area B10, located centrally at the foot of the cluster's SE-facing slope, and the highest spoil heap deposits in this area were found in B10's NW corner at a height of 18.6 m. From this point the spoil was found to slope down to the south-east for about three quarters of B10's surface area until it reached an overall height of 15.5 m.

The surface deposits of Cluster 2 (contexts 5400, 5401 and 5406) were made up of eroded dumped deposits that had been left there after the early French excavations. Archaeological deposits were found at a topographical height of 16.7 m in the north-west of B10 (5426 and 5414) and at heights ranging between 14.94 m and 15.39 m (5479) in the S part of the trench. The elevations of the undisturbed archaeological deposits showed that these layers were cut obliquely down from the north-west to the south-east, with the slope breaking from 15 m to 6.5 m diagonally across B10, parallel to the preserved structures in the central part of the tell. This topography had an effect on the drainage in this part of the site, as was evidenced by the erosional cuts created by gullies running from the north-west to the south-east, where they fed into wash deposits in the central depression. Indeed, towards the S side of B10, the uppermost level was found to be a wash layer (5409) characterised by the same banded deposits of powdery grey silt sands as were found in the run-off deposits seen generally in the centre of the tell.

The spoils forming Cluster 2 that were excavated in B10 contained 170 finds. Notable among them were sixty-five Lagash II and three Ur III cones (and fragments of cones). Three of the Lagash II cones were inscribed in the name of Ur-Bau and dedicated to Ningirsu, while twenty-seven contained Gudea's Standard Inscription for the New Eninnu, and a further seven were inscribed with the usual Gudea variant. Six Gudea cones celebrated his construction of the EPA, and ten more were dedicated to a variety of gods, including four to Gatumdug, four to Bau, one to Meslamtaea and one to Nindara. The inscriptions on fifteen cones and fragments of cones were indistinct or entirely abraded. Finally, the three Ur III cones were inscribed in the name of Shulgi

to commemorate the Esheshsheshegara of Nanshe. Remarkably, a poorly preserved cone (TG2611) that was found in the same spolia was inscribed with an otherwise unattested text commemorating a Gudea building: '[For…] Gudea, ruler of Lagash, built(?) his/her bedchamber(?)…' Other noteworthy artefacts recovered from these spoils included an Ur-Bau brick (TG2476) with a previously unknown stamped version of a text (RIME 3.1.1.6.6) recording the ruler's many building activities; an Akkad cylinder seal (TG3598; Fig. 142); a Seleucid iron arrowhead (TG3584); a bronze coin from the reign of Antiochus III with an image of a war elephant (TG2253); and thirty-five Sumerian and Hellenistic terracotta objects, among which were figurines, plaques, zoomorphic forms and models of furniture (TG2093, TG2095, TG2114, TG2117, TG2123, TG2145, TG2150, TG2151, TG2153, TG2162, TG2163, TG2166, TG2167, TG2168, TG2169, TG2170, TG2171, TG2172, TG2179, TG2184, TG2189, TG2190, TG2195, TG2222, TG2225, TG2248, TG2255, TG2609, TG2610, TG2680, TG3005, TG3393, TG3542, TG3567 and TG3589).

The spoil heaps of Cluster 3 are situated north-north-east of the main French excavation area (Fig. 138). The cluster occupies a tranche of ground measuring 880 m², of which an area measuring approximately 102 m² was excavated in areas B6 and B9, both located at the cluster's SW base. The spoil was found in the NE and SE parts of B6, where it covered about half or two-thirds of the trench's surface area. The excavated spoil was highest in B6's NE corner, where it reached a topographical height of 16.55 m, and from there sloped diagonally down and across the trench to a height of 15.4 m in the south-west. In B9 the spoil was found covering the entire trench, sloping down from 17.3 m in the NE corner to 15.1 m in the W part of the trench. Below spoil deposits 5000 and 5200, which ranged in thickness between 0.4 m and 0.85 m, undisturbed archaeology was found at various topographical heights along a line that sloped generally from the north-east to the south-west, from 16.2 m at context 5222 in the NE corner of B9, down to 15.3 m at context 5237 in the central S part of B9, and descending from 15.91 m to 15.38 m at context 5002 in B6. As indicated by the find heights, the archaeological deposits were obliquely truncated. For example, the spoil at 5002 was vertically truncated along its SW edge by French cut 5003, and the truncation and cut were filled and covered with spoil that consisted of dumped and eroded material (5000 and 5200), together with wash in context 5001 (beneath 5000).

The excavated spoil at contexts 5000 and 5200 in Cluster 3 contained seventy-one finds, notable among which were twenty-nine Lagash II cones and fragments of cones. One of these belonged to the old Eninnu of Ur-Bau (as it is called in the Gudea Cylinder Inscriptions), while seventeen contained the Gudea Standard Inscription, and one was inscribed with Gudea's usual variant. Of three further Gudea cones, one celebrated the EPA, another the Kasurra, while one cone was dedicated to Gatumdug. No dedications could be determined for the other seven. Among other noteworthy finds were: a circular brick (TG2520) with Gudea's Standard Inscription; a fragment of gold sheet (TG915); a fragment of a Lagash II diorite statue (TG1659); an Isin-Larsa, or possibly Old Babylonian cylinder seal (TG1999); a Middle Uruk stone amulet in the shape of a fish (TG2666); an incense burner (TG1871); a Hellenistic oil lamp (TG1993); and five Sumerian and Hellenistic terracotta figurines (TG1850, TG1851, TG1869, TG1773 and TG1991).

The spoil heaps of Cluster 4 (Fig. 138), which were located to the south-east of the central depression, were more spread out than those forming the clusters just discussed. They were found to cover a surface area of about 1,695 m², of which 265 m² were excavated in trenches B5, B8 and B11, all located at the base of the cluster's NW slope. The spoil was found covering the SE corner of B5, the entire W corner of B8 and the S half of B11. Several humps were observed in the spoils, the highest of which, in the SE corner of B5, reached a topographical height of 17.8 m. Other humps were noted in the NE part of B8 and slightly to the north of the S end of B11. From the highest point in B5 the spoil was found sloping down towards the centre of the trench, where it lay at an overall height of 15.61 m, spreading out for approximately 7.5 m to the north-west and for about 8.5 m to the west and north. In the central part of B11 another hump with an overall height of 17.5 m was found sloping down to 15.6 m in the north, where it merged with other humps in the cluster in the S part of B11. In the E sector of B8 a hump with an overall height of 17.81 m sloped down to 16.07 m in the central part of B8, where it met SH2 (part of Cluster 1).

Undisturbed archaeological remains, including those recorded as context 2160, were found at a maximum height of 17.22 m, about 0.5 m below the top of the high spoil heap in the SE corner of B5. The archaeological deposits were cut by French trench 2036 along the NW side, and they were found sloping down towards the central and NW part of B5, and also to the north-east, where the adjacent context (2035) was

preserved to topographical heights ranging between 15.66 m and 16.12 m. The spoil of Cluster 4 was made up of a mix of mud-bricks, fired bricks, occupation layers and wind-blown or melt layers (contexts 2028, 2078, 2126 and 2129). In B8 the soft spoil followed and covered the contours of archaeological contexts that had not been touched by the historic excavations. In the aftermath of the Gulf War many pits were dug in this part of the tell by looters, and one consequence of this was that deposit 2078 was found to contain significant materials that had originated deeper in the ground (at 2031, 2164, 2159 and 2116). Spoil 2126, which is an overburden layer that represents the maximum depth of the French excavations at this point, included the degraded surface of the French trenching that had been mixed with the by-products of the pits dug in the course of recent robberies. It was found to be made up of loose mid-grey and brown clayey silt with frequent mud-brick lumps and fragments of fired brick.

A total of 148 finds were unearthed in the excavated spoils of Cluster 4. They included twenty-six Lagash II cones and fragments of cones, of which all except one of the legible examples (nineteen in total) contained Gudea's Standard Inscription (the exception was a cone dedicated by Gudea to Dumuziabzu). No dedications could be established for the other six cones and fragments. Among other noteworthy finds were a Hellenistic group of thirty-one loom weights and seventy-six spindles, and a Sumerian votive anchor (TG1011).

Topsoil and Wash

The uppermost deposits encountered on Tell A appear to have resulted from the excavations of Sarzec and Genouillac. Broadly speaking, two types of deposit were identified. First, were layered surface deposits that had a very loose, fine consistency with very little density, compaction or coherence. Often exhibiting an aerated, brittle salty crust, the upper deposits became slightly more compact deeper down, and even approached a clay-like composition in parts, albeit still with a soft compaction. In the absence of a better designation, this material is referred to as 'topsoil', though the word might not be entirely accurate because it is not clear whether pedogenesis or soil formation has actually occurred anywhere on the tell, and it seems in any event not to have occurred uniformly. In reality, the material that was labelled topsoil was therefore probably formed through a variety of physical and chemical processes, including precipitation in the form of heavy seasonal rainfall, along with aeolian processes of wind erosion and the transport of sediment. Also notable is salt precipitation, which causes the distinctive whitish crust that is characteristic of surficial deposits right across southern Mesopotamia. These climatic causes were no doubt accompanied by the less immediately visible processes involved in the geochemical breakdown of mud-brick and clay building materials, and this applies not only to walls, but also to floors and to the rendered or plastered faces of walls. Since it is surficial, the topsoil deposit is still in the process of being actively formed, augmented and altered, and it therefore constitutes a dynamic geomorphological environment.

Secondly, underlying the surficial topsoil deposits, and most obviously on inclined surfaces, the team encountered deposits that are termed 'wash'. Probably originating as sedimentary deposits that had been transported and modified, mostly by precipitation during seasonal episodes of severe rainfall, this wash had much in common with the laminated deposits that were found infilling the deeper soundings generally on Tell A (most obviously in the W parts of Area B9). It exhibited a firmer compaction and a higher clay content than the overlying topsoil deposits, and it seemed to have derived mostly from an admixture of materials that originated in the higher parts of the surrounding spoil heaps and the exposed surfaces of mud-brick walls. It was only when this material had been removed that the courses of mud-brick walls became visible in plan, together with the erosion gullies that had incised themselves into the surfaces of these walls between seasons or subsequent to the abandonment of the cleared areas, trenches and deeper soundings.

In Area B1, in the deepest part of the rectangular crater in the middle of the tell, at topographical heights ranging between 14.98 m and 15.13 m, context 1000 consisted of firm laminating thin lenses of pale grey silty wash, together with compact purple-brown brick wash, that had been disturbed by animal burrows and shrub roots. The undisturbed deposits, which were found to be between 0.2 m and 0.7 m thick, consisted of several laminating lenses of sand, silt and clay, each between 0.01 m and 0.05 m thick. These lenses were consistent with waterborne deposits. Comparable with the identical lenses that can be observed across Tell A today, they suggest that the depression in which Area B1 is located periodically collected water that washed in from the adjacent French spoil heaps. Accordingly, each thin silty lens was

probably caused by a single episode of rainfall. This deposit contained three badly preserved Lagash II cones with barely any surviving cuneiform signs.

Similar wash was identified in Area B10, in the S part of the trench, where context 5409 consisted of powdery laminated deposits. This context contained nine small finds, of which the most notable were: four fragments of large Seleucid pythoi (TG3223, TG3224, TG3225 and TG3226); a Lagash II cone marked with Gudea's Standard Inscription (TG2991); a fragment of a zoomorphic object (TG2871); and a fragment of a Neo-Sumerian terracotta figurine (TG2992). In Area B9 a wash deposit (5207) was identified in the N part of the trench, where it covered an evident archaeological context (5222). This clayey silt deposit contained seven finds, the most important of which was a Neo-Sumerian figurative terracotta (TG1771).

Wash was found in Areas B2 and B5 at topographical heights ranging between 15.05 m and 16.08 m (context 2000). Varying in depth between 0.1 m and 0.4 m, it consisted of a mixed deposit of loose sandy silt with occasional pottery fragments and some large fragments of fired bricks and mudbricks. This deposit was formed by the gradual accumulation of wash and (or) run-off from the series of spoil heaps that are situated immediately above the northernmost extent of Areas B2 and B3. It was found covering an area of 34 m × 15m, and it contained the relatively high total of sixty-five mixed finds, the most noteworthy of which were: a Lagash II door socket inscribed with Gudea's Standard Inscription (TG951); a rare Early Dynastic sealing (TG585); and forty-four Lagash II cones and fragments of cones. Two of the cones were inscribed in the name of Ur-Bau to commemorate his building of the old Eninnu; thirty-five contained the Gudea Standard Inscription; one celebrated Gudea's construction of the EPA; and single cones were dedicated in Gudea's name to Gatumdug and Bau, respectively. The inscriptions on the other four were either completely worn away or too fragmentary to be deciphered.

It is probable that part of the same deposit (2000) was recorded in Area B6, where context 5001, which measured 7.3 m × 2.9 m, also consisted of alluvial deposits that must have resulted from slope wash. The context yielded an Ur III cylinder seal (TG1368; Fig. 142) and six Lagash II inscribed cones and fragments of cones, five of which contained the Gudea Standard Inscription. No preserved inscriptions were found on the sixth.

Topsoil was identified in Area B7 (context 6000) at an overall maximum height of 17.24 m. Between 0.6 m and 0.1 m thick, it consisted of mixed and loose silty sand. The highest section of the deposit was observed in the SE part of the trench, from where it sloped down equally in all directions, descending to a height of 16.3 m in the SE corner, and fanning out and down to 16 m in the west (where it met the foot of Cluster 4), while in the N and NE corners of B7 it descended to 15.45 m.

Re-Excavating the French Trenches

It was in some cases extremely difficult to differentiate clearly between the cuts made by Sarzec, Cros and Genouillac. Nonetheless, a thorough re-examination of the French documentation, including the plans, photos and reports, supplemented by the British Museum team's analysis of the topography of the tell and the meticulous re-excavations that followed, all combined to facilitate the identification of most of the successive French trenches and backfills that were encountered in the new excavation areas (Fig. 143). The work was aided by the fact that the individual French archaeologists used different digging techniques, which can be correlated with successive periods of exploration. For ease of reference, the signature cuts and soundings that each of the pioneers left in the fabric of Tell A (detailed in Chapter 28) can be summarised as follows:

- **Sarzec:** extensive ramped trenching from the edges of Tell A towards the centre of the mound.
- **Sarzec:** large-scale horizontal pitting and trenching in the central part of Tell A.
- **Sarzec:** long, narrow, deep trenches extending across the mound.
- **Cros:** especially deep soundings, but limited to the area around the Gate of Gudea.
- **Genouillac:** the names and locations of Genouillac's trenches were clearly recorded, so the ones that were re-excavated could relatively easily be described in more detail.

FIGURE 143. Aerial view of the French excavations on Tell A, showing extensive ramped trenching and large-scale horizontal pitting, together with a long, narrow, deep trench running north to south and some pits.

Ramped Trenches

The data relating to the varying heights of undisturbed archaeology below the spoil heaps and top layers indicated that the shallow ramped trenches excavated by Sarzec were still identifiable. In Areas B4, B5 and B8 collapsed bricks and structures were found *in situ* at a maximum topographical height of 17.59 m (contexts 3057 and 3062), running diagonally from the north-west to the south-east. The heights at which undisturbed archaeological deposits were found descended gradually on both sides of the exposed contexts. To the south-west, along the edge of the tell, previously unexcavated archaeological deposits were obliquely truncated down to about 16 m. To the north and north-east, towards the centre of the excavation area, the truncation could be traced into Areas B2 and B3, where archaeological deposits were found sloping down to heights of 15.09 m in B2 (3011) and 15.04 m in B3 (3006). In the latter the cut also truncated the archaeology obliquely from the south-east to the north-west. The broad SW–NE truncation also seemed to have affected the archaeology in B7 (6006), which exhibited a similar slope (from 16.24 m to 15.26 m) down towards the north-east.

In Area B5, following a SW–NE line, archaeological contexts 2035 and 2160 were found sloping down from a maximum topographical height of 17.22 m, and a more general height of around 16.2 m in the south-west, to a lower level of 15.8 m in the north-east. Contexts 2035 and 2160 were also observed to slope gently downwards to the north-west, while the NW side of these contexts was cut by a wide horizontal trench (2036) that was again found sloping gently down towards the centre of the tell, towards both the north-east and the north-west. Trench 2036 was also traced in places where it dissected contexts 2140 and 2162 in area B11, and the latter were found to be continuations of 2035 and 2160.

In Areas B6 and B9 a similarly broad, oblique truncation was identified, and undisturbed archaeology was found generally sloping down from the north-east to the south-west, from an overall height of 16.2 m in the NE corner of B9 (5222) down to 15.3 m in the central S part of B9 (5237), and from 15.91 m down to 15.38 m in B6 (at context 5002). It seemed probable that this cut levelled out in the south-west as a consequence of the wide horizontal shaving off and pitting that was carried out by Sarzec in that area, as recorded in his photos (Pl. 61 bis (top and bottom); Figs. 127 and 128).

A comparable truncation of archaeological deposits was observed in Area B10, where the levels again sloped down towards the centre of the tell, such that the archaeology was truncated from the north-west down to the south-east. Archaeological deposits were found at an overall height of 16.7 m in the north-west of the trench (5426 and 5414) and at heights ranging from 14.94 m to 15.39 m (context 5479) in the S part of B10. The cut exhibited a stepped break of slope, with the steps running diagonally across B10. This steeper cut related to the deeper sounding that was identified in the SE corner of B10 (cut 5429), which was probably made in the course of Genouillac's excavations in *Chambres* I, II and III, as marked on his plan.

Broad, Shallow Horizontal Pits

Towards the centre of Tell A the oblique and ramped trenches just described were seen to level out into broad horizontal excavations in places where Sarzec (as he did extensively across the site) shaved off the top layer of ground and carried out shallow pitting that affected archaeological deposits. The evidence of these activities was particularly clear in Areas B1, B2, B5, B6, B9 and B11. The widest horizontal cut, which was L-shaped, was identified in the greater part of B5, extending north-eastwards into B11 and north-westwards into B2 and B6, as can be seen in Sarzec's photos (Pl. 61 bis (top and bottom)). In Area B5 this broad rectangular trench (2036) was exposed over a distance of about 22 m along a SW–NE line and for about 9.65 m along a NW–SE line. It was found cutting through archaeological contexts 2035 and 2140, as well as through 2158, which lay below these structures along the NW side of the remains; it also broke through the ground surface, fill, other deposits and overburden (2034, 2134, 2146, 2150, 2151 and 2152). At topographical heights ranging between 15.24 m and 15.33 m, the general fill (2037) of cut 2036, which consisted of laminated clayey silt, filled the entire extent of cut 2036, where it was accompanied by numerous scattered fired bricks (2077) that might have collapsed, been dumped or been deliberately deposited as fill. Another dump or intentional fill (context 2128, which formed part of 2037) was found covering an area of 5.5 m × 5 m and reaching a maximum depth of 0.9 m; it was observed within the general fill (2037) of cut 2036 in Area B11. These fills and dumps together contained seventeen finds, of which the most noteworthy were nine Lagash II cones and fragments of cones. Six of these were inscribed with the Gudea Standard Inscription, while two others in the name of Gudea were dedicated to Shulshaga and Ninhursag, respectively. No inscriptions were preserved on the other fragment of a cone. Also among the finds were shell inlays and fragments of stone vessels.

The N extent of this shallow horizontal excavation was probably represented by a broad, shallow cut (5003) that was found in Area B6, where it truncated the SW face of context 5002. Exposed over a width of 6.6 m and to a depth of 0.3 m, cut 5003 was identified at topographical heights ranging between 15.38 m and 16.55 m. It was filled with the general dump of French backfill that was found extending across most of trench B6. This trench, which was first established as the continuation of the broad, shallow pitting that was conducted by Sarzec, extended north-westwards along the NE edge of Sarzec's excavation area, running between the spoil heaps and the NE façade of the Palace. It was later re-excavated by Genouillac in his East Trench (*Tranchée Est*), traces of which were observed in the NE corner of B2. Accordingly, cut 5003 contained evidence of work carried out by both Sarzec and his successor Genouillac. In the north-east of B6, covered with French dump 5000, an archaeological layer (5012) was found horizontally truncated at an overall height of 16.15 m to depths of between 0.2 m and 0.25 m. Context 5012 might also have been produced by the horizontal excavations that were carried out by the French in this location.

As is seen in the photographic evidence, these broad horizontal excavations were accompanied by extensive steep cuts at the limits of the excavation areas, a phenomenon that is particularly clear in Sarzec's photo (Pl. 61 bis (bottom)). A likely trace of this was picked up in Area B6, where a cut (5050) with a depth of 1.25 m was exposed over a length of 7.5 m, and it was found dissecting the SE side of contexts 5002 and 5237. This French trench can probably be related to the wide vertical cuts that can be seen behind and to the left of wall AB (as marked on Heuzey's New Plan; Fig. 114) in the Ur-Bau platform in Sarzec's photo (Pl. 61 bis (bottom)).

Deep, Narrow Trenches

The new excavations in the central part of the depression, namely in the middle of the upper part of the mound (B2, B3, B5 and B8), also exposed signs of the long, narrow sondages

that Sarzec dug on a N–S alignment. In B5, a long, narrow cut (2080), which measured approximately 15 m × 2.4 m and reached a maximum depth of 1.5 m, was identified as one of Sarzec's exploratory trenches. It was filled with redeposited and mixed materials that derived from mud-brick structures and occupation deposits (2076). The fill contained thirty-two finds, including twenty-nine Lagash II cones and fragments of cones, of which one was inscribed in the name of Ur-Bau to celebrate his building of the Eninnu of Ningirsu; twenty-four contained the Gudea Standard Inscription, while one celebrated Gudea's construction of the EPA, and three were indeterminate. The redepostion of material in the fill, accompanied by erosion and alluvial and aeolian deposition, had resulted in the gradual realignment of the trench with respect to the surrounding terrain. It was observed that trench 2080 possibly continued into B3 (where it was recorded as 3084) and perhaps also into disturbed context 3011, which was located further north in B2.

In B3, cut 3084, which measured 2.1 m × 1.5 m and had a maximum depth of 0.4 m, was filled with heavily mixed backfill (3083) that yielded no small finds. If cuts 2080 and 3084 were indeed both part of Sarzec's excavation trench, this would suggest that the total length of his original cut was at least 19 m, and that it must have become narrower and shallower towards its N end. It is visible on Sarzec's photo (Pl. 61 bis (top)), where it can be seen entering the tell from between the two smaller spoil heaps to the left of Mount Sarzec (Cluster 1).

In the central part of B8, at the S edge of the major crater on Tell A, the N edge of a large pit (2108) was exposed at a maximum height of 16.43 m. Measuring 5.8 m × 4.2 m × 1.1 m (deep), cut 2108 was found filled with clayey silt (2109) that was seemingly the melt of a mud-brick structure (2164 and 2167) that had been dissected by the cut. The fill contained a few fired bricks, as well as other mixed materials and one exceptional find: a rectangular brick (TG2573) that had been incised with secondary lines to create a board on which to play the Game of Twenty Squares. Cut 2108 represented the N extremity of another one of Sarzec's narrow exploratory trenches of the type that can be seen in his photo, Pl. 61 bis (top). Two deep, narrow trenches can be seen slicing into the tell in the background of the photo, and the extended trench that might also be associated with cut 2108 can be seen entering Tell A along the left side of the spoil heaps that form Cluster 1.

French Deep Soundings

The British Museum team's investigations of the broad, shallow horizontal excavations just discussed were focused on establishing a plan of the site. While this work was being carried out, and after it was finished, the team also targeted some of the deeper soundings that were dug by the French, particularly in the NW part of the so-called Palace. The locations of the deeper soundings were determined on the basis of the photographic evidence, and more particularly with the help of Genouillac's plan (Fig. 115), which indicates the positions of former trenches. All of this evidence, combined with the published excavation results, made it possible to identify individual trenches dug during the French campaigns.

In Area B1, in the deepest part of the major central depression, a complex sequence of large pits was identified. Cut 1022, in the NW corner of B1, exhibited a roughly SW–NE alignment, and it was recorded to a depth of about 1 m, seemingly sloping down towards the north-west. Directly south of this, and also visible in the W section of B1, was a broader, deeper cut (1011) with a similar alignment that deepened further towards the south-west, where, at a depth of 2.95 m, a dump of broken Gudea bricks was found on a flat horizon. Considered to be the base of the French trench, the subrectangular brick dump was found sloping gently down towards the south-west, from where it sporadically stepped down vertically. This roughly rectangular pit truncated, and also belled into, the S end of context 1021, which was found extending 10 m south-westwards from B1's NE corner. Cuts 1022 and 1011 were both visible in the W section of B1, where they were separated by a baulk with a width of approximately 1 m. Fills from the broader cut (1011) extended into cut 1022, but the two were otherwise remarkably different. Cuts 1022 and 1011 were found below context 1001, which was identified as backfill that was deposited by the French in their obsolete trench. Backfill 1001 extended over a large area of the French trench, where its thickness ranged between 0.3 m and 0.5 m, and it consisted of lensing dumps of varying consistency (fine pale-grey sandy silt and compact clayey silt with thin lenses of sand). The deposit, which was simply the topmost dump of several grey levels of sandy silt that ran across the trench, contained a number of Gudea brick fragments and twelve Lagash II cones and fragments of cones, eleven of which were inscribed with Gudea's Standard Inscription. The dedication on the other one could not be determined.

Cut 1022 was filled with wash levels, without any backfill or brick dumps, but only the top 1 m of the cut could be seen in Area B1, and it could have deepened considerably to the north-west, where its make-up might be entirely different, though this could not be determined. The fill deposits, consisting of several thin horizontal laminating wash lenses of silt, sand and clay that were laid down in water, were excavated collectively as context 1013, which yielded nine finds, most notably a rare Lagash II shell cylinder seal (TG300; Fig. 142). The carving on the seal shows a robed and bearded worshipper approaching Ningirsu, who is pictured in his shrine, where he is flanked by two nude, bearded heroes who hold ringed gateposts. Among the other noteworthy finds were four Lagash II cones and fragments of cones, one of which was marked with Gudea's Standard Inscription; no dedications could be established for the others.

Cut 1011 contained several mixed fills that were recorded as a single context (1010). The top fills rose upwards as they approached the W section of B1, and this suggested that the edge of the French cut might lie somewhere just beyond this part of B1. Exposed at a topographical height of 13.7 m and to a depth of about 2.6 m, context 1010 yielded hundreds of broken fired bricks that were mostly stamped with the Gudea Standard Inscription, along with chunks of black bitumen and occasional inscribed cones (both intact and broken). Twenty significant finds were also recorded, including ten Lagash II cones and fragments of cones, seven of which contained the Gudea Standard Inscription, while one was dedicated in Gudea's name to Bau and one was indeterminate. Among the other rare finds were a fragment of an Ur-Bau stone tablet (TG168) and three terracottas (TG218, TG241 and TG244).

Although the fill in cut 1011 was mostly excavated as one context (1010), a striking characteristic of its composition was the presence of several wash levels that were made up of a number of thin laminating bands of waterborne silt, sand and clay lenses, which were reminiscent of the wash levels that were found sealing the top of the French trench today (context 1000). These levels therefore indicated that the cut was exposed to standing water at some time in the past. Two distinct bands of wash levels were separated by a layer of dumped fills that was 0.5 m thick. The upper band of wash levels filled the gently sloping top of the cut, while the contrasting deeper band extended to a lower edge of the cut, at which point the wash deposits dropped vertically near the base of the trench. Since these deeper wash levels were found to lie over thicker fills, it was assumed that the lower vertical sides of the base of the French cut were partly filled before being left exposed and that they later started to collect wash. Subsequently, the cut was refilled, including with large quantities of dumped bricks, before it was once again left open, resulting in the accumulation of the second band of wash layers just mentioned. It is worth noting, however, that fired bricks uniformly stamped with Gudea's Standard Inscription were found at the very top and the very bottom of the trench, regardless of the intervening wash bands. The distribution suggested that, despite the different infilling events, the materials found in 1010 derived from much the same place.

When Area B1 was extended southwards in the autumn of 2018, additional pits were identified, including context 1081 (the continuation of cut 1011) that was visible in the S section of B1. It was filled with silt wash (1074) that formed horizontal banding to a depth of 2.75 m (descending from an overall height of 14.96 m down to 12.21 m). Notable finds in this deposit were: three Lagash II cones and fragments of cones, two containing the Gudea Standard Inscription, and one marked with Gudea's text for the EPA; a fragment of a stone vessel; and an Early Dynastic haematite weight (TG1676).

Below 1081, an even smaller subrectangular pit (1080) was exposed over an area measuring 3.6 m × 3.5 m × 1.4 m (deep), at topographical heights ranging between 11.1 m and 12.5 m. This cut was notable for its distinctive fill of broken fired bricks (contexts 1079 and 1078). The top fill (1079) consisted of packed fired bricks that were mixed with clayey silt. Seven finds were retrieved from the lower fill (1078), of which the most important were: a complete cuneiform-inscribed brick in the name of Ur-Bau (TG2265); three fragments of Lagash II cones, all of which were inscribed with Gudea's Standard Inscription; and a fragment of a stone vessel (TG2273).

Pit 1080 was found dissecting two broad rectangular pits (1076 and 1054). Pit 1076, which measured 4.2 m × 3.1 m × 0.89 m (deep), was found at heights ranging between 11.67 m and 12.5 m, while pit 1054, which was found at a topographical height of 12.21 m, measured 4.4 m × 3 m × 1.2 m (deep). Both pits were aligned north-east–south-west, and both had nearly vertical edges, rounded corners and irregular flat bases. They were filled with similar silt wash deposits (1077, 1069, 1057 and 1055). The N and (or) NE ends of these pits cut into archaeological context 1063.

The locations of these cuts and their particular characteristics suggested that they could be correlated with the various French trenches that were dug in the vicinity of the Gate of Gudea, and these could be reconstructed from the reports, photos and plans. The area was deeply excavated and re-excavated several times, firstly by Sarzec in 1895 (Season 9), followed by Cros in 1903 and finally by Genouillac in 1929 and 1930, when he opened his Trench of the Gudea Esplanade (*Tranchée de L'Esplanade de Goudéa*) and Central Trench (*Tranchée Centrale*), both marked on Genouillac's plan (Fig. 115). Accordingly, cut 1022, in the NW corner of B1, was probably associated with the Trench of the Well (*Tranchée du Puits*) in the middle of Genouillac's plan. The fact that its top layer of infilling consisted only of wash suggested that no dumping of spoil occurred here, at least during the final phases of infilling, with the possible further conclusion that excavations had ceased at this location by about 1930 (and Genouillac was, of course, the last excavator to work on Tell A until the arrival of the British Museum team). Furthermore, in view of their relative proximity and locations, it is highly likely that cut 1011 represented the NE edge of Genouillac's Central Trench, since its fill (1010) appeared to merge with the fill of cut 1081 (situated within 1074) in the southernmost part of B1. In all likelihood, this was part of the N corner of the Trench of the Gudea Esplanade on Genouillac's plan. One particular difficulty faced by the British Museum team was that of differentiating between Genouillac's Central Trench and the Trench of the Gudea Esplanade, since these trenches, which were laid out next to each other, were only separated by a very narrow baulk. The edges of the two Genouillac trenches were therefore not easy to identify in plan or in the S part of B1, perhaps because the baulk collapsed at some point, such that the fills of the two trenches merged (1010 being absorbed into 1074).

Below these trenches, subrectangular pit 1080 (mentioned above) was found cutting into the two broad rectangular pits (1076 and 1054), and this indicated that 1080 was the last of the three to be excavated. Rectangular cuts 1076 and 1054, which were very clearly recognisable, lay on a NE–SW alignment and were separated by a narrow baulk that ranged in thickness between 0.5 m and a maximum of 1 m, all of which agrees well with the recorded location of Cros's deep soundings in front of the Gate of Gudea, and the archaeological contexts also correspond with Cros's findings. As discussed in Chapter 23, at a depth of 3.4 m, below the W face of the

FIG 144. Fragment of a Lagash II stone statue, showing two hands clasped in prayer (TG3067).

Gudea Gate—in front of its threshold and on the same orientation as the gate's façade—Cros found a mud-brick wall made of archaic bricks that was resting on a layer of sand covered with a layer of sand and ash. This data is consistent with the discovery that cuts 1054 and 1076 truncated Early Dynastic structures 1036 and 1063. Consequently, if cuts 1054 and 1076 were indeed the ones that were dug by Cros then the later cut (1080) could well have been excavated by Genouillac as a deeper sounding at the bottom of his Central Trench and the Trench of the Gudea Esplanade. It is frustrating that Genouillac provided so little information about his findings at this location.

Significantly, the top of cut 1011 (the continuation of 1081) was also detected in Area B3, in a small sounding (3017) that was discovered 4.6 m south of Area B1. The NW part of sounding 3017, which had obliquely truncated a series of archaeological contexts, was filled with clayey silt that included broken bricks (3016), among which were twenty-one recorded fragments that mostly derived from Gudea's New Eninnu. The position and composition of cut 3017 and fill 3016 suggested that they were part of the continuation of Genouillac's Trench of the Gudea Esplanade, which was also found further north in the S section of B1. The edge identified in B3 might therefore have been close to the SE edge of the Trench of the Gudea Esplanade.

A broad cut (6119) was discovered in Area B7, where it partially truncated context 6006 along its N side. Based on its location to the south-east of Genouillac's narrow-gauge railway track (which was still visible in the topography) this was judged to be the S part of Genouillac's West Trench (*Tranchée Ouest*). Finally, a deep cut (5429) that measured 7.5 m × 3 m was found truncating the SE corner of Area B10. Filled with the material recorded as context 5428, it contained nineteen finds, including fifteen Lagash II cones and fragments of cones, six of which contained Gudea's Standard Inscription. A further three were marked with the usual Gudea variant text for the New Eninnu, while five commemorated his building of the EPA, and one was dedicated in Gudea's name to Ningirsu to celebrate an unknown construction project. Among the other rare objects were two fragments of stone vessels and a fragment of a Lagash II stone statue representing a hand on a folded arm (TG3067; Fig. 144). The base of cut 5429 was not encountered, but the pit dissected most of the SE face of structure 5479. The SW corner of another rectangular cut was identified in the NE corner of B10. These cuts were possibly made by Genouillac in the course of his work on *Chambre* III (cut 5429) and *Chambre* II (the cut in the NE corner of B10).

Wadis and Natural Gullies

As was revealed by the British Museum team's excavations and the way in which the French plans could be correlated with the topography of the site, the French initiated particularly deep excavations in the NW parts of the mound. These were targeted in Areas B1, B9 and B10, where the deep French trenches altered the tell's drainage patterns, resulting in the infilling of trenches with bedded alluvial deposits and the deposition of extended sheets of wash deposits. The water also carved erosion gullies through the archaeological remains. A significant gully (1037) with a width of 0.7 m was exposed in Area B1 over a length of more than 5 m and to a maximum depth of 0.9 m. Running deep inside B1, it sloped down from 13.93 m in the north-east to 13.23 m in the south-west, where it dissected a series of archaeological contexts (1033, 1036, 1043, 1038 and 1048). It was traced down to the N corner of 1011. The gully was found to be filled with loose red-brown silty clay (1023) that contained some small shards and a lower fill of loose silty sand (1047). The fills had been laid in thin lenses, probably due to standing water, while the gully was a direct result of the way the deep cut (1011) in the centre of the tell had changed the mound's topography, lowering the maximum depth at which water could accumulate. Water that would formerly have collected towards the north-east was therefore probably channelled to the NE corner of cut 1011 via structure 1036.

Another gully (3099) in Area B3 was identified running towards the S end of the deep French soundings (1011, 1080, 1081, 1076 and 1054), and evidence of its flow was observed in the hollows, water damage and erosion that it had caused in the NW part of context 2032, where 2032 met context 3006. In Area B9, below excavation dumps 5200 and locally above the natural wash deposits (5207) that were found generally in the trench, was a mixed deposit of sandy silt (5206 and 5216) that filled another gully (5217) that had cut through a series of underlying archaeological features (5203, 5215, 5223, 5237 and 5233). The fill contained lenses of fragments of fired bricks and four finds, the most important of which was a fragment of a Seleucid terracotta (TG1853). In addition, gully 5217 possibly fed the wash deposits that were found in the south-west of B9, and it might have caused the erosion damage that was seen in context 5235, the surface of which was found sloping down from the north-east to the south-west. The slope might have resulted from erosion that took place when water flowed down from the higher ground situated to the north-east.

The waterborne fill (5216) of gully 5217 probably merged with the wash and natural deposits recorded as context 5231, extending from B9 towards B1. It was observed as a light greenish-grey sandy silt, with frequent lenses of light grey sand, along with a few fragments of red and yellow fired bricks and pieces of charcoal. It contained five notable finds, including two indeterminate fragments of Lagash II cones and one fragment of a stone vessel. Context 5231, which measured at least 7.8 m × 3.5 m, was either the silted infilling of a wide French excavation pit, or the product of erosion in antiquity. The distinction is important because, if it was produced by ancient erosion, that would suggest that archaeological context 1063 represented a more or less intact surface, a conclusion that would have implications for the topography of the temple complex more generally, as is discussed in Chapter 31.

The SE corner of Area B10 was heavily truncated by early French deep sounding 5429 (mentioned above), which altered the drainage pattern on B10's W side, leading to severe localised erosion damage. Several gullies that cut through underlying archaeology were found running down from the north-west to the south-east towards the deepest part of Tell A's main crater in the vicinity of Area B1. Water erosion had split a substantial structure into three parts (5441, 5478 and 5479). The alluvial deposits and fills (5410, 5411, 5412 and 5430) contained in the erosional cuts consisted of sandy silt, while context 5411 contained material that had been transported from spoil heaps to the west, as well as material that had come from other parts of B10. Thirty finds were derived from these erosion deposits, including fifteen Lagash II cones and fragments of cones, four of which contained the Gudea Standard Inscription. A further two cones commemorated the same ruler's construction of the EPA, while one was inscribed in Gudea's name to celebrate the Eangursulum shrine of Nanshe. The dedications on the other eight could not be determined. Other notable finds included two fragments of stone vessels and six Sumerian and Hellenistic terracotta figurines (TG2868, TG2981, TG2982, TG2995, TG3001 and TG3044).

CHAPTER 29

The Effects of Modern Looting

AS THE PRECEDING DISCUSSIONS MAKE CLEAR, THE early French excavations had an extremely significant impact on Tell A, not only due to the digging and truncating that were carried out in order to explore and retrieve archaeological remains, but also because of the changes that were inflicted on the site's topography, both deliberately and unintentionally. The raising of large spoil heaps and the sinking of deep and extensive trenches led to significant alterations to processes and patterns of erosion, most notably where the processes were intensified and new patterns were established. Importantly, the alluvial deposits that eventually filled some of the original French trenches were carried away through newly formed gullies or wadis, while the unearthed archaeological remains that were discarded or could not be removed from the site were exposed to the elements and quickly deteriorated.

The spectacular finds that were excavated and removed also had a profound, if indirect effect on the fate of Tell A because they placed Tello in the spotlight. The allure of undiscovered treasures captured the public imagination, suggesting a kind of Mesopotamian El Dorado that inevitably attracted unscrupulous opportunists. After the arrival of Sarzec in the late nineteenth century, whenever Tello was left unattended the site was vulnerable to looters, who plundered the tells between the seasons of excavations and in the long intervals when no systematic work was conducted. Facilitated by conflict and instability, and spurred on by the insatiable appetites of international collectors, illegal excavators have repeatedly targeted the site for the past 150 years, and their rough and ready methods have left scars on the topography.

More understandable was the digging carried out over many centuries by people in search of building materials. Though less deliberately malign in intent, such activities have also left their mark on the site.

As a result of the investigations carried out by the British Museum team most of the large trenches can now be attributed with a reasonable degree of certainty to particular French excavation campaigns. Unfortunately, the additional pitting that has affected the site is far more difficult to date. Some cuts (occasionally visible in the early photos) were made by the French but not recorded on the published plans; some were dug by modern looters; others were excavated in antiquity, in the Hellenistic era, when bricks were collected from Tell A to be reused. In general terms, extensive pitting was carried out to retrieve building materials or in search of valuables in three main epochs: Hellenistic times, the period of the French Mandate and most recently after the Gulf War (Fig. 145). In some cases modern pits can be identified and even dated on the basis of datable pieces of material evidence that have been left behind, including old newspapers, torn pages of books, pieces of plastic and bottles (some of which were converted for use as night lamps; Fig. 146). In addition, the stratigraphic locations of unattributed pits can also yield useful information—for example, when they cut through the infills of French excavation trenches. Particularly with respect to the Hellenistic excavations, the make-up and stratigraphy of some pits can help to identify their origins. Sadly, however, the ages of a number of pits may never be established.

The work of the British Museum team indicates that modern pitting was probably carried out most extensively in the

FIGURE 145. An oval looting pit cutting through the mud-brick walls of the New Eninnu; re-excavated by the British Museum team.

SE and NE parts of Tell A (the SE corners of B5, B8 and B11, and the E sides of B6 and B9), and mostly along the edges of the clusters of spoil heaps. There are a couple of probable reasons why the spoil heaps were targeted, especially on their peripheries. First, the ground in these areas was no doubt looser and easier to dig than the compacted surface of the tell itself; secondly, as is exemplified by the results of the team's systematic excavations, the spoil heaps are especially rich in archaeological deposits. These circumstances might even have led looters to the mistaken belief that the heaps were not discarded spoil, but untouched archaeology. Nonetheless, despite the apparent attractions of the spoil heaps, pitting was also observed in Areas B1 and B2 on the NW side of the mound and in the deeper part of the central depression.

Multiple pits that had caused the truncation and churning of archaeological deposits were found at the foot of Cluster 4 in Areas B5, B8 and B11. An irregular pit (2070), which was composed of several intersecting pits, was found in the W part of B5. Measuring 6.9 m × 6.2 m, it descended to a depth of more than 1 m, cutting through structures 2031, 2058, 2059, 2066, 2068 and 2073. The fill (2049), which consisted of a mixed clayey silt deposit, together with collapsed spoil, was discovered below the general surface deposit (2000).

It included a great deal of eroded wash from the surrounding spoil heaps, and this might explain why numerous artefacts were found in fill 2049, since they could perhaps have been transported by flowing water. The pit contained thirty-three finds, most notably a fragment of a large Lagash II terracotta plaque or stele decorated with relief (TG855) and twenty-four Lagash II cones and fragments of cones, which were all inscribed with the Gudea Standard Inscription, except for one that was illegible.

In the same area, a long, narrow shallow robbing pit (2086) measuring 2.73 m × 0.85 m × 0.26 m (deep) was found truncating the W side of context 2066. Pit 2086, which had steep, straight sides that broke abruptly to form a flat base, was laid out along a line running from the south to the north-north-west, where its vertical face was rounded. It was filled with occupation deposits and structural materials, all of which appeared to have fallen back into the pit after it was opened or subsequently abandoned. Also dissecting context 2066, but on its E side, was robbing pit 2088, which measured 1.4 m × 0.6 m × 0.34 m (deep), and it also had steep, straight sides that broke sharply into a flat base. Running along a SW–NE line, its NNE face was rounded (again comparable with pit 2086). Pit 2088 was similarly filled with occupation

FIGURE 146. Objects discarded by looters, including plastic and glass bottles adapted for use as night lamps.

deposits and structural remains (2089). Pits 2088 and 2086 seemed to be related, as was further indicated by the merging of their S sections. Pit 2088 also cut through French trench 2080, part of trench 2076.

To the north-east of this heavily pitted area, in the central N part of B5, at a topographical height of 15.5 m, was found an oval pit (2044) with steep sides that broke through the tell's top layer (2000), cutting through archaeological structures and deposits (2068 and 3018). It measured 1.64 m × 1.22 m × 0.89 m (deep), while its fill (2045), which contained no small finds, consisted of very loose clayey silt and collapsed materials that were discarded by the robbers.

Archaeological deposits were widely and deeply pitted in the SE and E parts of Area B11, where the illegal digging had a heavy impact on lower archaeological remains. A robbing horizon (2127) was found on the SE side of B11, below the general overburden (2126), at topographical heights ranging between 14.94 m and 17.47 m. The overall dimensions of the horizon were 22 m × 5 m × 2.53 m (deep), and it cut extensively through archaeological contexts in the area (including 2035, 2159, 2160, 2137, 2139, 2134, 2136, 2141, 2148, 2116, 2117 and 2118). Displaying a mix of mud-bricks and occupation deposits, the horizon was made up of materials from the underlying ravaged archaeology. It yielded fifteen finds, among which were eleven Lagash II cones and fragments of cones, all containing Gudea's Standard Inscription.

To the north, also below overburden 2126, were the traces of another modern robbing horizon (2135) that was found at heights ranging between 15.75 m and 16.94 m; it measured 8.8 m × 2.8 m × 1.19 m (deep). Extending towards the northeast from the E side of Area B8, horizon 2135, which cut into contexts 2113 and 2138, consisted of redeposited and backfilled materials deriving from context 2113. The redeposited material contained twenty finds, including one complete Lagash II cone and three fragments of cones, all bearing the Gudea Standard Inscription, and a total of forty shell inlays (TG3126, TG3160, TG3162, TG3165, TG3166, TG3169, TG3170 and TG3176), mostly rectangular or shaped like teardrops. One square-cut shell had a centrally inlaid red stone (TG3536). Another noteworthy find was a fragment of inscribed stone (TG3167; Fig. 193) that was originally part of a hollow cylindrical object (presumably a cultic vessel, probably for libations) with a diameter of between 15 cm and 30 cm. The inscription was found running around the vessel rather than down it, but this was explained as the traditional reading orientation. The little that survived of the text confirmed that it related to the Ningirsu temple: é.ninnu ^{d}IM.MI/^{mušen} bar$_6$-bar$_6$-ra-ni ('his Fifty House, the White Thunderbird'). This line is contained in the Gudea Standard Inscription, and the presence of the suffix -ra-ni ('his') confirms that the text must have contained the name of Ningirsu and a statement about the construction of the New Eninnu.

In the W part of B5, a robbing pit (2130) was found cutting through context 2105. Pit 2130 was very irregular, such that its N and W sides were undercut, while its E side was more or less straight and its S side was stepped. Measuring 1.4 m × 1.1 m × 0.89 m (deep), it was discovered at a topographical height of 16.5 m, descending to 15.61 m at its deepest point. Its fill of sandy silt (2131) was the gradually accumulated product of run-off sediments. Another pit (5004), which measured 1.8 m × 1.2 m × 0.5 m (deep), was exposed in Area B6 at an overall height of 15.57 m. Cutting through context 5002, pit 5004 was filled with heavily mixed material (5007).

A smaller pit (5011), with dimensions of 1.05 m (l) × 0.75 m (deep), was found towards the NE corner of B6; its single fill (5010) yielded no finds. Cut 5011 was dissected by pit 5006 (with a depth of 1.25 m) that was filled with loose mixed backfill (5005 and 5009). Pit 5006 contained nine finds, notably including seven fragments of Lagash II cones, all containing dedications to Ningirsu in the name of Gudea, and a weathered stone cylinder seal of uncertain date (TG1479).

Two robbing pits (5213 and 5205) were identified in Area B9, where they lay at a topographical height of 15.91 m, below the topsoil and covered by material from the adjacent spoil heap (5200). Cut 5213 was 1.5 m long, with a minimum width of 0.4 m and a depth of 0.4 m. Its slightly scalloped sides showed the marks of the shovels that were used to dig it, while its base was rather uneven. Extending beyond the N edge of B9, it was filled with unconsolidated sandy silt (5212) that contained no finds. Cut 5213 dissected another modern pit (5205), measuring 1.35 m × 0.7 m × 0.5m (deep), which was discovered below spoil heap 5200 at a topographical height of 15.7 m. Cut 5205, which broke through a layer of underlying natural wash (5207) that appeared to cover context 5222 and other structures, was filled with loose sandy silt (5204) that contained no artefacts.

Pit 5225, which had a flat base and a NW–SE alignment, was found at topographical heights ranging between 15.19 m and 16.2 m. Measuring 2.25 m × 1.4 m × 1 m (deep), it bisected, and was therefore judged to postdate, context 5222, but its function and phase were otherwise uncertain. Its fill (5224) contained a small amount of Lagash II residual material, but the finds were mainly Hellenistic ceramics, all of which (as suggested by the stratigraphy) appeared to be residual. Unlike the fills in other apparently similar pits in B6 and B9, fill 5224 yielded ten finds, which perhaps suggested that the pit was not dug by looters, though the recovered items could also, of course, have been left behind or overlooked by thieves. The finds included five fragments of Lagash II cones: two bearing Gudea's Standard Inscription; one dedicated in Gudea's name to Bau in her Eurukug; one dedicated in Gudea's name to Ninhursag; and the end of a cone with no preserved signs. Among other notable finds were a large decorated Hellenistic pottery krater (TG2069), a Sumerian figurative terracotta (TG2009; Fig. 256) and an Old Babylonian chlorite cylinder seal (TG1994; Fig. 142).

CHAPTER 30

Coda: Objects from the Spolia of Tell A

THE BRITISH MUSEUM TEAM'S RE-EXCAVATIONS OF the spoil heaps and backfills that were left behind by the French excavators who worked on Tell A before the Second World War, together with the pits that were dug by looters, particularly in the aftermath of the Gulf War, produced a colossal hoard of artefacts, many of which were found in a fragmented state. The retrieved objects and sherds, which mostly originated in greatly disturbed archaeological contexts, were dated to a range of epochs spanning more than four millennia: from the prehistoric past of the ancient city of Girsu all the way through to modern times, represented by the Mandate era in the early twentieth century and latterly the Republic of Iraq. As discussed above, the site was affected by the actions of previous excavators and recent looters, as well as by locals in search of building materials, and also very significantly by the Hellenistic-era builders, who excavated the Sumerian Eninnu in order to construct a revived shrine on top of the mound. In addition, and principally as a direct consequence of the state in which Tell A was left by the French, the site has also been disproportionately damaged by ongoing erosion and other natural processes. The present-day characteristics of Tell A are analysed in detail in Chapters 27–9, and the objects are listed in previous chapters. In an ideal world, it would be of considerable interest to produce an additional comprehensive overview of the finds, reflecting on the objects themselves, their identities and uses, as well as their groupings, probable interrelationships and provenances. Especially with respect to the ancient artefacts, it would be fascinating to know whether certain items originated on Tell A or elsewhere in Girsu. Such a study, which

would need be carried out with the utmost care in order to be of genuine scientific value, would potentially add a wealth of detail to the general history of the Mound of the Palace, shedding light on particular unresolved or problematic questions. In practice, however, the sheer number and diversity of the British Museum team's finds makes it impossible to include an exhaustive account of them in this study. The exception to that rule are the Lagash II inscribed cones or clay nails that were found fragmented and intact in great quantities during the re-excavations. Their special importance demands closer attention.

The discussion of the clay nails must be prefaced with a number of caveats that apply generally to the British Museum team's discoveries. First and foremost, the battered settings in which most of the excavated objects were unearthed are indicators of indirect archaeological contexts. Countless newly exposed items had been previously uprooted and moved from the places where they had lain for millennia, before being discarded on spoil heaps, incorporated into backfills or left in the pits dug by robbers, who might have overlooked them or rejected them as worthless. To complicate matters still further, many of the often fragmentary artefacts that were mishandled in relatively recent times were displaced not from their original locations but from secondary or tertiary archaeological contexts because they had already been exposed, moved and discarded in antiquity. The use of salvaged materials to build the Hellenistic shrine in the fourth and third centuries BCE (as detailed in Part 4) is a clear instance of this, but significant displacements also occurred at several earlier times in the site's long history. A seminal example is the fragment of the Presargonic Stele of the Vultures that was exhumed in the Hellenistic complex on Tell A, having been previously removed from the ruins of the sacred precinct on Tell K at some unknown date after the Early Dynastic temple and its annexes were destroyed in the reign of Urukagina at the end of the twenty-third century BCE. As illustrated by this single carved fragment, the effort to define the provenance of the innumerable small remnants that were unearthed by the British Museum team in disturbed contexts on Tell A potentially represents an archaeological quagmire of uncertainty and confusion.

Nonetheless, the problems associated with the unstratified small finds from Tell A are considerably mitigated by the clearer understanding of the use and formation of the mound that results from the British Museum team's work. The meticulous re-excavations that were carried out on the Mound of the Palace offer a detailed picture of the history of the sacred precinct that derives from its complex stratigraphy. The salvage excavations examined the French spoil heaps and backfills, together with the modern looting pits, with the same care as was expended on all the other archaeological layers that were freshly exposed on Tell A. Every find was painstakingly contextualised, described and plotted on the team's comprehensive grid of the mound, from which detailed distribution maps were generated. Accordingly, though it might be almost impossible to trace the exact provenance of an individual fragment found on a spoil heap, analysis of the rigorously compiled database reveals that the enormous number of artefacts constitute coherent groups, including the Lagash II inscribed cones that are considered further below. In this regard, the conclusions laid out above about the formation of the Tell A spoil heaps and clusters of heaps should also be re-emphasised. Clear correlations exist between the large-scale digging that was carried out by the French pioneers and the formation of the spoil heaps and clusters that are prominent features of the present-day shape of Tell A, and the vast majority of the artefacts found in them were almost certainly discards from the trenches that were dug on the mound. Since Sarzec, later followed by Cros and Genouillac, focused mainly on the Hellenistic deposits on Tell A, and only to a much lesser degree on the Lagash II remains, the spolia they produced undoubtedly reflect a jumble of archaeological strata. Unfortunately, the situation is further complicated by the fact that a number of objects that were found in the spoil heaps must unquestionably have been brought to Tell A from other parts of the site, as can be exemplified by recalling one salient occurrence. In his first seasons, Sarzec established his site headquarters on Tell A (before later moving it to Tell K). It is therefore highly probable that, at this early stage of the excavations, finds made in other parts of the site were regularly brought to him at his working base on Tell A so that he could assess their importance. Accordingly, numerous finds that were then judged by Sarzec to be insignificant must have been discarded in the nearby dumps.

Those caveats notwithstanding, some insights into the layout and setting of the Temple of Ningirsu at the heart of Gudea's New Eninnu can be gained by examining the spatial distribution of one group of recovered objects in particular: the Lagash II inscribed cones or clay nails. The map of their find locations (Fig. 147) draws on the discussion of the formation history of the spoil heaps and clusters that is outlined in Chapter 28 above. It also plots the clay nails that were found in other tertiary contexts (including topsoil, wash, wadis, French backfills and looting pits) and therefore provides an exhaustive graphic record of exactly where the numerous cones were found on Tell A.

The Distribution of the Lagash II Clay Nails from the Historic Spoils

Though it is immediately and unsurprisingly apparent that most of the cones retrieved by the British Museum team (including the ones found *in situ*, which are discussed in Chapter 43) contained Gudea's Standard Inscription, subtle distinctions were noted between groups of cones, in particular between the respective examples that were found on different clusters of spoil heaps, and also between groups deriving from the various tertiary contexts. A close look at the contents of the heaps shows some qualitative (and not merely quantitative) variations. For example, the cones found in Cluster 1, on the SW side of Tell A, mostly contained Gudea's Standard Inscription, while SH3 and Cluster 2, on the W and NW sides of Tell A, respectively, yielded a more balanced proportion of cones dedicated to Ningirsu, on the one hand, and to the goddesses Bau and Gatumdug, on the other. Generally, the finds exposed in SH3 and Cluster 2 were also closely comparable with each other. A relatively high proportion of cones containing Gudea's EPA text emerged in all three dumps (Cluster 1, SH3 and Cluster 2).

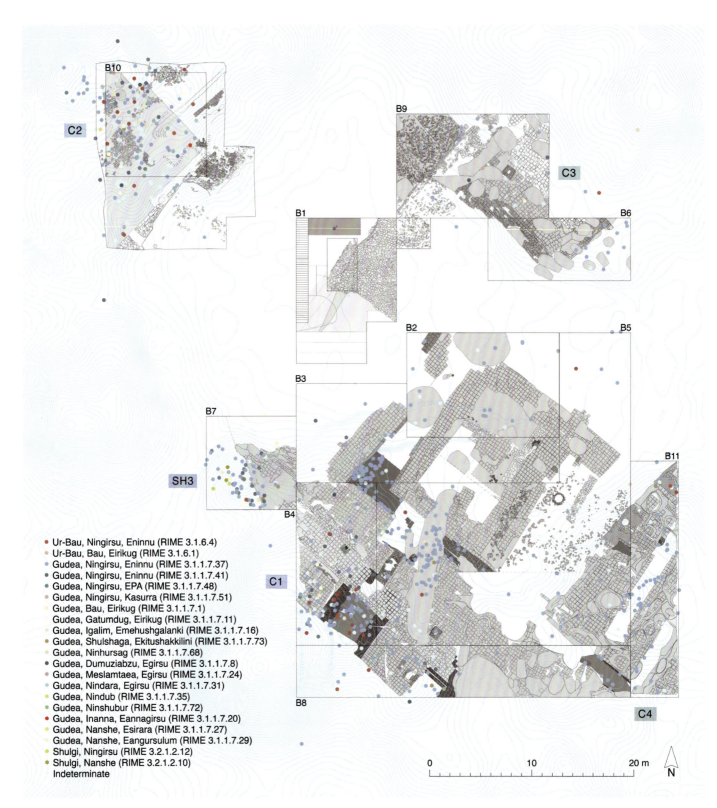

FIGURE 147. Plan showing the distribution of Lagash II and Ur III inscribed clay nails in the British Museum team's trenches.

men) who came from outside the region from rich, powerful countries that had well-honed traditions of scientific and historical research, including established museums that were both display rooms and also laboratories in which curatorial skills were constantly being refined. There was undoubtedly an unseemly scramble for treasure, with national and institutional rivalries being played out in the funding of excavations, but the picture was more complicated than this might suggest because numerous factors were in play—political, economic, historic, scientific and personal. The day-to-day economics of sales rooms and auction houses were also of considerable importance. Free-market attitudes and a burgeoning appetite among the buying public spawned a lucrative traffic in Mesopotamian antiquities. The problems associated with that often shadowy trade, not to mention the high prices that prized pieces commanded on the open market, gave national museums, particularly in the West, a still greater incentive to conduct their own excavations. They did so against the fluid backdrop of a constantly changing balance of power, such that individual sites were all too often seen as extra-territorial holdings of external national governments, with their effective ownership being underwritten by Ottoman or Mandate legal documentation. When the first French excavations took place in Tello at the end of the nineteenth century, the area was under Ottoman rule, but after the First World War direct Western political control over the Near East as a whole increased enormously. Ironically, that eventually led to the cessation of French excavations in Iraq and their relocation to neighbouring Syria. This complicated history meant that the significance of key sites was brought to the attention of the wider public, but the sites themselves were periodically left unguarded. The treasures that lay underground were therefore extensively looted before, between and after systematically organised seasons and campaigns of investigation. That situation has pertained and even been intensified right up until the present day, particularly in the wake of the Gulf War and the subsequent instability that beset the region at the end of the twentieth century, soon followed by the second American-led invasion in 2003.

These salient facts combine to explain the catastrophic damage that has been inflicted on Tell A (and other parts of Tello) over the past century and a half. The archaeology from the Hellenistic and later periods was undoubtedly affected most severely because many of those relatively recent remains were almost completely removed by archaeologists who were keen to dig down to third-millennium levels. In consequence, most of the Hellenistic fired-brick structures on Tell A were dismantled, and their bricks were reused by archaeologists to build their excavation HQs. More generally, extensive tracts of the tell were truncated by broad, shallow trenches that were cut obliquely from the periphery of the upper part of the mound inwards towards its centre. In the central area, as has been noted previously, considerable surface expanses were shaved off horizontally and hollowed out by Sarzec, who also carried out deep, narrow soundings on general N–S and E–W alignments, as well as locally in the spaces between the SW third of the British Museum team's Area B1, the NW part of B3 and the SE part of B10. Such deep pits were dug in the course of the repeated excavations around the Gate of Gudea that were started by Sarzec and later continued by Cros and Genouillac. The other deep trenches that Genouillac dug in the rooms inside the so-called Palace, along with his East and West Trenches (recorded on his plan), were identified by the British Museum team in Areas B7 and B10, and possibly also in B9. Again as is discussed above, these major excavations seriously mutilated stratified deposits, especially the mud-brick structures that were almost entirely overlooked, but the works also altered the tell's drainage patterns, causing additional secondary and ongoing damage. Finally, the scars of modern looting (some of which has taken place very recently indeed) are most obvious in the extensive dense pitting that is found in the south-east of Tell A and in the north-east of the site at large.

As explained above, all of these factors combined to invert Tell A's inherent profile to the extent that the convex mound that was shaped by natural processes, following the collapse and erosion of mostly clay-based structures and installations, now resembles a giant crater that is surrounded by a more or less amorphous mass of spoil heaps and unexcavated earth. It is understandable, therefore, that when the British Museum team's new campaign of excavations began in 2016, any hopes of uncovering intact third-millennium stratigraphy were extremely modest.

The Devil Is in the Details

The chapters above are devoted to an in-depth history of the unfortunately destructive digs that were carried out on the Mound of the Palace by the French pioneers in the late nineteenth and early twentieth centuries. The following sections and chapters detail the results of the British Museum team's salvage excavations on Tell A that were undertaken between 2016 and 2022. The account takes a chronological approach, working from the earliest to the latest periods, namely from the Early Dynastic through to Hellenistic times. The connecting thread that runs all the way through this study is the long history of the Temple of Ningirsu, from its origins on Tell K through to its later manifestation on Tell A, after the big move that was instigated by Ur-Bau and crowned with Gudea's New Eninnu. The book also details the temple's subsequent fate and legacy. Embedded in that overarching narrative is a crucial question that has a profound influence on how the entire sequence should be interpreted: which deity was worshipped in the temple complex on Tell A before it was made sacred to Ningirsu? The results of the British Museum team's work, which are laid out in the remainder of this chapter, provide evidence that helps to answer that question unequivocally.

Beneath the enormous religious precinct that was built on Tell A by Gudea in Lagash II times, the team's excavations uncovered the remarkable remains of a series of superimposed archaic cult platforms and associated temple buildings that date back to the beginning of the third millennium BCE (Fig. 148), contemporary with the Lower Construction on Tell K. The time span of the excavated structures, which covers the whole of the Early Dynastic and Akkad periods, is exactly parallel to the chief part of the long sequence on Tell K that is laid out in Part 2 above: from the erection of the Ur-Nanshe Building through to its later post-destruction phase. That succession of events, which begins with the founding of the Lower Construction (and even before that with the laying of pavement V), continues through the reign of Ur-Nanshe, the founder of the First Dynasty of Lagash, and extends beyond the end of the Presargonic era to include the Akkad interlude. The entire historical framework is outlined in Part 2.

The fact that the British Museum team's work on Tell A was necessarily a salvage operation reflects the dramatic changes in archaeological methodology that have occurred since the time of Sarzec, Cros and Genouillac. Despite some inherent drawbacks, it would be wrong to say that the methods employed by Sarzec et al. were entirely without merit. Excavating large expanses of archaeologically fertile ground, they exposed extensive remains and retrieved a hoard of

FIGURE 148. The sequence of mud-brick platforms excavated by the British Museum team on Tell A, showing (from bottom to top) the red and white platforms.

really exceptional objects, all of which gave fundamental new insights into how Sumerian culture developed in the third millennium BCE and the legacy that it left behind. But their way of working was marred by two highly significant defects: it was both extremely destructive and strikingly lacking in precision. The scale of the damage is still evident today in the topography of Tell A, which (as noted repeatedly) was transformed by the French from a towering ancient mound that was teeming with undiscovered archaeological relics into a deep crater surrounded by spoil heaps. The lack of precision was ubiquitous: among other things, it included Sarzec's much-observed failure to take any notice of mud-brick structures, the lack of a scientific system for recording the exact locations and heights of finds, the failure to note the exact composition of building materials, and the inattention to a wealth of small finds that were simply discarded. These flaws meant that the data was imperfectly recorded and interpreted, and the resulting record was peppered with gaps.

The new methodological frameworks and technological tools that have come into being since the last of the French pioneers left Tello in the 1930s allow a degree of precision that they would have found unthinkable (and also perhaps regarded as disproportionately time-consuming). The modern approach begins by conceiving of the site's history as a series of superimposed archaeological deposits that form strata or layers. The stratigraphic method means that excavated remains can be scrutinised in great detail and dated with ever-increasing accuracy because structural remains can be correlated with pottery assemblages and other remnants of material culture. All the recorded characteristics of even the smallest deposits, including their size, composition, colour, consistency and condition, together with their exact find locations and stratigraphic relations, contribute to a minute understanding of particular sequences of events. The data sets might sometimes appear dry, but it is vital to recall that they are nothing more or less than a systematised account of human actions and their consequences. The reconstructed events might be, for example: the raising of an artificial mound that formed the terrace platform for an array of buildings, including the temple to a god and its annexes (storehouses, a coach house, a brewery and so forth); the location of access points to individual buildings and to the mound itself, which are indicators of how people used the site at different periods; the closure and levelling of a temple, accompanied by the observance of rituals and ceremonial feasting; and the subsequent elevation of the mound to a new level prior to the construction of a successor temple. This short list is far from exhaustive, but it highlights the crucial fact that each and every recorded deposit represents an action that was carried out with the intention of achieving some particular purpose. That is the human and historical meaning of the stratigraphic data, and it is why the devil is incontrovertibly in the details, none of which are too small to be overlooked.

For the sake of clarity, and bearing in mind that even specialists can be deterred by exhaustive technical descriptions, the following accounts of the British Museum team's findings separate the stratigraphy from the associated pottery assemblages that were used to establish ceramic dating. To avoid descending into an ultra-abstract domain of strata that are not anchored in the real world of historical figures and events, however, indications of the chronological periods that the strata represent are included. In all cases, the exact rationales for the dating are laid out in separate sections that are devoted exclusively to the pottery.

The Early Dynastic and Akkad Sequence

The history of the Early Dynastic archaeological sequence on Tell A is laid out below in chronological order, beginning with the first two Early Dynastic temple platforms that were encountered in Area B1, along with their associated underlying and overlying layers (Fig. 149). This is followed by a discussion of the third platform (subsequently remodelled in the Lagash II period to create the NE entrance to Gudea's New Eninnu) that was found in Area B9, and it concludes with an account of cult buildings dating from the Early Dynastic IIIb era, Akkad times and the reign of Ur-Bau in the Early Lagash II period (in Areas B2, B3, B5 and B11); these remains were found beneath the most recent Lagash II Temple of Ningirsu that was built by Gudea. In summary, three superimposed platforms were exposed below the foundations of the New Eninnu: the red platform (1063) that was built at around the same time as the Lower Construction on Tell K; the white platform (1036) from the reign of Ur-Nanshe; and finally the grey platform (5235) of Urukagina, which was the last of the Early Dynastic additions to the mound.

The team's new excavations indicate that, for two main reasons, only parts of these older structural layers survived. First, because they were either buried or partly or entirely demolished during later construction phases. This was particularly noticeable with respect to the older Early Dynastic and Akkad walls that were obscured and mutilated during the construction of Gudea's Lagash II complex, which was built immediately on top of the earlier layers. Secondly, walls and terraces were removed indiscriminately by the French excavators, without being adequately recorded. Indeed, as a consequence of the shortcomings in their methods, some mud-brick remains were not even identified as buildings and installations before they were cleared.

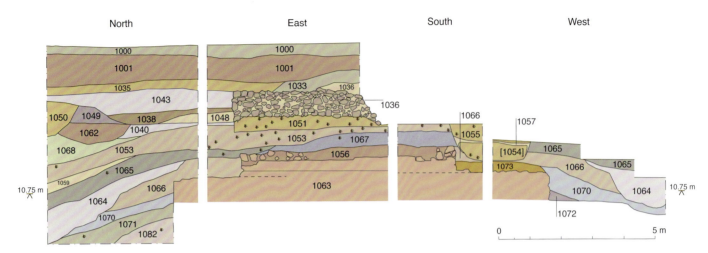

FIGURE 149. The principal sections recorded by the British Museum team in Area B1.

The Earliest Deposits

The earliest deposits and structures found on Tell A, which date back to the Late Early Dynastic I period (the ceramic dating is detailed below), were a reddish-coloured mud-brick platform (context 1063), together with the deposits (1082 and 1071) upon which it was built (Fig. 150). As the stratigraphy shows, layers 1082 and 1071 predated the red terrace platform (1063), which was the earliest structure encountered (as described below). The oldest layer (1082), which contained no artefacts, was identified at a topographical height of 9.96 m. It comprised a silty clay deposit with a surface that sloped uniformly down to the north-west, and it extended under the red platform (1063). The depth of layer 1082 meant that only a limited examination was practicable, but it appeared to have a homogeneous character and to contain very few inclusions. Extending beyond the floor of the deepest sounding in Area B1, it was recorded to a maximum thickness of 0.76 m.

Another deposit of silty clay (1071) that also extended underneath mud-brick platform 1063 lay directly on top of context 1082 at a maximum topographical height of 10.45 m. Like 1082, its surface sloped downwards from the south-east towards the north-west, and it was also devoid of objects. More extensive in plan than 1082, layer 1071 was exposed to a length of 3.3 m from the north-west to the south-east, and it was in excess of 0.61 m thick, though its maximum thickness could not be ascertained because it continued beyond the limits of the trench. Overall, the deposit was light greyish green in colour, with patches of reddish mottling throughout. Since the mottling was very similar in colour to the materials found in platform 1063 (above), it might have been caused by fragments that filtered down from the later deposit.

No horizontal layer that could be associated with the ground surface around red platform 1063 was recorded anywhere in the trench. Although context 1071 was found to be compact, it sloped downwards, away from the platform, and did not form a level surface. This might well suggest that platform 1063 was constructed on a deliberately prepared elevated artificial mound with sloping edges, and that the state in which the platform was found might be associated with the demolition and burial of this phase prior to the addition of deposits intended to raise the ground. Its condition was no doubt affected by erosion before the preparatory phase was complete.

The Red Platform

The oldest structure discovered on Tell A dated from the Late Early Dynastic I to the Early Dynastic IIIa periods and was therefore (as noted above) contemporary with the Lower Construction on Tell K. It comprised a monumental mud-brick platform (1063) that took the form of a two-stage stepped terrace that faced the north-west, with the body of the structure extending to the south-east beyond the excavation area (Fig. 151). It was constructed from brownish-red mud-bricks, formed by hand rather than in a mould, with dimensions ranging between a maximum of 0.35 m × 0.24 m down to a minimum of 0.15 m × 0.1 m. The lower step of the

FIGURE 150. (*top*) The two-step red platform (below) and white platform (above), excavated by the British Museum team on Tell A.

FIGURE 151. (*bottom*) Detail of the stepped red platform in Area B1.

terrace was 0.75 m high, while the upper step, which was set back by 1.15 m from the edge of the lower one, was preserved to a height of about 0.55 m. The height differential was due to damage and superficial erosion on the platform's upper stage (contexts 1056 and 1067) that had occurred when the platform was partially levelled during a subsequent construction phase. Red platform 1063 was exposed at a depth of about 2.5 m beneath the base of the later Early Dynastic IIIb white platform (1036), at a topographical height of 10.45 m. The excavated area measured 9.65 m × 6.9 m, but it certainly extended far beyond the limits of Area B1, spanning an overall surface of perhaps 3,000 m^2 or 3,200 m^2.

The absence of any non-trivial finds in platform 1063 made it difficult to date, but the pottery assemblage that was found in the levelling layers immediately above it indicated that it must have been laid down before the Early Dynastic IIIa period (see contexts 1064 and 1065), while its associated substructural layers were from Late Early Dynastic I times (1071 and 1082). The fact that no monumental stepped platforms dating from this epoch have previously been discovered anywhere in the region suggests that red platform 1063 might potentially be the earliest known example of this kind of structure in the whole of Mesopotamia. Other than a few sherds of pottery, no notable finds were made in context 1064, but context 1065 yielded a burnt fragment of a flint blade (TG1478) that was broken at both ends and exhibited inverse retouch on its left and right edges.

Red platform 1063 was also associated with a series of superimposed ground-raising deposits (1070, 1072, 1073 and 1066), mostly composed of sandy silt and ranging in thickness between 0.3 m and 0.76 m, that contained a well-stratified assemblage of datable sherds or diagnostic potsherds from a time span that extended from the Late Early Dynastic I to the Early Dynastic IIIa periods. Layer 1066, which exactly marked the transition between the two eras, projected over, and therefore embraced or encased, the red platform's lower step. Having a surface that sloped down from the south-east towards the north-west, layer 1066 was 0.6 m thick, and it was traced for 3 m from the north-west to the south-east. Though it was laid directly on top of the red platform's lower step, 1066 abutted onto the face of the red platform's upper step at a topographical height of about 11.85 m. The absence of mud-brick fragments as inclusions suggested that layer 1066 was simply another dumped deposit that was intended to raise the ground around the edge of the red platform and that it did not derive directly from the dismantling and demolition of structures on or around its summit.

The Levelling and Burial of the Red Platform

Layers 1064, 1065 and 1059, which appeared to have been deposited after platform 1063 fell into disuse, were presumably linked with the demolition of 1063 in preparation for the construction of the white platform (1036) above it, at a topographical height of about 12.95 m (Fig. 149). The three layers are described in order of deposition, beginning with layer 1064 (the oldest), which was found to be composed of brownish-red brick fragments that were of a similar or identical colour and composition to the bricks that were used to build red platform 1063, where many intact examples were found. Layer 1064 was 1.05 m thick, and it was exposed over a length of 4.4 m from the south-east to the north-west, extending beyond the limits of Area B1. Although it was not found directly in contact with platform 1063, it was placed immediately on top of layer 1066, which encased the red platform's lower step, and was therefore presumed to date from a time when the red platform was no longer in use. The presence of red mud-brick fragments suggested that 1064 was formed from demolished structures or a demolished higher terrace that must have been situated on top of 1063. Its position away from the edge of 1063, however, indicated that it was a dump of material that was used to raise the ground on the red platform's periphery.

Layer 1065, which was composed of silty sand, was found above both 1064 (just described) and deposit 1066 that encased the red platform's lower step. It was between 0.22 m and 0.58 m thick, becoming generally thicker towards the north-west, and it was exposed over a length of 5 m from the north-west to the south-east. It also extended beyond the limits of B1 to the north-west. Layer 1059 was a bedding and levelling deposit of loose pure sand that was laid over 1065 at thicknesses of between 0.08 m and 0.28 m, also becoming generally thicker towards the north-west. Stratigraphically, it represented an interstitial deposit between the demolition and construction levels below and above, respectively: the demolition of the underlying red platform, and the overlying deposits that were laid down when the white platform (1036) was built. The position and relative purity of 1059 suggested that it might have been deposited as part of the ritual cleansing and closing of the old temple terrace.

These distinct layers of sandy and clayey silts were rich in pottery remains that were unearthed in assemblages typical of the ceramic objects that were used in temples during Early Dynastic IIIa times. Such assemblages commonly included fine jug sherds as well as sherds of conical bowls and, to a lesser extent, goblet sherds (all detailed below). Apart from the scraps of pottery just mentioned, no significant artefacts were recovered from 1064 or 1059, but context 1065 yielded the blade fragment discussed above (TG1478), while 1053 contained a fragment of a stone vessel (TG1046) and the flat head of a decorative cone (TG2102). Context 1051 contained another fragment of a stone vessel (TG1015).

The White Platform

The later Early Dynastic temple platform (1036) was built above its red precursor (1063) at a topographical height of about 12.95 m as part of the comprehensive rebuilding of the complex at a higher level (Fig. 152). As a consequence, the later platform closely mirrored the earlier one in both shape and alignment. This construction phase does not seem to have involved the expansion of the entire temple precinct to the north-west to cover the upper terraces of earlier phases, but was rather focused more narrowly on the main temple establishment, elevating its base level above that of its predecessor by about 0.5 m.

White platform 1036 was constructed from planoconvex mud-bricks that were initially brownish grey when they were first uncovered, but soon weathered to a whitish colour when they were exposed to sunlight. The change in colour, which was doubtless intended by the manufacturers, was achieved by mixing limestone powder into the brick clay—a process that whitened the platform's external faces. Most of the bricks were subrectangular and subcircular in shape, with the variation probably indicating that the core of the platform was built in a slightly haphazard manner. It is likely that the platform's outer faces were originally finished with regular courses of uniformly subrectangular planoconvex bricks, such as were encountered immediately to the north-west in Area B9, in the uppermost terrace of the later Early Dynastic IIIb complex. Conversely, the dimensions of the bricks that made up the core of the white platform were heterogeneous, varying in size between 0.5 m × 0.23 m × 0.07 m and 0.13 m × 0.1 m × 0.08 m. They were laid in seven rough, semi-regular courses, bonded with a silty mud mortar that exhibited occasional pottery inclusions.

FIGURE 152. The white platform in Area B1, showing the truncation caused by French excavation trenches.

The upper surface of the white platform (at topographical heights ranging between 13.65 m and 13.85 m) was formed of small subrounded mud-bricks of various colours (brown, grey, white, yellow, green and salmon) that were set within a silty tan-brown matrix. The mixed nature of this surface, in terms of both colour and the small size of its constituent parts, was probably the result of erosion, though other damage was doubtless caused when the platform was still in use, including while structures and installations were being built on it, and when it was occasionally resurfaced and repaired during its lifetime.

A shallow silty deposit (1030) between white platform 1036 and the later Lagash II residual *pisé* (1033) contained some pottery, including an intact conical bowl that was dated to Early Dynastic IIIb times—a find that suggested that 1036 could not postdate this period. The platform was truncated to the south-west by a series of wide French excavation pits and trenches, including 1011 and 1022 (Genouillac's Central Trench and Trench of the Well); the deepest of the French cuts (traced in contexts 1054 and 1076), which was dug by Cros, descended down into the underlying red platform (1063).

The NW face of white platform 1036 had been further eroded by water that had flowed through a large gully (1037) that ran from the north-east to the south-west. Formed sometime after the French digs had come to an end in 1933, it had caused the partial collapse of the platform's westernmost side. When this area of 1063 was excavated, it appeared at first to have been built in a slightly different way from the rest of the platform, as it bulged out in a subcircular protuberance towards the south-west. On closer inspection, however, it became clear that this was not a deliberately designed feature of the original construction, but was rather due to accidental erosion and subsidence, perhaps resulting from the periodic flow of water across the compacted buried surface of 1036 into an adjacent French sounding (1011).

As a consequence of heavy rainfall, the NW edge of white platform 1036 suffered a further collapse during the British Museum team's excavations. The subsidence revealed that a single fired brick (uncovered in a broken state) had been positioned in the middle of the frontmost course of roughly shaped mud-bricks. The apparently purposeful placement of a solitary kiln-fired brick in the fabric of the platform was surely significant, but the absence of an inscription and the lack of any associated artefacts made it difficult to interpret

the anomalous brick as a foundation deposit in the usual sense of the term. It might perhaps have been installed as a functional marker to aid the construction process, possibly as a standard measure or to demarcate the platform's external edge. Signed with a thumbprint (the regnal mark of Ur-Nanshe), it appeared to date from the Early Dynastic IIIb period, around the same time as the assemblage of potsherds mentioned above. White platform 1036 was exposed over an area measuring 9.2 m × 7.6 m, but as with the red platform (1063) this represented only a tiny part of its original extent, which in all likelihood covered much of Tell A, perhaps measuring some 3,000 m² in total.

The base of white platform 1036 was identified after the removal of a series of contemporaneous deposits immediately to its north-west. Partially truncated by gully 1037 (described above), these hard deposits, which were exposed at an overall elevation of 13.95 m to a thickness of 1.4 m, included a hard-packed topmost concretion (1043), with a thickness of 0.7 m, that was composed of pinkish-tan clay with nodules of clay mixed throughout its loam. Other foundation fills were uncovered beneath concretion 1043, with a combined thickness ranging between 0.5 m and 0.75 m. They included other clay fills (1049), fills of sand (1050) and sand with clay nodules (1038 and 1048), all of which were superimposed on a bottom layer of clay (1040).

A fragment of the base of a stone vessel (TG844) that was probably made of limestone was recovered from context 1043. Context 1038 also contained a fragment of a limestone vessel (TG936), which was identified as part of the rim and body of an open receptacle, drilled with an 8-mm perforation that was placed 19 mm below its rim. A fragment of basalt was also found in context 1038, while no artefacts other than pottery were recovered from contexts 1049, 1050, 1048 and 1040.

A foundation fill (1051) that was rich in pottery and charcoal remains was uncovered beneath platform 1036, where it extended under the lowest course of mud-bricks and therefore confirmed the platform's lower limit. The excavation of 1051 facilitated the team's investigation of the immediate underlying layers, beginning with the partial removal of the white platform's westernmost section in order to create a cross-section through the platform on a N–S alignment. A small number of mud-bricks were removed from 1036, all of which were slightly textured with the imprints of the hands that had shaped the clay when it was still wet. Foundation fill 1051, which was 0.42 m thick, consisted of compacted clay that contained potsherds dating to the Early Dynastic IIIb period, though a conspicuous number of Early Dynastic IIIa sherds suggested the fill might have been laid down at the very beginning of the Presargonic epoch, during the reign of Ur-Nanshe. It was placed on a similar substructural fill (1053) that covered and sealed off the underlying levelling deposits, all of which were capped with the possibly purified layer of sand (1059) mentioned above that was associated with the demolition of the earlier red platform. Composed of sandy silt, fill 1053 was between 0.34 m and 0.76 m thick, and it sloped down towards the north-west. It also contained diagnostic pottery dating to Early Dynastic IIIb times, together with the Early Dynastic IIIa remnants just noted.

Whereas most, if not all, of the other pottery remains found in deposits associated with the white and red platforms were of types connected with religious ceremonies (notably conical bowls; Fig. 153), foundation fills 1051 and 1053 (both lying above sand layer 1059) exhibited an entirely different pattern of discards. By contrast with those other finds, these layers predominantly yielded the kinds of goblets that were used for divine offerings at communal ritual feasts, and it is therefore tempting to link these artefacts with the festivities that must have accompanied the consecration of the freshly raised sacred site prior to the building of a new temple. The celebrations would presumably have involved the ruler, in this instance almost certainly Ur-Nanshe, along with the royal household, cohorts of high priests and attendants, and representatives of the citizenry of Girsu.

On top of layer 1053 was found a subfloor packing (1068), with a maximum thickness of 0.92 m, that raised and levelled off the white platform and its immediate environs. Over this was a flooring horizon (1040) made of very compact clay that was laid flush with the base of 1036 at a topographical height of 12.95 m. At the same level was a pit (1061), with a width of about 2 m, that had been dug into layer 1040 to a depth of 0.62 m. It featured a concave base and gradually sloping sides, while its fill (1062), which exclusively contained Early Dynastic IIIb pottery, was distinguished by a notable absence of later sherds—the implication being that the deposit was laid down during a well-defined, self-contained period of activity.

The uppermost deposit (1043) that was associated with white platform 1036 represented a further general raising of the ground that corresponded with another comprehensive reconstruction of the sacred complex on a higher terrace (5235) that was partially identified in Area B9 (detailed

FIGURE 153. Early Dynastic ceremonial vessels from Tell A: four offering bowls (left) and a goblet (right).

immediately below). Potsherds from layer 1043 dated this rebuilding programme to the late Early Dynastic IIIb period, or possibly to a proto-imperial phase of the Early Akkad era. That being the case, it was almost certainly contemporary with the reign of Urukagina, the last Presargonic ruler of Lagash.

The Grey Platform

In Area B9, a very short distance to the north-east of platform 1036, and clearly closely connected to it in several respects, was found a stretch of poorly preserved planoconvex mud-brick masonry (5235) at a topographical height of 13.8 m, rising to an overall maximum elevation of between 14.7 m and 14.8 m (Fig. 139). The incompletely exposed part of grey platform 5235 comprised a stretch of mud-brick walling that was aligned north-east to south-west, with its NW face mostly visible in plan and only partially in section. Its poor state of preservation was due to a variety of factors that had been exacerbated by the fragility of the deposit's constituent parts. First, it had been used as the foundation for the later NE gateway that was built during the Lagash II period. Secondly, a pair of very closely spaced French trenches ran approximately perpendicularly through the face of 5235, contributing to the fact that its surface was found sloping downwards within the adjacent Area B1 for approximately 1 m from the north-east to the south-west, following the line on which it was unwittingly truncated by the French excavators. Thirdly, after the French excavations in Tello ceased altogether in 1933, processes of erosion (mostly caused by seasonal water channelling) carved the bed of a narrow stream through the soft deposits that filled the Lagash II gateway, but then fanned out beyond the inner side of the gate structure into one of the open excavation trenches that were found cutting through context 5235.

The result of this broadly threefold series of events was that all the regular courses of planoconvex mud-bricks that formed the core of structure 5235 were destroyed, leaving nothing more than the remains of the underlying mass of white platform 1036 to the south-west and the face of grey platform 5235 to the north-east, where platform 5235 was preserved only because it was encased in or bolstered by Gudea's Lagash II temenos wall and its associated platform at the point where those structures extended out to the north-east beyond the NE gateway (as is discussed below).

The rectangular bricks used in the construction of grey platform 5235 were about 0.06 m thick on average, and their visible sides measured about 0.2 m. They appeared to be typically planoconvex in shape, and they were probably handmade from a dark grey and dark brownish-grey matrix that was found to be very variable in composition, ranging from a firm silty clay to a more friable sandy silt, though no pattern was discernible in the distribution of the resulting variants. There were some indications in plan that the bricks were laid in different ways: some on their broad, flat sides; others on their narrower edges (particularly on the platform's NW face). This might reflect phases of repair, or possibly decorative or structural augmentation across the façade.

The function of platform 5235 was hard to ascertain, but it was clearly very closely associated with white platform 1036, as was most noticeable in Area B1, where its exposed NW façade was set back 1 m from the edge of 1036. It was built on top of white platform 1036, probably forming a terrace foundation for a new sanctuary or subsidiary shrine. Since only one face of 5235 was discovered (and in B1 the damage done by the French trenching meant that it was only encountered in the form of shapeless lumps), and since the colour and especially the composition of the mud-bricks differed somewhat from those used in 1036, it is most likely that 5235 formed the edge of a distinct platform, the interior of which doubtless extended inwards towards the centre of the mound. It might be further observed that the bricks used in 5235 were seemingly more regular in their shapes and dimensions than those found in 1036, again confirming that these were two separate structures belonging to different building phases. The overall height difference of 1 m between the highest preserved points of platforms 1036 and 5235 would also be consistent with the raising of a new stepped terrace.

Pottery from the Temple Platforms

The British Museum team's excavations yielded a mass of pottery data that was analysed to reconstruct the occupation sequence of the Tell A temple site. The oldest levels reached in the deep sounding in Area B1, together with the associated overlying strata, permit the reconstruction of a rare complete stratigraphic sequence that embraces a large part of the third millennium BCE. The most ancient ceramic materials, which were found in the basal levels of B1, can be linked with the earliest of the three superimposed Early Dynastic platforms that were detected on the mound: the red platform (1063), which was contemporary with the Lower Construction on Tell K. More specifically, the oldest ceramics were found in layers 1071, 1070 and 1066, all of which were associated with the red platform. Although the recovered repertoire of pottery shapes was rather limited, it nevertheless provided some chronological information. A total of 141 diagnostic fragments were found that pertain to this phase, and the breakdown of types was as follows: mass-produced pottery (less than 50%), including mostly conical beakers (37%) and a much smaller proportion of conical bowls (11%), along with large bowls (20%) and jars (19%) that were found in roughly equal quantities.

Layers 1071 and 1070 yielded numerous sherds that came from three kinds of deep bowls: vessels characterised by straight walls and plain rims (Fig. 154.2); those with straight walls and triangular rims (Fig. 154.3); and those with thickened rims and straight walls, with the addition of ribs that were made with the potters' fingernails (Fig. 154.4). Also found in these layers was a flat tray with an internal ring (Fig. 154.7). The deep bowl sherds recovered from layer 1066 are characterised by curving walls and a variety of rim morphologies, including a thickened rim with an incised external wavy line between the rim and the rib (Fig. 154.8), as well as a triangular rim accompanied by an outer-wall rib made with a fingernail (Fig. 154.9). Among the forms that were found in layers 1070 and 1066 were numerous fragments of beakers and bowls that are attested over a long period during the third millennium BCE (Fig. 154.1 and 154.6). Two specimens of large reserved slip jars without rims were also discovered in 1070 and 1060, and both were found coated with a yellowish slip that had been partly removed to create a geometric decoration. Both jars also feature a projecting ribbing rope located at the junction where the shoulder of each vessel meets its body (Figs. 154.5 and 155.1). The sherds of beakers and bowls from these layers are not conclusively diagnostic since they are attested from a range of periods that span almost the entire third millennium. Nonetheless, the assemblage as a whole compares well with pottery remains that can be securely dated to Early Dynastic I times. More exactly, when combined with the chronological data provided by the ceramic findings, the analysis of the stratigraphic sequence suggests that the red platform was built and used during the Late Early Dynastic I period. This is confirmed by

the absence of ceramic forms, including goblets with solid feet, that are typical of older Early Dynastic I phases.

Above layer 1066 was a homogeneous ceramic horizon represented by 303 processed diagnostic fragments that were recovered from layers 1060, 1064 and 1065. Examples of mass-produced pottery increased significantly in this phase, amounting to 63% of the diagnostic sherds, with beakers (43%) and bowls (20%) continuing to be the main forms (Fig. 155.2 and 155.3). By comparison with the earlier phase, the proportion of deep bowls decreased to 12.5% of the total, while jars became more numerous (21.5%). The open-shaped vessels included many deep bowls with triangular rims (Fig. 155.5), while two fragments of hollow stands with thickened rims and a rib on the outer wall were also found (Fig. 155.6). Among the plentiful closed forms that were uncovered were: a small jar with a short plain rim (Fig. 155.7); another short plain-rimmed jar (Fig. 155.4); a low-necked jar with an external angular rim (Fig. 155.8); and finally two jars with necks of medium size and a triangular rim (Fig. 155.9 and 155.10). Unlike the open forms, which, as mentioned above, remained in use over longer periods, these sherds probably derived from an Early Dynastic IIIa chronological horizon, as evidenced in particular by the ceramics with hollow stands, as well as the range of closed forms just described.

The pottery assemblage recovered from layers 1052 and 1053 included 529 diagnostic sherds, among which the proportion of mass-produced pottery rose to 66% of the total. Conical beakers (44%) made up about half of the finds from this phase, while the percentage of bowls (22%) hardly rose at all. The number of deep bowls decreased markedly to just 7% of the total, but jars (16%) registered a smaller decline. Although beakers and bowls continued to be two of the most attested forms (Fig. 155.11), the ceramic repertoire from these contexts also manifested some interesting innovations, of which the most distinctive diagnostic type were examples of carinated bowls with a plain everted rim (Fig. 155.13–15). Notable open forms included the lower part of a funnel with sinuous walls and a hole in the middle of its flat base (Fig. 156.7), and a hollow stand with a thickened rim and a lower external rib (Fig. 155.12). The repertoire of open shapes was completed by deep bowls featuring a triangular rim (Fig. 156.1) or a hammer rim (Fig. 156.2), with the outer walls of some of the specimens including a rib with a notched band, or a large rib with impressions made with a finger (Fig. 156.3 and 156.4). The repertoire of closed forms was largely dominated by jars of medium size with a short plain rim (Fig. 156.5 and 156.6). More definitely characteristic of the period was a type of jar with an elongated band rim (Fig. 156.8 and 156.9). Pottery from contexts 1052 and 1053 displayed some continuity with the assemblage from the previous layer. There was an increase in the proportion of deep bowls with notched bands on the outsides of the vessels, and new shapes appeared, in particular small carinated bowls. Chronologically, the repertoire retrieved from this phase can also be securely dated to the Early Dynastic IIIa period.

Context 1051 merits a separate discussion because this layer, which was connected with the white platform (1036) that was built during the reign of Ur-Nanshe, yielded very few pottery fragments. Only 127 diagnostic sherds were recorded, with 77% of the total being made up of mass-produced ceramics, including beakers (Fig. 157.1), which represented 46% of the total, and bowls (31%). Among the other diagnostic shapes were some short plain-rimmed jars. Analysis of the finds revealed that, in addition to the preponderance of mass-produced types, the sherds from this layer were very fragmented. Putting all these factors together, the repertoire in its entirety suggested a link between context 1051 and the building of white platform 1036. As such, it provided an important anchor point for the reconstruction of the relative sequence of Area B1 as a whole, and more specifically for the dating of the white platform. The fact that mass-produced pottery made up more than three-quarters of the diagnostic fragments from this phase confirmed the increased impact of these forms. More generally, the analysis showed that the layer was probably created while the white platform was actually under construction. When the stratigraphic sequence was correlated with the chronological periodisation provided by the pottery, it was concluded that context 1051 was laid down during a final phase of the Early Dynastic IIIa period, or was possibly part of a transitional phase between Early Dynastic IIIa and Early Dynastic IIIb times.

The levels connected with white platform 1036 that could be dated to the interval between the Early Dynastic IIIb and the Early Akkad eras returned very few ceramic fragments. Only seventy-one diagnostic sherds were recorded, with 80% of the total consisting of mass-produced pottery. A repertoire of diagnostic forms, including beakers and bowls (Fig. 157.2), was found in strata associated with the occupation and use of the white platform, notably contexts 1043 and 1038. Although mass-produced pottery accounted for 68% of the diagnostic

sherds, an interesting change was observed when the repertoire was compared with assemblages from previous phases. Whereas, in earlier strata, beakers were more numerous than bowls, in this phase the trend was reversed, with beakers and bowls making up 22% and 46% of the total, respectively. Open shapes comprised 13% of the finds from this level. Among them were large bowls with an external rounded triangular rim (Fig. 157.3), as well as deep bowls with a deep, upward-curving wall and an overhanging rounded triangular rim (Fig. 157.4), and also a deep bowl with a notched band below a triangular rim on its outside wall (Fig. 157.5). Another specimen (Fig. 157.6) with an overhanging hammer rim was probably a stemmed dish rather than a deep bowl. The closed forms from this level displayed reduced variety in the rims of the recovered jars (14%) compared to previous phases. The largest group of closed forms were sherds from short plain-rimmed jars (Fig. 157.7), while the small number of variants included a sherd from a jar with a medium-size neck (Fig. 157.8).

The trends discerned in the pottery repertoire from the lower layers of Area B1 were also observed in the layers that covered the upper surface of platform 1036, where mass-produced pottery represented 62% of the diagnostic sherds recorded for this phase. The proportion of beakers was further reduced to 14% of the total, while bowls increased to 52% of the recovered examples. In addition to conical beakers (Fig. 158.1) and beakers with curving walls (Fig. 158.2), conical bowls (representing 14% of the pottery assemblage found at this level) were still well attested (Fig. 158.3–6). Closed forms were limited to small jars and jars of medium size (18% of the diagnostic sherds that were processed), with two types predominating: short plain-rimmed jars (Fig. 158.8 and 158.9) and a kind of small jar with a plain rim (Fig. 158.7). The significant disturbances in the upper layers of Area B1 that were caused by the French pioneers added to the difficulty of establishing a stratigraphic sequence for this phase, but the data provided by the pottery indicated that the white platform remained in use continuously from Early Dynastic IIIb times through to the Early Akkad era.

Perhaps the most noteworthy feature of the layers above contexts 1040 and 1062 was the gradually changing ratio of two mass-produced vessels—beakers and bowls. The use of beakers declined considerably in this period, while bowls (representing about 50% of the recorded fragments) became the main form. Another interesting development was the progressive reduction in the variety of pottery shapes—a change that was particularly evident in the range of closed shapes, of which plain-rimmed jars, both small and of medium size, were almost the only attested forms. Despite the relatively limited information available, it seemed clear that these trends, which were initiated in the Early Dynastic IIIb period, extended through to Early Akkad times, and this further indicated that white platform 1036 was almost certainly occupied continuously in this time frame. It should be stressed that this does not mean that the Girsu pottery assemblages from the Early Dynastic IIIb and Early Akkad eras were indistinguishable. Rather, in this area of the mound, the recovered diagnostic fragments from these times were essentially limited in number, but the same types of pottery continued to be used.

A Temple Building and an Enigmatic Platform

Although the presence of walls and other structures from the later Lagash II period made it impossible to conduct extensive excavations underneath Gudea's Temple of Ningirsu, limited investigations were carried out in Areas B2, B3 and B5, below the cella, and further to the south-east, beneath the antecella (Fig. 139). They aimed to explore the physical remains that lay under a baked-clay formation deposit (contexts 2011 and 3024) that appeared to have been a foundation layer for the inner sanctum of Gudea's New Eninnu. The foundation was laid over a levelling deposit (3025, 3037 and 3050) that was formed of a loose greenish-grey clayey silt that contained large amounts of Late Akkad and Early Lagash II potsherds and charcoal flecks. Most notably, among many more damaged examples, context 3037 yielded a complete conical bowl (TG383), while context 3025 contained two complete conical bowls (TG319 and TG382); all were found upside down.

The removal of contexts 3025, 3037 and 3050 revealed structural remains from the Early Dynastic IIIb and Akkad periods at a topographical horizon defined between 14.6 m and 14.8 m, which was commensurate with grey platform 5235 in Area B9. This suggested that the horizon was a general feature of the central area, and that it was a foundational layer for the buildings that were erected on it. The uncovered structures included a NE–SW wall (2052) that was built of planoconvex mud-bricks. Measuring 3 m × 1 m, it was exposed to a height of 0.15 m, and its SW end featured a doorway (1.2 m wide) that was flanked on its SW side by traces of a similarly constructed wall (2064) that had the same alignment and orientation. Wall 2052 formed a corner with NW–SE wall 2053 of which a portion measuring 1.5 m × 0.86 m × 0.2 m (h) was uncovered. The extension of wall 2053 (context 3085) ran north-westwards for 3.7 m until it met structure 3091, which measured 0.8 m × 0.9 m. Wall 3085 was made of rectangular planoconvex bricks with dimensions of 0.25 m × 0.2 m. Since it was partly truncated by French trench 3084 and levelled horizontally in Lagash II times, it was unclear whether structure 3091 was a kind of foundational base or possibly a display bench. It was nevertheless observed that 3091 was positioned beneath the later Lagash II offering table (3039) of the Temple of Ningirsu's inner sanctum, and that it faced the overlying Lagash II cult podium (2073). These factors suggested that it might have been an earlier manifestation of the same type of installation. A NE–SW wall (2061), which ran north-eastwards for 2.85 m from the corner formed by 2052 and 2053, was exposed over a width of 0.9 m to a height of 0.1 m.

The structures just described were all built of rectangular planoconvex mud-bricks that were similar (if not identical) to the ones found in the façade of grey platform 5235. They measured 0.25 m × 0.2 m (on average), and they were interspersed with large subrectangular lumps of clay that were positioned in a rudimentary fashion. Although walls 2052, 2053 and 3085 were seemingly part of the same construction phase, wall 2061 might possibly have been built later. Nonetheless, they all (including 2061) partly defined two spaces that were identified as internal rooms of two subsequent occupation phases of a temple that extended out to the south-east: a NE annexe room that was delimited by 2053, 3085 and 2061; and a SW room made up of 2052 and 2053 (the corner), together with 2053 and 3085. The latter possibly contained a cult podium (3091) that was approached indirectly via an opening in the SW room's SE corner.

In the SW room, exposed over a length of 6.8 m and a breadth of 3.8 m, a series of superimposed layers (2050, 2055 and 3088) extended to a depth of about 0.2 m beneath the levelling deposit that was associated with the preconstruction phase of Gudea's project. Meeting walls 2052 and 2053, the upper surface of the room's flooring horizon (2050) was identified at a topographical height of 14.78 m, and it was exposed over an area measuring 4.25 m × 3.75 m. Rich in potsherds, organic materials, ash and charcoal, context 2050, which appeared to be an occupation deposit dating from the Late Akkad and Early Lagash II (Ur-Bau) periods, exhibited multiple lenses of activity. Similar to 2050, and exposed at the

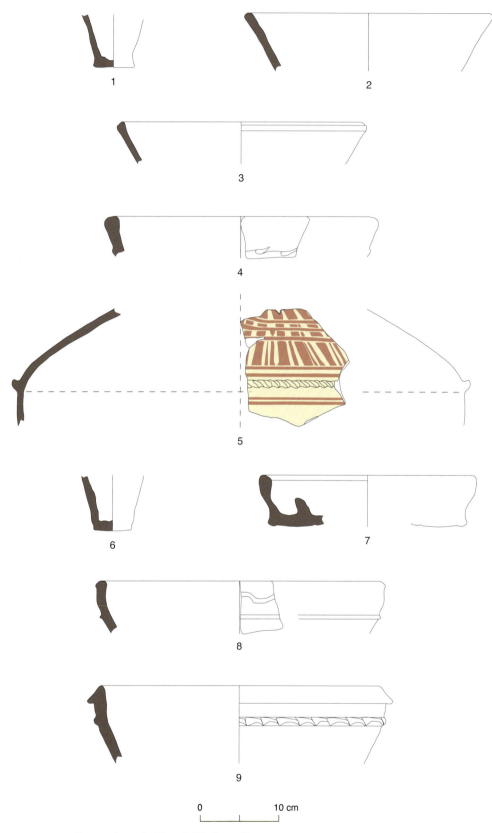

FIGURE 154. Pottery from the Temple Platforms I.

Before the Big Move: The Early Dynastic and Akkad Temple Complex 431

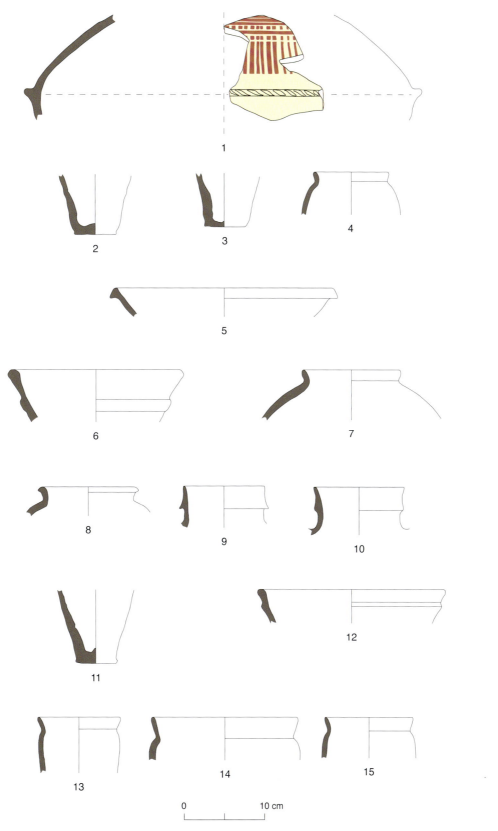

FIGURE 155. Pottery from the Temple Platforms II.

432　The Mound of the Palace

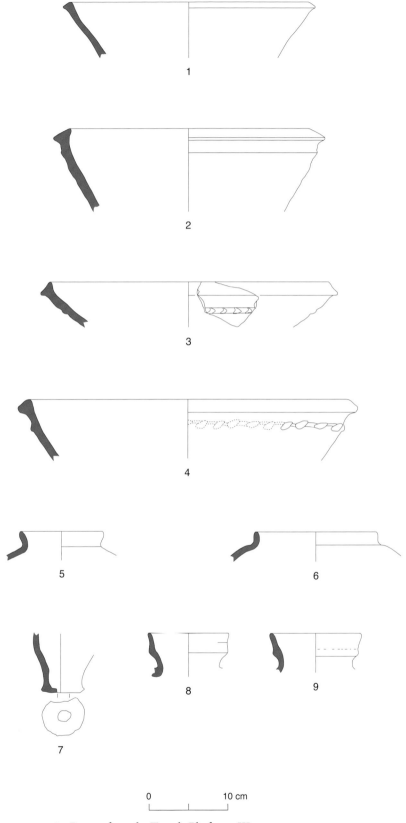

FIGURE 156. Pottery from the Temple Platforms III.

Before the Big Move: The Early Dynastic and Akkad Temple Complex 433

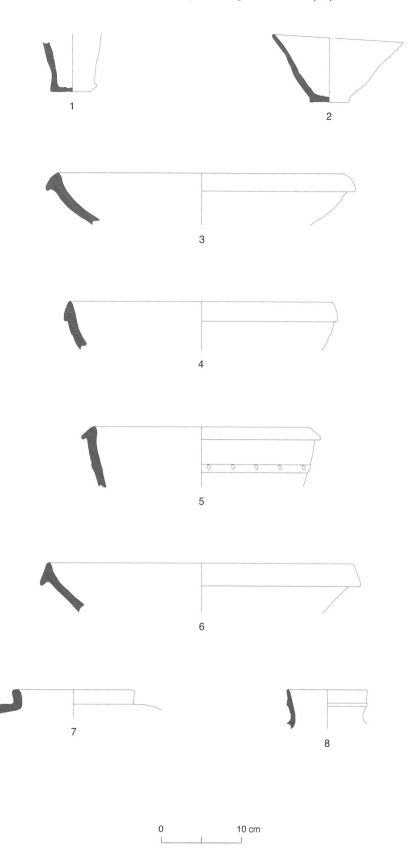

FIGURE 157. Pottery from the Temple Platforms IV.

434 The Mound of the Palace

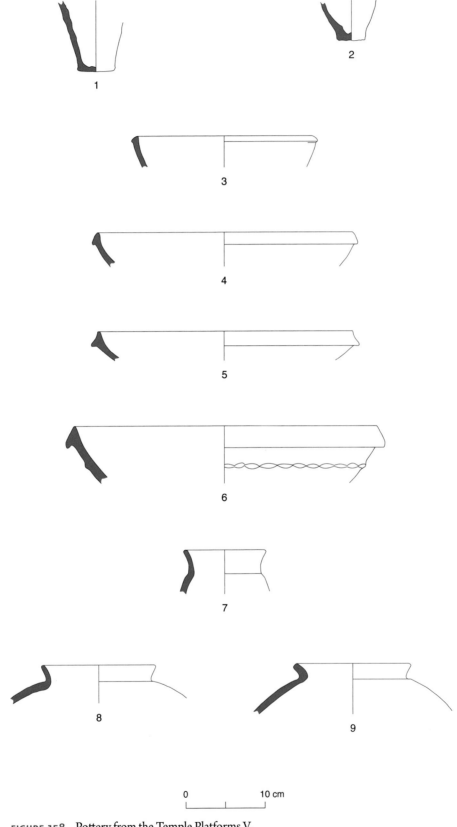

FIGURE 158. Pottery from the Temple Platforms V.

same topographical level, was layer 2055, the continuation of the SW room's occupation fill, which yielded a complete conical bowl (TG991). Fill 2055 was sealed off by layer 2054, the make-up of which differed slightly from that of the overlying levelling deposits. Made of a compact layer that contained large clay lumps, it was seemingly laid down when the room's walls were demolished.

Beneath flooring horizon 2050 and 2055, at a topographical height of 14.66 m, was an earlier occupation layer (3088) that was uncovered over an area measuring 4.20 m × 2.80 m, where it was found to be stratigraphically associated with walls 2052 and 2053, and platform 3091. Layer 3088, which was a very distinctive pale greenish-white colour, and composed of clay lime, was largely truncated by French cut 3084. It contained conical bowls, including one complete example (TG1605), that were typically found very close to the associated walls. Also found were other fragments of vessels characteristic of the Late Early Dynastic IIIb and Akkad periods.

In the NE room, exposed over an area measuring 6.2 m × 3.6 m (a total of 22.3 m²), a similar sequence of layers was excavated to a depth of 0.3 m. Flooring horizon 3087, with dimensions of 5.8 m × 2.5 m, lay at a topographical height of 14.6 m. It was identical to deposit 3088, and was therefore presumed to be part of the same occupation phase. Associated with wall 2053 and its 3085 continuation, context 3087 yielded a complete offering bowl (TG1606) together with many more fragments, all of which were found along the NE face of wall 3085. The flooring horizon (3087) was established on a subfloor bedding (3086) that was uncovered at a height of 14.51 m over an area spanning 5 m × 3.8 m. The latter consisted of a friable clayey silt composition that was rich in potsherds indicative of a backfilled preconstruction layer dating to the Late Early Dynastic IIIb and Akkad periods. A number of intact bowls (TG2350, TG2351, TG2435, TG2436 and TG2470) were found in bedding 3086, all deposited upside down along the substructural façades of the walls. The subfloor bedding also featured three pits (3082, 3095 and 3093), the most noteworthy being 3093, which was a rectangular favissa (1.7 m × 1.15 m × 0.33 m (deep)) with vertical sides and a flat base. The pottery retrieved from pit 3093's single fill (3096) was of the same type as that found in layer 3086, namely temple vessels (mainly conical bowls) of the type used to contain offerings of food and drink. The pots found in pit 3093 had seemingly all been deliberately broken into tiny pieces, however, and this was suggestive of a

ritual—perhaps a ceremonial closure. The pit also contained a fragment of a blade (TG2353) that was made of translucent brown flint and was broken at both ends. The left edge was irregularly denticulated or serrated, with approximately two teeth per 10 mm, and the denticulated edge showed the high gloss that is a characteristic of well-developed use-wear.

The two sacred rooms were both fronted on their SE sides by a large space, perhaps a vestibule or open-air court, that was 6 m wide and bordered towards the south-east by a façade wall (2145), which lay on a NE–SW alignment, parallel to inner walls 2052 and 2061. It was exposed over an area measuring 4.9 m × 1.02 m. The NE portion of wall 2145 exhibited two courses of rectangular planoconvex mud-bricks (measuring 0.24 m × 0.18 × 0.07 m) that were arranged as four rows of headers. Its SW side was constructed of a single course of large mud-brick lumps that were laid in an irregular fashion, perhaps as a foundation course. On top of wall 2145 was layer 2146, which was made primarily of mud-brick melt and collapse. It contained potsherds dating to the Late Akkad and Early Lagash II (Ur-Bau) periods that were similar in character to those found in the levelling deposits excavated over the remains of the two temple rooms. Layer 2146 was seemingly produced when the older building was demolished and levelled during the preparatory phase of Gudea's project.

Finally, further to the south-east of wall 2145 (directly beneath the walls of Gudea's Ningirsu temple) were found the remains of a large enigmatic platform (2158) that had been sealed off in Lagash II (Gudea) times at a topographical height of 15.57 m. Oriented on a NE–SW alignment, it was constructed of pale grey square bricks (0.24 m × 0.24 m × 0.07 m) that were bonded with bedding joints made of mud mortar. The combination of the later structures that were built on top of it, and the fact that it had been damaged by French cut 2036, meant that its original size could not be determined, but it was found to occupy an area of 10.4 m × 2.35 m and was exposed to a depth 0.35 m. Associated pottery complemented by an examination of its stratigraphic relationships with other attributable archaeological features suggested that it was a Late Akkad construction, contemporaneous with the later occupation phase of the two rooms of the nearby temple. This was probably also confirmed by the use of square bricks—an Akkad innovation—that in this instance were markedly smaller than the square bricks used by Ur-Bau and Gudea (with standard side lengths of 0.47 m and 0.32 m, respectively).

Pottery from the Temple Building

The layers representing pre-Gudea Tell A were all character-ised by the same types of pottery shapes and a high percentage of mass-produced ceramics—mostly conical bowls, but also goblets and a very small number of conical beakers. Two main occupation phases were distinguished that could be associated with the pre-Gudea temple and its associated annexes from the Late Early Dynastic IIIb and Early Akkad times to the Late Akkad period (coextensive with the Lagash II Ur-Bau horizon). The most ancient layers yielded the pottery found in context 3088 in the temple's SW room, and contexts 3086 and 3087 in the NE room, namely a few goblets and numerous bowls (Fig. 159.1–4), which together made up 90% of the sherds recorded. Among the rare examples of other types that were found in these contexts were some open shapes, including bowls of medium size with an over-hanging rim (Fig. 159.5) and a few sherds of deep bowls with a triangular rim (Fig. 159.11). The repertoire of closed shapes was especially limited, being almost entirely confined to short plain-rimmed jars (Fig. 159.7 and 159.10). Only one of the excavated specimens gave some insight into the overall form of these particular vessels, which were characterised by a flaring rim, an oval-shaped body and drooping shoulders (Fig. 159.8). Otherwise, the only other closed shape that was attested was a jar with a flaring neck and a thickened rim (Fig. 159.6).

Three ancient pits (3082, 3092 and 3095) that were exposed in the NE room under floor 3087 and its associated subfloor yielded valuable materials that helped with the reconstruction of the occupation sequence of this phase. The filling (3081) of pit 3082 produced the most varied repertoire of forms, in particular a large number of mass-produced bases that came from beakers and bowls. The diagnostic open forms were confined to medium-size bowls with an overhanging rim (Fig. 160.2 and 160.3) and a kind of deep bowl with a notched band below a hammer rim (Fig. 160.1). The repertoire of closed shapes, which was more varied, included more of the short plain-rimmed jars mentioned above (Fig. 160.4), together with two other types of collared jars: a double-rimmed jar (Fig. 160.5) and a jar with a hammer rim (Fig. 160.6).

The range of ceramics found in the filling (3095) of pit 3094 was more limited. Goblets were the most common open shape (Fig. 161.1), together with conical bowls, but two deep bowls were also found: one with a hammer rim and straight walls (Fig. 160.8), and one with a thickened rolled outside rim and curvilinear walls (Fig. 160.9). The repertoire of closed shapes was confined to just two sherds associated with the common type of short plain-rimmed jar (Fig. 160.7).

Finally, the filling (3096) of pit 3093 yielded numerous tiny pottery fragments. In common with the other two pits just described, the sherds suggested a high proportion of mass-produced vessels, mostly goblets (Fig. 161.2 and 161.3) and bowls, but the very poor condition of the retrieved pieces made it difficult to establish a repertoire. The nature of the damage, in particular the small size of the sherds, indicated that the pots were deliberately broken when they were deposited in the pit. Accordingly, only three other vessels could be reconstructed: a deep bowl with a triangular rim (Fig. 161.5), a strainer with a thickened rolled outside rim (Fig. 161.4) and a fragment of another short plain-rimmed jar.

Sherds from the second phase of occupation were found only in the temple's SW room, and they came almost exclusively from mass-produced vessels, mainly goblets (Fig. 161.6) and bowls (Fig. 161.7 and 161.8). The ceramic horizon that characterised this phase was supplemented with pottery shapes that were collected from contexts 2084 and 2085, which were located outside the SW and NE rooms. Mass-produced pottery types also predominated in these layers, though conical bowls (Fig. 162.2) were more numerous than goblets with a narrow base (Fig. 162.1). The other shapes found in these contexts, which compared well with finds from other pre-Gudea Tell A soundings, included bowls with an overhanging rim (Fig. 162.3), deep bowls with a triangular rim (Fig. 162.4 and 162.8) and a deep bowl with a notched band below a hammer rim (Fig. 162.9). Closed forms made up a very small proportion of the total, with short plain-rimmed jars being the most common type (Fig. 162.5) in both medium and small sizes. Among other closed shapes were a jar with a triangular rounded rim and a horizontal shoulder (Fig. 162.6), and a large jar with a vertical neck, a flat and angular outside rim, and sloping shoulders (Fig. 162.7). The latter type displayed three rows of incised fingernail markings at the intersection of the neck and shoulder.

The pottery that was found in the contexts that sealed the last phase of occupation of the temple's SW and NE rooms, prior to the construction of Gudea's New Eninnu, was also mostly mass-produced (70% of the total), with bowls (Fig. 163.4–7) being by far the most common form, followed by goblets with a narrow base and a very small number of conical beakers (Fig. 163.1–3). Other open shapes of medium size included bowls with an overhanging rim (Fig. 159.8), as well as examples of the kinds of deep bowls with a triangular rim (Figs. 163.9, 163.10, 164.1 and 164.2) that remained in production throughout the third millennium BCE. The most common of the closed forms were short plain-rimmed jars with two distinct shoulder types: sloping and rounded (Fig. 164.3–7). This kind of vessel was also manufactured over a very long period, and the same rim was used on jars of various sizes. Other types were only rarely recorded, but two that stood out were a jar with a rolled rim, a short neck and sloping shoulders (Fig. 164.8), and another short-necked jar with an oval rim and horizontal shoulders (Fig. 164.9). Also excavated were occasional sherds from a type of big storage jar with a thickened flat rim that had a rib just below the rim on the outside wall (Fig. 164.10).

The sequence as a whole was characterised by the presence of mass-produced pottery, mostly bowls (Figs. 159.1–4, 161.7, 161.8, 162.2 and 163.4–7), which were more numerous than goblets (Figs. 159.1, 161.1–3, 161.9, 163.1 and 163.2), and conical beakers (Fig. 163.3). All the pots had string-cut bases, though the manufacturing techniques varied. In particular, some examples had been coiled and had their outer walls roughly shaped before being subsequently finished on a turntable or wheel. The recovery of some intact goblets and conical bowls made it possible to calculate the respective volumes of the vessels. The goblets had a constant average capacity of about 0.35 l, while the average capacity of the bowls, which differed significantly from vessel to vessel, was between 0.45 l and 0.55 l.

Since mass-produced pottery was characteristic of all the occupation phases represented by the excavated layers, the occupation sequence could only be reconstructed by referring to the other recorded shapes, of which the most common open forms were deep bowls with a triangular rim (Figs. 8.5 and 9.4), including those with a rounded triangular rim (Figs. 159.11, 160.9, 162.8, 163.9, 163.10, 164.1 and 164.2), and deep bowls with a hammer rim (Fig. 160.8). All the ceramics of this kind, which were manufactured over a long period, were in use in the transition between Early Dynastic IIIb and Akkad times. Also noteworthy were the bowls with an overhanging rim (Figs. 157.2, 157.3, 159.5, 162.3 and 163.8), which were also found in Nippur, and are generally considered to be a diagnostic type for the early and late Akkad phases (McMahon 2006, pp. 70–1 (Type O-10)). Two open shapes that merit further attention were probably types of deep bowls displaying a notched band below a hammer rim (Figs. 160.1 and 162.9), but the condition

of the excavated fragments meant that they could also perhaps be described as stemmed dishes. Examples of this type of vessel, dating from Early Dynastic IIIb to Akkad times, were again excavated in Nippur, but the distinguishing feature of the Girsu specimens was the peculiarity of the hammer rim.

The most common closed shape was the short plain-rimmed jar, of which two especially noteworthy variants were found: a more prevalent kind with a straight short neck (Figs. 159.7, 159.9, 159.10, 160.4, 160.7, 164.3 and 164.4) and a less well-attested alternative with a flaring short neck (Figs. 159.8, 162.5 and 164.5–7). Vessels of this general type, which were manufactured in S Iraq over a long period in the third millennium BCE, remained in production even after the end of the Akkad period, but the two variants can be dated specifically to Akkad times (McMahon 2006, p. 69 (Type C-12) and p. 71 (Type C-14)). The type of jar with a narrow neck and a hammer rim (Fig. 160.6) might represent a variant of jars with an elongated triangular rim that were found in Nippur (MacMahon 2006, p. 66 (Type C-6)), while comparable examples of the jar with doubled ridges (Fig. 160.5) and the square-rimmed jar were both also excavated in Nippur, where the first kind was in production from the Late Akkad period through to subsequent chronological phases (MacMahon 2006, pp. 79–80 (Type C-25a)). Similarly, the jar with a rolled rim (Fig. 164.8) can also be dated to the Akkad period, as attested by diagnostic specimens found in Nippur (MacMahon 2006, p. 69 (Type C-12)). Two more types that were produced in the Akkad period were the jars with a rounded triangular rim, a slightly flaring neck and horizontal shoulders (Fig. 162.6), and the ones with an oval rim, a flaring short neck and horizontal shoulders (Fig. 164.9). Finally, the cylindrical strainer (Fig. 161.4) was also in use between Early Dynastic IIIb and Akkad times.

Though the range of recovered ceramic shapes was rather limited, they attested to at least two main occupation phases. The most ancient of the two, which is represented by the relatively small number of sherds collected in pits 3081, 3093 and 3095, was the transitional phase between the Early Dynastic IIIb and the Early Akkad periods. The subsequent occupation phase, which relates to the finds made in contexts 2084 and 2085 in the SW and NE rooms, and to the levelling layers that were established prior to the construction of the New Eninnu, was characterised by a mix of pottery types that were attested in Early and Late Akkad times (the latter being coextensive with the reign of Ur-Bau in the Lagash II era).

438 The Mound of the Palace

FIGURE 159. Pottery from the Temple Building I.

Before the Big Move: The Early Dynastic and Akkad Temple Complex   439

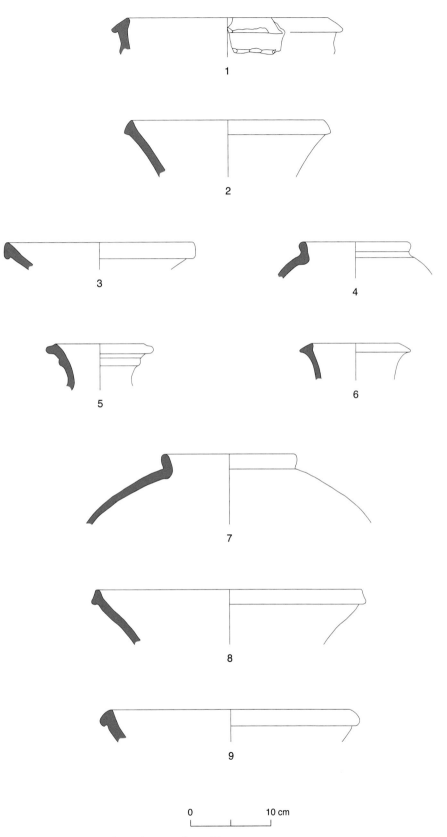

FIGURE 160. Pottery from the Temple Building II.

440 The Mound of the Palace

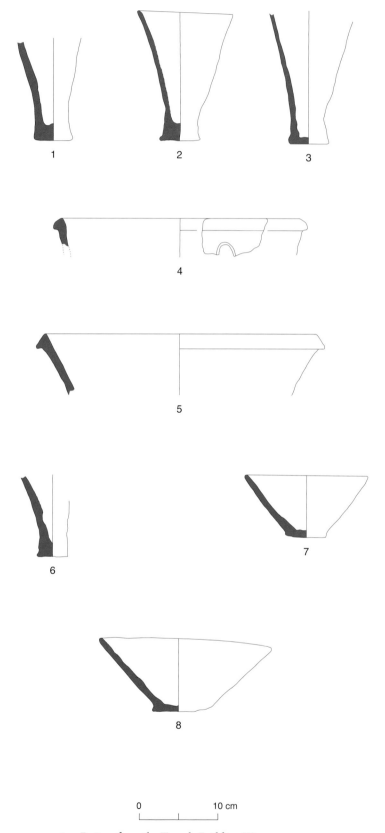

FIGURE 161. Pottery from the Temple Building III.

Before the Big Move: The Early Dynastic and Akkad Temple Complex 441

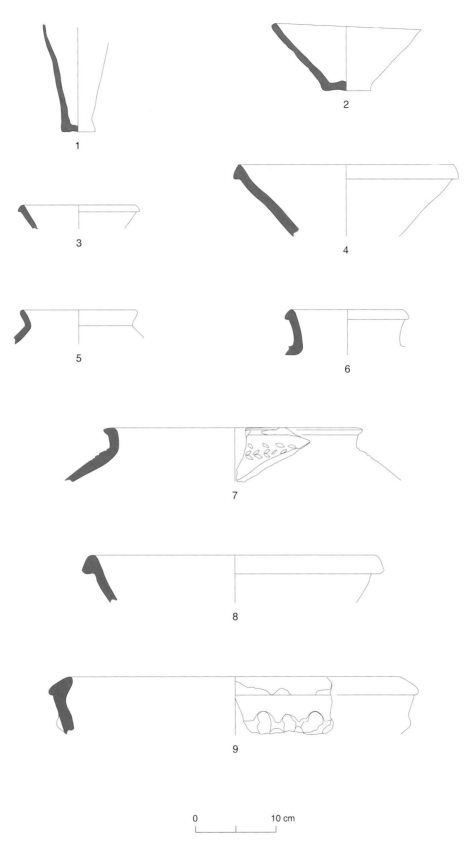

FIGURE 162. Pottery from the Temple Building IV.

442 The Mound of the Palace

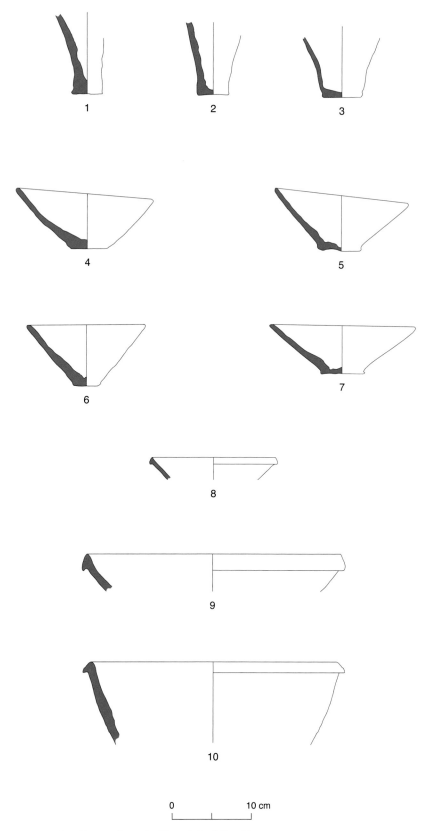

FIGURE 163. Pottery from the Temple Building V.

Before the Big Move: The Early Dynastic and Akkad Temple Complex   443

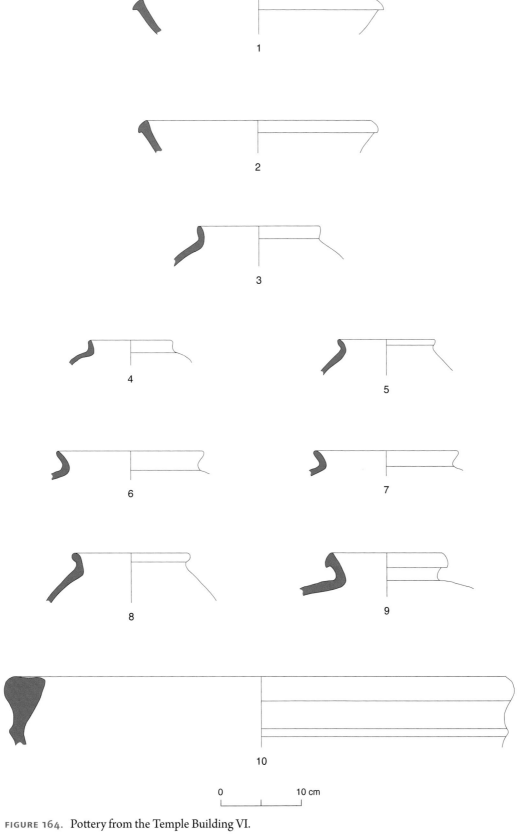

FIGURE 164. Pottery from the Temple Building VI.

CHAPTER 32

The Early Dynastic Sanctuary of the Goddess Bau

THE TEMPLE PRECINCT ON TELL A, WHICH WAS repeatedly renewed during the Early Dynastic and Akkad periods, was a highly significant feature of Girsu's sacred landscape for many centuries, as is evidenced by the massive superimposed terraces that supported its successive iterations. It is therefore all the more extraordinary that no inscriptions have so far emerged that explicitly identify the deity to whom Tell A's pre-Gudea temples were dedicated. A number of compelling arguments, principally deriving from the British Museum team's research, nevertheless indicate that it was the goddess Bau, the queen consort of Ningirsu (Fig. 165). Before the arguments are presented in detail, it is important to outline some particular problems that have so far been left unresolved.

The Curious Paucity of Dedicatory Bau Inscriptions

There can be no doubt that foundation figurines and probably also tablets must lie buried in the preserved mud-brick masses that make up the successive Early Dynastic and Akkad platforms on Tell A, but these deeper levels were not exposed by the French explorers, and the British Museum team was unable to access them without damaging or deliberately removing expanses of the mud-brick fabric. Despite the care that was taken, a limited portion of the NW edge of the white platform (1036) unfortunately collapsed during the course of the excavations on account of heavy rain, which led to subsequent erosion. As noted previously, the

only object of any significance that emerged was a solitary uninscribed brick bearing the thumbprint that was the regnal marking of Ur-Nanshe.

The absence of votive and dedicatory objects associated with the temple structures on the Urukagina grey platform (5235), the most recent of the pre-Gudea sequence, can be most convincingly explained by the fact that the complex on Tell A did not suffer the same fate as the one on Tell K, which was comprehensively razed to the ground by the army led by Lugalzagesi during Urukagina's reign at the end of the Early Dynastic IIIb period. The violent end that befell the Tell K shrine left behind traces of broken objects and structures that were absorbed into the mound's fabric. The main reason why the signs of the invasion survived so distinctly is that the Tell K complex was never again comprehensively rebuilt after Lugalzagesi's conquest. Instead, the facility was partially and presumably poorly refurbished, including under the subsequent Akkad overlords, until Lagash II times, when the sacred mound was finally closed and turned into a memorial shrine, leaving the destruction horizon buried beneath it (see Chapter 21). In stark contrast, Tell A was maintained and several times renovated through the Early Dynastic and Akkad eras all the way down to the reign of Ur-Bau in the Lagash II period. In traditional Sumerian fashion, every time the temple was renewed, and most notably when the ground level of the mound was raised, the key cult objects must have been either reverently transferred to their new homes or ritually processed and carefully interred, as happened in a number of observed instances on Tell K. The limited area of the British Museum team's deep excavations underneath Gudea's

FIGURE 165. Fragment of an Early Dynastic relief excavated by Sarzec between Tells J and K, showing Bau (left), enthroned and probably wearing a feathered crown, and Ningirsu (right), attacking an enemy with a mace. Musée du Louvre AO48.

New Eninnu on Tell A did not expose any foundation deposits or favissas containing deconsecrated ex-votos dedicated to the deity who was worshipped in earlier temples on the mound, but it is nevertheless highly likely that individual pieces and caches of sacred objects must exist in the underlying layers of the mud-brick matrix. Importantly, however, as is detailed in Chapter 31, the team did expose pre-Gudea layers beneath the Ningirsu temple at the heart of the New Eninnu in Areas B2, B3 and B5, where the evidence showed that the Early Dynastic walls were indeed maintained without interruption from Early Dynastic times, through the Akkad interval until the reign of Ur-Bau, and there were no signs whatsoever of a destruction horizon.

None of the rare Early Dynastic and Akkad dedicatory objects that were found in the ruins of the much later Hellenistic building gave any clue as to the name of the deity to whom Tell A was sacred before Ur-Bau relocated the Temple of Ningirsu, together with the cult statue (the primary religious symbol, which might conceivably have been refashioned, though that cannot be known) and vital appurtenances. It should also be noted that, if evidence had been found in the Hellenistic complex, it might in any case have been inconclusive because some votives that ended up on Tell A were in fact brought there from other parts of Girsu— an important example being a fragment of the Stele of the Vultures that originated on Tell K. If an inscribed Early Dynastic or Akkad ex-voto had been found in the ruins of the Hellenistic complex, therefore, it could very plausibly have been a stray, though the picture is further complicated by the later activities of Adadnadinakhe, who excavated artefacts from the third and second millennia in order to display them in his Hellenistic shrine.

Amidst the surprising lack of revealing remains, one object deserves special mention (Fig. 166). It is an inscribed calcite bowl dedicated to the goddess Bau by a legate of Urukagina (BM90902). The surviving part of the restored inscription (RIME 1.9.9.11) reads: 'For the goddess Bau, the gracious lady, Ningirsulumu, the emissary, for the life of his master, Urukagina, king of Lagash . . .' The three inscribed fragments of the bowl, which were discovered by Hormuzd Rassam on behalf of the British Museum in 1879, are fraught with complications, not least the fact that the museum's records state

FIGURE 166. Reattached fragments of an inscribed bowl dedicated to the goddess Bau. British Museum 90902.

that the object came from Sippar, and not Girsu. The likeliest explanation is that delays in the unpacking and cataloguing of items that were received by the museum in the late 1870s and early 1880s meant that a number of the pieces received from Rassam were wrongly registered as having come from Sippar rather than Girsu, and this doubtless included the bowl fragments. The problem was almost certainly exacerbated in the case of the bowl due to the very small number of finds that Rassam sent back from Tello, and because the limited work that he undertook there between 2 March and 5 March 1879 was not properly authorised (see Chapter 2). Rassam was frustrated by his lack of the requisite Ottoman licence to excavate, and his visit was portrayed in his published account as little more than a reconnaissance mission (Rassam 1897, pp. 275–9). Nonetheless, he employed several gangs of workers to open trenches on Tell A that almost certainly did reach pre-Hellenistic levels. Again as noted above, he unearthed and reburied the lower part of the Gudea Colossus (Statue D) that had previously been found by Sarzec in order to take a cast of the inscription, and his memoir records a number of other objects that were considered to be of interest, including one complete foundation peg, numerous fragments of pegs, a pit of inscribed clay tablets and some inscribed red granite weights (as Rassam calls them). One of the finds that Rassam avowedly did send back to London was a door socket made from a pebble that came from 'the remains of a temple', where he also found 'traces of the walls' (Rassam 1897, p. 276). The pebble socket was one of a pair, and the second one was presented to the regional Ottoman authorities to be sent to the Imperial Museum in Constantinople—perhaps suggesting that he was allowed to operate with a degree of impunity, despite the lack of formal permission. The three pieces of the inscribed bowl dedicated to Bau could, of course, have been picked up elsewhere on the site by one of the locally employed labourers, or bought from one of the local tribespeople, but if Rassam did find them on Tell A then it is quite possible that the fragmentary bowl was not a stray but was rather found either in, or in close proximity to, its final resting place. This might be further confirmed by the fact that the preserved base of the bowl was drilled with three dowel holes—a clear sign that it had been repaired in Sumerian times (the technique being well attested on statues and other votives). That would not necessarily be indicative of its later fate, but it would suggest that the object was in the condition in which it had been finally left by its Sumerian keepers. If Rassam had found only one of the pieces, it might certainly have been a stray—comparable to the portion of the Stele of the Vultures that was exhumed on Tell A, for example—but the discovery of three fragments in close proximity to each other indicates that the bowl was unearthed in a Sumerian context, in all probability on Tell A. As mentioned above, the conclusion must be treated with a degree of caution on account of the excavations subsequently undertaken by Adadnadinakhe, though it might be corroborated by some of the Sumerian finds made by the British Museum team, which were also unearthed in contexts that had not been disturbed by the Hellenistic soundings.

This is not the case for other surviving artefacts associated with Bau, which appear almost universally to be strays. For example, a sherd from another inscribed Early Dynastic offering bowl that was also dedicated to Bau during the reign of Urukagina was uncovered at the site of the bridge made of fired bricks (previously known as the Enigmatic Construction) during the British Museum team's first reconnaissance of Tello in 2015. Made of alabaster, the bowl's fragmentary inscription (RIME 1.9.9.11) begins 'For the goddess Bau, the gracious lady . . .' and is therefore closely comparable with the text contained on the bowl found by Rassam. Another important example (detailed in Chapter 15) of a similar kind of stray is the fragment of the cup dedicated to Bau by Ur-Nanshe that was found on Tell K (EŞEM427), with an inscription (RIME 1.9.1.27) that reads: 'To the goddess Bau, Ur-Nanshe, king of Lagash, son of Gunidu, dedicated (this cup)'.

Preserved examples of Early Dynastic ex-votos dedicated to Bau, including vases and other objects, are rare, and most if not all of them are of unknown or unclear provenance. At least two more instances can be associated with Ur-Nanshe, including another vase fragment (EŞEM4811) with an inscription that opens: 'To the goddess Bau, Ur-Nanshe . . .' (RIME 1.9.1.28). There is also a remarkable text of six lines on an Ur-Nanshe brick (EŞEM1538) that was inscribed to commemorate the construction of a shrine referred to as the E.TAR. It was excavated in Tello by Sarzec, who failed to record its find location, but it is likely that the reference is to the Etarsirsir temple of the goddess Bau in Girsu's holy precinct (the Urukug). The inscription (RIME 1.9.1.29) reads: 'Ur-Nanshe, king of Lagash, son of Gunidu, built the E.TAR'. In addition, a fragment of a now missing grey stone statue, dedicated to Bau and formerly in a private collection, bears (or bore) an inscription in the name of Enanatum I (RIME 1.9.4.11):

> For the goddess Bau . . . Enanatum, ruler of Lagash, son of Akurgal . . . when the god Ningirsu nominated him, granted him strength, and put all the foreign lands under his control, he named it [the statue]. For the goddess Bau, the gracious woman, he set it up in the temple . . . the gracious woman, the temple . . .

Finally, two fragments of stone vases (EŞEM2496 and one in another private collection) both bear part of a dedicatory inscription in the name of Enmetena (RIME 1.9.5.24): 'For the goddess Bau, the gracious lady, Enmetena, ruler of Lagash, chosen in the heart [by the goddess Nanshe] . . .'

The very fact that this corpus of inscriptions relating to the great goddess of Girsu is so small is extremely significant because it is unthinkable that the state's most important female deity, the wife and queen consort of Ningirsu himself, was not a pre-eminent focus of religious belief and practice. Since a large haul of dedicatory Bau artefacts is precisely what a trained archaeologist would expect to find on the site, its absence speaks volumes. Two things are certain, however: no remains of Bau's Early Dynastic temple complex were exposed on Tell A by the early French excavators, and the only possible trace of it that could perhaps have been unequivocally identified as such was the solitary bowl that was probably found on the mound by Rassam. Nonetheless, the lack of recorded finds does not mean that archaeological remains of Early Dynastic shrines, including a temple dedicated to Bau, do not (or in some cases did not) exist on Tell A. The very good reason for this is that the preserved parts of the earlier sanctuaries that are still buried deep inside Tell A—as confirmed by the British Museum team's findings—were not targeted by the French, who were content with the spectacular, mainly Lagash II and Hellenistic objects and structures that they found principally in the mound's upper levels. If Tell A's Early Dynastic shrines and annexes had been comprehensively uncovered in the same way as the successive temples to Ningirsu were on Tell K, there is little doubt that the French digging (together with subsequent looting) would have yielded a much larger trove of artefacts dedicated to the goddess, and that these would have been directly associated with the successive shrines to Bau that existed on Tell A prior to the construction of Gudea's New Eninnu.

A Shared Temple for Ningirsu and Bau on Tell K?

The suggestion made by two of the French excavators (Genouillac 1936, pp. 12–13; Parrot 1948, pp. 156–8) that the reincarnation of the goddess's temple in Lagash II times might somehow have been linked to structures exposed on Tells G or I (to the north-north-east and north-east of Tell K, respectively) is simply unwarranted. Another proposal that is sometimes put forward in the literature (Sallaberger 2018, p. 172, n. 4) is that the Early Dynastic temple of Bau was a component part of the Ningirsu temple on Tell K, but this idea can also be ruled out. The mistaken argument turns largely on two facts: first, that no named sanga or temple administrator for a temple dedicated to Bau is listed in the arguably incomplete archive relating to the household (é.mí) of Bau, the Lady of Lagash, that contains around 2,000 tablets covering a period of about twenty years in the reigns of Enentarzi, Lugalanda and Urukagina; secondly, that tribute was paid to the deceased temple administrators of Ningirsu, above all Dudu, the high priest of Enmetena, during the festival of Bau. These are interesting details and doubtless worthy of further study, though (as suggested by Prentice 2010, p. 191, n. 789) the supposed absence of the sanga might well be explained simply by the fact that the role was fulfilled by another high official, for example the overseer (nu.bandà), who acted on behalf of the queens Dimtur, Baranamtara and Shasha in the reigns of Enentarzi et al. But these shreds of disputable information in no way justify the conclusion that Bau was not venerated in a temple of her own throughout the Early Dynastic period and that she must therefore have had a cella in a purported separate wing in the Temple of Ningirsu on Tell K.

Similarly, the idea that Bau was worshiped in the Ningirsu temple (or an associated annexe) is contradicted categorically by the lack of even the slightest trace of any architectural or epigraphic evidence. The epigraphic finds from Tell K are detailed in Part 2 above, and the absence of any dedicatory Bau remains (with the exception of the anomalous cup inscribed in the name of Ur-Nanshe) is surely enough in and of itself to rule out the suggestion. No traces of a secondary cella were recorded in or around any of the Early Dynastic temples that were uncovered on the mound, dating all the way back to the Lower Construction. Nor is any mention of the removal of a joint Ningirsu–Bau establishment made in the Gudea Cylinder Inscriptions. A dual cult with adjacent shrines devoted to Ningirsu and Bau certainly came into being in later times, from the Lagash II period onwards, but it is anachronistic to project that back onto earlier periods without proof, especially when the argument pointedly disregards a wealth of negative evidence that flatly rebuts it. On the contrary, everything points to the fact that, in Early Dynastic Girsu, the large sanctuaries that were built on separate mounds were considered to be the dwelling places of individual gods and goddesses from the Lagash pantheon, such that the temples of Ningirsu and Nanshe (to cite a second verifiable instance) were on Tells K and L, respectively.

The incongruity is the seeming absence of a temple to Bau, Ningirsu's queen consort and the most revered deity in Girsu after the heroic god himself. It is inconceivable that she was not worshipped in a temple complex of her own that must unquestionably have been located in another important and commanding area of Girsu, and unquestionably raised on a tell.

This issue of a dual Ningirsu–Bau cult in Early Dynastic times is closely connected to another misleading idea that is sometimes advanced, namely that the hoard of Presargonic tablets relating to the goddess's establishment (the é.mí, mentioned above), which were looted between Sarzec's last season in 1900 and the arrival of Cros in 1903, originated on Tell K. Coming from the archives of the queens of Lagash, the tablets contain managerial records kept by the administrators responsible for looking after the queens', and therefore the goddess's, estates—the queens being the earthly counterparts of Bau, just as the kings were the earthly counterparts of Ningirsu. There is no reason to assume that the archive was kept on Tell K. With the exception of an enigmatic cache of eight Fara-era clay tablets and possibly a few oddments, no coherent sets of administrative tablets were found on Tell K at any time during the twenty seasons of organised excavations that were carried out by the French. The same can be said of Tell A, where archives were not found either by the French or during the British Museum team's work on the mound. It can therefore be said with a considerable degree of certainty that Tells K and A, the sites of the two principal temple complexes of Girsu, did not house state archives, but rather that they were stored entirely (or almost entirely) in a building on Tablet Hill (Tell V), in all likelihood the site of the royal palace of Girsu, which lay outside the confines of the city's most sacred inner district, the Urukug.

The Temple of Bau: The British Museum Team's Fieldwork and the Epigraphic Record

The British Museum team's excavations on Tell A shed a great deal of light on the probable history of Bau's temple, especially when the results are placed against the wider backdrop of what is known about the sacred landscape of Girsu in Early Dynastic times. The broken bowl dedicated to Bau by the legate of Urukagina (BM90902) that was found by Rassam provides a fascinating indicator, but many other clues point to the conclusion that the massive mud-brick terraces and the associated sequence of pre-Gudea temple buildings on Tell A formed the sanctuary devoted to Bau in the sacred heart of Girsu. First and foremost, it is important to recall the imposing character and location of Tell A, which, under Ur-Bau and Gudea, superseded Tell K as the highest and most expansive mound not only in the Urukug, which was isolated from the surrounding parts of the urban area by an enclosing temenos wall, but in the extended city of Girsu as a whole, including the administrative and communal quarters in which people lived and worked. Placed to the north-west of the Ningirsu temple on Tell K, at the opposite end of Girsu's sacred district, Tell A complemented Tell K as one of the two key points of an arrangement that was a microcosm of the Sumerian system of the world. The sacred buildings on the two mounds were both, of course, oriented towards the cardinal points, and that alignment, as has previously been demonstrated, dynamically generated two N–S axes that in turn defined parallel W–E axes. Derived from the fixed astronomical point represented by the north star, these axes together instantiated a spatial and temporal framework that linked the earth with the sky, and it was in this sense that the temple was conceived of as a divine compass. The result was the tessellated earth on which the spaces between similarly oriented temples could conceptually be filled or tiled, as it were, with an unbroken series of astronomically determined lines and rectangles. The relationship between Tells A and K, and especially the cardinal connections between the buildings on the two mounds, turned this divine dynamism into a living reality, such that every step taken within the confines of the Urukug must have been supercharged with the sense that the earth's place in the cosmos was being vividly and actively revealed (Fig. 167). Accordingly, the raised grounds of the holiest mounds were liminal, multi-dimensional settings in which earth, sky, time and space were integrated into a continuum, and although the Urukug was walled off from the world at large it manifested a pattern that was universally representative. The continuum was the founding cosmological principle, and the Urukug—the innermost sacred core of the state—was designed to be the significant part that unveiled the shape of the cosmic whole, including the entire state of Lagash with its similarly aligned major triad made up of Girsu, Lagash and Nigin, and also, by extension, the rest of the earth.

Secondly, not only the significant positioning, but also the scale and exceptional size of the monumental Early Dynastic terraces that have now been partially exposed on Tell A represented a huge investment of human labour, resources and planning that could only have been justified at a sacred site of the utmost importance. Occupying a surface area of some 3,000 m^2, and comparable in their size and general characteristics to the Ningirsu platforms of Tell K, the successive terraces on Tell A were the setting for a first-order sanctuary that must unquestionably have been established for the worship of one of the foremost deities in the Girsu pantheon. The British Museum team's fieldwork has established a chronological sequence for the construction of successively raised religious platforms on Tell A, together with their associated buildings and some important deposits. Beginning with the earliest structures, the stratigraphic sequence of red, white and grey platforms indicates a chronological series of events that ran from the Late Early Dynastic I era through to Late Akkad and Early Lagash II times. To complement this, thanks to the huge number of Early Dynastic royal inscriptions that were left behind by the rulers of Lagash from Ur-Nanshe to Urukagina, as well as many detailed inscriptions in the name of Ur-Bau in the Early Lagash II period, there is also a wealth of information about individual temples in Girsu. When the stratigraphic and historical records are put together, it becomes possible to identify the temple complex on Tell A and to establish the name of the deity to whom it was sacred. There is a caveat, however. The royal inscriptions of Girsu reference a huge number of sacred places, but not all of them were temples devoted to individual deities; nor were they all located in Girsu. It is therefore important to highlight some of the issues that arise from the preserved texts before attempting to collate the Early Dynastic textual information with the archaeological record of physical remains.

It is well known that translations of the Sumerian nomenclature of sacred places (é, èš and so forth) are sometimes problematic and need to be contextualised systematically in order to establish their exact designations. Thus, the Sumerian words that are principally taken to mean 'temple', 'sanctuary', 'religious complex', 'shrine' and 'chapel' can also connote parts of these places and structures (an inner sanctum or a temple annexe, for example), and this creates complications. As has already been highlighted with respect to the Ningirsu shrine on Tell K, the names of temples are not consistent in the epigraphic records, and a temple or sanctuary was often known by more than one name, including ceremonial and popular names (see George 1993, pp. 59–63), which were

450   The Mound of the Palace

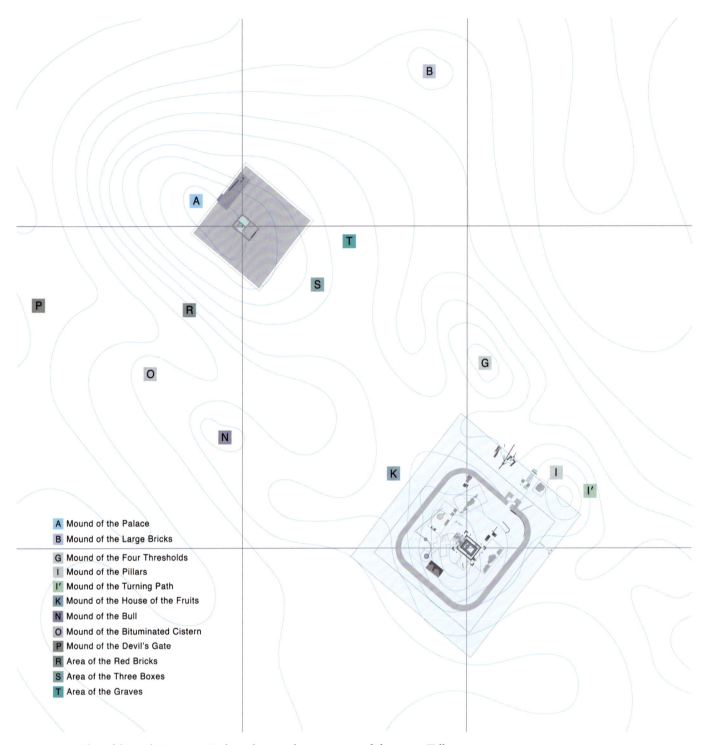

FIGURE 167. Plan of the Early Dynastic Urukug, showing the reconstructed shrines on Tells A and K, respectively. The contour lines, taken from Sarzec's Plan B, show the site as it was before the French excavations began; the letters A to T indicate mounds and areas named by Sarzec. The two N–S axes extend through the N corner of the Ningirsu temple on Tell K and the presumed N corner of the Temple of Bau on Tell A. In the Bau temple, as in the excavated shrines in Girsu from all periods, the N–S axis probably intersects with the E–W equinoctial line in the cella, close to the cult podium.

supplemented by a rich list of epithets and bynames. By the same token, different temples sometimes bore the same name, and individual gods were frequently worshipped in several temples that were known by different names.

The identification of temples is further complicated by the fact that not all of the names of sacred buildings include one or other of the sacred predeterminatives (é, èš and the like), while some nouns that begin with the temple predeterminative (é) were not necessarily attached to temples or cult centres but were instead used to name entirely different places and structures. A related problem arises because the name of the temple could apply just to the sacred building, and also, by extension, to the institution of which the temple was in a sense the headquarters, since Sumerian temples were the centres of large agrarian estates that were stewarded on a day-to-day basis by the temple officials (acting under the earthly authority of the ruler and the ruling class) on behalf of the presiding deity. In cases such as these, it is necessary to fall back on context. For example, a particular Sumerian word, é.Bau, which is found in the epigraphic texts, might refer either to the Temple of Bau or to the Institution of the Queens (the royal household that administered the goddess's properties)—two meanings that are, in an important sense, inseparable because the frames of reference invoke an established analogy between the divine and royal spheres of activity. For this reason, some of the names that are used in administrative documents for installations that 'belong to' the temple of Bau should not be taken to imply that the designated structure was part of the physical temple complex in the Urukug because such terms could also be used to denote buildings in the countryside or in other towns that were part of the goddess's landed estates. Sometimes, therefore, it is only by cross-referencing the available sources, including diverse texts from different periods, that the nature, function and location of particular sacred buildings and places can be determined. Furthermore, the use in royal inscriptions of a temple name in association with the verb 'to build' (dù) does not automatically imply that the respective ruler erected an entirely new temple. This is because the Sumerian word dù can convey a wide variety of meanings, ranging from the construction of a completely new temple to a little light repair work.

With these caveats in mind, a thorough cross-checking of all the documents makes it possible to identify the Early Dynastic temples and their annexes, together with their approximate construction dates and locations. From this, a hierarchy for the Early Dynastic and Early Lagash II sacred places of Lagash can be established that extends from major religious complexes all the way down to small rural chapels. This is outlined in the following paragraphs and laid out in Table 6.

The Early Dynastic cuneiform sources from Girsu–Lagash that pertain to the temple buildings erected by Presargonic rulers from the reign of Ur-Nanshe to that of Urukagina are extremely rich in information that offers a rare picture of the sacred landscape of the state of Lagash as a whole, with its main city temples and large sanctuaries in Girsu, Lagash and Nigin, together with its broad hinterland of towns, rural shrines and frontier chapels. More importantly for the present purpose, it also provides a diachronic perspective on the development of the network of religious sites through time, beginning with the overarching programme of the founder of the dynasty, Ur-Nanshe, whose establishments were honoured, maintained, refurbished and sometimes completely rebuilt by his successors. The evolution of religious institutions was also linked, of course, with historical events, notably a series of wars with the neighbouring rival state of Umma. Some conflicts resulted in the destruction of sacred places— by the ruler Urlumma, for example, and most significantly by Lugalzagesi—and in certain instances the destroyed shrines were rebuilt by charismatic rulers of Lagash, notably Enmetena and Urukagina. Additionally, outbreaks of war led to the boundaries of Lagash being expanded to incorporate newly conquered territories, and some of these events were marked by the building of new temples, for example in the city of Badtibira, which was annexed under Enmetena.

The texts relating to Girsu clarify repeatedly that, from the time of Ur-Nanshe to that of Urukagina, the state's sacred metropolis was laid out along the axis defined by the two chief sanctuaries devoted to Ningirsu on Tell K and Bau, presumably on Tell A, that were situated in the Urukug. Accordingly, two of the three monumental gates that gave access to the sacred precinct were unsurprisingly named after Ningirsu and Bau (a.bul₅.la.ᵈNin.ğír.sú and a.bul₅.la.ᵈBau), and there is little doubt that the term translated as the 'strong wall of Bau's house' (bàd.é.ᵈBau) designated the temenos wall of the entire hallowed enclosure or Urukug because Bau was the divine protectress of the sacred inner zone of the city of Girsu. The symbolism expressed in Bau's association with the wall can be compared with the mural crown worn by a goddess

452   The Mound of the Palace

TABLE 6. The Construction, Renovation and Rebuilding of Sacred Sites by the Early Dynastic Rulers of Lagash and Ur-Bau.

Ruler	Girsu	Lagash
Ur-Nanshe	**The sanctuary of Ningirsu** on Tell K, known as é.^dnin.ğír.sú (House of Ningirsu) and èš.ğír.sú (Shrine of Girsu). **A temple annexe** (the House of the Sceptre), known as é.ğidru. **A Ningirsu shrine** (the House of the Princely Path), known as é.ğír.nun.(na). **The sanctuary of Bau** in the Urukug on Tell A, known as é.tar.sír.sír (é.TAR). **A Bau shrine**, known as the é.mah, perhaps located in Bau's sanctuary. **The sanctuary of Nanshe** (the House Established by the Brothers) outside the Urukug on Tell L, known as é.šeš.šeš.e.ğá/ğar.ra.	**The sanctuary of Ningirsu**, known as (é).ba.gára. Desecrated by Lugalzagesi. **The temple of Inanna** on the route of divine processions from Girsu to Lagash, known as (é).ib.gal. **The sanctuary of Gatumdug**, known as é.ğá.tum.du₁₀. Desecrated by Lugalzagesi.
Akurgal		
Eanatum	**A sacred well** in the 'broad courtyard' (kisal-dağal) of Ningirsu on Tell K, known as pú-sig₄. **A sacred wall** around the Urukug, known as bàd-uru-kù.	**A shrine or storehouse** of Ningirsu (the House of Stone), known as é.za. **Inanna's shrine**, known as é.an.na (commemorated in Eanatum's name). The inner sanctum of the shrine was known as (é).ib.gal. **The restored sanctuary of Gatumdug** (as listed above).
Enanatum I	**Restoration of the Ningirsu Temple** (the 'roof of white cedars for Ningirsu') for the Ningirsu sanctuary (the é.ninnu) on Tell K. **A statue for Bau** 'to be placed in her temple', presumed to be in the Urukug on Tell A.	**Restoration of Inanna's shrine**, known as (é).ib.gal.
Enmetena	**Restoration of the sanctuary of Ningirsu** on Tell K, known as é.ninnu. The temple complex was also known as èš.gi gi.gù.na (the Reed Chamber of the Terrace Temple). **Chapel of the sanctuary of Ningirsu** (the Foremost Jar), 'where regular offerings were made', in the Urukug on Tell K, known as bur.sağ. **Ningirsu's brewery** (the Sacred Brewery), an annexe of the sanctuary of Ningirsu in the Urukug on Tell K, known as é.bappir. **Ningirsu's coach house** (the Coach House), an annexe of the sanctuary of Ningirsu in the Urukug on Tell K, known as é.^{ğeš}gigír.ra. **Renovation of the sanctuary of Nanshe** (the House Established by the Brothers), which was fitted with new doors of white cedar, outside the Urukug on Tell L, known as é.šeš.šeš.e.ğá/ğar.ra. **A quayside wall** (the Wall of the Girsu Ferry Terminal), the sacred quay of the Urukug, possibly on Tell B, known as bàd.kar.má.addir_x.	**A Nanshe sanctuary** (the House Chosen in the Heart), known as (é).šà.pàd.da. Desecrated by Lugalzagesi. **Renovation of the Gatumdug sanctuary**, known as é.ğá.tum.du₁₀ (details uncertain).

The Early Dynastic Sanctuary of the Goddess Bau   453

Nigin	Smaller Towns and Countryside
The sanctuary of Nanshe in Sirara, known as é.sìrara^{ki} (claimed by Inanna in an éš.dam hymn). Also known as é.^dnanše.	**A freshwater shrine,** known as abzu.bàn.da. Desecrated by Lugalzagesi. **A dike shrine** (the Apzu Dike), known as abzu.e or abzu.ég. Probably desecrated by Lugalzagesi. **A rural shrine** (the House of the Wife), known as é.dam. **A rural shrine** (the Steppe House), known as é.edin. **A civic shine** (the High Place) in the town of Kinunir, known as ki.nir. **A Ningirsu temple** (the House Founded by the Sister), known as é.nin₉.e.g̃ar.ra. **A Ningirsu shrine** (the House of Tirash) in the town of Tirash, known as (é).ti.ra.áš. Looted by Lugalzagesi. **A rural Ningirsu sanctuary** (the House that Twinkles from Heaven) in the Gu'edena or border area, known as (é).an.ta.sur.ra. **A restored shrine** (the House of Tirash) in the town of Tirash, known as (é).ti.ra.áš. Looted by Lugalzagesi. **A border chapel for Ningirsu** at Namnunda-kig̃arra, known as dais (bára). Destroyed by Urlumma of Umma. **A border chapel for Enlil** in Namnunda-kig̃arra, known as dais (bára). Destroyed by Urlumma. **A border chapel for Ninhursag** in Namnunda-kig̃arra, known as dais (bára). Destroyed by Urlumma. **A border chapel for Utu** in Namnunda-kig̃arra, known as dais (bára). Destroyed by Urlumma. **The temple of Amageshtin** in the town of sag̃.ùb^{ki} near Lagash, known as é.sag̃.ug₅. Desecrated by Lugalzagesi. **The temple of Nindara** in ke.ès.(sá)^{ki}, known as é.làl.ᴅᴜ. Desecrated by Lugalzagesi. **The temple of Lugal.ᴜʀᴜ×ᴋᴀ́ʀ^{ki}** (the Palace or Storehouse of g̃anun-mah) in ᴜʀᴜ×ᴋᴀ́ʀ^{ki}, often known as é.gal.ᴜʀᴜ×ᴋᴀ́ʀ^{ki}. Desecrated by Lugalzagesi. **A Ningirsu sanctuary** in Dugru, known as éš.dug.ru. Desecrated by Lugalzagesi. **A rural temple for Hendursag** (no further details).
Restoration of the Nanshe sanctuary in Sirara, known as gi.gù.na mah. The restoration possibly included the raising of the terrace platform.	**A rural Ningirsu sanctuary** (the Fearsome House), known as a.huš (which collates with é.huš). Other epithets include é.igi.zi.bar.ra (the House Seen with a Steadfast Eye) and é.huš^{ki} (a term used in the offering lists). Looted by Lugalzagesi. **The sanctuary of Enki** in Pasirra, known as (é).abzu. **The sanctuary of Enlil of Imsag̃g̃a** (the House of the Father), known as é.ad.da. **Reconstruction of Ningirsu's rural sanctuary** (the House that Twinkles from Heaven), known as (é).an.ta.sur.ra. Referred to by Enmetena as é.me.lám.bi.kur.kur.ra.a.dul₅ (the House whose Radiance Covers the Lands). Desecrated by Lugalzagesi. **The temple of Nanshe** in Sulum near Lagash, known as é.engur.ra. Desecrated by Lugalzagezi. **Reconstruction of the temple of Dumuzi (as Lugal-Emush), Inanna and Lulal** (the House or Foundation (of the Land)) in Badti-bira, known as é.mùš.(kalam.ma). Also known as é.múš.(kalam.ma). Rebuilt in cooperation with Lugalkineshdudu of Uruk. **A rural Ningirsu sanctuary** (the House of the Heart or Inner Chamber), known as é.šà. The shrine was furnished with a garden.

454   The Mound of the Palace

TABLE 6. (*continued*)

Ruler	Girsu	Lagash
Enanatum II	**Restoration of Ningirsu's brewery** (the Sacred Brewery), an annexe of the sanctuary of Ningirsu in the Urukug on Tell K, known as é.bappir.	
Enentarzi		
Lugalanda	**A stele for Ningirsu** (Ningirsu Is the Lord Eternally Exalted in Nippur), known as na.rú.	
Urukagina	**Restoration of the sanctuary of Ningirsu** on Tell K, known as é.ninnu. **Reconstruction of the chapel of the sanctuary of Ningirsu** (the Foremost Jar), 'where regular offerings were made', in the Urukug on Tell K, known as bur.saĝ. **Annexe of the sanctuary of Ningirsu** (the House of the Sceptre) in the Urukug on Tell K (probably a shrine), known as é.ĝidru. **The shrine of Shulshaga** (the Seat of Lamentation), probably in the Urukug, known as (é).ki.tuš.akkil.lé. **The shrine of Igalim** (the House of the Great Awesome Powers of Heaven and the Underworld), probably in the Urukug, known as é.me.ḫuš.gal.an.ki. (The difficult word me is here translated as 'power'.) **Ningirsu's chariot house** (the House whose Radiance Covers the Lands), probably in the Urukug on Tell K, known as é.me.lám.bi.kur.kur.ra.(a).dul₅. Also known as é.me.lám.kur.kur.ra (the House of the Radiance of the Lands). **Restoration of the sanctuary of Bau** in the Urukug on Tell A, known as é.tar.sír.sír (é.TAR). The sanctuary (é.ᵈba.ba₆) was enlarged with the addition of a food store and a sheep-shearing shed. **A temple for Ninshar**, probably in Girsu (no other information available). **A temple for Lammashaga**, including chapels for the minor deities Zazaru, Nipae and Urnuntaea. Location unknown. (No other information available.) **A wall for Ningirsu** (the Great Wall of Girsu), probably a renewal or restoration of the city wall, known as bàd.ĝír.sú.KI. **Ningirsu's winery**, probably in Girsu (no other information available.) **A sacred building for Ningirsu**, probably in Girsu and possibly part of the Ningirsu temple complex, known as the EPA (no other information available.)	

Nigin	Smaller Towns and Countryside
	A border temple for Dimgalabzu on the frontier between Lagash and Umma (no further information available). **Reconstruction of the border chapel for Enlil** at Namnunda-kiĝarra, known as dais (bára). Destroyed by Urlumma. **Restoration of the temple of Lugal.URU×KÁR**[ki] (the Palace or Storehouse of ĝanun-mah) in URU×KÁR[ki]. Desecrated by Lugalzagesi. **Restoration of the Ningirsu sanctuary** in Dugru, known as èš.dug.ru. Desecrated by Lugalzagesi. **Reconstruction of the border chapel for Ninhursag** in Namnunda-kiĝarra, known as dais (bára). Destroyed by Urlumma. **A sanctuary for Ninmah** (the Terrace House of Tir.ku: the Pure Forest), known as gi.gù.na tir.kù.ga. Plundered by Lugalzagesi. **Reconstruction of the border chapel for Utu** in Namnunda-kiĝarra, known as dais (bára). Destroyed by Urlumma.
Restoration of the sanctuary of Nanshe in Sirara, known as é.sìrara[ki].	**Restoration of the sanctuary of Enlil of Imsaĝĝa** (the House of the Father), known as é.ad.da. **Reconstruction of Ningirsu's rural sanctuary** (the House that Twinkles from Heaven), known as (é).an.ta.sur.ra. Referred to by Urukagina as é.ḫé.ĝál.kalam.ma (the House of the Abundance of the Land). Desecrated by Lugalzagesi. **Reconstruction of the Ningirsu shrine** (the House of Tirash) in the town of Tirash, known as (é).ti.ra.áš. Referred to by Urukagina as é.gal ti.ra.áš (the Palace of Tirash). Looted by Lugalzagesi.

TABLE 6. *(continued)*

Ruler	Girsu	Lagash
Ur-Bau	**Erection of a new temple for Ningirsu** (House Fifty (Eninnu): the White Thunderbird) on Tell A, known as é.ninnu.^{d}IM.MI^{mušen}.bar$_6$.bar$_6$ (é.ninnu.^{d}IM.DUGUD^{mušen}.bar$_6$.bar$_6$). **House of the Donkey Stallions** (the Stable of Ensigun, the Divine Herder of Donkeys) part of the Eninnu on Tell A, known as é.^{anše}du$_{24}$.ùr. **Restoration of the temple of Bau** in the Urukug on Tell A (House of the Holy City), renamed é.uru.kù.ga (é.iri.kù), which is a byname of é.tar.sír.sír. **A temple for Ninhursag**, known as é.maḫ, in Girsu. **Unnamed temple for Dumuziabzu** in Girsu. **Unnamed temple for Enki** in Girsu. **Unnamed temple for Geshtinanna** in Girsu. **Unnamed temple for** Ninagal, probably in Girsu.	

(probably Bau herself) in a terracotta relief, almost certainly dating from the third millennium BCE, that was found in the fabric of the Hellenistic shrine on Tell A (see Chapters 46 and 47). Other instances of the same motif include the portrait made somewhat less than 2,000 years later of Ashursharrat, the wife of the Assyrian king Ashurbanipal, and the walled crown that was an attribute of the Greek goddess Tyche in her role as a protective city deity (also discussed below). Further reflecting these meanings, the cult of Bau included important ritual processions at key locations in the border regions of Lagash, again recalling the way in which the innermost sacred space with its protective temenos wall was conceived of as the representative microcosm of the world at large. In a mystical sense that was expressed in many material forms, therefore, Bau was characterised as the perfect complement of her divine consort, Ningirsu. The heroic god, the 'warrior of Enlil', wielded the mace, while his wife, Bau, the 'beautiful lady', held the shield.

Outside the walled holy city lay other notable sanctuaries, most importantly the religious complex of Nanshe that was situated on Tell L (é.šeš.šeš.e.ğá/ğar.ra). Founded by the deity's royal namesake, Ur-Nanshe, the shrine was later renovated by Enmetena. Similarly, as detailed in Part 2, the Early Dynastic Ningirsu sanctuary on Tell K, referred to in the inscriptions by several names, including é.^{d}nin.ğír.sú, èš.ğír.sú and é.ninnu, was renewed by Ur-Nanshe after the decommissioning of the older Lower Construction, while the complex was later refurbished and reconstructed to varying degrees

by Eanatum, Enanatum I (possibly), Enmetena (under whom it acquired a new epithet, èš.gi gi.gù.na) and lastly by Urukagina.

The great sanctuary of Bau (é.tar.sír.sír), which, as the epigraphic records confirm, was also constructed by Ur-Nanshe, was renovated several generations later by Urukagina. This particular construction sequence correlates remarkably well with the two more recent chronological phases identified in the overall tripartite stratigraphy of Tell A: the white platform, which dates to the reign of Ur-Nanshe in the Early Early Dynastic IIIb period, and the grey platform (its later reincarnation), dating to the reign of Urukagina in the Late Early Dynastic IIIb or Early Akkad period. With regard to the connection, it should be stressed that no other historical temple building sequences recorded in the Presargonic texts match the remains excavated on Tell A by the British Museum team. Less important shrines indubitably existed within the confines of the Urukug, but the monumental character of the Early Dynastic religious platforms on Tell A provides a clear indication that it was the only other religious foundation that could compare in prominence and scale to the Ningirsu complex on Tell K. In consequence, in conjunction with Tell A's location to the north-west of Tell K, all the evidence confirms that Tell A was the site of the Etarsirsir complex that was sacred to Bau.

There is one final argument (presented in greater detail in Chapter 33) that should dispel any remaining doubts, and it relates to Ur-Bau's construction project on Tell A.

Nigin	Smaller Towns and Countryside
	A shrine for Ninmar, known as èš.gú.tùr (part of a byname of é.ab.šà.ga.lá) in the harbour town of Gu'abba. **A temple for Ninkununna**, known as é.URUXKÁR^{ki}, in the town of URUXKÁR^{ki}.

As has been highlighted already, it is apparent that, unlike the sacred precinct on Tell K, the Late Early Dynastic IIIb or Early Akkad religious complex on Tell A that was renovated under Urukagina was assuredly not destroyed at the end of Urukagina's reign. That being the case, the temple establishment on Tell A was retained in its age-old location, where it was repaired and serviced during the Akkad and Early Lagash II periods. As is described below, Ur-Bau's transfer of the Ningirsu temple from Tell K to Tell A did not involve the all-inclusive replanning of Tell A's existing complex. Instead, as is well known from inscriptions in Ur-Bau's name (now backed up by the archaeological evidence), he incorporated the new temple to Ningirsu within the confines of an older sanctuary that he also restored and to which he applied a new epithet: é.uru.kù.ga, or the House of the Holy City. This was none other than the temple of Bau, a fact that is proved by numerous cones and bricks that were stamped and inscribed with a text in Ur-Bau's name that commemorates the renovation of Bau's sacred building, which is referred to as already extant on Tell A.

For several reasons, the only possible counter-argument to this, which is the idea that Ur-Bau might have transferred both sanctuaries to Tell A, makes no sense. It would imply that the temple of Bau was removed from another location in the Urukug to Tell A, where it was brought together with the Ningirsu temple when the latter was transferred from Tell K. There is no written evidence to suggest that this is what happened, and indeed the inscriptions explicitly say that the Bau establishment remained in its current location when Ningirsu's temple was refounded in close proximity. The argument would also reopen the question of which deity, if not Bau, this pre-eminent mound might have been devoted to, with Bau being the only plausible candidate. Lastly, it would leave a gaping lacuna in the sacred landscape, namely the absence of Bau's sanctuary. Again, the only suitable location was Tell A, and it must therefore be concluded with a high degree of confidence that Tell A was the site of Bau's shrine, as it presumably had been for a very long period. Nor can it be a coincidence that one of the six gates that gave access to Gudea's later New Eninnu on Tell A—the Tarsirsir Gate at the NW end of the complex—and the nearby temple of Bau, 'Bau's inner room', which Gudea almost certainly sited close to the Tarsirsir Gate, were both named in honour of the old sanctuary of the goddess, no doubt as a way of paying homage to the time-honoured sacred locus.

CHAPTER 33

The Ur-Bau Complex: The Relocated Ningirsu Temple and the Restored Temple to Bau

THE SOPHISTICATED EPIC TEXTUAL APPARATUS THAT was put in place by Gudea to accompany his extraordinary redevelopment of the sacred complex on Tell A has inevitably tended to overshadow the achievements of his predecessor and father-in-law, Ur-Bau (Fig. 168). Despite that, it was probably not Gudea's intention to demote Ur-Bau (as it were), or to downplay his precursor's importance. This is confirmed by the fact that he conserved and repurposed the sanctuary that Ur-Bau had built on Tell A, and he conspicuously prayed in it on more than one occasion while his New Eninnu was being planned and built. As is touched upon in greater detail in Chapter 44, he also adopted several of Ur-Bau's ritual practices, particularly with regard to the installation of foundation deposits, and this might well have reflected the more general adoption of an evolving theology that was conceivably also instituted by Ur-Bau. In historical terms, it was Ur-Bau who dramatically and substantially reframed the religious architecture of Girsu, initiating and orchestrating the Sumerian renaissance that came about in Lagash II times after the fall of the Akkad colonial power that had controlled Lagash and the rest of Sumer from the time of Sargon of Akkad's conquest of the region a little less than a century previously. Above all, Ur-Bau revolutionised the basic principles that had shaped Girsu's sacred landscape since the beginning of the third millennium BCE by transferring the Temple of Ningirsu from Tell K to Tell A, the precinct that had previously been devoted exclusively to the god's queen consort, Bau. In so doing, he brought the divine couple together, presumably with the intention of permanently uniting them under one roof. The precise symbolism of the consolidation, which is

further discussed below, can only be guessed at, but in the changed circumstances of the post-Akkad restoration of full worship the move might have appeared, on the one hand, to be a natural development, perhaps like the rectification of an anomaly. Henceforth, seemingly like their royal human counterparts, the divine husband and wife would live and reign in close proximity, perhaps in a coordinated fashion. On the other hand, however, Ur-Bau's undertaking was absolutely extraordinary because it was perhaps the first and only time in ancient Sumer that the founding temple of a state's chief god had been moved from its original location to a new site. In transferring the cult of Ningirsu from its age-old setting on Tell K to Tell A, therefore, Ur-Bau did something that seemingly had no parallel in the Sumerian world.

The preserved royal inscriptions from the reign of Ur-Bau make no mention of his earthly filiation, stating only that he was the 'child of the goddess Ninagala', so any presumed dynastic links with his immediate predecessors, Ur-Ningirsu I and Pirigme, are unclear. Ninagala is repeatedly honoured as Ur-Bau's divine mother and also as his personal deity, but the fact that his human origins and lineage are not documented is in itself both highly unusual and of great interest. In terms of his successors, Ur-Bau's reign initiated a sequence of related rulers spanning three generations that was briefly interrupted for a period of about five years between the time of Ur-Ningirsu II and that of Nammahni (as noted in Chapter 3). The sovereignty of Lagash appears to have been hereditary after Ur-Bau, and it also seems, in principle, to have devolved exclusively to male members of the king's extended family, even in the absence of a blood relationship between fathers

FIGURE 168. Statue of Ur-Bau from Tell A. Musée du Louvre AO9.

and sons, as is witnessed by the role played in the succession by two of Ur-Bau's three prominent daughters: Ninalla, the wife of Gudea; and Ninhedu, the wife of Nammahni. Incidentally, the third notable daughter, Enannepadda, held the prestigious office of high priestess of the moon god, Nanna, in Ur. Ur-Bau's direct successor, Gudea, was therefore his son-in-law, as was Nammahni, who came to the throne some thirty-five years later, after the reigns of Gudea (who ruled for about twenty-five years), Gudea's son Ur-Ningirsu II, and three rulers who were seemingly not filially connected to Gudea or Ur-Bau (UrGAR, Urabba and Urmama). The complications in the descent, which includes five short reigns over a period of no more than about fifteen years (as shown in Table 4 in Chapter 3), are fascinating in themselves, and they might conceivably testify to a paucity of male heirs in a hereditary monarchy based on male primogeniture. As is discussed in Chapter 34 with reference to the rise of Gudea, however, there is another plausible explanation for the peculiarities evident in the lineage. That is that Ur-Bau and Gudea, together with Ur-Bau's shadowy predecessor, Pirigme, were all sons of the temple: children who were possibly born and brought up in the institution.

The quantity of royal inscriptions in the name of Ur-Bau, as well as the nature and number of his recorded activities, suggest that he enjoyed a long reign that might plausibly have lasted between twenty-five and thirty years. In addition to the epoch-making work devoted to the shrines of Ningirsu and Bau that he carried out on Tell A, he built or restored the temples of several other deities in Girsu, including those of Enki, Ninhursag, Inanna, Nindara, Ninagala, Ninmarki, Geshtinanna and Dumuziabzu. The fact that his name has been found engraved on a variety of stone vessels, mace heads and tablets suggests that the economy of Lagash flourished during his reign, and that the trading routes for imported raw materials, semi-precious stones and other valuable commodities were open and secure. He seems assiduously to have reinforced his political status and legacy by ensuring that his daughters were placed in institutional positions of high dynastic and religious importance. At first glance, this is most apparent with respect to Gudea's wife, Ninalla, and Enannepadda, the Ur high priestess, but the fact that Ur-Bau's daughter Ninhedu married Nammahni, who eventually (presumably about three decades after Ur-Bau's death) became the dynasty's last ruler might well provide further proof of his foresight, statecraft and lasting charisma. These matters are considered again in the context of Gudea's ascent to the throne in Chapter 34 below, but it is worth saying here that, if Ur-Bau was indeed born and raised in the temple, possibly

460   The Mound of the Palace

as the offspring of a sacred rite, then the succession of kings that came after him might not have been entirely dependent on his personal choice, prestige and power. That said, Ur-Bau's career in many ways recalls that of the Early Dynastic founder of the First Dynasty of Lagash, Ur-Nanshe, and it is even tempting to assume that Ur-Bau modelled his reign on that of his renowned forerunner. Like his illustrious antecedent, Ur-Bau fundamentally reshaped the religious landscape of Girsu, the sacred centre of the state of Lagash, by building and renovating shrines and commissioning monuments and sacred artefacts on a grand scale. He also created an innovative ritual apparatus to accompany his work, including horned deities holding foundation pegs and accompanied by tablets, as well as inscribed temple cones and commemorative bricks containing new ritual formulae, to name just three examples. The overall impression is that, again following the precedent set by Ur-Nanshe, Ur-Bau's aim was to establish a well-founded, long-lasting dynasty for the post-Akkad age in which he lived.

The motives that prompted Ur-Bau to reinstitute the Ningirsu temple in its changed location on Tell A must surely have been commemorated in inscriptions that were intended to preserve a record of the exceptional event in perpetuity, but no epigraphic or sculptural accounts of the circumstances surrounding Ur-Bau's momentous decision have yet been uncovered. Nonetheless, several speculative explanations have been mooted, and they are not mutually exclusive. First, there can be no doubt that the final destruction of the Early Dynastic Temple of Ningirsu on Tell K during the reign of Urukagina must have appeared utterly catastrophic to the restored Sumerian rulers and citizens of the Second Dynasty of Lagash. When the newly liberated inhabitants of Lagash looked back beyond the intervening years of Akkad subjection, Lugalzagesi's razing of Girsu's holiest place, little more than a century earlier, doubtless looked like a calamitous turning point. The scale and violent manner of the sacred precinct's destruction, including the sacrilegious defacing and desecration of Ningirsu's divine image and all the cult objects associated with the god and the state of Lagash generally, must have remained a matter of deep national regret.

An understanding of the period of Akkad occupation is complicated by Sarzec's discovery in the upper layers of Tell K of wall *Mur* (on Plan C (2)), the preserved corner of a building that seems to have followed the outlines of the final pre-Akkad version of the Temple of Ningirsu that was built in the reign

of Urukagina. In conjunction with the British Museum team's discovery, in 2021, in a spoil heap to the south of Tell K, of a fragment of a votive bowl that was dedicated to Ningirsu by the Akkad king Rimush, the existence of wall *Mur* positively confirms that a late version of the Ningirsu temple was rebuilt under Akkad imperial rule (as detailed in Chapter 21). Even so, the uncovering of just a single preserved piece of Akkad wall suggests that the reinstated shrine must have been little more than a sorry shadow of the sequence of magnificent sacred complexes that had graced Tell K for more than 700 years until the conquest of Lagash by Lugalzagesi and the subsequent Akkad invasion. More immediately, the suppression of two noteworthy uprisings against Akkad rule during the reigns of Rimush and Naram-Sin were commemorated by the creation of a victory stele (the Akkad Stele, also discussed in Chapter 21), some defaced fragments of which were found on Tell K. Announcing the final crushing of the Sumerian revolts and the forced submission of the nobility and high clergy of Lagash, the monument was doubtless displayed in close proximity to the Akkad iteration of the temple, conceivably on an adjacent podium or even inside its walls. The erection of the Akkad Stele on the state's holiest site must have magnified the fearful effects of Akkad imperial dominance, further reminding the people of Lagash that they had been subjected to yet another crushing humiliation. With this in mind, and despite the presumed existence of an Akkad temple, Tell K surely exhibited a godforsaken aspect during these dark times, and this fact perhaps helped to persuade Ur-Bau, presumably advised by his college of priests, that the cult of Ningirsu should be transferred from its ancient home on Tell K to a location in the Urukug that had been less severely desecrated, namely Tell A, the site of the shrine of Ningirsu's wife, Bau.

Beyond the desire to re-establish the native religious culture of Lagash on fresh foundations (an ambition that seems to have been vigorously embraced by Gudea, as is considered below), Ur-Bau probably also had another agenda that was associated with the changing times in which he lived. For whatever reason, from the Lagash II era onwards there was a growing interest in dual cults—a development that led to the construction of large sanctuaries that were devoted not to individual deities but to divine couples, notably Ningirsu and Bau, but also Ningishzida and Geshtinanna. Whether Ur-Bau inaugurated the trend, or whether he was just one of its most powerful early advocates is not certain, but his decision to bring Ningirsu and Bau together as divine husband

and wife in a joint household on Tell A was unquestionably in tune with the theological spirit of the age.

Ur-Bau's redrawing of the sacred map of Girsu might also have had combined emblematic and logistical ends because the removal of Ningirsu's shrine to Tell A brought the god nearer to the edge of the sacred precinct, not far from the wall of the Urukug, part of which, on the north-west side of Tell A, was excavated by the British Museum team (context 25021 in Area B12). The temple was thereby moved closer to the surrounding network of canals that facilitated the transport of people and supplies. There was important symbolism in this too. Situated to the north-west of Tell K, the new location recalled the path previously taken by Ningirsu when the cult statue was transported back and forth from his own temple on Tell K to that of his wife on Tell A, accompanied by the temple attendants and priests who brought the god's belongings, portable appurtenances and inscribed texts. It should also be recalled that the new principal approach that was built by Ur-Nanshe when he raised Tell K to construct his celebrated version of the temple, the Ur-Nanshe Building, was pavement F on Sarzec's Plan C (1), on the NW side of the structure. The innovative Ur-Nanshe Building was the basis for subsequent iterations of the temple that were created under Ur-Nanshe's Early Dynastic successors all the way down to Urukagina, and then in all likelihood also under the Akkad ruler Rimush. It seems credible to suppose that they all retained the main approach that had been inaugurated by Ur-Nanshe. In addition to its ceremonial functions on Tell K, therefore, pavement F (and any homologous successors) necessarily extended along, and might therefore also have called to mind, the line that connected Tells K and A: the respective homes, under Ur-Nanshe, of Ningirsu and Bau. There is, of course, no reason why this interwoven set of associations could not all have played a role.

Ur-Bau's Platform for the Temple to Ningirsu

The centrepiece of the architectural ensemble that embodied Ur-Bau's restoration of the religious site of Girsu was the relocated Ningirsu temple, which was placed on the newly established self-contained platform or monumental podium that was partly exposed on the Mound of the Palace by Sarzec and Cros (walls ABC on Heuzey's New Plan; Fig. 114). Ur-Bau's rectangular Ningirsu temple platform had its corners closely aligned with the cardinal points, with its shorter sides facing north-west and south-east, but as is discussed in Chapter 39 below, the correct orientation of the temple itself was the overriding priority. Situated on the NE side of the Temple of Bau, it raised the base of the new building by about 2 m above the general ground level of the rest of the sanctuary, ensuring that Ur-Bau's Ningirsu temple would dominate Tell A. In addition, as confirmed by the British Museum team's excavations, Ur-Bau refurbished, but did not dismantle, the existing temple dedicated to Bau, together with the sanctuary's annexes and ancillary structures. Finally, he also constructed a new enclosure or temenos wall around the entire sacred complex on the summit of the mound, where the two deities were now united.

The raised monumental podium on which the Ningirsu temple was built was a solid mass of sun-dried bricks that were encased in a thick skin of inscribed square fired bricks (with sides of 0.47 m) that were bonded with bitumen. Both kinds of bricks were mostly marked with the standard Ur-Bau inscription—the precursor to Gudea's royal cartouche—celebrating the construction of Ur-Bau's relocated Eninnu for Ningirsu. Covering a total area of around 200 m², the temple platform measured about 17.14 m × 11.17 m, and it was (as just noted) about 2m high. The corners of its SE wall (doubtless at both ends, though only one survived) exhibited corner buttresses, each capped with a decorative element in the shape of a three-step tower. This, according to Heuzey, was an architectural motif inspired by the form of the ziggurat. Presumably, these monumental square pilasters, with sides of 1.5 m and a recorded height of 1.4 m, were installed on either side of a broad flight of steps that was built into the fabric of the podium. The substantial raised platform was placed on a superficial foundation fill made of a layer of clean silty sand, which, according to Heuzey, was 'ritually sifted' (Sarzec and Heuzey 1912, p. 401). Beneath that was a solid mud-brick platform of small, hard compacted square briquettes measuring 0.2 m × 0.2 m × 0.1 m (t), which turned out to be closely comparable with, if not identical to, the mud-brick foundation layers on Tell A that dated back to the Late Early Dynastic IIIb and Early Akkad periods. Accordingly, the underlying mud-brick mass on which the Ur-Bau podium for the new temple was built was undoubtedly a continuation of the grey platform (5235)—the uppermost Early Dynastic layer that formed the raised summit of Tell A that was established by Urukagina. As previously discussed, the grey platform was uncovered during the British Museum team's excavations in Areas B1 and B9.

Sarzec's published report records the recovery of a supposed foundation deposit from beneath the W corner of the Ur-Bau podium (Fig. 169). It apparently consisted of a terracotta jar (AO451) that contained an inscribed stone tablet (AO261; RIME 3.1.1.6.6) and a copper deity holding a peg (AO311) of the type that was later adopted by Gudea (see Chapter 44). Although Sarzec's account has universally been taken at face value (first and foremost by Heuzey), the description raises several insoluble difficulties, not least because it states that the tablet and the peg were found inside the jar (Sarzec and Heuzey 1912, pp. 241–2; see also Pl. 8 bis (1–3)). In view of the objects' respective sizes, this could not have been the case. The medium-size jar has an outwardly rounded ledge rim, a short vertical neck, rounded shoulders, an ovoid body and a flat base that is pierced with three circular holes. It is 24 cm high and has a maximum diameter of 19.5 cm across its pronounced shoulders, while the diameters of the base and rim range between 6 cm and 9 cm, and 10 cm and 15 cm, respectively. The intact jar was therefore simply not big enough to contain the objects. The peg, which measures 29 cm (h) × 8.5 cm (w) × 13 cm (t), is at least 5 cm longer than the height of the jar, while the tablet, which measures 21 cm (h) × 18 cm (w) × 3 cm (t), is far too big, both lengthways and widthways, to have passed through the jar's mouth.

FIGURE 169. Inscribed copper foundation peg and inscribed stone tablet from the reign of Ur-Bau, together with the clay pot in which the objects were supposedly found by Sarzec. Musée du Louvre AO311, AO261 and AO451.

Remarkably, these basic facts have never previously been pointed out. Furthermore, when compared with the pottery finds made by the British Museum team, the supposed Ur-Bau jar can be securely dated to the Isin-Larsa period—200 years or so after the reign of Ur-Bau. None of this means that the three objects could not have been found together, or in close proximity, but they were certainly not three associated elements of a single Ur-Bau foundation deposit. The most likely explanation for the long-standing mistaken interpretation is that the broken Isin-Larsa jar, which was seemingly found by Sarzec close to the Ur-Bau deposits, was erroneously linked with the earlier remains merely on the basis of contiguity, without any attention being paid to the dimensions of the individual objects, or their possible histories.

A fragment of another foundation tablet (TG168), inscribed with the same Ur-Bau inscription (RIME 3.1.1.6.6), was uncovered during the British Museum team's excavations in Area B1 on Tell A, where it was found in the backfill (deposited between 1929 and 1930) from Genouillac's Central Trench. Made of a beige crystalline stone (possibly marble), it measures 0.105 m × 0.71 m × 0.03 m (t), and has a smooth, flat face, a slightly convex back and straight sides (the top left side and part of the right side are damaged). Although about a quarter of the tablet is missing, the broken edge is nevertheless regular and straight, while the fracture along the top of the stone is slightly diagonal. Some damage on the bottom right corner of the tablet has also removed part of the inscription, but thirteen lines are preserved, including the declaration: 'he built. For Bau, the beautiful woman, daughter of An, he built her Eurukug (House of the Holy City) . . . his lord, he built his house. For Ninagala, his (personal) goddess, he built her house.' Furthermore, along the Ningirsu temple platform's SW façade, and to a lesser degree on its NW side, the French pioneers also retrieved a large number of particularly big cones that were deposited in the name of Ur-Bau, and all contained the same text (RIME 3.1.1.6.4) commemorating the ruler's pious deeds: 'For Ningirsu, mighty warrior of Enlil, Ur-Bau, ruler of Lagash, child born of Ninagala, made things function as they should. He built for him his Eninnu, the White Thunderbird and restored it to its proper place.'

As these finds confirm, on top of the platform that was first exposed by Sarzec in 1880 (sadly razed to the ground between 1909 and 1929) stood Ur-Bau's Temple of Ningirsu, organised on the direct-approach principle, and probably with a single sacred chamber. Its high walls were studded with inscribed cones of the type just described. In addition to the cult image of Ningirsu, the temple no doubt contained a number of important votive objects, and it was probably fitted with a pedestal that supported the inscribed standing statue of Ur-Bau at prayer (AO9) that was found by Sarzec on the NW side of the Hellenistic complex, in the vicinity of Court B (on Sarzec's Plan A; Fig. 111). The surviving commemorative and dedicatory inscriptions meticulously describe the construction rituals and architectural design of Ur-Bau's Ningirsu shrine, together with the elaborate consecration ceremonies that were celebrated when it was officially opened. The details correspond remarkably well with the archaeological features that were exposed by Sarzec and reinterpreted by the British Museum team in the context of the team's work on Tell A. The inscription on Ur-Bau's statue (RIME 3.1.1.6.5) vividly describes the founding of the temple on its new site, as well as the accompanying purification rites that were overseen by the ruler:

> For Ningirsu, the powerful warrior of Enlil, my master, I, Ur-Bau, ruler of Lagash, the child born to Ninagala, chosen by Nanshe in her heart, given strength by Ningirsu, called by a propitious name by Bau, given wisdom by Enki; (Ur-Bau) who submits to the orders of Inanna, (who is) the beloved slave of Lugal-Uruba, the beloved of Dumuziabzu, dug a pit . . . kuš (deep). I sifted its earth as if (I were searching for) gems (and) brought fire as if it were (to be made ritually) pure. I had (the temple) stand wide like a bull. I returned the earth to (the pit), constructed its . . . foundation pit. On it I built a substructure 10 kuš (high, and) on the substructure I built Eninnu: the White Thunderbird (rising to a height of) 30 kuš for (Ningirsu).

The narrative states that Ur-Bau prepared the ground by digging a pit. He then sifted the excavated earth and further purified it with fire before replacing it in the cavity. Though the initial digging is subject to some philological uncertainty, the latter part of the operation is reasonably clearly expressed in the Sumerian sentence saḫar.bi šag$_4$.ba im.ši.gi$_4$, which speaks of returning the 'earth' to (or into) 'its heart', such that the -ba suffix ('its') after šag$_4$ ('heart') refers to thing that 'I (Ur-Bau) dug . . . for him' (mu.na.ba.al). The standard translation by Edzard (1997), which refers to strewing the excavated earth 'over a wide area as with a seeding funnel' is problematic, most importantly because the key

Sumerian word (gub) does not have the attested meaning of 'to spread', and also because the erroneous idea of scattering or strewing the purified clay (like casting seeds in a field), while introducing an idea of growth, does not refer specifically to the process of laying down a firm foundation as a necessary preliminary to the raising of a high building. For this reason, the imagery is here taken to connote the breadth (and by implication the depth) of the building's large podium or platform, which is substantial enough to allow the finished temple to stand on its underpinning like a mighty bull that supports its great weight on strong, outstretched legs.

Though there can be no doubt that the inscription describes Ur-Bau's temple and its self-contained podium of mud-bricks, the exact figures given in the text require careful scrutiny. On the one hand, the 3:1 ratio of the respective heights of the temple walls (of Eninnu: the White Thunderbird) and the monumental mud-brick platform with its retaining wall of fired bricks appears perfectly rational and surely reflects a Sumerian devotion to sacred proportions. On the other hand, if a Sumerian kuš is taken to be 0.52 m (the usual height attributed to a Sumerian cubit), the converted heights of 15.6 m (30 kuš) and 5.2 m (10 kuš) for the temple walls and the foundation platform seem very much exaggerated. With that in mind, there is little reason to suspect that the height of the Ur-Bau platform in Lagash II times was significantly greater than the section that was excavated by the French, and it should also be recalled (as described above) that one of its decorated corner buttresses might have been preserved to its full height of 1.4 m. If the Ur-Bau podium for the Ningirsu temple had a height of about 2 m, therefore (as calculated in Chapter 23), the temple walls themselves were perhaps around 6 m high, which would appear to be plausible. By comparison, Heuzey (Sarzec and Heuzey 1912, p. 401) theorises that the podium or *soubassement* rose to a height of 2.7 m. One further implication, it should be noted, would seem to be that the unit named as a kuš in the Ur-Bau inscription had a length of about 20 cm.

Finally, with respect to the Ur-Bau platform, the British Museum team's exploration of Tell A, particularly in and between Areas B2, B5, B11 and B6—the precise location of Ur-Bau's dismantled Ningirsu temple platform—revealed significant traces of extensive digging and looting pits, including fragments of large bricks inscribed in the name of Ur-Bau, all of which appear to have resulted from illegal digs that were carried out before World War II. These fragments are presumably all that now survives of the extremely substantial remains that lay under the ground when Sarzec began work on the site in the late 1870s.

The Restoration of Bau's Temple

As detailed in Chapter 32 above, a plethora of royal inscriptions bear witness to the fact that, after the downfall of the Akkad overlords, Ur-Bau was an indefatigable builder of religious buildings in the state of Lagash. In addition to his momentous repurposing of Tells A and K, the texts commemorate the restoration of the sanctuaries and smaller shrines of numerous deities from the Lagash II pantheon. Although none of the attested temples or cult places have been identified by archaeologists, they were probably located outside the innermost sacred enclosure on Tell A, either within the walls of the Urukug or on one of the lesser mounds of Girsu: Tell M, Tell N or Ningishzida Hill, for example. Some were doubtless also situated outside the religious centre, in rural chapels, border areas and other towns, particularly in the city of Lagash, as well as Nigin and URU×KÁR.

The British Museum team's deeper excavations below Gudea's New Eninnu, especially under the cella and antecella of Gudea's Ningirsu temple (at the SE end of the complex) in Areas B2, B3 and B5, confirmed that the antecedent set of Early Dynastic IIIb temple rooms were in use uninterruptedly before, during and after the Akkad interval, all the way down to the time of Ur-Bau's restoration. Delineated by surviving expanses of planoconvex mud-brick walls, these sacred spaces (as argued in the previous chapter) represented the ancient site of the cult of Bau, whose temple was eventually rebuilt, or perhaps rather extensively refurbished, during the reign of Urukagina. Unearthed in the course of the team's excavations, well-preserved parts of the shrine's uppermost floors (contexts 2050 and 2055) yielded an extremely coherent assemblage of ceremonial vessels and offering bowls that were securely dated to the Late Akkad and Early Lagash II periods—a time span that includes the reign of Ur-Bau.

It is equally clear that the nearby enigmatic Akkad platform (2158), facing the SE side of the podium that supported Ur-Bau's Ningirsu temple, was still standing when Ur-Bau carried out his architectural works, and that it was probably refurbished either by him or slightly before his time. The fill (2133) of a perfectly circular pit (2132), with a circumference of 0.82 m and a depth of 0.2 m, that was found embedded in the surface of this Akkad and (or) Ur-Bau terrace (2158), yielded diagnostic potsherds dating to the Late Akkad and Early Lagash II periods. The cavity, which was sealed off when Gudea subsequently built his new walls above it, was perhaps created as a low-lying shallow installation or more probably as the housing for a large pithos.

Occupying the same sacred setting, the restored shrine to Bau, together with Ur-Bau's transferred Ningirsu temple, were enclosed in a remodelled version of the presumed earlier temenos wall, where they formed the re-established heart of Girsu's pre-eminent religious complex on Tell A. Numerous cones and brick fragments inscribed in Ur-Bau's name were unearthed by the French explorers during Otto-man and Mandate-era digs, and the British Museum team's salvage operations produced many more. The majority were understandably dedicated to Ningirsu, but most, if not all, of the rest contained the ruler's standard Bau inscription (RIME 3.1.1.6.1), which records construction work carried out in honour of the goddess: 'For Bau, the beautiful woman, daughter of An, Ur-Bau, ruler of Lagash, child born of Nina-gala, built her House of the Holy City'. It is important to note that Bau was worshipped with particular fervour dur-ing the reign of Ur-Bau. The unbreakable bond between the ruler and the goddess was expressed in Ur-Bau's regnal name, while her importance in the state more generally is attested by a number of finds that were often fragmented and mostly exhumed in unrecorded or unclear archaeological contexts in other parts of the extended complex. With one exception (a mace head dedicated to the god Igalim), the recovered votive artefacts that were commissioned by Ur-Bau and other contemporary high-status individuals were all offering bowls dedicated to Bau and her ministering Tarsirsir, who acted as a protective spirit on the goddess's behalf. It might even be supposed that the Tarsirsir was conceived of as the goddess's avatar, in the same way as the Thunderbird was for Ningirsu.

Other architectural relics discovered on Tell A by the French pioneers that might perhaps have been built during the reign of Ur-Bau are more problematic. They include a pavement and some possibly associated brickwork structures that were uncovered by the French in the vicinity of Gudea's sacred well (structure M on Heuzey's New Plan; Fig. 114). A small portion of paving, measuring 2.4 m × 4.4 m, and made of uninscribed square fired bricks with sides of 0.4 m, was found at a similar topographical level as the base of Ur-Bau's terrace podium, and can therefore probably be dated to the time of the construction of his new Ningirsu temple. More difficult to contextualise are the remains of structures K and L (on Heuzey's New Plan) that the French dated either to the reign of Gudea or to the subsequent Ur III and Isin-Larsa periods. Made of reused brick fragments, the installations appear to have been poorly built, levelled in antiquity and truncated in Hellenistic times before being finally dismantled much more recently in the Ottoman and Mandate periods. Nonetheless, if structures K and L are superimposed on the plan of the British Museum team's excavations in Area B5, the conclusion seems to be that the fragment of purported Ur-Bau paving discovered by the French was perhaps aligned with the suite of temple rooms found in Areas B2, B3 and B5, and it might therefore have originally formed part of the adjoining exterior paved floor of the Bau temple when it was renovated by Ur-Bau.

Ur-Bau's Sacred Enclosure

Generally in Area B, the British Museum team's findings indi-cated that an ever-increasing number of architectural struc-tures should be ascribed to the reign of Ur-Bau, even though the attribution of the brickwork itself was often uncertain. In conformity with Sarzec's discoveries, some batches of fired bricks inscribed in Ur-Bau's name were found to be signifi-cantly larger than those used by Gudea—their long sides hav-ing standard measurements of 0.47 m, as opposed to 0.32 m for the Gudea bricks. With regard to sun-dried bricks, how-ever, the bricks used by both rulers were found to be roughly the same size, with sides measuring between 0.3 m and 0.32 m. In the absence of *in situ* dedicatory objects, the revised dat-ing was carried out on the basis of archaeological context and stratigraphy, complemented by typologically distinct pieces of pottery that were retrieved from associated deposits. These factors helped the British Museum team to distinguish between specific construction phases and events that could be assigned to one or the other Lagash II ruler, facilitating the creation of a chronological sequence for the work carried out on Tell A by Ur-Bau and Gudea, respectively.

As stated previously, Ur-Bau enclosed the newly built Nin-girsu temple and the refurbished Temple of Bau, along with any adjacent annexes and the enigmatic Akkad platform in a peripheral wall that was specially designed to demarcate the limits of the redefined sacred precinct. Archaeological vestiges of Ur-Bau's temenos wall were exposed by the team in Areas B2, B3 and B4, where they were found beneath structures associated with Gudea's New Eninnu or interred in its substructural fabric. In B2, for example, wall 2024, which was levelled in Gudea's time and recut horizontally in the Hellenistic era, was incorporated into the foundational structure of its successor (2001), which was built by Gudea. Exposed at a topographical height of 14.99 m, and preserved to a length of 2.1 m on a NE–SW alignment, wall 2024 was made of uniform square mud-bricks (with dimensions of 0.32 m × 0.32 m × 0.07 m) that presented a red-brown matrix with a grey-brown surface and inclusions of white lime flecks. The excavated section was formed of a single course of mud-bricks with an approximate depth of 0.1 m (including the mortar). Three rows of bricks were identified, meaning the wall was just a little less than 1 m wide (again allowing for the mortar). Notably, the wall also featured a buttress (or recess pattern) on its SW face that added a decorative element to an elaborate NW–SE gateway. Associated with this structure—though not physically adjoining it—was a clear floor horizon (2023) that was identified at a topographical height of 15.23 m, where it was sealed off by an overlying Gudea foundation fill (2022). The flooring contained diagnostic potsherds dating to the Late Akkad period and to the reign of Ur-Bau.

Context 3097 (in Area B3), which was oriented northeast–south-west and formed an alignment with wall 2024, was also identified beneath a successor structure (3006) that was built during the reign of Gudea. Like its counterpart in B2 (2024), wall 3097 was laid on bed (directly on the ground and not in a foundation trench) at a deeper topographical level (14.9 m) than Gudea's temple walls, and it was exposed over a length of about 9.5 m to an average thickness of 2.5 m. Despite the extensive truncation in this area, the NW face of wall 3097 appeared to have been strengthened by thick buttresses, of which only one survived (3080). Damaged by French trenching, the preserved buttress measured 0.83 m × 0.57 m, and its base lay at an overall height of 14.93 m. Further traced in B4, wall 3097 turned ninety degrees towards the south-east, where, at a topographical height of 14.92 m, it bonded perfectly with context 3098. Carefully levelled during Gudea's reign to a height of about two or three courses of mud-bricks, the excavated corner also served as the core of later walls that were part of Gudea's New Eninnu (3049 and 2032). A locus of good stratigraphy near the intersection

of pre-Gudea walls 3097 and 3098 revealed superimposed deposits containing diagnostic potsherds that helped the team to date the structure to the reign of Ur-Bau. At the top of the stratigraphic section was found a series of layers (3067, 3070, 3071, 2083 and 2084) that were dated to the time of Gudea and the Ur III period. With a total depth of 0.66 m, they were made up of subfloor packings that alternated with repeated gradual raisings of the floor level. Underneath this sequence was a clear occupation deposit (2085) that was exposed at a topographical height of 15.09 m. Associated with wall 3098, deposit 2085 contained an array of ceramic remains from both the Late Akkad period and the reign of Ur-Bau.

Shortly after it was built, Ur-Bau's innovative double temple complex, dedicated to the worship of the dual cult of Ningirsu and Bau, was extensively levelled and ritually interred by Gudea. In spite of that, and also, of course, thanks to the thoroughness with which Gudea ritually processed the structures that were built by his revered predecessor, the British Museum team found significant remains of Ur-Bau's undertaking preserved beneath the Gudea walls. Left relatively unscathed by the much later Hellenistic excavation and reconstruction, as well as by the massive trenches that were dug by the French pioneers, the surviving sections of the pre-Gudea structures that were exposed during the British Museum team's excavations shed an extraordinary light on Ur-Bau's buildings, refurbishments and overall reorganisation of the mound. The all-embracing character of his plan confirms that the pre-Gudea revolutionary change that was wrought on the religious landscape of Girsu, including the crucial removal of Ningirsu's temple from Tell K to Tell A, was first and foremost the realisation of Ur-Bau's vision. As repeatedly noted, however, the impact of his work was quickly overshadowed by the remarkable architectural achievements of Gudea, who left behind a wealth of inscriptions, including an unprecedented epic account of the origins and execution of his work, that almost erased Ur-Bau's achievement from the record. That was probably not Gudea's intention, since it seems highly probable that he regarded his predecessor with considerable admiration, but the fact remains that, with the significant exception of his deconsecrated and superseded Ningirsu temple building, Ur-Bau's innovations were almost immediately swallowed up in the foundations of Gudea's great exploit. Carried out on a scale and with a degree of grandeur that were previously unthinkable, the construction of the vast complex that is here referred to as the New Eninnu was an epoch-making event that irrevocably changed the shape of Tell A forevermore.

CHAPTER 34

The Gudea Sanctuary of Ningirsu: The New Eninnu

The Paradox of Gudea

Like many of the heroes, sages and prophets who have won lasting renown throughout human history Gudea's origins are shrouded in uncertainty, such that it is extremely difficult to distinguish myth from reality. As was the case with his father-in-law and predecessor, Ur-Bau, from whom Gudea took a great deal of inspiration, Gudea's human ancestry is conspicuous by its total absence from his royal inscriptions, which make no mention of his earthly parents and give no information at all about his role or status before he ascended the throne. According to the much later List of the Rulers of Lagash (an apologia for Gudea dating from Old Babylonian times, which is detailed in Chapter 35), Gudea was 'the younger brother of Ur-Bau . . . who was not the son of his mother nor the son of his father'. This fascinating statement, which apparently suggests that neither Ur-Bau nor Gudea were the natural offspring of the parents who raised them, is consistent with the texts found on artefacts commissioned during Gudea's reign, including statues of the ruler and the Cylinder Inscriptions, in which Gudea addresses the mother goddess, Gatumdug, as his sole parent, saying that she implanted the seed from which he grew in a womb in the temple (A3): 'For me, who has no mother, you are my mother; for me, who has no father, you are my father. You implanted my semen in the womb, gave birth to me in the sanctuary, Gatumdug, sweet is your holy name!'

The part played by Gatumdug in Gudea's conception might be less directly maternal than the text seems initially to suggest, however, because another passage implies that

Gudea's divine mother was actually Ninsun, 'the bearing mother of good offspring, who loves her offspring' (B23). It might be, therefore, that Gatumdug is introduced into the inscriptions in a mythical or poetic capacity, as the mother goddess—the cosmic divine agent—to whom all humans owe their existence, while Ninsun was his personal divine mother. Similarly, in poetic terms, the 'sanctuary' from which Gudea is born might be a vividly expressive metaphor for the 'womb' in which Gatumdug is said to plant the seed from which Gudea grows. In this context, it should again be recalled that Ur-Bau styled himself a 'child born of Ninagala', while Ur-Bau's obscure predecessor, Pirgme (historically the son of Ur-Ningirsu I), also called himself the son of Ninsun (RIME 3.1.1.2.1)—the divine mother of Gudea. As briefly mentioned above, a literal reading of these texts leads to the interesting idea that Ur-Bau, Pirgme and Gudea could all have been sons of the temple—children who were perhaps born and brought up in the sacred institution. That might also explain the fraternal relationship between Ur-Bau and Gudea that is mentioned in the List of the Rulers of Lagash: if both were raised in the temple (as is again intimated of Gudea in his Cylinder Inscriptions) then Ur-Bau could in reality have conceived of his junior contemporary as a 'younger brother' (see Emelianov 2016).

These caveats aside, the fact that Ur-Bau and Gudea claimed divine parentage and pointedly made no mention of their human origins in their official inscriptions is of some significance, as is the assumption that there was a fraternal bond between the two. The idea that a group of rulers might have risen to power in large part because they were, in reality

467

or even just in terms of their upbringing and education, children of the temple potentially helps to explain a number of oddities in the historical record. It might, for instance, explain why the natural sons of rulers were not necessarily adopted as their heirs, and this might account for the transfer of power from Ur-Bau to Gudea, as well as the later accession, three or more decades after Ur-Bau's death, of Nammahni, the second son-in-law of Ur-Bau to take power. Could Ur-Bau's prestige as the founder of the dynasty really have endured for so long, even eclipsing the spectacular eminence and status of Gudea? Or was there another mechanism at work that preferred children born in the temple over natural offspring? The answer cannot be known, but the thesis might also account for the seemingly tumultuous interval between the presumed death of Ur-Ningirsu II and the ascent of Nammahni, when three rulers successively occupied the throne in a span of just five years. Such quick transfers of power often indicate periods of conflict in human affairs, and if that was indeed the situation in Lagash at that time, it could also have been due to the festering resentment experienced by the natural sons of rulers who were conceivably overlooked in favour of institutionally appointed alternatives. Finally, the important roles played in the succession between the time of Ur-Bau and that of Nammahni by two of Ur-Bau's daughters is noteworthy and highly unusual in Lagash (as mentioned above). A surmised line of descent that favoured sons of the temple might also have added to the power and prestige of royal women in this epoch, with the lineage being strengthened and consolidated by the marriage of a temple heir to a daughter of Ur-Bau. In the absence of more definitive evidence such conclusions must, however, be treated with the utmost caution.

It should also be stated unequivocally that, even if the two rulers were conceived and raised in the institution of the temple, this would not have meant that they themselves were considered to be partly or fully divine, as has sometimes been averred. The deification of Gudea happened in the Ur III period (as is argued below in Chapter 35), while the connections that Ur-Bau and Gudea enjoyed with a variety of deities can be accounted for without conferring divinity upon either of them. In this regard, Ur-Bau's filial relationship with Ninagala seems almost commonplace by comparison with the abundance of divine associations ascribed to Gudea. The closeness of his bond with Ningishzida, his personal god, was such that the two were at times regarded almost as consubstantiate. In addition, Gatumdug was his

earth mother (as previously noted), Nanshe was said to be his sister, and the fact that he and the legendary divine hero Gilgamesh were both believed to be sons of Ninsun engendered a narrative that is intimated in a slightly fragmentary passage in the Cylinder Inscriptions (B23), according to which the two heroic figures were very closely related, and the great Gilgamesh was in some sense Gudea's fraternal alter ego. None of this means that Gudea was himself believed to be a god, however. There can be absolutely no doubt that his actions were seen as divinely inspired, and that he was perceived and represented during his lifetime as being closer to the gods than any of the rulers who had held the sacred seal of kingship before him. Similarly, his special status, together with his outstanding piety and charisma, allowed him to interact with the gods to an almost unprecedented extent, but to maintain that he was actually regarded as a divinity would be a step too far. As is demonstrated with respect to the Sumerian system of the world in Chapter 14, Sumerian thought did not deal in simple opposites, such that the sacred dimension could be played off against the secular or profane. All creation was sacred, but its sanctity was graded into countless shades that are difficult to describe or even to comprehend, though the temple was the terrestrial locus where the presence of divinity could be felt most intensely and visualised most clearly by the way in which the building was laid out and oriented, with the cult statue of the god at its sacred heart.

Intriguingly, the mystery surrounding Gudea's persona is infused even into his name, gù.dé.a, which is a most unusual Sumerian form. Its equivalent in Akkadian is *nabi'um*, meaning the one who is 'called', while in other Semitic languages the word *nabi* means 'prophet'. His full ceremonial name, sipa $^\text{d}$Nin.ğír.su.ke$_4$ gù.dé.a, as preserved on Cylinder B (B6), might be taken to mean the 'shepherd who is called by the god Ningirsu'. The prophetic connotations of his name, including the idea that he is the 'shepherd' of his people (an appellation that is repeated several times in the Cylinder Inscriptions), fit well with some of the mystical events that are narrated in the narrative. There is, for example, the theophany that he experiences, with its complex allegory and vision of a fabulous, quasi-tetramorphic creature whose vastness fills the cosmos; and also the sacred sleep that overcomes him in the temple, when the meaning of the theophanic visitation (previously expounded by Nanshe) is further clarified by Ningirsu himself, who refers to Gudea as the 'true shepherd'. The events and the manner in which Gudea receives information and instructions from the gods are all in accordance with later developments of the prophet figure.

The paradox of Gudea extends to his historical status because so little concrete information is known about him, in spite of the wealth of preserved objects and texts deriving from his reign. His material legacy, which far exceeds that of any other Sumerian ruler in both quantity and quality, comprises a huge corpus that is made up of a variety of temple fittings and appurtenances—inscribed and sculpted artefacts dedicated to particular deities, many of which were created to commemorate the construction or restoration of shrines devoted to members of the pantheon. Surprisingly, therefore, neither the length of his reign nor the precise dates of its commencement and conclusion can be established with certainty. The inscriptions included on the numerous portrait statues of Gudea that were found in mostly excellent condition (discussed below), as well as on figurines, steles, foundation tablets and pegs, ex-voto vessels and weapons deal almost exclusively with his religious activities. Couched in strictly ritual terms, they relate mainly to the construction work that he carried out in his native state, above all the building of the New Eninnu dedicated to Ningirsu. Excluding the Cylinder Inscriptions, the devotional formulae in the Gudea corpus name Nanshe (five times), Inanna (also five times), the goddess Bau (four times) and Gatumdug and Ningishzida (three times each). In addition, mention is made of his personal god, Ningishzida, and Ninazu, the god's father (for instance in RIME 3.1.1.7.30). The New Eninnu of Ningirsu takes centre stage, however, with more than fifteen mentions in a range of formulaic commemorative texts, to which may be added four dedicated year names that are attested on administrative tablets (Gudea's regnal years seven to ten) as follows:

> Gudea 7: the year the brick mould was made (AO31385; RTC 109).
> Gudea 8: the year the brick of Ningirsu was laid in the brick mould (BM18721; Kaskal 15 69).
> Gudea 9: the year following the year of the brick of Ningirsu (Ist L 11096; or AOAT 25 81 9).
> Gudea 10: the year the temple of Ningirsu was built (AO3367; RTC 221).

In total, more than ten year names are recorded for Gudea's term of office, but the vast corpus of Gudea inscriptions, and the extensive programmes of building works that they attest, all indicate that he must have reigned for a much longer period of between twenty-five and thirty years (see Chapter 3). The implication of the names of regnal years seven to ten is that it might have taken just four years to build the enormous and intricately planned New Eninnu, with its massive buttressed walls and the Ningirsu temple at its heart, surrounded by numerous rooms and internal courtyards. The speed at which this extraordinary feat of engineering could have been accomplished is also intimated in the Cylinder Inscriptions, where Gudea is indefatigable in his desire to complete the project. For example, though it took one year to carve the great stone steles of the New Eninnu, if the account given in the Cylinder Inscriptions is to be believed, it seems that they were installed in just seven days (A23):

> It took one year to bring the great stones in slabs and it took another year to fashion them, although not even two or three days did he let pass idly. Then it needed a day's work to set up each one but by the seventh day he had set them all up around the house.

The way the time frame is described might have allegorical overtones (perhaps like the seven days of creation at a much later period), but there is no doubt that the task was speedily achieved, and the importance attached to Gudea's completion of the sacred complex is further confirmed by the fact that, at least after his tenth regnal year (whose epithet is quoted above), the renowned achievement was incorporated into his official appellation. For example, the titular introduction to an inscription on a statue that was commissioned to commemorate the erection of a temple to Ninhursag in Girsu expressly styles Gudea as the builder of the new Ningirsu shrine (AO8; RIME 3.1.1.7.StA): 'Gudea, ensi of Lagash, he by whom the Eninnu of Ningirsu was built'.

Aside from the officially sanctioned texts that were produced under his authority, hardly any of the surviving sources relate Gudea's regnal years to events that occurred beyond the state borders of Lagash. Indeed, the only recorded political incident of any kind is his victory in a campaign against Elam (RIME 3.1.1.7), which was probably prosecuted in cooperation with Ur, and represented a stage in the formation of the Ur III hegemony that later became a defining feature of the region. The disproportionate paucity of executive or governmental texts inscribed in his name might suggest that Gudea's sphere of influence was rather limited, but the extremely ambitious construction programmes that he undertook could not have been embarked upon without ready access to imported commodities, including building materials (timber, stone and bitumen) and precious stones and metals. Many examples are named in the Cylinder Inscriptions, where it is explicitly said that they must be brought from foreign lands, and as was the case for Ur-Bau before him, Gudea's ability to obtain resources from abroad implies a degree of control over the important trade routes, which must have been kept open, free flowing and well protected. Girsu–Lagash became a hub for the import and distribution of precious items into and around Mesopotamia during the reign of Gudea, and this adds weight to the idea that he must have reinstated, or been instrumental in the restoration of, routes that were previously controlled by the Sargonic kings. In Lagash II times, long-distance trade was conducted eastwards and westwards, with goods perhaps being brought from as far away as the Indus valley to the east and the forested regions of present-day Lebanon, which was an important source of timber, to the west.

Beyond the borders of Lagash, the solitary conflict with Elam, the arch-enemy of Sumer, is referred to on a tablet (AO3385; RTC 249) that seemingly originated from Shushtar (ancient AdamDUN) in Iran (Steve 2001, pp. 5–21; Potts 2010, pp. 246–7; and Steinkeller 2014, p. 289, n. 20). The campaign can be more precisely dated on the basis of a reconstruction of the name of Gudea's sixth regnal year as it appears on an administrative tablet found in Girsu. This records the defeat of the Elamite city of Anshan, using the formula: 'the year that Anshan was smitten by weapons' (Gudea year 6; AO4303). The event is also mentioned on Gudea's Statue B, and it might again be referenced in an incomplete passage on Cylinder A. The inscription on Statue B (AO2; RIME 3.1.1.7.StB) states that Gudea 'smote the cities of Anshan and Elam and brought their booty to Ningirsu in the Eninnu'. The slightly more cryptic text on Cylinder A (A15), which reads 'The Elamites came to him from Elam, the Susians came to him from Susa', is difficult to clarify because the preceding lines are broken, but if 'him' is taken to mean Ningirsu, it surely means that representatives of Elam and Susa came to pay homage to the god. That being the case, the great interest of both documents is that they present the conflict not as a glowing account of Gudea's military success, but rather as a celebration of the contribution made by the spoils of

war, together with the subsequent tribute paid by defeated enemies, to the construction of the New Eninnu. There can be no doubt that the outcome was an important occurrence that had broad political ramifications, particularly so if it was carried out as a joint action involving forces from Ur, but Gudea's primary (if not only) reason for recalling the victory was because it facilitated his programme of religious building. It should also be noted that the war was concluded in Gudea's sixth regnal year, the year before he began work on the new sacred complex, so the timing adds yet more substance to the idea that Gudea was principally motivated by his desire to embark on his architectural masterwork in the service of Ningirsu.

The overall picture of Gudea that emerges is of an ultra-pious ruler who was concerned to the point of passionate exaltation to pursue what he doubtless saw as his vocation—his mission to honour Ningirsu and the other gods of the pantheon. As attested by the inscriptions in his name, this is seemingly how he wanted to portray himself and how he wanted to be remembered—as a man who lived his life in a state of perpetual adoration, solely dedicated to the service and promotion of the cults of Lagash. That said, it should not be presumed that his devotion was in any sense freakish. The range and quality of his achievements and the length of his reign both attest to an extended period of prosperity in Lagash, and there can be little doubt that he was a leader of extraordinary distinction who was able to inspire his subjects with the degree of fervour necessary to turn his sublime visions into concrete realities.

Nor should Gudea's reign, with its relentless emphasis on sacred rituals and the sense that every detail of human affairs was enacted in the immediate presence of the gods, be viewed as though it was somehow independent of historical frames of reference (see Steinkeller 2017, p. 32). In historiographic terms, and as is discussed below with particular reference to the Gudea Statues, Gudea seems to have presided over the ongoing rejection of the alien Sargonic values that had been imported and enforced by Sargon of Akkad and his successors. He might well have placed a renewed stress on the need for a return to a more authentically Sumerian world view, possibly in an intensified and cleansed form. In truth, this was probably another legacy that Gudea inherited from Ur-Bau, or perhaps even Puzurmama, the governor of Lagash in late Sargonic times, who eventually became the state's ruler when it regained its independence after being freed from

Akkad control. Puzurmama left behind at least one inscription (RIME 2: 271-272 P-M 1) in which he styles himself the lugal of Lagash, and there can be no doubt that the text was modelled on Early Dynastic documents from Lagash, as is corroborated by the fact that it borrows the royal epithets found in those materials. Even more revealingly, it states that Puzurmama's personal deity was Šul.MUŠ×PA, who is repeatedly identified in much earlier inscriptions as the personal god of Ur-Nanshe and his descendants (Volk 1992, pp. 28–9; and Steinkeller 2017, p. 32). Viewed in this context, it is clear that Gudea was perpetuating and intensifying an already existing trend by instituting a systematic programme of returning the state to its Sumerian roots—attempting to revive a version of the Early Dynastic ethos that had existed in Lagash prior to the Akkad takeover (Steinkeller 2017, pp. 32–4).

Gudea's aims and ambitions in this regard have to be carefully defined, however, because the evident idealism and zeal for a renewed and purified religious outlook went hand in hand with the retention of characteristic Sargonic practices in bureaucratic affairs. On a day to day basis, the business of the state in Lagash II times was administered in the same way as it had been under Sargonic rule (Maiocchi and Visicato 2020). A remarkable continuity exists in the Akkad and post-Akkad periods in matters of prosopography (naming conventions), as well as accounting, general bureaucracy and even aspects of material culture. Six hundred preserved Lagash II administrative tablets provide information about both local matters and political affairs, not just in and around the cities of Girsu and Lagash, but over a vast area that extended beyond the boundaries of the state. Mention is made of a variety of foreign visitors, including rulers, high dignitaries, soldiers, travellers and merchants, who came from places as far away as Ebla (in modern-day Syria) and Elam (modern Iran). On palaeographic grounds, the tablets can mostly be dated to the reigns of Gudea and his son Ur-Ningirsu II, though, as just mentioned, Gudea's name is not personally associated with the mundane running of the state. On the contrary, Gudea's inscriptions represent his world as a timeless, mythical dimension in which all that counts is the ruler's total self-abasement and submission to the divine will, as symbolised most prominently by the building of the New Eninnu. It is yet another fascinating aspect of Gudea's reign that the seismic shake up of the sacred landscape that he presided over in the course of his long kingship was somehow separated from the administrative practices of Girsu, which exhibit a remarkable degree of stability throughout the third millennium BCE. On the one hand, to paraphrase the words of Henri Frankfort (1954, p. 93), in the rejection of the Sargonic ethos and the restoration of a distinctively Sumerian outlook, 'piety replaced vigour'; while on the other, Gudea pursued his mission with an energy and determination that Sargon himself might have envied. At the same time, some key lessons of Sargonic imperial organisation were internalised and well learned.

The Origins and Rationale of the New Eninnu

The idea that Gudea and Ur-Bau might both conceivably have been sons of the temple in the context tentatively outlined above could help to explain why Gudea was nominated as Ur-Bau's chosen successor, either directly by Ur-Bau himself or as a consequence of an inferred line of descent that might plausibly have been determined by the sacred institution. The most likely possibility is perhaps a combination of the two: Gudea, who was the next in line according to whatever hierarchies were in place, also had a strong personal, even fraternal bond with Ur-Bau. In any event, the connection and the lineage were affirmed and consolidated through the marriage of Gudea to Ur-Bau's daughter Ninalla. Less explicable even than the rather speculative circumstances surrounding the transfer of the kingship are the reasons why Gudea took the remarkable decision to build the New Eninnu so soon after his enthronement, especially when the Ningirsu temple had only recently been transferred from Tell K to the remodelled Tell A by his predecessor. Gudea paid due tribute to Ur-Bau, as has been noted, but his motives for redesigning the state's chief sanctuary on such a grandiose scale just two decades or so after it had been consecrated in its changed location remains a mystery. As repeatedly observed, the Cylinder Inscriptions narrate Gudea's theophany and god-given dream, which together represent a divine command that issued from Ningirsu himself. It is possible that the ruler and his sacerdotal advisors deemed that the translation of the god's cult statue from its time-honoured spot to a new *locus sanctus* required a more thorough renewal of the theological rites and a more convincing divine sanction than had been thought necessary under Ur-Bau. As plausibly suggested by the great number of ritual texts that accompanied the decision, it was perhaps believed that the spiritual foundations of the cult needed some correction, and Gudea took the opportunity to create a shrine in Ningirsu's honour that would not only re-establish the state religion on the firmest possible footing, but would trumpet Ningirsu and Gudea's renown to the world at large (Fig. 170). Some of these matters must inevitably remain in the realms of surmise, but it should also be stated that, in several ways, Gudea emulated his predecessor, such that many of the key changes that he made were quantitative rather than qualitative in nature. He used much of the same ritual apparatus as Ur-Bau—including the praying statues, foundation pegs and tablets, and votive cones and so forth—but he increased their potency through the simple expedient of using many more of them. In the same way, he preserved the shrine that Ur-Bau had built, while incorporating it into a much larger and far more impressive architectural totality.

In terms of its archaeological recovery, the New Eninnu was found entombed by Sarzec within the terrace platform that was established to support Adadnadinakhe's Hellenistic complex. The later accretions were almost entirely removed by the French pioneers in the late nineteenth and early twentieth centuries, and the destruction that they inflicted on the site, followed by the subsequent erosion that they unwittingly caused and the scars left by looters, are matters of regret. Nonetheless, the way the early work was carried out eventually provided salvage opportunities for the British Museum team, who were able to reveal much more about Gudea's project than was previously known. Of overriding import is the fact that the layout of the New Eninnu clearly owed much to the architectural structures that existed on Tell A before the time of Gudea, and to the sacred topography of Girsu (especially the Urukug) and the layout of the state of Lagash more generally.

With regard to this bigger picture, it is important to note that the temenos was closely aligned not only with the cardinal points (slightly modified by the need to incorporate

FIGURE 170. A cutaway reconstruction of Gudea's New Eninnu, looking towards the E corner, with the stepped NE façade to the right. The two principal buildings are the temples of Ningirsu (left) and Bau (right); the smaller building on the NE side of the Ningirsu temple is the old Eninnu of Ur-Bau, retained inside the area known as the Ur-Bau plaza.

Ur-Bau's temple podium, as discussed in Chapter 39), but equally with widely dispersed geographical features, communication arteries and cultural buildings and installations that were pregnant with historical and symbolic meaning. First and foremost, as a busy religious institution the New Eninnu relied in significant ways upon the close proximity of waterways, processional approaches and service routes in the form of canals, harbours, reservoirs and ancient roads or pathways (preserved as hollow ways). Situated in a lofty position at the N edge of the holy city (iri.kù), Tell A overlooked the great wall of Girsu (bàd Gír.su^{ki}) on its NW side, and beyond that, far to the north-west, Ningirsu's 'beloved field': the Gu'edena border area with its no man's land facing the hoary arch-rival state of Umma (the domain of Ningirsu's nemesis, the warrior god Shara). To the north-east, the main watercourses of Girsu flowed south-eastwards; they included the Nigin Canal (i$_7$.Niğen$_6$^{ki}.DU.a), which was the principal nexus and lifeline that integrated the various sectors of the city-state of Lagash. To the south-east stood, most importantly, Tell K, the site of the god's former immemorial home, which was transformed into a memorial shrine that presumably housed the Gudea Cylinders. Finally, to the south-west lay a large plaza or ceremonial square (the sanctuary's civic counterpart) and beyond that the bustling residential quarters of Girsu, separated from the sacred complex inside the Urukug by a containing wall.

Building inscriptions commemorating Gudea's project record the ceremonial names given to the newly constructed gates in remarkable detail. Their precise locations, which are subject to a degree of uncertainty, are discussed in Chapter 40 below, but they include: the Battle Gate, 'where the weapons hang'; the City Gate 'in front of the city' (perhaps also known as the Flood gate or the Mighty gate); the 'awesome' Shugalam gate; the Sunrise gate; the Kasurra Gate (facing the god's sacred quay); and the Tarsirsir Gate, associated with Bau's shrine. The various toponyms and theonyms were chosen to reference the sacred geography of Girsu. Furthermore, together with the monuments to the Slain Heroes that were displayed in association with them (also discussed in Chapter 40), they expressed the ancient mythology of Ningirsu in condensed form. The gates and the many other named monuments that were exhibited in the New Eninnu defined the sanctuary as the material extension of Ningirsu's divine substance, placing special emphasis on his role as a warrior god and on the inextricable bond between Ningirsu and Bau

that was manifest in the revised placement of the Temple of Ningirsu on Tell A, facing the newly reconstructed Temple of Bau.

Gudea's account of the series of events that preceded the building of the New Eninnu makes explicit reference to the shrines dedicated to Ningirsu and Bau that already existed on Tell A. The Cylinder Inscriptions describe how Gudea prayed on at least two significant occasions in the building referred to as the old Eninnu of Ur-Bau—the Ningirsu temple that was built by Ur-Bau when he moved the sanctuary from Tell K, and which remained standing inside the temenos walls of Gudea's New Eninnu on the NE side of Gudea's divinely inspired sanctum sanctorum. Gudea prayed in the old temple in order to seek favourable omens after the construction rituals for the New Eninnu had been celebrated (A17–18):

> When the night fell, he went to the old temple to pray, so that the inclination of the one from the dais of Girnun (i.e. Ningirsu) would become favourable for Gudea. When day broke, he took a bath and arranged his outfit correctly. Utu let abundance come forth for him.

And he is said to have returned there after the consecration of the New Eninnu, when he brought divine offerings to the 'old house', as recounted at the beginning of Cylinder B (B2):

> The true shepherd Gudea is wise, and able too to realise things. His friendly guardian went before him and his friendly protecting genius followed him. For his master, Lord Ningirsu, Gudea gave numerous gifts to the house of yore, the old house, his dwelling place.

The inscription carved on Gudea's praying statue for Bau (Statue E: AO6; RIME 3.1.1.7.StE) records the lengths he went in order to please the goddess after he had relocated her temple, which is described as the 'House of the Shining City', to another 'ritually cleansed' spot on Tell A. The text stresses that the new arrangement has multiplied her 'bridal gifts':

> When for Bau, the child of An, the lady of Urukug, his lady, he built the Etarsirsir, her beloved temple, he built it in the same way as he did the Eninnu, (Ningirsu's) beloved temple for Ningirsu, his master. He purified

the city by carrying around fire. He made a drawing on the brick-mould's frame, (and) made a standard shine at the clay pit. He mixed the clay in a pure place, made the (first) brick in an undefiled place, and put the (first) brick into the brick-mould. He brought about perfection. He purified the foundation by carrying around fire, (and) anointed the foundation pegs with oil of princely fragrance. He built the temple in a pure place for Bau, his lady, the lady who fills Urukug with awesomeness.

He fashioned her lofty throne of ladyhood, (and) set it up at her place of rendering judgments. He fashioned her holy chest, (and) brought it into her lofty temple for her. He fashioned the balaj-drum (named) 'The lady, as prominent as An', (and) set it up it in her main courtyard for her.

At the turn of the year, at the festival of Bau, when the bridewealth is to be presented, the bridewealth for Bau consisted of these in the former, old temple: 1 grain-fed oxen, 1 fattened sheep, 3 grain-fed sheep, 6 rams, 2 lambs, 7 portions of dates, 7 jars of ghee, 7 palm hearts, 7 strings of figs, 7 baskets, 1 ti'uz-bird, 7 cranes, 15 geese, 60 small birds in strings of 15, 60 suḫurtun-carps in strings of 30, 40 gun turnip, 7 gun marsh reed, 60 gun manu wood.

After Gudea, ruler of Lagash built his beloved temple, the Eninnu, for Ningirsu, his master, and built her beloved temple, the Etarsirsir, for Bau, his lady, the bridewealth for Bau consists of these in the new temple, increased by Gudea, ruler of Lagash, the temple-builder: 2 grain-fed oxen, 2 fattened sheep, 10 grain-fed sheep, 2 lambs, 7 portions of dates, 7 jars of ghee, 7 palm hearts, 7 strings of figs, 7 baskets, 14 date spadices, 14 cucumbers in a basket, 1 ti'uz-bird, 7 cranes, 15 geese, 7 izi-birds, 60 small birds in strings of 15, 60 suḫurtun-carps in strings of 30, 40 gun turnip, 7 gun marsh reed, 60 gun manu wood.

To see that the temple of Bau is maintained, that its abundance is made visible, that the throne of Lagash is firm, that the sceptre of just words is in the hand of Gudea, ruler of Lagash, that the days of his life are lengthened, his personal god, Ningishzida, brings these (gifts) to Bau in her temple in Urukug.

Gudea's inscriptions grandiloquently record the programme of events that he carried out in his reign—the centrepiece being the construction of the New Eninnu. Although the scale and magnificence of the building was unprecedented, at least in Lagash, it is nonetheless clear from the texts that it was not conceived of as unconditionally novel—like the founding from scratch of a new cult, for example. Instead, Gudea respected the Sumerian belief in the permanence of the sacred: the fact that the holiest features of the site were, in essence, immutable. The unprecedented transfer of the deity's supreme locus had been accomplished by Ur-Bau. Accepting that as a fait accompli, and further legitimising it by gaining Ningirsu's sanction for the New Eninnu, Gudea duly absorbed and referenced the most sacred parts of the older complex that had been built by his father-in-law. In so doing, he also ratified connections between politics and myth, mortals and deities, new and old kingship, and between himself and his predecessor, Ur-Bau. These associations are outlined above, but it is important to note some of the ways in which they were expressed spatially. The self-contained elevated podium that Ur-Bau built on the summit of the mound to support the transferred Ningirsu temple was incorporated into the large precinct demarcated by Gudea's temenos wall, and in particular into the wide SE portion of the greatly extended complex that was specially devoted to Ningirsu (Fig. 171). In several ways the earlier building also acted as a direct prototype and inspiration for the later construction: both included foundation deposits in the form of kneeling gods and stone tablets, together with numerous inscribed cones, and both used stamped and inscribed bricks. Similarly, votive statues of the praying rulers with clasped hands were carved in dark stone and installed in both temples. Furthermore, the way in which the overall L-shaped walled enclosure that is carved on the architect's tablet on the seated statue of Gudea in his role as an architect (Statue B) can be seen to overlap with a series of walls and gates unearthed on Tell A, throws light on a number of difficult problems. These include some obscure toponyms mentioned in the statue's inscriptions and in the Cylinder Inscriptions, as well as issues associated with the religious, political and cultural programme as a whole. As is described in Chapter 38, crucial correspondences emerge when the sculpted blueprint is compared with the results of the British Museum team's excavations.

It is also important to note the possible political agenda that was implicit in the project because the statue of Gudea as an architect, which contains no explicit verbal acknowledgement of the role of his predecessor in its preserved text,

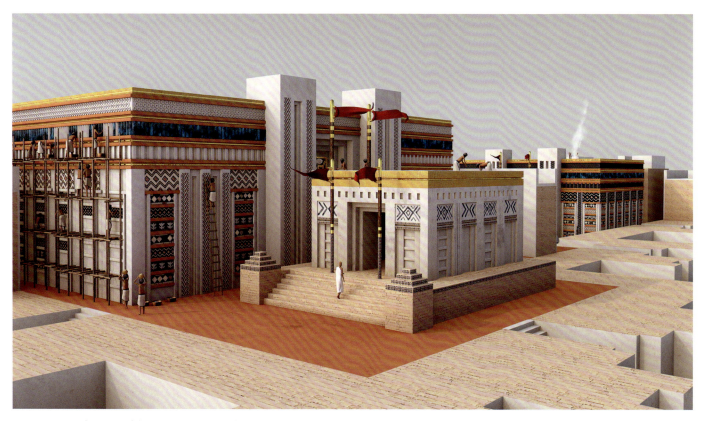

FIGURE 171. Close-up of the reconstruction of the Ur-Bau plaza, looking towards the E corner, with the old Eninnu of Ur-Bau (right) and Gudea's successor Ningirsu temple (left).

might ostensibly be taken to depict Gudea as though he were the originator of the sanctuary on Tell A and not just of the New Eninnu. The issue should not be oversimplified, however, because Ur-Bau's legacy was silently but strikingly recognised and referenced in the carved plan, where the language of architecture narrates a fascinating history. The irregular layout, most importantly the double protrusion or salient shown on the long NE wall of the New Eninnu, is an exceptional feature that was added to take account of the relationship between the old and new buildings. It is an acknowledged principle of Sumerian sacred architecture that asymmetries were only introduced to deal with particular spatial constraints or special pre-existing features of the construction site that were of the highest symbolic and religious importance, such that they could not be removed or otherwise surmounted. In the case of Gudea's temple plan, the protruding double salient that disrupts the otherwise rectangular temenos wall clearly reflects not just the physical location of Ur-Bau's old Eninnu, but also its symbolic inclusion in a new amalgamated whole.

It is helpful to have an explicit overview of exactly what all of this meant in practice. Prior to Gudea's accession to the throne, Ur-Bau had transferred Ningirsu's temple from Tell K to Tell A, where he placed it on the NE side of the latest iteration of the Temple of Bau on a specially raised foundation platform that was built on top of the massive terrace (here referred to as the grey platform) that had been elevated and extended by Urukagina almost two centuries earlier. Ur-Bau also built a thick rectangular temenos wall on the raised topmost surface of the mound that enclosed an area a little larger than that occupied by the two adjacent temples to Ningirsu and Bau, together with an enigmatic platform built in the Akkad interval. When Gudea came to power he made three hugely significant innovations (though not necessarily in this order): first, he moved the Ningirsu temple onto the site that had always until then been occupied by the temple to the god's wife, Bau; secondly, to clear the ground for the Ningirsu temple, he moved the old Bau temple out along the site's major, NW–SE axis to a new location to the north-west of its original position; and thirdly, having significantly extended the upper NW part of the mound in its entirety, he built the extended, irregular L-shaped temenos wall to enclose the two temples to Bau and Ningirsu, placing a new central courtyard between them and absorbing the now repurposed Ningirsu temple of Ur-Bau, which was left intact on the NE side of Gudea's new Ningirsu temple in an area that is referred to below as the Ur-Bau plaza. Finally, parts of Ur-Bau's temenos walls inside the Ningirsu section on the SE side of Gudea's L-shaped enclosure were levelled and used as the foundations of new envelope walls built by Gudea, even though they served no structural purpose.

The description of Gudea's New Eninnu that is laid out in succeeding sections begins with an explanation of how the site was prepared, followed by a detailed discussion of the higher areas of the new sacred precinct—the Ningirsu temple, together with its surrounding open-air ambulatories, and the adjacent Ur-Bau plaza. Next, comes an in-depth account of the inner wall, with its ascending platforms and monumental gateway, that separated the Ningirsu section of the complex from the rest. The discussion then moves onto the lower NW areas of the sanctuary, including the ceremonial central court. It concludes with an account of the huge outer walls that formed the L-shaped complex.

Clearing the Site and Refounding the Eninnu

Evidence of the preparatory phase for Gudea's construction of the New Eninnu was uncovered by the British Museum team across most of Tell A (in Areas B1, B2, B3, B4, B5, B9 and B11), where a series of levelling deposits were found that had been laid down over demolished structures from the Early Dynastic IIIb and Akkad periods (Fig. 139). Also discovered were signs of the ritual closing of Ur-Bau's extended sanctuary, with some of the Ur-Bau temenos walls and the Ningirsu temple building in its entirety being enclosed within the L-shaped outer walls of the new complex. Elements of the partly refurbished and partly new complex that was established by Ur-Bau for the dual cult of Ningirsu and Bau were uncovered in Gudea's New Eninnu itself, where Gudea's walls made significant reference to Ur-Bau's elevated Ningirsu temple and parts of his temenos layout. The planning of Gudea's New Eninnu thereby paid emblematic and material tribute to the tremendous step that Ur-Bau had taken when he moved Ningirsu's temple from Tell K.

Below Gudea's new sanctuary, a series of deposits of varying composition were found in association with compact clay deposits that were similar to, and probably derived from, mud-brick fragments that were obtained from structures that had been previously demolished. Most importantly, these were found in layers above the Early Dynastic IIIb temple platform and its reincarnation in Ur-Bau's reign (in B1 and B9), above the older temple rooms that lay underneath Gudea's Ningirsu temple cella (in B2, B3 and B5) and also above the enclosing walls of the older rooms (in B3 and B4). The implication of the findings is that there was a phased preparatory process, such that the mud-brick layers just mentioned were added towards the end. First came the decommissioning of superannuated sanctuary buildings (often accompanied by significant rituals), most notably the old temple to the goddess Bau. This was followed by the demolition of most of the older walls, and finally the levelling and compaction of the resulting debris to create a solid foundation for Gudea's new structures. Evidently, the stages were carefully executed. Earlier walls were not hastily demolished in their entirety, but carefully dismantled to leave truncated remnants that could serve as either a solid base for new walls on the same plan, or as a grid of cellular compartments that could be infilled. Sections of the old walls were used to contain the filling material and prevent it from spreading laterally when it was later compacted due to the weight of the extremely heavy structures that were built above. Particularly important features of earlier temples, including most of the Ur-Bau enclosure walls and the enigmatic Akkad cult platform, were ritually buried within the core of successor constructions, but the outlines of these symbolic spaces were left slightly higher than other run-of-the-mill walls to demarcate the layout of some inner Gudea walls.

Truncated pre-Gudea mud-brick elevations dating from the Late Early Dynastic IIIb to the Early Lagash II periods that were found in various sectors of Tell A helped the British Museum team to define the broad levelling horizons of Gudea's project. The complex as a whole was founded on the underlying superimposed platforms and other subterranean fills, which exhibited significant differences across the temple site. It became clear that well-identified staged levelling horizons dating to the reign of Gudea in the Mound of the Palace and the neighbouring area of the Gudea Steles (between Tells A and B) reflected the overall stepped character of the New Eninnu, which was built on a series of terraces that became progressively more sacred in proportion to their altitude. This again confirms that the Gudea sanctuary was not intended to be a categorically novel construction, but rather one that incorporated and developed elements from its precursors. In particular, its towering height was essentially cumulative, the consequence of a protracted history of building on the mound that culminated in Gudea's ritual interment of levelled older structures, followed by the partial raising of the ground to create an enlarged summit. At its very heart, the New Eninnu, including Gudea's temple to Ningirsu and the Ningirsu temple structure built by Ur-Bau, stood on the entombed white platform, dating from the reign of Ur-Nanshe, that had been subsequently capped and extended by the grey platform from the reign of Urukagina. Altogether, the assemblage represented a superimposed series of massive layers that elevated the core of the New Eninnu above the surrounding temple annexes and ancillary buildings.

In the area occupied by Gudea's Ningirsu temple (B2, B3, B5 and B11), including its cella and antecella, the perfectly levelled planoconvex mud-brick walls and structures of temple rooms 2052, 2053, 2061, 2064, 3085, 3091 and 2145 were found at maximum topographical heights of around 14.8 m (in B2 and B3) and 15 m (in B5). The temenos walls of the Ur-Bau precinct (contexts 2024, 3080, 3097 and 3098), which were founded at a topographical height of 14.9 m (as previously noted), were identified either beneath their Gudea successors or selectively rebuilt within the new walls to form an inner envelope that ran partly around Gudea's Ningirsu temple. The levelled walls were all truncated to a similar horizon of between 15 m and 15.3 m. Serving as a structural base for one of the Gudea shrine's façades, the enigmatic Akkad platform (2158) was identified at a higher elevation of about 15.5 m, and it had been carefully absorbed into Gudea's brickwork.

Fragments of brickwork from the old structures that were knocked down by Gudea were observed in Areas B1, B2, B3, B4 and B5, where several compacted layers were found that varied in constitution and mostly derived from demolished mud-brick walls. The observed differences between foundation fills across the temple site, with some noteworthy deposits being placed at significant and symbolically charged spaces, in all likelihood reflected the complex foundation and purification rituals that the construction of the New Eninnu necessitated. For example, in the Ningirsu temple's sanctuary chamber—the most sacred space of the entire complex—a rare foundation fill was identified in Areas B2 and B3 (contexts 2011 and 3024), at an overall elevation of about 15.1 m, where it lay above the levelled, infilled walls (3037 and 3050) of the Ur-Bau iteration of the ancient sanctuary of Bau. Exposed to a depth of about 0.15 m, the foundation fill (2011 and 3024) was composed of a red to pink compacted silt matrix and lumps of baked clay that resembled very lightly fired bricks. It appeared to extend over the whole area and beneath the walls of the cella, and it also showed signs of having been carefully processed because the individual mud-bricks had been broken into pieces of about the same size. The care with which this filling was prepared can be contrasted with the backfills found in later pits, including those associated with the abandonment and collapse of the Gudea temple in the Old Babylonian period, where much larger fragments of mud-brick were used, and there was a much greater variation in the sizes of the pieces. In merely functional terms, the homogeneous fill provided a foundation layer for the New Eninnu's inner sanctum, but the meticulous way in which it was produced suggests that it also served the symbolic purpose of screening the old Bau temple under a purified layer, creating a tabula rasa on which to work.

Contexts 2011 and 3024, which formed part of this purified reddish filling, yielded a coherent assemblage of diagnostic potsherds that were dated to the Late Akkad and Early Lagash II periods. It should be noted, however, that these layers had been disturbed by later cuts and recuts, and that their contents might therefore have been contaminated by strays. In context 2011 the most likely anomalies included a fragment of an inscribed brick (TG248) and a fragment of a Lagash II inscribed cone relating to Gudea's construction of the New Eninnu (TG222). Context 3024 contained a complete Lagash II cone (doubtless a stray) marked with Gudea's Standard Inscription (TG870), together with two heads of copper nails, a square nail fragment and an obsidian blade (TG879). Unearthed in context 3037 were the tip of a stray inscribed cone, probably in the name of Gudea and relating to the New Eninnu, as well as a fragment of a stone vessel and a complete conical bowl (TG383). No finds were made in 3050.

In Area B2, in the vicinity of the gate that was built into the inner NW wall that ran across the L-shaped compound (referencing the general layout of the gateway that led into Ur-Bau's enclosure), another sequence of rare deposits was recorded at a topographical height of 15.4 m, and with a thickness of about 0.3 m. Below a patchy layer of laminated white lime cement (2012) that was part of the earliest construction phase of the subfloor of the Gudea gate's porch, at the point where the subfloor merged on its NW side with one of the open-air corridors that ran around Gudea's Ningirsu temple, the team encountered a horizon of loose, dark ashy silt (2013), between 0.02 m and 0.05 m thick, that was exposed over an area measuring 2.8 m × 2 m. Immediately below this burnt deposit was a foundation fill made up of compacted friable clayey silt with frequent specks of white lime (2022) that contained Late Akkad potsherds. The fill had a thickness of 0.2 m, and it extended below inner wall 2001, where it sealed off remains associated with the earlier Bau temple (as detailed above in Chapter 33). It could not finally be determined whether deposit 2013 had been ritually burnt or whether its composition was indiscriminate, but it compared closely with other homogeneous backfills found on the site; in conjunction with its placement below the important inner gateway, this seemed to suggest that it had in fact been cleansed and sanctified. Apart from the Late Akkad potsherds, no artefacts were recovered from 2012, 2013 or 2022.

More generally, the foundation fills found in other parts of Tell A were like base layer 2022, which was composed of homogeneous deposits of compacted crumbly mud-brick fragments that exhibited frequent specs of white lime in the matrix. This was the most common mixture found in infillings and levelling horizons in the whole temple complex, all of which were dated to the Late Akkad and Early Lagash II periods on account of the pottery assemblages they contained. Contexts with this filling were identified in the Ur-Bau plaza in front of Gudea's Ningirsu temple (in B2, where context 2030 was found under part of the temple's main façade wall (2008)) and beneath its vestibule (2146 in Area B5). Exposed at topographical elevations ranging between 15 m and 15.2 m, the thickness of these deposits varied between about 0.1 m and 0.2 m. No notable finds were made in contexts 2030 and 2146.

It should be mentioned in passing that no indication was found anywhere on Tell A that Lagash II mud-brick walls were set in foundation trenches. Instead, they were all built directly on the beds provided by the prepared surfaces just described, and many of Gudea's temple walls were consequently fitted with wider foundation footings.

In addition to the enormous and extremely delicate task of levelling the state's principal sacred site, while refounding the temples of its two leading deities in a vast complex that had to be constructed according to a divinely inspired plan (and retaining some meaningful earlier features), Gudea

also had to enlarge the surface area of the mound. This was especially the case towards the north-west, where Tell A was extended far beyond the limits of the very old white platform that was built by Ur-Nanshe to an area associated with the Early Dynastic temenos wall of the Urukug (context 252021 in Area B12). The building of the extension was a colossal undertaking that necessitated terracing the adjoining landscape, levelling the sacred district's old precinct wall, and artificially raising the ground level to the north-west of the white platform on a massive scale to bring it into conformity with the NW side of the mound's summit. Signs of this work were discovered in the central part of Tell A in Area B1, beneath the main court of the New Eninnu that lay between the new temples to Bau and Ningirsu, where far-reaching levelling and ground-raising construction fills of superimposed compacted layers were encountered. These layers were found to embrace and entomb the NW façade of the archaic white and grey platforms (1036 and 5235) on which Bau's extended sanctuary had previously been founded. The fills consisted of a substantial layer of *pisé* or adobe (1018 and 1021) that was placed on a superficial layer of loose green silty sand (1033, continued as 1035) that extended over, and therefore sealed off, the levelled white and grey platforms (1036 and 5235). Further significant signs were found on the NW side of Tell A in Area B12, where similar ground-raising construction deposits (25013, 25024 and 25025) were found on either side of the levelled, and therefore almost certainly decommissioned Early Dynastic temenos wall (25021). The raising and levelling deposits were formed of subrounded and subrectangular lumps of clay (with average and maximum diameters of 250 mm and 400 mm, respectively) that were mid- to dark reddish brown and brownish red in colour. Although truncated by erosion, the deposits were found at a maximum topographical height of 13.35 m, and they were partially exposed to a maximum depth of 1.5 m. These Lagash II layers formed the solid foundations for the terrace platform that was built to support the NW extension of the New Eninnu.

The Design of the Temple of Ningirsu: The Cella, Antecella and Stairwell

Gudea's Temple of Ningirsu at the heart of Tell A (exposed in Areas B2, B3, B5, B8 and B11) rose above the associated service rooms and subsidiary sacred spaces, notably the new

Temple of Bau, that were also contained in the New Eninnu's enlarged enclosure. The re-established Ningirsu temple was placed on the ritually entombed archaic platform of the former Temple of Bau, where it faced the decommissioned old Eninnu that had previously been elevated by Ur-Bau (Fig. 139). Gudea's Ningirsu temple, which was conventionally rectangular, occupied a total area of 516.25 m² (30.12 m × 17.14 m). In common with all the principal temples to Ningirsu that had been built in Girsu since the time of the Lower Construction on Tell K, it was oriented north-west–south-east, and its corners were aligned with the cardinal points. Again like its predecessors on Tell K, the new temple's longer sides lay to the north-east and south-west, but in a significant departure from the Early Dynastic tradition its only external entranceway, flanked by buttress towers (of which just one was preserved), was positioned in its NE façade, overlooking the Ur-Bau plaza on which the old temple building still stood. The new temple's façade walls were extremely thick (2.3 m), while its isolation within the temenos walls of the huge complex was further emphasised by narrow ambulatories or open-air corridors that ran around its sides and back (Fig. 172).

Gudea's Temple of Ningirsu was organised on the indirect-approach principle, with a relatively wide cella that was accessed via a mediating anteroom. It contained a spacious brickwork podium that extended out from the shorter SW wall. The entrance was placed in the longer SE wall at the opposite (NE) end of the room, at right angles to the podium, so that the cult statue could not be seen from outside the cella, and this meant that officiating high priests and other worshippers had to turn through ninety degrees in order to face the deity. The temple also included another loculus or transitional space in the form of a stairwell chamber that extended across the width of the building. Accessed via another indirect-approach route through the central antecella, the flight of stairs led up to the temple's flat roof, which was doubtless conceived of as another highly charged point of interaction with the divine, and was probably also a celestial observation point, as is considered in Chapter 40 below. Reflecting this generic design, the ground plan divided the

FIGURE 172. The NE façade of the Ningirsu temple on the SE side of Gudea's New Eninnu, viewed from the Ur-Bau plaza, with the old Eninnu of Ur-Bau removed.

building into a parallel set of three internal rooms, each 11.5 m long, that were separated within the outer façades by two thick partition walls (at least 2.3 m, the same as the façades) that ran from the north-west to the south-east across the width of the temple. The two larger rooms, the cella and antecella, had widths of 7.1 m and 9.6 m, respectively, while the significantly narrower stairway chamber was just 2 m wide. The partition walls, which were constructed with generous foundation footings on both sides, exhibited the same extraordinary solidity as the temple's façades, suggesting a shared structural purpose, namely the need to support a heavy roof, almost certainly made of cedar beams, that probably rose to a height of between 8 m and 10 m.

In common with all the other walls in the New Eninnu, the walls of the Ningirsu temple were built of unfired square mud-bricks with standard side lengths of 0.32 m and a thickness of 0.07 m. As is considered in detail in Chapter 42, the square bricks must have been accompanied by great quantities of rectangular or half-bricks that were needed in order to create the bonding patterns that held the walls together, particularly at the corners, which had to be built up of half-bricks. All the bricks were made of a compact silty clay that varied in colour between light reddish-brown and light yellowish-brown with white flecks that were caused by the precipitation of salt. An abundance of equally distributed chaff impressions running all the way through each individual brick testified to the meticulous care with which they were manufactured. The bricks were laid on the prepared bed in regular stacked courses and bonded with bedding joints of mud mortar that were found to have a typical thickness of between 5 mm and 10 mm.

The Temple of Ningirsu: The Façades and Partition Walls

The NE Façade

The uncovered section of the NE façade of the Ningirsu temple was formed of four contexts (2008, 2017, 2048 and 2140) that were found split between Areas B2, B5 and B11, and separated by intervening truncations, including substantial Hellenistic and French trenching, as well as targeted investigation pits and holes made by looters. Wall 2008 (in Area B2) measured 5.2 m and ran from the north-west

to the south-east; it was bonded at right angles to the NE end of the temple's NW façade (2003), where the corner was truncated by Hellenistic pit 2027. The NE wall was preserved to a maximum height of 0.52 m, made up of five courses that were laid in a regular offset stretcher pattern. Preserved to an average thickness of 2.2 m (representing between five and seven rows of bricks), its interior SW face was slightly truncated by a large circular pit. The NE façade extended towards the south-east (context 2017), which was exposed to a length of 3.45 m and preserved to a maximum height of two or three courses (0.3 m). Its base thickness was measured as 2.7 m, made up of seven or eight rows of mud-bricks, with the lowest course being slightly thicker than the ones above due to an extra brick on the interior SW face that was added to form the wall's foundation footing. The higher parts of the wall, without the foundation footing, were 2.31 m thick. Formed of contexts 2008 and 2017, this part of the temple's NE façade had been partially levelled in antiquity at a topographical height of 15.4 m by a horizontal Hellenistic trench in which fired-brick fragments were found (2016), all bearing Gudea's Standard Inscription, and the fragments were scattered between, and on either side of, walls 2008 and 2017. This spacious pit, which was securely dated to the Hellenistic period, was probably dug at the command of Adadnadinakhe when he was searching for Gudea remains and associated votives prior to the construction of his revived shrine. The existence of this spoil heap of broken bricks suggested that Adadnadinakhe's workers were instructed to salvage the bricks that had been used to pave the floors of Gudea's Ningirsu temple.

Context 2017 continued into Area B5 as a NW–SE stretch of wall (2048) that was exposed towards the south-east over a length of 3.72 m. Like the adjoining section to the north-west (2017), the continuation was also thicker at its base, where it was fitted with a footing composed of one or two rows of square mud-bricks on its inner SW side. Accordingly, its maximum base thickness was 2.98 m, made up of a total of eight or nine rows, while its higher parts (without the footing) were about 2.3 m thick. Preserved to a height of between 0.13 m and 0.2 m (just one or two courses), wall 2048 had been unsparingly levelled by successive Hellenistic and French horizontal cuts, while its extreme SE edge had been completely truncated by a further French pit (2036) that sliced through it at an angle. In addition, it had previously been disturbed in the Old Babylonian period, either when the temple was decommissioned, or soon after it was abandoned, when three particularly abnormal-looking pits were dug; two of them were rectangular (2038 and 2040), while the other was subrectangular (2042). This portion of the temple's façade wall (2048) was pierced by a gateway. A single inscribed door socket (TG974; Fig. 173) was found on the inner SW side of wall 2048, and the opening itself was flanked on the exterior NE face of the wall by a substantial buttress tower that was placed on the gateway's NW side. Extensive trenching had eliminated any significant traces of a counterpart structure on the SE side of the gate, but there can be little doubt that buttress towers were built on both sides to create an appropriate effect of symmetrical grandeur. The preserved area of the buttress tower (2168) measured 2.07 m × 1.15 m.

The NE–SW passageway inside the gate, which had an overall length of 2.3 m (the thickness of the standing wall, discounting the foundation footings), ran through wall 2048 near to its interface with wall 2017. The passage was approximately three or four rows of mud-bricks wide (about 1.15 m). The stone door socket (TG974) bearing the Gudea Standard Inscription was found with its cuneiform signs facing upwards and oriented towards the south-east, so that it was easily read by someone entering the doorway and turning ninety degrees towards the south-west to face the temple's cella, where the cult statue was located. The placement of the fitting in the SW corner of the threshold indicated that the door passed through 180 degrees from the south-east into the antecella, where it could lie flat against the inner SW side of wall 2048. The socket was partially set into the foundation footing of wall 2048, where it was placed on a mud-brick socle or abutment (2065) that was built on a layer of bitumen. Made of pale beige limestone, the socket itself was rectangular, with dimensions of 0.51 m × 0.36 m × 0.15 m (h), and it was found more or less complete, though its smooth top surface was delaminated and fragmented. The cuneiform inscription, which was placed in a square or rectangular debossed frame, was carved along the stone's shorter right-hand side. To the left of the inscription, and centrally on the stone, was found a smooth hemispherical depression (123.5 mm in diameter) that held the door's pivot, as was confirmed by a series of circular striations that were found in the hollow. The foundation base or socle (2065) on which the stone door socket stood was found at a topographical height of 15.27 m, with preserved dimensions of 0.95 m × 0.73 m. It was made of a single course of brownish-grey mud-bricks (0.32 m × 0.32 m × 0.07 m) that were the same size as the Gudea bricks used generally on the site, and the brickwork was bonded with clay mortar. It is likely that this low

FIGURE 173. The inscribed stone door socket found by the British Museum team inside the main entrance in the NE façade of the Ningirsu temple.

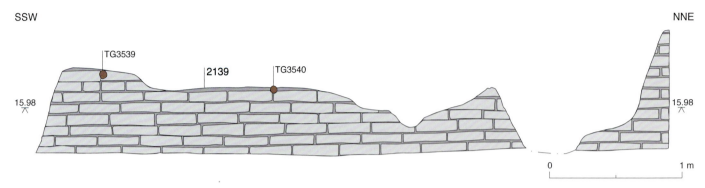

FIGURE 174. Section of the SE façade of the Ningirsu temple (wall 2139), showing the brickwork and the positions of the *in situ* clay nails.

installation formed the base of a dismantled and levelled subsurface box or compartment that originally encased the door socket and its pivot.

Interrupted by horizontal French pitting (2036), wall 2048 resurfaced in Area B11 as wall 2140, which was aligned with wall 2048 and therefore also oriented north-west–south-east. Wall 2140, which was exposed over a length of 5.5 m, extended south-eastwards beyond the limits of B1, where it would presumably have bonded at right angles with the temple's SE façade (2139). Greatly damaged by expansive ramped French trenching (2036), and further mutilated by post-Gulf War looting holes (2127), wall 2140, which was made up of between fifteen and seventeen courses of bricks, was preserved to a maximum height of 1.45 m. Its maximum thickness was recorded as 2.75 m (seven or eight rows of brickwork), though it also seemingly had a wider foundation footing that was constructed on top of the Akkad platform (2158). The thickness of its upper parts (without the footing) would have been approximately 2.3 m.

The SE Façade

The temple's SE façade was partially exposed in Area B11 (2139), though its NE corner lay beyond the limits of trench B11. Wall 2139 extended 12.64 m towards the south-west, where it contributed to the temple's S corner, bonding with wall 2159, which formed part of the SW façade. Despite having been severely damaged by dense pitting caused by post-Gulf War looters, wall 2139 was preserved to a maximum height of 1.56 m, made up of between seventeen and nineteen courses of bricks. Its upper parts were 2.3 m thick, representing between six and seven rows, while its inner NW face exhibited a foundation footing that was two bricks wide and two courses high; the base thickness of the wall was 2.9 m. The outer SE face of wall 2139 contained two cones marked with Gudea's Standard Inscription (TG3539 and TG3540), both of which were found just below the point where the surviving wall had been truncated by looters (Fig. 174). Cone TG3539 was found at a topographical height of 16.24 m, between two bricks in the eighth course up from the base of the wall. The complete cone measured 97 mm long, with head and shaft diameters of 46 mm and 34 mm, respectively. Cone TG3540 was found about 1.3 m to the north-east of TG3539, and 0.12 m lower, at an overall elevation of 16.12 m. It was placed between the sixth and the seventh courses up from the base of the wall, and partly between two bricks in the sixth course. The complete cone was 102 mm long, with head and shaft diameters of 45 mm and 34 mm, respectively.

The SW Façade

The SW façade of the temple was formed of two contexts (2068 and 2159) that were found split between Areas B5 and B8. The two sections of the wall were separated by wide French trenching (2036 and 2080) and truncated by frequent pits dug by post-Gulf War looters (2127). Wall 2068 (in B5), which bonded at right angles to part of the NW façade wall (3011), ran from the north-west to the south-east over a length of 12.08 m. Its upper parts had a thickness of 2.35 m, increasing to 3.05 m with the addition of an inner footing on the NE side. It was made up of a total of eight or nine rows of bricks, and preserved to a maximum height of 0.85 m, or ten

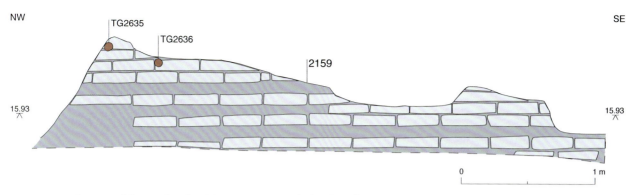

FIGURE 175. Section of the SW façade of the Ningirsu temple (wall 2159), with two *in situ* clay nails.

courses. The wall was heavily truncated in its central part by a trench (2080) that lay on a N–S alignment, while its SE end was completely bisected by another large French pit (2036). About 6 m further to the south-east, wall 2068 formed an alignment with wall 2159, which was exposed over a length of about 10.3 m, as far as the temple's S corner in Area B8, where it bonded at right angles with wall 2139 (part of the SE façade, as discussed above).

Three cones marked with Gudea's Standard Inscription were preserved *in situ*, all in the outer SW face of wall 2159—the section of the SW façade that lay closest to the S corner Fig. 175). One cone (TG1603) was found at the NW end of wall 2159, where it was placed in the tenth course up from the base at an overall height of 16.19 m, inserted directly into the corner of one of the bricks, rather than in the space between the bricks. The complete cone measured 114 mm long, and its head and shaft diameters were 48 mm and 39 mm, respectively. About 4.7 m to the southeast (also in wall 2159's outer SW face), cone TG2635 was found at an overall height of 16.41 m. The courses of bricks were less distinct in this part of the wall, which was built using the regular offset pattern, but in this area the bricks were varied with the inclusion of brick-like deposits. Cone TG2635 was found inserted directly into the corner of a brick (not between bricks) in the tenth course up from the base of the excavation trench. Almost complete, with only a small part of its tip missing, cone TG2635 was 97 mm long, while its head and shaft diameters were 48 mm and 34 mm, respectively. At a distance of 0.3 m to the southeast of cone TG2635, and 0.12 m below it, at a topographical height of 16.29 m, another cone (TG2636) was found in the SW face of wall 2159. It was set in the eighth course up from the base of the trench (two

courses below TG2635), and also in the corner of one of the bricks rather than in the space between bricks. This complete cone measured 118 mm in length, with head and shaft diameters of 43 mm and 35 mm, respectively.

The NW Façade

Running from the south-west to the north-east, the exposed section of the temple's NW façade was formed of two contexts (2003 and 3011) that were split between Areas B2 and B3. Wall 2003 (in B2) ran 4.8 m north-eastwards towards the temple's N corner, where it bonded with wall 2008, which formed part of the building's NE façade. Wall 2003 was preserved to a maximum height of 0.65 m, made up of between three and five courses of bricks, and it was partially cut or truncated by two Hellenistic pits (2020 and 2027). It had a maximum thickness of 2.3 m that was formed of between six and seven rows of bricks; no foundation footing was observed. Wall 2003 continued into Area B3 (context 3011), which was exposed over a length of 5.57 m to a maximum height of 0.77 m (or ten courses of bricks). It extended towards the W corner of the building in the south-west, where it bonded with wall (2068), part of the SW façade. With a thickness of 2.3 m, wall 2003 was made up of seven rows of bricks, and again no evidence of a foundation footing was found. Two cones (TG372 and TG373), which were marked with Gudea's Standard Inscription, were found in the outer NW face of wall 2003. The whole façade (2003 and 3011) showed significant signs of having been extensively renovated in the Ur III period.

The two cones, which were found 0.46 m apart, were placed in the wall just below its levelling height at an overall elevation of 15.7 m. The head of cone TG372 was slightly damaged, but it was otherwise complete and measured 101 mm in length, with head and shaft diameters of 54 mm and 40 mm, respectively. Cone TG373, which was found 0.46 m south-west of TG372, was also complete. It was 112 mm long, with head and shaft diameters of 47 mm and 36 mm, respectively. Remarkably, part of the cuneiform text inscribed on cone TG373 was found impressed into the underlying bonding of mortar. Although this might, at first glance, indicate that the cone was fitted into the wall while the brickwork courses were being laid, it appeared more likely—as also evidenced elsewhere—that it was inserted into a specially drilled hole in the wall at a later stage and then fixed with mud mortar.

The NW Partition Wall between the Cella and the Antecella

Inside the temple, the excavated part of the inner NW wall that separated the cella from the antecella was formed of context 3026 (identified in Areas B3 and B5), which was oriented on a NE–SW alignment and extended over a length of 13.3 m. At both ends wall 3026 bonded perfectly at right angles with the temple's NE and SW façades (contexts 2017 and 2048, and 2068, respectively). The partition wall featured wider foundation footings on both sides: one row of bricks on its NW side, and two or possibly three on the SE side. This gave it a maximum thickness of 3.5 m, made up of a total of ten or eleven rows, with the thickness decreasing to 2.34 m in its upper parts, above the foundation footing. Although it had been considerably levelled by French horizontal trench 2036, and before that by Hellenistic pit 2046, the wall was preserved to a height of between 0.39 m and 0.52 m (between three and five courses of bricks).

In Area B3 the NE extent of partition wall 3026 was pierced by an opening or short passageway that connected the antecella with the cella. Running through the wall from the north-west to the south-east, the opening was 2.34 m long (the same as the thickness of the wall), and it had a width of 1.15 m, representing three or four rows of mud-bricks. The opening indicated a bent-axis approach to the cella, meaning that anyone entering would have had to make a ninety-degree turn in order to face the cult statue, which stood on its podium against the short SW wall (as noted above). The position of the entrance was confirmed by the discovery of a single inscribed stone door socket (TG366) that was found inside the cella on the NW face of wall 3026 (Fig. 176). The

TG366

TG318

0   10 cm

FIGURE 176. The inscribed stone door socket (left) and copper pivot (right) found by the British Museum team inside the entrance to the cella of the Ningirsu temple, on the NW wall (3026).

socket was fitted on top with a copper pivot shoe (TG318), and its inner edge was contiguous with both the wall and also with a kerb or sill that was laid across the inner face of the threshold (towards the cella). The sill was formed of a single course of rectangular (half-size) mud-bricks that were laid as stretchers across the opening.

Made of bicoloured limestone (pink and beige), the door socket (TG366) measured 442 mm × 325 mm × 250 mm (h), while the diameter of the depression was 87 mm. Two of its sides were observed to be somewhat rounded, possibly reflecting the natural shape of the stone, while the other edges were cut and smoothed to form more or less straight sides. The top of the socket was smooth in the centre and pitted towards the sides. Centrally on the top was a smooth hemispherical hollow in which were found traces of copper. To the right of the hollow (when the socket was viewed from inside the cella), and further to the right along the edge of the stone, was the ten-line cuneiform inscription, which was placed in a frame. The text was oriented towards the south-west, in the direction of the cult podium, so that the characters could notionally have been read by the god's statue on its display bench, as it looked towards the north-east. The hemispherical pivot shoe (TG318), which was made of copper alloy, was found placed on top of the door socket. It had a maximum diameter of 170 mm and a total height of 70 mm (inside the depression of 87 mm). The base of the pivot shoe was 6 mm thick, while its walls or sides narrowed to a thickness of 2mm towards the rim, which was found to be pierced all around with rivets or nails whose spikes pointed inwards towards the centre of the shoe. Presumably they had been hammered through the sides of the pivot shoe into the wooden door post that turned on the socket. Possibly related to this pivot shoe was a copper alloy nail (TG356) that was recovered from the fill (3027) of 3028.

Although the stone socket was inscribed in the name of Gudea, there were reasons to believe that it had probably been altered at a later date, presumably during the Ur III period (as is discussed later in Chapter 36). Finally, despite clear signs that the area around the entrance to the cella had been disturbed, the presence of just one door socket echoed the arrangement that was observed in the entrance to the antecella, which had almost certainly been fitted with a single-leaf door. The door to the cella, which probably also included just one leaf, must have opened into the cella by pivoting through 180 degrees from the south-west to the north-east.

The SE Partition Wall between the Antecella and the Stairwell

The exposed section of the SE partition wall that divided the antecella from the stairwell was formed of two contexts (2160 and 2162) that were split between Areas B5 and B11, separated by a passageway with a width of 1.15 m. Wall 2160 (in B5), which was oriented on a NE–SW alignment and bonded perfectly at right angles with the temple's SW façade wall (2159), extended for a length of 8.5 m north-eastwards into Area B11. Like the partition wall (3026) between the cella and the antecella, wall 2160 also featured wider foundation footings (made up of one or two rows of bricks) on both its NW and SE sides that gave it a maximum base width of 2.75 m, representing seven or eight rows. It was preserved to a maximum height of 0.6 m, or eight courses of bricks, and its higher parts were 2.3 m thick. Wall 2160 had been extensively damaged and truncated by French trenching and Hellenistic levelling, and also by post-Gulf War looting, evidenced by robber pits (2127). The wall continued in B11 as wall 2162, which was exposed over a length of 1.6 m to a height of 1.45 m (or seventeen courses). Wall 2162 ran south-west to north-east, where it bonded at right angles with part of the temple's NE façade (2140). It had a maximum thickness of 2.75 m (the same as 2160), made up of seven or eight rows of bricks, including foundation footings on each of its NW and SE facings.

The NW–SE passageway that ran through the partition wall was 2.3 m long (the same as the thickness of the upper parts of the partition). It was exposed in Area B11, where it was perfectly aligned with its counterpart in the other partition wall to the north-west that gave access to the cella. Again mirroring the access point to the cella, the position of the opening between the antecella and the stairwell suggested a bent-axis approach from the antecella to the interior of the stairwell corridor, and its layout and fittings also reflected those found in the entrance to the cella. The inner SE edge of the threshold (inside the stairway corridor) was again fitted with a single door socket, evidenced by a semicircular compartment that abutted onto the SE corner of wall 2162, where it lay partly on top of wall 2162's foundation footing. In all likelihood, a single-leaf door opened through

180 degrees into the stairwell space, pivoting from the south-west to the north-east. The passageway displayed significant traces of later renovation work that was dated to the Isin-Larsa and Old Babylonian periods. It also appeared to have been blocked when the temple was taken out of service and probably (as argued in Chapter 36) deconsecrated before it was finally abandoned.

The Temple of Ningirsu: The Inner Rooms

The Layout of the Cella

The cella or inner sanctum of the Ningirsu temple, which was the most secluded part of the entire L-shaped complex, measured a little more than 11.5 m in length (along its SW–NE axis, which ran widthways across the building) and about 7.1 m in breadth, making a total of 81.65 m². Established on a foundation layer of compacted red clay that had been ritually cleansed by fire (2011 and 3024), the cella included the two most highly symbolic architectural elements that were generally found in such innermost spaces, namely an altar for divine offerings (3039) and a podium or display bench (2073) that was used to exhibit the cult statue of the god. The offering platform (3039), which was built lengthways in the middle of the cella's long SW–NE axis, measured 3.55 m (north-east to south-west) × 2.95 m (north-west to south-east), and it was made of square mud-bricks (with recorded measurements of 0.3 m × 0.3 m × 0.06 m) that were laid on bed in regular courses. The bonding patterns for Gudea bricks are discussed in Chapter 42, but single rows of half-bricks must have been needed all the way along the beginnings and ends of successive alternating courses of the installation's short and long faces, including at the corners, which would have been formed entirely of half-bricks. For practical purposes, the exact order in which the sequence was executed would not have mattered, but for symbolic reasons the builders might usually have preferred to begin with a half-brick. The extensive use of half-bricks was evidenced by the half-brick stretchers that were observed on the construction's exposed edges. Levelled in Hellenistic times, the altar survived to a maximum height of 0.36 m, though the fact that it was so poorly preserved meant that details of its construction were unfortunately hard to make out. Nonetheless, its NE face, where the possible remains of steps might have been noted, seemed to provide an access point to its upper surface, with the impression being further enhanced by the presence of shallow buttresses. Its foundations lay directly on the preparatory layer (3024) of crushed red mud-bricks, which was noted all the way across the room (2011), including directly underneath Gudea's Lagash II walls.

Found to the south-west of offering platform 3039, the brickwork of the podium for the cult statue (2073) was bonded to the cella's SW wall (2068). As for the altar just described, the podium would have been constructed with single rows of half-bricks alternating on the long and short sides of each course, such that the corners were again made entirely of half-bricks. In the case of the podium, which was bonded to the SW wall, the alternating rows of half-bricks on the structure's SW edge must have been incorporated into the fabric of the temple's SW wall in order to tie the podium to the building behind it (probably by keying it only into the wall's first row). Unfortunately, the poor condition of the structure meant that little evidence of this had survived. Like the altar, the podium had also been levelled in the Hellenistic period and was further truncated by a French excavation trench (2080). When it was built, it therefore probably extended much further to the north-west, closely following (or perhaps determining) the proportions of other features in the room, particularly the offering table (3039). Its SE face had the same alignment and orientation as the SE face of the offering table, but the original extent of podium 2073 could not be established because of the truncation. It was nevertheless thought highly likely that its NW face had the same orientation as the NW face of platform 3039. Podium 2073 was found preserved to its original NE–SW length of 2.09 m, while its truncated width was 1.66 m, and it survived to a height of 0.65 m. Its position within the cella, and particularly its placement at the end of a series of bent-axis approaches, left little doubt that podium 2073 was the support for the chief cult statue of Ningirsu in the New Eninnu's sanctum sanctorum (Fig. 177). Characterised by its remoteness, it was the only location in the complex that was entered via such a complicated, maze-like access route.

The Layout of the Antecella

The temple's antecella, which served as both a libation or ablution room and a vestibule (Fig. 178), was slightly more than 11.5 m in length (along its SW–NE axis) and about

The Gudea Sanctuary of Ningirsu: The New Eninnu   487

FIGURE 177. Artist's impression of the cella in the Temple of Ningirsu at the heart of Gudea's New Eninnu. The cult podium is situated on the SW wall, so the statue of Ningirsu faces north-east.

9.6 m wide, giving a total area of 110.4 m². It had been significantly disturbed by Hellenistic levelling and subsequently recut by extensive French trenching that affected the whole area (2036). This was the part of the mound that housed the related set of structures that were exposed by the French: a well (M), together with a platform (K) and its associated water containers (L), as marked on Heuzey's New Plan (Fig. 114). Designed to be used for ritual libations and ablutions, these installations were in all likelihood built by Gudea and subsequently renovated in the Ur III or Isin-Larsa period, and it is clear from the new excavations that they were originally positioned in a key sacred location inside the antecella.

Only the substructure of the well had survived (re-excavated as context 2143; Fig. 179). The other fixtures had been completely dismantled, and a hundred or more fragments of bricks and pieces of bitumen were found scattered all across the vestibule (2077). The well's lower-lying brickwork (2143) was discovered inside a cylindrical cut that was filled with brick fragments. The context was unearthed just 0.1 m beneath the large French trenching horizon (2036), at a topographical elevation of about 15.3 m, where the previous excavations had left off. The base of the well was found in a highly symbolic place inside the antecella, aligned with the main entrance to the temple and close to the door that led into the cella, thus marking the exact spot where the

FIGURE 178. Artist's impression of the antecella in Gudea's Temple of Ningirsu, looking towards the southwest, with the entrance to the cella (right), some seated Gudea Statues on the podium on the SE wall (left) and the well (M) and double cistern (KL) in the centre.

officiating priests and high-status worshippers who came in through the temple's main entrance would have had to turn through ninety degrees to proceed into the cella. The preserved construction was formed of a circular ring of rectangular fired bricks, five courses high, with an external diameter of 1.3 m. The pale yellow bricks, which were laid flat, measured 0.24 m × 0.18 m × 0.07 m, and they were bonded with thick, black bitumen. The limited depth of only five courses meant that the shaftlike construction could certainly not have reached the water table, which lay perhaps 15 m below, so it could not have been a proper well, but was probably rather a soakaway for the disposal of the water that was used in ritual libations. These ceremonies were no doubt carried out in the antecella, as is also confirmed by the reference in the Cylinder Inscriptions to a 'place where water can be drunk' (ki.a.nag), indicating a set of water features that were used sacramentally for the worship of the temple's divine proprietor, Ningirsu. The features alluded to in the inscriptions might well relate to the installations just described and discussed further below.

Despite the large-scale pitting caused by the previous excavations that were carried out in this area, the SE end of the vestibule had survived more or less intact, truncated only obliquely by a ramped French trench on a SE–NW alignment. The room contained another large display bench

FIGURE 179. The remains of the well (M) in the antecella of Gudea's Ningirsu temple. The well cuts through the underlying Early Dynastic layers; the low wall in the background belongs to the latest iteration of the Early Dynastic shrine.

or low platform (2035; Fig. 180) that was found engaged with the antecella's SE and SW walls (2160 and 2159). The display platform, which measured 6.89 m × 2.30 m, and was preserved to a height of about 0.6 m, was doubtless used to exhibit large votive artefacts of particular importance, among which were almost certainly one or more of the Tell A statues of Gudea—a suggestion that is corroborated by the observed archaeological findings, as well as by the Cylinder Inscriptions and the text found on Statue B. Similar to the cella podium for the divine cult image (2073), display platform 2035 was bonded to the temple's structural fabric, though in this instance it was tied to two walls, rather than just one. Like the podium and offering table in the cella, it must have been planned from the outset as an essential architectural element and cultic appurtenance. Its location is particularly significant in this respect because it was placed in the S corner of the antecella or libation room, in front of the sacred font (L on Heuzey's New Plan), and directly facing the plinth supporting Ningirsu's statue, which lay on the other side of the water installations and the cella wall.

Together with other especially holy temple fixtures and fittings (detailed in Chapter 36), the display platform had been reverentially deconsecrated when the New Eninnu was decommissioned. Accordingly, a black layer was found evenly spread laterally across its whole surface (2081), but since there was no sign of fire damage on any of the bricks that actually made up the platform, it was clear that the black deposit must have been produced and raked out somewhere else on the site before being transported to the antecella. The fact that the burnt material was found deliberately processed and meticulously dispersed over the entire platform, rather than being piled up in one place, tended to confirm that it was part of a deconsecration ritual.

The Stairwell Chamber

The Ningirsu temple's stairwell chamber was again more than 11.5 m long (along its SW–NE axis), but only about 2 m wide, and it too had also been ritually decommissioned (as is argued in Chapter 36) when the sanctuary was finally closed. In this case the deconsecration included the removal of the fired-brick steps, followed by the ritual interment and capping of the whole stairwell, as represented by contexts 2113 and 2094. In addition, strong archaeological evidence suggested

FIGURE 180. The podium, presumably for one or more of the Gudea Statues, on the SE wall of the antecella inside the Ningirsu temple.

that the single flight of steps (originally spanning a length of about 9 m on a NE–SW alignment) that extended from the room's threshold, was renovated at least twice before it was finally taken out of service. The renovations took place in the Ur III period and subsequently in Isin-Larsa times.

The Ambulatory Walkways, Transitional Walls and Entrances

The Ambulatory Walkways

The walls of the Ningirsu temple were surrounded by a rectangular peribolus or sacred circuit, 100 m in length, which was made up of open-air corridors with an average width of 1.6 m that met at right angles outside the building's corners (Fig. 181). Merging with the Ur-Bau plaza, in which stood Ur-Bau's decommissioned or repurposed Ningirsu temple building, the NE walkway was oriented north-west–south-east. It was uncovered over a length of 32 m along the temple's main façade wall, from the north-west in Area B2, where it intersected with the NW open-air corridor, to the south-east (beyond the limits of Area B11), where it doubtless formed a right angle with the SE ambulatory. The latter extended for 18 m towards the south-west along the SE façade wall, where it was found to intersect at right angles with the SW corridor in Area B8. The long SW walkway, exposed over its entire length of 32 m in Areas B3, B4, B5 and B8, merged with the inner porch of the sanctuary's SW gate. Thereafter, it extended to the temple's W corner, where it formed a right angle with the NW open-air ambulatory, which ran 18 m north-eastwards along the temple's NW façade wall, merging in Area B2 with the portal in the inner NW wall, and intersecting at right angles with the NE ambulatory (and the Ur-Bau plaza). Despite the extensive damage that was caused by Hellenistic and French trenching or pitting, as well as by more recent looting, the peribolus around the Ningirsu temple was found to contain a series of undisturbed stratigraphic locations, providing a complete matrix of occupation build-up that stretched continuously from the time of Gudea to the Isin-Larsa and Old Babylonian periods, as is discussed in Chapter 36.

The NW Inner Wall and the Inner Gate

The temple's NW ambulatory was fronted on its NW side by a wall that extended across the interior of the L-shaped

FIGURE 181. The internal walkway on the SW side of the Ningirsu temple, looking towards the north-west. The head of an *in situ* clay nail can be seen in the inner envelope wall (2031) on the left.

complex, separating the Ningirsu section of the New Eninnu that lay in the south-east from the rest. Running along the NE side of the peribolus and the Ur-Bau plaza, the inner NW wall was pierced by a gateway that referenced the earlier gated temenos wall that was built by Ur-Bau. The gate was approached on the NW side of the wall via a monumental entranceway composed of the two elaborate ascending platforms, decorated with niches and fired-brick stepped recesses, that were identified by Sarzec as H and H', with the higher parts subsequently labelled DEGH (on Heuzey's New Plan; Fig. 114).

Rising above the uppermost platform (DEGH), and set back by about 3 m from the NW edge of platform H, two sections of Gudea's inner NW wall were identified in contexts 2001 and 3006. They were split between Areas B2 and B3, and separated by a gateway passage that had been partly damaged by Hellenistic pit 2020. The two preserved parts of the wall had been truncated in various ways. Context 3006 was mainly affected by a French ramp that sloped down from the south-east to the north-west, where it gave access to the deeper excavations carried out by the French in and around the outer and lower parts of the monumental entrance in Area B1. In addition, the NE end of wall 3006 appeared to have been truncated by Hellenistic pit 2020, which had been driven through the gateway. By contrast, the upper courses of wall 2001 had been truncated horizontally at a topographical height of 15.17 m, while its NE end had been wholly removed by Hellenistic pit 2027.

The surviving parts of walls 2001 and 3006 were both constructed using regular courses of standard square Gudea mud-bricks (with sides of 0.32 m and a thickness of about 0.07 m) that were laid flat. They were manufactured using an extremely compact clay silt matrix that had been heavily tempered with a carefully prepared coarse chaff composed of similarly sized pieces of straw. The colour of the resulting bricks varied from reddish brown to yellowish brown. Both walls were aligned north-east–south-west, with wall 3006 located to the south-west (in Area B3) and wall 2001 to the north-east of that (in Area B2). Wall 2001, which was traced over a length of 4.8 m, had a thickness of 2.3 m that was made up of between six and seven rows of mud-bricks, and it was preserved to a height of three courses. At its SW end, its external NW face was articulated with a pronounced thick buttress that extended the wall's façade outwards towards the north-west by three rows of mud-bricks. This allowed the adjacent entrance to be accented with decorative recesses. Wall 2001 was bordered to the north-west by a level deposit of compacted mid-greyish-brown clay silt (2004) made up of crushed fragments of mud-bricks. Deposit 2004 had an average thickness of 0.16 m, and it was directly covered by a top-soil deposit (also extending over wall 2001) that had been formed following the cessation of the French excavations. As previously discussed, wall 2001 sealed off a short section of Ur-Bau's temenos wall (2024), which was preserved to a height of only one course of mud-bricks. Wall 3006 and its continuation (3048), which was built over Ur-Bau's wall 3097, was 2.3 m thick and preserved to a maximum height of 1.13 m. Aligned north-east–south-west, it was traced over a distance of 9.7 m. Its NE termination formed the SW edge of the gateway, which was accented with both internal and external buttresses that increased the thickness of this part of the wall to 2.75 m. The width of the opening between walls 3006 and 2001 was approximately 3.6 m. A larger Lagash II buttress (3045) was identified as having been built against the inner SE face of wall 3006, which also showed traces of renovations that were carried out in the Ur III and Isin-Larsa periods.

The inner SE face of Gudea's wall 3006 appeared to have been studded with numerous inscribed cones commemorating his project. Four cones were discovered *in situ* (TG374, TG375, TG376 and TG378), while one cone (TG381) was possibly *in situ* or very close to its original place in the wall, and twenty-one partial or complete cones were recovered from the bulk fills (3008) that were found just in front of wall 3006 in the open-air corridor. These fills must certainly have been formed by the partial collapse of the adjacent superstructure, prior to the renovation of the complex in Isin-Larsa times. The cones that were found *in situ* in context 3006 were placed in the central part of the SE wall. Furthest to the south-west, 0.6 m above the base of the wall, cone TG375 was inserted in the space between two adjacent bricks in the eighth course (at a topographical height of 16.15 m). The complete cone was 120 mm long, with head and shaft diameters of 50 mm and 41 mm, respectively. Cone TG374 was found at the edge of the French cut, 0.6 m north-east of cone TG375 and at an overall height of 16.23 m, where it was embedded in the space between the bricks and courses, one course above TG375, at a height of 0.67 m above the base of the wall. Also

complete, TG374 measured 121 mm in length, and its head and shaft diameters were 48 mm and 39 mm, respectively.

Cone TG381 was again found at the edge of the French excavation cut that had truncated wall 3006. Uncovered at a topographical height of 16.15 m, TG381 had probably been disturbed by the cut, but it was nonetheless judged to be approximately *in situ*. It was found 0.2 m to the north-east of cone TG374 and one course of bricks lower than it. Broken at the tip, cone TG381 measured 78 mm in length, while its head and shaft diameters were 63 mm and 49 mm, respectively. About 0.2 m below TG374 and 0.14 m below TG381, in a rare mud-plastered portion of wall 3006, cone TG376 was found at an overall height of 15.97 m. It was 101 mm long, with head and shaft diameters of 48 mm and 41 mm, respectively. At a distance of 2.4 m to the north-east and one course down from TG376, cone TG378 was also discovered at the edge of the French excavation cut, at a topographical height of 15.93 m. In this part of the wall the mud plaster was preserved only between the courses so it did not cover the bricks themselves. Cone TG378 was found 0.3 m above the base of the wall, just above a structure (3021) that was built into the wall at this point. Cone TG378, which was slightly damaged at the tip, measured 97 mm in length, and its head and shaft diameters were 50 mm and 40 mm, respectively.

The Inner SW Enveloping Wall

Lying on the SW side of the gateway that pierced the complex's monumental inner NW partition, wall 3006 turned through ninety degrees from the south-west to the south-east to join wall 3049 in Area B4 (continuing as 2032 in B5). Wall 3049 made special reference to Ur-Bau's earlier sacred enclosure by following the levelled line of the older temenos wall. Accordingly, wall 3049 was an envelope (or wrapping) wall, with a thickness of 2.3 m, that stood between the external SW wall of Gudea's L-shaped enclosure and the ambulatory inside the complex on the SW side of the Ningirsu temple. Adjacent to the SW part of Gudea's temenos wall, enveloping wall 3049 marked the outer side of the NW–SE stretch of the peribolus. This was the section that led to the vestibule in front of the SW gate and extended south-eastwards on the same side of the gateway (context 2031 in Areas B5 and B8).

The internal face of the inner SW envelope (3049 and 2032), which was excavated to a length of 5.75 m in Areas B4 and B5, was decorated with votive clay nails that were

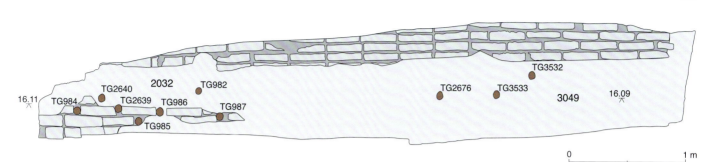

FIGURE 182. Section of the NE façade of the inner envelope wall (3049 and 2032) on the SW side of the Ningirsu temple, showing the positions of the *in situ* clay nails.

inscribed in the name of Gudea and dedicated to Ningirsu (Fig. 182). The findings confirmed that the envelope was substantially the work of Gudea, despite the fact that it was later repaired in the Ur III period (context 3069), since the placement of these clay nails could only have occurred either when the sanctuary was being built or during the activation rituals that must have been celebrated when it was consecrated. Their presence again demonstrated the intimate connection between ritualised acts and the building of the sanctuary. A total of ten clay nails were found *in situ* in the NE face of the envelope wall (3049 and 2032). At its SE end, close to the point where the wall formed a corner with the gateway vestibule, cone TG984 was discovered between the bricks in the third course up from the base of the trench, at a topographical height of 16.05 m. TG984 had some damage at the tip that seemed to have occurred before the cone was inserted into the wall, but it was otherwise complete and measured 74 mm in length, with head and shaft diameters of 58 mm and 43 mm, respectively. A fragment of another inscribed cone (TG2640) was found inserted in the wall at a distance of 0.21 m to the north-west of TG984, at an overall height of 16.13 m. Measuring 76 mm in length, its maximum diameter along the broken central part of the cone was 34 mm; its tip, which was also broken, had a minimum diameter of 17 mm.

Another broken fragment of a cone (TG2639) was found 0.14 m north-west of TG2640, and just below it, at an overall elevation of 16.06 m. With a preserved length of 79 mm, the fragment's broken end had a maximum diameter of 32 mm. Additionally, 0.16 m north-west of TG2639, and 0.11 m below it, at a topographical height of 15.95 m, cone TG985 was found *in situ* in the space between adjacent bricks, one course down from TG984 and TG986. The fourth cone found *in situ*, TG985, which was complete, was 122 mm long, with head and shaft diameters of 54 mm and 40 mm, respectively. At a distance of 0.19 m to the north-west, cone TG986 was also found placed between bricks, at a topographical height of 16.03 m, and therefore 0.08 m higher than TG985. It was found at roughly the same height as TG2639 (which was placed to the left of it), and TG986 was inserted in the same course of bricks as TG984. Also complete, TG986 measured 129 mm in length, with head and shaft diameters of 51 mm and 37 mm, respectively. To the north-west, at a distance of 0.33 m, in the fifth course up from the base of the trench, at an overall height of 16.19 m, cone TG982 was discovered in a part of the wall that was plastered with mud. Preserved intact, it was 117 mm long and the diameter of its head was 57 mm. Close by, at a distance of 0.18 m to the north-west of TG982, and 0.21 m lower than it, at a topographical height of 15.98 m, cone TG987 was found *in situ* in the same course of bricks as TG985 (described just above), where it was inserted into the mortar bonding between two bricks. Also found intact, TG987 was 142 mm long, with head and shaft diameters of 59 mm and 42 mm, respectively.

Cone TG2676 was found *in situ* 1.87 m to the north-west of TG987, at a topographical height of 16.11 m. Broken approximately halfway down from the head, so its narrower end was missing, its preserved length was 57 mm, while the head and shaft diameters were 49 mm and 37 mm, respectively; the diameter of the broken end was 27 mm. Cone TG3533 was set into the face of the wall, 0.5 m to the north-west of TG2676, and at a similar overall height of 16.12 m. Since it was also broken, only the tip of TG3533 was recovered. The preserved part measured 62 mm in length, and the maximum diameter of the cone's broken central part was 29 mm. The tenth cone retrieved from this stretch of wall was TG3532, which was found 0.31 m north-west of TG3533, at a topographical height of 16.28 m. The cone, which was complete, measured 106 mm in length, with head and shaft diameters of 43 mm and 34 mm, respectively.

On the SE side of the vestibule associated with the SW gate, the envelope wall (3049 and 2032) was further traced as context 2031 in Areas B5 and B8. It was exposed over a length of approximately 20 m and had a maximum thickness of 2.3 m. Wall 2031 must also originally have been studded with cones that were inscribed in the name of Gudea, but significant truncations and looting (2080 and 2127) meant that only two were recorded *in situ*. Cone TG979 was found in the NE face of envelope wall 2031 at a topographical height of 16.19 m. It was unbroken and measured 122 mm in length, with head and shaft diameters of 47 mm and 34 mm, respectively. Approximately 19.85 m to the south-east, cone TG2637 was also found *in situ* in the NE face of wall 2031 (Fig. 183), where it was placed in the fifth course up from the base of the wall, at an overall height of 16.06 m, and it was inserted into the bottom right-hand corner of one of the mud-bricks (in the brick itself rather than in the mortar). The tip and a section of the shaft of TG2637 were missing, but it had a preserved length of 81 mm, while its head and shaft diameters were 57 mm and 40 mm, respectively; the narrower broken end of the cone had a diameter of 30 mm.

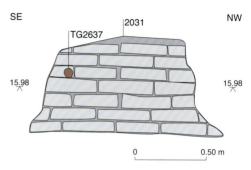

FIGURE 183. Section of the continuation of the façade of the inner envelope wall (2031), showing a single *in situ* clay nail on the SE side of the New Eninnu's SW entranceway.

The L-Shaped Complex: The Central Courtyard

The latest distinct archaeological feature found in Area B1 that could be dated to the time of Gudea's New Eninnu was a *pisé* or adobe surface (contexts 1018 and 1021, associated with 1002 and 1012), which was identified at a topographical height of about 14 m, extending at least 25 m towards the north-west, as was confirmed by further traces of it that were discovered in Area B10 (5505), beyond French cut 5429. The *pisé* surface was judged to form the substructure of a large courtyard (Fig. 184) that was located between the higher Ningirsu temple that occupied the SE part of the complex (in B2, B3, B5, B8 and B11) and the presumed Temple of Bau at the NW end of the complex (Fig. 185). The courtyard probably fronted the gateway and two-stage monumental sloping ascent (H and H′ on Sarzec's Plan A) that were associated with the inner NW wall (discussed above) that cut across the L-shaped complex on the NW side of the Ningirsu temple. In Area B1 the *pisé* surface (1018 and 1021) was formed of a level, very compact dark purplish-brown clay deposit that was made up of superimposed layers (1014, 1015, 1016, 1017 and 1019), with a total thickness of 0.5 m. No evidence was found of any internal structuring. Its continuation in Area B10 (5505) comprised a tough deposit of compacted light reddish-brown and light yellowish-brown clay that exhibited patches of repair represented by deposit 5517. Present in the N part of Area B1, where the surface had been truncated by large French excavation pits (1011, 1022, 1054, 1076, 1080 and 1081), and in the W part of Area B10, the original extent of the *pisé* surface could not be determined, except to say that it must certainly have extended over a length of at least 25 m from the north-west to the south-east and for about 10 m from the north-east to the south-west.

The SE edge of the *pisé* surface in Area B1 was noticeably straight, and this suggested that it had abutted onto an earlier feature, which, as indicated by the spatial arrangement of this part of the complex, was probably the NW face of the uppermost stage of the previous, Early Dynastic IIIb temple platform (5235). With regard to structure and symbolism, it seemed reasonable to compare it with the foundation of adobe boulders that was established to support the Lagash II precinct wall (5234) in Area B9 to the north-east. For structural and symbolic reasons both deposits reinforced and buttressed the faces of earlier terraces. The architectural association between the courtyard's adobe substructure and Gudea's programme was underscored by the recovery of a mixed but coherent assemblage of Early Dynastic IIIb and Akkad potsherds in most if not all of the fills (1018, 1021,

FIGURE 184. Reconstruction of the central courtyard inside Gudea's New Eninnu, looking towards the south-east. The raised entrance in the facing wall is the Gate of Gudea, or the King's Gate, as it is probably called in the Cylinder Inscriptions. The Ningirsu temple stands on the other side of the monumental partition, screened from the rest of the complex. A throne is placed on the first level of the stepped ascent to the gateway, and some of the Gudea Statues can be seen on a series of inferred composite bases like the Pillar of Gudea (left and right).

1012, 1014, 1015 and 1017). These dated from the same periods as the pottery that was associated with the foundation fills of the Ningirsu temple in Areas B2, B3, B4 and B5.

The L-Shaped Complex: The Temenos Gates and Walls

The SW Temenos Gate and Inner Porch, and the SW and SE Temenos Walls

Significant archaeological remains of the SW temenos wall, which was pierced with a gateway (Fig. 186) fitted with a towered gatehouse, were found nearly intact in Areas B4, B5, B7 and B8, where they were enclosed within the Hellenistic platform and other associated substructures that were parts of the successor complex built by Adadnadinakhe in the late fourth century BCE. The SW temenos wall formed a right angle with the Gudea enclosure's SE wall, traces of which were found in Area B11. It is a remarkable fact that portions of Gudea's SW temenos wall, in particular contexts 2058 and 3100 (in B4 and B5), and contexts 2059 and 2164 (in B5 and B8), embraced and complemented the inner SW envelope wall (3049 and 2032, and 2031), which seemingly served no structural purpose, as was also the case for other sections of envelope wall that were incorporated into the L-shaped complex on the NW and NE sides of Gudea's Ningirsu temple. Symbolically, the SW envelope wall paid homage to the precursor enclosure built by Ur-Bau, and it had the practical consequence of doubling the New Eninnu's SW façade, thereby creating an additional screen between the Ningirsu temple and the busy residential quarters of Girsu that were situated to the south-west, beyond the confines of the Urukug. Raised above the rest of the Gudea

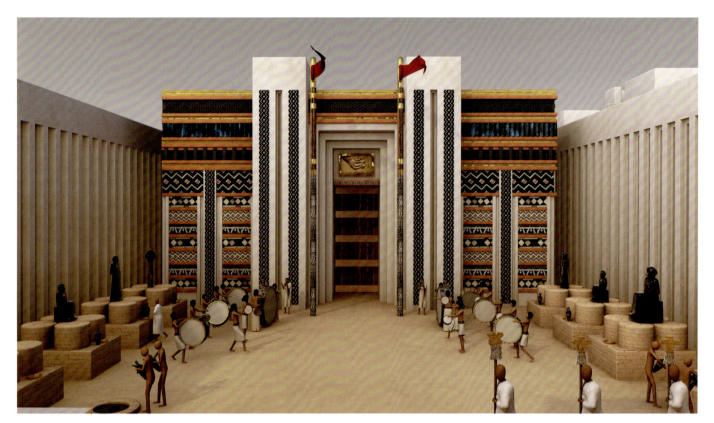

FIGURE 185. Reconstruction of the central courtyard inside Gudea's New Eninnu, looking towards the north-west, where the entrance to the Bau temple can be seen. More statues are placed on composite bases (left and right), and the ceremonial space reverberates with the sound of drums.

complex, the Ningirsu temple lay inside the SW wall of the inner sanctum, with the divine statue of Ningirsu placed on its podium (2073) inside the cella, where it faced north-east, with its back to the populated areas of the city. Accordingly, the arrangement of the three SW walls (the outer façade of the temenos, the inner envelope and the façade wall of the Ningirsu temple) combined with the orientation of the god's statue to accentuate a special sense of isolation and security.

Exposed portions of the SW face of the L-shaped compound were identified as a series of walls, including 2164 and 2059 (in Areas B5 and B8), together with 2058 and 3100 (in Areas B4 and B5), and their continuation as context 6006 (in Area B7). All were found oriented on a NW–SE alignment, and all had thicknesses of between 3.68 m and 4.08 m, representing between nine and twelve preserved rows of standard Gudea mud-bricks. The combined length of all the excavated walls was about 35 m. Like the inner SW envelope (2031) by which the temenos was shadowed, so to speak, the SW façade of the L-shaped complex had been extensively damaged by broad French trenching (2080 and 2108), as well as by looting that was carried out after the Gulf War. Nonetheless, significant traces of large-scale renovation works, dating in all likelihood to the Isin-Larsa period, were found in Area B8, where a buttressed façade (2125) was added to reinforce Gudea's Lagash II temenos wall (2164). This refurbishment had been undertaken in conjunction with other extensive repairs from the same Isin-Larsa period that were identified more generally in the vicinity of the SW gateway.

In Area B11 the SE end of Gudea's SW temenos wall joined wall 2137 at right angles to form the L-shaped enclosure's S corner. Oriented on a NE–SW alignment, wall 2137, which was part of the sanctuary's SE façade, extended for 5.51 m towards the north-east, beyond the limits of Area B11. Heavily pitted by robbers (2127), it was preserved to a height of 0.97 m, made up of fourteen courses of mud-bricks, and although its inner NW face had been subject to extensive

FIGURE 186. Artist's impression of a gate in the external façade of the New Eninnu, with relief sculptures commemorating one of the Slain Heroes killed by Ningirsu on either side. Above the entrance is a relief showing the Thunderbird grasping the backs of two stags.

oblique truncation, it nevertheless showed signs of having been fitted with a foundation footing made of one row of bricks. Excluding the possible footing, the preserved thickness of wall 2137 was at least 3.67 m.

In Area B5 the inner porch of the SW gateway, which was found partly truncated by French trench 2080 (running north to south), was placed on a NW–SE alignment, with its long side (measuring more than 5 m) extending out to the south-west towards the gate itself in the external SW wall; it was about 2.3 m wide. The long SW side of the vestibule, merging on its NE side with the SW walkway that ran around the temple, was formed of walls 2058 and 2059, and these were separated from each other by the narrow passageway that gave access to the SW gate. The vestibule's short sides were formed of wall 2032 to the north-west and wall 2031 to the south-east. Four cones inscribed in the name of Gudea were found in the inner NE face of wall 2059, on the SE side of the entrance (Fig. 187). Cone TG980 was placed between two bricks in the fifth course up from the base of the trench, at a topographical height of 16.17 m. Remarkably, the two bricks that flanked the cone were half-bricks that were laid side by side with their short sides positioned along the face of the wall. The use of half-bricks in this way seemed highly unusual, above all because the two were placed side by side, and they do not appear to have been associated with a corner or buttress, though even in those cases it is hard to see

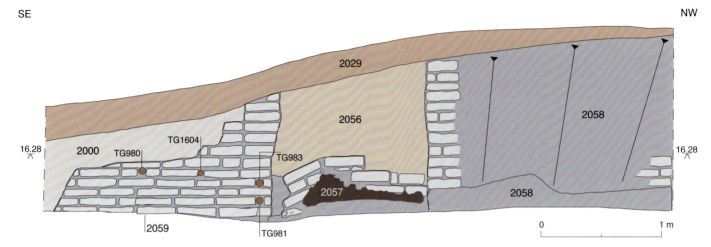

FIGURE 187. Section of the NE wall (2059) inside the SW gateway passage in the temenos wall of the New Eninnu, showing four *in situ* clay nails.

a structural reason for the use of adjacent half-bricks. Since the other bricks in the wall were generally of the standard square Gudea kind (with sides of 0.32 m), this almost certainly meant that the two half-bricks performed no bonding function, and it might be that they were laid to replace a single square brick, or in order to facilitate the placement of the cone, though neither of these ideas could finally be confirmed. The broken end of cone TG980 was missing, but the preserved part was 106 mm long, while its head and shaft diameters were 56 mm and 42 mm, respectively.

Cone TG1604 was found 0.42 m north-west of TG980, in the same course of bricks, at a topographical height of 16.12 m. Since it was broken, only the tip was recovered, and its preserved length measured 82 mm. A third cone (TG983) was discovered *in situ* to the north-west of TG1604, where it was placed between two bricks in the course below TG980 and TG1602. It was found 0.44 m north-west of the latter, at an overall height of 16.04 m, in the fourth course up from the base of the wall. The head of TG983 was missing, but its surviving length was 102 mm, while its broken end had a maximum diameter of 37 mm; the shaft was fractured into two pieces. The fourth cone (TG981) was uncovered just below TG983, at a topographical height of 15.92 m, two courses down from TG983, where it was inserted between two bricks. Cone TG981 was broken at the point where the shaft began, just below the head, such that the damage might have been done when the object was fitted into the wall, or when it was reinserted into the brickwork after a wall repair. Its overall length was 43 mm, while the diameter below the missing head was 60 mm, and the diameter of the rest of the shaft was 43 mm.

Excavated in Area B5, the narrow passage leading to the gate, which was an important feature of the external face of the SW wall, ran through the fabric of the SW temenos wall. It was 4.08 m long (the same as the thickness of the wall) and 1.15 m wide, the same width as the openings between the rooms inside the Ningirsu temple. The sides of this entrance passage were formed by wall 2058 (preserved to a maximum height of 1.24 m) to the north-west, and wall 2059 to the south-east, where a single cone inscribed in the name of Gudea was found. Cone TG1602 was uncovered in the NW face of wall 2059, where it was inserted directly into a mud-brick in the first course above the pavement, at a topographical height of 16.19 m. The cone, which emerged intact, measured 125 mm in length, while its head and shaft diameters were 51 mm and 39 mm, respectively. The brickwork in this part of the wall was coated with mud plaster, and when a very fine layer of the plaster was removed in order to expose the shaft of the cone and the courses of mud-bricks, it seemed that a round hole had been dug or drilled into the mud-bricks to create a space into which the cone could be inserted. The cone appeared to have been fixed with a mud plaster similar to that which had been used to cover the walls. The mix was notably more resilient and less crumbly than the material used to make the mud-bricks themselves.

The inner NE edge of the threshold of the gate probably featured a single door socket that was possibly enclosed in a compartment (2066) abutting onto the N corner (or NE face) of wall 2059. In all likelihood, the socket was associated with a single-leaf door that opened into the space of the inner porch, passing through 180 degrees as it pivoted from the south-east to the north-west. A socket stone (TG951) bearing the faded signs of a framed inscription in the name of Gudea was retrieved from nearby French pitting 2080, and it seemed likely that this originally belonged to the doorway. The subrectangular limestone socket (TG951), with dimensions of 0.49 m × 0.37 m × 0.22 m (h), was beige to light brown in colour, with some red colouring along its shorter left-hand side and the lower part of the long side. It exhibited rounded corners and more or less straight sides, while its top surface, which was pitted, laminated and fragmented, was rather rough. Centrally on the top, was found a hemispherical depression (rather rough and marked with black traces), with a diameter of 105 mm, in which the door (or more exactly its copper shoe) would have pivoted. Vestiges of the cuneiform inscription were found to the right of the central depression, along the socket's shorter right-hand side.

The passageway and the probable door socket compartment showed signs of having been extensively renovated during the Isin-Larsa and Old Babylonian periods. Unfortunately, an old pit that was dug by robbers had caused considerable damage to the middle of the entry to the passage on the SW side, and this made it impossible to determine whether or not the original brickwork formed a flight of steps that ascended towards the north-east. On its SW side, in Areas B4 and B5, the passage was fronted by a wider open-air ceremonial walkway that was fitted with two low square platforms (or display benches) that looked as though they were made to support votive artefacts or steles. The benches were placed on the two sides of the entrance, which originally had a width of 5.75 m and was exposed over a length of 6.65 m. It too underwent significant remodelling in the Isin-Larsa period.

The gateway featured two substantial rectangular towers: 3060 (in Area B4) in the external wall on the NW side of the grand entrance, and 2105 (in Areas B4, B5 and B8) on the SE side. Having been severely truncated during previous excavations, they were exposed to a preserved height of only two or three courses of bricks on their external SW faces, though the massive area occupied by each of the mud-brick structures (as recorded on Fig. 139) indicated that they were tall and imposing installations. They were both found with their short sides running along the temenos wall's SW façade. Tower 3060 was exposed over an area measuring 6.9 m ×

5.53 m, though its W corner lay beyond the limits of B4. A facing wall (3102), with a thickness of 1.6 m, was built all the way across tower 3060's SE side as part of the Isin-Larsa renovations. Tower 2105 was preserved over an area measuring 7.35 m × 5.51 m, and like its NW counterpart it had also been subsequently reinforced in the Isin-Larsa period, in this case with wall 2165 (mirroring wall 3102), which was built against its NW face. The addition of the two reinforcing walls meant that the outer entrance of the gateway was significantly narrowed to about 3 m.

The towers were both fitted with generously sized foundation boxes at all four corners. For the most part, the boxes had either had their contents stolen (2110 and 2123) or been completely dismantled in antiquity (as evidenced by robber pits 2130 and 2101 at the N corner of tower 2105 and the E corner of tower 3060, respectively). Some were probably emptied, damaged or destroyed when the New Eninnu was excavated in Hellenistic times, while others were probably affected quite soon after the sanctuary was decommissioned and subsequently abandoned in the Old Babylonian period. Fortunately, box 2092 had survived more or less intact. Located in the E corner of tower 2105, and set within the tower's mudbrick fabric, where its top surface was found at a topographical height of 16.5 m, box 2092 had been partially opened in antiquity. Its copper figurine (presumably a kneeling figure with a horned tiara holding an oversized foundation nail) was missing, but it still contained, *in situ*, the second conventional component of a Gudea foundation deposit: a stone tablet bearing Gudea's Standard Inscription. The box was not square but rectangular, with its long axis aligned north-east–south-west. It was made of square bricks (with dimensions of 0.35 m × 0.35 m × 0.065 m) and half-bricks that formed a container with sides measuring three bricks long by two and a half bricks wide. The central cavity was one brick long by half a brick wide. Built on a brick base, it rose to a height of eight courses, and the top was closed with a pair of enlarged capping bricks. Since the box had been opened and robbed, only one of the two capping bricks was found (TG1534, which measured 503 mm × 496 mm), but both had been laid on a bitumen-soaked reed mat, which was used instead of mud mortar to bond them to the topmost course of bricks. The capping bricks were marked with Gudea's Standard Inscription, and the text was placed face down (Fig. 188). Inside the box, the inscribed tablet (TG1501) was a squarish rectangle made of beige to white limestone, with sides of

FIGURE 188. One of the oversized fired bricks that formed the cover of the foundation box (2092) installed in the E corner of the tower on the SE side of the SW gateway that gave access to Gudea's New Eninnu.

FIGURE 189. The stone foundation tablet (TG1501) seen *in situ* inside the rectangular foundation box (2092).

85 mm × 94 mm (Fig. 189). The cuneiform text was found on its smooth upper face, divided into two columns with a single vertical line. Six rows of cuneiform signs were placed on the left, and four on the right. The tablet was very slightly planoconvex, with a shallow convex reverse that was not as smooth as the inscribed obverse. Traces of bitumen showing the imprint of a reed mat were found adhering to the top left corner of the tablet's reverse, suggesting that it had been fixed or glued to the bottom of the box, such that the cuneiform signs were oriented towards the north-east, facing the cult podium of Ningirsu in the temple cella. Significantly, therefore, the tablet was not neatly placed in line with the sides of the box, but slightly and deliberately misaligned so that the inscribed text pointed towards the podium in the cella.

The NE Temenos Gate and the NE Temenos Wall

The excavations in Areas B6 and B9 uncovered extensive remnants of Gudea's NE temenos wall, which was also pierced by a towered gateway that gave access to the sanctuary's central court (in Area B1). Considerable disruptions were caused in this part of the complex by Hellenistic pits, French excavation trenches and consequent water damage, while the archaeology was also badly affected by a broad horizon of post-Gulf War looting holes. Despite that, and although they were often poorly preserved, several structural elements were identified in the NE part of the New Eninnu, where sufficient remains were exposed to enable a reconstruction of the sequence of building phases. To begin with, a large foundation for the thick mud-brick precinct wall (5234) was constructed. It adjoined the NW face of the late Early Dynastic IIIb platform (5235 in Area B9) that was made of planoconvex mud-bricks, such that the new foundation formed a clear edge that marked the NW side of the narrow entrance of Gudea's Lagash II gateway. From there, it extended north-westwards, beyond the limits of Area B9, where it seemingly established a NW–SE edge that could perhaps have formed the inner SW side of the NE temenos wall. The foundation was composed of artificial boulders formed of subspherical masses of clay that were laid down as a bulk fill to create the foundation for the upper part of the wall, which was built of square mud-bricks. Unfortunately, the wall itself had entirely disappeared, either because it was dismantled during the previous excavations or because it was subsequently destroyed by erosion. One possible clue as to its fate was the fact that, in Area B9, it was generally observed that the upper surfaces of all the walls sloped downwards from the north-east to the south-west (just as the top surfaces of the walls in Area B3 sloped down from the south-west to the north-east). The slope provided clear evidence of the activities of the earlier excavators.

A disturbed pit (5243) was encountered in the area of the inner entrance of the NE temenos gate. Measuring 1.65 m × 1.6 m (along its NE–SW and NW–SE axes, respectively), the pit was 0.45 m deep, and its fill (5242) contained several sun-dried clay spheres or balls (both partial and complete), together with Early Dynastic IIIb and Akkad potsherds. It was difficult to determine the function of pit 5243, which appeared to have been interfered with and backfilled after it was first excavated, perhaps in order to remove objects that had originally been placed in it, and its location suggested that it might have been dug to contain a foundation deposit of some kind. No signs of a box of either fired bricks or mud-bricks were found, but the fact that the pit had subsequently been disturbed made the observation inconclusive.

The enclosure's superstructure (5223) was encountered a short distance to the south-east, beyond the gateway, at a topographical height of 15.37 m. Since the erosion in this area was less severe, the wall had survived to a height of about 0.7 m, made up of as many as ten courses. The mud-bricks formed the SE side of a partly preserved, wider outer passageway, which was bounded on its SE side by the remains of a tower (5245) that had been extensively levelled and covered with a later retaining structure (5222). On stratigraphic grounds, combined with the ceramic evidence, the retaining structure was identified as the terrace platform that supported the Hellenistic complex. Fronting a narrower entrance, the open-air passageway mirrored its counterpart in Areas B4 and B5 in the SW temenos wall on the other side of the L-shaped complex. It was traced over a length of 6.3 m

from the north-east to the south-west, extending beyond the limits of Area B9 to the north-east.

As suggested by the evidence found in the towers on the SW side of the complex, two foundation boxes would normally have been placed at the intersections between the enclosure wall (5223) and the projecting tower (5245): one at the tower's S corner, and the other at its W corner. In fact, the truncated remains of just one box (5203) were found at the tower's W corner, at an overall elevation of 16.6 m, and they consisted only of the base and one course of the box's walls. It is highly likely, however, that the second box had been looted, as was attested by a subrectangular pit (5211) that was found next to the tower's S corner. Box 5203, which was square (with sides of 1.1 m) was made of square fired bricks (measuring 0.36 m × 0.36 m × 0.06 m). It was found empty, its contents having been removed either in antiquity or by the French excavators. Its SE counterpart had probably been removed in Hellenistic times, when dense pitting was carried out in the area, perhaps immediately prior to the construction of the revived complex.

From Area B9, the excavated part of the temenos wall (5223) extended south-eastwards into Area B6 (contexts 5002 and 5237), spanning a total exposed length of 11.8 m. Its preserved width was 4.48 m, including foundation footings, and its NE façade was enclosed within Adadnadinakhe's substructural platform (5222). Constructed with distinctive, very hard light pinkish-orange to light reddish-brown mud-bricks (measuring 0.36 m × 0.36 m × 0.07 m on average), which contained a very high proportion of chaff inclusions, the SE edge of wall 5223 had been completely truncated by substantial French trenching. Despite that, it seemed reasonable to assume that the NW enclosure of the New Eninnu's outer walls probably turned abruptly through ninety degrees to the northeast in B6 in order to incorporate the older temple platform that was built by Ur-Bau. This was indicated by traces of later structures dating to the Ur III or Isin-Larsa periods (5042, 5043 and 5044) that seemingly abutted onto the damaged original face of a Lagash II structure that ran north-eastwards. Wall 5223's SW façade (5237), which was seemingly rebuilt in sandy green bricks in Isin-Larsa times, had also been damaged by French trenching that extended across and probably into the renovated face. The excavations had removed any signs of a visible connection between wall 5223 and other structures in the temple complex, notably the relationship between wall 5223 and the inner NW inner wall (2001) in Area B2.

CHAPTER 35

The Historical Significance of the New Eninnu from Lagash II Times to the Old Babylonian Period

The New Eninnu from Gudea to Nammahni

From the time of the rediscovery of Girsu by Sarzec and his successors it has regularly been assumed that the magnificent sanctuary built by Gudea in honour of Ningirsu was a short-lived marvel. Part of the reason for this is that the renown of the complex is so closely bound up with the reign of its architect, Gudea (Fig. 190), who left his mark on every detail of its conception and construction in the plethora of archaeological finds that have come to light since Sarzec made his first tour of Tell A in 1877. The spectacular Cylinders of Gudea, the Gudea Steles and the Tell A diorite statues are accompanied by a great wealth of more unassuming, but cumulatively impressive survivals, including countless Gudea bricks, many clay cones and numerous other fixtures and fittings, all of which reinforce the message that is proclaimed explicitly in thousands of cuneiform inscriptions that range from the repeated formulae stamped on mass-produced objects to the sublime poetry of the Cylinder Inscriptions—the immense and splendid New Eninnu was Gudea's personal achievement. It came into being thanks to his exceptional intelligence, his special closeness to the gods and his unbending determination to turn the dream vision that was vouchsafed to him by Ningirsu into a reality. The lasting effect of Gudea's seemingly hitherto unprecedented public information campaign was to establish an umbilical link between the ruler and his masterwork that has made it extremely difficult for researchers to detach the history of the shrine from the life and reign of its creator. In consequence, it has remained all too easy for archaeologists and historians

of Girsu to assume that the New Eninnu somehow died along with Gudea—that its splendour faded almost immediately when the link between the sacred complex and the ruler who built it was severed by his death.

The inference is contradicted by the archaeological evidence, and it also clashes with a key theme in many of the Gudea texts, especially those found on the Tell A statues, which threaten the direst punishments for later rulers or other rash individuals who might dare to wreck or dishonour Gudea's legacy. Implicit in the command that his statues must not be moved, or that the offerings made to them must not be revoked, is the idea that the New Eninnu in which they were housed would survive forever. In reality, and notwithstanding the fact that they were expressed in standard formulae, Gudea's statements about the imperishability of both his sacred complex and his reputation were impossible illusions, but in a Sumerian setting his aspirations and curses were charged with a religious aura that was doubtless reinforced by his prestige and the inherent grandeur and monumentality of the architecture, which was executed in a style and on a scale that was unquestionably intended to endure. The prominent buttresses and towers of the massive temenos wall (built with nearly a million bricks, as is explained in Chapter 42) must surely have announced unequivocally to all who saw them that Gudea's accomplishment was not only durable but insurmountable—the ne plus ultra of human achievement. Aptly, therefore, the fact that the New Eninnu was not only intended to be a lasting institution but that it was actually kept in service for a considerable period after Gudea's reign is attested by a number of texts inscribed in the names

FIGURE 190. Reconstruction of a cylinder seal belonging to Gudea, showing the ruler, preceded by Ningishzida, his personal god, as he is led into the presence of Enki (enthroned on the right). Musée du Louvre AO3541.

of his successors from the Second Dynasty of Lagash and the Third Dynasty of Ur. Though they record the continued existence of the sacred complex in Girsu, sometimes making mention of refurbishment schemes, the ineradicable bond between the New Eninnu and Gudea has led scholars to conceive of the inscriptions as mere epiphenomena, reflecting the perhaps understandable desire of later rulers to associate themselves, their periods in office and their building projects with the charismatic and idealised figure of Gudea—the ruler whose life and reign were enveloped in the aura of perpetual prayer that was the foundation of his celebrated exploits.

Gudea's special identity as an architect king (*roi-bâtisseur*, as the French pioneers called him), which was enthusiastically acknowledged immediately after his death, became a source of great pride for his successors, including his son, Ur-Ningirsu II (*c*.2100–2095 BCE), whose short reign seems to have been discharged in the shadow of his celebrated predecessor's pre-eminence. One sign of this is the fact that Ur-Ningirsu retained Gudea's personal god, Ningishzida, as his own. Most notably, his inscribed royal titles declare his filial relationship with Gudea, but they also refer to Gudea, using Gudea's own formula, as the builder of the Eninnu: 'he by whom the Eninnu of Ningirsu was built' (BM90845; RIME 3.1.1.8.1). Ur-Ningirsu's royal inscriptions, which deal exclusively with his religious activities, are mostly records of votive offerings, among which is an alabaster statue of himself that he dedicated to Ningishzida (AO9504 and MMA47.100.86, for the body and the head, respectively; and RIME 3.1.1.8.6 for the inscription), and at least two other statuettes (one made of diorite) that were both created in honour of the same god.

Ur-Ningirsu did not entirely neglect the building activities that preoccupied his father, but his projects were inevitably carried out on a much-reduced scale. Inscriptions found on two pieces of round bricks (AO11947 and AO26693) state that he enlarged the Temple of Nanshe so that it abutted onto the city gate of Girsu (RIME 3.1.1.8.3). Of potentially greater significance is the text found on a number of inscribed bricks that speaks of the giguna that Ur-Ningirsu built for the state's patron deity (RIME 3.1.1.8.2): 'For Ningirsu, mighty warrior of Enlil, his lord, Ur-Ningirsu, ruler of Lagash, son of Gudea, ruler of Lagash, who built Ningirsu's Eninnu, built his beloved giguna, amidst the scent of cedars'.

Although the enigmatic word giguna is of exceptional interest in the history of the successive shrines that were created for Ningirsu, its use here surely does not imply that Ur-Ningirsu undertook the restoration of the uppermost terrace that had so recently been completed by his father. None of the Girsu bricks on which the text was inscribed or stamped were excavated in the vicinity of the Mound of the Palace. On the contrary, they were all part of a large-scale renovation of the acclaimed Girsu bridge (excavated by Genouillac in 1929 and then by Parrot between 1930 and 1933) that was carried out in Isin-Larsa times, and all therefore originated in a tertiary archaeological context. The probable conclusion is that the bricks, which might never have been used for the project described in the inscription, were repurposed, possibly because Ur-Ningirsu died before his intended programme of works had even begun or perhaps before it was completed. These hypotheses can never finally be proved, but in either case it is plausible to think that Ur-Ningirsu's plans were abandoned, and the already commissioned bricks were stored or otherwise disposed of until they resurfaced in the Isin-Larsa period. Similarly, it is extremely difficult to determine exactly what kind of project Ur-Ningirsu had in mind: was it a comprehensive overhaul of the complex or a much more modest makeover of some restricted area? Coming so soon after Gudea's death, the former is highly improbable (and no archaeological evidence would support the idea), and it should again be stressed that the word giguna has a wide range of possible connotations. It might have been introduced as a way of referring to the terrace platform on which the complex was built. Alternatively, it could perhaps in this particular instance have been used to denote the sacred grove that was presumably planted in the vicinity of the sanctuary walls in the environs of Tell A.

The Lagash II rulers who came after Ur-Ningirsu left little or no mark on the history of Girsu, and if that is because they were outshone by the lasting radiance of Gudea—a kind of Sumerian sun king—it is all the more reason to suppose that his New Eninnu remained fully operational and in good repair. Incidentally, if that was indeed the situation, it would add further force to the likely surmise that the giguna building work planned by Ur-Ningirsu was a walled grove or garden that needed some refurbishment (and perhaps replanting) rather than a wholesale reconstruction project. The other dominant strand in the history of post-Gudea Lagash that might have eclipsed the endeavours of Gudea's successors was the rise of the powerful Third Dynasty of Ur, which gradually established far-reaching military and bureaucratic dominion over Mesopotamia and some foreign regions, eventually taking control of Girsu in the reign of Nammahni. It was conceivably due to a combination of these factors that the local ensis who ruled the state of Lagash after Ur-Ningirsu II appear to have been modest figures on the political scene. The only noteworthy information concerning Ur-Ningirsu's three immediate successors—UrGAR, Urabba and Urmama—is that they continued to receive funerary offerings in Ur III times, while the most salient fact about Nammahni, who left a number of inscriptions in Girsu, is that, as mentioned in the so-called Urnamma law code, he was probably appointed to the governorship of Girsu by the king of Ur, after Ur achieved hegemony.

Nothing is known about the origins of UrGAR, Ur-Ningirsu's immediate successor, because no explicit filiation is recorded in the very few inscriptions that can be dated to his reign, none of which can be directly attributed to UrGAR personally. His kingship is attested only by votive inscriptions that were dedicated on his behalf by third parties. The documents intimate that UrGAR might have had familial ties with other Lagash II rulers, while one text (RIME 3.1.1.9.1) mentions that he was married to a certain Ninkagina, but whether this was the woman named in later records as the mother of Nammahni is unclear. The reference, which occurs on a mace head that was dedicated to Shulshaga by Ninkagina on behalf of UrGAR, mentions that Ninkagina was the wife of UrGAR and the daughter of a somewhat obscure figure named Kaku, who might have been the predecessor of Ur-Bau (see RIME 3.1.1.3–5), though the lacuna in the text makes Kaku's name extremely difficult to decipher. To complicate matters further, another votive inscription (RIME 3.1.1.9.2), which was apparently dedicated to an unknown deity by an unnamed daughter of Ur-Bau for the sake of UrGAR, might suggest that UrGAR was another of Ur-Bau's sons-in-law. The text is fraught with difficulties, however. It was seemingly found on a fragment of a lost stone figurine of a woman that is known only from an unpublished photo taken by Sarzec. Its existence is recorded by Heuzey (Sarzec and Heuzey 1912, pp. 348–9), who also provides a sketch of the piece, including the cuneiform characters, but the object itself is unfortunately missing.

Urabba and Urmama, the two rulers who are presumed to have followed UrGAR, appear in the famous Ur III list of offerings that is inscribed on the Maeda Tablet (named after the scholar who deciphered it), which is a key text for the reconstruction of the Lagash II dynasty (see Chapter 3). Otherwise, no inscriptions survive from the time of Urabba, apart from the name of his first regnal year (RIME 3.1.1.10), which is noted on a poorly preserved administrative tablet (ITT 4 7573). Urmama's first year name is also recorded on a fragmentary official document (AO3306, RTC 184), but further evidence of his kingship appears in a few words from a text inscribed on an onyx bowl from Girsu (AO3284) that was seemingly dedicated to the goddess Ninmarki on behalf of 'Urmama, ruler of Lagash' (RIME 3.1.1.11.1).

Much more evidence exists about the reign of Nammahni (c.2090–2085 BCE), who was the last in the sequence of Lagash II rulers, and it was during his reign that Lagash went from being a sovereign city-state to a vassal province under the control of the kings of Ur III. Married to Ur-Bau's daughter Ninhedu, Nammahni was, like Gudea, a son-in-law of that influential leader. This seems at first glance to suggest that he was of the same generation as Gudea, who had ascended the throne more than thirty years earlier, and it leads to the further inference that, on account of Nammahni's presumably rather advanced age, the reigns of UrGAR, Urabba and Urmama must have been very short. While the latter assumption seems in any case highly likely, the situation regarding the relative ages of Gudea and Nammahni is complicated by the possibility that they, along with some of the other Lagash II rulers, probably including Ur-Bau, were born and brought up in the temple, which might have been the source of an alternative order of succession that was distinct from that based on bloodlines (see Chapter 34). As previously noted, a votive inscription that records a dedication on Nammahni's behalf identifies him as the son of a woman named Ninkagina (RIME 3.1.1.12.6), but whether she was the wife of

UrGAR and the daughter of the earlier Lagash II ruler Kaku is unclear. The text (RIME 3.1.1.9.1), which was found on a stone figurine, records the dedication of the statuette to Bau (see Marchesi 2011, p. 158; and Sallaberger et al. 2015, p. 31). Even if it could be established that the two Ninkaginas were one and the same person, and that Nammahni was her son, however, it would not resolve the vexed question of Nammahni's filiation because no further evidence exists to confirm a blood relationship between him and UrGAR. Nor would it clarify whether Ninkagina was the daughter of Kaku, the postulated pre-Ur-Bau ruler of Lagash.

With particular regard to the sacred architecture of Girsu, and especially Gudea's New Eninnu, the obscurity that prevails in the historical record after the death of Ur-Ningirsu II is somewhat dispelled with the accession of Nammahni, who left a number of inscriptions that refer to building works that were almost certainly undertaken on and around Tell A. First, a door socket of dark grey stone (AO101) carries a dedication to Bau (RIME 3.1.1.12.1): 'For Bau, the beautiful woman, daughter of An, the lady of the Shining City, his lady, Nammahni, ruler of Lagash, her mighty steward, turned (this stone) into a door-socket'. The provenance of the piece is unfortunately unknown, but the text leaves little doubt that the socket was installed in Bau's temple in the Eninnu complex. Furthermore, if the Bau socket was an isolated survival then it might be presumed that the works carried out on the temple were limited in scale, but this is a matter of conjecture.

More remarkably, at least two bricks inscribed in the name of Nammahni also mention the giguna of Ningirsu (BM123338 and AO26690). The most notable find (BM123338) was excavated far from Girsu in the region of Ur, probably in the vicinity of modern Diqdiqqa, though its archaeological context is sadly unknown. With the exception of the changed name of the ruler, however, its text is exactly the same as the Gudea inscription (RIME 3.1.1.7.45) that was found on a stone threshold associated with the stairway that gave access to the sacred summit of Tell A in the area of the Gudea Steles between Tells A and B (RIME 3.1.1.12.2): 'For Ningirsu, Enlil's mighty warrior, his master, Nammahni, ruler of Lagash, built his Eninnu, the White Thunderbird. Therein he caused to be planted (built) his giguna beloved grove(?), (in) the scent of cedars.' The translation of the important word giguna as 'grove' is again open to question, while the fact that another of its potential meanings is temple terrace (as mentioned above) might suggest a link with the massive substructural

platform that was fitted with stone stairs by Gudea. Furthermore, since the inscription on the brick is intact, this might be the best way to account for the clearly erroneous announcement that Nammahni built Gudea's Eninnu, which was indubitably not the case. Alternatively, if the word giguna is taken to refer to a grove or garden in the sacred precinct then the interesting possibility arises that Nammahni's work might have had something to do with Ur-Ningirsu II's probably aborted refurbishment of the giguna that was discussed above. It is conceivable that Nammahni undertook a programme of work that was planned by Ur-Ningirsu, but either left unstarted or not finished by him, and this might have related to the refurbishment or rebuilding of the walls of an enclosed sacred garden, or to its replanting—both meanings potentially being conveyed by the Sumerian term giguna. The matter is, of course, fraught with uncertainty.

The inscriptions on many other votive objects dedicated to the gods of Lagash by members of the court and the royal household entreat the deities to preserve Nammahni's life. The artefacts and texts combine to indicate that the cult and court were flourishing institutions in Nammahni's reign. For example, his wife, Ninhedu, the daughter of Ur-Bau, commissioned a round slab of speckled alabaster (EŞEM481) with an inscription (RIME 3.1.1.12.5) that reads: 'To Ningirsu, Enlil's mighty warrior, Ninhedu, daughter of Ur-Bau, ruler of Lagash, his (Nammahni's) wife, dedicated (this object) for the life of Nammahni, ruler of Lagash, and (also) for her (own) life'. Similarly, a statuette dedicated to Bau by Nammahni's mother, Ninkagina (RIME 3.1.1.12.6), was inscribed with a text that reads:

> To Bau, the beautiful woman, daughter of An, lady of the Shining City, her lady, Ninkagina, dedicated (this object), a sacristy object, for the life of Nammahni, ruler of Lagash, (saying) 'When the protective spirit of Tarsirsir is about to enter the courtyard of Bau, this statuette here will turn to my lady there (whispering?) into her ear; let it say my prayer to her'.

A year name preserved for Nammahni's period in office suggests that he might have been installed as governor of Lagash by Urnamma, king of Ur, after Lagash lost its independence and became subject to Ur's hegemonic control: 'Year: Nammahni (became ruler), following . . .' (AO3309, RTC 187; see Sallaberger 2015, pp. 120–1). An older reading of some lines in the Urnamma Code (RIME 3.2.1.1.20) that was propounded in particular by Samuel Kramer (1954) was taken to imply that Nammahni was defeated in battle and killed by Urnamma, and the fact that Nammahni's name was perhaps deliberately erased from a number of his inscriptions seemed to lend the thesis further support—the name being presumably cancelled as an act of *damnatio memoriae* in the wake of Urnamma's victory (see, for example, RIME 3.1.1.12.7 and Edzard's introduction to Nammahni's inscriptions (1997, p. 194)). More recently, however, the relevant lines in the Urnamma Code have been interpreted quite differently, as an indication not that Urnamma fought and killed Nammahni, but that he chose him to take charge of what had by then become the province of Lagash in the region ruled by Ur: 'I had Nammahni to follow in the governorship of Lagash' (RIME 3.2.1.1.20; see Sallaberger 2015, p. 120). The idea of Nammahni's peaceful accession to power in the context of a reasonably respectful relationship between a weakened Lagash and the supreme power vested in the king of Ur would also help to account for the reverence later shown by Ur towards some of the late Lagash II rulers, notably Gudea. As is discussed in greater detail below, this took the form of a cult of ancestors, the worship of Gudea and the restoration of his Eninnu, together with the adoption by Ur of Girsu's calendar (for which see Widell 2004).

If Nammahni's name was indeed obliterated as an act of *damnatio memoriae*, but not by forces from Ur, that would leave open the question of when and why the erasure might have taken place. One tentative proposal is that it could have happened after the fall of the Third Dynasty of Ur, when the Girsu high priests who conceivably took control of Lagash in the hope of re-establishing it as an independent political entity (Lagash III, which is considered further below) perhaps attacked the name and legacy of Nammahni as the Lagash II ruler who had treacherously allowed the state to be absorbed by Ur. This might well have been regarded as a base betrayal of Ningirsu, but the general uncertainty surrounding this period in the history of Girsu makes it extremely difficult to advance the argument with confidence.

Gudea's Deification and Posthumous Influence

Paradoxically, despite the loss of its independence, Girsu achieved unprecedented eminence as a religious centre when it fell under the sway of the Third Dynasty of Ur from about 2102 to 1995 BCE. The twofold core of the new esteem enjoyed by Girsu were Gudea and his Eninnu, which held a special fascination for the kings of Ur. Regarding Gudea with reverence and devotion, the rulers of Ur elevated their charismatic forebear to the status of a divinity, turning the familiar pious images of him in the pose of a worshipper into the focus of a cult that venerated Gudea as a god. The lists of offerings previously mentioned bear witness to the high regard in which their illustrious Lagash II ancestor was held by the kings of Ur, but the addition of the divine determinative DINGIR ([d]) to Gudea's name in Ur III inscriptions (by contrast with texts from Gudea's own lifetime in which the sign of divinity is never bestowed upon him) seems to confirm his deification. The situation regarding the use of the determinative has been seen as inconstant, particularly with respect to the distinction between ancestor worship and actual deification, and a further possible contrast exists with the lifetime divinity accorded to Naram-Sin (see Sallaberger 1993; and Edzard 1997, p. 26). In the case of Gudea, however, his outstanding achievements—and perhaps also his character and the sense that he was exceptionally close to the gods during his lifetime—magnified his status beyond that of any comparable figures from the period. Accordingly, he appears in lists of deities alongside major gods and goddesses, including Inanna, and in the company of other deified rulers, notably Shulgi.

The posthumous veneration of Gudea attests to the special standing with which Lagash was endowed in the political structures that allowed Ur III to exercise and maintain its supremacy in the region. It also fits well with the suggestion that some Ur III high-ranking ministers (those occupying the second-highest office of state after that of king) might well have been chosen from prominent Girsu families (see Michalowski 2011, pp. 66–7). In any event, Gudea became a heroic figure in Lagash (see Sallaberger 1993, p. 94; and Fischer 1996, pp. 223–4). After he was deified, his name was incorporated as a theophoric element into personal names (as, for example, Ur-Bau and Ur-Ningirsu were partly named after deities), in the same way as the names of exalted Ur III kings were used. Similarly, priests were appointed to celebrate rites that were posthumously associated with him, just as members of the clergy were assigned to deified Ur III kings (gudu$_4$ and NIN.diĝir), and special Gudea cupbearers (sagi) are also attested for him (Fischer 1996, p. 224).

Lots of evidence from Girsu has survived relating to the offerings made in honour of deceased rulers in the Ur III cultic calendar (Sallaberger 1993, p. 277). After his death, in addition to his daily offerings, Gudea received extra gifts twice a month on moon holidays, and further donations were added almost every month as part of the annual cycle of festivals. His statue was reanimated annually, though it is not clear whether the ceremony was performed on one or more of his likenesses, and in late Ur III times his image was also taken out in procession to the fields during the festival known as ezem še.íl.la, or 'carrying the grain', which took place in the twelfth month (Sallaberger 1993, pp. 294–5), when the same ceremonies were performed in honour of the deceased governor Urlamma.

More specifically, during the reigns of Amar-Sin and Shu-Sin, Gudea's image was presented with offerings of beer and flour every new moon and full moon—the same gifts as were offered to Arad-Nanna's personal god, Shulpa'e, as well as to Urlamma and the deceased king Shulgi (Sallaberger 1993, p. 94). The donations are recorded as ki.a.nag offerings, with the word ki.a.nag denoting a place 'where water is drunk'. As argued in Chapter 38, this probably means that the presentation ceremonies took place in the antecella of the Ningirsu temple—a libation room that was equipped with a well, water tanks and a large display platform (see Chapter 34). During the reign of Shu-Sin, Gudea also received gifts of sheep during the feasts of ga.kú è.a, or 'bringing out the sucklings', which probably took place four times a year, namely in the first, fifth, ninth and eleventh months, when donations, presumably of young animals, were made to the city gates, the boathouse of Nigishzida's barge, Shulpa'e and again to Urlamma (Sallaberger 1993, p. 299). In early Ur III times further ki.a.nag offerings of sheep were provided for Gudea during the festival of the mourning of the mother goddess, Lisi, which took place in the third month, when Gudea was honoured alongside other deceased Lagash II rulers, together with two Lisi goddesses and his personal god, Ningishzida (Maeda 1988). In the early Ur III period, in company with other deceased Lagash II rulers, a number of deities, some articles of temple furniture, certain priests and Ninhedu (the living wife of Nammahni), Gudea received ki.a.nag offerings of butter in the sixth month, which was named after Dumuzi (Perlov 1980). Similarly, in the eighth month, during the reigns of Shulgi and Shu-Sin, he was honoured along with his wife by the priestess of Bau, presumably because the relevant festival (é.kas₄, meaning 'roadhouse', and referring to the hostelries that catered for the many messengers who were employed on state business) was a celebration of Bau's marriage to Ningirsu (Sallaberger 1993, pp. 290–1). Finally, together with two Lama deities and Dumuziabzu, Gudea's likeness was presented with beer in later Ur III times during the ú.šim festival of Bau (literally meaning the feast of 'greenery', and referring principally to the vegetation sprouting in the plains), which was celebrated in the eleventh month (Sallaberger 1993, p. 293).

The reason it was considered proper to make posthumous offerings to statues of Gudea, in company with the gods and other venerated figures, was because they were animated through the performance of mouth-opening rituals when they were sculpted, and such ceremonies could be repeated, especially on the images of posthumously deified individuals, in order to keep the artefacts spiritually alive. The preserved records confirm that Gudea's likeness was regularly reanimated, and that mouth-opening rites were celebrated annually in the third month during the reigns of Amar-Sin and Shu-Sin. The ceremony was probably connected with the lamentation procession that was held for Gudea's personal god, Ningishzida, in the same month (Sallaberger 1993, pp. 281–3). Though this seems inherently plausible because of the close connection between Ningishzida, on the one hand, and Gudea and his extended family on the other, it cannot finally be confirmed, but the yearly repetition of the ritual as a reawakening of the statue was perhaps also linked with Ningishzida's role as a protector of natural and agricultural cycles, in which context the god was seemingly regarded as a Dumuzi figure.

The relationship between the rituals performed on the Gudea statue (or statues) and the attested existence of such ceremonies in the first millennium BCE, when they were first described in detail in Akkadian texts, is noted in Chapter 37. The surviving inscriptions relate a series of actions that were carried out to breathe spiritual life into divine images and other sacred statues after they were created, and they culminated in two rituals that are conventionally referred to, using their Akkadian names, as *pīt pî* and *mīs pî*—the 'mouth-opening' and 'mouth-washing' sacraments, respectively. Called ka.du₈ in Sumerian, the mouth-opening rite is seemingly mentioned in the inscription on Gudea's Statue R, but the text is unfortunately damaged (see Selz 1997, p. 177). The ceremony is nevertheless referred to explicitly in Ur III texts,

FIGURE 191. Reconstruction of a cylinder seal belonging to Ur-Sharura, a servant of the deified Gudea; the impression, which shows Gudea enthroned on the right, was found on a tablet dating from the eighth regnal year of the Ur III king Shu-Sin.

FIGURE 192. Reconstruction of a cylinder seal belonging to Lu-Dumuzi, a cupbearer to the deified Gudea who is shown on the right, enthroned and holding a sceptre. The impression was found on a tablet dating from the reign of the Ur III king Shu-Sin.

in which context Gudea's name is prefixed with the divine determinative (ᵈ). As discussed in Chapter 37, the vivified statues were believed to be capable of mediating between the human and divine realms. This is made clear in the inscription on Gudea's Statue B, where the order to speak to Ningirsu is given by Gudea himself, who seems personally to have overseen the installation of the statues in the newly completed Eninnu (RIME 3.1.1.7.StB): 'Gudea "gives word" to the statue: "Statue, would you please tell my lord...".' There follows a short account of the steps taken by Gudea in order to purify the city prior to the construction of the temple complex, after which comes further confirmation of the ability of the likeness to communicate with Ningirsu: 'He installed the statue (in order) to convey messages'. The role of statues as intercessors is also explicit in the performative ceremonial name given to the carved likeness of a woman (described above) that was dedicated on Nammahni's behalf to the goddess Bau by Ninkagina (RIME 3.1.1.12.6).

The imagery on some seal impressions from the Ur III period provides further insights into the ways in which Gudea was venerated. One example is dedicated to Gudea as though he were the reigning king of Ur (Fig. 191), while another depicts him not only in a spot that was otherwise reserved for deities and Ur III kings, but also holding a sceptre (Fig. 192)—a distinction that was accorded to no other Sumerian ruler who did not belong to the Ur III line of succession (Suter 2012, p. 62). From shortly after the time of his death, Gudea was regarded with a reverence that outshone the esteem conferred upon other members of his dynasty.

In early Ur III times it is evidenced in the offerings he received, such that his image was presented with first-class butter made from cow's milk, while all the other Lagash II rulers were given a second-class product made of ewes' milk (Perlov 1980). By the late Ur III period, by which time Gudea had been deified, a personal $gudu_4$ priest took care of the rites associated only with his statue, while all the other Lagash II ancestors were collectively served by a sole functionary.

Gudea was almost certainly lauded in a number of later copies of the superb Ur III mythical and devotional composition, Lugale ('O king!'), which tells of Ningirsu's conquest of the mountainous regions at the ends of the earth, where he dramatically releases the life-giving waters from the ice in which they are trapped and (among other things) makes a variety of stones available to humankind. When the battle is well won, Ningirsu speaks to the different stones, enumerating their several uses, and when he addresses diorite ('you' in the following quotation) he seems to refer particularly to the famous diorite statues of Gudea that were installed in the New Eninnu: 'When a king who is establishing his renown for perpetuity has had its [the temple's] statues sculpted for all time, you shall be placed in the place of libations—and it shall suit you well in my temple Eninnu, the house full of grace'. Interestingly, as also indicated in the offerings lists, according to the text of Lugale the statues in question were displayed in the ki.a.nag—the place 'where water is drunk', previously identified as the temple's antecella. The fact that Gudea's name is not stated, and that his identity is invoked only through his masterwork, the Eninnu, together with the diorite statues that were found on Tell A, speaks volumes. It signals that the glory of Gudea's achievements was sufficient in and of itself for those who read or heard the poem to know that he was the subject of the allusion. It also places Gudea as one of a select cohort of sometimes semi-legendary deified heroes, all of whom belonged to an emerging Ur III roll-call of ancestral figures who had won eternal fame. Repeatedly copied by scribes from Sumerian times all the way down to the age of Hellenistic Babylonia, the poem was in all likelihood composed in Girsu, either in the Ur III or late Lagash II period (Jacobsen 1987, p. 234), as is attested by the archaisms found in the preserved texts, notably the rather wordy, rhetorical manner in which the god's martial prowess is described—a style that has been compared with that of the Gudea Cylinder Inscriptions (see Bottéro and Kramer 1989, p. 339). The sophistication of the composition points to the existence of a flourishing literary tradition, with an associated scribal school in Sumerian Girsu, while the fact of its long survival indicates the work's importance, presumably as an admired early classic, throughout Mesopotamian history.

Gudea's prominence in the cultic calendar in Ur III times, as well as the necessary and noteworthy periodic reanimation of his statues, leaves little doubt that his New Eninnu was in a flourishing state during the Ur III period, when it is also fair to presume that the most important of his statues continued to be housed in their allotted place in the temple's libation room or antecella. The assumption is in accord with Ningirsu's speech in Lugale, and, as is further detailed below, the Gudea likenesses continued to be preserved and worshipped in the subsequent Isin-Larsa and Old Babylonian periods.

The Later Governors of Lagash in Ur III Times

The history of Girsu in the post-Gudea period is further enriched by a wealth of royal, votive and administrative documentation that records the state's successive governors. Some are styled ensi Lagash, while others are referred to as ensi Girsu, and though the significance of the respective titles remains unclear, the texts provide some important insights into the way the province was administered under Ur III rule. As noted above, Nammahni was seemingly appointed to the governorship by Urnamma, who ruled Ur from 2102 to 2085 BCE. The kingship of Ur then passed to

Shulgi, who remained in office for almost fifty years, from 2084 to 2037 BCE, but surprisingly only one governor of Girsu is recorded for Shulgi's long reign. His name was Lugirizal, and evidence for his period of office is found in votive inscriptions, including the text on the stone disc that he dedicated to Ningirsu for the life of Shulgi. As described above, it was found on Tell K, in or around the walls of the building that was constructed on the mound by Gudea, probably as a memorial to commemorate the sequence of old temples that had stood on Tell K for nearly a thousand years before its removal to Tell A. Lugirizal is also attested on a series of seals that date to Shulgi's reign (see, for example, AO190; RIME 3.2.1.2.2010). Finally, he is mentioned on a stone tablet from Girsu (AO16650) that was dedicated to the goddess Inanna by Lugirizal's son Nammahnidug to commemorate the building of her temple in the city (RIME 3.2.1.2.2011). A new counterpart of this inscription was found by the British Museum team on a fragment of an unidentified ceramic object (TG39; Fig. 193), which was in all likelihood a ceramic vessel that was dedicated as an offering by a daughter of Lugirizal. The fragmentary text reads: 'For ... (epithet), his lady, for the life of Lugirizal, governor of Girsu, Geme- ... servant of ... Lugirizal, lady ... dedicated this ...'

It is of great significance that the first certainly attested large-scale restoration works were carried out on Gudea's Eninnu during the reign of Shulgi, who also constructed temples for Nanshe and Ninmar in Girsu. The works on the New Eninnu are commemorated in a royal inscription (RIME 3.2.1.2.11) that is repeated on copper canephors (figurines with baskets on their heads) and stone tablets from Girsu: 'For the god Ningirsu, mighty hero of the god Enlil, his lord, Shulgi, mighty man, king of Ur, king of the lands of Sumer and Akkad, built for him Eninnu, his beloved temple'. A variant of the text (RIME 3.2.1.2.12) was found on some clay cones that were unearthed on Tell A by the French pioneers, and one cone bearing the same inscription came to light on Tell A during the British Museum team's excavations. The cone text reads: 'For Ningirsu, mighty warrior of Enlil, his lord, Shulgi, mighty man, king of Ur, king of Sumer and Akkad, built his House for him'. Though none of the cones were found *in situ* in the brickwork of the complex, they are an important testament to the renovations that Shulgi carried out on Gudea's Eninnu, and they must indubitably have been inserted into the faces of repaired walls inside the complex (as is detailed further below). The foundation deposits

510   The Mound of the Palace

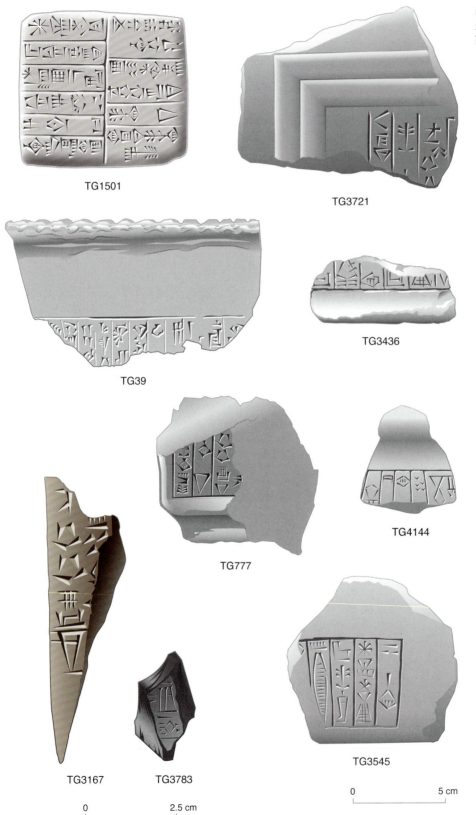

FIGURE 193. Inscribed fragments from Girsu unearthed by the British Museum team.

in the form of figurines with baskets of bricks on their heads (discussed in Chapter 44) were found in areas of the Urukug other than Tell A, but always associated in some way with the New Eninnu, and always alongside foundation deposits that were interred in the name of Gudea himself—most importantly, on Tell K, below the walls belonging to the Gudea memorial shrine to the former temple (see Chapter 21), and in a sector on the S and SE side of Tell A (for which see Chapter 44). The use of the inscribed cones and the meticulous fashioning and placement of the foundation deposits provide telling testimony of the extent to which Shulgi, the great king of Ur, wished to honour and even to imitate his illustrious forebear, Gudea, who by that time was considered to be a god. Shulgi followed Gudea by installing inscribed cones to commemorate his work on the Eninnu, as the Lagash II ruler had done when the complex was first constructed, and he also reaffirmed the timeless symbolic link between the New Eninnu on Tell A and the site of the age-old temple on Tell K by renovating the presumed cenotaph that Gudea had created after the temple was transferred from its ancestral home.

The particular devotion that Shulgi seems to have felt for Girsu is further attested by a rare object that was discovered by the British Museum team, but unfortunately on the surface of the ground and therefore in a tertiary archaeological context. This fragment of a clay vessel (TG41) is highly unusual in that it bears a stamped inscription naming it the 'Fruit jar of king Shulgi', and it is the duplicate of another stamped object that was excavated by Genouillac and is now in the Louvre (AO12227; RIME 3.2.1.2.46). The two ceramic sherds bearing the text are surely representative of a copious store of luxury goods considered fit for a king. The further interesting question that cannot currently be answered is whether the goods were kept in a building that stored products that were consumed by the king himself, or by his official representative, while one or both of them were resident in Girsu, or whether the items were sent by Shulgi as offerings to the gods of Girsu.

After Lugirizal, three governors held office in Lagash during the reign of the Ur III king Amar-Sin (2036–2028 BCE): Urlamma, who is varyingly styled ruler (ensí) of Lagash or Girsu, and Nannazishagal and Sharakam, who are always referred to as the governors of Girsu alone. The sequence of succession can be reconstructed on the basis of administrative documents found on seals and tablets that are marked with Amar-Sin's regnal years. Accordingly, Urlamma was

active from Amar-Sin 1 to Amar-Sin 4, while Nannazishagal's name appears on a tablet dated to Amar-Sin 4 (BM17824), and Sharakam is attested on two tablets (AO3455 and BM17801) dated to Amar-Sin 5 and Amar-Sin 6, respectively. Whether Sharakam remained in office until the end of Amar-Sin's reign or whether he was succeeded by an as yet unidentified governor is not known.

A further three governors are associated with the next king of Ur, Shu-Sin (2027–2019 BCE): Aradmu, who is styled ensi Girsu on a tablet dated to Shu-Sin's first year regnal year (1st L 6359), and his two successors, Alla and Arad-Nanna, who both bore the title ensi Lagash. Alla's name appears on two seals, one of which (S005786) is dated to Shu-Sin 3. Interestingly, Arad-Nanna is known from an informative votive inscription (RIME 3.2.1.4.13) that was found preserved on four door sockets from Girsu: AO3298 (A and B) and AO3298 (A and B), the whereabouts of which are currently unknown. They reveal that Shu-Sin had by that time been deified, since the texts dedicate the artefacts to him while commemorating the construction of a chapel or temple (é) that was sacred to him in his divine guise. The dedicatory inscription also lists the many offices that were held by Arad-Nanna. In addition to his post as governor of Lagash, the text records that he was also the state's chief minister (sukkalmah), the temple administrator (sanga) of Enki and the governor of Sabum, Hamazi and Karhar (on the office of sukkalmah see Sallaberger and Westenholz 1999, pp. 188–90). Arad-Nanna's rich array of titles indicates that he must have enjoyed a successful career in the higher echelons of the Ur III hierarchy, but also that he served under Shu-Sin's successor, Ibbi-Sin (2018–1995 BCE), the last king of Ur. This is proved by the circumstantial evidence contained in the door-socket inscriptions, which indubitably show that Shu-Sin had passed away by the time they were dedicated. The timeline is further confirmed by a votive inscription (RIME 3.2.1.5.2004) that was found on an agate eyestone that was dedicated to Bau for the life of Ibbi-Sin by Arad-Nanna's wife, Amanili (the object itself is unfortunately missing).

Some undated votive inscriptions attest to two more governors of Lagash about whom very little is known: a certain Ur-Ninmar is named in an inscription preserved on a mace head (DUROM 2264), while the name and title (ensi Lagash) of a governor called Ur-Ninsun are recorded on a tablet from Girsu (FAOS 9/2, Urninsun 1). More importantly, and on the assumption that it is the same person who

512   The Mound of the Palace

is referred to, Ur-Ninsun is mentioned on a votive stone disc dedicated to Ningirsu that was found on Tell K alongside two comparable objects (both mentioned above): the disc inscribed in the name of Ur-Bau's daughter Ninhedu for the life of her husband, Nammahni, and the one dedicated for the life of Shulgi by the governor Lugirizal. The text on the Ur-Ninmar artefact reads: 'For Ningirsu, mighty warrior of Enlil, his lord, Ur-Ninsun, governor of Lagash, for his life, dedicated this. The name of this disc is "O my lord, may my life be long."' The circumstances of the object's discovery on Tell K and the nature of the inscribed text mean it is possible that Ur-Ninsun held office (before or after Lugirizal) under Shulgi. This is all the more likely because, as previously noted, it is strange that the name of only one governor is preserved for the entirety of Shulgi's extremely long reign, while the object's find location on Tell K, close to a foundation box in the name of Shulgi, might further confirm the connection. Nonetheless, it should also be recalled that more than one Ur-Ninsun from Girsu bequeathed his name to posterity in the Ur III period, notably a son of Amar-Sin, so the identity of this particular Ur-Ninsun remains subject to doubt.

After the Third Dynasty of Ur: Lagash III or Isin-Larsa?

The weakening and eventual collapse of the hegemony enjoyed by the Third Dynasty of Ur took place in the reign of Ibbi-Sin (2018–1995 BCE), the last of the dynasty's rulers. The territory of Lagash may have been one of the earliest to liberate itself from Ur's power, perhaps in Ibbi-Sin's sixth regnal year (Sollberger 1980, p. 2), though an unpublished tablet (BM85129) suggests that the move might have come five years later in the eleventh year of his reign. Seeing an opportunity in the waning of Ur III, some leading figures conceivably tried to re-establish Lagash and the sacred city of Girsu as an independent state. The evidence for this is associated with a possible ruler or governor called Ur-Ningirsu, whose name appears in votive inscriptions spanning a period of some twenty to twenty-five years from the latter part of the reign of Shulgi (2030s BCE) through to the early years of Ibbi-Sin's reign (2010s BCE). For reasons that are not clear, Ur-Ningirsu is often given the further epithet or byname, Enmeziana—an appellation that would appear to suggest he was a type of priest. His inscriptions can be divided into two

groups: those that acknowledge the supremacy of the kings of Ur, and others that pointedly do not mention Ur. Among the first group are votive objects dedicated by Ur-Ningirsu on behalf of either Shulgi or Ibbi-Sin, notably: a statuette (HMA 9-16476) dedicated to Ninmarki for the life of Shulgi (RIME 3.2.1.2.2032); a model wig (BM91075) dedicated to Lamma for the life of Shulgi by Babaninam, Ur-Ningirsu's cupbearer (RIME 3.2.1.2.2030); and a statuette (VA8787) dedicated to Nindar for the life of Ibbi-Sin (RIME 3.2.1.5.2005). The inscriptions that are silent on the subject of Ur's supremacy include a brick (TG1370) found by the British Museum team (a duplicate of one found by Sarzec (AO26694)) that bears Ur-Ningirsu's name, epithet and priestly titles, but includes no reference whatsoever to the reigning king of Ur (RIME 3.2.2.1.1). In both types of inscription, Ur-Ningirsu is not named as the governor (ensí) of Lagash or Girsu, but rather as the priest (en) of Nanshe and the priest or minister (shennu) of Enki. Although he is not referred to as ensi, the absence of any mention of the overlordship of the kings of Ur in the brick inscription is highly significant because the commissioning of inscribed bricks was a ruler's prerogative (see Heimpel 1981, p. 103). It therefore tends to suggest that Lagash no longer acknowledged the authority of Ur, and that the state had gained its independence. That being the case, a further inference is that Ur-Ningirsu might have been a priestly ruler of the freed state, perhaps in the context of a hierocratic government. The idea is conceivably lent further credence by another votive inscription (RIME 3.2.2.2.1) that is preserved on a stone vessel (IM13829). The object was dedicated to Nanshe by a person named Ur-Bau for the life of an otherwise unknown figure called Ur-Nanshe, who, like Ur-Ningirsu, is styled the priest of both Nanshe and Enki (en and shennu, respectively). As with Ur-Ningirsu's brick inscription, even without the traditional title of governor (ensí), the dedication of a votive object for the life of this latter-day Ur-Nanshe, with no mention of a current king of Ur, suggests that Lagash could conceivably have become an independent power.

If Lagash did achieve some form of independence during the inferred reigns of the priestly rulers that are tentatively styled U-Ningirsu III and Ur-Nanshe II, no evidence of any other executive activities or additional information about the chronology of the epoch has survived. In any event, Lagash III, if it existed as a distinct political entity, must have been a short-lived interregnum between the demise of the centralised sovereignty of the Third Dynasty of Ur and the rise, first of Isin and then of Larsa as regional powers. Jointly giving their names to the Isin-Larsa period (*c.*1995–1750 BCE), the two dynasties successively gained ascendancy in the region, and each absorbed the state of Lagash into their governmental and administrative structures. Looking still further ahead in time, the very last chapter in the history of Lagash and Girsu is inextricably associated with Babylon, the third regional power that emerged after the fall of the Third Dynasty of Ur. At the end of the Isin-Larsa period the state of Lagash fell into the hands of Hammurabi of Babylon (1792–1750 BCE) until it was eventually abandoned during the reign of Hammurabi's son Samsuiluna (1741–1704 BCE), when the illustrious history of Sumerian Lagash and Girsu was finally brought to a close; in the second half of the eighteenth century BCE the historical record peters out.

The idea that Lagash achieved temporary independence after the collapse of Ur III is by no means certain, however, and a direct transition from Ur III to either Isin or Larsa governance is also credible. Very few records relating to Lagash and Girsu have survived from the Isin-Larsa and Old Babylonian periods—the total number of texts amounting to about 170. This limited corpus, which contains little historical information on the political situation in Girsu in the early second millennium BCE, is in stark contrast to the abundant wealth of documents that chart the history of the state of Lagash, with the sacred city of Girsu at its spiritual core, throughout the third millennium BCE. The later scarcity might well reflect the loss of the former great political and cultural power's first-order regional status, and this might be further confirmed by the nature of the later corpus, which reveals an important shift of emphasis. Whereas the earlier administrative texts were almost invariably associated with a centralised Lagash authority, the documents from the second millennium BCE, which are mostly contracts, receipts and letters between individuals, belong to the private sphere.

While these developments were being played out, the literary tradition of Girsu during the early part of the second millennium BCE remained in good health. The divergence of literary and political circumstances is indicative of a trend that can be observed in many parts of Mesopotamia, but two aspects of it especially reflect the situation of Girsu. On the one hand, the likelihood that literary texts were being composed in Girsu at this period would point to the existence of a continuous scribal tradition, while on the other, the enduring

renown of Girsu, Gudea and the New Eninnu is confirmed in literary compositions from around the region that celebrate and recall the city's former glories. If, therefore, in the context of a decline in the importance of the state of Lagash generally, Girsu forfeited its status as an economic and administrative hub, it seems at the same time to have retained its spiritual aura as a great cult centre. In addition to the political consequences of the rise and fall of successive political powers, the former trend was probably exacerbated by natural changes in the watercourses in the territory, combined with the problem of maintaining the extremely complex network of canals on which the cities of Girsu and Lagash depended. All of these factors were further compounded by the increase in salinisation that affected farmlands at this period.

Documents from the early second millennium BCE were found in Girsu in the early 1900s CE and again in the 1930s. The first group included eight administrative and epistolary texts, together with nineteen hymn fragments (Thureau-Dangin 1910, pp. 186–212), while sixteen documents in total were unearthed in the 1930s, three of which were explicitly dated to the reign of Rim-Sin of Larsa (Genouillac 1936, pp. 128–34). Another twenty-eight texts were published in the 1980s, including a handful from the Larsa period and the First Dynasty of Babylon (Arnaud 1981, pp. 70–4). With respect to the entire corpus of about 170 inscriptions, it is not always possible to say whether particular texts come from the Isin-Larsa or Old Babylonian periods, and the provenance and archaeological context of many of the documents is unclear.

Apart from the inscriptions relating to the two possible hierocratic rulers, Ur-Ningirsu III and Ur-Nanshe II, there is a hiatus in the preserved records from Girsu from the sixth regnal year of Ibbi-Sin (2013 BCE), the last Ur III king, through to the time of Ishme-Dagan of Isin, who reigned from 1947 to 1929 BCE (Sollberger 1980, p. 2), and Lipit-Ishtar (1928–1918 BCE), who succeeded him. Royal inscriptions that are thought to have originated in Girsu tentatively suggest that the city was under the control of Ishme-Dagan and then Lipit-Ishtar in the second half of the twentieth century BCE, and the fact that the kings of Isin ruled the southern part of Sumer during these years increases the likelihood that Isin supremacy extended into the region of Girsu. Problematically, however, the absence of a substantial and convincing body of evidence confirming the presence of the Isin rulers in Girsu and the territory of Lagash more widely makes it impossible to corroborate the assumption, particularly since the evidence that has survived is scant. An Ishme-Dagan royal inscription (RIME 4.1.4.5), which commemorates the construction of the great wall of Isin, was found on approximately fifty clay cones that were mostly unearthed in Isin, with the exception of one cone (now in a private collection) that is thought to have come from Girsu. Similarly, an inscription in the name of Lipit-Ishtar (RIME 4.1.5.3) was found on about a hundred clay cones from Isin, with just one cone probably coming from Girsu (ROM 991.207.001).

To complicate the picture still further, the third possibility is that Girsu, together with the province of Lagash as a whole, fell under the control not of Isin but of Larsa immediately after the fall of the Third Dynasty of Ur, during the reign of Naplanum, king of Larsa, who ruled from 2017 to 1997 BCE (Edzard 1997, pp. 64, 100–2). The Larsa thesis gains credence due to an increase in the amount of epigraphic evidence. Accordingly, whereas the surviving documentation for the decades between the end of the twenty-first century BCE and the middle of the twentieth century is sparse and inconclusive, inscriptions from the later part of the twentieth century BCE onwards provide a fuller impression. One of them is an inscribed dog figurine (AO4349) that was dedicated in Girsu to the goddess Ninisina by a certain Abbaduga for the life of Sumu-El (1887–1859 BCE), the king of Larsa (RIME 4.2.7.2001).

From about the same time, royal inscriptions in the names of two more kings of Larsa, Warad-Sin (1827–1815 BCE) and his long-reigning successor, Rim-Sin (1814–1755 BCE), make explicit mention of the city of Girsu and its renowned Eninnu. This is in stark contrast to the inscriptions of Ishme-Dagan and Lipit-Ishtar, in which Girsu and the Eninnu do not appear. In particular, in the Warad-Sin and Rim-Sin texts, Girsu and Lagash are said to form part of the territories ruled over and protected by the two kings of Larsa. Thus, a Warad-Sin inscription (RIME 4.2.13.14) styles the ruler as: 'Warad-Sin, prince, favourite of Nippur, provider of Ur, who looks after Girsu (and) the land of Lagash, who reverences the Ebabbar, king of Larsa, king of the land of Sumer and Akkad'. Two Rim-Sin inscriptions (RIME 4.2.14.6–11 and RIME 4.2.14.6.13) extol the king of Larsa in similar terms:

> Rim-Sin, prince who reverences Nippur provider of Ur, who looks after Girsu (and) the district of Lagash, who perfectly executes the mes and rites of Eridu, who

is in awe of Ebabbar, king of Larsa, king of the land of Sumer and Akkad, who renovated the temples of the gods, who perfectly executed the rites and great lustration ceremonies, who stands daily in supplication and entreaty.

Most notable of all is an inscription in the name of Warad-Sin (RIME 4.2.13.16) in which the ruler declares that he has kept up the programme of offerings for the Eninnu and has carried out restoration works in the cities of Lagash and Girsu:

> I, Warad-Sin, provider of the Ekur, shepherd who looks after the Ekishnugal, the one who reverences the shrine Ebabbar, who perfectly executes the mes and rites of Eridu, the one who abundantly makes offerings for the Eninnu, who restores Lagash and Girsu, I, who renovated the cities of the gods of their lands (and) put the gods Nanna and Utu in a good, peaceful residence, reverent prince who stands for his life at the house of his lord.

These clearly expressed references to Girsu and Lagash seem to confirm the ascendancy of Larsa over the former Ur III province, but the texts are relatively late, and it is difficult to know what bearing they might have on the earlier period, immediately after the fall of Ur, when the situation seems to have been fluctuating and uncertain.

The Ascendancy of Babylon and the Literary Afterlife of Girsu

Towards the middle of the eighteenth century BCE the kings of Babylon superseded the rulers of Isin and Larsa, taking control of the region of Sumer along with the rest of Mesopotamia. Historical sources that directly relate to Lagash or Girsu remain scant, though the twin cities and the Eninnu do appear in several literary compositions. In particular, the renowned Eninnu of Ningirsu is mentioned in a lexical list of temples and shrines, and in the prologue of the epoch-making law code of Hammurabi (1784–1742 BCE): 'I am Hammurabi, the wise one, the noble one, who allots pasturage and watering place for Lagash and Girsu, who provides plentiful food offerings for the Eninnu'. Some time later, a handful of administrative texts from Girsu are expressly dated to the reign of Hammurabi's successor, Samsuiluna (1741–1704 BCE). They include a tablet (AO21953) containing a rental contract that is dated to Samsuiluna's fourth regnal year, and another (AO21952) from the tenth year of his reign that contains records of a legal dispute. It is likely that Girsu came under Babylonian rule in Hammurabi's thirtieth regnal year, after he defeated Larsa and subsequently annexed the conquered territories. The city remained in the control of Babylon during the reign of Samsuiluna, but after that there are no further written documents whatsoever for a period of fifteen centuries until the Hellenistic period.

The discovery by the British Museum team of a particularly significant and rare fragment of a clay tablet (TG1639) containing a tabular account that dates to the Isin-Larsa period tantalisingly hints at the ongoing existence of a sophisticated bureaucracy in Girsu even after the region's decline in post-Ur III times. Despite that, the paucity of royal, administrative, legal and economic texts relating to the cultural and political history of Lagash and Girsu during the Isin-Larsa era and the Babylonian ascendancy contrasts with the number of attested literary works. As noted previously, they indicate that a rich scribal tradition continued to flourish in Girsu in the second millennium BCE. Most of the surviving texts, which are passages from hymns dedicated to the goddess Bau, are similar to contemporary works from Nippur (Thureau-Dangin 1910, p. 200). Their fragmentary nature has hindered attempts at commentary and interpretation, but it is noteworthy that one fragment (AO4332) contains a work in Sumerian and Akkadian that is one of the earliest examples of the bilingual texts that subsequently became increasingly common.

Perhaps the most significant survival is a highly sophisticated composition known as the Rulers of Lagash that is preserved on a clay tablet (BM23103) dating to the mid-Old Babylonian period (see Edzard 1983, pp. 84–5; and Glassner 2004, pp. 74–5, 147–9), the colophon of which provides clear evidence of the existence of a scribal centre (conventionally known as the 'house of tablets') in Girsu: 'Written in the house of tablets. Glory to Nisaba!' The text itself (ETCSL 2.1.2) was indubitably produced in response to the Sumerian King List, from which Lagash rulers are signally absent. Following the pattern established by certain iterations of its better-known counterpart, which survives in several versions, the Rulers of Lagash begins with a mythological prologue that narrates the slow revival of humankind after the

great flood. At first, there was no organised agriculture, and humans existed in a state of misery, but things improved markedly when Ningirsu invented agricultural tools and irrigation techniques, both of which were made available to humanity. The final part of the prologue is sadly missing, but it doubtless gave an account of the descent of kingship from heaven to earth—a decisive moment in the history of humankind. Thereafter, the main body of the text presents a sequential list of the kings of Lagash, and as in the Sumerian King List they are said to reign for long periods (often for many centuries). Most of the kings in the Rulers of Lagash are seemingly fictional, but some historical figures are listed, perhaps because their names were familiar from inscriptions and from the history of Girsu as it was transmitted locally from generation to generation. Dating back to Early Dynastic times, the verifiable rulers include Ur-Nanshe, Eanatum (or Anetum, as his name is written), who is wrongly identified as Ur-Nanshe's son, Enentarzi, Puzurmama (who reigned after the Akkad interval), followed by Ur-Ningirsu I, Ur-Bau and Gudea. Significantly, the historically attested kings are listed in correct chronological order, and the roster culminates with Gudea.

The Rulers of Lagash has been deemed fanciful or satirical, partly because of the introduction of otherwise unheard-of kings, but also on account of the unrealistic lengths of the reigns of many of them. As Sollberger (1967, p. 279) describes it, the composition is: 'a politico-satirical work written by a Lagash scribe in answer to the author(s) of the Sumerian King List who had ignored the rulers of Lagash'. A contrasting interpretation (Steinkeller 2017) is that the text is not satire but an example of inferior, wildly inaccurate historiography that was genuinely inspired by the Sumerian King List: 'a pathetic jumble of factual information haphazardly extracted from earlier materials which was expanded and embellished by the addition of various fictitious data'. According to this view, it is nothing more than 'bad history writing . . . a desperate and uninformed attempt to produce a local history out of deficient data'. Whether it was intended as satire or as an authentic history that was based on inadequate information, however, the Rulers of Lagash was indisputably the work of an educated writer who knew the Sumerian King List and was well able to imitate its structure and style. As Jacobsen (1973, p. 76) notes, the Lagash scribe even borrowed the first line of the postdiluvian section of the version of the Sumerian King List that is contained in a manuscript

(Ashm1923.444) produced in the eleventh regnal year of Sinmagir of Isin. Though the Rulers of Lagash was arguably meant in part as a retort to the Sumerian King List, therefore, the fact that it concludes with Gudea, whose reputation as a ruler of the highest piety and industry was widely acknowledged throughout the region in the Old Babylonian period, indicates that the composition was probably also intended as an apologia for the true virtues and blessings of kingship, as exemplified by perhaps the greatest king of all, Gudea.

During Isin-Larsa and Old Babylonian times, Girsu was slowly engulfed in historical obscurity, but the memory of its former glory was kept alive in Mesopotamia thanks to the ongoing renown of Gudea and his New Eninnu, which was extolled in inscriptions. An especially rare example from a private collection (MS 2814; CUSAS 17 22) is found in an Akkadian translation of an original Sumerian Hymn to Nanshe (Wilcke 2011). According to its syllabary and orthography, this bilingual version of the hymn can be dated to the reign of Rim-Sin, and it might have originated in Larsa, which was an active scribal centre at the time. Alternatively, with its focus on Ningirsu, Nanshe and Gudea, the text could have been produced in Girsu, though by the time of its composition the fame of Gudea had become a well-used literary trope. In any event, like other texts from the Larsa period that were inspired by Sumerian examples, it was doubtless an imitation of a Sumerian original that was written in Girsu during the Isin-Larsa period. Unfolding over five or six columns (faint traces of cuneiform characters can perhaps be made out in the possible sixth column on the reverse), the text is couched in the style of Lagash II royal inscriptions, and it employs patterns that, with some significant exceptions, are relatively familiar from the inscriptions found on the diorite Gudea statues from Tell A. It therefore exalts two of the main gods of Lagash (Nanshe and Ningirsu), celebrates a victory over Elam (a military theme that is generally absent from Gudea's inscriptions), records the building of the Ningirsu temple, mentions the sourcing of raw materials from Magan, Meluhha and Dilmun, and finally reports the installation of the statues of Gudea in the Eninnu. It has been suggested that the hymn was perhaps copied from an actual monumental inscription in the name of Gudea (Wilcke 2011), but this is highly unlikely. In addition to the mention of a successful armed conflict, which is uncharacteristic of genuine Gudea texts, the hymn is dedicated for the life of Shulgi of Ur, while Gudea is initially presented as the one 'who is enthroned in the Ekur' (the name for the temple of Enlil in Nippur)—all factors that strongly contradict the idea that work was reproduced from a Lagash II original.

The lines describing the introduction of Gudea's statues into the New Eninnu are of special interest: 'The diorite was destined for my statues. I (Gudea) formed the diorite for my statues. These statues, 537 of them, I brought to the Eninnu, inside the house of Ningirsu.' As discussed earlier, the placing of the Gudea statues in the temple is a narrative element that is found elsewhere, notably in Lugale, in the passage in which Ningirsu addresses the diorite that he has liberated from the cosmic mountain (quoted above). The introduction of the topos in the Hymn to Nanshe is further proof of the awe that Gudea's sublime achievement continued to inspire long after his death. The number of statues mentioned in the hymn must, of course, be dramatically exaggerated (537 compared to the preserved total of nine that were found on Tell A), but that very fact adds to the sense that Gudea was viewed by later generations, as indeed by his contemporaries, as a ruler of superhuman energy whose legacy and attainments far outstripped those of other Sumerian kings.

Gudea is also celebrated in a song (tigi) composed in honour of Bau (ETCSL 2.3.2 (Gudea A)) and in a superb hymn to Nanshe (ETCSL 4.14.1 (Nanshe A)), where he is associated with a figure named Ur-Nanshe, who has been identified as the celebrated Early Dynastic ruler. Though this might at first glance seem almost incredible, the possibility that Early Dynastic Ur-Nanshe is a prominent figure in the Rulers of Lagash perhaps indicates that he too had acquired a legendary status that lived on in the popular mind:

Lagash thrives in abundance in the presence of Nanshe. She chose the shennu in her holy heart and seated Ur-Nanshe, the beloved lord of Lagash, on the throne. She gave the lofty sceptre to the shepherd. She adorned Gudea with all her precious divine powers. The shepherd chosen by her in her holy heart, Gudea, the ruler of Lagash, placed the lyre (?) Cow-of-Abundance among the tigi drums and placed the holy balag drum at its side.

The Eninnu is mentioned in a number of other literary compositions that are known from mostly Old Babylonian manuscripts. In one of the Temple Hymns it is the centrepiece of an epic passage that is distinguished by its poetic grandeur (ETCSL 4.80.1):

O Eninnu, right hand of Lagash, foremost in Sumer, the Anzu bird which gazes upon the mountain, the sharur weapon of . . . Ningirsu . . . in all lands, the strength of battle, a terrifying storm which envelops men, giving the strength of battle to the Anuna, the great gods, brick building on whose holy mound destiny is determined, beautiful as the hills, your canal . . . your . . . blowing in opposition (?) at your gate facing towards Urukug, wine is poured into holy An's beautiful bowls set out in the open air.

Whatever enters you is unequalled, whatever leaves endures . . . terrifying façade, house of radiance, a place of reaching judgment which Lord Ningirsu has filled with great awesomeness and dread! All the Anuna gods attend your great drinking-bouts.

Your prince, a raging storm which destroys cities in hostile lands, your sovereign, a terrifying wild ox which will manifest its strength, a terrifying lion which smashes heads, the warrior who devises strategies in lordship and attains victory in kingship, the mighty one, the great warrior in battle, the lord without rival, the son of Enlil, Lord Ningirsu, has erected a house in your precinct, O Eninnu, and taken his seat upon your dais.

Gudea's Eninnu also provides a focal point for a song (adab) to Bau that was commissioned on behalf of Ishme-Dagan of Isin (ETCSL 2.5.4.02 (Ishme-Dagan B)):

Your own father, An, the highest god, clothed you in the ba garment. He gave you the warrior of Enlil, Ningirsu, as your husband. He bestowed on you the Eninnu and Urukug, the shrine which brought forth the seeds of mankind. He has set up your lofty throne-dais in Lagash, in Girsu the mooring post of the Land, in Egalgasud, your beloved residence, in Tarsirsir, the temple of ladyship; and now all the gods of the land of Lagash bow down before your august residence.

The few preserved historical sources suggest that, in the early second millennium BCE, Girsu did not share the fate of numerous other Sumerian cities over the centuries by being conquered and razed to the ground, but rather slowly faded

away. Girsu lived on in the development of a Gudea motif in the literature of the period, and its memory was kept alive in other, sometimes contradictory narratives. In the Lament for Nigru, for example, as in the Temple Hymns just quoted, the city (with the Eninnu as perhaps an unnamed but nonetheless significant presence) is presented as a stabilising force in the relationship between heaven and earth, and a favourite locus of the gods (ETCSL 2.2.4): 'An and Enlil have looked with their beneficent gaze on Lagash, the mooring-pole of heaven, and the shrine Girsu, established long ago'. By contrast, in the work known as Gilgamesh, Enkidu and the Netherworld, the 'son of Girsu', whoever that might be, is presented as a wrongdoer in a Dante-like passage from the version contained in the Ur manuscript (UET 6.58) that describes the fate of those who do not fare well in the afterlife, including one who did not respect the 'word' of his parents, another who did not receive 'funerary offerings', and someone else who 'lied to the gods while swearing an oath'. The main body of the text is structured as a series of questions that Gilgamesh poses to Enkidu, who has successfully descended into the underworld and returned unscathed:

Did you see the citizen of Girsu who refused (?) water
    to his father and his mother?
I saw him.
How does he fare?
In front of each of them are a thousand Martu, and his
    spirit can neither . . . nor . . . The Martu at the liba
    tion place at the entrance (?) to the nether world . . .

The well-known city laments (the very earliest of which, from the Early Dynastic period, is discussed in Chapter 20) give some idea of the fate that possibly befell Lagash and Girsu as a result of their being abandoned by the gods. Sometimes, as when Lagash is introduced in the Lament for Ur, the mere departure of the gods is considered sufficient to bring about the city's sorry end. Four thousand years after the piece was composed, the melancholy imagery that pervades the Lagash section of the Ur lament still retains a vivid poignancy (ETCSL 2.2.2): 'The mother of Lagash has abandoned it and has let the breezes haunt her sheepfold. Gatumdug has abandoned that house Lagash and has let the breezes haunt her sheepfold. The lady of Nigin has abandoned it and has let the breezes haunt her sheepfold.' In other examples, notably the Lament for Sumer and Ur, the divine repudiation of

Lagash is symbolised with the metaphor of a violent invasion (see Michalowski 1989), and the end of Girsu is described in terms of a hostile conquest, even though there is no historical or archaeological evidence to suggest that this actually happened. As is discussed further in Chapter 36 below, therefore, the descriptions probably reflect the ritual closing of the holy city (ETCSL 2.2.3):

> Girsu, the city of heroes, was afflicted with a lightning storm. Ningirsu took an unfamiliar path away from the Eninnu. Mother Bau wept bitter tears in her Eurukug. 'Alas, the destroyed city, my destroyed house', she cried bitterly. On that day the word of Enlil was an attacking storm. Who could fathom it? The word of Enlil was destruction on the right, was ... on the left. This is what Enlil, the one who determines destinies, did: Enlil brought down the Elamites, the enemy, from the highlands. Nanshe, the noble daughter, was settled outside the city. Fire approached Ninmarki in the shrine Guaba. Large boats were carrying off its silver and lapis lazuli. The lady, sacred Ninmarki, was despondent because of her perished goods. On that day he decreed a storm blazing like the mouth of a fire. The province of Lagash was handed over to Elam.

Contradictory Histories: Girsu in Literature and Archaeology

The abiding impression created by the later sources is that, from the beginning of the second millennium BCE, in the Isin-Larsa and subsequent Old Babylonian periods, the Eninnu of Gudea was no longer regarded principally as a material entity. Instead, its substantial presence was seemingly transformed into a phantasmal literary topos that, together with other Gudea-related motifs, expressively encapsulated some formative ideas that permeated the thinking of the period: the praise of a model ruler (Gudea); the importance of the magnificent temple (the New Eninnu) as the sign of a properly established, harmonious relationship between humanity and the gods; and the ineluctable

transience of human wishes and achievements as represented in the melancholy imagery of the destroyed city, especially Girsu, in the laments. The power of the literary transformation led to the belief that the Eninnu, the city of Girsu and indeed the state of Lagash in its entirety, entered into an inexorable spiral of decline sometime after the death of Gudea that accelerated greatly after the fall of the Third Dynasty of Ur. The force of the literary texts is undeniable, but the resulting historical assumptions, which view the fate of Girsu through a prism made up of metaphorical meanings, is incorrect. This is confirmed by the completely different picture of Girsu that is preserved in the archaeology, but further complicated by the huge discrepancy between the few inscriptions that have survived from the early second millennium BCE and the abundant wealth of material culture that has been unearthed. The consequent misreadings have unquestionably been compounded by the unparalleled quantity and quality of surviving texts from the Gudea era. The sheer number of inscriptions from Gudea's reign has cast a distorting shadow not only over the periods in office of the rulers who came after him, but also over the subsequent life of the New Eninnu. Simply put, Gudea's achievement was so surpassing that the reigns of the rulers who followed him seem by comparison to be marked by inactivity and decline.

The British Museum team's excavations shed new light on these neglected and misunderstood periods in the history of Girsu, illuminating the long lifespan of the New Eninnu all the way down to its decommissioning in the Old Babylonian period. For four hundred years after the death of Gudea the complex was maintained under successive regimes. Relatively minor, almost deferential repairs were carried out in the Ur III era, and from Lagash II times right through to the Old Babylonian period some floors were occasionally raised. In between, major renovations were undertaken in Isin-Larsa times. As is discussed in great detail in the following chapter, in the case of the New Eninnu the contradiction between the reality on (or under) the ground and the inscriptions provides an illuminating example of the way in which archaeology sometimes reveals a more granular and fascinatingly complex history than the one that is found in the surviving texts.

CHAPTER 36

The New Eninnu from Lagash II Times
to the Old Babylonian Period

The Stratigraphy of the Sanctuary

The Ningirsu Temple

Raised above the rest of the sanctuary at the SE end of the L-shaped complex, Gudea's Ningirsu temple was eventually truncated in Hellenistic times, in the late fourth century BCE, when Adadnadinakhe excavated the site in order to create his renewed shrine. As emerged during the British Museum team's work on Tell A, the Hellenistic levelling that affected large portions of the extended Gudea complex preserved much of the original architecture (repeatedly refurbished down to the Old Babylonian period) beneath the levelling horizon because the French explorers only engaged in very limited digging below that topographical height (Fig. 194). Consequently, French trenching 2080 and 3084, at the SE end of the complex in the vicinity of the Ningirsu temple, had hardly disturbed the temple's walls and fixtures. The team's new excavations in Areas B2, B3 and B5 revealed the mainly untouched Hellenistic levelling horizon at topographical elevations that extended from 15.51 m, where it covered the podium (2073) in the cella, down to 15.47 m, where it covered the offering table (3039) that was also in the cella. Still deeper, at a topographical height of 15.42 m, it sealed off parts of the temple's NE façade (2008 and 2017), as evidenced by a heap of fired-brick fragments (2016) that formed a component of the sealing layer.

Preserved subfloor packings (contexts 3010, 3012 and 3018) that were laid down as part of Gudea's original construction project were identified in Areas B2, B3 and B5, where they were found under the cella of the Ningirsu temple at topographical heights ranging between 15.19 m and 15.49 m. These infilling layers, which were composed of compacted sandy silt and clay, were placed on top of the cella's red foundation layer (2011 and 3024), and they abutted onto the lowermost parts of the sides of the offering table (3039) in B3 and the podium (2073) in B5.

The Gudea foundation layers below the cella floor were exposed under a series of later subfloor infillings that were judged to date from the Ur III and Isin-Larsa periods. In the cella's N corner, in Area B2, two overlying subfloor packings (2005 and 2015) were uncovered at maximum heights of 15.42 m and 15.5 m, respectively, beneath a shallow deposit of the backfill that was laid down by Adadnadinakhe. The same kind of packing was also found under Court A (on Sarzec's Plan A; Fig. 111). Contexts 2005 and 2015, which were composed of a homogeneous matrix of grey-brown clayey silt and compacted mud-brick debris with frequent flecks of white lime and specks of dark ash, contained a series of diagnostic potsherds dating to the Ur III period. Pieces of two cones inscribed in the name of Gudea with a New Eninnu text were found in context 2005: the head of one cone (TG192) and the end of another (TG103). A third cone fragment (TG193) from subfloor packing 2005 was inscribed in Gudea's name to commemorate the Emehushgalanki shrine (associated with the New Eninnu) that was built for Ningirsu's son Igalim. Subfloor packing 2015 yielded a noteworthy find in the form of a complete cuneiform-inscribed cone (TG136) in the name of Gudea and commemorating the New Eninnu.

520 The Mound of the Palace

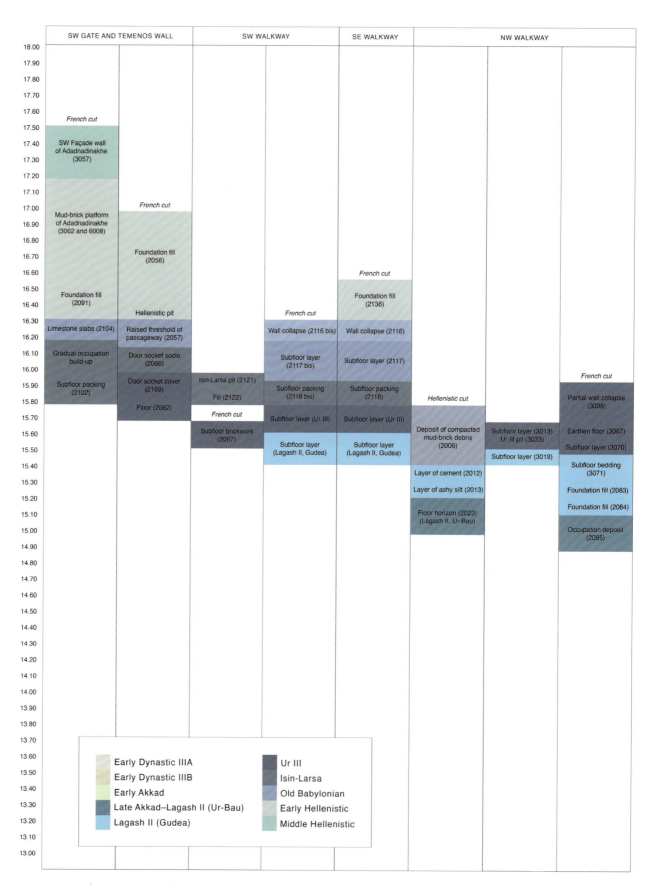

FIGURE 194. The Stratigraphy of Tell A from Early Dynastic times to the Hellenistic era.

NE WALKWAY (UR-BAU PLAZA)		TEMPLE CELLA	ANTECELLA	STAIRWELL	CENTRAL COURTYARD		NE GATE
					AREA B1	AREA B10	

NE WALKWAY (UR-BAU PLAZA)

French cut
- Fired-brick soakaway (2149)
- Degraded bricks (2150)
- Floor (2151)
- Substructural fill (2152)
- Subfloor packing (2153)
- Subfloor packing (2153)

Hellenistic cut
- Subfloor packing (2014)
- Foundation fill (2030)
- Akkad platform (2158)

TEMPLE CELLA

Hellenistic levelling
- Subfloors (2005, 2015)
- Subfloor packings (3010, 3012, 3018)
- Foundation layers (2011, 3024)
- Levelling deposits (3025, 3037, 3050)
- Flooring horizon (2050, 2055)
- Floors (3087, 3088)
- Subfloor packing (3086)

ANTECELLA

French cut
- Earthen floor (2034)
- Layers of gradual subfloor infilling
- Akkad platform (2158)

STAIRWELL

French cut
- Capping wall (2094)
- Blocking wall of passageway (2141)
- Redeposited burnt layer (2113)
- Raised threshold of passageway (2142)
- Substructural fill (2114)
- Substructural fill (2115)

CENTRAL COURTYARD — AREA B1

French cut
- Layer of *pisé* (1018, 1021)
- Layer of silty sand (1033)
- White platform (1036)

CENTRAL COURTYARD — AREA B10

French cut
- Fired-brick rubble (5414, 5426)
- Paving floor (5404)
- Foundation layers (5436, 5439)

French cut
- NW façade wall (5403)
- Precinct wall (5441, 5478, 5479, 5518)
- Burnt patches
- Layer of sand (5477)
- Deposit (5517)
- Layer of *pisé* (5505)

NE GATE

French cut
- Mud-brick platform of Adadnadinakhe (5222)
- NE temenos wall (5223, 5002, 5237)
- Grey platform (5235)

In Area B3, close to the doorway in the cella's E corner, the small box or compartment (3028) that was built to enclose Gudea's door socket was found to have been altered, probably in the Ur III period, when the original installation was replaced by a semi-circular structure made of broken bricks. Mostly bearing the regnal cartouche of Gudea, the fragments were laid with their dedicatory texts facing downwards, perhaps to express a sense of reverence towards the ruler, who by that date was deified. Box 3028, which was found levelled at a topographical height of 15.4 m, measured 0.9 m × 0.68 m. It was made of fragments of fired bricks (with dimensions ranging between 0.15 m × 0.22 m × 0.07 m and 0.25 m × 0.23 m × 0.08 m), some of which had been fired excessively, or perhaps deliberately refired, and then laid on bed in rough courses over a brick-paved floor. The highly symbolic restoration of the temple's holiest doorway was dated to the Ur III period, based on the stratigraphy in combination with a set of characteristic potsherds that were found in the backfilling of a regular semi-circular pit (3029) that had been cut into the Lagash II subfloor layer (3010). The evidence suggested that the restoration was probably carried out in the reign of Shulgi.

Pit 2046 was found in Area B5, in the S corner of the cella, close to the podium that supported the cult image. It was filled with lenses of ashy deposit and sandy silt that contained nodules of mud-brick material (2047). Measuring 4.14 m × 1.99 m × 0.3 m (deep), the pit was another archaeological vestige of the Hellenistic digging that was carried out in this part of the New Eninnu under Adadnadinakhe.

From the time of the publication of Sarzec and Heuzey's first interpretations of the archaeological remains that were found in this area, it has been generally assumed that the installations excavated in the antecella had subsequently been refurbished in the Ur III or Isin-Larsa period. The structures, as labelled on Sarzec's Plan A and also on Heuzey's New Plan (Fig. 114), included the shallow well M (context 2143 on Fig. 139), which is now assumed to have been a libation well, platform M (perhaps a low dais or ancillary altar) and basin L, which must presumably have been a receptacle for holy water. Originally constructed by Gudea, their remains were all found scattered across the anteroom (2077), and although well M in particular was re-exposed and re-evaluated during the salvage excavations, the team did not find enough evidence to establish a reliable chronology for

its post-Gudea history or its post-Lagash II fate more generally. This was principally due to the magnitude of the destructive French trenching (2036) that had affected this part of the complex.

In Areas B5 and B11, however, in the E corner of the antecella, close to the passageway that led into the stairwell, a locus of good archaeology had fortunately survived the French excavations, even though it had been obliquely truncated by a ramped SE–NW French trench and suffered further damage on account of the horizontal pitting (2036) that was mentioned above in connection with the well. The locale included a surface (2034) that was coated with an earthen mix of pale brownish-grey compact silty clay that was identified at a topographical height of 15.77 m over an area measuring 2.42 m × 1.62 m × 0.03 m (t). Lying over of a series of occupation layers, and abutting onto the NE face of display bench 2035 and temple walls 2140 and 2162, surface 2034 was found associated with a mud-brick construction (2033). Oriented on a NW–SE alignment, the structure, which was probably the remnant of a light partition wall, was built of a single row of square bricks (0.32 m × 0.32 m × 0.07 m) and presumably also half-bricks, though none were observed. It was preserved to a height of three courses over an exposed length of 1.52 m. Despite the scarcity of diagnostic potsherds in these contexts, the stratigraphy of this part of the site suggested that the surviving earthen floor (2034) and the associated screen-like partition wall (2033) dated from the Ur III period. Below these levels, the underlying Lagash II layers of gradual subfloor infilling, with a depth of about 0.17 m, sealed off the circular installation (2132) dating from the reign of Ur-Bau that was set into platform 2158. A single fragment of a cuneiform-inscribed cone (TG947) was found in context 2034. It was the head and part of the shaft of a cone containing Gudea's Standard Inscription.

Thankfully, the stairwell chamber in Areas B5 and B11, which was not disturbed by the French pioneers, was also preserved more or less intact, in spite of the large-scale Hellenistic digging and subsequent backfilling that was carried out under Adadnadinakhe, followed by the extensive looting that occurred after the Gulf War (signs of which were observed in context 2127). Renovation work was carried out in the stairwell in the Isin-Larsa period, when the ground level of the original entranceway in B11 was raised to a topographical height of 15.95 m, and a new brickwork floor (2142) was laid. Floor 2142 was made of recycled fired bricks (measuring 0.31 m × 0.31 m × 0.07 m) and half-bricks that were exposed to a height of three courses, over a length of three and a half bricks, with another single line of bricks parallel to that which was one course high.

The rebuilt fired-brick steps that formed the single flight of stairs that led up to the temple roof had not survived in B5 and B11 because they were almost certainly deliberately removed during the deconsecration rites that were performed when the New Eninnu was taken out of service in the Early Old Babylonian period (discussed below), but the stairway's substructural fills (2114 and 2115) were found preserved over the whole area. Fills 2114 and 2115, which were separated by a layer of ashy, silty dark grey clay with a thickness of 20 mm, provided a complete stratigraphic sequence from the Ur III period to Isin-Larsa times. Base layer 2115 consisted of compacted homogeneous beige silty clay that was very similar in colour and composition to the mud-bricks that formed the neighbouring temple walls. The surface of context 2115 was also found to be flush with the top of the chamber's particularly high footings, at a topographical height of 15.7 m, and this was consistent with the idea that the layer was part of the underfloor of a post-Gudea iteration of the stairwell corridor. Containing a good assemblage of Ur III potsherds, fill 2115 probably formed a replacement bedding for an Ur III fired-brick staircase that was subsequently removed. Placed above bedding layer 2115, at a preserved topographical height of 15.99 m, layer 2114 shared many of the characteristics of 2115, and it also yielded diagnostic potsherds dating to the Isin-Larsa period. The evidence combined to suggest that it was probably another (perhaps third and final) substructural fill for a renewed or refitted fired-brick stairway, of which no trace was found. With regard to the stratigraphy, it should also be noted that infilling layer 2114 was seemingly deposited in conjunction with the raising of both the chamber's brickwork threshold and the ring of fired bricks that formed the refurbished door socket cover (all discussed above).

Among the noteworthy objects discovered in context 2115 were an almost complete cuneiform-inscribed cone with a Gudea text commemorating the New Eninnu (TG3412) and a fragment of a large fired-clay plaque (TG3504). The most important finds from context 2114 were a complete Isin-Larsa pot (TG3177) and a group of thirty-six carved or cut shell inlays (TG3395).

The Ur-Bau Plaza

A number of sectors outside the Ningirsu temple that were found to have been left mostly or entirely undisturbed helped the team to reconstruct a comprehensive chronological sequence for works that were carried out in the investigated areas between the end of Gudea's reign and the Isin-Larsa and Old Babylonian periods (Fig. 194). This, in turn, made it possible to establish an unbroken stratigraphic matrix for the post-Gudea New Eninnu in its entirety. The freshly excavated sectors included the Ur-Bau plaza in front of the Ningirsu temple on its NE side, in Areas B2, B5 and B11 (extending into B6 in the vicinity of the NE temenos wall), together with the open-air ambulatories that ran around the sides and back of the temple in Areas B2, B3, B4, B5, B8 and B11 (described below).

As previously noted, some of the walls and installations in the Ur-Bau plaza were extensively levelled in the Hellenistic period, before being further truncated in the course of Ottoman and Mandate-era digs. The remains were also repeatedly looted after the long succession of French seasons on Tell A finally came to an end in the 1930s. Despite that (and indeed partly because of it), the structural make-up of the Ur-Bau plaza was found to have survived below the general levelling horizon, where it was excavated in at least two locales (B2 and B11) that both lay close to the Ningirsu temple's NE façade. In Area B2 the substructure of the plaza was made of a horizon of very compact reddish-brown clayey silt (2014) that was identified as a mixture of decayed mud-bricks, with frequent flecks of white lime and dark ash. Set above foundation fill 2030, where it extended under the adjacent temple walls, subfloor packing 2014 had been truncated horizontally at a topographical height of 15.5 m, and soon afterwards recut by Hellenistic pit 2027. It spanned an area measuring 6.9 m × 3.8 m that was excavated along and against the NE face of walls 2008 and 2017 (parts of the temple's NE façade), where it was exposed to depths of between 0.37 m and 0.47 m. It contained some of the finest examples of potsherds from the reign of Gudea and the Second Dynasty of Lagash that the team found anywhere on the site. Other notable objects recovered from this context included two fragments of the ends of cones: one weathered and eroded (T237), and one with enough preserved signs to show that it had been inscribed in the name of Gudea to commemorate the New Eninnu (TG301). Also found in deposit 2014 was a finely worked Akkad flint arrowhead (TG299) that was leaf-shaped and denticulated.

A series of superimposed deposits and archaeological structures was found in Area B11, extending over an area measuring 3.2 m × by 2.8 m, adjacent to the NE face of wall 2140 (part of the temple's NE façade), and exposed to a total depth of 0.94 m. Marked by intervening cuts and recuts, the remains spanned a long chronological sequence that stretched from the Early Dynastic IIIb and Akkad eras all the way down to Hellenistic times. Despite the extremely long period of occupation, the various truncations that were carried out at different times had resulted in a scarcity of diagnostic potsherds. In conjunction with the limited area in which the preserved layers were found, the absence of pottery remains meant that the archaeology could only be dated stratigraphically, as was the case more generally for this part of the Ur-Bau plaza (adjacent to the NE face of 2140), where the chronology from Lagash II times through to the Isin-Larsa and Old Babylonian eras was based purely on stratigraphic analysis.

Above the Akkad platform (2158), which was refurbished probably in the reign of Ur-Bau and then ritually interred by Gudea in the foundation levels of his Ningirsu temple (2140 and 2162), an initial deposit (2153) was identified at a topographical height of 15.84 m. With a thickness of 0.42 m, it consisted of superimposed layers of hard silty clay containing frequent lumps of mud-bricks that probably represented a series of overlapping subfloor packings that were laid at a range of dates between the time of Gudea's original project and the New Eninnu's subsequent refurbishment in the Ur III period. The uppermost surface of 2153 was sealed off by another substructural infilling (2152) that was exposed at a topographical height of 16.02 m. Made from grey clay material placed on top of a thin layer of lumps and grains of yellow bricks (altogether 0.18 m thick), it represented a further raising of the Ur-Bau plaza in the Isin-Larsa period—an operation that was almost certainly carried out at the same time as the other Isin-Larsa renovation works evidenced across the entire complex on Tell A.

Above deposit 2152 a clear layer of gradual occupation build-up (2151) was identified at a topographical height of 16.14 m. It consisted of a hard clay deposit (0.15 m thick) that was stained grey with charcoal, and it was covered by a thin reddish-brown layer of degraded mud-bricks (2150). Exposed at an overall height of 16.22 m, the latter, which was

0.07 m thick, was identified as either a subsequent (and final) subfloor packing dating from the Late Isin-Larsa or Early Old Babylonian period, or as rubble that was produced when the adjacent temple walls collapsed. Alternatively, it could also have been part of a backfill for the construction of the Hellenistic complex. It was capped with a fired-brick structure (2149), identified at a topographical height of 16.51 m, that belonged to Adadnadinakhe's later building. Made up of a single curving line of bricks, and built on a patch of elevated ground, the Adadnadinakhe construction was preserved to a height of four courses that were possibly the remnants of a soakaway. The only finds made in these layers were in context 2152, which yielded two fragments of cuneiform-inscribed cones, both in the name of Ur-Bau to commemorate the construction of his Eninnu for Ningirsu (TG3414 and TG3415).

The SE and SW Circumambulatory Walkways

As noted above, the walkways that ran around the sides and back of the Ningirsu temple, which were exposed in Areas B2, B3, B4, B5, B8 and B11, produced a further series of diversely located but complementary stratigraphic deposits (Fig. 194). Fortunately, the excavations in these areas also yielded coherent and robust assemblages of diagnostic potsherds that enabled a secure chronology to be established. Good archaeological deposits were excavated in the SE open-air corridor (in B11) and in a strip of its SW counterpart (in B8), at the point where the two walkways met at right angles (Figs. 195 and 196). Although these sectors of the complex were greatly affected by recent looting, they had previously been left relatively unscathed by the nearby French trenching because they were protected by the large spoil heaps that also preserved the temple's stairwell chamber. The lower fill (2118) in Area B11 was identified at a topographical height of 15.95 m. Composed of silty clay, it represented the gradual accumulation over time of a set of superimposed subfloor packings and infillings with a total thickness of 0.44 m. Containing a wide selection of potsherds from a range of dates between the Lagash II and Isin-Larsa periods, fill 2118 provided evidence of a sequence of partial rebuilds that were carried out between the time of the temple's original construction through to its renovation after the fall of the Third Dynasty of Ur. On top of 2118, at a topographical height of 16.2 m, was another subfloor layer (2117), with a thickness of 0.25 m, that displayed similar characteristics to context 2118. It appeared to have performed the same

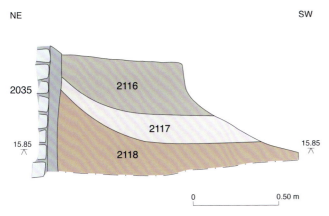

FIGURE 195. Section of the SW ambulatory of the Ningirsu temple, showing a sequence of fills deposited from the Lagash II period through to Old Babylonian times.

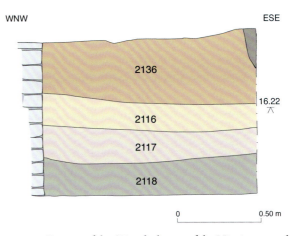

FIGURE 196. Section of the SE ambulatory of the Ningirsu temple, showing the early sequence of fills capped with Hellenistic foundation fill 2136.

function as its predecessor, and was therefore considered indicative of a subsequent refurbishment carried out either in Late Isin-Larsa or Early Old Babylonian times. Deposits 2117 and 2118 were both formed principally of degraded mud-bricks or mud render from which very little ash, organic content or other finds were recovered. This suggested that the temple's subfloor fills and floorings were carefully prepared and kept clean while the work was being carried out.

Context 2116, which was exposed on top of layer 2117, at an overall elevation of 16.3 m, contained many large lumps of baked clay that seemed to indicate the partial but rapid infilling of the open-air corridor space. Since no signs of occupation build-up were found, the filling probably resulted from the collapse of one or more adjacent walls. It was sealed by a Hellenistic foundation fill (2136) that was preserved to a thickness of 0.36 m, at a topographical height of 16.66 m. Composed of lumps of mud-brick and melt from disintegrated structures, the fill contained a wide range of fragmentary artefacts, including mixed pottery. No artefacts were found in contexts 2117 and 2116 (disregarding the potsherds) or 2136, but fill 2118 yielded four complete cuneiform-inscribed cones with New Eninnu texts in the name of Gudea (TG2449, TG2481, TG2482 and TG2483).

In Area B8 parts of the lower archaeological layers that formed the SE edge of the SW ambulatory were identified as continuations of the various subfloor packing layers (2116, 2117 and 2118) exposed in B11. Area B8 had been severely affected by French pitting, which had drastically truncated the preserved overall elevation, removing much of the Late Isin-Larsa and Early Old Babylonian destruction layers, along with the entire Hellenistic horizon. In consequence, only the first three deposits discussed above (2116, 2117 and 2118) were preserved *in situ*. Additionally, the sides of the SW walkway in Area B8 had been carefully replastered with a smooth mud render, of which two superimposed layers were found: one on the end of wall 2159 (the Ningirsu temple's SW façade, which formed the walkway's inner wall); and the other across the corridor on wall 2031 (the inner envelope wall that was placed on the inside face of the SW temenos wall). Wall 2159 (the SW temple façade) contained two inscribed cones (TG2635 and TG2636), while envelope wall 2031 contained one inscribed cone (TG2637).

The topmost fill of the deepest deposit (2118 bis), which was laid down in the Isin-Larsa period, extended laterally underneath the bottoms of the thin coats of mud render on the walls on both sides of the ambulatory. This showed that the replastering of the walls was carried out during the later stages of the Isin-Larsa refurbishment phase, when the protruding cones must have been deliberately covered. Fill 2117 bis was exposed above the earlier subfloor packing (2118 bis) and must therefore have formed a Late Isin-Larsa or Early Old Babylonian subfloor horizon that was associated with the replastering of envelope wall 2031. Thin laminated lenses of fine sand found at the base and top of this deposit suggested that it might have been affected by water erosion, and this probably further confirmed that the walkway was exposed to the open air. The top layer that was uncovered in the ambulatory space (2116 bis) was created by the final, wholesale collapse of the upper parts of the inner SW temple facade and the outer envelope wall.

Also in Area B8, immediately to the north-west of the series of deposits just discussed, was another locus of relatively good archaeology, notably a subrectangular pit (2121) containing a fill (2122) from which pieces of some large jars from the Isin-Larsa period were retrieved. Measuring 1.06 m × 0.38 m × 0.46 m (deep), the pit had straight vertical sides that broke very abruptly into short slopes and a flat base, suggesting that it probably accommodated at least two big ceramic storage vessels. Placed stratigraphically below deposit 2117 bis, pit 2121 was in all likelihood filled in the course of the extensive restoration works that were carried out after the fall of the Third Dynasty of Ur. Fill 2122 contained one complete cone that was inscribed in the name of Gudea to commemorate the New Eninnu (TG2574).

To the north-west, in Area B5, in the vicinity of the SW gateway's inner porch, the SW walkway included a stretch of subfloor brickwork (2067), exposed at a topographical height of 15.7 m, that was composed of a single course of three to four rows of grey square mud-bricks with sides of 0.32 m and a thickness of 0.07 m. Oriented on a NW–SE alignment, the brick subfloor covered an area of 2.4 m × 1.6 m (the width of the corridor), and it structurally linked the bases of the two walls that enclosed the ambulatory at this point, namely the SW façade of the Ningirsu temple (2068) and the SW envelope wall (2031). Subfloor 2067 had been truncated on its NW side by the long N–S French trench (2080) and on its SE side by the expansive horizontal French trench (2036). This substantial, carefully laid subfloor, which bore the hallmark of an Ur III renovation, seemed to have served as the structural base for a well-crafted wall repair—a footing or low bench (2069), found at an overall elevation of 16.15 m, that was built of a single row of mud-bricks (0.32 m × 0.32 m × 0.07 m) and presumably also half-bricks, though none were observed. Preserved to a height of four courses over a length of 1.64 m, the narrow structure was set against the NE face of envelope wall 2031. These archaeological features mirrored a series of similar Ur III repair works that were identified by the British Museum team at several points in the peribolus of the Ningirsu temple.

The NW Circumambulatory Walkway

The special care with which the Ur III restoration of the New Eninnu was carried out in the reign of Shulgi was evident in the way the Gudea door socket inside the cella was preserved and reinstalled, complete with a newly fashioned cover. This was the temple's religious and symbolic heart, but similar pains were taken with the refurbishment of the NW ambulatory corridor (in Areas B2, B3 and B4), where the L-shaped complex's inner NW dividing wall, with its dual access ramps and splendid gateway, shielded the holiest part of the sanctuary containing the Ningirsu temple at the SE end of the complex. Despite the Hellenistic levelling and pitting that affected Area B2 (contexts 2020 and 2027), together with the widespread, albeit superficial French trenching in B3 and B4, three significant portions of the NW open-air corridor were found intact. They consisted of a series of superimposed subfloor packings dating from Lagash II to Ur III times that were uncovered in the vicinity of the inner NW gate (in Area B2), where the Lagash II foundation deposits (2022 and 2013) were capped with a layer of white plaster, specifically lime cement (2012). The later fill (2006) that was found immediately above that, at a topographical height of 15.83 m, was formed of a deposit of compacted mud-brick debris with a total thickness of 0.63 m.

An exposed strip of ground close to the interface between Areas B2 and B3 provided a complementary stratigraphic sequence of floors and walls, beginning with an underlying Gudea subfloor (3019) that was identified at a topographical height of 15.54 m. It was associated with structure 3045: a pilaster with a base height of 15.45 m that was found against the inner SE face of the NW dividing wall (3006 and 3048), flanking the SW side of the gateway. The pilaster, which was probably added during Gudea's reign, perhaps shortly after the New Eninnu was originally completed, or possibly in a later Lagash II phase, was 3.15 m wide × 0.65 m (deep), and it was preserved to a height of four courses of square mud-bricks (with dimensions of 0.32 m × 0.32 m × 0.06 m) and half-bricks. The bricks were regularly laid, with the four courses of the pilaster's long SE face seemingly made up of a pattern of single courses of full-size bricks that sandwiched double courses of half-bricks.

Subfloor 3019 was found to have been subsequently levelled and cut by a square Ur III favissa pit (3033) with sides of 0.5 m that contained a foundation deposit (TG331) in its fill (3032). The deposit was a single brick that was inscribed in the name of Gudea with a New Eninnu text, and it was found in the middle of the open-air corridor's short NW–SE axis. The text, which was facing upwards, was legible for a reader looking towards the north-east, while its original stamped epigraphy seemed to have been carefully reinscribed by hand in order to restore the worn and broken parts of the text's closing words, namely the section that refers to Gudea's construction of the New Eninnu. This highly significant action seemed undoubtedly to confirm that the brick had been deliberately saved, overworked and relaid in a key position in the ambulatory floor.

Favissa 3033 was sealed by a homogeneous Ur III subfloor packing (3013), preserved to a topographical height of 15.66 m, that was associated with the comprehensive refacing and refurbishment of the walls (specifically the wall footings) on both sides of the NW ambulatory: the NW façade (3011) of the Ningirsu temple, where structure 3044 was placed against the NW face of 3011, and the L-shaped complex's inner NW dividing wall (3006), where structure 3021 was placed against the SE face of 3006. Both of these notable repairs were found on top of deposit 3013, at a topographical height of 15.68 m. Structure 3044 was a low wall made of a single row of square mud-bricks (0.3 m × 0.3 m × 0.06 m) that rose to a height of three courses and was exposed over a length of 5 m; its upper surface and its NW face appeared to have been plastered. Structure 3021, which was situated on the opposite side of the open-air corridor, abutting onto buttress 3045, was built of a single row of square bricks and half-bricks, exposed over a length of 6.15 m, that were preserved to a height of between three and four courses. Like its counterpart on the other side of the walkway, its top surface was plastered with very compact light greyish-brown plaster, but it could not be determined whether plaster had also been applied generally on the upright surface of wall 3021. Three fragments of inscribed cones and one complete cone were found in context 3013. The barely legible fragments appeared to be inscribed in the name of Gudea to commemorate the New Eninnu for Ningirsu (though the god's name could not be made out on one of them). No artefacts were found in association with wall repairs 3044 and 3021.

Another remarkable sequence of deposits relating to the repaired walls on the NW side of the temple were found in an extensive section of the NW ambulatory, at the interface of Areas B3, B4 and B5. Having a maximum thickness of a little more than 1 m, the deposits were situated above the levelled occupation layer (2085) that was dated to the reign of Ur-Bau. Immediately on top of this pre-Gudea horizon was base layer 2084: a Lagash II foundation fill that was identified at a topographical height of 15.22 m. Above this, at a topographical height of 15.33 m, layer 2083 was formed of a gradual build-up of various construction materials, including numerous pottery fragments and wind-blown dust, possibly combined with the remains of a series of temporary earthen floors. Above 2083, at an overall height of 15.53 m, layer 3071 was the Lagash II subfloor bedding that was also the continuation of subfloor 3019 (discussed above). On top of subfloor bedding 3071, at a topographical height of 15.61 m, layer 3070 represented the Ur III continuation of subfloor 3013 (also discussed above), and above that, at an overall height of 15.73 m, was layer 3067, which was the Ur III earthen floor that was laid in association with the refacing (3069) of the lower portion of the NE façade of the inner SW envelope wall (3049). The refacing (3069), which took the form of a replacement footing (or perhaps one that was newly added), had its base at an overall height of 15.7 m, and it met wall 3021 at right angles. Made of a single course of mud-bricks (0.3 m × 0.3 m × 0.07 m) and half-bricks, the low plinth-like structure, which was exposed over a length of 1.25 m, was possibly added to consolidate the base sections of 3049 and 2032, and also to frame and perhaps symbolically to accentuate the upper wall surface, which was studded with Gudea cones. The new footing or plinth (3069) and its associated Ur III floor (3067) were covered at a topographical height of 16.03 m by layer 3008, which yielded a large number of inscribed cones and must have resulted from the partial collapse of the upper parts of wall 3049. The presence of French (and possibly also Hellenistic) pitting made it extremely difficult to date the collapse, but it might have occurred between the end of the Third Dynasty of Ur and the large-scale renovations that were carried out during the Isin-Larsa period. The notable finds from wall collapse layer 3008 included twenty-one cones and fragments of cones, all of which were inscribed in the name of Gudea to commemorate the construction of Ningirsu's Eninnu.

Remarkably, floor 3067 included a commemorative relic of Gudea's project in the form of an inscribed cone (TG988) with a preserved length of 121 mm and head and shaft diameters of 50 mm and 39 mm, respectively. It was found to have been carefully embedded in the floor's clay surface, with the name of the temple in the uppermost line of the inscription facing upwards. Like the reinscribed brick (TG331) that was found ritually deposited in the favissa fill (3032) in the walkway, the cone was positioned very precisely, in this case in the centre of the NW ambulatory corridor (at the meeting point of the NW and SW corridors), with its head located to the south-west and its tip pointing north-eastwards towards the dedicatory brick. It seemed to have been meticulously deposited at the point where visitors who walked around the peribolus would have had to turn through ninety degrees as they passed the Ningirsu temple's W corner—a highly symbolic juncture in the temple's outer ambulatory. The placement of the sacred artefact, which would have been visible in the surface of the floor, might have affected the way people progressed along the walkway, perhaps causing worshippers or high priests to adjust their paths to avoid stepping on the object. This would have taken them out from the middle of the corridor towards its sides, bringing them very close to the surfaces of the walls that were fitted with a great number of dedicatory cones. Whatever the rationale behind the placement in the floor of the cone and the single brick, it seems clear that relics from Gudea's reign were specially incorporated into the new surface (3067) and its associated bedding (3013), if not elsewhere. Related pottery finds suggested that the renovation was carried out in the Ur III period, and this might further imply that the inclusion of Gudea artefacts in the restored building could have been linked with the religious veneration and deification of Gudea that was a feature of the reign of Shulgi. The worship of Gudea is known textually from the records of ceremonies that were directly linked to the diorite statues of the ruler that were found on Tell A, and it is feasible that other, more minor rituals were associated with the commemorative objects that were found in the fabric of the refurbished sanctuary.

The SW Gate and the Adjacent Temenos Area

The stratigraphy of the New Eninnu's SW gate and the adjoining parts of the interior of the sacred enclosure yielded important insights into the sanctuary's post-Gudea history, highlighting the extent of the renovation works that took place in the Ur III and subsequent Isin-Larsa periods (Fig. 194). A large portion of the chambered gateway, including substantial sections of its flanking towers, were found to have been completely rebuilt from the ground up (Fig. 197). These archaeological features, extending over Areas B4, B5, B7 and B8, were entombed within the huge Hellenistic terrace platform (3062 and 6008) that was established to cap off and infill the SW gate's outer passageway in B4, along with its narrow inner portal and porch in B5. In spite of the considerable French trenching in this area (2080, 2108 and 6002), a sizeable extent of the SW gate was preserved intact,

FIGURE 197. Repairs and fills inside the New Eninnu's SW gate, viewed from inside the gateway passage.

protected beneath the colossal spoil heaps of Cluster 1, including the aptly named Mount Sarzec (SH1).

In Areas B4 and B5, bordered by tower 3060 to the north-west and tower 2105 to the south-east, the approach that led into the gateway passage on the gate's SE side was completely sealed off by a Hellenistic foundation fill (2091). Identified at a topographical height of 16.63 m, the fill was made up of small fragments of mud-bricks in a clayey silt matrix (50%), larger mud-brick lumps (40%) and pieces of fired bricks (10%). The mixture was laid down over layers of gradual infilling, melt, collapse and wind-blown deposits. Forming a component of the infrastructure of Adadnadinakhe's Graeco-Babylonian platform (3062 and 6008), it yielded a miscellaneous assemblage of Ur III to Isin-Larsa potsherds. Other notable finds included two complete cones (TG2133 and TG2134), both inscribed in the name of Gudea to commemorate the New Eninnu, and one head of a cone (TG2132) that was inscribed in the name of Ur-Bau with a dedication to Ningirsu (no further details were legible).

Layer 2091 covered a series of archaeological strata (2102, 2104, 2095 and 2103) that belonged to later stages in the SW gate's history, all of which were dated to the Isin-Larsa and Old Babylonian eras. The lowest deposit (2102), which was a very homogeneous compacted silty clay subfloor packing that contained potsherds diagnostic of the Lagash II and Ur III periods, was exposed at a topographical height of 15.98 m, spanning an area measuring 4.2 m × 2.95 m that extended over the entire breadth of the entrance area. This carefully processed infilling, which displayed a constant character across its whole extent, appeared to have been added to deal with the significant narrowing of the open space in front of the gate that resulted from the earlier construction of large buttress walls (3102 and 2165) on either side of the gate's outer approach. Built against the SE face of tower 3060 and the NW face of tower 2105, the new buttresses each measured 1.6 m × 5.8 m, and they were both formed of five rows of square mud-bricks with sides of 0.32 m and a thickness of 0.07 m, and half-bricks. One complete cone (TG1596) inscribed in the name of Gudea to commemorate the New Eninnu for Ningirsu was found in 2102, but no finds were recovered from 2104, 2095 or 2103.

Layer 2102 was covered with a paving of large limestone slabs (2104) that was preserved in a limited area (1.31 m × 1.22 m) of the entranceway, near to the intersection of B4 and B5, at a topographical height of 16.31 m. The flat, irregularly shaped stone tiles, which were pale grey in colour, ranged in size from 0.19 m × 0.1 m to a maximum of 0.76 m × 0.46 m, and the paved floor was sealed with a coat of lime cement. Fitted during the final phase of occupation build-up in the gateway in the Late Isin-Larsa and Early Old Babylonian periods, before the sanctuary was finally deconsecrated, the floor was stratigraphically related to the rebuilding of two low platforms (2095 and 2103) that were found on either side of the gate's narrow inner portal. Fronted by bitumen revetments that separated the courses of bricks from the associated fills (2106 and 2107, respectively), pedestals 2095 and 2103 had clayey silt cores, while their preserved dimensions were 0.98 m × 0.49 m × 0.3 m (context 2095) and 0.91 m × 0.74 m × 0.39 m (context 2103). They were both built along the interior walls of the gateway passage, with their SW sides, which faced the opening of the gateway in the temenos wall, sloping down towards the south-west by ten degrees. The faces of the two features were formed of a mixture of bitumen stones and brick fragments, plastered with a thick layer of bitumen.

Despite the extensive French trenching that had affected this area, especially in front of the gate's open-air approach on its SW side, archaeological traces of the raising of the platform terrace outside the L-shaped complex in Isin-Larsa and Old Babylonian times were identified in the form of a substructural backfill (2112) that was found extending uninterruptedly across the SW corners of Areas B4 and B8. The two rectangular display benches (2095 and 2103) that were placed inside the gateway passage, which were almost certainly designed to support votive objects or gateway steles, were stratigraphically associated with the raising of the narrow brickwork floor (2057) in Area B5, inside the SW gateway passage. Preserved to a maximum topographical height of 16.24 m, the newly raised floor was made of a loose fabric of fragmentary and recycled fired bricks—some bearing Gudea's Standard Inscription—that were bonded with bitumen or mud-mortar bedding joints.

The passageway area had been partly looted in antiquity, in all likelihood in the Hellenistic period, around the time of Adadnadinakhe's large-scale excavations. Indeed, a Hellenistic pit in the middle of the passageway, probably targeting a ritual deposit beneath the brickwork, was found sealed off by a substantial backfill (2056). The latter contained a wide range of mixed artefacts, but not a single potsherd that dated from Tell A's Hellenistic occupation phase—a telling lack that meant the pit must have been opened and filled during the initial stages of Adadnadinakhe's project. Noteworthy artefacts found in backfill 2056 included two cones (TG1278 and TG1198) containing the Gudea Standard Inscription and one fragment of a cone that was possibly inscribed in the name of Gudea to commemorate the EPA (TG892).

The inner NE side of the entranceway passage was fitted with a raised brickwork feature, presumably a floor, that spanned its entire width of 1.15 m, rising to a height of three courses of bricks. Coated with a layer of bitumen, it was laid in association with the more limited raising of the floor to the south-west (2057) that consisted of just one course of fired bricks. Traces of bitumen found on the surface of the raised floor along the edge of the NE side of the passageway and at its NE threshold might have been remnants of additional fixing materials that were used where the floor met the surrounding walls. It seemed unlikely that there was a fired-brick skirting along the floor's edges because no traces of further bricks were found above the level of the three-course pavement, while a single course of square bricks (with sides of 0.32 m) laid on bed would have left the passageway impossibly restricted, and even half-bricks laid as stretchers would have narrowed the space considerably. Although the three-course structure was judged to be a floor, it bore some resemblance to the foundation boxes that were found elsewhere, notably concealed in the corners of the mud-brick towers, but the placement of such a feature in the middle of one of the complex's most important access points would have been extremely disruptive. The three courses of fired bricks were therefore added, in all probability, to form a step that led up into the entrance passage of the inner porch, and there is every reason to believe that stepped levels and spaces were a key feature of this part of the temple complex.

As previously noted, the Late Isin-Larsa or Early Old Babylonian pavement floor (2057) featured a socle (2066) for a door socket that was placed close to the threshold's E corner, against the NE face of wall 2059, inside the gate's inner porch, at a topographical height of 16.14 m. Alternatively, the feature could conceivably have been a foundation base for a cultic feature, perhaps a libation vessel, but this seemed far less likely. Composed of square bricks (with sides of 0.26 m and a thickness of 0.06 m) that were strikingly different in size from the Lagash II mud-bricks used by Gudea, the structure was found covering a Gudea cone that was preserved *in situ*. The surviving part of the fragmentary masonry had overall dimensions of 0.89 m × 0.82 m × 0.41 m (h), but the

extent of the truncation in this area (evidenced in contexts 2080, 2086 and 2088), together with the removal of most if not all of the softer archaeological deposits that doubtless formed superimposed layers associated with the raising of floor 2057, made it difficult to determine the feature's function with complete certainty. Nonetheless, it was comparable with another recovered door socket compartment (2169), made of reused pieces of inscribed bricks and found underneath socle 2066, that was installed in the passageway at an earlier stage of the Ur III renovations. The two fittings probably therefore performed the same function. It should also be recalled that a Gudea socket stone (TG951) that might have been an original fixture was recovered from a neighbouring French sounding (2080), and this might further confirm the assumption. The placement of the presumed door socket socle suggested that the entrance was fitted with a single-leaf door that pivoted through 180 degrees from the north-west to the south-east into the inner porch.

Also found in this heavily disturbed sector of the inner porch, where the passageway merged with the SW part of the temple's peribolus in Area B5, were the remains of an Ur III floor (2062) that survived as a narrow strip of hard lime cement that was exposed beneath the Hellenistic foundation layer at a topographical height of 15.82 m. With preserved dimensions of 0.92 m × 0.1 m × 0.1 m (t), it was associated with a replastering of the L-shaped complex's inner NE façade (2058), where two layers were applied to the exposed face of the wall: a coat of mud plaster (0.11 m thick), finished with a wash of white lime. Despite the extensive pitting carried out at later periods, the plastered and whitewashed wall survived to a maximum height of 0.11 m above the level of the floor. The presence of a shallow depression between the coated floor and the inner NE façade (2058) suggested that the wall might have been more substantially refaced at a later date, perhaps with wood panelling or a stone dado. Stratigraphically, the strip of floor and the plastered portion of wall were contemporary with the wholesale restoration works that were carried out generally across the sanctuary in the Ur III period.

More evidence of a complex stratigraphy spanning the subsequent Isin-Larsa period was also recorded in the vicinity of the gate in Area B8, around the inner S corner of tower 2105. Two partially preserved fired-brick foundation boxes were found in the brickwork fabric of the tower: 2110, which was uncovered close to the tower's S corner, and 2123, which lay a little to the south-east of 2110. Exposed at maximum topographical heights of 16.44 m and 16.36 m, respectively, both had been looted in antiquity, while their upper parts had been subjected to further disturbance during earlier excavations, and extensive erosion had also taken place. Despite that, sufficient brickwork survived to show that the two boxes differed from each other in their overall sizes, as well as in their construction materials and manner of construction. Box 2110, which was the smaller of the two (measuring 1.09 m × 0.48 m × 0.42 m (h)), was found further away from the outer edge of the tower than 2123, and it was only partly built of fired bricks. The brickwork on the SE side of 2110 (the side closest to box 2123) was formed of the mudbrick core of tower 2105 (though the box's original wall might have been removed), while its other sides were made from reused, often fragmentary fired bricks that were bonded with bitumen. Just to the south-east of 2110 (still within the brickwork fabric of the tower), box 2123 was larger and squarish in shape, with measurements of 1.27 m × 1.31 m × 0.32 m (h). It was built exclusively of the standard square fired bricks and half-bricks that were used by Gudea, which were found to be generally more complete than the pieces of bricks used to build box 2110. Box 2123 was nonetheless in a poorer state of preservation than its counterpart, since it had been truncated and largely dismantled, probably at one of three possible moments: perhaps when the sanctuary was finally closed during the Late Isin-Larsa and Early Old Babylonian periods; or during the preconstruction phase of the Hellenistic complex, when artefacts from the earlier temple were systematically sought out and salvaged; or during the late nineteenth and early twentieth centuries, when the French excavators were working on the mound.

The differences between the two boxes provided some inferred insights into their dates and about the more general construction sequence around the S corner of tower 2105. The absence of fired bricks on the SE side of box 2110 might at first glance suggest that it was built before box 2123, and that 2123 might have subsequently truncated it, but this order of events would surely have left box 2110 neatly cut and showing no other signs of disturbance. It would also raise the question of why box 2123 was not simply shifted slightly to the southeast, thereby avoiding any overlap with 2110 (though 2123 was already very close indeed to the SE side of the tower). A close examination of box 2110 revealed an alternative possible explanation. It was noted that 2110 was made of reused fired bricks, including one bearing the royal inscription of Ur-Bau, that were mostly either slightly damaged or even fragmentary. Since a similar use of materials was observed in later features elsewhere on Tell A, and especially in structures built during the Isin-Larsa period, it was therefore tentatively assumed that the SE side of 2110 was not finished with fired bricks because of the close proximity of 2123 in this direction. It also seemed probable that any foundation deposits that were placed in the box were intended to commemorate the refurbishment of the monumental SW entrance to the sanctuary during this later period.

The idea that a significant portion of tower 2105 was rebuilt in Isin-Larsa times was further supported by the discovery that renovation works were carried out on the adjacent SW temenos wall (also in Area B8). Despite extensive French pitting (2108), a new wall (2167) with a thickness of about 3.7 m was found adjoining the SW face of the Lagash II wall (2164), where it was strengthened with a projecting buttress (2125) measuring 1.56 m × 1.32 m. Buttressed wall 2167 doubled the thickness of the original structure and seemingly abutted onto the restored SE face of tower 2105, all of which indicated that it was also built during the Isin-Larsa period. Noticeably, its SW face included a protruding row of half-bricks that formed a foundation ledge (coated on its outer face with mud plaster), which was laid at an angle of forty-five degrees, giving it an overall depth of 40 mm (from front to back).

The Central Courtyard; the NE Gate and the Adjacent Temenos Area

With regard to the stratigraphy of both the central courtyard in Areas B1 and B10, and the NE sanctuary gate and temenos wall in Areas B6 and B9, most if not all of the archaeological structures that originally belonged to the New Eninnu were found at, or very rarely slightly above, the foundation level of the complex as it was established under Gudea (Fig. 194). This is because the Lagash II structures were extensively levelled in Hellenistic times, before being considerably truncated by French digging and then further damaged by recent looting, particularly after the Gulf War. The ground surface of the courtyard in Area B10 (5505) included patches of repair (5517) that were identified in the NW corner of the trench and tentatively dated to the Isin-Larsa period. Two layers (5507 and 5508) encountered above the courtyard surface were made essentially of windblown weathered material resulting from the long period when the New Eninnu was abandoned, prior to the Hellenistic epilogue. These layers, which appeared to have been deposited naturally, included slightly compacted lenses that were caused by localised erosion and the presence of short-lived weathering surfaces. Traces of a renovation (5237) of the inner SW façade of the Gudea wall (5223 and 5002) in Areas B6 and B9 might have been left by restoration works that were carried out during either the Ur III or Isin-Larsa periods. Remnants of the renovation (5237), which used bricks of a roughly uniform size that were all manufactured from a distinctive light green clayey material, were found along the entire SW facing of 5223, where the renovated section measured about 11 m in length and had an average width of 1.6 m.

In Area B6 some indeterminate, but clearly later archaeological features (5042, 5043 and 5044) were seemingly superimposed adjacent to a structure that might have been the exterior NW façade of the NE precinct wall. Turning through ninety degrees towards the north-east, the superimpositions lay outside the temenos, directly over the continuation of its platform terrace, and they probably dated either to Ur III times or to the Isin-Larsa or Old Babylonian periods. Mud-brick walling (5042) was exposed over a length of 4 m to a width about 2.5 m, though the wall was certainly longer. Its exact dimensions could not be determined because its NW side was obscured by later Hellenistic brickwork (5222), while its NE side extended beyond the limits of B6, but it was undoubtedly laid in a construction trench (5043) in which a fire had been deliberately kindled, probably during a purification rite that was performed before the courses of mud-bricks were laid, as evidenced by the fact that the latter showed no signs of fire damage. For two reasons the observed characteristics of wall 5042 suggested that it was built after the temple was originally completed in the Lagash II period, but before the Hellenistic reconstruction was carried out: first, because the wall could clearly be seen cutting through the Lagash II platform terrace; and secondly (as just noted), the trench in which the bricks were laid had been subject to controlled preparatory burning—a procedure that is consistent with Ur III and Isin-Larsa practices, but there is no indication that the Hellenistic builders carried out such rituals anywhere on Tell A.

The function of wall 5042 was unclear, and any hypotheses about its use were impeded by its incomplete exposure in Area B6. It might perhaps have formed part of the articulation of a raised post-Gudea platform that was established on top of the original Lagash II platform terrace; alternatively,

it might have been built during a subsequent construction phase in conjunction with the addition of external features to this part of the complex (conceivably including display benches and altars). The only certainty, which is a point of some significance, is that the ritual purification of the foundation trench in which the wall was built showed that it was an especially sacred enhancement.

Another later stage of rebuilding (5044) was evidenced by the discovery of some regular courses of greyish-green sandy silt mud-bricks (noticeably lacking in vegetal inclusions), the quality of which was markedly inferior to the bricks used in the Lagash II and subsequent Ur III phases. Though the date of structure 5044 could not be determined, the fact that it was found unmistakably behind, and to the south-east of, the Hellenistic construction (5222) indicated that it was possibly earlier than the walls built by Adadnadinakhe. It could therefore have formed part of the Isin-Larsa and Early Old Babylonian renovations and repairs that were carried out in and around the temple precinct—the further corollary being that these later refurbishments might have involved the construction of a newly raised platform. Conversely, however, it might have formed part of the substructural layers of Adadnadinakhe's Hellenistic complex.

The Deconsecration and Closure of the New Eninnu

The New Eninnu remained in use continuously from the time of its completion under Gudea in the Lagash II period down to Isin-Larsa and Old Babylonian times—a long history that included significant renovations and repairs. Finally, however, it was meticulously deconsecrated and decommissioned. In the process, its most highly revered architectural features and sacred spaces were interred, as was much of its votive content, notably the many statues of the original temple builder and lately deified ruler, Gudea. Signs of the deconsecration of the holy of holies, the Temple of Ningirsu itself, were found in at least two liminal (or transitional) locales that represented significant mediating points in the approach to the building's most sacred spaces: the portal of the inner sanctum in Area B3, and the stairwell chamber that gave access to the roof in Areas B5 and B11. In both cases the principal structures and fittings, in particular the doors and the flight of stairs, were removed, and a closing deposit of burnt material was laid down. Additionally, in the cella, the door's copper pivot shoe (TG318) was found reburied in the door socket's cover box (3028), which had been converted into a sarcophagus for both the copper shoe and the inscribed socket stone (TG366). The ensemble, which was buried down to its top course of bricks, was entombed in a carefully processed deposit of sandy silt (3027) that was thoroughly clean and homogeneous, with no signs of silting lenses. The area was then further sealed with a redeposited black layer (3022) that extended over the interred door fittings and out into the adjacent passageway. Containing lots of ash, charcoal and lightly burnt material that had been brought into the temple from elsewhere, the black layer was clearly specially produced during a purification rite. Layer 3022 was found continuously between topographical heights of 15.38 m and 15.32 m, while the sandy silt deposit (3027) was found between heights of 15.39 m and 15.32 m.

Evidence for the decommissioning of the stairwell chamber (partly considered above) was provided by a similarly processed layer (2113) of burnt material that was found deposited over the room's entire surface area (measuring 11.5 m × 2 m) to a thickness of more than 1 m. Made up mostly of fine ash (90%), mixed with sand that could be described as thin beige tip lines of silty clay (10%), the sheer volume of this tertiary and final fill (amounting to more than 20 m^3) must have required a controlled conflagration of some considerable size. Combined with its general character as a rapid backfill, the way the deposit was produced seemed consistent with an inclusive desanctification. Furthermore, it was sealed with a mud-brick capping (2094) that had been drastically mutilated by Hellenistic and French trenching, as well as by post-Gulf War looting. Made of rectangular mud-bricks measuring 0.24 m × 0.16 m × 0.07 m, the capping layer, which was aligned with the stairwell chamber's long NE–SW axis, must have extended across the entire breadth of the room. The preserved part of the deposit, which was laid in a rudimentary fashion to a height of two courses of bricks and a width of two headers plus a stretcher, was associated with another contemporary closing event, namely the blocking of the doorway (2141) leading into the chamber. Constructed entirely of large square mud-bricks (0.34 m × 0.34 m × 0.09 m), the blocking wall was preserved to a height of 0.7 m or seven courses, and it completely sealed off the infilled entrance passage to the stairwell (with dimensions of 1.15 m × 2.3 m) between walls 2160 and 2162. It should be recalled that a distinctive black layer (2081) similar to those just discussed was also found evenly spread over the whole surface of the display bench (2035) in the temple's antecella (as noted above).

Several finds were made in two of the closing deposits. One cone fragment that appeared to have been deliberately burnt was discovered in the mud-brick capping (2094); it was a piece of the head of a cone (TG3323) that was inscribed in the name of Gudea to commemorate the New Eninnu. Burnt deposit 2113 contained twenty-seven artefacts, among which were: twelve cones and fragments of cones, all marked with Gudea's Standard Inscription; two Lagash II cylinder seals—a broken one made of bitumen (TG3254) and a complete one made of stone (TG3326); a sealing impression of a Lagash II cylinder seal (TG3319; Fig. 198); and thirteen shell inlays, some of which appeared to have been burnt.

FIGURE 198. Impression of a Lagash II cylinder seal found inside the layer of burnt materials that were ritually deposited in the stairwell chamber of the Ningirsu temple.

Finally, some fascinating connections can be made between the materials that were ritually deposited during the deconsecration of the complex and the imagery of violent devastation that is contained in the Lament for Sumer and Ur (quoted in Chapter 35). The layers of ash that covered the temple's most sacred features in the cella and the antecella clearly evoke the idea of destruction by fire that is a key feature of the lament, in particular when Enlil sends down a storm that blazes like the 'mouth of a fire'. Similarly, the treatment and ritual interment of the many statues that were displayed in the Eninnu were doubtless procedures that shattered and thereby metaphorically ejected the divine aura with which the carvings had been ritually animated. The consequent reduction of the sacred spaces and objects to mere bricks, mortar and stone, together with the expulsion of the local deities from their ancestral home, were seemingly conceived of as a kind of alienation, which is expressed in the lament by the imagery of foreign invasion and occupation. Whether or not the Elamites did indeed take possession of Girsu, therefore, the events depicted in the lament are not framed as simple history, but as the fulfilment of a cosmic destiny that was ordained by Enlil. Taken together, the sacramental manner in which the Eninnu was desacralised and the imagery of the lament both express the sense of profound rupture that was felt when the sacred spaces and objects were secularised.

Pottery from the New Eninnu

As confirmed by the stratigraphic data, the ceramic materials derived from the New Eninnu were associated with four chronological phases: the Gudea (Lagash II) era, represented by finds from layers that were sealed by later floors and Ur III restoration works; the Ur III occupation phase and the beginning of the Isin-Larsa period; the Isin-Larsa occupation phase that came after an extensive renovation of the complex; and lastly, the Old Babylonian period. With respect to the first two phases, limited pottery assemblages were found, including some diagnostic fragments. Conversely, sufficient data was collected for the post-renovation Isin-Larsa period to enable an exhaustive reconstruction of the pottery repertoire for this phase. Finally, although numerous Old Babylonian sherds were

recovered, analysis of them was hampered by their generally poor archaeological provenances.

Despite the relative sparseness of the data relating to the Lagash II period, it was possible to reconstruct a compelling and evocative picture of the repertoire of vases that were used in the New Eninnu's Lagash II phase. The most interesting vase sherd was a pedestal with a triangular overhanging rim that was decorated internally and externally with multiple incised wavy lines (Fig. 199.1). This rare vessel is scarcely attested in any of the ceramic assemblages that have been identified from this period anywhere in Sumer. Amongst the Lagash II open forms found on Tell A, a variety of large bowls predominated. The type most commonly found had a triangular rim and curvilinear walls (Fig. 199.2), while less frequent finds included deep bowls with an overhanging triangular rim and straight walls (Fig. 199.3), as well as large carinated bowls (Fig. 199.4). Of the recovered closed shapes, a type of jar with a triangular rim and ridged shoulders (Fig. 199.5 and 199.6) was found that is also well documented in the previous Late Akkad period, while the short plain-rimmed jars that were common in the third millennium BCE remained in production in Lagash II times (Fig. 199.7).

The Ur III occupation phase was also defined by a small number of diagnostic fragments, but they were supplemented by stratigraphic and architectural data from Ur III and early Isin-Larsa times, notably the renewal of some temple floors and other features described above. The limited repertoire of open forms from the Ur III period was represented mainly by bowls with an inward round-folded rim (Fig. 200.1 and 200.2) and carinated bowls (Fig. 200.3). Closed forms, which were much more numerous, presented a greater variety of edge shapes, sizes and other morphological characteristics. The small and medium-size jars that were excavated included two vessels with short plain rims (Fig. 200.5 and 200.6), one fragment of which displayed rounded shoulders and a globular body. Also found was a hole-mouth jar with an outwardly folded thickened rim and a rounded body (Fig. 200.4). Two kinds of medium-size jars were uncovered: some with a triangular rim (Fig. 200.7), as well as short plain-rimmed jars with ridged shoulders (Fig. 200.8). Both kinds had shoulder profiles that suggested the vessels were probably ovoid in shape. Large storage jars were represented by a sherd of a triple-ridged rim jar (Fig. 200.9).

The pottery repertoires associated with the Lagash II and Ur III occupation phases indicated that the temple was used continuously during this time frame and that the ceramic sets were periodically renewed. By contrast, the assemblage from the Isin-Larsa period was much richer and more heterogeneous. A numerous and diverse batch of diagnostic sherds from the Ningirsu temple was found in the subfloor packings of the shrine's stairwell corridor. Open forms made up about 35% of the recovered fragments, consisting mainly of a group of deep bowls with a conical profile, together with small bowls with a plain rim (Fig. 201.2 and 201.3) and bowls with an inward round-folded rim (Fig. 201.4). Although all the deep bowls with a flat and thickened rim (Fig. 201.5–8) presented similar body shapes, they featured differently formed rims, albeit of a well-attested type. The repertoire of open shapes was completed by a large vessel with a cylindrical body that displayed a variety of well-spaced ribs on its exterior and an outwardly expanded rim (Fig. 203.8). The more prevalent closed shapes, which accounted for 65% of the diagnostic sherds found inside the stairwell chamber, came from medium-size jars, supplemented by a solitary example of a small jar with a plain rim and a rounded body (Fig. 202.4). Numerically, the most common vessels formed a homogeneous group of jars with a tall and narrow flaring neck and a band rim (Fig. 202.3, 202.5 and 202.6). Also well documented was a group of ovoid jars with a wide base and upwardly narrowing body, on which the rims were consistently flat and everted, while the shoulders featured a protruding ridge at the intersection between the neck and body (Fig. 202.1 and 202.2).

Among the jars with a tall, narrow neck was found a sherd of a jar with an external short thickened band rim (Fig. 202.12). Variants of the necked jars with a flaring rim were distinguished according to the changing shapes of the rims, namely whether the rims were flat and externally expanded (Fig. 202.9), triangular (Fig. 202.10) or everted and rounded (Fig. 202.11). Other sporadically attested forms were a kind of necked jar with a bulbous rim and rounded shoulders (Fig. 202.13), while types of short-necked jars included occasional examples of jars with an inverted triangular rim (Fig. 202.7) and band-rimmed jars (Fig. 202.8). Just one kind of neckless jar was found: a hole-mouth jar with a thickened rim and a rounded body (Fig. 202.14); it was distinguished by the finish, known as textured slip, which was applied to its

exterior surface. Various fragments from this kind of jar were collected from non-primary contexts in the course of the excavations, and it was observed that, of all the many different kinds of vessels recovered, this was the only type that was treated with textured slip. To date, this is the only pottery shape from Girsu that has been found with this kind of finish, but it should also be noted that examples of the vessel were discovered with and without textured slip.

Three other *in situ* batches of pottery were unearthed: one in the SW gate area, one in the NW ambulatory, and a third in the SE and SW ambulatories. Although the ceramics found by the SW gate yielded the smallest number of diagnostic fragments, it was the only one of the three batches that presented a preponderance of open forms (55%). Open forms from the SW gate and NW ambulatory included many bowls, mostly carinated (Fig. 203.1 and 203.2), though inward round-folded examples were also recovered (Fig. 203.3). With respect to deep bowls from these two areas, the only retrieved specimen had an external expanded rounded rim and a curved body profile (Fig. 203.7). As regards closed forms from the SW gate and NW ambulatory, only sherds of three related kinds of medium-size jars were recovered: some with a tall, narrow neck; some with a flaring neck and a band rim (Fig. 203.5); and a type of necked jar with a bulbous rim and stepped shoulders (Fig. 203.6).

The third large batch of *in situ* ceramics was excavated in the SE and SW ambulatories, where closed forms were again more frequent than open ones (the latter amounting to 30% of the total). The open forms, mostly types of bowls, included more examples of small conical bowls (Fig. 204.2), carinated bowls (Fig. 204.1) and bowls with an overhanging band rim (Fig. 204.3). Noteworthy among the open forms was a large, deep vessel whose profile could be entirely reconstructed: grooved on the outside, and featuring an expanded rim, it presented five ribs on its outer walls (two just below the rim, two in middle section of the vase and one close to the base), and a ring base with a central hole (Fig. 204.8). The closed forms in this batch were more numerous and varied. The only small jar found was a specimen with a short plain rim (Fig. 204.4). Jars of medium size, which made up the largest group, included necked jars with a flat external expanded rim, an ovoid profile and a horizontal comb decoration on the shoulders (Fig. 205.3). Also found were necked jars with an external expanded rim, a vertical neck and rounded shoulders (Fig. 205.2), and a type of jar with a bulbous rim and stepped shoulders (Fig. 204.6). One of the jars with a short neck was a specimen with an outside rounded rim (Fig. 204.5). Two other short plain-rimmed jars were found that featured either plain shoulders (Fig. 204.7) or shoulders with multiple ridges (Fig. 205.1). The large shoulders that were characteristic of both of these types seemed to suggest that they had a greater cubic capacity than the other specimens described above. Two large jars were also excavated in this area: one with a rim with multiple ridges (Fig. 205.5); the other with a drooping rim (Fig. 205.4). The neck of the latter type was lined internally and externally with bitumen, while the former was marked with a sinuous line on its shoulder. These two types were found together, along with the large, deep vessel with a perforated ring base described above.

With regard to the Old Babylonian period, the paucity of sherds found in primary contexts prevented a detailed analysis of the ceramic materials (as noted at the outset), but the assemblage from this phase could be partially reconstructed with the help of the post-Isin-Larsa stratigraphic sequence. The most striking feature of the later phase was the appearance of new shapes. In particular, many more goblets were in use during the Old Babylonian period than in previous epochs, which yielded only occasional examples. Most attested was a kind of goblet with cylindrical or slightly sinuous walls and a ring base (Fig. 206.4 and 206.5), but others were also found, including goblets with a button base (Fig. 206.1) and examples with a flat stump base (Fig. 206.2). Among other shapes were vessels with a solid pointed base (Fig. 206.3) and a vessel with a cylindrical body and a ring base (Fig. 206.6). The bowls associated with the Old Babylonian phase were almost exclusively of small sizes, notably small bowls with a plain rim and others with a thickened inwardly bevelled rim (Fig. 206.7). Two additional open forms were large, shallow bowls with a thickened inwardly bevelled rim and curved walls (Fig. 206.8), and a type of deep bowl with curvilinear sides and an outwardly expanded flat rim (Fig. 206.9). Notable among the closed forms was a specimen of a jar with a vertical neck and a plain rim that was decorated in several places with dark paint (Fig. 206.10). It displayed a painted narrow horizontal band inside the rim, a wide horizontal band of paint extending over the rim and the neck, and a row of dots in dark paint along the junction between the neck and the shoulder. In addition, the outer walls featured a large circular motif in dark paint, but the

fragment was unfortunately not sufficiently well preserved to clarify whether this was an isolated figure or whether it was part of a more elaborate geometric design. Also attributable to the Old Babylonian phase was a large vessel with a thick triangular rim and straight vertical walls featuring multiple thick ribs (Fig. 206.11).

The way the pottery types evolved in the four occupation phases identified for the New Eninnu during the British Museum team's excavations (outlined above) was reflected in a series of discernible trends, the first of which was clarified by the marked contrast between the immediate pre-Gudea phase and the earliest occupation of the New Eninnu. This related particularly to the mass-produced vessels that predominated overwhelmingly in the period prior to Gudea's construction of the complex. During the Late Akkad or Early Lagash II and Ur-Bau eras the mass-produced repertoire was composed of goblets (Figs. 161.1–3, 162.1, 163.1 and 163.2) and above all conical bowls (Figs. 159.1–4, 161.7, 161.8, 162.2 and 163.4–7), but pots of this kind were completely absent from the few contexts in which ceramics associated with the first (Gudea) occupation phase of the New Eninnu were recovered. Characteristic of the Gudea era were other forms that continued to be used in the Ur III and Isin-Larsa phases. They included a slightly smaller kind of conical bowl (Figs. 201.1, 201.2 and 204.2), carinated bowls (Figs. 200.3, 203.1, 203.2 and 204.1) and bowls with an inward round-folded rim (Figs. 200.1, 200.2, 201.4 and 203.3). It is noteworthy that very few examples of conical bowls with an overhanging band rim (Fig. 204.3) were found in the early New Eninnu phase, though they were attested in Late Akkad times, in contexts associated with the period prior to the construction of Gudea's Ningirsu temple (Figs. 159.5, 160.3 and 162.3).

Two vessels that were in use continuously from the pre-Gudea phase through to the early occupation of the New Eninnu were large bowls with a triangular rim and short plain-rimmed jars. Production of large bowls of this type (Figs. 159.11, 160.2, 160.9, 161.5, 162.4, 8, 163.9 and 163.10) was discontinued in subsequent phases, and the form was seemingly replaced in the Isin-Larsa period with a kind of deep bowl with a flat thickened rim (Fig. 201.5–8). Although the short plain-rimmed jars that were widely attested in the pre-Gudea phase (Figs. 159.7–10, 160.4, 160.7, 161.5 and 164.3–7) remained in use in subsequent periods, they were no longer the most common kind of jar in the repertoire. Indeed, they decreased in numbers dramatically in the Ur III period (Fig. 200.5) and were only poorly attested in Isin-Larsa times (Fig. 204.7). A related form that should be mentioned is the small jar with a short plain rim (Figs. 200.6, 202.4 and 204.4), which was a significant numerical presence in the Ur III and Isin-Larsa repertoires.

Typical of the Late Akkad pottery repertoire from Tell A were large carinated bowls (Fig. 199.4) that were also found frequently in Late Akkad contexts in Nippur (and might have been in use in earlier periods; see MacMahon 2006, p. 77 (Type O-15)), together with jars with a triangular rim and ridged shoulders (Fig. 199.5). The latter form, which was found only in the Late Akkad layers on Tell A, is generally considered to be a hallmark of the Late Akkad and Ur III periods (MacMahon 2006, pp. 72–3 (Type C-16b); and Armstrong and Gasche 2014, pp. 65–6 (Group 255A2)). The characteristic form of jar in the post-Gudea occupation phases was a jar with ridged shoulders and a short plain rim (Figs. 200.8 and 205.1), which was also found in Girsu by the French excavators (see Genouillac 1936, p. 99 (Pl. XXVIII, no. 3483)). The evidence currently suggests that this type of jar was a regional or local variant that was probably first produced in Ur III times (Fig. 200.8), though it continued to be used during the subsequent Isin-Larsa era (Fig. 205.1).

Finally, some more general conclusions can be drawn. First, the pottery repertoires of the pre-Gudea and Lagash II phases (Figs. 159–164 and 199, respectively) displayed both continuity and divergences that were attributed to the changing use of the mound before and after the construction of the New Eninnu. With respect to forms that remained in use during the two phases, the recovered materials were classified on the basis of comparisons with Late Akkad ceramics. Secondly, contrasting with the degree of continuity in the ceramic repertoire that was evident between the pre-Gudea and Gudea phases, the following eras saw the introduction of some completely new shapes. The move away from Lagash II forms (Fig. 199) began in the New Eninnu's second occupation phase in Ur III times (Fig. 200), when novel pottery types began to emerge, notably carinated bowls with an inward round-folded rim and jars with triple-ridged rims. Both types were also part of the subsequent Isin-Larsa repertoire (Figs. 202–6). Little can be added about the retrieved sherds from the Old Babylonian period (Fig. 206), except to say that, compared with examples from other sites in the central part of southern Iraq, the finds made in Girsu suggest that

Tell A was occupied until at least the beginning of the Old Babylonian era.

Ritual Pits for the Burial of the Statues of Gudea

The procedures for the decommissioning of the Temple of Ningirsu included the burial of its sacred votives, notably the impressive statues of Gudea that were unearthed on Tell A. Four atypical pits that might have contained such ritual interments were discovered by the British Museum team in the fabric of the temple walls, where they were dug laterally (like spacious niches) into the faces of the walls that formed the temple's symbolically charged doorways. All were found truncated horizontally at a similar topographical height of around 15.35 m, corresponding to the Hellenistic levelling horizon in this area. Moreover, they had all been carefully re-excavated in antiquity, again probably under the authority of Adadnadinakhe, and subsequently backfilled prior to the construction of the Hellenistic complex.

A series of three particularly abnormal-looking pits, two rectangular in shape (2038 and 2040) and one subrectangular (2042), were found in the NE façade of the Ningirsu temple. Situated on the NW side of the temple's main entrance (leading into the antecella), pits 2038 and 2040 were cut directly into the NE façade wall on either side of the buttress tower (2168). Pit 2042, which was hollowed out in the wall that formed the NW side of the passageway of the main entrance leading through the NE façade (2048), was subrectangular, with a NW–SE length of 1.94 m and a NE–SW width of 1.49 m. Filled with clayey silt material that was derived from mud-brick melt and redeposited occupation layers (2043), it was excavated to a depth of 0.28 m below the levelling horizon. Rectangular pit 2040, which had straight vertical sides, was cut to align with the exterior NE face of wall 2048. Measuring 2.04 m along its NW–SE length, it was 0.98 m wide, with an exposed depth of 0.42 m, and it contained a compact clayey silt fill (2041), together with seemingly redeposited materials and a few brick fragments and mud-brick melt. Pit 2038, which had the same NW–SE alignment as its counterpart on the SE side of the buttress tower (2040), was also rectangular with vertical sides, and it was dug directly into the NE face of wall 2048, respecting the line followed by the wall. Having a NW–SE length of 1.92 m and a width of 0.91 m,

538 The Mound of the Palace

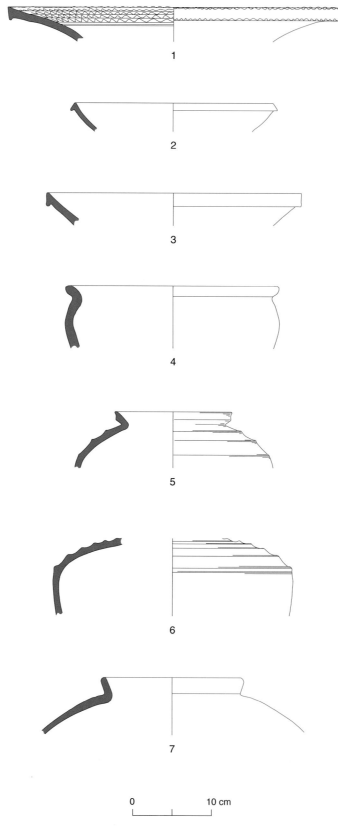

FIGURE 199. Pottery from the New Eninnu I.

The New Eninnu from Lagash II Times to the Old Babylonian Period   539

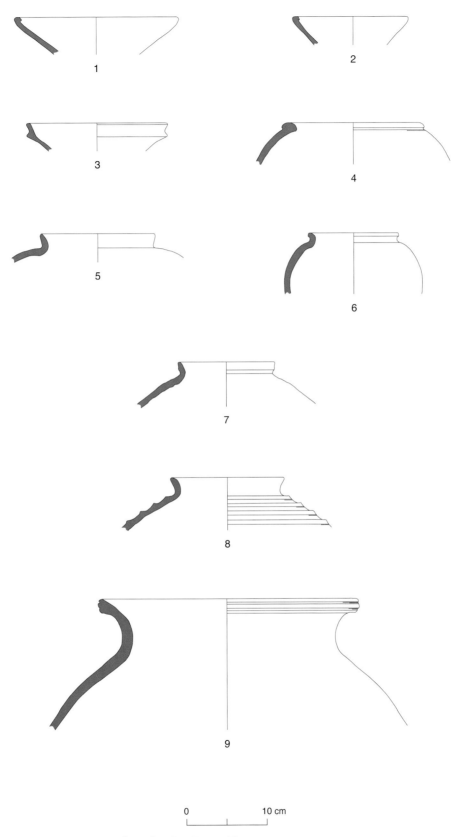

FIGURE 200.   Pottery from the New Eninnu II.

540 The Mound of the Palace

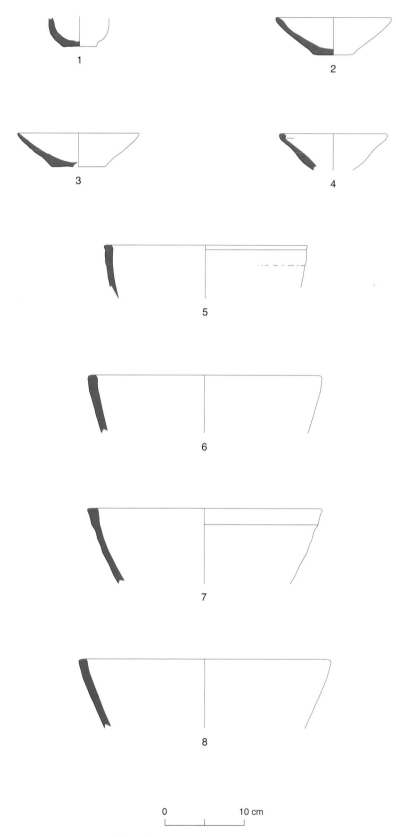

FIGURE 201. Pottery from the New Eninnu III.

The New Eninnu from Lagash II Times to the Old Babylonian Period 541

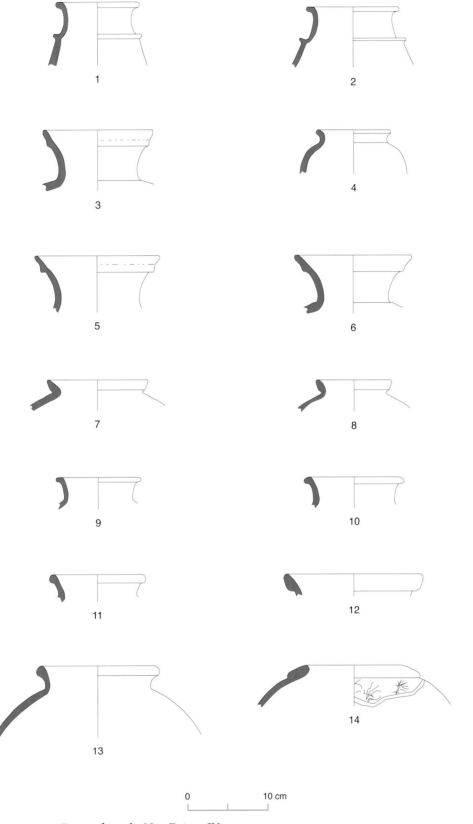

FIGURE 202. Pottery from the New Eninnu IV.

542　The Mound of the Palace

FIGURE 203. Pottery from the New Eninnu V.

The New Eninnu from Lagash II Times to the Old Babylonian Period 543

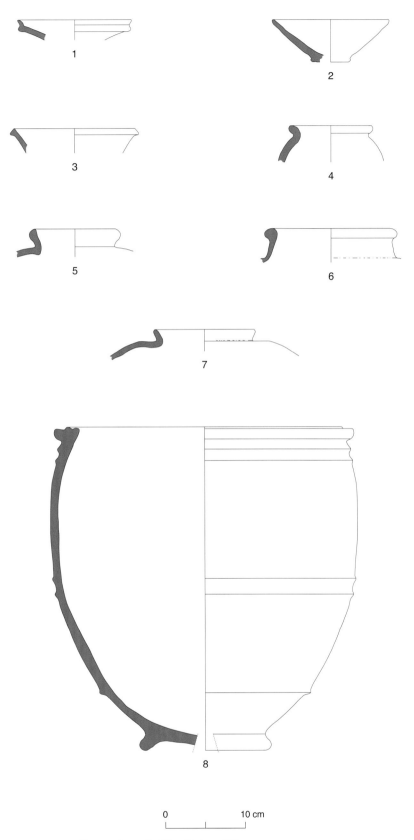

FIGURE 204. Pottery from the New Eninnu VI.

544 The Mound of the Palace

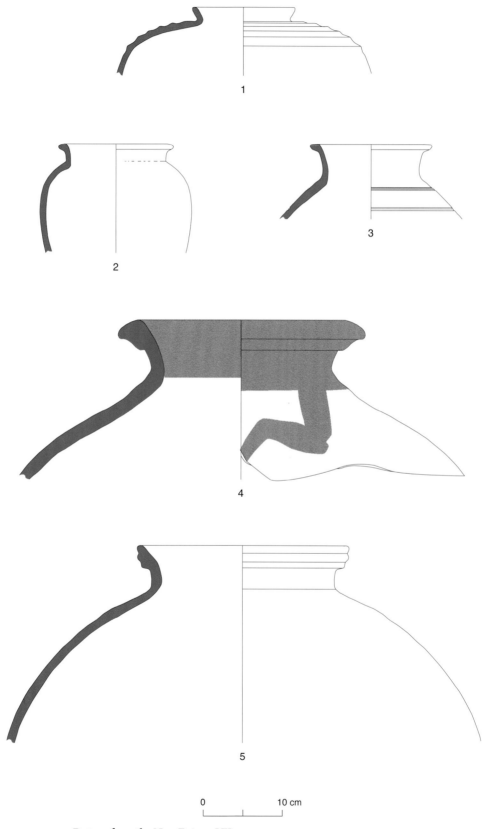

FIGURE 205. Pottery from the New Eninnu VII.

The New Eninnu from Lagash II Times to the Old Babylonian Period 545

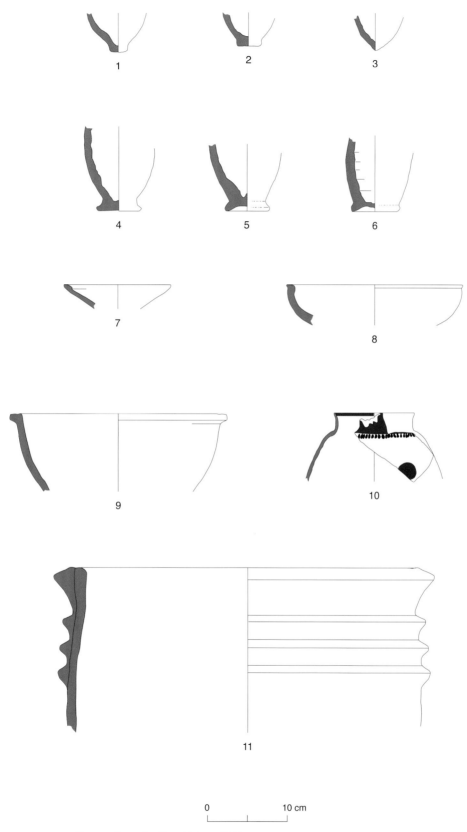

FIGURE 206. Pottery from the New Eninnu VIII.

it was excavated to a depth of 0.4 m, and it too contained a deliberately laid backfill (2039) of clayey silt and compact non-specific site deposits that were seemingly a mix of mud-brick melt and degraded occupation layers. Notably, no finds whatsoever were retrieved from any of these pits.

A fourth subrectangular pit (3031) of a very similar character to those just described was found centrally placed in the wall that formed the SW side of the passageway that led into the Ningirsu temple's inner sanctum, where it was aligned with the passageway's long axis through the partition wall between the antecella and the cella. With a NW–SE length of 1.55 m and a width of 0.95 m, it was excavated to a total depth of 0.89 m. As was also noted with respect to the three pits found in the temple's NE façade and its main entrance, pit 3031 was filled with a sandy silt deposit (3030) that

appeared to be a tertiary backfill of very homogeneous material, including mud-brick fragments and melt. It had been opened in antiquity with a degree of care that did not suggest either chance or haphazard looting. On the contrary, since its top and sides were distinct and well preserved, it seemed to have been excavated with the intention of retrieving some precious object (or objects) that had been buried inside it, no doubt when the temple was deconsecrated and closed. Similarly, if it had not been backfilled soon after it was re-excavated, its side walls would certainly have shown signs of at least partial collapse. Noticeably, since it contained no potsherds dating to the Hellenistic occupation phase of Tell A (after the shrine was built and in use), it was probably exposed during the digging stage of Adadnadinakhe's project. No artefacts were recovered from pit 3031 or fill 3030.

CHAPTER 37

The Statues of Gudea from the New Eninnu

The Origins and Meaning of the Gudea Statues

The pits in which the Lagash II statues dedicated to Ningirsu (Statues B, G, D and K, described below) were presumably buried when the complex was decommissioned evince all the characteristics of favissas that were specially created for the ritual interment of precious sacred artefacts. Their sizes and locations help to confirm their purpose: they were hollowed out in the thick walls of the Ningirsu temple's inner sanctum, in the walls of the antecella or libation room, where at least some of the statues of Gudea were originally installed and subsequently worshipped in the Ur III period. The stratigraphically reconstructed sequence of events indicates that the pits were dug during the temple's desacralisation phase, in the last days of its active life, and then almost certainly re-excavated centuries later in Hellenistic times, when the artefacts were removed and the cavities immediately backfilled during the preparatory works that were carried out prior to the construction of the successor complex built by Adadnadinakhe. The stratigraphy correlates extremely well with the probable narrative history of the statues, according to which they were ritually deconsecrated and placed in the favissas in the Old Babylonian period, remaining there for a millennium and a half, until the Hellenistic epoch, when they were unearthed and displayed in niches in Adadnadinakhe's shrine. Finally, when the Hellenistic building was burnt to the ground around 150 BCE, the carvings were malignly displaced, violently mutilated and beheaded. The Hellenistic history of the renewed building and the ultimate fate of the

Sumerian statues are detailed in Part 4 below, but it is vital to understand the early history of the Lagash II Tell A statuary to determine which carvings were originally housed in the Ningirsu temple itself and which of them might therefore have been deliberately and carefully entombed in the pits found in the walls of the antecella. Equally, although actual evidence of the existence of favissas has only been uncovered in the Ningirsu temple that lay at the heart of Gudea's New Eninnu, it is reasonable to assume that the Gudea statues devoted to other deities were similarly treated and interred in the Old Babylonian period, when the complex was taken out of service.

A crucial point that must be stressed at the outset is that, if the statues were indeed ritually treated and buried in Old Babylonian times, they should show traces of the desacralisation processes that they underwent prior to their interment. As is demonstrated in Part 2 with regard to the sacred objects that were formally deconsecrated and entombed on Tell K, deconsecration rites were customary procedures in Sumerian times. It should also be noted, however, that the Lagash II statues, which endured unusually long and eventful lives, met violent ends when the Hellenistic complex was destroyed, and the very fact that they were on display in the building constructed by Adadnadinakhe made them especially vulnerable to the hostile forces who eventually overran the site. This long and checkered history makes it difficult to assess their condition and to distinguish between categories of damage, including: deliberate, but pious acts of defacement that were carried out during decommissioning and deactivation rituals; natural wear and tear consequent

547

upon the long passage of time; programmatic or symbolic mutilation inflicted by hostile forces (such as was demonstrated with respect to the Stele of the Vultures on Tell K, for example); and finally, the destructive effects of wanton acts of pillage and plunder. The Lagash II statues from Tell A bear the scars of their history as palimpsests of marks that must be systematically and forensically scrutinised in order to distinguish between different types of damage and to recover the valuable information that might be encoded in them.

Sarzec unearthed a total of ten Lagash II royal statues from the ruins of the Hellenistic complex that he encountered in the upper layers of Tell A: nine of Gudea (AO1–AO8 and AO10) and one of Ur-Bau (AO9). The Gudea carvings are traditionally referred to alphabetically as Statues A to K, following their display locations in the Louvre in the early 1900s, and the alphabetical ordering of other Gudea statues has become a widespread convention. All made of diorite, the sculptures range in height between about 1 m and 1.5 m, with the exception of the depiction of Ur-Bau, which is only 0.68 m tall, and they all show the subject—whether standing or seated—wearing a long robe like a toga, with his hands clasped at his chest (Fig. 207). The rulers are depicted in a standardised manner that relates to formal conventions displayed in votive statues from the third millennium BCE in the Early Dynastic period and Akkad times, though the Lagash II style is less naturalistic, more synthetic and more formalised than that preferred by the Akkad sculptors.

One element that ostensibly links the Ur-Bau and Gudea carvings with earlier portrayals of Akkad rulers (Fig. 208), for example, is the treatment of the hands. In all cases, the right hand, which is placed laterally across the torso, is held in the upward-facing left palm, with the fingers of the left hand reaching up almost perpendicularly across the back of the right hand and the two thumbs interlocked horizontally above. Iconographically, the stylised position signifies an act of worship, supplication or prayer, and it is also found on the diorite statue in the Louvre (SB47) of the Akkad ruler Manishtusu that was looted in antiquity by the Elamite king Shutruk-Nakhunte I. Manishtusu's hands are far more realistically carved than those of Ur-Bau and Gudea, however, as can be seen in the fingers and joints of the left hand, and overall in the contoured detail that is applied to the left hand to show its muscularity and to give it an individualised character. Those features are notably absent from the hands of Ur-Bau and Gudea, which are by and large much more stylised,

as is especially evident in the smooth, elongated fingers of the right hand, and this raises an important point of interpretation. With respect to the pious gesture, it should be noted that, although at first glance it seems unexceptional, this precise way of holding one hand in the other, including the positions of the fingers of the clasping hand and the interlocked thumbs, is extremely unnatural, as can easily be verified by an attentive observer who tries to replicate it. Unless people of that epoch had incredibly long fingers and thumbs, it is impossible for the fingers of the left hand to reach up over the back of the right hand such that the thumbs can be crossed above in the way they are shown on the statues. Accordingly, the realistic detail in the hands of Manishtusu tends not to complement but rather to contradict and work against the stylisation that is inherent in the pose, suggesting that Akkad realism might have been an alien addition to a native Sumerian tradition. As with other features of the revival of Sumerian culture under Ur-Bau and Gudea, therefore, the precise way in which the gesture was interpreted in the Lagash II statuary from Tell A was perhaps not a modification of an Akkad practice, but a return to much older conventions, as are apparent, for example, in the extremely stylised hands of the praying figures on the Ur-Nanshe Plaques (discussed in detail in Chapters 16 and 19). It is speculative to suggest that the Akkad importation of realistic ingredients into a sacred gesture such as this might have struck a trained Sumerian eye as somewhat barbaric, but it would not be surprising if that had in fact been the case.

Two variants of the statues of Gudea were produced that show him both standing (Statues A, C, E, G and K) and seated (Statues B, D, F and H), and both have antecedents in Akkad and Early Dynastic times: for instance, two standing statues of Manishtusu (SB47 and SB48) and one of him seated (SB49) from the Akkad period; together with a seated Early Dynastic statue of an unidentified subject from Tell A (AO11) and a standing statue of Enmetena that was discovered in Ur (IM5 (U805)). On both types of Gudea statues the ruler is shown wearing a long, plain robe that wraps around his body, covering his left shoulder and arm (with a long strip of cloth hanging down from his left forearm), and passing diagonally downwards over the chest to leave his right arm and shoulder exposed. The garment seems to be secured below the figure's right armpit, where the fastening creates several pleats or folds. The arrangement is reproduced on all the statues of Gudea and on that of Ur-Bau, and it can also be

The Statues of Gudea from the New Eninnu 549

FIGURE 207. The diorite statues of Tell A, including Statues A–F of Gudea and the portrait of Ur-Bau. Musée du Louvre, AO8 (A), AO2 (B), AO5 (C), AO1 (D), AO6 (E), AO3 (F) and AO9 (Ur-Bau).

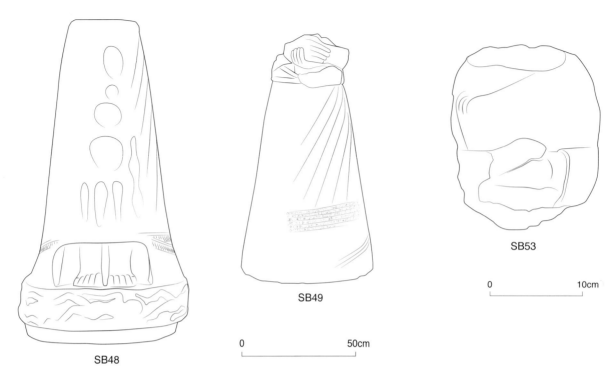

FIGURE 208. Statues of the Akkad rulers Manishtusu (standing and seated) and Naram-Sin. Musée du Louvre, SB48, SB49 and SB53.

observed on a rather worn fragment of a diorite statue of the Akkad king Naram-Sin that was discovered in Susa (SB53); it should be noted in passing that Naram-Sin's hands are also shown in the praying pose, but they are so badly damaged that no details are preserved of how they were carved. By contrast with the clothing worn by Gudea and Ur-Bau, Early Dynastic carvings often show priests, soldiers and high-status individuals (including divinities) wearing just a kaunakes or skirt that covers only their lower bodies, leaving their torsos bare (as on the Ur-Nanshe Plaques and the mythological obverse of the Stele of the Vultures, for example), though early versions of the Gudea-style robe are also attested, notably on the historical reverse of the Stele of the Vultures, where Eanatum is distinguished by the fact that he wears a toga-like garment that is made of the same lanceolate flounces as his kaunakes. As on the Gudea statues, it also covers his left shoulder and bicep and the left side of his chest, leaving his right arm and shoulder bare.

With regard to the way the Lagash II figures are posed, a further comparison between the way the hands are portrayed in the Early Dynastic carvings and the Gudea statues reveals a possible pattern. On the historical side of the Stele of the Vultures, for example, Eanatum wields his spear in his left hand on Fragment E, and almost certainly also on Fragment D, where it is only partially preserved (on Fragment A), just as Ningirsu on the obverse holds the net of prisoners and the reins of his chariot in his left hand (Fragments D and E, respectively). For the ruler, as for the god, that is, the left hand is engaged in immediate action—a correlation that is reinforced by the fact that the hands are in apposition on the two sides of the preserved pieces. In his right hand, by contrast, the god rather passively—or perhaps ceremonially—holds his divine mace (on the obverse of Fragments D and E), while on the reverse of the stele Eanatum comparably holds a limp-looking enigmatic weapon on Fragment D, and the manner in which he is shown holding another unidentified weapon close to his chest on Fragment E is similarly unassertive. The contrasting ways in which the hands are shown seem to point to a distinction between the left, which is used for active, worldly purposes, and the right, which is more closely associated with sacred and symbolic objects and gestures. In the reconstruction of the obverse, therefore, Ninhursag is shown raising her libation cup and blessing her son with her right hand (in the restorations associated with

Fragments C and B, respectively), while the reconstruction of the inferred burial scene on the historical side (associated with Fragments F and G) depicts Eanatum sanctifying the Lagash dead with a sacred mace that he holds in his right hand. Analogously, the Lagash II carved likenesses of Gudea, and indeed that of U-Bau, show the left hand emerging from the part of the robe that falls down from the left forearm in order to grasp and support the right hand. It is as though the left hand is ancillary to the right, which is held in a state of readiness to perform whatever sacred gesture might be required, and the distinction is positively maintained on all the carved likenesses of Gudea, including the seated ones.

The feet of the standing statues of Gudea are set into a kind of niche that is formed as an extension of the pleated length of cloth that falls from below the figure's right shoulder. The train, as it might be described, descends down the right flank of the body, wrapping around the back of the figure to create the enclosure. The feet of the standing statue of Enmetena are also placed in a recess, but in this case there is no attempt to contextualise it, and when the carving is viewed from behind, it can clearly be seen that the base that forms the back and sides of the niche is just plain polished stone that is not descriptively connected with the bottom of the skirt, either as an undergarment, for example, or as a short ceremonial train. This contrasts with the feet of the Akkad standing statue of Manishtusu (SB48), the feet of which are also placed in a recess that is formed as an extension of his elongated robe. In this instance, however, the garment is highly decorated along its hem and where it falls down from the shoulder, as can again be most clearly seen when the sculpture is viewed from behind. Similarly, the pleats that are only visible below the right shoulder of the Gudea statues are developed in the Manishtusu carving as soft undulations (beautifully formed, it must be said) that extend down the back of the garment. As with the marked dissimilarity between the hands of Gudea and those of Manishtusu noted above, in this respect the Akkad portrait also exhibits a much greater interest in sculpted realism than the Sumerian statuary. This is further confirmed by the fact that the Gudea sculptors treated one or more parts of the garment (and sometimes the right shoulder) non-representationally as blank spaces that could be used to contain cuneiform inscriptions. Conversely, the symbolic import of the Manishtusu portrait is focused on the base on which the ruler stands, which is decorated with the outstretched figures of vanquished enemies whose torsos are inscribed with cuneiform texts in Akkadian indicating that they are princes supplicating for mercy. Since the Sumerian sculptors who made the Gudea statues must have been well aware of the more naturalistic approach taken to figurative carvings by their Akkad forebears, the reversion to a more stylised mode might once more be taken as a sign that the Sumerian sculptors working under Ur-Bau and Gudea consciously rejected Akkad practices.

The feet of the seated Gudea statues are largely released from the niche or enclosure. Just a part of the cavity remains that is formed by the sides and seemingly also the back of the ruler's bench or stool, though it is not entirely clear whether the filled area between the legs at the back of the seat is supposed to be a mimetic representation or not. The anonymous seated statue from the Early Dynastic period mentioned above (fragment AO11 from Tell A) seems also to include a rudimentary indication of a stool, but as with the base of the standing Early Dynastic figure of Enmetena it is not descriptively developed, and the feet are contained in the same kind of artificially formed space as on the standing sculpture. The feet of the standing figure of Ur-Bau (AO9) are too badly damaged to be interpreted, but a stylistically similar diorite fragment that shows two feet (AO38B) was unearthed in room 8 (on Sarzec's Plan A) of the Hellenistic shrine on Tell A. This compares well with the feet of the Gudea statues, which are bare (as is seemingly the case for all free-standing figurative sculptures from Early Dynastic, Akkad and Lagash II times) and smooth, and characterised by solid ankles with long slender toes and well-formed toenails. In certain instances there is also some schematic contouring along the bridge of the foot that is perhaps intended to represent the metatarsals.

Ur-Bau and Gudea are not shown carrying any evident symbols of kingship, such as a sceptre or a mace, and unlike Manishtusu they are not placed on bases or socles adorned with images that bear witness to their high status. Nonetheless, the stools on which the seated figures are shown are presumably a kind of throne, and it seems fair to assume that they would have been interpreted as seats of power by early viewers of the works. Perhaps most importantly, though, all the figures (including Manishtusu) are shown wearing the same style of long robe or toga, and this garment was surely indicative of their rank. Another emblem of office on some preserved sculptures is almost certainly the brimmed hat that Gudea is seen wearing. It cannot be known how many of the Tell A carvings included this feature because the heads of all the Tell A sculptures were violently removed, but the brimmed hat surely represented a meaningful alternative to other kinds of regal headgear or crownlike emblems—the horned helmet worn by Naram-Sin on his victory stele, for example, or the basket loaded with bricks that Ur-Nanshe carries on his head on Plaque A. Other detached heads that have long been thought to derive from Gudea statuary (notably AO12, which was also found on Tell A) show the ruler with a shaven head—a sign of piety that was much used in Early Dynastic times, including (again) on the Ur-Nanshe Plaques. Interestingly, the preserved heads of Gudea, with and without the brimmed headgear, are consistently beardless, and while beards were sometimes used as evident symbols of virility (conspicuously by Naram-Sin) and also of divinity (in the case of Ningirsu on the obverse of the Stele of the Vultures, for example) it is also common for rulers to be portrayed with clean-shaven faces in the Early Dynastic period—not only in pious contexts, as on the Ur-Nanshe Plaques, but also in warlike situations, as on the historical reverse of the Stele of the Vultures, where Eanatum is beardless.

Especially in the exposed parts of the upper bodies, the statues of Ur-Bau and Gudea exhibit softly modelled curves representing the musculature of the chest, arms (the bare right arm in particular) and shoulders. Similarly, when the statues are seen from behind, the curvature of the spine is not hidden by the long robe, and the hips are noticeably rather broad—a feature that is most evident on the statue of Ur-Bau, but not lacking on the portrayals of Gudea. It has been argued that the way the torsos are carved signals physical strength and a capacity to rule, albeit in an idealised representational mode (Winter 1989), and there can be no doubt that the added interest in the musculature represents a new emphasis that was hardly present in depictions of Early Dynastic rulers, where the limbs, which are not depicted with any attention to realism, are generally rather shapeless. Nevertheless, the Gudea statues evince only a small interest in anatomically precise depictions of physiology, and the overall softness of the contours tends to downplay any focus on pure muscularity, doubtless as a way of further accenting the pious connotations of the portrayals.

Though they are not usually larger than life (the biggest standing statues of Gudea being a little less than 1.5 m tall, without the lost heads), the physical presence of many of the

works is, of course, extremely impressive, not least because of the weight and hardness of the imported stone. This conceivably adds an air of magnificence to the representations, though the idea should again not be overstated, and it should also be noted that Ur-Bau and Gudea are patently displayed without material adornments that might enhance their grandeur, and without clear or elaborated attributes of kingship (as mentioned above). Similarly, while the positioning of the arms with respect to the torsos might suggest a dependable solidity of form, and in the case of the standing statues the shape is almost columnar, which might symbolise the ruler's ability to sustain and govern the state, it also minimises the sense that there is a potential for action. Consequently, the portraits are essentially contemplative, such that any suggestions of strength are at one remove from the physicality of the sculpted bodies and the raw materiality of the stone, which is extremely highly polished, emphasising the play of light on its surface rather than its inner substance. To focus on Gudea, the implication is that the ruler's qualities of strength and leadership derive not from his mere physical presence, but from his piety and the unstinting obedience he has shown to the will of Ningirsu and the rest of the Girsu pantheon, and this is also the message of the texts inscribed on the statues (considered below). In particular, it is an outlook that is perhaps further confirmed by a suggestive connection that can be made between the preserved Gudea heads and the inscription on Statue B (RIME 3.1.1.7.StB), which refers to a 'legitimate head made to stand out gloriously in the assembly by Ningishzida'. Special value is accordingly given to intellectual qualities: the prominent ears, perhaps suggesting attentiveness and wisdom, as well as an ability to heed the call of the divine (as explicitly narrated in the Cylinder Inscriptions), while the large percipient eyes (also a significant feature of Early Dynastic carvings) add to the mood of devoted composure that is signalled most clearly by the hands.

Despite the many carved portraits of himself that Gudea commissioned, therefore, it is probably correct to say that the implied aesthetic was not one of aggrandisement, but rather the regal self-abasement of a supreme king who saw clear continuity between his spiritual devotion and his leadership qualities—a ruler who was confident in the knowledge that when strength was needed it would be supplied by the gods. Indeed, as is also discussed below with reference to their inscriptions, it is perhaps not going too far to say that the carvings aim to inhabit a liminal dimension that is characterised by sanctity and divine service, and this would doubtless have been made apparent in the way the lustrous forms were displayed and illuminated within the holiest rooms of the Ningirsu temple at the core of the New Eninnu, as well as in the shrines of any other deities to whom statues were dedicated (not least Ningirsu's wife, Bau, whose temple was also in the New Eninnu on Tell A). The expression of these traits might once again represent a partial reversion to native Sumerian traditions, though the Gudea statues probably invoke a newly sophisticated version of the ethos—locating the renaissance of local beliefs in a modified approach to sculptural form that might represent the earliest hints of transcendental philosophical and religious ideas. In any event, the style of the Lagash II carvings contrasts starkly with the way in which, for instance, Naram-Sin portrayed himself on his victory stele as a man of heroic action to the point of bombast, and even with the superficially similar sculpted portrait of Manishtusu, which stresses magnificence in the costume and political and military might in the symbolism of the carved socle.

The statues retrieved from Tell A are made of greenish dark grey diorite, a relatively rare plutonic rock that is hard and therefore difficult to sculpt, but capable of taking a high polish. Not easily salvaged or reworked, it is also extremely durable—characteristics that doubtless contributed to the survival of the Lagash II carvings. The inscription on Statue B (RIME 3.1.1.7.StB) indicates that the material was chosen for its special qualities: 'For this statue nobody was supposed to use silver or lapis lazuli, neither should copper or tin or bronze be a working (material). It is (exclusively) of diorite.' Similarly, in the epic poem Lugale (475–8) diorite is declared to be suitable for the statues of great rulers because the carvings must endure for as long as their subjects are remembered. The Gudea inscriptions also stress the provenance of the material, for example in the text on Statue A (RIME 3.1.1.7.StA), which states that (like the Akkad rulers who came before him) he ordered the stone to be brought from the 'mountain of Magan' (probably somewhere in modern Oman), and the statement is repeated on all the other preserved Gudea statues with the solitary exception of seated Statue F. In addition to its material properties, the stone was also prized on account of its exotic origins, which increased its value and subtly added to the prestige and implied influence of a ruler who was able to obtain it with relative ease. Small differences in the stone are observable, perhaps indicating that they were from different batches, or even different

quarries, though no mention of that is made. Statue K is a slightly lighter green than the others, while Statue G is mottled with tiny light-coloured spots, and the more homogeneous blocks from which Statues B and D were sculpted are respectively dark green and dark grey. Additionally, there are some perceptible variations in the carving. For example, the folds of the robe are more prominent on Statue B (particularly by the left armpit), when it is compared with Statues D and G, while the torso of Statue B exhibits a thicker profile than that of Statue D (the Gudea Colossus), which is rather slender. The heights of the bases also differ: that of Statue D is the tallest, while the base of Statue G is both the lowest and the least well polished.

The statue of Ur-Bau (AO9), which measures 0.68 m (h) × 0.37 m (w) × 0.29 m (t) and creates a solid or stocky impression, is a little more than half the size of the large standing Gudea figures from Tell A. The rounded outlines are softer than those of the Gudea statues, while the robe is simpler: it has no fringes, and only the upper oblique part of the edge is incised on the back of the figure. Ur-Bau's thumbs appear bigger than his other fingers, which are flattened, and the fingernails are incised, but no attempt is made to represent the knuckles, which sometimes appear on the Gudea pieces (Statues B, D, E and H). The inscription is placed on the upper part of the back of the Ur-Bau figure, where it is set within a rectangular frame. The text (which is cited more fully in Chapter 33) gives an account of Ur-Bau's construction of the relocated Ningirsu temple on Tell A, including a description of the associated rituals, while mention is made of a number of shrines in Girsu that were commissioned by the ruler in honour of other deities (Ninhursag, Bau, Inanna, Enki, Nindara, Ninagala, Ninmarki, Ensignun, Geshtinanna and Dumuziabzu). After dedicating the statue of himself to Ningirsu, Ur-Bau stresses his closeness to the gods. A 'child born of Ningala', he is also the favourite of Nanshe, the executor of orders given to him by Inanna, the 'beloved slave' of Lugal.U and the 'beloved' of Dumuziabzu. Similarly, his good qualities are said to be gifts from the gods. For example, Ningirsu gave him strength, Bau gave him his auspicious name, while Enki made him wise (RIME 3.1.1.6.5).

As previously noted, most of the standing statues of Gudea that were discovered on Tell A are a little less than 1.5 m high, excluding the now missing heads, but including the heights of the socles, so they might have been life-size (or nearly life-size) representations (Statues A, C, E, G and K). The seated depictions are generally less than 1 m high, again without the missing heads (Statues B, F and H), with the notable exception of Statue D (the Gudea Colossus), which is about 1.58 m tall, making it at least 0.5 m taller than the other seated likenesses, and the biggest of all the Gudea statues found on Tell A, including the standing portrayals. All the sculptures depict the ruler in the conventional pious pose, with his hands clasped in front of his torso, and without any other attributes, but two of the seated portrayals (B and F) show Gudea with a tablet resting on his lap, together with a graduated measuring rod and an object that is probably a surveying peg. Whereas the tablet on Statue B contains the L-shaped plan of the New Eninnu, however, the one on Statue F is blank (as is considered further below).

The detached shaven head (AO12) that was unearthed on Tell A, and which has dimensions of 0.265 m (h) × 0.19 m (w) × 0.25 m (t), might possibly have come from a life-size portrayal, though it could not be reattached to any of the retrieved headless torsos. The bald head appears to have been one of two variants (as also mentioned above), the other being carvings of Gudea wearing a brimmed hat that is seemingly fashioned from wool or sheepskin. The preserved faces of the Gudea figures adopt a standard form. He has a low forehead and prominent arching eyebrows that meet at the bridge of the nose, while the curved brows are carved in relief and marked with an incised herringbone pattern. The large recessed eyes feature thick lids and protruding blank eyeballs, without any indications of the pupils. Looking straight ahead, with his eyes wide open, Gudea appears alert and focused. A vertical groove between the nose and the lips represents the philtrum, while the lips themselves are full and closed. Overall, the face is rather square, with soft cheekbones, a wide chin and a broad neck that is so short it almost allows the head to sit directly on the shoulders. The elongated ears, which are shown flat against the sides of the head, are represented with an attention to detail. Their outer edges are carved in relief, while the interiors are somewhat hollowed out, and the ear lobes are sculpturally described, as is the central cartilaginous protrusion (the tragus).

Gudea's robe generally recalls the style of the garment worn by Ur-Bau, but it is slightly more elaborate. On Statue A, for example, it features an incised fringe-like strip of oblique lines on the edge below the right armpit, together with modelled pleats, including on the upper left arm and the left forearm. The cloth falling down from the left hand is hemmed and further finished with the same vertical band of oblique lines, which curves all the way around the back of the garment, down towards the bottom (but with some distance maintained between it and the edge of the robe) and back up towards the right forearm. The upper hem on the back of the robe is generally shown running obliquely across the right shoulder (except on the broken Statues K and H). The standing statues are placed on low truncated socles (slightly conical in shape) that are completed at the back with the bottoms of the respective robes, while the socles of the seated figures are generally rounded at the front but straighter at the back. The backless seats are shown as narrow benches or stools that are just a little wider than the figure. They have well-formed details at the sides, with two broad, inward-curving legs that are finished with flat, rounded feet and blank hollows placed above and below a stretcher that suggest an overall A-shape inside the thick outlines of the legs. The stone that forms the cavity in which the feet are placed is polished, as is also usually the case with the standing statues. There is some ambiguity (noted above) about whether or not the filled space at the back of the seat, between the two legs, is intended to represent the way the item of furniture was constructed.

The carved figures excavated on Tell A are dedicated to Ningirsu (Statues B, D, G and K), Ninhursag (Statue A), Inanna (Statue C), Bau (Statues E and H) and Gatumdug (Statue F). The identity of the god or goddess to whom each sculpture was devoted is recorded in the respective inscriptions that were added to all the statues. The texts differ considerably in length and content, though there are some overlaps, especially in the formulaic proclamations. Standing Statue A and seated Statues D, F and H have cuneiform characters only on their fronts, while standing Statues C, E, G and K are inscribed only on their backs. Statues A, D, E and F have a rectangular block of text on their bare right shoulders that contains Gudea's name and other epithets linking him with the commemorated deity. In these self-contained labels Gudea styles himself as the ruler (ensí) of Lagash and the builder of the New Eninnu. The texts on Statue B, which are discussed in greater detail in Chapter 38, form the longest of all the inscriptions on the preserved likenesses (RIME 3.1.1.7.StB). In this instance the cuneiform characters are divided into nine columns that are placed around the robe on the lower part of the body (exclusively below the waist) and all around the stool or throne on which Gudea is seated, including on the blocklike parts at the rear and at the sides that do not seem to belong to its legs or form other parts of its structure. The socle itself is uninscribed. In addition to the text on its right shoulder, the Gudea Colossus (Statue D) has a further seventy-seven lines (divided into five columns) on the front and the right-hand side of the skirt—the part that covers the figure's right leg (RIME 3.1.1.7.StD). The inscriptions on the robe on the back of Statue G, which are placed between the shoulder blades and the tops of the thighs, make up 107 lines that are divided into six columns. A rectangle made up of ten lines that have been left conspicuously blank in the third row of text might have been intended to contain the statue's ceremonial name, which is not otherwise inscribed. Part of the text found on Statue G is repeated on Statue E, which is dedicated to Ningirsu's wife, Bau. The fragmentary Statue K is engraved with text on the back above the waist, but its broken condition means that only parts of the inscription are preserved, and they do not include Gudea's name (RIME 3.1.1.7.StK).

A distinctive feature of the texts on Statues B and D is that they include a lengthy, almost identical quasi-biographical note about Gudea that explains the relationship between him and the gods. In both cases he is said to have a 'treasured name' and to be the 'shepherd' chosen in the heart of Ningirsu. It is also mentioned that he serves other gods. For example, he is obedient to Bau and is the child of Gatumdug, while he was given prestige and a lofty sceptre by Igalim, and richly provided with the breath of life by Shulshaga. On Statue D he is called the one 'who tows Enlil's boat', while Statue B makes mention of Nindara, who gave him strength, and Ningishzida, his personal god. His connection with Nanshe is recorded on Statue B, where she is said to regard him in a 'friendly manner', and on Statue D, where he is described as her 'mighty steward'. Uniquely, Statue B contains a lengthy account of Ningirsu's nomination of Gudea as the ruler of Lagash, together with details of the preparatory phase of the construction of the New Eninnu, in particular the purification rituals and oracular communications. Statues B and D use the same formula to celebrate the completion of the work: 'Gudea made things function as they should for his lord Ningirsu, he made and restored for him his Eninnu, the White Thunderbird'. Interestingly, both also refer to the building of a giguna in the 'scent of cedars'.

More generally, the inscriptions record the construction of whichever temple the statues were made for, and much of the basic information is expressed as a repeating formula that notes the fact that the diorite for the carving was imported (as mentioned above). The text describes the process of making the statue in terms of 'giving birth' to it, using the Sumerian verb tud that literally refers to parturition, but metaphorically has connotations of forming and creating (see Steinkeller 2017, pp. 110–11). Other information included in the formula are the naming of the statue and the fact of its introduction into the temple where it was displayed. Partly on account of the use of the verb tud, it has been suggested that the formulaic passage alludes to rituals that endowed the human-made artefacts with a cultic life, enabling them to commune with the divine (Winter 1992, pp. 21–4; and Winter 2000). Mesopotamian statues of divinities and royal figures were infused with life in the ceremony known as the mouth-opening ritual (touched upon in Chapter 35). Since the oldest confirmed written instructions for this ritual date from the first millennium BCE (Walker and Dick 2001), the possible allusion to it with reference to the opening of the mouth of a Gudea statue in the Ur III offering list cited in Chapter 35 might constitute the earliest mention of the rite prior to the Neo-Assyrian period. More uncertainty surrounds the broken remains of the Lagash II text inscribed on Gudea Statue R (RIME 3.1.1.7.StR), including the inferred reconstruction of the Sumerian word for the mouth-opening ritual, ka.du$_8$ (Selz 1997, p. 177). Even in the absence of unequivocal epigraphic evidence, however, there can be little doubt that animation rituals were performed on dedicatory statues in the Lagash II period (Winter 1992, pp. 13–42). Similarly, as discussed in Chapter 19 above, during Early Dynastic times many kinds of artefacts were solemnly imbued with a divine essence before being placed in the holiest rooms of the successive temples that were built on Tell K. What this meant with regard to the animation of the Gudea likenesses is that, like the cult statues of deities, they underwent a ritual transformation that turned them into substantial manifestations of their subjects. Consequently, the statues were endowed with the power to speak on the ruler's behalf and to make his wishes known to the populace.

In addition to the stress that is placed on his special proximity to the divine sphere, Gudea's personal characteristics are also described in some of the longer inscriptions, and particular emphasis is placed on his intelligence. In the inscription on Statue F, for instance, where he declares that he is the servant of the 'god', Gudea's exceptional intellect is explicitly associated with the fact that he 'drew a design in the shed of the brick mould' (RIME 3.1.1.7.StF). The interest of the statement is increased exponentially by the fact that the tablet that Gudea holds in his lap on Statue F is blank, as though it has not yet been inscribed with the temple plan that had presumably already been executed by the time the statue was carved and installed within its walls. Maybe the *tabula rasa* was therefore an implied challenge to those who viewed it, asking them to consider whether they would be able even to draw the blueprint of a building that was already in existence, let alone have the necessary imaginative power to design one from scratch, as Gudea had done in the brick-making shed. Given the inclusion of the finished design for the temenos of the New Eninnu on Statue B, the relationship between the two statues, with their contrasting tablets, is intriguing. The transition from the blank slate to the worked-out design seems to depict two closely connected states—before and after. Similarly, although Statue F was made to honour Gatumudug, the opening lines of the inscription laud Gudea as the ruler who 'built Ningirsu's Eninnu, the White Thunderbird' (RIME 3.1.1.7.StF). It is therefore difficult not to see the two sculptures as, in some sense, companion pieces, even if they were not displayed side by side. Statue B must undoubtedly have been placed in the Ningirsu temple on the SE side of the complex. As is detailed further below and previously in Chapter 11, Gatumudug, the dedicatee of Statue F, was probably identified with Bau during the reign of Gudea, and Bau's sanctuary was, of course, located in the NW part of the New Eninnu, so the two carvings might well have been displayed in complementary locations within the L-shaped complex—in the two most sacred spaces devoted to Ningirsu and Bau, respectively.

The exact relationship between the two artefacts cannot finally be confirmed, but the broader theme of Gudea's special intelligence is also broached in the Cylinder Inscriptions, where the intellectual creativity that sparked the design of the New Eninnu is portrayed as a divine gift. With respect to Statues B and F, this intimates the bigger question potentially posed by the carvings: namely, whether viewers of the two tablets could rely for inspiration on their closeness to the gods in the way that Gudea unquestionably could, as clearly evidenced by the built structure in which the likenesses were displayed. As ever in Sumerian thinking, it is essential to take account of the inherent breadth of the conceptual parameters. There may, of course, be other explanations for the contrast between the blank tablet and the one with the

design, and it is perhaps relevant to recall that the plan shown on Statue B depicts only the outline of the New Eninnu's L-shaped temenos wall (considered further in Chapters 38 and 39), not the shrine of a particular god or goddess.

The ceremonial names that were bestowed upon the carvings in procedures closely associated with the mouth-opening or animation rituals and the rites performed prior to the induction of the statues into the temples are another highly significant feature of the inscriptions. The formal appellations (stressed in the listing and presentation of offerings) were not simple titles, such as are conventional in modern times ('Gudea Statue A', for example), but rather sentences and clauses that provide a performative record of actions that the likeness was intended specially to commemorate, together with the resulting recompense. Statue B (RIME 3.1.1.7.StB) provides a characteristic instance: 'I built his House for my lord, (so) life is my reward'. Most of the names are preserved, including that of Statue D: 'The master whose heavy hand the foreign countries cannot bear, Ningirsu made a favourable firm promise for Gudea, the builder of his house' (RIME 3.1.1.7.StD); and the name of Statue K (RIME 3.1.1.7.StK): '[As for me] whom his master loves, let my life be long'.

The inscriptions also narrate stages in the fabrication of the New Eninnu, and Statue B again provides the most interesting details, including information about the nature and origins of the materials used (also mentioned on Statue D): different types of wood were brought from the mountain of Amanus, as well as from Ursu, Ibla and Gubin (Statue B), while Statue D further records that wood was transported by water from Magan, Meluhha and Dilmun (RIME 3.1.1.7.StD). Statue B gives precise information about the kinds of stone that were used (as noted above with respect to the diorite from which the statues were carved), as well as various metals, notably copper and gold. Among the other substances mentioned are bitumen and even clay. The same text mentions that the spoils of Gudea's successful campaign against Anshan and Elam were brought back to Lagash to be used in the construction of the complex (RIME 3.1.1.7.StB), while the extensive transportation networks between the 'Upper and Lower Seas' are said to have been opened by Ningirsu himself, and the inscription confirms that the building was constructed in accordance with the divine decree communicated to Gudea. A fairly full description of the New Eninnu is also contained on Statue B, with references being made to the doors, the roofs of the various subdivisions of the complex, including its retaining walls and foundations, and the shrines and objects most closely associated with Ningirsu, above all his divine weapons and steles. Statues D and G mention the enigmatic EPA building (for which see Chapter 38), while tribute is paid to Bau and her House of the Holy City, otherwise known as her Tarsirsir—as it is described on Statue G (RIME 3.1.1.7.StG). Statue D records the building and dedication of a sacred barge to Ningirsu. It is noteworthy that the inscription on Statue B is the only text that unequivocally proclaims the exceptional nature of Gudea's achievement, reserving special praise for his unconditional piety (RIME 3.1.1.7.StD).

The inscriptions on Statues B, D and K explicitly mention that the likenesses were installed in the New Eninnu. With respect to their exact display locations, Statues B, D, G and K, which are all dedicated to Ningirsu, were presumably placed either within or adjacent to the inner sanctum of the complex. The group includes the two seated portrayals (B and D) and two of the standing likenesses, Statues G and K, the latter of which is in a very poor state of preservation, but its text indicates that it was dedicated to Gudea's 'master', who is presumed to be Ningirsu. The inscription on Statue B informatively states that the carving should not be removed from its proper display location, which is described as the ki.a.nag, a term that can be translated as the 'place where water can be drunk' (RIME 3.1.1.7.StB). As argued in Chapter 38, the ki.a.nag should not be taken to refer to a funerary or mortuary chapel inside the New Eninnu, as has sometimes been proposed, but rather to one of the libation wells that were situated in the complex, in both the main courtyard, and more importantly in the antecella of the Ningirsu temple, where some of the Gudea statues were almost certainly placed. Religious libations in honour of deceased rulers and their statues were indubitably performed inside the New Eninnu, but there is no reason to think that the relevant sacred rooms were mortuary chapels. Two further fragments of statuary, known as W (AO20) and Y (AO26633), seem also to have been dedicated to Ningirsu. Only the neck and shoulder are preserved of fragment W, with a single preserved column of text (RIME 3.1.1.7.StW) that reads: 'he built for him the Eninnu'. Fragment Y, from a statue made of limestone, contains two columns that seem again to confirm that it was made in honour of Ningirsu (RIME 3.1.1.7.StY). With respect to likenesses that were sanctified in honour of other deities,

there can be little doubt that Statues E and H, which are dedicated to Bau, were installed in her personal shrine inside the New Eninnu. Similarly, as mentioned above, it is likely that the pieces created for Gatumdug and Ninhursag (Statues F and A, respectively) were also placed inside the complex, or perhaps (especially in the case of Statue A) in nearby chapels. This is indicated by their inscriptions, which refer to their being displayed in the 'House of the Urukug' (Statue F) and the 'House of Girsu' (Statue A). As argued in Chapter 11 above, it is likely that Gatumdug and Bau were syncretised before or during the reign of Gudea, and that would help to explain why Statue F, which is devoted to Gatumdug, is said to have been sited in the 'House of the Urukug' because the latter term is a synonym for Gudea's re-established Temple of Bau in the New Eninnu. Finally, the carving dedicated to Inanna (Statue C) is exceptional in that it was probably not housed in or immediately adjacent to the Gudea complex, but in her Eanna temple, which was almost certainly outside the confines of the Urukug.

Of special import are the curse formulae that some of the inscriptions contain. It is well known that Gudea was so anxious about the fate of his statues that their inscribed texts often incorporate extremely menacing imprecations that are meant to deter ill-intentioned people who might seek to modify, remove, damage or destroy the likenesses at some later date. In particular, as proclaimed on Statue B, Gudea was concerned about malign future rulers (RIME 3.1.1.7.StB), and not only enemy kings, but also legitimate rulers of Lagash—men 'chosen by Ningirsu', as Gudea himself was, who might contemplate making changes to the cult. The actions that Gudea wished to safeguard against (also made explicit on Statue B) include replacing his name with that of a future king in the temple hymns and renouncing the holy sites. The same inscriptions go on to list particularly virulent threats. Nobody must 'forcibly damage (the stone)', and Gudea condemns any future ruler who might try to cancel the offerings that are consecrated to his likeness in the New Eninnu, defining the gifts as the 'rights of Ningirsu'. A king who dares to defy Gudea's execrations will, in turn, have the offerings he himself receives in the Ningirsu temple annulled, while his mouth will be made to 'stay shut', so that he will be prevented from eating and therefore die. Nor will the reckless miscreant be able to pray or have his wishes heard by the god. The end of the inscription on Statue B contains several further curses that are directed against anyone who might seek to damage the statue. First of all, no fewer than eighteen major gods of the Sumerian pantheon are called upon to punish the wrongdoer. The threat is so all-inclusive that no guilty parties could hope to escape divine retribution for their misdeeds, and any blameworthy future ruler must suffer both physically and politically. The promise previously made to the wrongdoer by the gods, namely that he would enjoy a long life and a prosperous reign, will be nullified, and he will be immediately 'slaughtered like a bull', or captured like a wild ox. His power will melt away, and he will find himself sitting in the 'dust' instead of on the throne. Then the curses are redoubled: the name of anyone who removes Gudea's inscriptions will be erased from both the temple and the 'tablet' (presumably the tablet of destiny). That person will forfeit all divine protection, and the actual consequences of the malefactor's spiritual banishment are enumerated. His personal god will ignore any uprisings against him on the part of his citizens, abandoning him to a humiliating death at the hands of his own people, and nature itself will fail: there will be no rain, and the watercourses will run dry; there will be a dearth, and his country will be afflicted with famine. Finally, presumably in order to dispel any lingering doubts that even the most stubborn potential offenders might entertain, a ruler who dares to carry out any of the actions condemned by the curse will have committed an unjust criminal act, and he will therefore be taken prisoner and made to suffer legal consequences for his offence.

Though the proscriptions and sanctions vary interestingly from statue to statue, the message remains fundamentally the same: woe betide the person who dishonours the carvings in any way. On a personal level, there can be no doubt that Gudea was eager to preserve his legacy and his reputation, but that is not the only point to stress about the maledictions. As noted above and discussed in greater detail below, once their mouths were metaphorically opened and they were formally inducted into the temple, the statues themselves acquired a kind of divine nature, similar to that which was attributed to the chief cult image, which was believed in a real sense to embody the deity's substance. A crime committed against the statue was therefore an offence against the very principles of sanctity or divinity that were the bedrock of the Sumerian system of the world: it was an outrage against creation. Perhaps Gudea's protests were a little more vehement than was warranted by the facts, as though he believed his special closeness to the gods might somehow allow him

to defy the course of history, such that his name and works would be preserved unmodified in perpetuity. But even if that was the case, the assertion was connected with basic beliefs about the essential character of divinity and its transference into sacred artefacts. Accordingly, malign actions aimed at the statues, as distinct from proper desacralisation rites, would injuriously deactivate them, or perhaps even worse, release their formidable powers in an uncontrollable manner, possibly also causing harm to the person portrayed as well as to the vandal or hostile agent. For them to operate as animated spiritual forces, the carvings not only needed to be intact, they also had to be kept in the specific place to which they were assigned when they were made sacred. To retain its ability to commune with the temple deity—to ensure the god's protection and the steady receipt of offerings—the statue had therefore to be displayed in a particular shrine or chapel. Furthermore, as the texts also indicate, the carvings were not to be moved from their pedestals or stands (not the integrated socle but the structures inside the temple on which they were placed) because that was not an interchangeable base, like the exhibition cases in a modern museum, but a unique spot that had precisely defined, inalienable associations with the divinity.

Offerings were made to both the standing and seated likenesses, as is recorded in the inscriptions. Moreover, since the statues were spiritually animated through some form of mouth-opening ritual, and because their quasi-divine powers were effective while they were in their intended places, they were to some degree considered to be actively involved in a number of ceremonies that took place in the temple, including the presentation of offerings. Some of the inscriptions give precise details about the gifts made to the statues, and as just noted the curses on many of them threaten dire consequences for wrongdoers who might seek to annul or divert the scheduled offerings. Seated Statue B (RIME 3.1.1.7.StB) and standing Statue K (RIME 3.1.1.7.StK) both mention the regular offerings that should be brought to the likenesses. Some doubts have been expressed about whether the amounts listed on Statue B might have been added after the work was originally carved because the cuneiform signs, which are smaller than the rest of the text, are unusually placed on the fringes of the robe (Braun-Holzinger 1991, p. 229), but the named foodstuffs in the texts on Statues B and K were standard Sumerian fare: 'beer, bread, flour for spreading, emmer groats' (RIME 3.1.1.7.StB). Both statues also give details of the amounts that should be brought, stipulating that half a litre of flour and half a litre of emmer groats should be offered. By any measure, these are rather small quantities, and it is it surely conceivable that the presentations made to the statue were symbols of larger amounts that were paid to the court and temple. The emmer groats in particular give pause for thought because such roasted whole grains can be used to add flavour to beer (as mentioned in Chapter 19), but the amounts of mixed grain needed for brewing (more than 400 kg of the chosen mixture, including the famed Sumerian barley cakes, for a batch of beer made in the brewhouse in the Enmetena Esplanade on Tell K in the Early Dynastic period) might further confirm the symbolic character of the offerings listed on the Gudea statues.

Nonetheless, the possible economic (or even fiscal) aspect of the offerings should not detract from the inherent spiritual meaning of the statues, because during the life of the ruler and after his death the likenesses were believed to be able to mediate between temple priests and worshippers (and by extension the citizenry at large) and the gods. As often noted, Gudea himself was subsequently deified, but even before that point—before and after his death—his statues could be asked to intercede on behalf of worshippers and the community to seek divine protection or aid. Statue B, for example, is expressly requested to inform Ningirsu of the ruler's good deeds and to 'convey messages' to him (RIME 3.1.1.7.StB). The communication channels also worked in the opposite direction. Accordingly, the text on Statue B notes that the eyes of the statue are the eyes of Ningirsu, who ceaselessly observes and is ever ready to punish any miscreant who dishonours or harms the likeness.

The Condition of the Diorite Figures

In common with other ancient artefacts excavated in Tello, in particular the sacred objects unearthed on Tell K (see Chapters 19 and 20), the Ur-Bau portrayal and the Gudea Statues from Tell A exhibit four kinds of damage that are not mutually exclusive (Figs. 209 and 210). They include natural erosion and accidental breakage, marks consequent upon the objects' ritual deconsecration and burial, and the more extreme effects of malign defacement. The statues are all broken to a greater or lesser degree, and it is undoubtedly exceptionally difficult to isolate the causes of the various

fractures and impairments with forensic precision, not least on account of the extreme age of the figures. Two interrelated factors provide a basis for any discussion, however. First, and as noted at the outset, is the fact that they were carved from an extremely hard stone that is very difficult to work and therefore highly resistant to chance fractures, scratches and natural erosion, but also to targeted disfigurement. To decapitate or otherwise mutilate the figures would unquestionably have required consolidated action involving the use of tools and many heavy blows. Incidentally, the word diorite that is conventionally used to describe the kind of rock from which the figures were carved is a catch-all term that refers to a number of hard, dark igneous stones (often greenish or grey in colour), including diorite, dolerite, olivine gabbro and other associated composites (see Reade 2002). The second point to stress is that the unelaborated style of the carvings made them robust and well able to withstand natural or incidental damage. Irrespective of their overall sizes, they are compact in form, with no fragile or slender protrusions, and it is hardly an exaggeration to say that they probably reflect the original shapes of the slabs or blocks of imported stone from which they were carved. The standing statues are generally like distended columns or heavy posts, while the solid shapes of the seated depictions of Gudea seem to have been cut from almost rectangular cuboids. The standing and seated figures' carved hands and arms are not separated from their torsos, and the feet are set into protective niches. Nor do any of the robes include semi-detached or trailing elements that might have snapped off relatively easily. In every case, the main projecting form was the head, but as previously noted the necks of the statues seem usually to have been rather short and broad, such that the heads were almost set into the shoulders, and this would have afforded them a high degree of protection from accidental or natural breakage. The points where the torsos of the seated statues meet the solid bases formed by the lower bodies might potentially have represented structural stress lines, but the arms and clasped hands, which are placed just above the laps of the seated figures, thicken the solid stone around their waists considerably, affording this area some protection. The test case for the robustness of the seated likenesses is Statue D, the torso of which was detached from the lower body, as is considered below, but the fact that none of the seated statues were found fractured across their chests, which is the narrowest part of those carvings, attests to the strength of the material and the inherent stability of

560   The Mound of the Palace

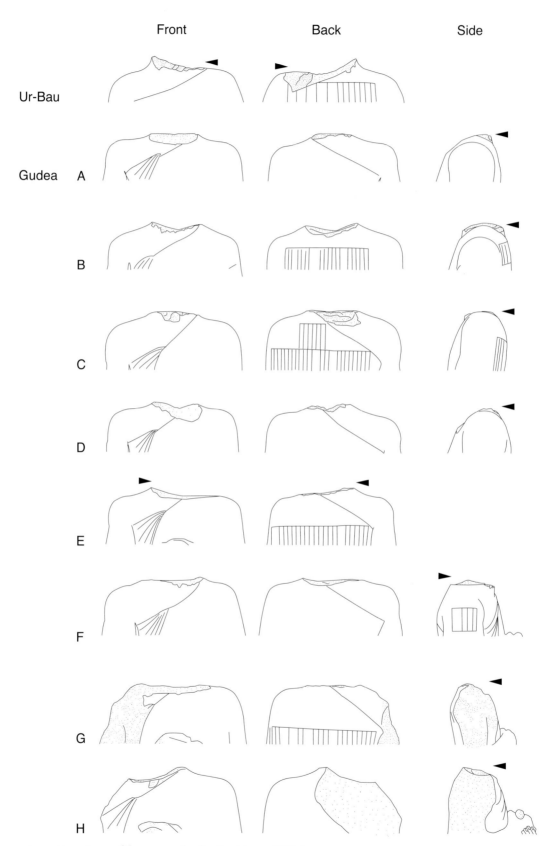

FIGURE 209. Areas of damage on the diorite statues of Tell A.

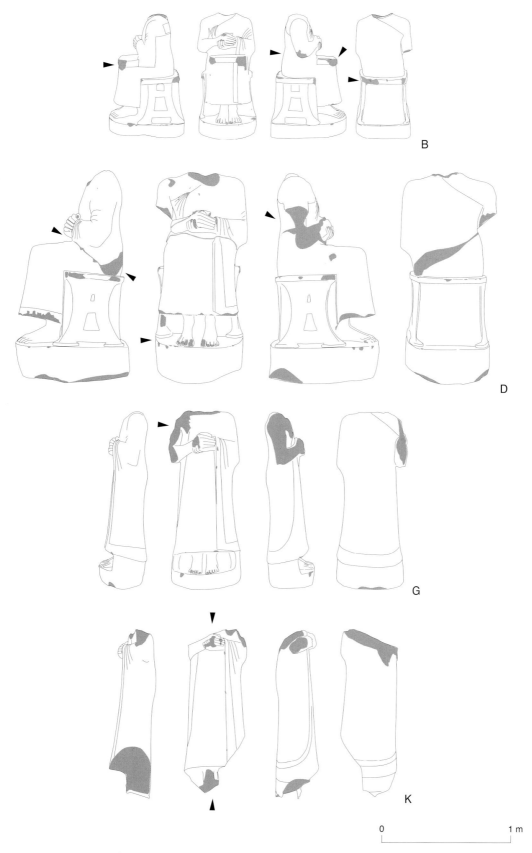

FIGURE 210. Areas of damage on the diorite statues of Tell A.

the sculpted forms, even where the upper and lower masses are less balanced, as in the case of the seated figures.

The overall shape of the statue of Ur-Bau (AO9) is particularly compact and thickset, which means that the ratio of its height with respect to its width, on the one hand, and thickness on the other (1:1.8 and 1:2.3, respectively) is low. To take a benchmark contrast, the height to width and thickness ratios of the tallest of the Gudea figures (Statue C) are much higher: 1:2.5 and 1:3.2, respectively. Whereas the Ur-Bau figure is short, broad and stocky, therefore, Statue C is elongated and relatively slender, and the same is more or less true of the proportions of all the Gudea likenesses compared to that of Ur-Bau. This might reflect the fact that, in real life, Ur-Bau was rather heavier than his son-in-law, but it would also tend to make his diorite portrayal more intrinsically durable. Despite that, the Ur-Bau statue is remarkably badly damaged. In common with all the other statues found on Tell A, it has been decapitated, but more particularly in this case substantial portions of it have been lost altogether. An approximately cylindrical wedge, with a height of at least 0.25 m, is completely missing from below the right arm, and a fracture extends from its narrow inner edge up towards the hip on the opposite side of the figure (under the left elbow). Further substantial breaks emanate from the bottom of the wedge, above the partial left foot (when the statue is viewed from the front) and from the bottom of the oblique fracture on the other side of the carving. In addition, the base of the piece is missing, with the exception of a small section on the right (as we look), though a three-toed fragment that was also recovered on Tell A (AO9B) seems originally to have belonged to it. The whole surface of the statue is also marked with numerous tiny chips, but the inscription on the back is largely untouched. A chunk of text is missing below the left shoulder, and this seems clearly to have been consequent upon the removal of the head; the corner at the bottom right on the back (as we look) is also missing, and again this would appear to have resulted from more obvious fractures, especially the formation of the cylindrical wedge; and there is a relatively limited patch of abrasion in the second row from the top (on the left as we look). Otherwise, the text is crisp, and it does not seem to have been maliciously or intentionally targeted. The same cannot be said for the head, which was evidently deliberately removed, as is evidenced by the clear, sharp points of impact around the base of the neck on the front and back: there are several jagged edges on the front, and grooved lines running through the neck (from front to back) that seem to have been made with a chisel of some kind, while the surface of the stone along the back of the base of the neck (especially above the figure's left shoulder) seems to have been cleanly and intentionally cut or snapped off. At the back on the right (at the bottom of the right side of the neck) a squarish shallow patch is missing from the polished surface of the carving, and in view of the regularity of the cut it seems likely that this mark was also made with a square-bladed chisel.

The wedge-like damage below the figure's bare right forearm is difficult to account for. Given the compactness and solidity of the diorite slab that makes up the surviving part of the sculpture, which roughly approximates a cuboid with proportionate sides that can be rounded off to 1:1.2:1.2, it seems highly unlikely that the stone would have broken under its own weight simply by being pushed or pulled off a display platform. That might have been the case if the block from which it was carved had been flawed in some way, but this is improbable, partly because any structural weak spots in the stone would surely have affected the work of the sculptors, but also because it would be apparent on the inner surfaces of the rock that were exposed when the carving was broken, and yet no anomalies have been recorded. It should further be recalled that the walls and floors of the later Hellenistic building on Tell A in which the statue was eventually displayed (as indeed of the New Eninnu) were made of fired and unfired mud-bricks—much softer materials than the diorite of which the statues were carved. This makes it even less likely that the dense, heavy rock might have been broken by a chance fall onto the relatively forgiving floors and walls. Arguments about the resilience of the torso and the relative hardness of the stone compared to its surroundings apply equally to the original base of the statue (including the feet), which was not intrinsically fragile or liable to snap off from the rest of the figure. On the contrary, it was an integral part of the block from which the piece was made—the only sculpted reductions in the slab's overall volume being the niche area and the feet at the front. For all these reasons, the strong likelihood is that the statue was struck on its left side (when seen from the front), underneath the right arm, probably when it was lying on the ground, and also fractured obliquely on the right side (again when it is viewed from the front). In this regard, it should also be recalled that, despite its weight, the Ur-Bau statue was rather small and therefore more movable that many of the other Tell A diorite sculptures. Although the main cuts on the top and bottom of the cylindrical wedge are surprisingly clean, this is probably the only way to explain a removal of this nature, since it is hardly feasible to suppose that the missing solid portion under the right arm could have become haphazardly detached as the consequence of a fall onto an earthen or fired-brick floor or against a mud-brick or fired-brick wall. The fact that none of the more slender and therefore theoretically more vulnerable torsos of the Gudea figures were damaged in this specific way tends to reinforce this conclusion.

More generally, and for reasons that are explained in detail below, it should be repeated that the Tell A statues were ritually treated or brutally harmed and broken at two distinct moments: in the Old Babylonian period, when Gudea's New Eninnu was taken out of service and the statues were in all likelihood piously processed in religious ceremonies, prior to being interred in a manner similar to that in which sacred objects from Tell K were dealt with at various times in the history of the earlier iterations of the Ningirsu temple; and in the second century BCE, when Adadnadinakhe's Hellenistic temple was finally overrun by hostile forces, and the sculpted figures displayed there were subjected to extreme violence.

The critical framework that emerges from the discussion of the kinds of damage found on the figure of Ur-Bau provides a useful starting point for an analysis of the Gudea statues from Tell A. All nine of them were found decapitated, while the badly damaged head that was excavated separately on the mound (AO12, which was also found by Sarzec) could not be reattached to any of the torsos, as noted above, suggesting that the heads of Statues A–K were taken away from the site. As further discussed below, this would tend to differentiate the Tell A figures from some of the other notable Gudea pieces that were found elsewhere in Tello by Sarzec and his immediate successors: for example, the small seated diorite statue of Gudea (considered in more detail below) that is usually referred to as Statue I (AO3293 and AO4108 for the body and the head, respectively), that was found in two pieces on Tell V at different times by Sarzec and Cros, but in a remarkably complete state, including its head; and the large diorite head of Gudea (AO13) that was uncovered by Sarzec on Tell H (though the context is uncertain). In both cases, although the figures—for whatever reason—were broken, the heads were clearly not targeted for special treatment or removal.

By contrast, as in the case of the Ur-Bau likeness, it can be stated with a very high degree of confidence that the heads of at least eight of the nine Tell A Gudea statues were systematically removed. The single exception is Statue K, from which the entire upper portion above the shoulders is missing, such that no evidence of what happened anywhere around the base of the neck was preserved, though the clean breaks across the torso and on the right shoulder strongly suggest that it was treated comparably to the rest. Almost from the moment of their discovery it was presumed by Heuzey that the heads of Statues B, D and G (all dedicated to Ningirsu) were premeditatedly severed (Sarzec and Heuzey 1912, pp. 136–40). For example, speaking of the seated Statues B and D (Gudea with the plan of the New Eninnu and the seated Gudea Colossus), he states that the heads did not simply snap off by chance, but were carefully excised with a chisel and probably preserved in a more or less intact state, as indicated in both cases by the well-defined edges of the cavities between the shoulders. Comparably, like the Ur-Bau figure, the bases of the necks of Gudea Statues A–H all exhibit clear impact marks, which are mostly at the rear or sides of the sculpted figures, while the breaks at the front above the chest are clean (see Fig. 209). The implication is that chisels or sharp points were used in conjunction with hammers or mallets to cut into the stone at the backs and sides of the necks so that the heads could be broken off by being pushed from behind or pulled from the front without being randomly broken—a manoeuvre that explains the sharp, smooth lines of the frontal fractures. The points of impact are clear on the side of the Ur-Bau figure, above the left shoulder, as well as on the backs of the necks of Statues A–D and Statue F, above the right shoulder of Statue E, and at the base of the neck on the fronts of Statues G and H.

It is often presumed that statues such as those found on Tell A were smashed by being pushed or pulled off their stands. The idea, which is superficially attractive, reflects a fear commonly expressed by Mesopotamian rulers. An explicit example is found in the text inscribed on Statue E (see Suter 2012, p. 72), which cautions would-be iconoclasts against damaging the inscribed statues by knocking them off their pedestals (RIME 3.1.1.7.StE): 'The statue of him who built Bau's house nobody will lift from its pedestal'. The straightforward inference is that, since the necks were supposedly 'narrow', the heads must have been separated from the bodies, and the noses broken, when the statues, which usually had their backs against temple walls, were pushed or pulled off their display bases and fell forwards onto their faces (Suter 2012). With respect to other ancient statues, there may well be some truth in this, but as an explanation for the particular kinds of damage found on the diorite statues from Tell A it is unconvincing. First, as noted above, and as is clear from the breadth of the cavities left between the shoulders by the missing heads, the necks of the diorite statues were noteworthy for their thickness, which is also attested by the relative width of the base of the preserved neck of the small seated depiction of Gudea from Tell V mentioned earlier (Statue I). The reason the necks seem to have been made proportionally wide might be due to the special attention that was paid by the sculptors to the heads of the Gudea likenesses, and again this can be confirmed by looking at Statue I, where the breadth of the head is further accentuated by the brimmed hat. The heads were not only important as portraits of the ruler, however. Their presumed size and prominence also reflected the pride that Gudea took in his wisdom (a function of the ears in Sumerian thinking) and his intellectual faculties more generally, as is stated in the inscriptions on Statues C and F, where he is said to be 'very intelligent' (RIME 3.1.1.7.StC and StF). The significance of the head in particular as the seat of inspiration or imagination (Gudea's self-proclaimed intelligence) is also clear in the Cylinder Inscriptions. Accordingly, when Ningirsu speaks to Gudea in the ruler's second dream vision, offering the ruler insights into his divine nature and urging Gudea to construct the New Eninnu, it is expressly mentioned that the god approaches the sleeper's 'head' (A9). In addition, as also mentioned previously, the necks seem to have been particularly short and set into the gap between the bones of the shoulders—a feature that is again apparent on the intact seated depiction (Statue I).

Both of these factors would no doubt have considerably reduced the vulnerability of the diorite heads, making them much less likely to snap off after falling from a display base that, particularly in the case of the large sculptures in the Sumerian Eninnu, might reasonably be supposed to have been rather close to the ground, not least because of the weight of the statues themselves. Furthermore, and yet again as argued above, the Hellenistic temple in which the statues were displayed when they were finally destroyed was made mostly of fired and unfired mud-bricks that were much softer than the extremely hard diorite of which the figures were carved, and this must further have lessened

the chances of extensive damage being caused only by a fall. One more piece of circumstantial evidence that should not be overlooked is this: if the heads of the Tell A statues were broken off by accident in the way sometimes suggested, and therefore not specially targeted, why was not a single one of them found? Even if some had fallen and been smashed into unrecognisable pieces (which is unlikely given the inherent hardness of the stone) and some of them had been randomly found and taken away, it is improbable that the Ur-Bau figure and the Gudea statues from Tell A were all affected in precisely the same manner and that, without exception, the heads were either completely destroyed or found and carried off. Added to these general points, the clinching piece of evidence in the case of the Tell A statues is the fact that they show very clear signs of having been struck with tools in a targeted way, expressly in order to detach the heads. Furthermore, and as is considered in detail in Chapter 48, no distinctions can be drawn between the treatment of statues that were sacred to different gods: the heads of the statues dedicated to Ningirsu (B, D and G, and seemingly also the more mutilated Statue K) were cut off with tools in the same way as the rest. Added to the fact that the inscriptions were left largely untouched (showing only signs of accidental damage), the implication is that the decapitators made no attempt to discriminate between the chief god of the cult and the other members of the pantheon.

A different type of damage is associated with the right arms of several of the sculptures, a group that includes all the ones devoted to Ningirsu and two more besides: Statues A, B, D, G, H and K. The upper right arm of Statue K has been completely severed, while the right forearm and elbow of Statue D are missing (though this is complicated by the fact that the hands of the Gudea Colossus were subsequently cut off and reaffixed). The right arm of Statue G is battered along its entire length, and the right elbow of Statue B is broken. By contrast, the left arms of Statues B, D and G (all dedicated to Ningirsu) are intact, though the left shoulder and the upper part of the left arm are missing from fragmentary Statue K. The hands—and especially the left hands—of Statues B, D, G and K are all damaged. The left thumb and the tips of the index and middle fingers of the left hand of Statue B are chipped, with the thumb exhibiting more extensive damage, while the hands of Statues G and K are more disfigured, but in both cases the damage done to the thumbs and fingers of the left hands appears more marked, and the back of the right hand and the fingers of the left hand of Statue G, which are badly abraded, appear to have been struck. The right elbow of Statue A, dedicated to Ninhursag, is missing, as are the tips of the right and left thumbs, though the rest of the sculpture is in extremely good condition. Statue H, in honour of Bau, has lost its right shoulder, upper right arm and elbow, and the tips of the right and left thumbs again appear to have been removed. The right arm of Statue C (dedicated to Inanna) appears unharmed, as do those of Statue E (devoted to Bau) and Statue F (devoted to Gatumdug), though the left hands of Statues C and E show signs of damage, and the tips of the thumbs of Statue F are missing. The left arms of Statues A, H, C and F are otherwise largely unharmed.

With respect to Statue D (the Gudea Colossus), the torso was detached from the seated lower part of the body and the hands were removed, probably in antiquity. The clasped hands were then rediscovered, presumably by looters, at some unknown point in the nineteenth century and eventually sold to George Smith of the British Museum in 1876 (the rediscovery of the Colossus and the history of the hands are outlined in Chapter 2 above). Regarding the condition of the now reattached hands of Statue D, the thumbs are badly damaged, as are the tips of the left fingers, especially the left index finger, and it is probable that these breaks, which follow the same pattern as can be observed on several of the other pairs of hands, were present when the fragment was rediscovered in the nineteenth century.

The areas of damage found repeatedly on the right arms and the left and right hands (especially the fingers) of so many of the statues cannot be explained away as the results of chance breakage or hostile action. The damage is too limited to have been part of the extreme violence associated with the decapitations, and the pattern is too consistent. Furthermore, though the prominent knuckles of the right hands in particular might have been vulnerable in the event of a fall (not forgetting the important caveats about the built environments and the relative robustness of the statues stated above), they are generally in good (sometimes very good) condition, while the much better protected fingers, and especially the crossed thumbs, which are placed very close to the torsos, exhibit marked mutilations. The same is true of the toes. The feet of all the statues are damaged (excepting Statue K, about which nothing definite can be said because the front of the base is completely missing). With respect to the sculptures dedicated to Ningirsu, both of the big toes

and the second toe on the left foot of Statue B are chipped; the toes of Statue D are all chipped, especially the ones on Gudea's right foot; and all the tips of the toes of Statue G are chipped, apart from the little toe of the left foot. A similar pattern is observable on Statues C, E, F and H, all of which have snicked or partly chiselled-off toes. The breaks are not explicable as random occurrences, not least because the feet of all the figures are placed in protective niche-like cavities: those of the standing sculptures in the spaces created between the front hems of the robes and the sides and backs of the garments; while the feet of the seated portrayals are set into hollows that are framed at the sides by the legs of the stools and at the fronts by the hems of the robes.

The very fact that the feet of these statues were carved with such extreme care is easy to overlook, but it is a notable feature of all the Tell A carvings, including the depiction of Ur-Bau from which the bottom section was removed. In practical terms, it would have been far less laborious for the sculptors simply to have extended the fronts of the various robes down to the integrated base of the statues, and little would have been lost in terms of verisimilitude or potential aesthetic appeal. Indeed, when viewed in the context of portrayals of rulers from other times and places, it is not at all obvious why so much attention was paid to the feet in Sumerian figure carvings more generally, and even why the persons portrayed were seemingly invariably shown without footwear. This is perhaps understandable in the sacred setting of a temple, where worshippers might commonly have removed their shoes or sandals, but it is also the case on the Stele of the Vultures, for instance, not only on the image of Ningirsu on the obverse, but even more noticeably in the martial scenes on the historical reverse. Is it conceivable that soldiers went into battle with bare feet? The exact symbolism of the foot is not known, and perhaps the only clue that is at least distantly related to the Tell A sculptures is the object that looks like a sandal that is carried in the left hand of one of the high-status individuals on the Circular Bas-Relief unearthed on Tell K (see Chapter 13), where the enigmatic shape—interpreted as a sandal—is assumed to have been a symbol of sovereignty. That being the case, however, it is difficult to know why the actual rulers shown in figurative sculptures, including the two main figures on the Circular Bas-Relief and Eanatum on the Stele of the Vultures, are always shown with bare feet. With respect to the damage done to the feet of the statues, one more obvious possibility is that, since the likenesses were thought to have been spiritually animated, the toes might have been targeted to deprive the statue of mobility, even if that was conceived of emblematically. The idea might have been further nuanced by the belief that impairing the feet would prevent a statue from asserting its formidable spiritual power and dominating or subduing those in its presence by metaphorically placing its foot on their necks—a common emblem of mastery (also discussed in Chapter 13). The image occurs in a climactic passage towards the close of the Cylinder Inscriptions (B18; also referred to above), in which, among his many other worthy actions in the service of the gods, Gudea is said to have 'set his foot on the neck of evil ones and malcontents' before Ningirsu enters the New Eninnu.

The symbolism of the arms and hands on the Tell A carvings makes the meaning of the limited defacements in these areas more immediately apparent. The bare right arms and hands seem to have been regarded as appropriate for carrying out sacred or sacramental actions, and the left hands seem to have been ancillary (as discussed above). The right arms and fingers might specifically have been associated with, for example, the giving and receiving of offerings, while the strength of the right arm is fundamental in many human cultures, where right-handedness is often privileged. The special significance of the right hands on the Tell A figures is perhaps a Sumerian variant of that widely attested, though fundamentally arbitrary norm. In any case, the hands and feet both appear to have been important features of the statues' religious significance, and that could well be why these extremities evince quite clear patterns of damage. Accordingly, the fingers and toes could presumably have been chipped as part of the desacralisation rites that were carried out before the statues were interred in Old Babylonian times, and it is noteworthy that a number of comparable ritually applied fractures (detailed in Chapter 19) are discernible on the figures on the Ur-Nanshe Plaques. Similarly, though it cannot be stated categorically because of their disappearance, it seems probable that the lost heads of the Tell A sculptures would also have exhibited traces of ritual damage relating to the statues' deconsecration, and that the signs might have been particularly discernible around the mouth, forehead and ears—the intellectual and sensory centres that were treated on the Ur-Nanshe Plaques.

It is noted more than once above that none of the cuneiform inscriptions show signs of having been deliberately erased or spoiled, and the same is generally true of the fronts, backs and sides of the robes of the statues. The garment of Statue B is lightly chipped on its left lower hem and around the damaged corners of the tablet containing the blueprint of the outer wall of the New Eninnu, held in the figure's lap. Otherwise, the tablet itself is well preserved, apart from some damage to the corners, and the plan is intact. The hem at the bottom of the robe on Statue D is chipped, and there is some slight damage to the cuff at the left wrist—though the removal of the hands might well have had a role to play in this, as might the fact that the torso was separated from the seated section of the body prior to their recovery in the nineteenth century, since the fracture line that divides the upper and lower parts runs from the bottom of the left cuff, below the forearm down to the left hip and around the back of the figure. The pleats by the right armpit of Statue G are terribly pitted, but much of the right shoulder is missing, and the upper right arm and forearm all show signs of the same kind of mutilation. The numerous small cavities on the right side of the chest look as though they might have been made with a metal punch, but the damage is so extensive that it is extremely hard to be sure. In addition, there are many tiny chips on the surface of the robe and along its edges, particularly at the lower hem, but once again the inscription is in good condition. Although Statue K is very badly disfigured, such that large chunks of it are missing, the robe is surprisingly polished and clean. There are just a few tiny chips at the left elbow and down the vertical edge of the cloth as it falls from the left wrist, and there is an abraded patch in the middle of the back, below the inscription, though the surviving parts of the text are sharp and unharmed. The bases of Statues B, D and G are nicked along their upper edges, close to the feet, and irregularly worn below, while the socle of Statue K has been entirely destroyed. The smooth concave curve visible on the base of Statue B probably resulted from breakage followed by some natural erosion and polishing that happened gradually over time. The socle of Statue D presents a similar concavity, while that of Statue A is damaged on the left (when the piece is seen from the front), but otherwise the integrated bases are generally formed into smooth projecting curves that were clearly carved as such by the sculptors.

Comparable instances of miscellaneous damage that have not been described in detail can also be observed on Statues A, C, E, F and H, where the many observable nicks and chips, especially on the hems of the garments and other protruding corners and edges (including the tablets, measuring rods and surveyors' pegs on Statues B and F) can in all likelihood be largely attributed to the passage of time, particularly because the sculptures were exhumed from their protective favissas. Nor should it be forgotten that the protruding corners and straight edges of the works could quite feasibly have been damaged after the likenesses were unearthed by the French pioneers, perhaps while the objects were in transit to the Louvre. The right upper arm and shoulder of Statue G might be an exception to this general rule about probable accidental damage, and it could be that the disfigurement in these areas on Statue G was caused by hostile forces. The fact that the Gudea Colossus (Statue D) was split in two along a line around the waist area also gives pause for thought: was this oversized figure—the most physically imposing of all the Gudea likenesses—broken deliberately while the head was being removed, or did the weight differential between the upper and lower parts create a stress fracture when the carving was displaced, after which the torso was eventually thrown down the side of Tell A at some point in time before the arrival of Sarzec? Unless further evidence emerges, this must remain an open question.

It would be beneficial to be able to confirm the nature and causes of the various kinds of damage found on the Ur-Bau and Gudea likenesses from Tell A by comparing them with Sumerian artefacts that have more readily traceable provenances. The immediate archaeological context of the Tell A statues was, of course, Hellenistic, since they were removed from their Sumerian resting places and displayed in Adadnadinakhe's revived building, which was built in the late fourth century BCE. Prior to that, they were originally commissioned by the portrayed Lagash II rulers and installed in the respective temples that were successively constructed by Ur-Bau and Gudea, before eventually being ritually processed and buried in the Old Babylonian period. Their tortuous and inescapably obscure post-Sumerian history, following their disentombment, radically complicates any straightforward appraisal of their condition. With respect to the Gudea statues in particular, comparisons with works that were possibly unearthed in Sumerian contexts are also fraught with difficulties because the provenances of most if not all of the other purported Gudea statues from Girsu are unclear—either because their archaeological contexts were not well recorded or because they surfaced in the art market, often after being looted, in which case their authenticity is open to question.

Furthermore, it is conceivable that, even if some of the uninscribed statues that derive from uncertain contexts are genuine Sumerian pieces, they might be likenesses of other kings, or they might have been commissioned long after Gudea's death, for example in the Ur III period, when a cult grew up around the revered ruler, and Gudea statues might have been in demand.

Statue I, which is referred to briefly above, is the only attested Gudea likeness that was unquestionably discovered in a Sumerian archaeological context, namely Tell V (or Tablet Hill), an institutional complex that included administrative, political and cultic areas. The exact setting in which Statue I was found cannot be established with any precision, but one thing that can be positively affirmed is that it was not placed in a favissa or otherwise ritually buried within, or in the environs of, a temple. This small seated portrayal, with overall dimensions of 0.46 m (h) × 0.33 m (w) × 0.225 m (t), has the distinction of being the only complete likeness of Gudea that was exhumed in the course of legal excavations. It was found in two parts: its head was uncovered by Sarzec on Tell V in 1898 (Sarzec and Heuzey 1912, Pl. 21 bis 1 (a and b)), while the body was recovered by Cros in 1903 on the S side of his Trench CE (marked on Cros's Plan A), on the W side of Tell V, topside down among a mass of debris (Cros 1910, p. 9). More specifically, the lower part of the statue was uncovered in a deposit of ash that also contained cuneiform tablets from the Ur III period, 4 m away from a door socket inscribed in the name of Arad-Nanna (see Suter 2012, p. 70). It is therefore assumed that the floor associated with this layer belonged to a second building phase of a temple that Arad-Nanna dedicated to Shu-Sin in the Ur III period, and that the Arad-Nanna construction was destroyed by fire (Huh 2008, pp. 165–9 and 189). Since the head, which was found nearby, shows no traces of impacts to indicate that it was deliberately severed, it is conceivable that the diminutive sculpture (which was perhaps more vulnerable than the Tell A sculptures, simply on account of its size) was fractured accidentally when the Arad-Nanna building catastrophically collapsed. Incidentally, the possible timeline is that the shrine was destroyed after the fall of the Ur III regime, and its destruction was conceivably linked with the hypothetical re-emergence of Lagash as an independent state (Lagash III)—occurrences that might in turn be associated with the erasure of the name of Nammahni in a number of his inscriptions (discussed in Chapter 35), though this must remain speculative. The alternative suggestion, outlined by Suter (2012, p. 72), according to which the small Gudea figure was purposefully decapitated as a hostile act of *damnatio memoriae* or reprisal that was carried out by the Elamites when they brought an end to the era of Ur III domination in the region, is built on uncertainty and tentative circumstantial evidence. As an explanation of the statue's fate it is in any event unconvincing, primarily because there are no impact marks around the base of the neck to support the idea that the carving might have been maliciously mutilated in the way that the Tell A likenesses clearly were.

Made of black diorite, Statue I depicts Gudea on a stool that is very much in the same style as the low benches found on the Tell A seated likenesses. His hands are clasped in the conventional attitude of prayer (with the left hand supporting the right from below and the thumbs crossed above), while his garment is also like those found on the Tell A figures. The robe covers his left shoulder in the conventional manner, leaving the right shoulder and arm bare, and a long strip of cloth falls down from the left forearm. The preserved headwear, which seems to represent an item that was, in reality, made of sheepskin or wool, has a high brim that features six rows of tight curls. An inscription containing three columns of text (divided into thirty-seven lines) is carved below the figure's lap, along the front and the right side of the skirt, and two further columns (divided into fifteen lines) are inscribed in the panel between the legs at the back of the stool. The text (RIME 3.1.1.7.StI), which is intact, mentions a 'courtyard' in the city, and agricultural lands that were given by Ningirsu to Gudea's personal god, Ningishzida. It goes on to record that, after Gudea had finished building a number of temples, including the New Eninnu and EPA of Ningirsu, and the Sirara temple of Nanshe, he then constructed the shrines of some unnamed deities, together with the 'House of Girsu' for Ningishzida. The inscription expresses Gudea's hope that future rulers will cherish the Ningishzida temple, as well as Gudea's name, and finally it states the statue's ceremonial title and the fact that it was installed in Ningishzida's shrine: 'Ningishzida gave life to Gudea, the builder of the house—(this is how) he named (the statue) for his sake, and he brought it to him into (his) house'.

On account of its small size and relatively intact state, Statue I must surely be the most bewitching of all the preserved Gudea likenesses, and it doubtless gives some sense of the mesmeric power that the larger statues must have exerted

in their presumably darkened temple settings, illumined only by flickering torchlight. The head, with its contemplative eyes, was reattached to the body without any significant losses because the two fractured pieces fitted together seamlessly. There is some damage to the nose, and the top of the brim of the hat is slightly broken (above the right eye), and there is a small chip on the outside of the bottom of the left eyelid. Significantly, however, none of these marks represent the kind of systematic impairment of the sensory and intellectual centres that is outlined above with respect to other carvings. Nor are there any signs of impact damage caused by tools around the base of the neck. The body is cracked down the length of the right arm, and some stone has broken away from the top of the left arm below the covered left shoulder. The upper edge of the stool is chipped around the back corner on the right side (when the statue is viewed from behind), and the base has a piece missing at the front on the same side, but the tips of the toes, as well as the fingers and thumbs of both hands, all of which are in remarkably good condition, have not been deliberately cut or snicked in the manner in which the extremities of the Tell A statues probably were. The damage to the front of the head might have occurred because of the sheer weight of debris and other materials that fell upon it, gradually stabilising around it over many centuries (and the possibility of earth tremors and the weathering effects of geological and climatic events should not be disregarded). Despite some of the uncertainties in the sculpture's archaeological provenance, therefore, it can be stated with a high degree of confidence that the statue was fractured around the end of the third millennium BCE, and there is no evidence to indicate that it was ritually processed prior to being ceremonially interred or that it was deliberately decapitated at a later date. This would tend to confirm that it lay in the ground undisturbed from the time of the collapse of the Arad-Nanna shrine until its rediscovery by Sarzec and Cros, while the absence of any signs of ritual deactivation would differentiate it from the Tell A likenesses.

Two other carvings provide further points of comparison. They are the two detached Gudea heads that were unearthed by Sarzec: AO12, found on Tell A, which shows Gudea with a shaven head; and AO13, which features the familiar brimmed hat, and for which no clear provenance was recorded. Both have damage to their sensory centres, though with respect to AO12 in particular, it is not easy to discriminate between accidental damage and intentional acts of ritual impairment.

For example, the nose of AO12 has been entirely severed, while that of AO13 has been cut back along a line descending from between the eyebrows, leaving the bases of the nostrils well preserved. Overall, AO13 is in reasonably good condition, and when it is viewed in profile it can be seen that the brim of the hat, which protrudes beyond the damaged upper part of the nose, might well have originally extended beyond, or at least as far as, the very tip of the nose. In any event, it seems likely that the front of the hat could have provided the nose with more protection from accidental breakage than the brim of the hat on Statue I, not least because the angle of the head of Statue I is more upright: the chin, for instance, is noticeably higher than that of AO13, where the chin angles downwards. Consequently, the hat brim of AO13 projects further forward over the nose than the lower front edge of the hat of Statue I. It is therefore significant that the lower part of the brim of the hat on AO13 is chipped but still relatively intact compared to the severed nose below it because it raises the likelihood that the nose was deliberately broken. If it is then assumed that the noses of heads AO12 and AO13 were both ceremonially snicked or severed, it would seem reasonable to suppose that AO12, with its shaven skull,

suffered further damage when the carving lay underground, after having been possibly removed from any ritually sanctioned resting place in which it might previously have been deposited. Of course, these are highly speculative matters, and the difficulties are compounded by the uncertainty surrounding the find location of AO12. Nonetheless, it can be observed that AO12 and AO13 both have chipped lips (especially the upper lip of AO12), and both exhibit damage to the eyelids. Part of the back of the skull (on the statue's right) and the right ear of AO12 are missing, and its left ear is badly abraded or worn. Furthermore, the chins of both AO12 and AO13 are abraded, while the left cheek of AO13 shows some superficial chips. The very survival of the two heads must, in and of itself, be regarded as extraordinarily fortuitous, but it might tentatively be argued that the marks found upon them reflect patterns of ritually administered disfigurement that are more clearly attested elsewhere, and that they might both have subsequently suffered more random damage when they lay buried under the ground. The poor state of AO12, together with the rather plain style of the portrait, means that any attempt at a forensic analysis of its condition is inherently subject to doubt, however.

CHAPTER 38

Gudea's Temple Plan and the Physical Remains

The Significance of Statue B

Statue B might with some justification be regarded as one of the great achievements of creative human endeavour from any period in history (Fig. 211). Portraying the seated Gudea with the freshly designed ground plan of the New Eninnu's temenos walls in his lap, it brings together the several conceptual planes on which Sumerian thinking operated. Gudea holds his hands in the familiar Sumerian attitude of perpetual prayer, signalling his pious submission to the will of the gods. The meaning of his piety with respect to the planning of the New Eninnu is expressed in narrative form in the Cylinder Inscriptions. Just before Gudea is about to begin actually marking out the walls of the Ningirsu temple on the earth, it is made clear that his agency is guided by two important deities (A17): 'Nisaba opened the house of understanding and Enki put right the design of the house'. Nisaba, the goddess of grain, accountancy and numbers provides the necessary mathematical enlightenment; Enki, one of the Sumerian pantheon's three first-order gods and (together with his many other strengths) a protean genius of the imagination, ensures that the temple's layout is free of human flaws. When Gudea subsequently lays the first brick, the importance of Nisaba is restated in the broader context of the New Eninnu's overall shape (A19): 'He put down the brick, entered the house and as if he himself were Nisaba knowing the inmost secrets (?) of numbers, he started setting down (?) the ground plan of the house'. A moving narrative transition then immediately takes place. Once the shape of the complex is acknowledged to be the instantiation of a divinely inspired

form, Gudea, the instrument of the gods' wishes, responds with unabashed human passion (A19):

> As if he were a young man building a house for the first time, sweet sleep never came into his eyes. Like a cow keeping an eye on its calf, he went in constant worry to the house. Like a man who takes but little food into his mouth, he went around untiringly.

The celestial sublime here comes together with everyday human emotions in a thoroughly Sumerian manner. The ground plans are inspired by the gods, but the job of laying out the walls and then actually building the sanctuary draws on commonplace human practices, including the fundamentally important operations of building a domestic home and dividing up agricultural land into plots using surveyors' ropes and pegs. Indeed, that is surely the significance of Nisaba's role in this stage of the construction process. As the goddess of grain and numbers, she personifies the principles that underlie the systematic management of the land and society. She is nonetheless only one part of the larger meaning that is embodied in the temple, which is nothing less than the material sign of the proper ordering of life on earth in its cosmic setting. With regard to that greater context, when the institution of the temple is soundly established—when Gudea makes things 'function as they should' for Ningirsu, to quote the evocative phrase that is used repeatedly in the ruler's inscriptions, including on Statue B—then the state will prosper. Ningirsu makes this promise at the outset, when he appears to Gudea in a second dream to give the ruler his

Gudea's Temple Plan and the Physical Remains 571

FIGURE 211. Statue B. Musée du Louvre AO2.

instructions (A11). Attached to the heavens above and to depths of the Abzu below, the mountainous temple stands in the midst of things, where it acts as the stabilising anchor in a universe that is otherwise incessantly mobile (B1): 'House, mooring post of the Land, grown so high as to fill the space between heaven and earth ... The house is a great mountain reaching up to the skies.' Accordingly, as is discussed in Chapters 43 and 44, the temple links the domains of An (the sky), Enlil (the mountainous earth) and Enki (the subterranean Abzu).

Perhaps the most important point to take from the many meanings with which the structure is invested is that the cosmic layers—comprising the sublime realms of the gods, including the sky and the Abzu, and the mundane world of humanity—together form a continuum. Envisaged as liminal entities within this chain of being, the worshipping statues of Gudea occupy a transitional space between the terrestrial and the exalted. Similarly, the architectural plan in the ruler's lap is both a divinely ordained sign—even a cipher—and at the same time (as is detailed below) the practical instruction manual for how the complex should be shaped and built. It therefore features emblems of the tools needed to create such blueprints and to turn the plan into a constructed reality: a surveying peg and a graduated ruler or measuring rod that is placed upright on the easel or board on which the tablet rests. The missing component that was used to transform the measured distances between the points defined by the pegs into lines on the ground (and perhaps on the tablet) is the surveyors' rope or cord, but this might be notionally present on the statue—wound around the long, sharp pin of the surveying peg. That is perhaps the only way to make sense of the peg's unusual conical or spindle-like shape. Though Statue B has been the object of countless studies since its discovery in the late nineteenth century, no convincing account has hitherto been advanced of its metrology—the principles of measurement that are encapsulated on the rod that was used by Gudea to draw out the design of the temenos and later to transfer the inscribed plan onto the ground and make it into a constructed reality. The work carried out by the British Museum team not only shows the conspicuous extent to which the New Eninnu's outer walls were actually built in conformity with the design inscribed on the tablet, it has also made it possible finally to make sense of Gudea's metrology—to understand the system of ancient measurement that is marked on the graduated rod.

Exceptional in its length and the diversity of its contents, the inscription on Statue B (RIME 3.1.1.7.StB) begins with a list of the regular food offerings that were brought to Gudea's stone surrogate, together with the consequences for any future ruler who might try to discontinue them. Next comes the formulaic dedication, which is followed by an enumeration of the ruler's epithets—titles that stress the special regard in which he is held by the gods:

Gudea, (whose) name is everlasting, ruler of Lagash, the shepherd chosen by Ningirsu in the heart, the one looked upon favourably by Nanshe, given strength by Nindara, who submits to the orders of Bau, the child born by Gatumdug, entrusted with authority and a lofty sceptre by Igalim, provided richly with vigour by

Shulshaga, and made to emerge as the true head of the assembly by his personal god, Ningishzida . . .

The text goes on to describe the construction rituals that were performed by the ruler in preparation for the building of the temple, including the cleansing of the city, after which comes the procurement of precious materials from foreign lands (under the aegis of Ningirsu) and the fabrication of the god's weapons, including Mow-down-a-myriad and Mace-with-a-three-headed-lion. The ruler is said to have suspended punishments to the extent that mothers abstained from slapping their children, while no lawsuits were prosecuted at the 'place of oath-taking' and debt collectors refrained from pursuing those who failed to meet their obligations. After Ningirsu opened the roads between the Upper and Lower Seas, Gudea procured cedar and boxwood planks of different lengths, some of which were seemingly used to make the shafts of the divine weapons, while others were manufactured into doors and roof beams. More roof beams were made from pine, plane and gishkur wood, which was shipped by river, and a variety of other types of wood and stone slabs were brought from far and wide. Gudea is said to have mined copper and transported ebony, along with at least two kinds of gold ore, bitumen and ha'um earth. In addition, 'huge ships' delivered gravel that was used to reinforce the New Eninnu's foundations.

At the climax of the inscription is a vivid recollection of the divine commission that was sent to the ruler as a dream omen—the epiphany detailed at the beginning of the Cylinder Inscriptions (A1–5)—followed by a passage that emphasises the performative role of the statue, which is said to be sculpted in unbreakable stone that can never be reused for any other purpose. The carving is then consecrated with a ceremonial name ('I built his House for my lord, life is my reward') and ordained as the ruler's perpetual substitute in the presence of the divine. It is also instructed to tell Ningirsu that the completion of the Eninnu was celebrated with a special holiday—seemingly a kind of devout Saturnalia, when the 'slave girl was equal with her mistress and the slave and his master were peers'. Lastly, it is said to have been displayed in the ki.a.nag, which, as previously noted, was not a mortuary chapel (the usual interpretation), but a libation room, or a 'place where water can be drunk':

He imported diorite from the mountains of Magan, fashioned from it his statue, named it for his sake 'I have built his temple for my master, (thus) well-being is my reward', and brought it before him into the Eninnu. Gudea entrusted the statue with a message: 'Statue, tell my lord: When I built the Eninnu, his beloved temple for him, I remitted all debts, I pardoned everyone. For seven days, no grain was ground, the slave girl was equal with her mistress, and the slave and his master were peers. The ritually unclean was allowed to sleep only outside my city. I banished (all) wickedness. I observed the laws of Nanshe and Ningirsu. I provided protection for the orphan against the rich, and provided protection for the widow against the powerful. I had the daughter become the heir in the families without a son.' He made the statue convey this as a message. As this statue is neither of silver nor lapis lazuli, and neither of copper, nor tin, nor bronze, no one may reuse it. It is of diorite. It is set up for the place where water can be drunk. No one may destroy it by force, as if it were a statue of Ningirsu.

The text concludes with ritual incantations and the enumeration of a list of malevolent spells and magic curses that are invoked to defend the statue against acts of *damnatio memoriae*—desecration or oblivion. Perhaps most impressively, any would-be malefactors (future rulers, in particular) are threatened with reprisals from a veritable army of deities: An, Enlil, Ninḫursag, Enki, Sin, Ningirsu, Nanshe, Nindara, Gatumdug, Bau, Inanna, Utu, Hendursag, Igalim, Shulshaga, Ninmarki, Dumuziabzu and Gudea's personal god, Ningishzida.

The Incised Temenos Plan

The blueprint that is the distinguishing feature of Statue B has given rise to the carving's familiar name: the Architect with a Plan. The inscribed tablet features the ground plan of the walls of the complex, including details of its gates, towers, pilasters or buttresses and two added protrusions, one at each end (Fig. 212). It shows is a clear orthogonal projection that depicts the outlines of the extremely thick temenos walls of Gudea's L-shaped sanctuary, demarcating the boundary between the innermost sacred spaces and the less sacred outer areas on the highest levels of Tell A. If the points of the compass were marked on the edges of tablet, with the N point placed in line with the middle of the stepped façade opposite Gudea's hands, then the plan roughly approximates the New Eninnu's orientation. In reality, and as detailed further below, when it was laid out on the ground, the entire structure was turned clockwise (from Gudea's perspective) by forty-five degrees so that the stepped façade faced the north-east, and the long, plain façade on the other side of the complex faced south-west. Additionally, the N–S axis that fixed the placement of the inner Ningirsu temple did not run through the middle of the long façades as they are marked on the plan, but rather along a line connecting the SE gate tower of the middle gate in the NE façade with the short stretch of plain wall between the two buttresses at the SE end of the SW façade (Fig. 219). At the SE end of the plan (referring to the building's final orientation) is an unusual feature that looks like a horned altar, with the horns turned inwards towards the walls of the complex. As is explained below, this is probably an astronomical observatory. The function of the second addition, which is adjacent to the W corner at the NW end of the complex, is less certain. Close to Gudea's right hand is the miniature or emblematic peg that might conceivably be shown with a length of rope or cord wrapped around its bottom section. Finally, next to the side of the tablet that is closest to the viewer, is a rod or straight-edged device that is marked with units of linear measurement—a graduated ruler that represents the oldest metrological system ever recorded. The rod, which is quite badly damaged on Statue B, also appears on Statue F (showing Gudea with a blank tablet in his lap), where it is in a much better state of preservation. Here it can be seen that the rod, which is shaped like an elongated triangular prism, has two graduated sides: one facing Gudea and one facing the viewer.

In Sumerian thought, metrology, or the art of measurement, was considered to be the source of all languages, or the language of the gods. A similar idea is intimated in the Cylinder Inscriptions, in the passage quoted above, when Gudea lays the first brick and is said to understand numbers as though he were Nisaba herself (A19). When Nanshe interprets Gudea's dream for him, Nisaba is also said to take readings from the stars, and only after they are found to be propitious does Nindub inscribe the ground plan on a tablet of lapis lazuli (A5–6). Nanshe also promises that the design or plan of the complex will subsequently be communicated to Gudea 'in every detail' by Ningirsu himself (A7), and later on, in a passage also quoted above, Enki corrects the

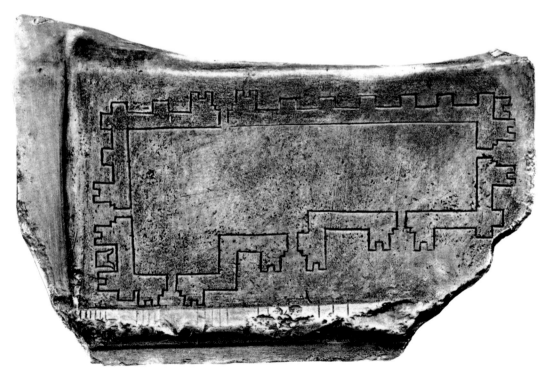

FIGURE 212. Close-up of the tablet on Statue B, showing the ground plan of Gudea's temenos, with the measuring rod (bottom) and the surveyor's peg (left). Musée du Louvre AO2.

design (A17). Accordingly, the plan occupies the same liminal space—exists on the same plane of the Sumerian chain of being—as the statue. It is a reciprocal votive interchange between the gods, who are acting on behalf of Ningirsu, and Gudea, who wishes to serve them. The gods bestow the design of the temenos upon Gudea as a divine gift, and he responds in the fullest way possible by realising the plan in a manner worthy of Ningirsu. Thus, the statue encapsulates the accomplishment of the pious work as it progresses from the first sign that Gudea saw in his dream through to the finished construction—from the divinely sent vision (a gift to Gudea) to the votive gift of the New Eninnu that Gudea finally offers to Ningirsu.

Since it was first published by Sarzec and Heuzey (1912, pp. 45, 136–40; and Pls. 15 and 17–19), and particularly with reference to the more complete example contained on Statue F, it has been thought that the graduated ruler records a standard measuring system in which the marks represent an infinite series of equally spaced units: 1, 2, 3 . . . Translated into historical lengths, each unit would then presumably represent a Sumerian cubit. As is demonstrated below, however, the gradations refer to a closed arrangement that is worked out in the context of the Sumerian sexagesimal system (base 60), but with a key further component, namely the standard unit used by Gudea in the planning of the New Eninnu's temenos, which is defined as a real-world quantity. All the architectural features carved on the temple plan, from the lengths and widths of stretches of the temenos down to the sizes of the gates, towers and buttresses, can be measured on the device as fractions of the standard unit, and the scaled measurements can then be closely correlated with the actual dimensions of the built structures. The deciphering of Gudea's metrological system provides important insights into the sanctuary's principal construction stages, shedding light on how—supervised by Gudea—the ancient Sumerian architects and surveyors must have laid out the walls on a grand scale, precisely following the measurements set out in the plan. As previously stated, therefore, the temple blueprint on Statue B was not intended simply as a symbolic representation of the sanctuary's outline, or even as an impressionistic sketch of it, but as the worked-out diagram of the shape and dimensions of the temenos. This was confirmed during the British Museum team's excavations, which showed that there is indeed a remarkably exact correspondence between the plan and the built structures (Fig. 213). The team was able

to establish some defining congruences, notably on the long walls running from the north-west to the south-east and on the shorter NW and SE walls (with the horned altar on the SE façade). The SW and NE temple gates towards the SE end of the complex and the SE temenos wall, all of which were unearthed by the British Museum team, were found to correspond extremely well with the blueprint. More generally, the layout and positioning of the L-shaped complex was found to be well accommodated by the overall shape and dimensions of the Mound of the Palace, which displays an unmistakable topographical signature.

With the diagram on Statue B confidently correlated with the British Museum team's excavation plan, it became possible to link some of the physical remains with the architectural descriptions recorded in the text on Statue B and in the Cylinder Inscriptions. This is a matter of some delicacy since several scholars have previously tried to correlate features of the plan with temple areas and structures that are described in the ancient inscriptions (see, for example, Parrot 1948, p. 161; Falkenstein 1966, p. 121; and Heimpel 1996, pp. 17–29), but the lack of properly verified layouts of the archaeological remains unfortunately hampered past studies, rendering their interpretations largely hypothetical.

Another recurring problem that has impeded attempts to match some of the ancient epithets with architectural features in Gudea's complex is that the meaning and use of the structures described in the Sumerian texts are often unclear. It is an issue that has been highlighted in previous chapters of this book, especially with regard to the several names by which the Ningirsu temple was known, including its main titles and other more evocative appellations. More specifically, the meaning of the primary compound name, Eninnu: the White Thunderbird (e_2.ninnu ^{d}anzud$_2$ babbar$_2$), has been repeatedly subject to exegesis, but there is now no doubt that in this composite form the terms Eninnu and White Thunderbird both refer to one and the same thing, namely the sacred complex. Though philologists occasionally continue to argue that the word 'fifty' (ninnu in Sumerian) connotes fifty Anzus or Thunderbirds, there is a passage in the Cylinder Inscriptions that seems unequivocally to clarify that the Sumerian wording signifies the fifty 'powers' or 'forces' that Enlil bestows upon Ningirsu (A10): 'Because of his great love, my father who begot me called me "King, Enlil's flood, whose fierce stare is never lifted from the mountains, Ningirsu, warrior of Enlil", and endowed me with fifty powers'. The word 'fifty' in

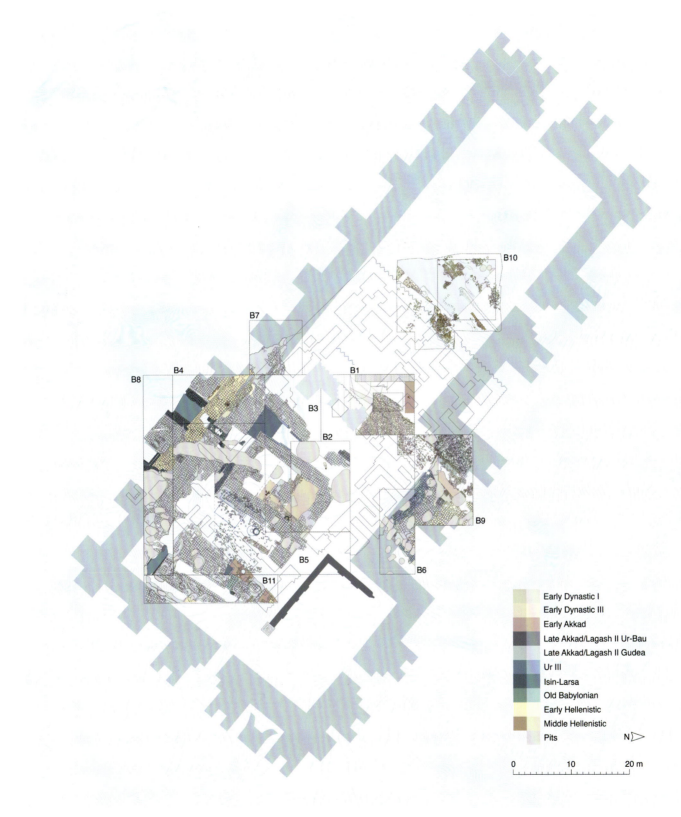

FIGURE 213. The ground plan from Statue B superimposed on the plan of the British Museum team's excavations and Heuzey's New Plan. The most important overlapping areas are: well M, together with the NE and SW façades of the temenos on Heuzey's New Plan and the British Museum team's excavations; and the SW gate, the gate in the middle of the NE temenos wall and a short section of the SE temenos wall on the plan from Statue B and the British Museum team's excavations.

the composite name of the Eninnu can therefore plausibly be linked with the fifty powers that Enlil grants to Ningirsu in the narrative, and it might be further assumed (perhaps with some caution) that the powers acquired by Ningirsu are not only physical, but that they also include broader meanings of personal, social and political dominance, and intellectual brilliance. Consequently, the Sumerian term e_2.ninnu ^{d}anzud$_2$ babbar$_2$ does not mean the Eninnu 'of the' White Anzu bird, but instead equates the two parts of the compound: the Eninnu 'is' the White Thunderbird. The point is further confirmed by the general rule that the copula connecting the elements in such composites is not usually included when the meaning is a proper or common name (see Zólyomi 2014, pp. 22–3; and Jagersma 2010, pp. 715–18).

Exacerbating the difficulty, it is highly likely that some key areas inside the religious complex, notably including the cella, the antecella and the main courtyard, were also known by more than one name, while some of the core sacred features—the cult podium and its associated offering table and libation well, for example—are referred to in the texts by appellations that were also used metonymically to designate the rooms in which they were situated. As mentioned repeatedly, the term ki.a.nag, which is usually wrongly taken to mean a 'mortuary chapel', was literally (as the Sumerian word implies) a place 'where water can be drunk' and should therefore be linked to the libation wells that were installed in the antecella and great courtyard of the Eninnu (see Chapter 34). With respect to ki.a.nag, the problem has arisen because the precise connotations of the term are complicated. The word can pertain to offerings that were seemingly dedicated to deceased royals, but this would presumably include (or perhaps refer principally to) gifts that were made to the statues of the departed. Examples of offerings to the Gudea Statues are considered in detail in Chapter 37, but such gifts are widely attested in inscriptions from Early Dynastic Girsu and again for the Lagash II and Ur III periods, with donations being made daily and extras being provided during certain festivals (Jagersma 2007). In some literary texts the deceased receive their gifts at the entrance to the netherworld, and the deathly associations acquire further credence by the fact that the ki.a.nags of the great gods are sometimes said to have been desecrated in times of war. Similarly, as detailed further below, when completing the New Eninnu, Gudea is said to install monuments to the Slain Heroes (the mythical warriors or forces subjugated by Ningirsu) at important

locations all around the complex, but he ensures that their mouths are always turned towards the ki.a.nag, precisely because they were 'warriors slain by Ningirsu' (A25–6). The etymology of ki.a.nag is generally understood to refer to the idea of a funerary or mortuary chapel that could be located above a tomb (Jagersma 2007, pp. 294–8), but the meaning of the word is much more nuanced. It incorporates a broad signification relating to the places where offerings (funerary, or in fulfilment of the protocols inscribed on statues) were administered, and it can also denote the offerings themselves or the ceremonies during which they were consumed (Sigrist 1992, pp. 182–4). Consequently, as argued in Chapter 37, Statue B was almost certainly displayed, together with some of the other Gudea statues, in the antecella of the New Eninnu, where they were placed on a specially built platform facing a libation well. With regard to Gudea's actual life history, no tomb has been identified among the remains found in Girsu, either for him or for any member of his dynasty, and no evidence exists to suggest that the sepulchres or sarcophagi in which such important figures were laid to rest were located inside the religious complex. Though libations in honour of deceased rulers and their statues were indubitably performed inside the New Eninnu, therefore, there is no reason to think that the sacred rooms in which they were celebrated were dedicated mortuary chapels.

Also problematic are the puzzling discrepancies between parts of the complex that are named repeatedly on inscriptions on clay nails, for example, but which are not mentioned at all in the Cylinder Inscriptions. A chief instance is the enigmatic EPA, which was commemorated on numerous recovered clay cones, presumably as an important feature of the New Eninnu, but no further information about it has come to light. One possible meaning of EPA emerges when it is identified with (or read as) e_2.gidru (in the genitive case), which can be translated as the 'house of the sceptre'. A structure by that name, and associated with Ningirsu, is mentioned in Lagash I royal inscriptions dating back to the time of Ur-Nanshe, while texts from the same period record the existence of buildings with the same name in the neighbouring province of Umma (see RIME1.12.7.1). The term EPA also appears in Lagash I administrative texts, for example in a wool ledger, and also with reference to the origins of oil and dates that were offered to Ningirsu. In other instances, the word EPA seems to have been used in connection with the goddess Nanshe, while buildings or installations that went by that name existed not only in Girsu but also in Lagash and Nigin. The EPA is said to have a doorkeeper, for example, and other texts introduce it as a place where sheep can be sheared. A little later in the history of Girsu, an EPA is mentioned in Old Akkad administrative texts, and one is recorded in Adab, where it was seemingly entitled the EPA 'of the palace' (see Such-Gutiérrez 2005–6, p. 43).

With regard to its composite make up (E, meaning 'house', plus PA) the definition of EPA hinges on the interpretation of the difficult word PA, which (as indicated at the outset) can be read as gidru ('sceptre'), though the meaning of gidru is not as straightforward as might first appear. Texts from Early Dynastic times, for instance, mention the idea that a sceptre could be presented to a ruler by Enlil and Ningirsu, while the inscription on Statue B tells how Gudea is given a 'lofty sceptre' by Igalim. The image of the sceptre as a sign of the human king's divine right to rule is perhaps reinforced in the Cylinder Inscriptions, where Ningirsu is said to be the possessor of a 'sceptre' of 'distant' or 'never-ending' days (B6), presumably referring to his everlasting kingship or authority, but several variant meanings of PA are attested. In other contexts it can be translated as the 'branch' of a tree, the 'frond' of a date palm and the 'wing' or 'feather' of a bird. Finally, there was also an Early Dynastic deity known as ^{d}PA.

The word EPA does not feature in any of the preserved inscriptions from the reign of Gudea's predecessor, Ur-Bau, but that does not mean that it could not have been used in texts that have not survived. It reappears under Gudea, where it is consistently modified by the epithet e$_2$.ub.imin.a.ni, meaning his 'house' with (or associated with) 'seven corners'. The Sumerian word UB typically equates to the Akkadian word *tubqu*, which means '(outer) corner'; additionally, depending on the specific context, it can connote the idea of a 'niche' or even a 'region'. For whatever reason, it sometimes designates a location where demons can be found, and the demonic connection adds the sense of a place that is a source of apotropaic materials. Furthermore, the inclusion of the number seven in the modifier should not be taken too literally because—in related contexts—a reference to the four corners of a space can be a way of indicating the space in its entirety, and the number seven can act in a similar manner, being used to allude to the totality of an entity or setting.

The way in which the term is applied by Gudea implies that the EPA was not identical with the New Eninnu. On the contrary, as is also confirmed by the archaeological findings,

it was something other than a byname for the complex, but nevertheless closely associated with it. It has been repeatedly suggested since at least the time of Parrot (1948) that the word might refer to a ziggurat with seven stages (James and Van der Sluijs 2008, p. 64), but scholars over the years have cast doubt on this (Falkenstein 1966), and no traces of a structure grand enough to fit this description have been unearthed in Girsu. It is also noteworthy that neither the EPA nor a ziggurat is mentioned explicitly in the Cylinder Inscriptions. Alternatively, the name has been taken literally to refer to a building with seven corners, but no heptagonal structure is recorded anywhere as a feature of ancient Sumerian architecture, and a ground plan of this shape therefore seems highly unlikely. Given the importance of the number seven in the EPA epithet, it might perhaps be connected with the seven 'squares' that Gudea is said to mark out inside the building (A21), for example, but (as noted above) seven was a number with a broad significance that could denote a totality, in which sense it occurs in many contexts, without necessarily meaning literally 'seven' of something. Similarly, the 'seven-cornered house' is a name found elsewhere in the preserved inscriptions, where it is applied to the Eanna of Inanna in Uruk (see George 1993). The reference occurs in Old Babylonian literary texts, for example in the Temple Hymns (201): 'Eanna, house with seven corners, with seven fires lifted at night-time, surveying seven pleasures(?)'; and in the Eridu Lament (226): 'Inanna, the queen of heaven and earth, destroyed her city Uruk. Fleeing from the Eanna, the house of seven corners and seven fires . . .' Lexically in these contexts, the city of Uruk is given as the explanation of the various uses of seven.

With respect to the archaeology of Tell A, the British Museum team's findings show that clay nails marked with Gudea's EPA inscription were predominantly found among materials dumped by the French pioneers in peripheral areas on the W side of the mound, specifically in Cluster 1 and SH3 on the SW side of Tell A, and in Cluster 2 on the NW side (Fig. 138). These examples came from tertiary contexts, but it should also be noted that not a single EPA inscription was found among the undisturbed archaeological remains that were excavated at the heart of the complex, and this would tend to confirm that the enigmatic EPA was indeed located on the periphery of the New Eninnu, probably towards the west. The slight caveat is that the British Museum team's excavations were focused mainly on the W areas of the tell so it is possible that more EPA cones might be concealed in the E spoil heaps. Also of great importance, however, is the fact that the EPA text, which was found by the British Museum team on sixty-five cones between 2016 and 2021, is the second most numerous after Gudea's Standard Inscription. Very tentatively putting some of these possibilities together, the idea that it was a building of some kind (the 'house of the sceptre', for example) and that the word EPA is invariably used in association with the number seven, which perhaps connotes the sense of a totality rather than a structure with seven walls or elements, might imply that it was a self-contained construction somewhere on the W side of the complex. It is strange that nothing of the sort is mentioned in the Cylinder Inscriptions, unless it is referred to in the form of a synonym that has not yet been deciphered, but the fact that its existence was recorded on so many cones might further suggest that it was a relatively large structure, or at least that it was of particular importance as a feature of the New Eninnu. Alternatively, it might not feature in the Cylinder Inscriptions because it was an addition that was built after the Eninnu was completed, but its inferred importance makes that idea difficult to sustain. In connection with the seven 'squares' (or spaces) that Gudea is said to lay out in the Cylinder Inscriptions, it is perhaps feasible that the word EPA refers to the platform terrace itself—the raised mound on which the New Eninnu was built—and this might help to explain the relatively large numbers of EPA inscriptions that have been recovered, though it does not, of course, account for the fact that they were found on the W side of the complex. Furthermore, it should again not be forgotten that no statistical data exists for the E side of the mound, but no EPA cones were found in the undisturbed archaeology in the central areas. Similarly, the texts clearly refer to the Eninnu and the EPA as two distinct constructions: 'Gudea, who built Eninnu, built EPA', and the way the inscription is phrased might further suggest that the self-standing EPA was built after the New Eninnu was completed. It seems, moreover, to have been a long-standing generic feature of temples, though the term EPA drops out of the lexicon after the Lagash II period, perhaps intimating either that such structures were no longer in use or that their traditional form and function changed to the extent that they were referred to by different names in later periods.

One final possibility that deserves consideration is that the word refers to the annexe close to the W corner of the New Eninnu. With respect to the possible sense of completeness conveyed by the use of the number seven, the plan suggests that this was indeed a self-contained addition to the exterior of the NW façade of the temenos. Nesting in the niche formed between two buttresses, it must have been built after the temenos walls were finished (and conceivably after the complex in its entirety was built), so this would accord with the order of events indicated in the EPA inscriptions. Furthermore, as it appears on the plan, it was shaped like a square U (open on its NW side), and it could therefore be said to have had a multitude of corners (as many as eight, depending on how they are counted), which might signal the idea of a plenitude of constituent parts that together form an integrated whole. No evidence exists to show how high it was, but the plan shows that it was shaped like the nearby buttresses, which might imply that it was at least as high as them, and the fact that it was self-standing might also suggest that its upper levels were accessed by an internal stairway (emphasising its separateness from the main structure), though this is in no way verifiable, and it would depend on whether the tops of the temenos walls were fitted with ramparts. With the idea of a sceptre or other similarly shaped object in mind (the branch of a tree, a palm frond, or the wing or feather of a bird), could it have been an elevated display point for a standard or some other tall symbolic post? The idea is attractive, not least because it could also incorporate the idea of a sceptre-like artefact, perhaps as a symbol of human or divine sovereignty, but it is conjectural. The potential mismatch between the high number of EPA cones and the rather limited surface area of the U-shaped annexe might militate against it, as would the possibility that many more EPA cones might lie buried in other parts of the mound, not to mention the difficulties posed by the examples found by the French pioneers.

A number of much more robust suppositions about the construction and shape of the Eninnu emerge when the results of the British Museum team's work are correlated with the preserved texts. It is helpful to note that, despite the inherently poetic nature of the text, the Cylinder Inscriptions detail the preconstruction and construction phases of the complex systematically and in considerable detail, starting with the divine revelation and instruction communicated to Gudea in his dream vision, and continuing with the decipherment of the dream, the preparation of the ground and the procurement of materials. Next come the actual construction phases (after Gudea has marked out the ground and laid the first brick in the initial wall of the inner Temple of Ningirsu), followed by exhaustive descriptions of the manner in which the complex was finished and the subsequent enthronement of Ningirsu and Bau. More specifically, the phases enumerated in the text of Cylinder A can be broken down into clearly demarcated stages:

1. The theophany: Gudea is sent a dream in which he is instructed to build the Eninnu.
2. The verification of the revelation: Gudea travels to Nigin to have his dream interpreted by Nanshe.
3. The incubation and confirmation: Ningirsu confirms his message to Gudea.
4. The preconstruction phase: the purification of Girsu generally and the construction site in particular.
5. The recruitment of the workforce and the sourcing of building materials.
6. The construction rituals: the marking out of the Ningirsu temple's walls and the moulding and laying of the first brick.
7. The building of the Eninnu: the work is described step by step, together with the accompanying rituals.

Remarkably, the British Museum team's excavations uncovered some material traces of the preparatory work and purification rituals, including the levelling of the old religious complex on Tell A, which is perhaps alluded to in the passage that begins 'He levelled what was high . . .' (A7). Here and throughout the discussion of the parallels between the texts and the archaeology it should not be forgotten that the poetry of the Cylinder Inscriptions could well add a layer of metaphor to the descriptions, so the language functions on more than one level. With that caveat stated, other clear traces of ritual actions were found in the form of particular deposits—burnt materials, for example—that were placed at symbolically charged spaces (see Chapter 36). Some of the presumably associated purification rites that were carried out under Gudea's authority are described in the text (A13): 'The citizens were purifying an area of 24 iku for him, they were cleansing that area for him. He put juniper, the mountains' pure plant, onto the fire and raised smoke with cedar resin, the scent of gods.' Similarly, the creation of the superimposed series of massive layers that raised the core of the New Eninnu above the surrounding temple annexes and ancillary

buildings is repeatedly alluded to in poetic terms (A21): 'They made the house grow as high as the hills, they made it float in the midst of heaven as a cloud, they made it lift its horns as a bull and they made it raise its head above all the lands, like the gishgana tree over the abzu'. Also noticeable is the correspondence between the surface area of purified ground mentioned in the text (24 iku) and the actual size of the site occupied by the Urukug: $24 \times 3,600$ m^2 (the conversion rate for 24 iku) amounts to 86,400 m^2 or 8.64 ha, which correlates extremely well with the surface area of the sacred precinct, as established by the British Museum team's measurements. With regard to the size of the L-shaped complex itself, the following passage indicates another very close correspondence between the text and the footprint of the temenos walls (A17):

Towards the house whose halo reaches to heaven, whose powers embrace heaven and earth, whose owner is a lord with a fierce stare, whose warrior Ningirsu is expert at battle, towards Eninnu-the-white-Anzu-bird, Gudea went from the south and admired it northwards. From the north he went towards it and admired it southwards. He measured out with rope exactly one iku. He drove in pegs at its sides and personally verified them. This made him extremely happy.

This passage refers specifically to the laying out of the inner Ningirsu temple, but if the figure of 1 iku (3600 m^2) is compared with the overall surface area occupied by the L-shaped sanctuary, it is again in agreement with the extrapolated size of the area enclosed by the temenos walls on the summit of Tell A.

A fascinating feature of the way the text of the Cylinder Inscriptions is presented relates to the order in which spaces are enumerated. In particular, an idea of inversion seems to be at work, such that, in some cases, there is a progression towards the most sacred space or feature, while in others the most sacred space or point is listed first. The clearest example of the latter procedure is when Gudea, having previously received enlightenment from Nisaba, pegs out the N–S line and subsequently lays the first brick in the N corner of the Ningirsu temple at the heart of the complex. This precise locus, it should be stressed, was also the N corner of the cella, and this was the geometrical point of inception from which the placements of the other sacred features inside the New Eninnu were logically derived. Indeed, this might explain the connection between the N–S line and the area of 1 iku that is mentioned in the quote above. Though the inner Temple of Ningirsu did not occupy 1 iku, its primary N–S axis determined the way in which the new sacred buildings were positioned in that space. Conversely, towards the end of Cylinder A, when the construction phases are complete, the progression is from outside to in, from the overall shape of the complex—poetically described in terms of the spectacular impression it makes on a wondering observer—to the most sacred or intimate sacred spaces at its heart (A24–5). Accordingly, the complex, which fills the 'space between heaven and earth', comes into existence like the sun emerging from behind the clouds, and it appears like hills of lapis lazuli and 'white alabaster':

> He built his master's house exactly as he had been told to. The true shepherd Gudea made it grow so high as to fill the space between heaven and earth, had it wear a tiara shaped like the new moon, and had its fame spread as far as the heart of the highlands. Gudea made Ningirsu's house come out like the sun from the clouds, had it grow to be like hills of lapis lazuli and had it stand to be marvelled at like hills of white alabaster.

The huge building is like a fabulous landscape, and when the focus then shifts from the panorama to some of the details of the New Eninnu's construction (its fixtures and fittings), they are conceived of as the fantastic creatures that inhabit the world that Gudea has brought into being:

> He made its door-sockets stand like wild bulls and he flanked them with dragons crouching on their paws like lions. He had its terraced tower (?) grow on a place as pure as the abzu. He made the metal tops of its standards twinkle as the horns of the holy stags of the abzu. Gudea made the house of Ningirsu stand to be marvelled at like the new moon in the skies. The built-in door-sockets of the house are Lamma deities standing by the abzu.

More epic comparisons follow: the New Eninnu's stores of 'timber' are like the waves of an 'enormous lagoon where snakes have dived (?) into the water'. Then the point of view shifts again, this time to focus on the King's Gate, which, as is detailed in Chapter 41, is almost certainly a reference to the monumental entranceway that connected the main courtyard with the most sacred area occupied by the Ningirsu temple at the SE end of the complex. The gate is ornamented with an 'eagle' that is 'raising its eyes toward a wild bull', and it is crowned with a wooden arch that is like a 'rainbow stretching over the sky'. This is the gateway through which the god later enters his personal abode at the heart of the sanctuary, and the progression towards the most sacred culminates with a description of Ningirsu's dining hall and his sleeping quarters: 'They installed the great dining hall for the evening meals: it was as if An himself were setting out golden bowls filled with honey and wine. They built the bedchamber: it is the abzu's fruit-bearing holy meš tree among innumerable mountains.' The movement from outside to in, from the panoramic landscape that is an image of the complex in its entirety to its innermost features, leads to the holiest space of all: the 'bedchamber' of the god, which might be identified as the cella.

The descriptive passage just cited is preceded by the enumeration of the Gudea Steles (A23–4) and followed by a list of the monuments to the Slain Heroes (A25–6). The probable display locations of the steles are discussed in Chapter 41, and those of the Slain Heroes, many of which are explicitly said to be located at gates in the temenos wall, are detailed in Chapter 40, but in terms of the progression from less sacred to most sacred or vice versa, it is interesting to note that the central terms in the two lists are exactly reversed to create a chiasmus. The significance of this, which is tentatively adumbrated below, remains elusive, but the repeated mentions of the sun and moon in the epic similes that are used to describe the New Eninnu help to draw attention to the role of the sacred complex in the demarcation of local and universal time frames, specifically the lunar months and the seasonal or agricultural cycle, which is a function of the solar year. The shrine was carefully laid out with respect to the north star, but (as argued in Chapter 40) its overall NW–SE orientation was also determined with respect to solar and lunar motions. An insight into these relationships provides a vitally important context for the naming and placement of the temenos gates that were associated with the Slain Heroes—an understanding that feeds into the arguments about the positions of the Gudea Steles that are laid out in Chapter 41.

CHAPTER 39

The Metrology of Statue B

PERHAPS THE MOST INTRIGUING ICONOGRAPHICAL element contained on Statues B and F is the measuring rod that appears on both. Shaped as a triangular prism, the graduated rulers are similarly placed (from Gudea's perspective) at the top of the tablet that he holds in his lap—the one with the plan of the New Eninnu on Statue B and the blank tablet on Statue F. The rods, which stand proud of the tablets' flat surfaces, are probably not represented as being parts of the tablets themselves, but rather shown as separate objects that sit adjacent to them, in a position that would allow them actually to be used and referred to by Gudea—or a living counterpart—while he was working on the blueprint of the complex. There must surely be some significance in the contrast between the completely marked-out temenos on Statue B and the empty tablet on Statue F, but the meaning of the distinction is obscure. The identities of the two gods to whom the statues are dedicated might provide a clue. Statue B, with the completed plan, is sacred to Ningirsu, the intended divine owner of the New Eninnu, while Statue F is devoted to Gatumdug (probably syncretised with Bau at this period), the guardian of the city walls of Girsu. The blank tablet might therefore be a record of the fact that Gudea correctly sought the approval and protection of Gatumdug even before embarking on the process of marking out the sacred precinct's temenos walls. In any case, as with every detail of the construction and completion of the New Eninnu, each phase of the process, including the planning, had a sacred aspect that was integral to the work. On the one hand, therefore, the statues give some insight into the way in which the historical planner of the New Eninnu actually operated, but

on the other, they affirm the overarching truth that the making of a building (this one and possibly any other) owed everything to the gods.

The measuring rods have not before now been deciphered, but they provide some interesting evidence about the state of Sumerian mathematics during the reign of Gudea, who reigned for a period of approximately twenty-five years from about 2125 BCE to 2100 BCE. The time frame is vital because it is all too easy to forget that mathematics, like all other aspects of Sumerian culture, evolved over a very long period. A broad-brush approach to the topic (detailed in Robson 2007, pp. 57–186) can be briefly summarised: the ancient Mesopotamians used the sexagesimal system of counting (based on the number sixty), which remains familiar down to the present day in the reckoning of time and angles; they were able to approximate the square root of two (the diagonal of a square with sides of one unit)—later enshrined as a crossroads in mathematical history by Pythagoras, who was rumoured, according to a tradition that emerged nearly a thousand years after his death, to have spent time in Babylon; they knew about Pythagorean triples—the series of right-angle triangles whose three side lengths are all whole numbers (3, 4, 5; 6, 8, 10; 5, 12, 13 and so forth); and they had developed some algebra.

For various reasons the generalities must be treated with great caution. First, when stated in this summary fashion, the basic information is misleading. For example, the sexagesimal system, which evolved over centuries, if not millennia, seems only to have become standard (if that is the right word) by about 2050 BCE (Robson 2007, p. 63), roughly a century after Gudea's reign, when school tablets, including one from Girsu from the Ur III period (AOT304; RTC 304), start to show fractions of sixty as lists of integers (whole numbers) that are expressed using the sexagesimal place value system (explained further below). Something very similar can be said about the famous tablet (YBC7289 at Yale University) that demonstrates the square root of two (Fig. 214). It dates from about the nineteenth or eighteenth century BCE (some three or four centuries after the reign of Gudea), by which time such calculations had gained currency and were being taught to trainee scribes. Secondly, therefore, it is paramount to approach Sumerian mathematics (including Gudea's measuring rod) on its own terms and not treat the subject teleologically, as though it exclusively relates to some higher-order mathematical truths that were established later or elsewhere, in different cultural settings. Thirdly, before the sexagesimal system became established, the Sumerians seemingly had no formalised concept of 'abstract numeration' (Robson 2007, p. 75). On the contrary, numbers were not thought of as existing in isolation (in a dimension of their own, as it were), but always in relation to real things: the length of an actual rope and the number of sheep in a flock (to cite just two examples). Indeed, as discussed further below, the inclusion of the measuring rod on Statues B and F might well signal a revolutionary moment in the transition from numbers as attributes of things to numbers as self-standing entities. That is conceivably why a sacred aura is bestowed upon what is—to the modern eye—merely a straight edge marked with units of measurement.

One structure that exemplifies the need for circumspection when approaching the geometrical principles at work in Gudea's reign has already been touched upon in this study. That is the design of the composite Pillar of Gudea, which is discussed in Chapter 9. As outlined there, the entire construction was probably based not on an abstract calculation, but rather on a unit size represented by the sides of one of Gudea's standard square bricks (0.32 m). The four circular pillars that made up the monument were placed on a large brickwork square with sides of five bricks. The diagonal of that large square, when calculated according to the sorts of maths that can comparably be used to find the value of root two for a square with sides of one unit, is 7.071, and the length of the diagonal on the square base of the Gudea pillars (spanning the diameters of two circles plus the space between them and the small spaces at the corners of the square) was

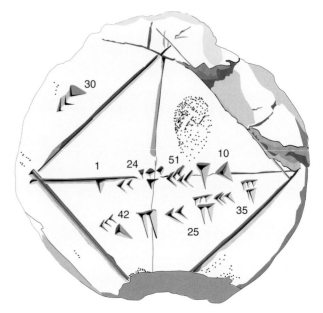

FIGURE 214. Old Babylonian tablet demonstrating a method for working out the square root of two, or the length of a diagonal of a square with sides of one unit. Yale University YBC7289.

equal to the sides of seven bricks (Fig. 53), therefore roughly approximating 7.071 units. But that surely does not imply that, perhaps three or four hundred years before the calculation of the square root of two was regularly taught to young scribes in Babylonia, the planners of the Gudea monument needed to perform an abstract sum in order to work out the most convenient size for the sides of the large brickwork square that supported the four columns. Decades or even centuries of experience of using square and rectangular bricks could presumably have told the builders that only squares of certain sizes could be used for a construction of this type, which depended on a particular relationship between the size of a square's sides and that of its diagonal, with both lengths referring back to a unit length defined by the side of a square brick. Those practically determined values could have been remembered or recorded in a list, without the need for recourse to complex maths. Such a list might have informed them, for example, that squares with sides of seven, twelve and fourteen units would also produce workable results because their diagonals are very nearly whole numbers: 9.9, 16.97 and 19.8, respectively. Nor should it be forgotten that further margins for error were inevitably built into the construction process by the need to bond the bricks with clay mortar. The everyday maths that the builders needed, in other words, would not necessarily have been framed as a higher-order conceptual discipline, but as a set of pragmatic skills that gave workable results in the situations they were faced with. A similar point can feasibly be made about the Sumerians' knowledge of Pythagorean triples. Since they had been building rectangular temples for centuries, their knowledge of such interesting shapes could have been derived experientially rather than being based on the now familiar theorem of Pythagoras.

As argued below, the marks on the measuring rods on Statues B and F seem to represent values in the sexagesimal system, which is also called base 60 because that is the number that provides the criterion for counting and calculations that are carried out within the given parameters. Sixty, in other words, plays the same role in the sexagesimal system as ten does in the now common decimal system. The overwhelming advantage of using sixty as a base is that it has a total of twelve factors: 1, 2, 3, 4, 5, 6, 10, 12, 15, 20, 30 and 60. Compare that to base 10, which has only four factors: 1, 2, 5 and 10. This makes sixty a much more useful framework in real-world situations than ten because it allows a person very easily and quickly to perform a great many calculations without having to phrase solutions in terms of decimal places or non-whole numbers. Underlying this principle is the easily verifiable point that all of the listed factors of sixty are multiples of just three numbers: 2, 3 and 5. From about 1900 BCE, Babylonian scribes copied lists of regular numbers and their reciprocals—the number by which a number must be multiplied to make the base unit of sixty. They did this because they were memorising (using the typical Mesopotamian devices of lists and rote learning) numbers that could be written in the sexagesimal system without resorting to fractions or decimal places—a practice that is exemplified with reference to a particular set of circumstances on Gudea's measuring rod.

More fundamentally, the factors of sixty and the regular numbers made with multiples of 2, 3 and 5, together with their reciprocals, were of the highest significance precisely because Sumerians and Babylonians did not represent numbers using fractions such as ½ and ⅔. That does not mean that halves and thirds did not exist, of course, but that they could be understood as whole numbers, such that ½ in base 60 equals 30, and ⅔ equals 40. This was apparently so from the outset, and increasingly the case as the system became firmly established in the course of the second millennium. Consider, by contrast, the decimal system, with its limited range of factors and regular numbers that are only multiples of two and

five. These constrictions mean that, for example, a third of ten cannot be resolved into a whole number because, in the decimal system, it is an irregular number that cannot be made by multiplying two and (or) five. Furthermore, when it is notated as a decimal (0.333 . . .), a third of ten cannot even be written with a finite number of digits. Conversely, as just noted, in the sexagesimal system a third is a very straightforward quantity because it is calculated as a third of sixty, which can be written as a whole number (twenty), without recourse to fractional values or a recurring decimal. This also exemplifies the utility of tables of reciprocals: they tell the user that (in the sexagesimal system) ½ = 30 subunits, ⅓ = 20 subunits, ¼ = 15 subunits, ⅕ = 12 subunits and so forth. All of the values in the fractions just listed are regular numbers (made of multiples of 2, 3 and 5), and that is why the fractions resolve into whole quantities (30, 20, 15, 12 and so on). Correspondingly, a fraction such as ⅐, which is not a regular number in the sexagesimal system, would have a qualitatively different status in ancient Sumerian calculations (and maybe also in later times) because it cannot be rewritten as a whole number. It is conceivable that Sumerian scribes had methods of dealing with such irrational quantities (as presumably later Mesopotamian mathematicians eventually did), but that fraction does not occur in the system that is represented on Gudea's measuring rod. On a day to day basis, this way of doing maths allowed ancient Mesopotamian scribes to represent a great many numerical values using a finite number of digits, and to carry out a wide range of calculations with extreme ease and precision.

The literate use of base 60 evolved in the context of the sexagesimal place value system, which can again be explained by comparison with the familiar decimal system, in which digits are ordered in columns that indicate powers of ten. The numeral 108 can therefore be parsed (from left to right) as: $(1 \times 100) (0 \times 10) (8 \times 1)$; or $(1 \times 10^2) (0 \times 10^1) (8 \times 10^0)$, where the superscript digits indicate powers of ten, or places in the sequence of columns, and each column can contain the digits one to nine. In the sexagesimal system, where the columns can contain the digits one to fifty-nine, the numeral 108 would be written (using modern notation) as 1.48, meaning: $(1 \times 60) (48 \times 1)$; or $(1 \times 60^1) (48 \times 60^0)$. The dot or point in sexagesimal 1.48 (sometimes replaced with a colon) is a modern convention that is used separate the digits (1 to 59) from the powers of sixty expressed in the other columns. In ancient Mesopotamia the digits (1 to 59) were written as

1 (SU)	60
2	30
3	20
4	15
5	12
6	10

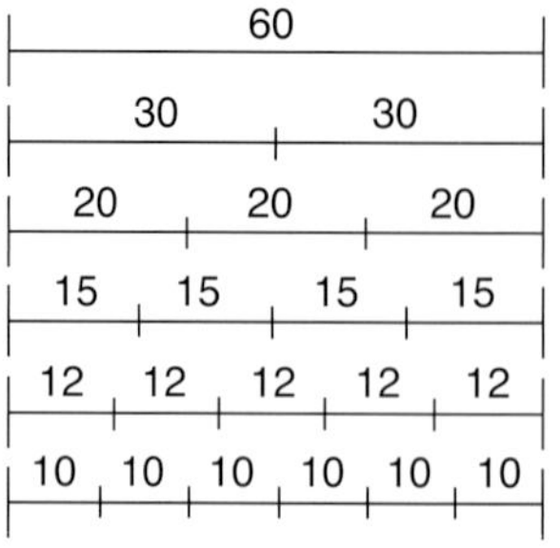

FIGURE 215. The standard unit on Gudea's measuring rod expressed as fractions of sixty and as a table of reciprocals.

multiples of ten and multiples of one, so the number eighteen, for instance, was written as a ten followed by eight ones. Finally, it is also worth noting in passing that, in terms of scribal practice, numbers were only determined as multiples of sixty, without the power (superscript 0, 1, 2 and so on) being specified. What this means in practice is that the number 1 (in the sexagesimal system) could imply that the base value 60 was raised to any given power: $60^1, 60^0, 60^{-1}$ or 60^{-2}, for example. Accordingly, in this very simple case, the symbol representing 1 could mean 60, 1, $\frac{1}{60}$, $\frac{1}{3600}$ and so forth. In real-life situations, the ambiguity of the written notation could usually be straightforwardly resolved with reference to the context.

This is the broad (and in some respects later) background against which the measuring rod on Gudea's lap in Statues B and F should be understood. The graduated markings are almost certainly defined with reference to base 60 in a manner comparable to that in which modern metric rulers, when divided into metres, centimetres and millimetres, represent values in base 10. If the graduated rule on Statue F is read from right to left (as we look) then it is apparent that the system of mensuration is based on a standard unit (1SU) that is repeated six times on the right before being successively subdivided into smaller fractions, each separated from its neighbour by an interpolated standard unit:

1SU | 1SU | 1SU | 1SU | 1SU | 1SU | ½ | 1SU | ⅓ | 1SU | ¼ | 1SU | ⅕ | 1SU | ⅙ | 1SU

It is relevant to note that the successive subdivisions of the standard unit (2, 3, 4, 5, 6) are all regular numbers in the sexagesimal system, and that the main sequence on this face of the measuring rod breaks off at ⅙, presumably (for one thing) because the next fraction in the series (⅐) is an irregular quantity that cannot be rewritten as a whole number

in the sexagesimal system. With respect to base 60, the rod can perhaps usefully be thought of as a simple table of reciprocals. In other words, if the value of the unit is taken to be sixty (of whichever thing or quantity is being measured and divided) then the subdivisions (2, 3, 4, 5, 6) tell the user of the instrument that those fractions can be rewritten as subunit values (30, 20, 15, 12, 10). Consequently, the rod is a graphic representation of a table of reciprocals (further clarified in Fig. 215). It is also worth noting that the subunit values on the measuring rods on Statues B and F have been carved with a high degree of accuracy (such that the standard units and their subdivisions are well correlated with each other).

The measuring rule on Statue F, which is much less damaged than the one on Statue B, includes additional marks, especially towards the left end (as we look), on the face of the triangular prism that is not visible from where Gudea is seated. Some of the unit demarcations that can notionally be seen by Gudea are also continued onto the front face of the prism (from the spectator's point of view), but they do not seem to add extra functionality. Conversely, the additional marks towards the extreme left on the dark side (so to speak) add further subdivisions of the standard unit, namely into twelfths and eighteenths. This can be seen on the far left of the rod on Statue F, where the first of the ⅙ divisions on Gudea's side of the ruler is further divided into two on the dark side to indicate 2/12, while the third of the ⅙ divisions on Gudea's side is divided into three to indicate 3/18, and both of these denominators (12 and 18) are, of course, regular in the sexagesimal system. The severe damage to the rod on Statue B makes it difficult to know whether it also contained twelfths and eighteenths (or any other subdivisions), but it does appear that some standard unit indicators were carried over from Gudea's side onto the dark side. These can just about be made out in at least three places: facing the NE side of the E corner; facing the NW tower on the gate leading into the Ur-Bau plaza at the SE end of the NE façade (on the horizontal bar of the L of the L-shaped complex); and facing the SE tower of the gate at the other end of the same façade. It is not unusual to find modern measuring rods intended for technical purposes that are shaped as triangular prisms and furnished with various subdivisions on their different faces, but in this case the fact that the divisions into twelfths and eighteenths are so minimally indicated, and also invisible from Gudea's point of view, might well suggest that such fractions were very rarely used, at least at that period and in the context of a large-scale project like the design for the ground plan of the New Eninnu.

How, then, do the standard unit and the various fractions marked on the measuring rod relate to the plan? It might be tempting to conceive of it primarily as a Sumerian exercise in geometry, and therefore to approach it as an exemplum of some of the Mesopotamian mathematical concepts listed at the beginning of this discussion. On the contrary, however, in a profound but slightly counterintuitive sense the plan is not really concerned with geometry at all in the way in which that science was later developed and used. The plan and the measuring rod express proportional quantities that are defined as fractions of a standard unit. Taken together, they visually describe much of the information that the builders needed in order to carry out Gudea's instructions and construct the temenos walls of the New Eninnu according to his design. The process by which Gudea might have created the actual design of the temenos is discussed in greater detail below, but in general terms the lines of the outer walls of the New Eninnu were marked out with ropes on the ground, as is stated in the text of the Cylinder Inscriptions (A19–21), and those lines, including the thickness of the various features, are proportionally represented on the incised diagram on Statue B. This can be verified with reference to Fig. 213, which correlates Gudea's plan with the archaeology by superimposing it over the structures at the SE end of the complex that were excavated by the British Museum team. The superimposition confirms that the gates are correctly positioned, and the length and thickness of the temenos wall are accurately indicated, as are the widths of the gate towers and buttresses. Gudea's plan therefore represents a scaled-down diagram of the lines of the temenos walls and the positions of the various elements that were built into the façades, but in conjunction with the measuring rod it also provides more detailed information. It indicates the exact sizes of the features, including

the gateway towers and their passageways, the buttress towers and all the expanses of blank wall.

The high level of detail embedded in the plan can be demonstrated by further comparisons with the rod (Fig. 216). When the standard unit recorded on the measuring rule is applied to the New Eninnu's SW façade (the one closest to Gudea), it measures almost exactly 12SU from the inside faces of the temenos walls at the NW and SE ends, respectively. The temenos wall is exactly half a unit thick (½SU)—the same as the width of the eight buttress towers that extend along the whole length of the SW façade. The width of the gateway towers and the interposed blank sections of wall is ¾SU, while the entranceway passages are ⅓SU wide, and the width of the recess between the two sides of each gate tower is ⅙SU. The total length of 12SU can be confirmed by adding up the dimensions of the various elements: (8 × ½SU = 4SU) for the buttress towers + (11 × ¾SU = 8¼SU) for the other elements, which gives a total of 12¼SU. The extra ¼SU can probably be accounted for by the size of the gateway, which has been treated as ¾SU at its widest point, but might in reality be a little less. In any case, the margin of error is extremely small. Other SU values are marked on Fig. 216.

Once the SU values of the temenos and its features are established, the question then arises: what was the real-world length to which the standard unit referred? There is no absolute answer to that question, of course, because a standard unit and its subdivisions can be used to handle any measurable quantity of countable things, just as nowadays, when using the standard unit in the decimal system, we can refer to ten (or any power of ten) of anything—metres, litres, bottles or people, for example, and any given group of ten can be subdivided or multiplied. A great deal of fascinating work has been done on the history of Mesopotamian mathematics (see Robson 2007), but it is expedient to approach the problem of Gudea's standard unit in terms of data that can be derived from the plan and the measuring rod, together with the archaeology of the New Eninnu. Accordingly, the thickness of the temenos wall, as measured on Tell A by the British Museum team, was 4 m (see Chapters 34 and 42; and Fig. 213). Dividing the thickness by the length of the side of a standard square Gudea brick (4 m ÷ 0.32 m = 12.5) gives 12.5 bricks. This seems to suggest that the walls were twelve and a half bricks thick, but the number includes the mortar in the vertical joints (the perpends) between adjacent bricks in each course. If the perpends are taken to be 2 cm wide, that would

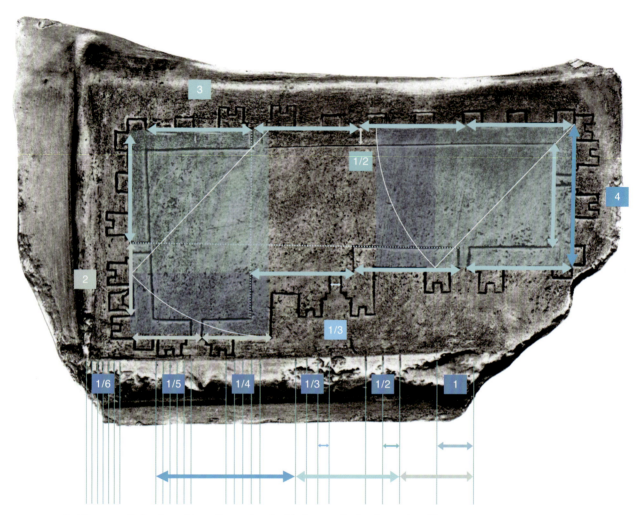

FIGURE 216. The ground plan from Statue B correlated with the standard units on the adjacent measuring rod. The numbers and fractions indicate multiples of Gudea's standard unit.

indicate that the thickness of the wall was made up of twelve bricks with sides of 0.32 m plus the total width of the mortar: (12 bricks × 0.32 m = 3.84 m) + (11 perpends × 0.02 m = 0.22 m) = 4.06 m. This is already extremely close to the measured thickness, but it becomes still closer if the perpends are taken to be the width of a finger, or 17 mm, which was a metrological unit dating back to Uruk times in the fourth millennium BCE and still current in late third millennium Sumer (Robson 2007, pp. 70–1): (12 bricks × 0.32 m = 3.84 m) + (11 perpends × 0.017 m = 0.187 m) = 4.027 m. Given the inescapable margins of error surrounding measurements of such ancient mudbrick structures, this degree of accuracy is perhaps unwarranted, but the fundamental point, namely that the temenos walls were twelve bricks thick, can be confirmed by looking at Fig. 139, where the number of bricks can be counted.

Since the thickness of the temenos is equal to half a standard unit on Gudea's measuring rod (½SU = 12 bricks), it follows that 1SU = 24 bricks. This means that the buttress towers (½SU, the same as the thickness of the temenos) were all 12 bricks wide (or about 4 m when the mortar is factored in), and this can be verified on Fig. 139. Similarly, with respect to the SW façade, the other features shown on the plan (the blank sections of wall and the elements of the gateway), which all measure ¾SU, were 18 bricks wide, or 5.76 m plus mortar. The excavated widths of the gate towers are problematic because they were heavily restored in Isin-Larsa times, so the original dimensions of the Gudea-era structures cannot be stated unequivocally (see Chapter 34). Nonetheless, the recorded total widths of the NW and SE gate towers in the SW façade were 5.53 m and 5.51 m, respectively, which is reasonably close to their predicted dimensions as recorded on Gudea's plan. No measurements were taken for the blank sections of wall between the buttress towers and on either side of the SW gateway, but a further extrapolation can be made, which is that the total length of the SW façade (12SU) was 12SU × 24 bricks = 288 bricks. This would indicate a measurement of 288 bricks × 0.32 m = 92.16 m for the SW façade plus mortar. If, for the sake of argument, the perpends are again taken to be 17 mm wide, that gives an additional length for the mortar of 288 perpends × 0.017 m = 4.896 m, which results in a measurement for the SW façade of 92.16 m + 4.896 m = 97.056 m, which is again very much in line with the length shown on the combined diagram of Gudea's design and the British Museum team's excavations (Fig. 213). Incidentally, the reason why the calculation includes 288 perpends and not 287, as might be expected, is because every other course of bricks must have started and finished with a half-brick (such that its length was made up of 287 whole bricks plus two half-bricks) and this would add an extra perpend, giving a maximum of 288 in every other course, which is the number used in the calculation. Conversely, as can be verified by looking at the archaeological plan of the outer façades (Fig. 139), and for reasons explained in Chapter 42, the thickness of the temenos (as opposed to its length) was made up entirely of whole bricks.

An initial conclusion that can be drawn is that, together with the measuring rod, the plan shown on Statue B is the graphic representation of a table of numerical values that could be used to inform the Lagash II builders how to fulfil Gudea's intentions. It is not obvious how Gudea's standard unit might have related to any measures that were commonly used in the Lagash II period, or indeed how it might have been associated with the sexagesimal system, even though the chosen fractions on the rod are determined with respect to base 60. Furthermore, the fact that the determining base was indeed sixty and not twenty-four (the number of bricks in Gudea's standard unit), can be confirmed by the presence on the rods of divisions into fifths because five, which is a regular number in the sexagesimal system, is irregular with respect to twenty-four (whose factors are all multiples of 2 and 3). The answer perhaps lies in the measured value of twenty-four bricks (24 × 0.32 m = 7.68 m), or in some quantity that can be derived from, or specially associated with, that value, but this is not at all clear. Much more fundamentally, the use of the measuring rod as a kind of graduated scale bar is now so familiar that it might be difficult to see the interest of it, but

Gudea felt so strongly about its importance that he ordered his sculptors to inscribe it on Statues B and F, thereby commending it to the gods. The special thing that he glimpsed might well lie in the fact that, by defining it with respect to twenty-four of his standard bricks, he chose what was in effect an arbitrary standard unit that was fitting for his purposes and the local cultural context in which the New Eninnu was created. In so doing, he realised the flexible power of a unit, which is not, in and of itself, a particular fixed quantity, but an envelope that can be used to define and contain any given number, whether that be twenty-four bricks or (say) the early ancient Mesopotamian unit known as a rod, which was equal to 12 cubits (1 cubit = 30 fingers; 1 finger = 17 mm, as introduced above). His achievement in this respect might therefore have been a seminal contribution to the developing concept of 'abstract numeration': the realisation that numbers could be treated as 'independent entities', and not purely as 'attributes of concrete objects' (Robson 2007, p. 75).

The degree of accuracy with which the plan is shown engenders another intriguing conundrum: why are the temenos walls—and specifically their corners—irregular? The overall shape might be defined as a trapezium, with equal base angles of 88.5° and a stepped top (at the SE end of the NE façade). The instinctive reaction might be to say that, in reality, the angles at the corners of the complex must have been right angles, but this is not convincing. It would imply that the ground plan was carved on the statue as a picture that did not aspire to complete accuracy, but that idea is decisively contradicted by the use of the graduated ruler to define the lengths of the various elements in proportion to the standard unit. Alternatively, therefore, the overall shape of the temenos walls must be regarded as an accurate diagram of the way the complex was built.

One matter that is beyond dispute is that the temenos was designed around some existing features, most importantly the old Ur-Bau Ningirsu temple, which was retained inside the short NE façade at the SE end of the L-shaped complex. No remains of the walls of Ur-Bau's shrine were found by the French, but they did find the fired-brick facings of the podium on which it was constructed (see Chapters 23 and 25), while the British Museum team unearthed traces of the original Ur-Bau temenos wall, particularly on the SW side of the Ur-Bau plaza (Chapter 33). Gudea either retained Ur-Bau's walls directly inside the façades of his New Eninnu, or he built envelope walls inside the new façades, following the lines laid out by Ur-Bau. The extent to which the Ur-Bau temenos walls were incorporated or redeveloped by Gudea is not clear from the archaeology, but it is conceivable that most of the lines of the New Eninnu's façades at the SE end of the complex followed the footprint that had been previously demarcated by Ur-Bau. Most significantly, the angle of the NW wall on the protruding NE section at the SE end of the temenos (the NE–SW wall that joined the short NE façade that was pierced by the gate at the SE end of the NE façade) to the central area of the façade containing the gate giving access to the central courtyard followed the line of the podium on which the old Ur-Bau temple was raised. Crucially, as measured by Cros (see Chapter 23), the podium was slightly offset with respect to some of the surrounding features, and this is the angle that defines the line of Gudea's façade at this point (Fig. 212). It has the effect of very slightly increasing the angle of the corner of the temenos from 90° to about 91.5°, but this small addition is a defining factor in the overall shape of Gudea's temenos, which (as noted above) closely approximates a trapezium with base angles of 88.5°. In other words, the lines defined by Ur-Bau's temple podium, and presumably followed by his original temenos walls (exemplified by the traces found on the SW side of the Ur-Bau plaza), provided Gudea with a fundamental parameter when he planned the façades of the New Eninnu, as represented on the diagram incised on Statue B, and that is why the corners shown on the plan are not right angles.

One issue that must be further clarified is that the lines of Ur-Bau's podium do not necessarily reflect the precise orientation of the temple that was built on it. Like all Sumerian temples, his shrine would have been very carefully positioned with respect to the north star and the other cardinal points, in the same way as Gudea's later Ningirsu temple was. There might have been any number of reasons why the podium and the temenos were not angled in exactly the same way as the temple. Perhaps the slope of the ground made it tricky, or maybe the nature of the massive substructural platforms on which the temple podium was built caused problems, but in any case there was self-evidently no structural or theological reason why the angles of the temenos had to be congruent with the corners of the temple. Notably, therefore, in this as in several other matters, Gudea was content to follow his father-in-law's lead.

The unusual footprint of Gudea's plan was thus presumably created as a solution to some practical problems, including the need to incorporate the old and new Ningirsu temples, while the decision to retain the angles given by the Ur-Bau temple podium and his temenos might have been taken partly as a matter of expediency and partly out of respect for an illustrious predecessor. The ground plan could well have been roughed out on the mound with ropes and pegs before being subsequently rationalised in the exceptional form of the finished plan as it is recorded on Statue B. Similar ad hoc methods must have been used for generations to mark out plots of land, for example, and there can be little doubt that Sumerians were skilled at accurately measuring out the areas of parcels of land. As demonstrated in Fig. 217, however, it is also possible to construct the design for the temenos geometrically, by first drawing out three rectangles (R1–3) and refining their dimensions, before adjusting the angles at the corners to create the finished shape. This includes the notional line that runs across the complex from the corner adjacent to the N corner of the Ur-Bau podium on the NE side (referred to above) to the SE gate tower of the gate in the SW façade. Two things become apparent when the design is considered in this more abstract way: first, the position of the gate in the SW façade is well aligned with the angles of the opposite NE façade; secondly, the area occupied by the Ningirsu temple at the SE end of the complex (R3 on Fig. 217) is almost exactly the same as the area that was almost certainly occupied by the Bau shrine and its associated annexes at the NW end (R1 on Fig. 217), and the dimensions of the two areas remain unaffected when the base angles of the notional trapezium are reduced from 90° to 88.5° because the change is the same on both sides. One caveat is that the position of the Bau shrine, which has not been verified by excavation, is no more than an inference that is very strongly supported by circumstantial evidence. That does not change the geometrical relationship between the two rectangles, however, and there is, of course, a pleasing symmetry in the idea that the principal deities were plausibly housed in congruent spaces.

Finally, a question that inevitably arises when looking at the plan is: why is its focus on the temenos alone, in isolation from the sacred buildings? Even more specifically, why is the ground plan of the Ningirsu temple not included? With respect to the temple, the answer is that the walls of the inner sanctum were almost certainly not planned as expressions of the standard unit. This can be verified by referring to the measurements that were taken by the British Museum team

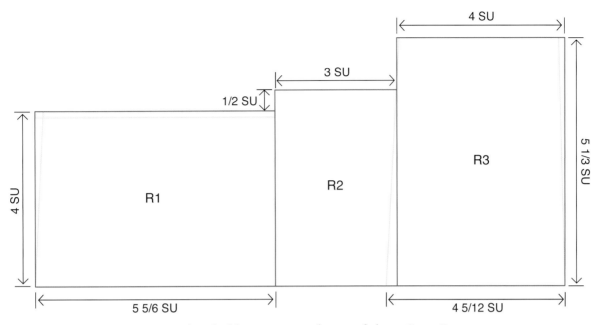

FIGURE 217. A two-stage geometrical method for constructing the ground plan on Statue B.

(presented in Chapter 34). The bricks used to construct the walls were standard Gudea square bricks (with sides of 0.32 m), and the building's footprint measured 30.12 m (north-west–south-east) × 17.14 m (north-east–south-west). The NE façade contained the main entrance, while the long SW façade, which was blank, must in all likelihood have been constructed of ninety bricks, as the following calculation shows: (90 bricks × 0.32 m = 28.8 m) + (90 perpends × 0.017 m = 1.53 m) = 30.33 m. An even closer match (30.17 m) is obtained if the calculation is performed with 89.5 bricks, and the same total thickness (1.53 m) is assumed for the perpends. Though there may be no reason why 89.5 bricks could not have been used, the round number is surely more likely. Nor should it be forgotten that the perpends might have differed a little in thickness from the presumed measurement of 17 mm, and that all the measurements are inescapably subject to a small margin of error due to the nature of the ancient materials. More to the point, however, neither of these numbers is close to being a straightforward multiple of Gudea's standard unit (1SU = 24 bricks): 90 bricks = 3 ¾SU; 89.5 bricks = 3.729SU. The same is true of the width of the building, represented by the blank NW and SE façades, which were probably made of fifty or fifty-one bricks, producing total lengths of 16.85 m and 17.187 m, respectively, including 17 mm perpends. Again, it would seem intuitively more likely that a round number of bricks was used, though that was not necessarily the case. In any event, the same circumstance applies, which is that neither figure is a simple multiple of Gudea's standard unit: 50 bricks = 2.0833SU; 51 bricks = 2⅛SU. The probable number of bricks is given for the sake of precision, but the calculations are, in practice, much more straightforward for built structures: 1SU = 8 m (8.088 m to be exact); ½SU = 4 m (or 4.044 m to be exact).

The thickness of the Ningirsu temple's walls is slightly more problematic because they were often fitted with foundation footings of various sizes. Nonetheless, an indicative thickness of 2.3 m was recorded repeatedly by the British Museum team (as noted in Chapter 34). It is interesting to recall that the figure is the same as the thickness of the envelope walls built by Gudea above Ur-Bau's old temenos, which were measured to the south-west of the Ningirsu temple, on both sides of the gate that pierced the SW façade of Gudea's temenos. Whether this implies that the walls of the sanctum sanctorum and the enveloping walls were both built to the same thickness as their Ur-Bau predecessors is speculative, but in any event the reference figure of 2.3 m for the thickness of Gudea's Ningirsu temple walls does not express a relationship with Gudea's standard unit. This can be generally confirmed by the overall figure of 2.3 m for the built walls, which bears no clear relation to 8 m (the guideline length of 1SU for built structures). More precisely, a thickness of 2.3 m would indicate the use of seven Gudea square bricks: $(7 \text{ bricks} \times 0.32 \text{ m} = 2.24 \text{ m}) + (6 \text{ perpends} \times 0.017 \text{ m} = 0.102 \text{ m}) = 2.342 \text{ m}$. Despite the poor condition of the temple walls, this is largely in accord with the British Museum team's findings (see Fig. 139). If the figure is assumed to be correct, it adds considerably to the basic argument because seven is an irregular number, with respect to both Gudea's standard unit (1SU = 24 bricks) and indeed to the sexagesimal system generally, which is why $\frac{1}{7}$ths are not marked on the measuring rod. It would seem to imply that, as a matter of mathematical principle, the thickness of the walls of Gudea's Ningirsu temple could not have been marked on the temple plan on Statue B with reference to scale shown on the measuring rod. That said, it is extraordinarily difficult to be categorical about these measurements (as indeed for the temple's overall length and width), not only because of the presence and absence of foundation footings in a range of sizes, but also because of the extreme age of the bricks. Inevitably, therefore, there could be some relatively minor variations in the measured thicknesses of the walls. Nevertheless, even if they had been recorded as being, for example, 2.2 m or 2.4 m, instead of 2.3 m, it would have no bearing on the important conclusion that they were not planned with respect to the measuring rod because none of these numbers relates in any clear way to Gudea's standard unit.

There could be several reasons why the temenos was planned independently of the temple walls, and presumably of the other sacred buildings that were inside the complex but not marked on the plan on Statue B. One possibility is that the measuring system was deliberately not used on the temple walls, maybe for historical reasons or on account of some symbolism that was associated with their dimensions, or perhaps because Gudea was following a precedent set by Ur-Bau, but none of these theories can be confirmed. It might also be that the metrology recorded on Statue B was only brought into being at a particular stage in the construction sequence, but again this is difficult to verify. The one thing that seems unequivocally clear is that the standard unit was used only on the temenos.

CHAPTER 40

The Gates of the New Eninnu and the Monuments to the Slain Heroes

The Positioning of the Complex with Respect to Solar and Lunar Cycles

A factor that has been largely overlooked in the various arguments that aim to correlate the names of the New Eninnu's gates given in the Cylinder Inscriptions with the physical remains is the way the complex was located with respect to the celestial events that must have determined some of the key divisions in the annual local time frame. It is a truism to say that the corners of ancient Sumerian temples pointed towards the cardinal points, but as is detailed in the discussion of the tessellated earth in Chapter 14, that apparently straightforward observation conceals several complexities. The Sumerian idea of the tessellated earth stressed the fundamental importance of the N–S line that was established with reference to the north star when a temple was laid out. The E–W line, or lines to be more precise, were also of primary significance, though not in the same way as in societies that base their sense of direction on the magnetic compass, or in cultures that spotlight the historical or religious importance of places that are said to be due east or due west, for example. When directions are plotted with respect to the rising and setting of the sun, without special priority being given to any other direction than north, then due east and due west are not necessarily conceived of as universal constants in the familiar sense.

Fig. 218, which for simplicity's sake is centred on the Ur-Nanshe Building on Tell K, shows the path of the sun over Girsu as it changes day by day during the course of the year. The vertical line bisecting the diagram is the N–S line.

The broad band containing a sequence of elongated skittle shapes (called analemmas) shows the range of positions in the sky through which the sun passes annually and day by day. Beginning in the north-east, at the top right of the band of analemmas, position A shows the point on the horizon at which the sun rises at the summer solstice (20 or 21 June), while position B to the north-west (on the top left of the band) shows the point at which the sun sets on the same day in June; position E (due east) shows sunrise at the spring and autumn equinoxes (around 21 March and 23 September, respectively), and position W (due west) shows sunset at the equinoxes on those same days in March and September; finally, positions C and D, on the SE and SW sides of the diagram, show sunrise and sunset at the winter solstice (21 or 22 December), respectively. The date ranges are indicative because the actual annual dates are subject to small variations. The thick curving line (E–W) that bisects the band of analemmas from east to west is the path of the sun through the sky at the spring and autumn equinoxes, with the times marked from 06.00 hrs in the morning on the right, via 12.00 hrs (noon) in the middle, through to 18.00 hrs on the left. The equinoctial timeline shows that on those particular days (21 March and 23 September) the sun rises over Girsu at around six o'clock in the morning, reaches its highest point in the sky at noon, and sets a little after six in the evening. The half of the band of analemmas that lies above the equinoctial line shows the range of sun paths in the spring and summer months, while the section below it shows their positions in the autumn and the winter. The skittle shapes or analemmas illustrate the path that the sun traces through the sky day by

591

day during the year at the times represented on the equinoctial line. Starting at noon in midwinter, therefore, when the sun lies almost due south, at the bottom of the skittle that is nearly bisected by the N–S line, the sun initiates this phase of its annual midday journey by moving up the right side of the bulbous form, before crossing from right to left (around mid-April) then continuing up the left side of the slender top part of the skittle until it reaches the apex at midsummer (in June). It then continues down the right side of the slender top before crossing over from right to left (towards the end of August) and tracing the left side of the bulbous form down to the base of the skittle at midwinter. At that point the sequence recommences. The sun's motion is, of course, only apparent; in truth, its seeming trajectory is caused by the earth's orbit around it and the earth's rotation on its own axis.

If, for the sake of argument, with respect to points A to D, E and W on the diagram, the start of the year is taken to be 21 March (the spring equinox), the dates (and points) succeed each other in the following order, after which the cycle begins again:

Date	Sunrise–Sunset
Spring equinox (21 March)	E–W
Summer solstice (20 or 21 June)	A–B
Autumn equinox (23 September)	E–W
Winter solstice (21 or 22 December	C–D

Between the spring equinox in March and the summer solstice in June the daily path of the sun moves gradually northwards from the equinoctial line to the top curve of the band of analemmas and then returns slowly southwards from the curving line (A–B) that joins sunrise and sunset at the summer solstice back to the equinoctial line (E–W), which it reaches at the autumn equinox in September. Between September and December the sun's diurnal path moves gradually southwards to the winter solstice (C–D) before returning gradually northwards between December and March, when the annual cycle restarts. The angles subtended at the centre of the circle by the arcs A–C and B–D (on the right and left of the diagram, respectively) each measure about 56°. Since the sun traces these arcs twice annually (from the equinox to the northernmost point and back, and from the equinox to the southernmost point and back), the total angle through which it passes is about 112°, which means

that, on average, the daily change in the position of the sun for successive sunrises and sunsets is about 0.31° (dividing 112° by 365). The average figure must be treated with great caution because the observed diurnal changes in the positions of sunrise and sunset vary according to the different lengths of the days and nights at different times of the year, but the smallness of the average daily change is a useful indicator of the difficulty of recording precise observations and making predictions. It is also worth pointing out that the sun passes twice annually through every point on the arcs (including E and W) except for the points it reaches at the summer and winter solstices (A, B and C, D, respectively). Consequently, in terms of the yearly sun path, the solstices are singular moments—exceptional by definition—that mark the end (and renewal) of the solar year in midwinter and the climax of the solar year (followed by a slow decline) in midsummer.

An in-depth discussion of the extremely intricate ways in which ancient Sumerians correlated the solar year with the lunar year, which is based on the monthly cycles of the moon, is beyond the scope of the present study (see Cohen 1993, pp. 3–8). With regard to the temple's role in the organisation of the Sumerian calendar, it is nonetheless vital to add a word about how solar and lunar time frames were coordinated, and some basic facts about the moon, in particular about the appearance of the new moon at the beginning of the lunar month, the waning of the moon at the end of the month, and the period in between, when the moon is briefly invisible. The moon's seeming disappearance actually signals the advent of a new moon that cannot be seen because it rises in the east at sunrise and is obscured during the day by its proximity to the sun's diurnal path. The slender crescent shape that is popularly referred to as the new moon occurs a day or two later, when it is seen in the west, shortly after sunset, as the setting moon reflects a glimmer of the sun's light after the sun has descended below the horizon. The waxing crescent (strictly speaking, a young moon rather than a new moon) is the part of the natural satellite that is lit up by the sun while the rest of the orb is in shadow. Since the moon, which has no light of its own, is illuminated only because it reflects sunlight, the appearance of the new moon on the W side of Fig. 218 is ineluctably tied to the changing position of the sun at different times of the year. Accordingly, at the equinoxes, the waxing crescent appears almost due west (W on the diagram), while at the summer and winter solstices it is visible in the

The Gates of the New Eninnu and the Monuments to the Slain Heroes   593

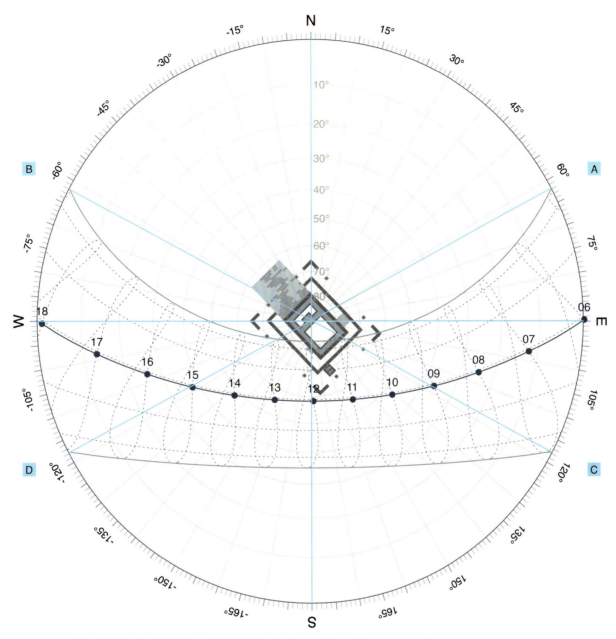

FIGURE 218. The Ur-Nanshe Building on Tell K, showing its position with respect to the cardinal points and the path taken by the sun as it passes over Tello in the course of a year.

north-west (B) and south-west (D), respectively. With reference to the E side of the diagram (on the right), the changing place of the waning crescent, or the last appearance of the old moon at the end of the month, before it temporarily disappears, is a mirror image of the variations that affect the new moon. The waning crescent is visible somewhere in the E sector at sunrise, but it changes its diurnal location according to the sun's shifting position: it appears due east at the equinoxes (E on the diagram), in the north-east at the summer solstice (A), and in the south-east at the winter solstice (C). The Sumerian lunar year began in March or April (the first month), a variable number of days after the spring equinox, with the appearance of the new moon soon after sunset in the west. There was also a second main annual festival that was celebrated in September, in the seventh month, which began with the appearance of the first new moon after the autumn equinox. Indeed, the seventh month was in some instances apparently regarded as the equivalent of another new year, as though the solar year was divided into two shorter lunar years (Cohen 1993, pp. 6–7). In any event, at these two junctures, around the times of the vernal and autumn equinoxes, the evening sky to the west of Girsu must have been conscientiously scoured for the first glimpse of the waxing crescent.

The further matter that should be briefly addressed is the discrepancy between calendars that are based on solar and lunar cycles. Since a lunar month is about 29.5 days long, a twelve-month lunar year amounts to 354 days, which is eleven days shorter than the 365-day solar year. The differential is more than a notional matter because the seasons are regulated by the key turning points in the solar year, but the Sumerian calendar that guided human activities, above all with respect to the agricultural cycle, was lunar. The eleven-day difference therefore meant that the named months, with their important agricultural and ritual associations, gradually drifted out of sync with the seasons to which they were fundamentally related, and the divergence had to be corrected with the periodic addition of extra days. The standard way of doing this (but perhaps not the only way) was by intercalating an extra month every three years to create a thirteen-month lunar leap year that restored the correspondence between the pattern of the seasons (fixed by the sun) and the lunar calendar. The principle is similar to the modern leap year, when an extra day is inserted at the end of February every four years to deal with the fact that the time it takes for the earth to orbit the sun is in reality a little longer than 365 days. The lunar differential is far greater, however, and the intercalary month was apparently inserted at a range of times during the year—varying at different historical periods and from city to city (see Cohen 1993, pp. 4–5). Without dwelling unnecessarily on the resulting complications, the problem of mensual drift in the lunar calendar means that the correlation between the fixed points in the solar year and the more flexible Sumerian months was subject to a degree of latitude.

In order to establish some basic principles of placement, the Ur-Nanshe Building on Tell K is shown at the centre of Fig. 218, such that its N and W corners are bisected by the N–S and E–W lines, respectively. The four further radii extending from positions A, B, C and D demarcate imaginary lines extending from sunrise and sunset at the two solstices to the centre of the diagram (created by the intersection of the NS and EW axes), where all the lines cross. Sunrise and sunset would naturally have been visible to an observer from the temple, which was elevated above the surrounding plain, and the radii themselves would have been partially manifested if, for example, a post or standard had been placed at an appropriate position in front of the temple, like the gnomon of a sundial, in order to create a shadow, either when the sun rose above the horizon or just before it descended below it. Whether or not one or more tall poles were actually used in this way cannot be confirmed, but the very possibility that, in principle, they could have been indicates that the radii drawn on the diagram are not merely theoretical. On the contrary, they represent a vivid physical reality. It should also be pointed out that the size of the building is inordinately exaggerated by comparison with the surrounding horizon line (the circle of the earth), but that does not change the geometrical relationships between the parts of the building and the key points on the circumference because the precise siting of the building is fundamentally determined by the fact that its N corner (a right angle) is bisected by the N–S line (see Chapter 14). Thereafter, the placement of the other right-angled corners with respect to the cardinal points follows geometrically, irrespective of the lengths of the walls. The W corner points due west on the primary E–W axis; the S corner points due south on another N–S line (not drawn on the diagram) that is parallel to the first N–S axis; and the E corner points due east on a second E–W line (again not represented on the diagram). In this regard, it is important to emphasise that the circle of the earth, with its unique NSEW points, is misleading in terms of the Sumerian system of the world since the Sumerians seem to have conceived of the earth as being divided up into an innumerable series of parallel (non-converging) N–S and E–W lines that interlocked to create a notional grid pattern on which temples and other sacred buildings could be correctly positioned. A routine analogue that helps to visualise the resulting grid patterns might be the division of farmland into regular agricultural plots.

Perhaps the first thing that might catch the eye about the relationship between the temple, the N–S line and the other radii (extending from points A to D, E and W) is that they all converge in the cella, exactly on the cult podium, which is drawn on Sarzec and Heuzey's plan as a NW-facing dentil in the NE–SW wall that separates the cella from the antecella (see Chapter 5). It is impossible to know how exact the placement of the point of convergence was in the physical structure, but the intersection of the lines at the point where the statue of the god was positioned is not forced for the purposes of illustration. It is an automatic geometrical consequence of the laying out of the temple, beginning with the bisected N corner on the N–S axis, together with the relative sizes of the two rooms—the smaller cella and the larger antecella. The second noteworthy thing (an axiomatic feature of the ground plan) is that the W corner of the temple points directly due west, to the point on the horizon at which the sun disappears from view at the spring and autumn equinoxes—the same direction in which the new moon was observed by Sumerian sky watchers in the first and seventh months. However it was done, an astronomer at the W corner (or directly in line with it, presumably within the confines of the temple complex) must have looked for the disappearance of the equinoctial sun at a point due west—an event that was followed by the emergence of the crescent moon at a nearby point some evenings later (all subject to the problems of mensual drift outlined above). The special importance of the W corner of the Ur-Nanshe Building was marked by the installation of inscribed bricks (see Chapters 5 and 16), while elaborate deposits were placed under the W corner of the Lower Construction (see Chapter 12). It would seem reasonable to assume that in both cases the W corner was especially linked with the equinoxes, corresponding with the first and seventh months, which were essential turning points in the year and in the agricultural cycle. As also noted in Chapter 12, however, whether the W corner of the Lower Construction was associated with the observation of the new moon is less certain, and the same caveat would apply to the Ur-Nanshe Building. The third feature of particular interest with respect to the placement of the temple is the NW radius that extends from B to the cult podium. There was a door in the NW façade of the Ur-Nanshe Building, and pavement F extended out from it, as can be seen on the diagram, following the extended lines determined by the NE and SW façades. The door could doubtless have been offset to one side of the façade to reflect the line linking the temple with sunset at the summer solstice (B), should that have been considered desirable, but the pavement was oriented directly towards the north-west, such that its centre was in line with the point marked as −45° on the circumference of the circle. How these relationships were worked out in practice, and how much weight was placed upon them, are hypothetical matters, but it should also be recalled that the Ur-Nanshe

Building was set within a portico, and that the sacred summit of Tell K was enclosed inside a temenos wall. Entrance points could therefore theoretically have been built at appropriate points in surrounding structures in order to instantiate some of the relationships shown in Fig. 218. Finally, the SE radius (C) leads towards the antecella, which was accessed via a door in the SE façade. Subject to the caveats just mentioned, an approach on the SE side of the building could have reflected this relationship. Nothing further can be said about points A, E and D, but they potentially also had special meanings, as might well be confirmed by the layout of Gudea's New Eninnu.

Fig. 219 shows the New Eninnu at the centre of the circle, with the same key points marked on the circumference and the same lines extending through its centre. The placement of the complex depends upon the positioning of the N corner of the Ningirsu temple at the heart of the complex, towards the SE end of the L-shaped temenos. This is the spot that is referred to in the Cylinder Inscriptions when Gudea lays the first brick, and as on the Ur-Nanshe Building, the right-angle is bisected by the N–S axis, such that the W corner of the temple axiomatically points due west, while the S corner is offset eastwards along a parallel (but non-converging) N–S line, and the E corner is offset slightly southwards along a parallel (and again non-converging) E–W line. Comparable to the Ur-Nanshe Building, the radii from points A, B, C, D, E and W on the edge of the circle meet in the cella, though in this case the cult podium was built into the cella's SW wall, and the god's statue faced north-east. That being the case, the lines apparently meet somewhere in the centre of the sanctum sanctorum, perhaps on the offering table, and not directly on the podium. Except to say that it was almost certainly inside the cella, however, the exact point of convergence is somewhat conjectural.

Needless to say, the actual placements of the features shown on the plan must also be subject to a degree of uncertainty, but the walls of the L-shaped complex, including the irregular extensions on the NE façade (namely, the Ur-Bau plaza in front of the Ningirsu temple and the gateway area on the NE side of the main courtyard) are in accord with the lines established by the positioning of the temple. Within that overall scheme, the lengths of the temenos walls and the siting of the entrances and other features could be varied to suit the intentions of the planners, principally Gudea himself, who took the decision to retain Ur-Bau's old Eninnu

596 The Mound of the Palace

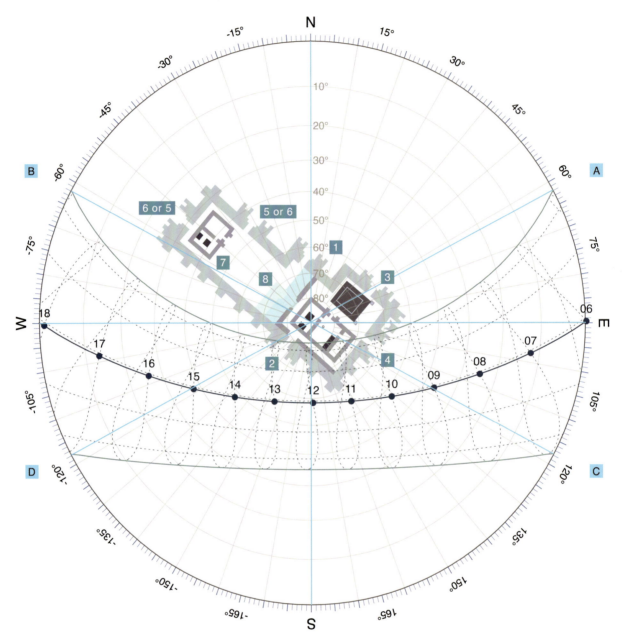

FIGURE 219. The New Eninnu of Gudea on Tell A, showing its position with respect to the cardinal points and the annual path of the sun. The added numbers show the probable locations of the gates and Bau's 'inner room', as named in the Cylinder Inscriptions: 1. Battle Gate; 2. City Gate; 3. Shugalam Gate; 4. Sunrise Gate; 5. Kasurra Gate; 6. Tarsirsir Gate; 7. Bau's 'inner room'; 8. King's Gate.

at the SE end of the L-shaped complex, at the NE end of the horizontal bar of the L. With the dimensions of the basic L shape established, the orientations of the main walls were determined by the placement of fixed features, most importantly the Ningirsu temple (as discussed in Chapter 39), but other attributes of the complex were a matter of deliberate choice for the designers. Noteworthy among these is the line A–D that runs all the way across the diagram, from the point associated with sunrise at the summer solstice (A) to the point where the sun sets in midwinter (D). The line conspicuously passes through (or extremely close to) the gates on the NE and SW sides of the complex, such that the NE gate was presumably a focal point at midsummer, while the SW one—the only entrance in the extremely long SW wall—was probably prominent at midwinter. In connection with this NE–SW line, it should be mentioned that all of the four lines that extend from one side of the circle's circumference to the other (N–S, E–W, A–D and B–C) are diameters, namely straight lines that pass exactly through the centre of the circle. Secondly, the radius extending from position C (associated with sunrise at the winter solstice) leads almost directly to the gate in the SE façade. This gate, it should be pointed out, is not in the centre of the façade, but rather offset towards the E corner, where it was carefully placed, perhaps partly in order to instantiate the connection between the midwinter sunrise and this side of the complex. The same might be said, incidentally, of the single gate in the SW façade, which was sited at the only position in the SW wall that was both directly in line with the midwinter sunset and diametrically opposite its midsummer sunrise counterpart in the NE façade.

On the SE façade, close to the E corner of the temenos, is a strange fixture that has been described as a horned altar. As is discussed in the following section, other artefacts in the complex indicate that the imagery of horns can be connected with the waxing and waning crescent moons, and this might suggest that the addition of this altar (if that is the correct way to describe it) to the temenos could have been a lunar observation post from which the waning moon could be detected at sunrise in the winter months. Conversely (as also discussed below), the second addition to the temenos on the NW façade, close to the W corner, might have been a counterpart lookout that was used to spot the midsummer new moon, but this is less likely, not least because the extension does not obviously display symbolic horns, and seems instead to be shaped rather like one of the nearby recessed buttresses. Clearly, however, the W corner of the Ningirsu temple is self-evidently in line with due west on the circumference of the circle (W), as is to be expected, but it is of great interest that there is no indication of any related observation post in the SW façade, not even the high gate towers of the SW gate, which do not align with the extension of the temple's W corner to the point due west on the horizon (W). The probable reasons for this are explored in detail below, but there is every indication that a W-facing lookout was sited on the roof of the temple. Finally, the N–S line, which bisects the N corner of the temple, also runs through the SE

tower that is associated with the gate in the middle of the NE façade. This conjunction, which was not inevitable, depends on the highly unusual stepped arrangement of the wall in this section of the NE façade that creates a transition between the narrower part of the L-shaped complex to the north-west and the protrusion that housed the old Eninnu of Ur-Bau at the NE end of the horizontal bar of the L. If, for example, the NE wall in the area of the middle gate had continuously followed the NE line indicated by the top part of the vertical stroke of the L (towards the NW end of the complex), there would have been no correlation between the middle gate and the N–S axis; conversely, if the middle gateway façade had followed the line of the wall on the NE side of the Ur-Bau plaza (at the SE end of the complex), the intersection would have occurred at the NW tower. Since the central one of the three NE gates led directly into the New Eninnu's main courtyard, there were undoubtedly very good reasons why the planners wished to widen the building (the vertical stroke of the L) in this area, but the choices they made might well have reflected the cardinal importance of the N–S line.

The Gates of the New Eninnu and the Slain Heroes

A fascinating passage in Cylinder A lists a series of places around the complex where memorials were displayed to honour the mythical heroes or 'warriors' who were vanquished by Ningirsu (A25–6). For clarity's sake, the sites are numbered in the following quotation, and the short coda stating that the figures can be identified as the Slain Heroes is included:

1. In the inner room (?) where the weapons hang, at the Gate of Battle he had the warriors Six-headed wild ram and . . . head take their stand.
2. Facing the city, its place laden with awe, he had the Seven-headed serpent take its stand.
3. In Shugalam, its awesome gate, he had the Dragon and the Date palm take their stand.
4. Facing the sunrise, where the fates are decided, he erected the standard of Utu, the Bison head, beside others already there.
5. At the Kasurra gate, at its lookout post, he had the Lion, the terror of the gods, take its stand.

6. In the Tarsirsir, where the orders are issued, he had the Fish-man and the Copper take their stand.

7. In Bau's inner room (?), where the heart can be soothed, he had the Magilum boat and the Bison take their stand.

Because these were warriors slain by Ningirsu, he set their mouths towards libation places. Gudea, the ruler of Lagash, made their names appear among those of the gods.

It has often been assumed that only six places are mentioned in the list and that they enjoy a one-to-one correspondence with the six main gates in the temenos. Some of the sites are explicitly called gates, and it is reasonable to assume that all six gates are included in the inventory, but the idea that only six places are enumerated is a clear mistake, which is based on the unfounded assumption that Nos. 3 and 4 refer to the same location. Heimpel (1996, p. 19), for example, elides Shugalam (3) and Sunrise (4), which is here capitalised to indicate its status as a place name, as though the Dragon, the Date palm, the standard of Utu and the Bison head were all situated together in association with the site identified as Shugalam (a problematic term that is explicated below). Apart from the wish to associate six places with six gates, it is difficult to understand why the elision has met with acceptance because the separation of Shugalam and Sunrise as two distinct sacred loci is clearly established in another important passage that comes earlier in the text (discussed in detail in Chapter 41), where the Gudea Steles are itemised (A23–4):

> The stele which he set up facing the rising sun he named as 'The king, the roaring storm of Enlil, the lord without rival, Lord Ningirsu, has chosen Gudea with his holy heart'.
>
> The stele which he set up facing Shugalam he named as 'The king, at whose name the foreign countries tremble, Lord Ningirsu, has made Gudea's throne firm'.

The precise locations of the steles are examined in Chapter 41, but it is self-evident that two monuments are here referred to and that, like the other named steles, they were 'set up' in two distinct places: respectively, 'facing the rising sun' and 'facing Shugalam'.

With the separation established, and assuming that the two sacred loci are indeed gates in the temenos of the New Eninnu, a further difficulty can be addressed, which is that the Sunrise Gate (4) could not have faced due east because there were no east-facing walls that could have been pierced with entranceways. Having elided places 3 and 4, and supposing that Shugalam faced sunrise, Heimpel (1996, p. 19) goes on to state that the Shugalam Gate was on the 'east facade'— an argument that is reinforced graphically in a schematic diagram of the New Eninnu's ground plan (p. 21), where the orientation of the complex is simplified, such that the main façades face the cardinal points, and the NE wall in front of the Ur-Bau plaza at the SE end of the temenos faces east. There can be no suggestion that Heimpel takes this to be the way the complex was actually laid out, but this particular schematisation tends to obfuscate matters. In truth, as can be seen on Fig. 219, there were two gates in the temenos that faced sunrise: the one in the NE façade, in front of the Ur-Bau plaza at the SE end of the L-shaped complex, which directly faced sunrise at the summer solstice (A on the diagram), and the one in the SE façade, which directly faced sunrise at the winter solstice (C on the diagram).

The question of whether the Sunrise Gate (4) faced northeast or south-east is best approached by considering the meaning of the difficult word Shugalam. Towards the beginning of the narrative of the Cylinder Inscriptions, when Gudea is ritually preparing the ground for the construction of the New Eninnu, he sacrifices a 'fattened sheep' and a 'grain-fed kid' (and possibly one or two more such animals) at a spot 'Facing Shugalam, the fearful place, the place of making judgments, from where Ningirsu keeps an eye on all lands' (A8). The sacrificial altar was almost certainly in Ur-Bau's old Eninnu, as Heimpel argues (1996, p. 21), and the term Shugalam doubtless refers to a focal point inside the shrine to which offerings were brought, as attested by an administrative text from the time of Gudea (RTC 247), while a hymn to the Eninnu from Old Babylonian times, which describes Shugalam as the 'awful façade, gate of splendour' (Heimpel 1996, p. 26), confirms that one of the temenos gates was also originally known by that name. Another inscription indicates that Shugalam was a source of ecclesiastical revenue (RTC 288), doubtless from lands administered on behalf of the temple, and it is described in a passage that immediately precedes the account of the carving and installation of the Gudea Steles as being close to the sacred podium, which (as explained below) is here identified as the 'dais' of Girnun (A22):

He planted the pleasant poplars of his city so that they cast their shadow. He embedded its Sharur weapon beside Lagash like a big standard, placed it in its dreadful place, the Shugalam, and made it emanate fearsome radiance. On the dais of Girnun, on the place of making judgments, the provider of Lagash lifted his horns like a mighty bull.

Ningirsu's divine mace, Sharur, is said to have been set up like a 'standard' at the 'dreadful' place of Shugalam, 'beside' Lagash, where it emits its 'fearsome radiance'. Shugalam is also associated in this passage with the processional route of Girnun and a place of 'judgments', where Ningirsu symbolically brandishes his 'horns like a mighty bull'. With regard to these allusions, one interpretation of Shugalam is that it was a site where executions were carried out. The argument (Heimpel 1996, p. 21) draws on documents showing that, in Ur III times, oaths of allegiance to Girsu were administered at a place linked with the 'dagger' (gir$_2$.an.na) of Ningirsu, which could be further referenced in the etymology of Shugalam, a composite term that might connote an artful, or artfully fashioned hand (šu, meaning 'hand', and galam signalling a range of meanings focused on 'artful'). The idea brings together references to the binding religious and civic laws of Girsu–Lagash, and to Ningirsu himself as the enforcer of justice, whose divine hand was ever ready to strike down malefactors and transgressors of the sacred oath. Taking the passage just quoted (A22) to mean that the main site associated with the term Shugalam was a point outside the temenos, the argument supposes that Shugalam itself was beyond the confines of the Eninnu. This is difficult to sustain, however, in large part because the sacrifice that Gudea makes facing Shugalam inside the old Eninnu seems clearly to indicate a place that was a feature of Ur-Bau's old temple. Similarly, after the construction of the New Eninnu, the sacred locus of Shugalam was transferred to Gudea's new Ningirsu temple, as is affirmed by the administrative text noted above (RTC 247). When these various hints are correlated, Shugalam can be connected with a focal point for offerings in the Ningirsu temple at the heart of the New Eninnu that is directly linked with the former sacred spot inside Ur-Bau's old Eninnu (which was, of course, intact inside Gudea's complex) and with a gate in Gudea's temenos wall. When the points inside the New Eninnu and the old Eninnu are joined and connected with a gate in the wall of the complex, the resulting

line corresponds almost exactly with the one on Fig. 219 that extends from the heart of Gudea's New Eninnu to position A on the horizon on the NE side of Tell A. This line joins the cella inside Gudea's Ningirsu temple with the NW side of Ur-Bau's old Eninnu—the part of Ur-Bau's Ningirsu temple that (as in Gudea's temple and the earlier Ur-Nanshe Building and the Lower Construction) must also have housed the cella. Indeed, the line might be said to connect the three points that are said in the Cylinder Inscriptions to be closely associated with Shugalam with an almost irrefutable degree of geometrical accuracy. The NE gate in front of the Ur-Bau plaza at the SE end of the L-shaped complex can therefore be fairly confidently identified as the Shugalam Gate (as Heimpel also maintains, despite his problematic argumentation). That being the case, it was here that the Dragon and the Date palm monuments were displayed.

Consequently, it seems correct to assume (with all due caution) that the word Shugalam was a byname for the cella inside both the old Eninnu of Ur-Bau and Gudea's New Eninnu, and this can be linked with the second enigmatic term, Girnum. The etymology of Girnun connotes the idea of an 'exalted road'—hence the assumption that it was one way of referring to a particularly important processional route—but from the earliest times it was also fundamentally connected with the Temple of Ningirsu, where the Girnun processions terminated. As mentioned in Chapter 11, in the Fara period (Early Dynastic IIIa), the word appears in a temple hymn, where the shrine is named as the 'House of Girnun', a term that can be regarded as an ancestral synonym for the Ningirsu temple. Consequently, the 'dais' of Girnun was almost certainly a long-standing cognomen for the cult podium (the procession's objective at the end of the 'exalted road') inside the respective cellas of Gudea's New Eninnu and Ur-Bau's old Eninnu, or the House of Girnun, as the Lagash II shrines were formerly known. This is presumably corroborated by another passage in the Cylinder Inscriptions (also cited above) that relates how, after laying out the ground plan of the Eninnu, Gudea returns to Ur-Bau's old Ningirsu shrine in order to seek the approval of the god, who is again said to be stationed on the 'dais of Girnun' (A17–18): 'When the night fell, he went to the old temple to pray, so that the inclination of the one from the dais of Girnun would become favourable for Gudea'. More generally, the processional route could have approached Gudea's New Eninnu from the northeast of Tell A, entering the complex via the Shugalam Gate in the section of the long NE façade that fronted the Ur-Bau plaza. It is also worth recalling that the stone stairway uncovered by Cros between Tells A and B lay to the north-east of the SE end of the complex, directly in line with what can now be termed the Shugalam Gate, such that the stairway and the shrine might well have formed a key stage on the processional route. Furthermore, the placement of the gate and the presumed orientation of the 'exalted road' might imply that an area to the north-east of Tell A had special associations with the Ningirsu temple when it was referred to metonymically as Shugalam. There might perhaps have been a scaffold for executions to the north-east of Tell A (as argued by Heimpel), and it is not inconceivable that revenues from lands that lay in this direction were set aside as Shugalam offerings (recalling RTC 288). More immediately, and referring back to the etymology of Shugalam, however, the principal meaning of the god's 'mighty hand' was probably a reference to Ningirsu's overarching role as the originator and executor of justice in the city-state, as would also be confirmed by the description of the 'dais of Girnun'—the cult podium—as the 'place of making judgments', which in this context would connote the divine determinations of Ningirsu.

With the Shugalam Gate (3) sited in the short section of the NE façade in front of the Ur-Bau plaza at the SE end of the complex, the Sunrise Gate (4) can be securely located as the one in the SE façade that faced sunrise at the winter solstice (C on Fig. 219). This is where the 'standard of Utu, the Bison head' must have been placed, together with other monuments that were 'already there'. The standard of Utu seems clearly to refer to a pole or post that was ornamented with a sun motif, but what was its relationship with the Bison's head? Did the latter artefact form part of the sun standard or was it a separate monument that stood by it? The answer might well be that the image of the Bison's head relates to the animal's horns, which, in turn, connote the waning crescent moon that is observed at sunrise. The standard was perhaps, therefore, a single pole that was fitted with sun and moon motifs, and its location could have expressed a connection between the waning moon and the end of the solar year. Actual observations in this direction were conceivably not carried out at the Sunrise Gate itself, but in the nearby horned structure that might perhaps have functioned as a dedicated observatory (depending on the actual size and shape of the construction, which is not clear from the diagram), thereby separating the gate's rhetorical

symbolism from the uncertainties of empirical astronomy. This is speculative, however. Furthermore, if the idea of the waning moon can then be linked with the dying Bison, as one of the Slain Heroes killed by Ningirsu, it would imply the existence of a Ningirsu myth relating to the cyclical death of the moon–Bison, which is subsequently reborn, only to be slaughtered again. This would connect with Ningirsu in his role as a second sun god (a substitute for Utu) because the annual sequence of sunrises at the end of the lunar month results in the moon's repeated slow death.

These are hypothetical matters, but the emblematic Bison is mentioned again, in an analogous context, at the end of the list of sacred places associated with the Slain Heroes, when Bau's 'inner room' (7) is introduced, and Gudea is said to have installed the Magilum boat and the Bison there. It should be noted that, unlike in the entry for the Battle Gate (1), where the 'inner room' (probably a porch, as discussed below) is expressly described as being part of the gateway, Bau's 'inner room' is not said to be a component of a larger structure, but rather appears to be an entity in and of itself. As is almost certainly confirmed by the British Museum team's findings, Bau's personal shrine was probably situated at the NW end of the L-shaped complex, on the NW side of the main courtyard that lay between the NW sectors and the SE area that housed both Ningirsu's temple and the old Eninnu. In addition to Bau's 'inner room' (7), two more of the seven sacred places can be associated with the NW part of the New Eninnu: the Kasurra Gate (5) and the Tarsirsir (6). The Kasurra Gate, which was probably linked to the Kasurra quay on a watercourse situated to the NE or NW of Tell A (as discussed below), can be provisionally set aside, leaving the Tarsirsir and the 'inner room' of Bau—two loci that are closely linked with each other. The exact meaning of the Tarsirsir is uncertain (see also Chapter 33). On the one hand, the word connotes a divine agent, who was seemingly Bau's minister and in all likelihood her principal go-between, who carried prayers or messages from worshippers to Bau, as implied by the word 'angel', a translation of the Sumerian word Lamma, that is sometimes associated with her (Heimpel 1996, p. 22). On the other hand, the term Tarsirsir is also used in the formulation, the Tarsirsir house, which was a cognomen for Bau's shrine, for example on Statue H: 'The lady, beloved daughter of shining heaven, mother Bau, gave life to Gudea out of the Tarsirsir House'. The set of interrelationships is also brought together in an inscription on a statuette from the reign of Nammahni (RIME 3.1.1.12.6): 'When the protective spirit of Tarsirsir is about to enter the courtyard of Bau, this statuette here will turn to my lady there (whispering?) into her ear; let it say my prayer to her'. Incidentally, the idea that the Tarsirsir was a divine agent or 'spirit', in which guise she was previously invoked by Ur-Bau in an inscription on a bowl (RIME 3.1.1.6.8), was not new. In the particular context evoked by the Nammahni inscription, however, the composite byname, the Tarsirsir house, might reflect the fact that access to Bau was obtained, perhaps exclusively for the majority of petitioners, only indirectly through the agency of the Tarsirsir—and for the same reason the Tarsirsir can be reasonably securely identified as the name of one of the gates in the temenos of the New Eninnu, in particular an entrance that was close to Bau's temple at the NW end of the complex, as discussed above.

The repeated reference to Bau's shrine as her 'inner room', reinforced by the heuristic contrast between this most sacred internal locus and the Tarsirsir gateway (the province of Bau's divine messenger and gatekeeper), would suggest that the Magilum boat and the Bison were displayed not at an entrance in the temenos wall, but rather in, or very close to, Bau's temple inside the complex. Incidentally, as is discussed further in Chapter 41, this also sheds light on the placement of the Bau stele, which is named last in the roll-call of the Gudea Steles, and is also said to be positioned 'by the inner room (?) of Bau'. These are conjectural matters, but in contraposition to the Bison at the Sunrise Gate, the placing of a Bison motif in Bau's 'inner room' conceivably refers to the waxing crescent—the new moon that appears at the beginning of each month. It might be further conjectured that Bau was believed to be instrumental in the moon's resuscitation or rebirth, after its symbolic death and monthly period of absence, maybe as the archetypal divine mother (recalling her maternal relationship with Gudea), or as midwife or supplier of the breath of life, in which case the nights of lunar darkness could plausibly have been characterised as a short term of gestation that took place in her 'inner room'. The description of Bau as the 'beloved daughter of shining heaven' on Statue H confirms the established association between her and the night sky that is repeated elsewhere, including in the passage relating to the installation of the Bau stele, where her father, An, is mentioned. In this respect, it is also worth recalling the passage at the beginning of the Cylinder Inscriptions in which Ningirsu refers to the monthly festival of the new moon as his 'Festival of An' (A10). With these allusions in mind, the Magilum boat might connote another celestial body, a planet or possibly a cluster of stars, that can be associated with the rising of the new moon. Venus or Mars might be credible options, and the image of the boat could presumably have been a half-circle, or perhaps a disc, like a round coracle seen from the side or face on. Analogous to the sun and moon standard by the Sunrise Gate, the two motifs could feasibly have been placed together on a long pole—with a crescent above (indicating the Bison's horns and the new moon) and below that a circle (for the boat or planet) perhaps making most sense.

The exact position of the Tarsirsir Gate, either on the short NW façade or at the NW end of the NE façade, is considered further below, but it is worth dwelling for a moment on another important crescent motif that appears in the Cylinder Inscriptions, directly after the enumeration of the Gudea Steles (A24):

> He built his master's house exactly as he had been told to. The true shepherd Gudea made it grow so high as to fill the space between heaven and earth, had it wear a tiara shaped like the new moon, and had its fame spread as far as the heart of the highlands.

The passage, which confirms the tallness of the structure, also indicates that it was fitted with a horn-shaped 'tiara' or crown, specifically to represent the crescent of the waxing moon, and in the following section of the text the metaphor is extended to incorporate the New Eninnu as a whole (A24): 'Gudea made the house of Ningirsu stand to be marvelled at like the new moon in the skies'. The inferred placement of the moon emblem on top of the building can perhaps be tentatively linked with the lack of a W-facing observation post in the temenos wall—one that might logically have been situated directly in line with the W corner of the Ningirsu shrine inside the complex. The British Museum team discovered a stairway that led up to the roof of the Ningirsu temple itself, and this might tend to confirm that the new moon associated with the spring and autumn equinoxes, when the sun set due west of the complex, was observed from the roof of Ningirsu's shrine, presumably from a place above the cella, at the central point of the complex (indicated by the intersection of the four diameters on Fig. 219). Indeed, depending on the function of the addition to the NW façade of the temenos, near the W corner, it is conceivable that all the months in the year were inaugurated following an observation made from this point. Replacing the motif of the Bison in this pivotal position, the image of the tiara might conceivably have expressed the lasting triumph of the god over the changeable moon that repeatedly dies and revives. The equinoctial new moons of the first and seventh months in particular signalled the culminating events in the year, when two of the most important feasts took place, and the possibility that they were observed from the roof of the Ningirsu temple would further stress the god's ultimate sovereignty over the interchange between solar and lunar time frames—a meaning also made manifest in the metaphor of the crown. Nor, it should be stressed, would this preclude the idea that the beginning of every month might have been proclaimed from this vantage point. As with other symbolic meanings built into the temple, notably Ningirsu's association with the north star, the god guarantees the stability of a cosmos that is otherwise characterised by ceaseless change.

With this in mind, the elemental association between Ningirsu and the N corner of the temple might confirm that the first of the seven named places, the Battle Gate, should be identified as the one in the centre of the NE façade, though the evidence is circumstantial and other possibilities cannot be categorically ruled out. Nonetheless, the celestial axes that the New Eninnu instantiated came into being as secondary functions of the N–S line that, first and foremost, fixed the New Eninnu's position on the earth. That primary axis— the single constant in the celestial system as it is manifested in the temple's design—connected the heart of the complex with the N corner of the Ningirsu temple (most importantly, the N corner of the cella) and with the gate in the middle of the NE façade, where it ran approximately through the gateway's SE tower and cut through the entrance passage. The 'inner room' or porch of the Battle Gate is described as the place where Ningirsu's divine weapons are kept, and the gate itself is distinguished as the display location for images (presumably statues) of at least two of the Slain Heroes (referred to in the plural as 'warriors'): the Six-headed wild ram and (following an ellipsis) the name of a second creature of which only the word 'head' is preserved. According to its presumed location, the Battle Gate led directly into the New Eninnu's main courtyard, which was the venue for a range of important public ceremonies (as discussed further in Chapter 41), and the gate and the courtyard are both named first in the inventories of sacred places associated with the Slain Heroes and the Gudea Steles,

respectively. Their equal prominence in the two lists combines with their assumed contiguity (each leading into the other) to confirm, albeit with an inescapable degree of uncertainty, that the Battle Gate in the middle of the NE façade gave access to the main courtyard. The name of the Battle Gate, and the fact that Ningirsu's weapons were displayed there, plausibly pays homage to Ningirsu's primary characterisation as the warrior god (considered further below), in which capacity he subjugated the forces of primordial chaos and brought order to the cosmos. It may not be correct to regard any of the temenos gates as being the main entrance to the complex, since all of them probably served distinct functions, but there is little doubt that the long NE wall, with its three entrances and complicated stepped arrangement, was the principal façade. This was the front of the building, and the central gate—Ningirsu's front door, as it were—gave access to the largest public space inside the complex.

That being the case, it can cautiously be assumed that the third gate in the NE façade—the one at its NW end— can be identified as the Kasurra, where the image of the 'Lion, the terror of the gods', was installed. Another Gudea inscription (RIME 3.1.1.7.51) commemorates the restoration of a second Kasurra entranceway, one in the city wall, presumably close to the quay: the 'Kasurra city-gate (with its) marvellous façade, (through which) sumptuous goods are transported'. Additionally, Statue D mentions that Gudea 'moored' Ningirsu's newly constructed boat at the 'Lapis Lazuli Quay' of Kasurra. The Cylinder Inscriptions provide further details, confirming that the landing stage of Kasurra was the reception point for materials that were transported by river from abroad (A15). The timber, for example, which was driven downstream 'like a giant serpent floating on the water', before being brought to shore at the 'main quay' of Kasurra, includes: 'logs of cedar wood from the cedar hills, logs of cypress wood from the cypress hills, logs of zabalum wood from the zabalum hills, tall spruce trees, plane trees, and eranum trees'. The ability of Gudea to bring these materials from beyond the borders of Lagash ultimately depends upon Ningirsu's mastery of other nations, such that 'sumptuous goods' can be safely transported from afar. In a later part of the narrative (B7) the god's triumph over troublesome or 'rebellious' foreign countries is directly associated with the weapons that are kept at the Battle Gate, and in the list of Gudea Steles the name of the Shugalam stele refers to Ningirsu as: 'The king, at whose name the foreign countries tremble'. The installation at the Kasurra Gate of the 'Lion, the terror of the gods', might therefore also tentatively be associated with Ningirsu's power over foreign countries, guaranteeing his hard-won ascendancy over the pantheon of gods that were principally worshipped in other city-states (and no doubt further afield), and explaining why Gudea was given ready access to the necessary international trade routes in order to obtain the resources he needed to build the New Eninnu.

The waterway that was served by the Kasurra quay has generally been located on a canal to the north-east of Tell A, but more recent information uncovered by the British Museum team shows that canals also existed to the northwest. Accordingly, the position of the gate cannot be stated categorically, but if it was placed at the NW end of the NE façade, it would have been a counterpart to the Shugalam Gate at the SW end of the same wall, and both can be closely linked to the central Battle Gate, which was arguably Ningirsu's arsenal and war machine (so to speak), and the principal emblem of the god's indomitable martial prowess. Finally, on a more practical level, if the Kasurra Gate was in reality the principal entry point for any of the building materials and other supplies that were unloaded at the quay before being transported to the New Eninnu, it might have been more convenient to bring them into the complex through an entrance that was closer to the main courtyard and therefore to the centre of the structure than the gate in the NW façade. The apparent absence of service entrances on the plan of the complex might lend further credence to the idea that, even after the completion of the New Eninnu, this was an access point for all kinds of equipment, materials and provisions. In this regard, it should not be forgotten that the internal route from the NW façade to the main courtyard would probably have taken visitors through or past the Bau area of the complex, which was seemingly considered to be a particularly private enclave, as confirmed by the repeated characterisation of Bau's temple as her 'inner room' and the fact that her devotees and supplicants communicated with her at one remove, via the ministering agent, Tarsirsir.

According to this rationale, the Tarsirsir Gate—again with all due circumspection—might be identified as the gate in the NW façade, close to the Temple of Bau at the NW end of the complex. Though these arguments seem inherently persuasive, it has to be said that they cannot finally be verified, and it is possible to make a case for the Tarsirsir Gate,

with its inextricable Bau connections, being the third one in the main NE façade (at its NW end), in which case the Kasurra would be reciprocally relocated to the NW façade, facing the canals to the north-west of Tell A that are mentioned above. By the same token, it might be argued that the Kasurra Gate—associated principally with the transport of goods by water and their presumed delivery to the sacred complex—was probably not placed in the centre of the NE façade that led directly into the main ceremonial courtyard, though this is not finally provable. Similarly, the close connection between the Tarsirsir and Bau's 'inner room' would perhaps confirm that the former was not linked with this pivotal position that would appear to have had a communal function.

Finally, the gate in the city façade (2), the site of the Seven-headed serpent, was in all likelihood the one in the long SW façade. This was the direction in which the civic area of Girsu was situated, with its residential quarters and urban districts, and it is usually linked with the Euruga stele, the fifth of the Gudea Steles (see Heimpel 1996, p. 21). One meaning of Euruga might confirm the link with the city of Girsu, but it has also been argued that it was connected with an outlying shrine to Ningirsu and Bau that lay in the direction of Uruk (Sallaberger 1993, p. 297). This might be less inherently likely, and it should be noted that the translation of URU_{18} (the central element of E.uru.ga) is not straightforward. The word URU_{18} connotes a concept of power or mightiness that is further associated with the image of a flood. Sallaberger argues that the rural shrine was located in the steppe between Girsu and Uruk, in which case the idea of a mighty flood might betoken the uncontrolled energy of the wilderness. Much more evident, however, is the possible association between the SW gate and sunset at the winter solstice—the longest night of the year, when the world is singularly engulfed in darkness. The symbolism of the longest night as a turning point from which the earth cyclically emerges, eventually to blossom into new life, might link the position of the gate with the metaphor of a flood, either the primordial flood or the seasonal flooding of the alluvial plain. On the basis of these arguments the numbered gates are shown on Fig. 219, together with the 'inner room' of Bau.

As a postscript to the preceding discussion, a further word should be added about another contextual framework that might help to clarify the meaning of some of the Slain Heroes. The narratives of Ningirsu's battles with those fearsome foes were part of his mythology, which was presumably retold on the Lost Cylinder, but the stories must have been more than just action-packed adventures. On the contrary, since Ningirsu was the divine agent who gave form to the cosmos (an epic undertaking that was eventually developed in great detail with respect to his Babylonian avatar, Marduk), his deeds had cosmological significance as ways of explaining the structure of the world. This is true of the myth of his taming of the Thunderbird, which, among other things, illuminated the origins of humankind's ability to harness the waters of the region's mighty rivers, the Tigris and the Euphrates (also noted in Chapter 1 above). With that in mind, the missing components in the foregoing interpretation of the way the New Eninnu was situated with respect to the seasonally changing skyscape are the constellations linked with the annual passage of the sun—later known as the zodiac constellations. Any consideration of the problem (also briefly touched upon in Chapter 12) faces several impediments: data on the named constellations in third-millennium BCE Sumer is scarce (see Rogers 1998); their precise identities and astral make ups are culturally determined and therefore changeable at different periods and places; and there is currently no way of knowing how many constellations were recognised in the third millennium BCE because the equal division of the sky into twelve parts associated with twelve signs only came into being in Babylonian times. Nonetheless, it seems a fair surmise that at least some of the Slain Heroes, notably the Seven-headed serpent (most clearly relating to the Greek Hydra and therefore to the sign of Cancer) and the Lion ('the terror of the gods'), might be Sumerian precursors of constellations whose identities were established by Marduk in the Babylonian creation myth and subsequently associated with the labours of Ningirsu's Greek descendant, Heracles (see Rochberg 2007; and Van Dijk 1983, vol. 1, pp. 17–18; connections between Ningirsu and Heracles are detailed in Part 4 below). Currently fraught with uncertainty, it is a subject that requires further study, but the detection of links between some of the Slain Heroes and constellations that were later widely recognised would shed more light on the positioning of the New Eninnu with respect to the seasonal time frame.

Approaching the Cult Podium: The Gates and the Bent-Axis Approaches

An unanswered question remains about the ordering of the gates in the Cylinder Inscriptions. Such lists seem generally to have had a special significance in Sumerian thinking, though the ordering principles were doubtless highly complex, as is indicated by the chiastic relationship between the list of the gates and the enumeration of the Gudea Steles. With all due caution, however, a relatively clear rationale might inform the sequence in which the City, Shugalam and Sunset Gates are introduced in the text. They apparently define the key points in the solar year, indicating a repeating cycle that might read as follows (with the added numbering and the two equinoxes included):

2. The City Gate: sunset at the winter solstice.

The spring equinox: Sumerian new year.

3. The Shugalam Gate: sunrise at the summer solstice.

The autumn equinox: the Sumerian seventh month.

4. The Sunrise Gate: sunrise at the winter solstice.

A complete solar year would thus be neatly delineated, and this might connect with the more mobile lunar months, such that the entire sequence could then be correlated with the important festivals that were held at these key junctures. At these turning points in the year, it might be supposed, the cult podium was approached via the respective gates with which they were linked. One evident problem is that, after the Sunrise Gate in the list just given, the cycle would continue with sunset at the winter solstice (associated with the City Gate), meaning that the end of one solar year and the beginning of the next would be marked by two winter solstice events (sunrise and sunset) that both took place on the same day, namely 21 or 22 December. One credible solution is to envisage a relatively long winter festival that started and finished at the beginning and end of a midwinter lunar month, so that the solstices events were incorporated into a protracted ceremonial interval that created a notional separation between the end of one solar year and the beginning of the next. (A similar principle is exemplified in some modern religious calendars, notably the Christian one, in which the entire Christmas and New Year period extends from the beginning of Advent in early December to Epiphany on 6 January.) The precise start and end dates of the festive period might have been flexible, depending on the way in which the lunar months overlapped with the solstices, and it is conceivable that the intercalary leap month might also have played a role in the way the calendar was worked out in practice, though this is far from certain. More generally, it might be presumed that the Battle Gate was an important focus at other times, while the Tarsirsir Gate (especially associated with Bau) and the Kasurra Gate presumably had particular cultic significances of their own. The complications are dizzying, and the fact that very little clearly extrapolated data exists about the cultic calendar in Gudea's reign makes it extremely difficult to propose a solution, though it seems reasonable to assume that a threefold sequencing principle was at work, probably based on the interactions between the solar and lunar years, together with other fixed points in the calendar.

The most secluded area of the whole complex was the Ningirsu temple, where the cult podium was built into the SW wall, and a rectangular offering table stood in the centre of the room. Like the room, the table was oriented north-east–south-west, and its proportions mirrored that of the space. Similarly, the statue looked to the north-east, along the same SW–NE axis, towards the old Eninnu of Ur-Bau and the inferred Shugalam Gate in the NE façade. The relative proportions of the table and the room appear to have reflected the harmonious distribution of space within the complex as a whole, while the innermost SW–NE axis that was stressed by the location of the cult statue and the offering table inside the cella was in counterpoint to the major axis of the whole complex, which ran from the north-west (the area of the precinct that was especially sacred to Bau) to the south-east, where the Ningirsu temple was positioned. This adds another noteworthy chiasmus to others that have been mentioned, for example in association with the listing of the gates and Gudea Steles.

Overall, the complex seems to have had a maze-like character that was rationally derived from the series of geometric and temporal frameworks that were expressed in its layout and orientation. The sense of labyrinthine intricacy was probably also embedded in the bent-axis approaches that led to the cult podium, concluding with the ultimate

turns that were made by priests or high-status worshippers as they entered the antecella from the NE walkway, before turning right into the cella and finally left to face the podium itself. The number of ninety-degree turns required to progress through the complex in order to face the cult podium when entering from certain gates can be precisely calculated. Entering from the City Gate, for example, the visitor would make a total of six turns: first turning left (or right to go anticlockwise—the end result is the same) to follow a clockwise path around the internal ambulatory to the W corner, before turning right and right again (at the N corner), then making another right turn into the antecella, turning right again to enter the cella and finally turning left to face the cult statue. Exactly six turns would also have taken the visitor from the Shugalam Gate, around Ur-Bau's old Eninnu and then into the antecella and cella (as above), and as with the entry from the City Gate, the effect would have been the same whether the visitor turned left or right (clockwise or anticlockwise) when passing through the gate.

Conversely, the Sunrise Gate that was probably located in the short SE façade presents a number of possibilities, while further complications arise because of the uncertain relationship between the gate and the SE façade of the Ningirsu temple, which formed one of the walls of the internal ambulatory. It seems reasonably likely that the gate opened directly into the Ur-Bau plaza, in which case only three ninety-degree turns were needed for visitors to proceed to the cella and the cult podium: passing through the gate, they would have walked straight ahead (with the Ur-Bau plaza on their right) before turning left into the antecella, right into the cella and finally left to face the cult statue. If, however, the gate opened onto the SE wall of the internal walkway, then visitors who turned right would have needed five ninety-degree turns to face the cult statue. In this case, proceeding anticlockwise, they would have turned right and then navigated around the E corner of the internal ambulatory before approaching the antecella and the cella. The uncertainty about the exact position of the gate would not affect the number of turns needed by visitors who passed through the gate and then turned left. In this clockwise direction, a total of seven turns would be required in order to circle around the temple and then turn right into the antecella before turning right again and finally left to face the cult statue in the cella.

It cannot be known what obstacles might have been negotiated by visitors who entered from the Battle Gate, presumed to be in the middle of the NE façade, or by the two gates (Tarsirsir and Kasurra) at the NW end of the complex, but all of these approaches eventually led through the main courtyard to the King's Gate (No. 8 on Fig. 219; see Chapter 41) in the internal SW–NE wall (parallel to the axis of the cella) that separated the Ningirsu temple from the rest of the New Eninnu. The number of turns needed to proceed from the King's Gate to the cult podium would have been either five or seven, depending on whether visitors turned right or left, when, having passed through the entranceway, they accessed the internal ambulatory that ran around the Ningirsu temple. If they turned left towards the N corner of the ambulatory then only five turns would have been required, but if they turned right towards the ambulatory's W corner then they would have had to turn seven times. This introduces a possible symmetry (or even another chiastic relationship) with the clockwise approach from the Sunrise Gate, which also required seven ninety-degree turns. It is not clear whether the King's Gate was diametrically opposite the Sunrise Gate (on line BC on Fig. 219), and the likelihood is seemingly rather low, but the two approaches were potentially linked by the equal number of turns required to reach the cult podium from either of them, depending on the respective directions of approach. The Shugalam and City Gates, which were diametrically opposite each other, seem to have been expressly linked in this way. The resulting correspondences are as follows:

City Gate and Shugalam Gate: $6 \times 90°$ turns.

Sunrise Gate: $3 \times 90°$ turns (if the gate gave access directly to the Ur-Bau plaza); $5 \times 90°$ turns (if the gate led into the internal ambulatory and visitors turned right); $7 \times 90°$ turns (if visitors passed through the gate and then turned left to take a clockwise route around the internal walkway).

King's Gate (providing access via the main courtyard from the Battle, Tarsirsir and Kasurra Gates): $5 \times 90°$ turns (if visitors entered the internal ambulatory and turned left, or clockwise); $7 \times 90°$ turns (for the anticlockwise path around the walkway).

The sense of seclusion that is stressed by the labyrinthine approaches to the Ningirsu temple raises a more general point about the layout and design of the New Eninnu that is worth briefly addressing. In common with other ancient Sumerian temples, and as is expressed in the reconstructions (Figs. 171, 172 and 185), the façades of the Ningirsu temple were almost certainly lavishly decorated, and the innermost holy rooms were surely accessed via a ceremonial gateway. Surprisingly, however, the resulting splendour was very much concealed inside the enclosing temenos walls and shielded by the internal SW–NE partition that contained the King's Gate. Furthermore, the temple's main entrance in the NE façade was screened by the old Eninnu of Ur-Bau, which stood in the Ur-Bau plaza, directly in front of Gudea's new structure. Since the open-air walkways that surrounded Gudea's Ningirsu temple had an average width of just 1.6 m on the building's SE, SW and NW sides, it cannot have been possible to step back and see the walls in their entirety. On the NE side, where it extended into the Ur-Bau plaza, the ambulatory was perhaps a little wider, but it should also be recalled that the old Eninnu of Ur-Bau was raised on a platform (Fig. 171), so the space in front of the entrance to Gudea's successor temple was still restricted. Therefore, irrespective of the route visitors used to approach the shrine, they could never enjoy the kind of panoramic view of it that is shown in the cutaway reconstructions because its elaborate façades were very closely surrounded by the thick, high temenos walls, while its main entrance was hidden behind the old Eninnu. The majestic inner construction, which was built at enormous expense and with the most extreme attention to detail (all minutely described in the Cylinder Inscriptions), was consequently not intended for display per se. On the contrary, the complex seems to have been designed in a way that consciously avoided ostentation or showiness.

The aesthetic decision to enclose the Ningirsu and Bau temples in a fortress-like temenos might, of course, have been influenced by the historical memory of the invasions and occupations of Girsu that happened during and after the reign of Urukagina. Nonetheless, the way in which the impressive buildings with their costly decorations and fittings were embedded in the core of a formidable set of enclosing walls and structures recalls the ethos that inspired the Lower Construction on Tell K, where the holiest spaces were literally buried in the ground. The focus in both cases appears to have been on the sacred power of the structures, rather than on their ability to impress. The Ur-Nanshe Building, which was elevated on a podium above the surrounding landscape, appears at first glance to contradict that pattern, but a more fundamental continuity is perhaps evidenced in the ground plans of the three temples. In all three the cella was not only the smallest room, it was noticeably small. Room U in the Lower Construction measured 4.5 m × 1.4 m (see Chapter 5), and the podium for the cult statue must have occupied much of the cella's 1.4 m depth, so the space in front of the statue was unquestionably remarkably confined; room B in the Ur-Nanshe Building had maximum dimensions of 4.6 m × 2.3 m (see Chapters 5 and 16), and again the cult podium, which probably measured about 1.6 m (w) × 1 m (deep), must have taken up most of the space. The cella in Gudea's Ningirsu temple was certainly more spacious than its Early Dynastic counterparts, measuring 11.5 m × 7.1 m (see Chapter 34), but the headline dimensions are deceptive. First, the doorway from the antecella, which gave access at the NE end of the cella, was 1.15 m wide, but it was at right angles to the podium, so that visitors had to turn left to face the statue,

effectively transforming the area inside the entrance into a transitional space that was presumably at least as wide as the doorway; secondly, the cult podium extended into the room for 2.09 m (from the north-east to the south-west). These two factors must have reduced the length of the room in which worshippers could actually pray to about 8.26 m (calculated by subtracting 1.15 m and 2.09 m from 11.5 m), but the centre of the room was also occupied by an offering table, albeit of uncertain dimensions. Accordingly, secreted at the almost inaccessible core of the vast New Eninnu, which had overall maximum dimensions of perhaps 100 m (NW–SE) × about 50 m (NE–SW at the SE end), the holiest locus was no more than a few square metres. The historical and cultural reasons why the most important rooms in the temples were so small, and why display for its own sake was not considered especially desirable, are too complex to discuss here, but it appears that the immense power of the deity was believed to be condensed into a single point that governed everything.

CHAPTER 41

The Steles of Gudea

THE GUDEA STELES, WHICH WERE CREATED TO COM-memorate Gudea's sacred building activities, were commissioned during the construction of the New Eninnu to be exhibited in and around the epoch-making complex. The surviving fragments indicate that they were all carved in bas-relief in a homogeneous style on light-coloured limestone, and that they portrayed or narrated a diverse series of subjects relating to the planning and building of the New Eninnu. Using a common set of sculptural conventions, they divided their contents into four or five registers, and some if not all of them featured rather narrow, shallow relief frames around their perimeters. The bottommost sections of at least two were probably unworked and unpolished (Suter 2000, p. 164), but whether that was the case for all of them is unknown. Those with unfinished base zones were seemingly set into slots, perhaps in the Eninnu's paved floors or in specially built brickwork display platforms, depending on their locations. Alternatively, if their entire surfaces were carved or polished all the way down to their bases, they might have been erected on pedestals or placed on the ground as self-standing objects. Only some of the preserved fragments are inscribed, but it is highly likely that they all included textual elements.

The scholarly debates have usually assumed that Gudea commissioned seven steles for the New Eninnu, even though a total of only six are definitively listed and named in the text on Cylinder A (A23–4), and despite the fact that the six named steles can all tentatively be assigned to a range of locations associated with the complex on the basis of various references in the inscriptions (detailed below). The idea that

there were seven originates with Heuzey (Cros 1910, p. 297), who based his opinion on Thureau-Dangin's (1905, p. 173) translation of another passage in the text of Cylinder A. The lines in question (A29) have recently been rather neutrally rendered as 'seven stones surrounding the house are there to take counsel with its owner', but Thureau-Dangin took the key word 'stones' (na in Sumerian) unequivocally to mean 'steles', thereby wittingly or otherwise adding an unlisted seventh stele to the six named ones. The further consequence would be that the text of Cylinder A must contain an error or an omission, but it is perplexing to imagine why the meticulously executed narrative would have permitted such an anomaly to stand, and why a seventh stele was not itemised if one was made. Yet another highly significant passage (A25), which is referred to again below, enumerates seven places in and around the temple where other sculptures and monuments intimately associated with Ningirsu were displayed. They include: an 'inner room' (the translation is uncertain) related to the Battle Gate; a place 'facing the city'; the Shugalam Gate or façade; the place (again almost certainly a gate) 'facing the sunrise'; the 'lookout post' at the Kasurra Gate; the Tarsirsir; and Bau's 'inner room'. As detailed in Chapter 40, among the statues and emblems displayed there were, respectively: the Six-headed wild ram; the Seven-headed serpent; the Dragon and the Date palm; the standard of Utu and the Bison head (conceivably two motifs on a single standard), and some other unnamed artefacts; the Lion; the Fish-man and the Copper; and finally the Magilum boat and the Bison. Named steles were also erected in five of these places, and the sixth was closely associated

608

with another of them, as is discussed below, but the overlap between the six steles and the seven sacred places where steles and other sculptures were displayed is incomplete. Bearing all of this in mind, it is surely conceivable that the 'seven stones' introduced in the passage mentioned above (A29) might signal carvings or sculptures, such as some of the ones enumerated in the list of seven sacred places (A25–6), that were more closely connected to Ningirsu's personal mythology than the steles. With a particular stress on Gudea himself, the steles narrated the history of the New Eninnu, and they were not always dedicated exclusively to Ningirsu, but rather honoured several deities who played roles in the Eninnu's conception and construction, and one was expressly devoted to Bau (A24). Additionally, the idea that the seven 'stones' could 'take counsel' with Ningirsu (the 'owner' of the Eninnu) might tend to imply figurative representations, or statues that were ritually animated, possibly like the fabulous creatures, together with the Fish-Man (but perhaps not the Copper, which might signify a copper vessel), that were installed at seven holy places in and around the complex, or indeed like the statues of Gudea (closely discussed in Chapter 37), which were animated and believed to be capable of communicating with Ningirsu and receiving his instructions and advice (taking 'counsel' from him).

Given these uncertainties, it is hard to see any obvious reason why an unnamed seventh stele must automatically be presumed to have existed, as it commonly has been (see, for example, Suter 2000, pp. 164 and 275). That does not mean, of course, that no other steles existed apart from the six named Gudea Steles because a distinction must also be drawn between the clearly listed ones that were very closely connected with the original design and shape of the New Eninnu itself, and monuments that could well have been erected in nearby locations, but which might have been regarded as adjuncts to the complex or even been commissioned at later dates. There can surely be little doubt that the six named steles that were associated with Gudea's design as it is described in the Cylinder Inscriptions do not represent an exhaustive inventory of all the steles that existed in the Urukug, or even all of the ones that were installed in the immediate vicinity of Tell A, but that does not justify the assumption that there is a mistake or even an anomaly in the text on Cylinder A.

It is difficult to give an exact figure for the preserved number of Gudea Stele fragments because their classifications and ascriptions are often problematic, but as many as sixty-four catalogued pieces are known. Six of them feature horizontal relief bands, indicating that the carved scenes were ordered into registers, together with figures that are identified as Gudea in their accompanying captions. Twenty-five further fragments that include portions of a dividing horizontal band or a sculpted perimetric frame can be said with some confidence to have derived from the Gudea Steles on account of their iconography and style. In terms of subject matter and the dimensions of the figures, the remaining thirty-three fragments show strong stylistic connections with the documented pieces of the Gudea Steles, but they cannot be attributed to them with complete certainty, and some of them might alternatively have been parts of plaques or other sculpted objects. Five fragments in the latter group bear inscriptions that expressly name Gudea. In addition, several unpublished fragments are known to exist, and the Museum of the Ancient Orient in Istanbul has charge of some boxes containing around 200 sherds that have not been fully documented (Suter 2000, p. 161). The poor condition of these sherds (many of which are tiny) makes it generally unlikely that they could be combined with any of the larger confirmed fragments of the Gudea Steles or meaningfully integrated into a reconstruction, and any number of them could have derived from other monuments or artefacts.

The provenances of the often poorly documented pieces that were unearthed by the French pioneers are included in a comprehensive catalogue compiled by Suter (2000, pp. 337–91). In total, Sarzec retrieved thirteen stele fragments (twelve prior to 1881 and one in 1893) as well as six further pieces of relief that probably came from door plaques. Unfortunately, the find locations of only two of the pieces of stele relief (AO52, here called the 'music stele', and AO63) were noted, and both came from Hellenistic contexts (see Sarzec and Heuzey 1912, pp. 37 and 48). The rest were probably also found associated with the Hellenistic Palace in the upper layers of Tell A, or possibly picked up as surficial remains in the area later excavated by Cros between Tells A and B (as suggested by Heuzey in Cros 1910, pp. 283 and 285).

Heuzey mentions that more than a hundred fragments were collected in this locality by Cros in 1905 and 1909 (see Cros 1910, p. 283), but since they were not well recorded, it is not clear how many were subsequently joined with other pieces, while some of the sherds in this group might well have been absorbed into the unpublished material in Istanbul (see Suter 2000, p. 167). Situated at the base of Tell A on the

NE side of the mound, the area between Tells A and B was the site of the shrine fitted with three external pedestals, and perhaps more display platforms inside, that was almost certainly built to house and exhibit a number of sacred objects, perhaps including a stele, though probably not one of the six that are named in the text on Cylinder A, as is explained below. On the SW side of the shrine was the stone stairway that led up to the higher terraces of Tell A, and between the building and the stairs was a smaller self-standing pedestal that seems to have supported an artefact shaped like a pole or a column. Significantly, the supposed column base (B on Cros's Plan H) showed the remains of a circular cavity (containing traces of bitumen and with a diameter of about 0.5 m or 0.6 m) in which the bottom section of the associated column or post (or some other monument) was probably secured, and a comparable rectangular slot could well have been built into the upper brickwork of the central pedestal (C on Cros's Plan H), which was the only one of the three (measuring approximately 3 m × 1.85 m) that was big enough to support a stele (Suter 2000, p. 164). The situation is complicated by the discovery in this area of fragments belonging to more than one stele. The assumption must be, however, that at some point in time after the New Eninnu was decommissioned, the patch of ground became a repository for the broken sculptures (Suter 2000, p. 164). Conversely, the existence of the various display platforms, together with pieces of other carved objects that were found nearby (including mace heads), would confirm that the structural ensemble was originally designed to bring together a range of commemorative artefacts. According to Heuzey (Cros 1910, p. 283), all the stele fragments found by Cros between Tells A and B exhibited stylistic similarities, and at least ten were inscribed with Gudea's name. In addition, Cros found one piece of a stele (AO4584) on Tell H (the Mound of the Necropolis).

Genouillac (1936, p. 34) discovered a relief fragment that he attributed to a 'large stele', together with a door plaque, in the preparatory fill of a wall inside the Hellenistic Palace. The supposed piece of the stele (AO12764) features a presentation scene in which the missing figure of Gudea is introduced to the goddess Bau by Ningishzida. Though it contains an inscription in Gudea's name dedicating the carving to Bau, the relief sherd almost certainly came not from a stele but from a door plaque, as is indicated by both the unparalleled thickness of the dividing band and the presence of a carefully made perforation, comparable with the hole found in

an associated sherd that was confidently identified as part of a door plaque (AO12763; Fig. 109). Also important is the fact that the mostly lost main scene on AO12764 (the presentation of Gudea to Bau) is not contained in the curving uppermost register of the carving, as is seemingly invariably the case for the principal scenes on the Gudea Steles, but in the one below it, leaving the top segment of the carving unusually blank, and this would also tend to confirm that the piece did not come from a stele.

Three more possible stele fragments are listed by Genouillac (1936, p. 37). No information whatsoever is given about TG4081, not even its size, so it must effectively be discounted. The other two, which were extremely worn and also rather poorly recorded (such that even their find locations were not noted), can only be interpreted very tentatively. Fragment AO13028 seems to show a kneeling figure with outstretched arms who is wearing a cap on his head. Presumably belonging to a male, the muscled torso might compare with the bodies of the musicians and workers depicted on the Gudea Steles, while the general positioning of the lower body conceivably recalls that of the standing figure with bent knees shown in fragment VA2896 (also discussed below). The long pleated skirt worn by the figure in VA2896 is characteristic of the garments worn by musicians and people carrying poles of various kinds (for instance in VA2902–4) rather than those worn by workers, who tend to be shown with short skirts. Though the dress worn by the person depicted on AO13028 is unclear, it nonetheless seems unlikely that the scene represents someone involved in, for example, laying bricks or installing foundation deposits. The positions of the outstretched arms and the feet conceivably suggest a fighter—a god or a wrestler, perhaps—or alternatively a boatman seated in a barge or raft, possibly transporting building materials along a watercourse. It can therefore be cautiously assumed that AO13028 did indeed derive from one of the Gudea Steles. A second fragment (AO11872) is described by Genouillac (1936, p. 37) as a relief carving of a crouching lion that appears as a decorative motif on an image of a divine throne. No photo of the piece is recorded, but AO28543, which is listed as having been found by Sarzec, and is of a very similar size (18.7 cm × 15.2 × 4.5 cm (t), as opposed to 19.2 cm × 14.9 cm for the Genouillac sherd), might provide a comparison. Despite its eroded state, the Sarzec piece shows a horned animal (not a lion) on the side of a throne, while the partly preserved flounced robe of a seated deity can still be made out. Accordingly, it is not impossible that AO11872 and AO28543 both derived from the same Gudea Stele. Lastly, in 1933 Parrot (1948, p. 184) excavated inscribed fragment AO16649 on Tell Y, between Tell A and the Eastern Tell (as Parrot labels it), in an archaeological context associated with a residential district dating to Ur III or Isin-Larsa times. The piece, which includes a horizontal band separating two registers, shows (in the upper register) the feet of three right-facing workers (including the short skirt or banded loincloth of the middle one of the three), with some cuneiform characters in thinly incised frames occupying the otherwise blank spaces between them (the text between the middle figure and the person on the right is better preserved than the one on the left). The lower register shows the remains of a shaven head (again facing right), which Parrot compares with the heads of the standard bearers depicted on some of the fragments of the Gudea Steles found by Cros.

Apart from the pieces that were directly accessioned into museum collections after being excavated by the French pioneers, some additional fragments of the steles (undoubtedly mostly looted) filtered through to the art market, especially in the early part of the twentieth century, between 1901 and 1926 (see Parrot 1948, pp. 184–6; and Suter 2000, p. 162). About twenty such sherds (some joined together to make composite representations) were acquired by museums, and fifteen of those fragments are inscribed. Eleven of the preserved inscriptions are labels that identify Gudea as ruler (ensí) of Lagash, and almost all of them are placed on Gudea's robe, though interestingly the label on a related fragment in Baghdad (IM14178), which did not come from a Gudea Stele, is placed next to Gudea's head. One caption (EŞEM5842) refers to a 'raft of cedar', the image of which is partly preserved. Three commemorative inscriptions apparently celebrate the construction of the New Eninnu, together with the fashioning and dedication of a stele. One (on fragment AO26634), which mentions the making of bricks and the purification of foundations, recalls the texts on the Gudea statues, in particular Statue C. It is placed in the upper section of a register, below a higher register that contains some preserved feet. The second commemorative inscription, which refers to a ruler (EŞEM5843, EŞEM5851 and EŞEM5989), is again placed in the upper part of a register, with a higher register above it, though very little remains of the text. The third (AO16649), which is in two framed texts between three male figures wearing short skirts or loincloths (as described above), speaks of someone praying to Gatumdug.

The passage that describes the Gudea Steles in the text on Cylinder A (A23–4), which, as argued above, should be taken at face value in terms of the number of commissioned monuments, is of great interest for a host of reasons. It records that six steles were installed on six successive days, and that the entire induction process was completed 'by the seventh day', when Gudea 'had set them all up around the house'. In terms of the construction sequence given in the text, the induction of the steles comes directly after the extremely important passage (A21–2) that describes the installation of the foundation deposits and the inscribed clay nails (discussed in detail in Chapters 43 and 44), and following the planting of shade-giving poplars and the erection of Ningirsu's Sharur weapon (or a standard representing it) in a place associated with Shugalam (discussed in Chapter 40). The sourcing of the raw stone is then said to have taken one year, after which the sculptors took another year to complete the carvings. It does not say at this point in the inscriptions when those events took place, but the acquisition and transport of the slabs (under the auspices of Ningirsu), together with other raw materials, is previously said to have occurred in the preconstruction phase of the complex, prior to the marking out of the foundations (A16). Having referred back to those earlier stages in the process, the narrative states that the carvings were fitted in six days (as just mentioned), after the completion of the Eninnu, and that the stone 'trimmings' or leftovers were used to make basins and stairs for the complex. Finally, the ceremonial names and placements of the six steles are carefully itemised (A23–4). As in the discussion of the sacred places associated with the Slain Heroes in Chapter 40, the steles are here numbered for ease of reference:

1. The stele which he set up in the great courtyard he named as 'The king who . . . the courtyard, Lord Ningirsu, has recognised Gudea from the Girnun'.
2. The stele which he set up at the Kasurra Gate he named as 'The king, Enlil's flood storm, who has no opponent, Lord Ningirsu, has looked with favour upon Gudea'.
3. The stele which he set up facing the rising sun he named as 'The king, the roaring storm of Enlil, the lord without rival, Lord Ningirsu, has chosen Gudea with his holy heart'.

4. The stele which he set up facing Shugalam he named as 'The king, at whose name the foreign countries tremble, Lord Ningirsu, has made Gudea's throne firm'.
5. The stele which he set up facing Euruga he named as 'Lord Ningirsu has decided a good fate for Gudea'.
6. The stele which he set up by the inner room (?) of Bau he named as 'The eyes of An know the Eninnu, and Bau is the life source of Gudea'.

The listing of the steles adopts a repeating formula, stating the fact that each carving is erected by Gudea in a particular place, and recording their respective ceremonial names. The performative epithets confirm that Ningirsu (five times) and Bau (in the sixth instance) approve of Gudea's actions, and they record particular blessings and benefits that the deities bestow upon the ruler. It might also be tentatively observed that the epithets progressively enhance Gudea's status and guarantee the security of his reign, before assuring him of ongoing good health and well-being, including into the future. Accordingly, in the first he is officially 'recognised' by Ningirsu, while the god is stationed at the Girnun, or cult podium (as explained in Chapter 40), which is elsewhere described as a 'place of making judgments' (A22), presumably indicating that Gudea's legal right to rule is ratified by the god; in the second, Ningirsu, as the agent or 'flood storm' of Enlil, looks favourably upon Gudea; thirdly, and again as Enlil's stormy agent, Ningirsu still more warmly takes Gudea to his 'holy heart'; fourthly, the god secures and defends Gudea's rule by making potential foreign enemies 'tremble'; fifthly (after the respective monument is installed facing the Euruga), Ningirsu determines that Gudea shall enjoy a 'good fate' or future destiny; and finally, in the ceremonial name of the sixth stele, which is dedicated to Bau, the Eninnu is blessed by An, while Bau is said to be Gudea's 'life source', presumably as the guarantor of his health and longevity. In addition to Ningirsu and Bau, it is significant that Enlil and An are both mentioned in the names because the supreme god Enlil is said at the very beginning of Cylinder A to have instigated and blessed Gudea's project (A1), and it is only after the conclusion of that event of cosmic significance (which is conceivably the fitting fulfilment of other happenings relating to Ningirsu's mythology that were probably described on the Lost Cylinder) that Gudea experiences his dream vision. Correspondingly, when the complex is finished, but before Ningirsu takes up residence, the Eninnu

is twice placed into the safekeeping of An: when the clay nails are installed (A21), and when it is said to have been painted with the 'splendours of heaven' (A27). Conspicuous by his absence from the epithets is Enki, the third member of the New Eninnu's cardinal trinity of senior deities who are explicitly mentioned together in the Cylinder Inscriptions (B12–13). Since he is a key figure in the critically important passages relating to the design of the complex (A17) and the placing of the various foundation deposits (A22), it is surprising that he is not introduced in the names of the steles, which seem to sum up the theology of the New Eninnu. Despite that notable absence, one of the steles was specially devoted to him, as is argued in the discussion of the reconstructions below, and it might therefore be supposed that he is alluded to periphrastically in an obscure term in one of the other stele names, but this is conjectural.

The text states that the steles were installed 'around the house', and though this should not be taken too literally, it would seemingly confirm that the itemised monuments were very closely associated with the layout of the New Eninnu as it is described in the Cylinder Inscriptions and illustrated in the plan on Statue B. It is extremely tempting to assume that one of the named steles must have been displayed in the shrine that was found by Cros between Tells A and B, but that was probably not the case. The positioning of the shrine with respect to the stone stairway that gave access to the top of the mound was undoubtedly of great significance (see Fig. 16). The stairs ascended along a line that led to the Shugalam Gate (No. 3 on Fig. 219) in the NE façade at the SE end of the L-shaped complex (which is not marked as such on Cros's plan because it had not yet been identified). Nonetheless, Cros's detailed plan does include the Ur-Bau corner (or *Angle d'Our-Baou*, as Cros refers to it), which was retained inside the New Eninnu, and this would confirm the alignment. The relationship between Cros's shrine and the Shugalam Gate can therefore be fairly confidently defined, and when the Gudea Steles are correlated with other identifiable locations in and around the New Eninnu itself, it is reasonable to assume that none of the ones named in the inventory was installed at the shrine outside the temenos. The likely display locations of the steles are summarised in Table 7, which shows them in relation to the positions of the gates and sacred places associated with the Slain Heroes, as detailed in Chapter 40 and marked on Fig. 219. As above, the sacred places and steles are numbered in the

TABLE 7. The probable locations of the Gudea Steles, correlated with the gates of the New Eninnu and the monuments to the Slain Heroes, all as detailed in the Cylinder Inscriptions.

The Sacred Places associated with the Slain Heroes (A25–6)	The Gudea Steles (A23–4)
1. The Battle Gate	
	1. The great courtyard (entered via the Battle Gate)
2. The City Gate (Flood or Mighty Gate)	5. Facing Euruga
3. The Shugalam Gate	4. The Shugalam Gate
4. The Sunrise Gate	3. The Sunrise Gate
5. The Kasurra Gate (positioned either at the NW end of the NE façade or in the NW façade)	2. The Kasurra Gate
6. The Tarsirsir Gate	
7. Bau's 'inner room' (associated with her cella at the heart of her personal shrine)	6. Close to ('by') Bau's 'inner room', probably on the NW side of the main courtyard

table, according to the order in which they appear in their respective lists.

Perhaps the first thing to notice about the correspondence between the seven sacred places (six gates and Bau's 'inner room') and the Gudea Steles is that both lists begin with an allusion to the principal public space associated with Ningirsu, and both end with a place that was especially devoted to Bau. The Battle Gate, with its weapons porch, where Ningirsu's divine arsenal was kept, appears to have led into the main courtyard. Bau's 'inner room' was where her Magilum boat and Bison emblems were displayed, while the Bau stele was positioned nearby. The other interesting feature is that, if the Euruga stele (5) can be correlated with the City Gate (2), it becomes evident that the steles placed respectively at the City, Shugalam, Sunrise and Kasurra Gates are listed in reverse order (5–2) to that of the gates (2–5). The discussion in Chapter 40 of the locations of the gates and sacred places with respect to the interconnected cycles defined by the solar year and the lunar months would seem to intimate that at least three of the gates (City, Shugalam and Sunrise) were enumerated in an order that reflected key turning points in the year (relating to the winter and summer solstices). Such occasions were doubtless associated with festivals, and it seems reasonable to assume that the calendar of feasts played a role in the way all of the gates and sacred places were placed around the temenos and in their ordering in the Cylinder Inscriptions. This is a matter of extreme complexity, however, which involves finding relationships between the fixed points in the solar year (namely, the changing seasons) and the lunar months (with their numerous uncertain names and a leap month intercalated at varying places every third year), and

interpolating any other festivals that might not have been directly connected with these cycles. It is therefore currently impossible to say why the ordering of gates 2–5 and steles 5–2 is reversed in the two lists.

Examined more closely (and with repeated reference to the discussion of the gates and Slain Heroes in Chapter 40, and to Fig. 219), the first stele (1) was placed inside the 'great' courtyard. Though it is surely inconceivable that the stele was the only ornament in this important public space, no information is offered in the inscriptions about other artefacts that might have been exhibited there. Indeed, the great courtyard per se is only named once in the entire text, though the same sacred locus is probably referred to more simply as the courtyard of the Eninnu, and in certain instances it is said to be a venue for celebrations and ceremonies, where sacred music is played (A28), and where Gudea confirms the appointments of the god's divine council (B6). The stele's ceremonial name is unfortunately not fully preserved, but it seemingly recorded some action undertaken by Ningirsu in the 'great courtyard', and it might very tentatively be assumed that this related to the receiving or approval of the various divine operatives who were introduced by Gudea. The second stele was 'set up at the Kasurra Gate', in the company of a statue of a lion, the 'terror of the gods', and the gate is associated with a 'lookout post'. The Kasurra Gate, which was probably located either at the NW end of the principal NE façade or towards the W corner of the NW façade, was associated with the shipment of goods from far-off places, which were brought to shore at the Kasurra quay and entered the city (as distinct from the sacred complex) via another Kasurra portal in the city wall. The symbolism of the lion and the lookout (conceivably referring to sentries stationed in the gate tower) seem jointly to connote the power that Ningirsu was believed to exercise over foreign states, such that the necessary international trade routes were kept open and secure, and the god's universal supremacy is appropriately the subject of the stele's ceremonial name, which describes Ningirsu as the 'king, Enlil's flood storm, who has no opponent'.

The third stele (3), 'facing the rising sun', can be located with a fair degree of confidence. Though the word 'gate' is not expressly used in the description of the stele (or in the description of the gate, for that matter), the carving was presumably installed at (or very close to) the Sunrise Gate in the SE façade, which was plausibly aligned with sunrise at the winter solstice. The monument's official name again refers to Ningirsu, in terms that seem to parallel those used for the Kasurra stele, as the 'roaring storm of Enlil, the lord without rival'. This might confirm that the Kasurra and Sunrise steles and gates were positioned at diametrically opposite points in the temenos, but this is speculative and subject to a host of qualifications (see Chapter 40). The position of the fourth stele (4), which was 'set up facing Shugalam' can also be identified with respect to the arguments made above. Again, no gate is explicitly mentioned in the listing of the stele, but the Shugalam Gate was almost certainly situated at the SE end of the NE façade, in line with the Ningirsu cella in Ur-Bau's old Ningirsu temple and the one in the New Eninnu (Shugalam being an inferred byname for the sanctum sanctorum), and on that basis it can be supposed that the stele was displayed in a relatively public space close to the gate. The stele's ceremonial name, which describes the god as the 'king at whose name the foreign countries tremble', again mentions Ningiru's international pre-eminence. As argued in Chapter 40, this might confirm that the Kasurra Gate (if it was placed at the NW end of the NE façade) and the Shugalam Gate (at the SE end of the same façade) were counterparts that pivoted (as it were) on the central Battle Gate, where Ningirsu's weapons were displayed, but this is hypothetical.

No gate is mentioned in the description of the Euruga stele (5), but the word Euruga was formerly directly linked with the idea of the city, and that association has led to the widely accepted assumption that the stele should be associated with the City Gate in the SW façade. The more recent interpretation of Euruga as connoting the idea of a mighty flood (outlined in Chapter 40) might tend to confirm the positioning of the stele and the gate on the SW side of the complex,

precisely facing the point at which the sun set at the winter solstice. This potentially introduces associations with the longest nights of the year (when the world is metaphorically flooded with darkness), and the imagery might, in turn, be linked with the 'good fate' that Ningirsu ordains for Gudea in terms of the final fixing of an individual human destiny that comes at the end of life, for example. The exact meanings are inevitably speculative, but the placement of the Euruga stele by the City Gate in the SW façade seems credible.

Finally, the Bau stele (6) was probably sited not at a gate, but inside the complex, close to ('by') Bau's 'inner room'. The Nammahni inscription quoted in Chapter 40 (RIME 3.1.1.12.6) speaks of the 'protective' Tarsirsir, interpreted as Bau's messenger and gatekeeper, entering the 'courtyard of Bau'. It seems unlikely that Bau's temple was furnished with its own major courtyard, partly because her worshippers seem usually to have communicated with her only indirectly, via the ministering Tarsirsir. That being the case, the Bau stele was perhaps displayed on the NW side of the great courtyard, in a position that would complement the symmetry of beginnings and ends that seems to be a key feature of the respective lists of steles and sacred places. The Bau stele's ceremonial name associates the New Eninnu with the 'eyes of An', Bau's father, the sky god, and this might link with the goddess's inferred role in the appearance of the new moon and the putative myth of the death and rebirth of the horned Bison (a symbol of the lunar crescent), which is sketched out in Chapter 40. The 'eyes' of the sky might refer to celestial bodies, but there might also be an association with the inscribed clay nails that were inserted into the walls of the New Eninnu, symbolically fixing the temple to the sky (see Chapter 43). The further description of Bau as the 'life source' of Gudea would seemingly reference her role as the archetypal divine mother (also a feature of the surmised Bison myth).

The locations of the steles can be correlated with the positions of the gates and Bau's 'inner room', as marked on Fig. 219, together with an entrance that has not been discussed previously, the gate through which the 'King' (Ningirsu) enters his abode (A24–5):

On the Gate where the King Enters an eagle is raising its eyes toward a wild bull. Its curved wooden posts joining above the gate are a rainbow stretching over the sky. Its upper lintel of the gate like (?) the Eninnu stands among rumbling, roaring storms. Its awe-inspiring eyebrow-shaped arch (?) meets the admiring eyes of the gods.

This gate (No. 8 on Fig. 219), which is not linked with any of the Slain Heroes, but with Ningirsu himself, would appear to have been the most spectacular of all the gates in the complex. It was decorated with the image of an eagle and a wild bull (presumably a doorway relief, but this is speculative), and according to the text its wooden gate posts extended high above the opening to form a rounded arch like a 'rainbow' or an 'eyebrow'. The entire gate seems to be situated at a very high point in the complex, such that its top crossbar or 'lintel' metaphorically penetrates the storm clouds that lie in the sky above the New Eninnu, and the 'eyebrow' of the gate is on the same level as the 'admiring eyes' of the gods that inhabit the empyrean domain. The description does not fit with any of the gates in the temenos wall, which were situated at ground level, at the bases of fortified towers. Similarly, the eagle and the bull emblems do not correspond with any of the motifs associated with the temenos gates. Such links cannot be categorically ruled out, but it would seem probable that the King's Gate was the one between the main courtyard and the SE end of the complex, where the Ningirsu temple and the old Eninnu were located. It was presumably on the highest level of the stepped arrangement of stairs and floors that led up from the courtyard to the platform that supported the Ningirsu temple, which was raised above the rest of the New Eninnu, and it can therefore be associated with the elaborate structure known as the Gate of Gudea (DEGH and FIJ on Heuzey's New Plan; Fig. 114), which (as detailed in Chapter 23) led up to an elevated monumental entrance (Fig. 184) that was much wider than the temenos gates. The evidence would therefore tend to confirm that the upper gateway was indeed the unique and magnificent King's Gate.

The Steles Reconstructed

Based on a comprehensive analysis of the preserved fragments, together with a thorough reassessment of earlier sketches dating back to the time of Heuzey, Suter (2000, pp. 161–275 and Pls. A–C) proposes possible designs for three of the Gudea Steles. The preserved fragments are apportioned to the various representations on account of their respective thicknesses, the widths of the dividing bands, the relative sizes of the figures and the provenances of the sherds. The results are reconsidered below, followed by fresh reconstructions of nine relief faces. First, however, it is important to outline some general principles about the probable form of the steles, even though the extremely fragmentary nature of the remains makes any conclusions necessarily hypothetical. The Gudea carvings were shaped like upright rectangular arched windows, with curving tops and width to height ratios of somewhat less than 1:2 (Suter 2000, pp. 209–10). The presumed proportions are based on a range of comparisons, among which the Early Dynastic Stele of the Vultures was considerably squarer (with a width to height ratio of 1:1.12). Based on the scant information available (Suter 2000, p. 225), a larger stele from the set might have had dimensions of around 2.56 m (h) × 1.7 m (w) × 0.225 m (t), but some were certainly considerably smaller, and it is impossible to say whether the stated measurements represent a maximum size. One of the sherds (AO4581, to which EŞEM5802 has been joined) shows an installed stele surrounded by monumental weapons on plinths, and this exceptional survival, which is unique in the archaeology of ancient Sumer, provides further confirmation of the indicative size, shape and positioning of the objects (Suter 2000, p. 189–90).

Of extreme importance for any attempt to reconstruct them is the fact that the steles could have been carved on both of their principal faces (front and back) and also around their edges or thicknesses. A few of the fragments—mostly composite pieces that have been rejoined since they were excavated—have imagery on a main side and an edge. The composites in this group include: AO4573, AO4580, EŞEM5837 and EŞEM 6117; VA2902, VA2903 and VA2904; and AO4579 and EŞEM5805. There are also two intact fragments that exhibit a main face and an edge, namely AO52 (the music stele) and EŞEM6016. Whether the obverse and reverse (if those terms can properly be applied) were both carved is of fundamental importance because if there were indeed six named Gudea Steles, as is indicated in the Cylinder Inscriptions, that would imply a maximum of twelve main relief surfaces (fronts and backs). If any were carved on just one face, that would reduce the total, but it would also in all likelihood be indicative of the steles' display locations. Those with carved fronts and backs (all of which might have had carved edges) were clearly intended to be seen in the round, but any single-sided steles must have been viewed from one side only, no doubt because they were positioned against a wall or some other architectural or sculptural back-drop. This was probably the case for the object—perhaps a stele, though seemingly not one of the six principal Gudea Steles—that was displayed on the pedestal in front of the Cros shrine, for example. Unfortunately, these matters are impossible to resolve, but it is vital to bear them in mind, especially when attributing the reconstructed surfaces to one or two individual monuments.

Furthermore, as stated at the outset, horizontal relief bands were used to divide the main faces into four or five registers, while some of the Gudea Steles had narrow relief frames all around their perimeters, and some or all had uncarved zones towards their bases that meant they could be slotted into display mounts. In terms of their sculptural programmes, the culminating scene of each face (or possibly each stele, depending on how the two main sides of a single monument related to each other) was contained in the taller uppermost register, framed by the arched top. The extant examples suggest that this was generally focused on an enthroned deity, and that the rather shorter registers below were filled with narrative or thematic vignettes that paved the way for the crowning climactic tableau. The steles that were carved on four sides appear to have developed the sculptural content of each register continuously all the way round the stone, though there are instances where scenes with figures facing one way appear to break off, at which point figures facing in the other direction are introduced. Since this happens only on preserved fragments associated with the edges of steles, it might be that the two main faces of four-sided carvings were sometimes (or even always) intended to be read somewhat independently of one another, but the limited evidence makes this impossible to confirm. It should also be stressed that several fragments, including those featuring main faces and carved edges, are composite pieces that were joined after their accession into their respective museums by scholars and curators, notably Eckhard Unger (see Suter 2000, p. 167). Taken together, the whole series told the story of the conception and building of the New Eninnu, making reference to the mythical or theological framework, which was inseparable from the chronology. Within that framework it is nevertheless difficult to be sure exactly how the individual steles related to each other, and in particular whether they each expressed self-contained, unabridged chapters of the overall narrative, or whether some other organising principle was at work. Unlike the Stele of the Vultures, which was designed

with a mythological obverse and a historical reverse, the Gudea Steles seem to have juxtaposed mythological and historical subject matter in a more fluid way. As a set, the steles were in all likelihood conceived as a pictorial complement to the Cylinder Inscriptions, comparable to the way in which a painterly or sculptural programme in a church might relate to the Bible, for example. One limitation to this obvious comparison would be that the steles, which were exhibited in a diverse range of locations around the sacred complex, were not designed to be contemplated side by side in an unbroken sequence.

Suter's rather conservative sketches differ markedly from the new reconstructions, mainly because the latter propose a much more complete sculptural programme that takes in a broader iconographical frame of reference. As with Suter's work, the preserved fragments are linked on the basis of the sizes of the sculpted figures and other represented objects, while some reliance has been placed on the sizes of the dividing bands, though many fragments do not contain any such indications of their places in a register. The various thicknesses of the fragments are less helpful, in large part because most of the dimensions generally relied upon in the literature are derived from secondary publications and museum catalogues. In the absence of a detailed compendium of all the surviving sherds, including verified measurements, it seems unwise to regard the published thicknesses as definitive. Nine principal relief faces have been reconstructed, though only two (Fig. 226) have been attached to form a single monument. This should not be taken to imply that there were eight named Gudea Steles in total, referring to the list in the Cylinder Inscriptions and including the seven single faces and the two-sided reconstruction (Fig. 226), but only that definite associations between particular faces and preserved carved edges are extremely difficult to establish. Several of the reconstructions nevertheless include carved edges, and this would considerably reduce the total number of represented monuments, but for the present purpose it has been judged better to focus on the sculptural programmes than to advance conjectures about how the relief faces fitted together. As noted previously, some of the Gudea Steles featured perimetric bands, though some seem only to have included them on the curved tops (Suter 2000, p. 226), and some if not all of the monuments had unworked base zones.

Fig. 220, which is a relief devoted to Enki, features four registers, the bottom three of which each have heights of

The Steles of Gudea 617

FIGURE 220. Reconstruction of the Gudea Stele devoted to Enki.

around 30 cm, while the top one is rather taller. They are divided by relief bands measuring about 2 cm (h), and the surface includes a perimetric band that also measures about 2 cm (or possibly a little more). If the uppermost register is judged to be around fifty per cent or sixty per cent taller than the ones below (measuring to the apex of the curve), that would suggest a total height of around 1.5 m (disregarding an unpolished base zone) and a base width of around 1.1 m. This would in turn indicate a width to height ratio of the order of 1:1.4. The subject of the relief is the design and laying out of the ground plan of the shrine, with a particular stress on the role of Enki in those decisive events. Accordingly, an inscribed fragment (AO26634, formerly AO56) that relates to the fashioning of bricks and the purification rituals associated with the pegging out of the ground or the laying of the first brick is placed in the bottom register, where the depicted events begin. The top of this sherd includes a dividing band on which can be seen two opposite-facing feet belonging to different characters. The foot on the left is therefore considered to be that of a worker who is carrying a basket or other heavy object on his right shoulder, while the right-facing foot is cautiously ascribed to Gudea on account of the sliver of the hem of a long robe that can be made out above the middle of the top of the foot. Approaching the ruler on the right are two priests, one of whom carries a Gudea foundation deposit in the form of a kneeling figure (AO4581 bis). Behind him on the same fragment is a missing figure who is assumed to be carrying a brick, or more probably the inscribed tablet that was the second object that made up the two-part deposit. The register above that (the third from the bottom) features a seated deity (AO60), conceivably Nisaba, who, when she appears in Gudea's dream, is said to read the 'holy stars' that augur well for the construction of the temple's ground plan (A5–6), and to be the goddess who knows the 'inmost secrets' of the 'numbers' that Gudea depends upon in order to mark the plan out (A19). A libation is provisionally placed between Gudea and Nisaba, who opens the 'house of understanding' for the suitably devout ruler (A17). Finally, Enki, who is associated with Nisaba in the same passage, where he is said to 'put right the design of the house', is introduced as the principal subject of the uppermost register. His key role as one of the three high-ranking gods who watch over the whole project is discussed below (in Chapters 43 and 44), and before Ningirsu takes up residence he is said to make 'oracular pronouncements' (B3–4). On this relief he is seen enthroned on the right of the top register, in a reconstruction that derives from a sherd with a streaming vase and fish (a motif expressing the life-giving power of water) that was found by Sarzec in Court A (AO63). To the left, Gudea is ushered into Enki's presence by his personal god and another divine attendant, Enki's double-faced minister, Isimud (VA2890).

The four lower registers of the second reconstruction (Fig. 221), which can be described as the Ningirsu and Bau relief, each measure about 0.3 m, but in this case the topmost one is considerably taller, with a maximum height (at the apex of the very shallow curve) of approximately 0.56 m. Incorporating four slightly thicker dividing bands of about 5 cm, but no perimetric margin, the total height of the relief is therefore about 1.96 m (disregarding an unpolished support zone), while its base width is about 1.11 m. This suggests a width to height ratio of around 1:1.76, which makes the monument tall and rather narrow compared to the Enki relief. The bottom

register contains a very poorly preserved commemorative inscription that forms the lower section of three joined fragments (EŞEM5843, EŞEM5851 and EŞEM5989). What little remains of the text mentions a 'ruler' (Suter 2000, p. 165). Above that, on the same composite piece, the second register from the bottom shows two men transporting a slab of stone on a wheeled cart, while the intervening dividing band on which they stand is filled with a schematic representation of a mountainous region (the similar forms on EŞEM5842 almost certainly show water). The theme of sourcing building materials from abroad is continued on the left of the second register from the bottom, where the control exercised over foreign lands is symbolised by a depiction of the god Ningishzida (Gudea's personal god), who is shown overpowering a fighter who is depicted with the horns of a bull, either on his helmet or directly on his head. The bottom of the same sherd (VA2896) includes two more vertical scale-like forms, probably stressing that the scene takes place far from Lagash. On the extreme left of this register is a more complete combat scene (VA2905) in which another divine figure (Ningishzida) can be seen grasping the beard of another horned warrior and cutting his throat with a long blade. The third register from the bottom features a procession of divine standards belonging to different deities and therefore signalling the contributions of the deities' respective peoples. The emblem of Inanna, a lion with a disc on its back (AO4577), might recall the 'levy' that is said on Cylinder A (A14) to be exacted from the 'clans of Inanna', who are described as carrying a standard fitted with another of Inanna's symbols, namely the 'rosette'. In front of the Inanna standard on the reconstruction can be seen the water bird of Nanshe and Lugal.kur.dub, the falcon of Ningirsu (elsewhere identified with Sharur, Ningirsu's divine mace (B7 and A14). The upper part of fragment AO4577 contains a dividing band, and on the fourth register from the bottom there is the rounded underside of a large circular drum. The rest of the register is accordingly filled with a ritual dance or fight, including fragment AO243A, and a libation scene (BM95477) in honour of Ningishzida, who is seen on the extreme right, carrying a mace (VA2897). Fragment BM95477 includes a dividing band, above which, on the top register, are a set of overflowing vases and (to their left) the foot of a deity. The vases, which continue towards the extreme right of the top register (AO4584), are understood to be the carved lower section of a throne that is decorated with seated lions, one of which can also be seen on AO4584. The scene

The Steles of Gudea 619

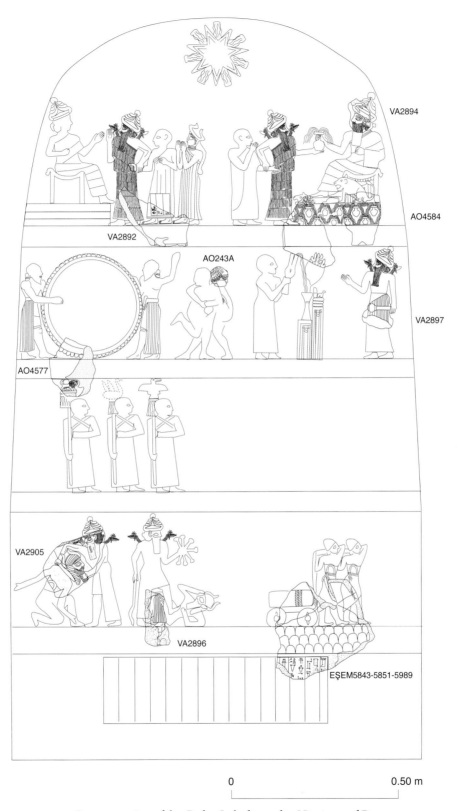

FIGURE 221. Reconstruction of the Gudea Stele devoted to Ningirsu and Bau.

depicts Ningishzida presenting Gudea to the seated Ningirsu, who grants the ruler the gift of prosperity that is symbolised by an overflowing vessel. On the left side of the same register sits an enthroned goddess, probably Bau, who faces her husband. Gudea is therefore shown being presented to her by Ningishzida, though this time the group (including a horned attendant standing behind Gudea) proceed in the opposite direction, away from the figures who approach Ningirsu. The fragment (VA2892) associated with the Bau presentation includes Gudea's name in an inscription above the hem of the ruler's long robe.

The relief with the seven-headed mace (Fig. 222) includes three carved registers, each with a height of 0.26 m, and a top one that is about twice as tall (0.52 m). Completed with three dividing bands that each measure about 7 cm, the total height of the main carved surface would be around 1.3 m, but a baseline dividing band with an empty register below it have also been provisionally added, bringing the total height of the carved face up to around 1.66 m and giving a reasonable width to height ratio of about 1:1.3 for a relief with five registers and four dividing bands. The fragments grouped on this reconstruction were selected on account of the relatively small figures. Above the empty base register, the second register from the bottom shows a procession of divine standards that are connected with the teams of workers preparing to build the New Eninnu. The lion, which can be made out on the left, is included on a fragment that was joined with others to create the dividing band and the ornate divine chariot that can be seen on the third register from the bottom (AO4586, EŞEM5808 and EŞEM6150). Above that, on the second register from the top, is a timpanist playing a large drum. This is part of an important composite fragment (AO4579 and EŞEM5805, which were joined by Unger) that includes a front face and also a carved thickness, where a standard-bearing figure can be seen taking part in the procession, in front of the musician. The top register features Gudea, who is carrying a palm branch (AO10867), being led (from left to right) by Ningishzida into the presence of Ningirsu. Behind Gudea is a divine attendant. Ningirsu, who is represented only by his seven-headed mace (VA2901), is seen enthroned on the right edge of the carving in the act of receiving the ruler.

The sculptural programme of Fig. 223 is devoted to Bau and Gatumdug, whose name appears in the commemorative inscription on fragment AO16649, in which someone is said

to have 'praised' her. Accordingly, the fragment has often been thought to derive from a stele devoted especially to Gatumdug (Suter 2000, p. 165), but that judgement is complicated by the argument made previously, namely that, by the reign of Gudea, she and Bau were syncretised, such that the two goddesses were to all intents and purposes regarded as one and the same. Consequently, the Bau–Gatumdug relief incorporates motifs that relate to both deities. The reconstruction again includes fragments that can be connected on the basis of their respective sizes and the dimensions of the portrayed figures. The dividing bands on this relief are rather thicker than on the previous ones (measuring about 7 cm), while the four lower registers are each about 0.35 m high. If the height of the uppermost register is estimated to be around 0.65 m (a little less than twice the size of the lower ones), that gives a total overall height for this monument of approximately 2.33 m, while an estimated base width of around 1.26 m would suggest a width to height ratio of around 1:1.85. The reconstruction tapers markedly towards the top, and no relief margins are included. The bottom register, which was presumably filled with construction scenes, shows only the remains of a shaven head on the extreme right. Above that, on the same sherd (AO16649), is the dividing band, on which can be seen the feet of three right-facing figures (interpreted as workmen carrying heavy loads), together with the Gatumdug inscription. In the middle of this register is a left-facing surveyor, perhaps the ruler himself, who carries a coiled rope (incorporating VA2893) and addresses or encourages a procession of teams of standard-bearing workers (EŞEM5828 and AO4576). The bird on the rightmost standard might be an eagle, but it could also be a sea bird—an emblem of Nanshe that is possibly attested on EŞEM5824, as discussed below— while the sherd containing the disc-bearing lion, which is extremely damaged and therefore very difficult to decode, is included in this position only with the utmost caution. The middle one of the five registers shows the divine chariot of Ningirsu (AO4583 and EŞEM5847), which Gudea is advised by Nanshe in the Cylinder Inscriptions to commission for the god (A6–7). Towards the end of the text (B13–14) it is also described as the chariot of the 'house' or temple and referred to by its ceremonial name: 'It makes the mountains bow down'. The chariot is followed on the reconstruction's left-hand edge or thickness by a figure holding a monumental mace, an interpolation that suggests that the Bau–Gatumdug stele might have been carved on three or four sides.

The Steles of Gudea 621

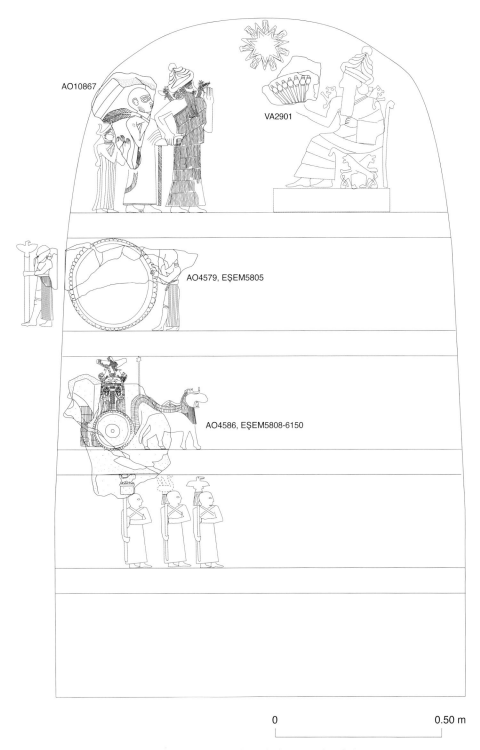

FIGURE 222. Reconstruction of the Gudea Stele with the seven-headed mace.

622 The Mound of the Palace

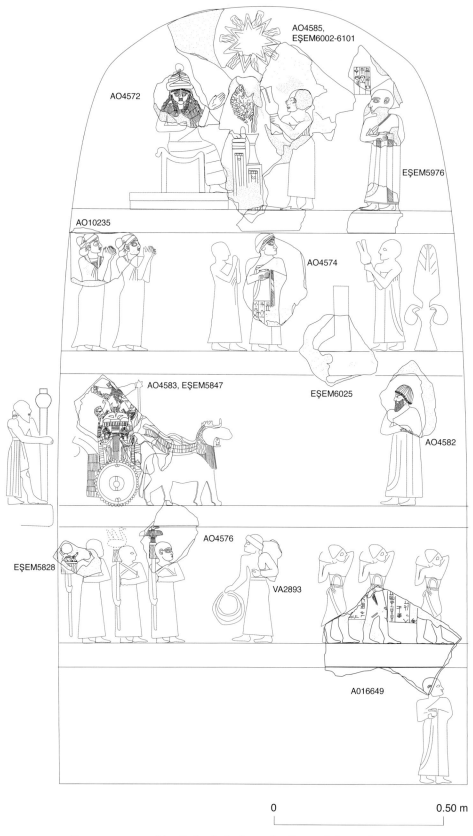

FIGURE 223. Reconstruction of the Gudea Stele devoted to Bau and Gatumdug.

On the right-hand side of the middle register of the main face is a left-facing figure with a beard (AO4582), who also appears on the music relief (Fig. 227). The clapping women (AO10235), who are placed on the left of the second register from the top, seem particularly appropriate for a sculpture that is devoted to Bau. In front of them, also facing right, Gudea (AO4574) is seen taking part in a libation, which is celebrated in front of an enigmatic object (EŞEM6025) that might be the leg of a monumental altar, a piece of furniture with substantial feet (Suter 2000, p. 206) or possibly some other kind of footed shaft. Finally, the top register is filled with a variation of the impressive Istanbul reconstruction created by Unger (Suter 2000, p. 167) in which the god has been replaced by the goddess (AO4572), who was judged by Heuzey (Cros 1910, p. 295) to be Bau. The figure performing the libation might tentatively be identified as Gudea instead of a priestly celebrant (AO4585, EŞEM6002 and EŞEM6101). That being the case, however, the portrait of the ruler with clasped hands, which, following Unger, is here positioned on the extreme right of the upper register, would be incorrectly placed (EŞEM5976). As detailed above, the last of the six named steles is said in the Cylinder Inscriptions to be displayed close to Bau's 'inner room' (A24), together with the Magilum boat and the Bison (A26), so it is probable that those motifs would also have been included on the original Bau (or Bau–Gatumdug) stele.

The sunrise relief (Fig. 224) features four lower registers with heights of about 0.34 m, plus an upper register of around 0.63 m, which is again almost twice the height of the ones below, and four dividing bands that each measure about 6 cm. This gives a total height for the monument of around 2.23 m, and a width to height ratio of around 1:1.9 (assuming a base width of 1.17 m). The bottom register features the libation that is represented on EŞEM6088 by the head of a celebrant, above which is a dividing band, and above that (on the second register from the bottom) is an inscribed robe that identifies its wearer as 'Gudea, ensi of Lagash', who is here shown taking part in a generic ritual. The middle register of the five again depicts the divine chariot that the ruler is said in the Cylinder Inscriptions to offer to Ningirsu, in a scene that includes the figure with a monumental mace on the edge of the monument (also shown on Fig. 223)—a fragment that indicates a three- or four-sided stele. The second register from the top shows Gudea with a coiled surveying rope (EŞEM1558), not in the act of laying out the ground, but rather taking part in

a procession that involves men clapping their hands (AO55). Fragment AO55 is said by Heuzey (Sarzec and Heuzey 1912, p. 221) to be a scene of war in which the central figure is a warrior who raises his hands in a plea for mercy, but the attitudes of the three figures (in so far as they can be made out) seem rather to recall the clapping women on fragment AO10235. The procession has therefore been construed as a scene of rejoicing. Finally, the top register shows Gudea carrying a palm branch (AO4575) as he approaches an enthroned god (AO53), who is identified by Heuzey as Ningirsu (Sarzec and Heuzey 1912, pp. 211–12). Two divine auxiliaries are in attendance, including a deity with a staff (AO4571), as well as the figure shown on EŞEM6106, who is positioned behind Ningirsu. The side of the god's ornate throne is embellished with carvings of horned figures (the horns of one can be seen on AO53) that are here associated with bison. That being the case, the relief can tentatively be identified as the sunrise stele, the third of the six named steles, which is erected alongside the standard of Utu. As noted above, the standard of the sun is further connected with (or possibly fitted with) a bison motif (A26).

Fig. 225, which might be described as the relief of abundance, features four lower registers, each with a height of about 0.28 m, and a significantly taller top one that measures about 0.65 m, giving a total height for the relief of around 2.09 m (including dividing bands of about 7 cm and a top margin of approximately 4 cm), and a width to height ratio of about 1:1.98. The two lower registers are filled with building scenes. On the extreme right of the bottom register is an interesting fragment that shows a man with outstretched arms and wearing a conical cap. Identifiable as a worker, he appears to be holding a rope in each hand (AO10236), possibly indicating that he is using a kind of pulley to hoist building materials up to higher parts of the construction. Complementing this idea, the ladder in front of him extends up past the dividing band to reach the second register from the bottom. If this was indeed how the scene was originally composed, it would represent a fascinating play on the correspondence between the registers of the monument and the heights of the walls or even the different levels at which parts of the finished building were meaningfully used (for example, ground level and the roof of the temple that was accessed via a stairway). The ladder forms part of a composite fragment (EŞEM5999 and EŞEM6001) that shows three workmen in the middle of the second register from the bottom. They are

624 The Mound of the Palace

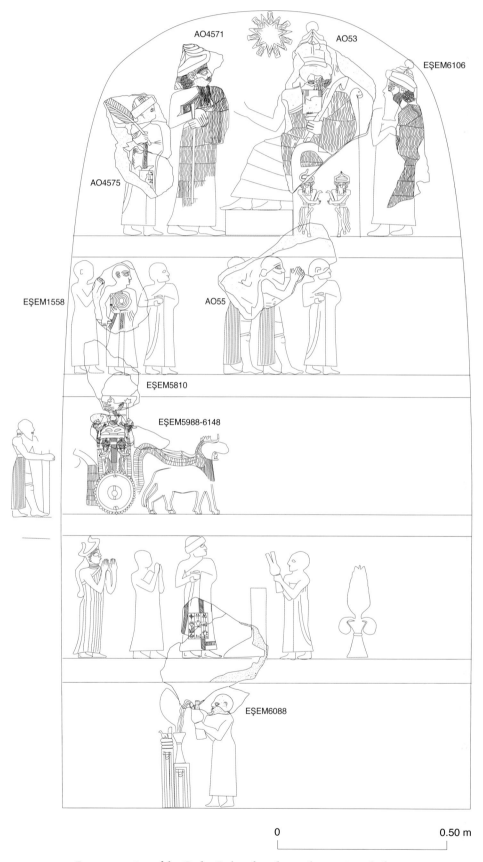

FIGURE 224. Reconstruction of the Gudea Stele referred to as the sunrise relief.

The Steles of Gudea 625

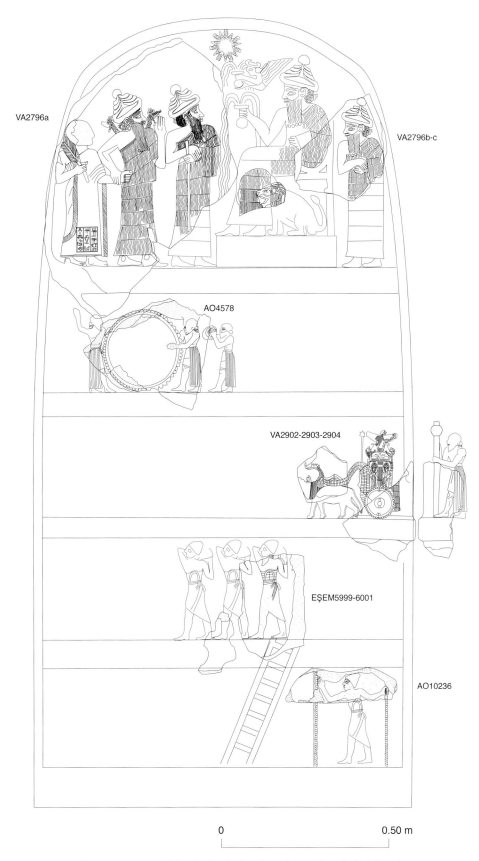

FIGURE 225. Reconstruction of the Gudea Stele referred to as the relief of abundance.

carrying heavy loads and walking from right to left. Above them, in the third register from the bottom, is the divine chariot of Ningirsu (also inserted into some of the previous reconstructions), while a figure supporting a monumental mace appears on the associated edge of this face (indicating a three- or four-sided stele). Above the chariot, on the second register from the top, are musicians, including a drummer and a man who is seemingly playing cymbals (AO4578). The crowning scene at the top of this monument is based on a reconstruction combining three pieces (VA2796a–c) that was created by scholars at the Vorderasiatische Museum in Berlin (Suter 2000, p. 168). It shows Gudea, who is carrying a palm branch, being led into the presence of Ningirsu by his personal god, together with another deity who carries a staff. Ningirsu, who is seated on a leonine throne, holds out an overflowing vase that is a symbol of the abundance that is promised to Gudea as a reward for his completion of the New Eninnu in the Cylinder Inscriptions (for example in A11). Behind Ningirsu is a divine attendant with the characteristic crossed hands that are familiar from the Gudea statues. Finally, the higher part of the space between Ningirsu and Gudea is filled with a sun emblem, reflecting the deity's partial identification with Utu, along with a horned goddess who carries another overflowing vessel.

The stele with two main faces (Fig. 226), which is the most complete of the reconstructions attempted here, can be tentatively associated with the Shugalam Gate, the Kasurra Gate or the Battle Gate (as marked on Fig. 219). Featuring four carved sides, the reconstruction has dividing bands of around 7 cm that separate three lower registers, each with a height of 0.34 m, and a rather taller upper register of 0.57 m. Its total height is therefore around 1.93 m (including a margin of about 7 cm, but excluding a possible fifth register or uncarved base at the bottom), and its width to height ratio is approximately 1:1.7. In this instance it is worth noting that the maximum recorded thickness of any of the incorporated fragments is around 27 cm, a figure that might be indicative of the width of the monument's carved edges. The bottom register of Fig. 226 (left) shows the transport of goods on a labelled cedar raft (on joined fragments EŞEM5842 and EŞEM6016). The delivered items are being carried away by workers, who move from right to left, while the edge of the monument associated with EŞEM6016 shows two robed figures walking in the opposite direction. Above the raft, on the second register from the bottom, is a shaven-headed man

who carries a Lugal.kur.dub falcon standard (EŞEM5811) as he approaches the stele that is shown displayed among a number of divine weapons on joined fragments AO4581 and EŞEM5802. Behind the group of monuments (on the right edge of the relief) is another figure with a raised hand who might be Gudea, though it should be noted that Suter (2000, p. 189) interprets the shapes that include the figure's arm as a bow with two arrows, or possibly a quiver. The second register from the top features two large drums, one on either side of another possible Gudea figure, who has his hands clasped. The drum on the left is interpolated to complete the upper part of EŞEM5811 (the character with the Lugal.kur.dub standard), while the top edge of the drum on the right is found on a composite of joined fragments (AO4573 and AO4580; EŞEM5837 and EŞEM6117) that extends into the top register (including part of the associated edge relief), where a robed divine attendant stands behind the enthroned Ningirsu, with sun and crescent moon emblems above. On the left of the top register, facing Ningirsu, is Gudea, who carries a palm branch as he is ushered by his personal god, Ningishzida, into the presence of the divine owner of the New Eninnu. Most importantly, the huge mace head on the right is probably Sharur, Ningirsu's divine mace, that is also identified with Lugal.kur.dub. On the other side of the stele (Fig. 226 (right)) the bottom register shows a procession of standard bearers (referring to composite fragment EŞEM5824) with emblems related to Ningirsu, Nanshe and Inanna—the tutelary deities of the respective clans that gather to contribute to the New Eninnu's construction. To their right is Gudea, holding a coiled rope and standing in front of the entrance to a shrine (EŞEM6000). Above that, on the second register from the bottom, are two praying figures, and on the third register from the bottom of the same composite fragment (AO4587 and EŞEM6115) are the remains of one or two stools or thrones (shaped like the sides of the stools seen on the seated statues of Gudea), together with a lion sculpture that is being wheeled to its display location in the shrine on a low trolley. Finally, the rather empty top register shows Ningishzida escorting Gudea towards an unknown deity who is not represented (EŞEM6087, EŞEM6089 and EŞEM12383).

Finally, the music stele (Fig. 227), as it is here referred to, features three tall registers, each with a height of 0.51 m, that are separated by thick dividing bands with heights of about 10 cm each. Lacking perimetric margins, the total height of the stele is therefore approximately 1.73 m, and its width to

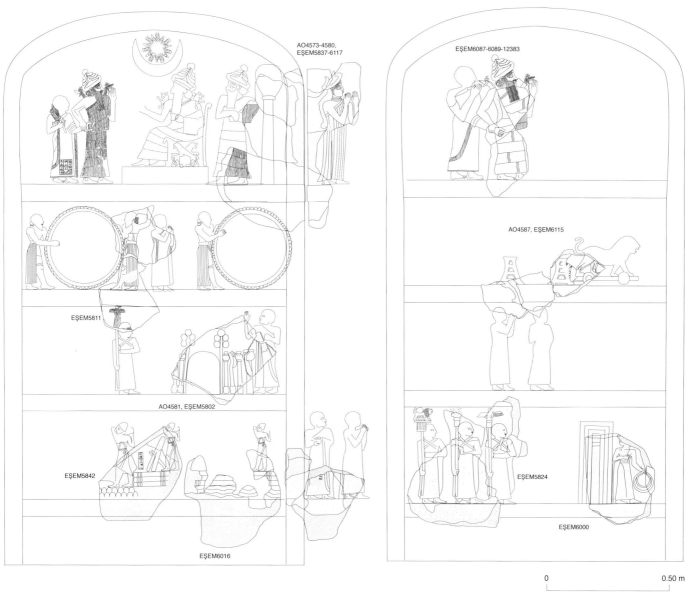

FIGURE 226. Reconstruction of a two-sided Gudea Stele.

height ratio is about 1:1.5. The subject of the relief is taken from a large fragment (AO52) that extends over three registers. Suter (2000, pp. 184–5) doubts whether this impressive survival (the largest single fragment found on Tell A) can be attributed to the Gudea Steles on account of (in her view) its crude carving and the exceptional height of the registers, as well as the unusual portrayal of the possible ruler figure on the associated edge, where he is seen wearing a beard. It has nevertheless been included here, partly on account of its subject, which is typical of comparable Sumerian artefacts (notably the Standard of Ur), and also because

of its find location on Tell A, close to gate M, where it was unearthed by Sarzec. The lower register shows a right-facing figure with clasped hands in front of a right-facing musician (identified as a woman by Heuzey (Sarzec and Heuzey 1912, pp. 219–20)), who is playing a lyre with eleven strings. The front of the instrument's soundbox seems to be decorated with a bull's head that might be turned slightly towards the viewer (as noted by Heuzey), and another complete bull statuette (proportionally smaller than the head) stands on top of the resonator, where it supports a vertical post that holds the crossbar over which the strings are stretched. The

628 The Mound of the Palace

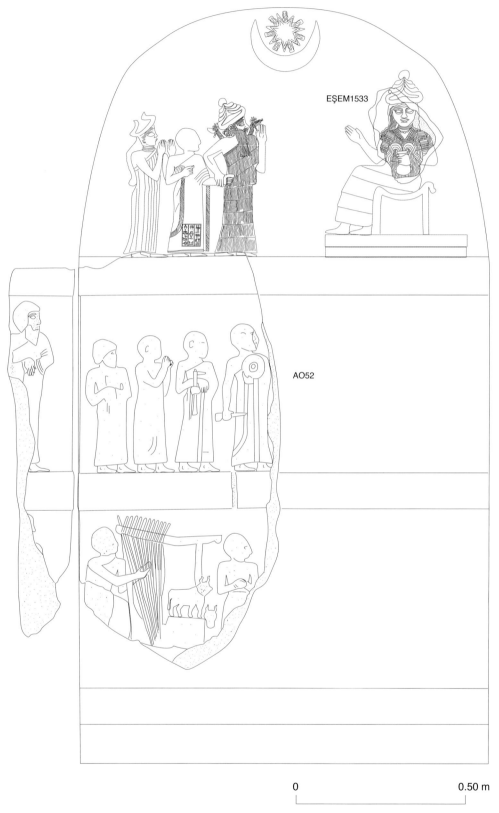

FIGURE 227. Reconstruction of the Gudea Stele referred to as the music stele.

second register from the bottom features a procession of a further four right-facing figures, led by a shaven-headed man (perhaps Gudea), who holds a coiled rope close to his chest in his left hand, and in his right he carries a surveying peg. Closely following him is a man carrying a pickaxe or an adze, and behind him is a third figure whose hands are clasped together in front of his chin. Unlike the front three figures, who are all bald and beardless, the fourth member of the group appears to have a short pointed beard and a thick head of hair (unless he is wearing a hat). He has his hands clasped at his waist in a gesture comparable with that used on the Gudea statues. The edge of the fragment includes the over-sized man with a beard mentioned above, while the bottom of the uppermost register on the main face (on the same frag-ment, above the dividing band) shows three sets of human

feet, also facing right. The culminating scene at the top of the carving features Gudea (with an attendant behind him) being led by Ningishzida into the presence of an enthroned goddess, probably Bau, who is holding an overflowing ves-sel (EŞEM1533). The size of the depicted goddess is propor-tionate to the other figures on this reconstruction, but it is not clear whether the thickness of the fragment correlates well with the other pieces used (even though, as mentioned above, the presumed thicknesses of a great many of the pieces cannot be entirely relied upon). Nonetheless, like AO52, frag-ment EŞEM1533 was also found close to gate M at the top of Tell A, and this might help to confirm the association. The top register of the reconstruction is completed with a sun and a crescent moon.

CHAPTER 42

The Bricks of the New Eninnu

THE NUMBER OF BRICKS THAT WERE USED IN THE construction of the New Eninnu is staggering to contemplate. The representative calculations are contained in Table 8, which shows the amounts that were laid to build the parts of the walls that were excavated by the British Museum team between 2016 and 2022. These relatively short and low expanses of uncovered brickwork (some of which include thicker foundation footings and narrower upper parts) make it possible to estimate fairly accurately the approximate number of square bricks that were required per metre of wall generally, taking into account the walls' respective thicknesses and heights. In Table 9 the findings are applied to the New Eninnu as a whole, with estimates of the lengths, thicknesses and heights of the many walls made using a combination of empirical data and inferences based on the British Museum team's plan of the complex (Fig. 139). The final figure of 1,445,049 square bricks does not deal separately with the many rectangular half-bricks that were needed (as detailed below), or the bricks used to make smaller features of the complex, including display platforms and offering tables, for example. Nor does it estimate the huge quantities of bricks that were used to consolidate, expand and raise the mound in the preconstruction phase, but it does include fired and unfired bricks. Their manufacture implies the need for a veritable army of clay diggers, brickmakers and assistants, straw cutters, water carriers, kiln operatives and transport personnel, while another army of bricklayers (probably including master builders who were trained to interpret the plans of the walls, towers, buttresses, gates, passageways and other features), hod carriers and mortar mixers would have been active directly on the site.

Given the extreme importance of clay bricks in the building of Gudea's Eninnu, as in Sumerian culture at large and throughout its history, it is little wonder that so much care was taken over the manufacture of the very first example, which was made by Gudea himself, in conformity with long-standing traditions, and meticulously following the instructions given to him in his dream vision. As described in the Cylinder Inscriptions, precious substances were added to the batch of clay from which this particular brick was made, and music was played to accompany the fabrication ceremony, which was a joyful public occasion (A18–19):

He poured clear water into the . . . of the brick mould—adab, sim and ala drums were playing for the ruler. He prepared the excavated earth for making (?) the brick, and hoed honey, ghee and precious oil into it. He worked balsam (?) and essences from all kinds of trees into the paste. He lifted up the holy carrying-basket and put it next to the brick mould. Gudea placed the clay into the brick mould and acted exactly as prescribed, bringing the first brick of the house into existence in it, while all the bystanders sprinkled oil or cedar perfume. His city and the land of Lagash spent the day with him in joy.

The New Eninnu was conceived and executed on an altogether massive scale, and it is little wonder that, in the Cylinder Inscriptions, the finished complex is more than once compared to a mountain, for example in a passage in the middle of the text (B1): 'The house is a great mountain reaching up to the skies'. Furthermore, as noted in Chapter 34, the names of Gudea's seventh to tenth regnal years suggest that the project might have been finished in just four years, from the manufacture of the mould for the first brick in Gudea's seventh regnal year ('the year the brick mould was made') to the completion of the sanctuary in the tenth year ('the year the temple of Ningirsu was built'). Moreover, the description of events in the Cylinder Inscriptions (A13) implies that the brick mould in which the first brick was formed was created at the very beginning of the project, before the ground was ritually prepared by the citizens of Lagash (A13–14), before taxes were collected to pay for the project (A14), and before vast quantities of more exotic materials were sourced from abroad (A15–16).

The account of the making of the brick mould for the first brick, which is one of the preliminary steps Gudea takes when he starts to plan and build the complex, raises some fascinating questions. He begins by taking a young goat, on which he performs a divination. The text does not say whether the procedure was an extispicy, and nor does it give any hint as to what precisely the ruler was looking for, but there is no doubt that the omens were favourable because Gudea then goes on to design and make the mould before using it to manufacture an initial sacred brick (A13):

> In respect of the . . . of the brick-mould he had a kid lie down, and he requested from the kid an omen about the brick. He looked at the excavated earth (?) approvingly, and the shepherd, called by his name by Nanshe . . . it with majesty. After making a drawing on the . . . of the brick mould and . . . the excavated earth with majesty, he made the Anzu bird, the standard of his master, glisten there as a banner.

The text is doubtless a little obscure, but the single brick that Gudea apparently made with the mould was clearly marked with a Thunderbird motif. No information is given about what happened to this brick, but the fact that it seems to have turned out well presumably confirmed that the mould was fit for purpose: sacramentally cured, as it were, and ready for use during the public ceremony of the moulding of the first brick that was to come later. Again, the text says nothing about where the mould was subsequently stored (though as a religious object of the first order it must have been very carefully looked after), but it subsequently reappears, just before

Gudea performs the brick-making ritual, when he seemingly heads a procession in which the 'holy basket and true fated brick mould' (A18–19) are brought to the place where the rite is celebrated (there is a slight lacuna in the text at this point, but this seems to be the meaning). The words 'true' and 'fated', which are used to describe the object, indicate that this particular mould has confirmed its sacred worth (it is 'true' in the sense of being the precise one that has been shown to be fitting and correct) and it has also passed the necessary divinatory tests that were carried out by Gudea earlier (in which sense it is 'fated').

In a society in which so much weight was placed on propitious omens, it makes sense to read that the rightness of the brick mould was formally established before the lavish state ceremony because any hiccup in the proceedings at that latter stage could presumably have been viewed as a disastrous setback for the whole enterprise. The further interesting consequence is that the crucial brick that was manufactured on that second momentous occasion was actually not the first brick to come from the mould, but the first brick from the 'true fated' mould to be laid in the building's walls, at the N corner, after Gudea had laid out the N–S axis, as described in the Cylinder Inscriptions (A17). The preordained identity of that epoch-making brick is confirmed by Enlil at the very beginning of the text, even before the narrative of Gudea's dream, when the great god states that he wishes a new temple for his son Ningirsu to be built by Gudea (A1): 'It is for him [Gudea] the fated brick is waiting. It is by him that the building of the holy house is to be done'. The 'fated' brick, as it is also called when Gudea tells his dream to Nanshe (A5), and again when the goddess interprets its meaning for him (A6), was perhaps not a Thunderbird brick—at least no hint of that is given in the text—but rather a more conventional building brick (though made from a mix that included special additives, as noted above), which was in all probability stamped or inscribed with the standard Gudea formula that is considered below. Since it came from the same mould, it would, of course, have been the same shape as the original Thunderbird brick, and since the bricks used to build the New Eninnu were mostly square, it might automatically be assumed that this was also a square brick, but that was not the case. As described in the latter part of this chapter, in order to create a stable bonding pattern for walls made predominantly of square bricks, every other course must begin and end with a row of rectangular half-bricks—but this is only for the simplest of structures, namely a single expanse of wall. Conversely, for reasons that are clarified later, the bricks that form the corners of walls made with square bricks all have to be rectangular in order to create the necessary two-way bonding pattern. This means that the mould that was designed by Gudea (he drew it out before making it, as the text says), and then manufactured in advance of the public ceremony, was rectangular. Consequently, the initial Thunderbird brick and the 'fated' brick that was laid at the temple's N corner were also rectangular (or half-bricks) rather than squares.

This does not definitively mean that no square Thunderbird bricks were made, but any that were produced must have been intended for other purposes, and it might tentatively be thought that Thunderbird bricks were exclusively rectangular. All in all, very few Thunderbird bricks have been recovered from Girsu, and there can be no suggestion that one of them was the very brick that Gudea is said to have made to test and consecrate the mould, but the extant examples are nevertheless intriguing. A rectangular Thunderbird brick (AO398) was found by Sarzec at some point prior to 1881 (the year in which it was accessioned by the Louvre), and could therefore have come from Tell A, but no information about its provenance was documented. It is assumed from its appearance to be archaic, perhaps Early Dynastic (as mentioned above in Chapter 1), and this seems to be further confirmed by its preserved dimensions of 0.3 m (l) × 0.185 m (w) × 0.06 cm (t), which are close to those of the bricks used by Ur-Nanshe (for which see Chapter 10). It is also presumably too wide to be a standard Gudea rectangular brick or half-brick because their maximum width must have been about 0.16 m (half the width of a standard Gudea square brick with sides of 0.32 m). The British Museum team found five more Thunderbird bricks (TG77, TG1202, TG1685, TG2965 and TG3239), all of which appear to have been rectangular, but sadly none of them came from good archaeological contexts (Fig. 228). One possible exception is a brick (TG1685) that was found in a Hellenistic context on Tell A and could therefore have originated in the New Eninnu, but the paucity of the evidence makes it impossible to reach such a conclusion with any confidence.

The rectangular shape of the 'true fated' brick mould is a matter of some consequence because the brick that Gudea made with it in the ritual of the manufacture of the first brick was the unitary starting point for the entire construction—the seed, so to speak, from which the whole complex grew. It is a matter of profound regret that the N corner of the Ningirsu temple, which was exposed during the course of the British Museum team's excavations, had been truncated by a Hellenistic pit that destroyed the original brickwork at the momentous starting point. Even if it had been feasible to dismantle the surviving parts of the walls in that area, therefore, it would not have been possible to retrieve the first brick. As argued in Chapter 14, however, rectangles seem to have been regarded as a primary shape in Sumerian

FIGURE 228. The rectangular Thunderbird bricks found by the British Museum team.

geometrical thinking because they were associated with the way temples were laid out with respect to celestially determined axes. Consequently, though Gudea mostly built with square bricks, the fact that the first brick that was laid at the N corner of the Ningirsu temple had to be rectangular might indicate that the complex was, of necessity, begun in a way that consciously respected the long-standing Sumerian principle that apparently prioritised rectangles over squares.

The vast majority of the bricks used in the New Eninnu, whether square or rectangular, were unfired. The baked bricks (square and rectangular, inscribed and uninscribed) were used for particular features of the fabric of the complex, including the façades of the substructural platforms (as evidenced by the finds made by Cros in the area between Tells A and B—for which see Chapter 23), the Gate of Gudea (exposed first by Sarzec and then by Cros, as also described in Chapter 23), the foundation boxes (which seem usually to have been incorporated into the thick brickwork of the Gudea walls rather than being buried underneath them, as detailed in Chapter 34) and the floors and passageways. With respect to the paved ground surfaces, it should be stressed again that no original brick pavements deriving from the reign of Gudea survived because the fired bricks that were used to tile the walkways were salvaged and reused during subsequent renovations of the New Eninnu in the Ur III and Isin-Larsa periods, before being retrieved in the fourth century BCE by Adadnadinakhe, who incorporated them into his Hellenistic shrine (see Chapter 46). It is also worth observing that the preserved examples of fired half-size Gudea bricks were not simply cut by the bricklayers but rather made in separate moulds—as the Thunderbird brick and the first brick were. The fact that they were moulded is evidenced by the small ridge that runs all the way round their perimeters, which was created when the moulds were slid upwards to release the shaped raw clay, as is discussed further below. Since the unbaked half-bricks found in the walls during the British Museum team's excavations were compacted and therefore not well preserved, it is impossible to say conclusively whether they were made in dedicated rectangular moulds or cut on site, but their importance—indeed, the fact that in a strict sense they notionally took priority over the square bricks—together with the sheer numbers that were required, might tend to suggest that both square and rectangular bricks (or half-bricks) were moulded, but that cannot be confirmed (as is also considered further below).

By comparison with the much more common square Gudea bricks, very few half-bricks were inscribed, but it should also be repeated that the vast majority of the bricks used in the New Eninnu were square, and the weight of numbers must play a role in this observation. According to Sarzec and Heuzey (1912, pp. 27), the inscriptions on the bricks that were retrieved from the Gate of Gudea (DEGH and FIJ on Heuzey's New Plan) were always found facing upwards. Similarly, the bricks that were used to build the sides and bases of the foundation boxes were laid with their texts facing upwards, but the inscriptions on the oversized capping bricks that formed the covers of the boxes were placed face down. Since none of the numerous bricks that were used to form the various pavements were found *in situ*, it is not known whether they were laid with their texts facing up or down, but it might be logical to assume that the inscribed sides were placed face down so that the words were not visible, meaning users of the complex did not have to tread directly on the names of Ningirsu, Gudea and the Eninnu, all of which were included in the inscriptions.

In view of the astronomical number of bricks that had to be manufactured, it is unsurprising to find that most of the bricks that contained texts were stamped, even though others were clearly inscribed by hand. Furthermore, and for reasons that are not clear, two texts were applied to them: Gudea's Standard Inscription plus a variant, and this necessitated the use of two distinct stamps. Almost all the bricks that carry the standard text commemorating Gudea's construction of the New Eninnu (RIME 3.1.1.7.37) seem to have been made with a single stamp, while only a handful of retrieved examples were clearly marked with a second implement. What is referred to as the Standard Inscription for the New Eninnu (RIME 3.1.1.7.37) was found on inscribed objects as well as bricks, and it is by far the most common of all the preserved Gudea inscriptions:

> For Ningirsu, mighty warrior of Enlil, Gudea, ruler of Lagash, made everything function as it should. He built for him his Eninnu, the White Thunderbird, and restored it to its (proper) place.

Found in huge numbers, this is the best-attested inscription in all of cuneiform literature. Indeed, there are more preserved examples of this text than of all the other surviving Lagash II building inscriptions put together, and even of all known Lagash II and Ur III building inscriptions combined. This is partly a matter-of-fact result of the particular sites at which extensive excavations have been carried out, but it is probably also a consequence of the size of the Gudea complex and the quantity of bricks that were needed to build it, though whether the frequency of the Standard Gudea Inscription is in reality unusually high cannot be determined unequivocally due to the lack of comparative evidence. The variant text (RIME 3.1.1.7.41), which is closely related to the Standard Inscription, is also well attested on bricks and on various kinds of objects. It differs from the Standard Inscription only in its inclusion of an expression that explicitly hails Ningirsu as Gudea's master, while the presence of the dative suffix in the standard version of the two texts (RIME 3.1.1.7.37) shows that the variant was a deliberate choice rather than a simple error or an ellipsis. It reads:

> For Ningirsu, mighty warrior of Enlil, his lord, Gudea, ruler of Lagash, made everything function as it should. He built for him his Eninnu, the White Thunderbird, and restored it to its (proper) place.

The significance of the small difference between the two texts is unclear, but the wording of the Standard Inscription closely follows the usual text used by Ur-Bau to commemorate his construction of the older Ningirsu temple, the only difference being the removal of Ur-Bau's epithet and the replacement of his name with Gudea's (RIME 3.1.1.6.4): 'Ur-Bau, ruler of Lagash, child born of Ninagala, made things function as they should, (and) he built and restored for him his Eninnu, the White Thunderbird'. The standard Ur-Bau building inscription does not refer to Ningirsu as the ruler's lord or master, but that addition is found on another Ur-Bau text that relates to the construction of Ur-Bau's Ningirsu shrine—the inscription on the diorite statue from Tell A (AO9), where Ur-Bau (speaking in the first person) states that he excavated the plot on which the temple was built for 'Ningirsu, my master' (RIME 3.1.1.6.12).

Linguistically, the texts used on the Ur-Bau and Gudea bricks are mostly predictable and common to all Sumerian building inscriptions. The opaque expression níg du₇.e pa mu.na.è ('for him he made everything function as it should') is, however, almost exclusively found in the Ur-Bau and Gudea inscriptions that record the construction of their respective Eninnus. The only exceptions to this are the text that commemorates Gudea's construction of Nanshe's Sirara House in Nigin (RIME 3.1.1.7.25–7) and two other instances of broader interest: the inscription on Statue E, marking Gudea's completion of Bau's temple (known as the Etarsirsir), which was inside the New Eninnu and therefore inextricably linked with the Ningirsu complex (RIME 3.1.1.7.StE), and his construction of Gatumdug's temple in the 'Shining City', as commemorated on Statue F (RIME 3.1.1.7.StF). The latter text, which describes Gudea as Gatumdug's 'beloved slave', who 'made everything function as it should, who built Ningirsu's Eninnu, the White Thunderbird', confirms an extremely close association between the goddess and Ningirsu, and this adds further substance to the argument that Bau and Gatumdug were assimilated during the reign of Gudea, when the two goddesses seem essentially to have been regarded as one and the same. In more concrete terms, the idea of making everything 'function as it should' might refer to some aspect of the ritual procedures that were followed at a very early stage in the construction of a temple, but it might also perhaps relate more generally to the fact that the ruler was able to harness the full resources of the state in order to carry out the commemorated sacred building project, in which sense the society that was founded on the worship of the chief god and the local pantheon was properly governed and worked correctly in accordance with the requirements and commands of the main deity. The cosmic significance of the phrase is further substantiated by its appearance in a slightly modified form in the very first lines of Cylinder A, where it comes after Enlil looks upon Ningirsu with approbation (A1): 'On the day when in heaven and earth the fates had been decided, Lagash raised its head high in full grandeur, and Enlil looked at Lord Ningirsu with approval. In our city everything functioned as it should'. Enlil's reaction to his son, which is fascinatingly communicated with a look rather than a word, affirms the well-being of the universe, and that, in turn, is the catalyst for the divine commissioning of the Eninnu, as Enlil states in the lines that immediately follow.

The broad context sheds some light on the enigmatic phrase that comes at the end of the next sentence in Gudea's Standard Inscription and in his variant: 'He built for him his Eninnu, the White Thunderbird, and restored it to its (proper) place'. The statement that Gudea constructed the New Eninnu is not controversial. It is both a formulaic confirmation of Gudea's historical agency, and also (in this particular instance) an implicit acknowledgement that the ruler executed the instructions that were divinely vouchsafed to him, as detailed in the Cylinder Inscriptions. The wording of the dedication in its entirety was adopted by Gudea from Ur-Bau, while the last part of the sentence, 'and restored it to its (proper) place' (ki.be$_2$ mu.na.gi$_4$ in Sumerian), was seemingly an innovation that was expressly introduced by Ur-Bau, presumably to account for his momentous transfer of the Temple of Ningirsu from its age-old site on Tell K to Tell A. Gudea moved the temple again, when he rebuilt it a little to the south-west of Ur-Bau's old Eninnu, on the site that was formerly occupied by the Temple of Bau (a conclusion confirmed by the British Museum team's findings; see Chapter 33). But Gudea was not merely following a precedent set by his father-in-law. His work was expressly carried out under the aegis of Ningirsu, whose request for a new 'house' was supported by the supreme authority of Enlil (as just noted). In Gudea's case, therefore, the idea of restoring the temple to its 'proper' place would probably indicate that it was being relocated at Ningirsu's behest because the 'proper' place was the one ordained by the warrior god (backed by Enlil). The circumstantial evidence derived from the Cylinder Inscriptions might further intimate that Ur-Bau formerly fulfilled the god's wishes in a similar way, but none of his surviving texts explicitly say that. Nonetheless, the opening lines of Cylinder A, which insinuate that the divine decision to build the New Eninnu was taken when the celestial and terrestrial 'fates' were decided, and after Enlil looks with favour upon Ningirsu, would presumably indicate that the restoration of the temple to its 'proper' place was an affirmation of cosmic well-being.

The inscriptions discovered on the preserved remains of the oversized bricks that were expressly manufactured to act as the lids of foundation boxes are especially interesting. All the boxes were made in the same way, but the best-preserved example (box 2092) was found by the British Museum team in the E corner of tower 2105, in the SW gate of the New Eninnu. It was inserted into the mud-bricks of which the wall was made, and although it had been opened antiquity, when some of its contents (namely, a kneeling god wearing a horned tiara and holding a foundation nail) were presumably removed, it still contained a key element of the foundation deposit: a stone tablet bearing Gudea's Standard Inscription. The cuneiform signs used on the inside covers of the boxes are remarkable for several reasons. When a sign contains a cluster of repeated wedges, such as at the start of DÉ (part of Gudea's name), the cluster always contains four wedges, and the regular use of four strokes per cluster is a characteristic feature of brick stamps and lapidary script (see, for example, TG168). Handwritten instances of such clusters do not display the same degree of regularity. Compared to contemporary inscriptions on clay cones, moreover, four is a relatively low number of wedges to make up an initial cluster. The fact that the writing on the undersides of the foundation box lids is unusually large (each line being between 36 mm and 38 mm high compared to a typical height of between 20 mm and 21 mm for standard bricks) makes the formation of the initial cluster even more noteworthy.

The manner in which the wedges were inscribed onto the foundation box covers also merits attention. The depth of the wedges is constant, as is their width—characteristics that differ markedly from impressed wedges, whose depths and widths are generally tapered. In addition, heads are evident only on some of the wedges, while many wedges appear not to be straight, even though no cause of the distortion is evident. This applies to the wedges of the cuneiform signs and to the line rulings that frame the inscription. The inscription does not therefore appear to have been made by impressing a stylus into moist clay, but nor does it seem to have been made with a stamp (perhaps on account of the large size of the text). Instead—and extraordinarily—the text seems to have been incised into dried clay. Setting aside the idea that this was simply due to bad planning, and taking into account that it would have been possible to add the texts by hand using a stylus, the most likely conclusion is that, for practical or ideological reasons (or perhaps a combination of the two), the dedicatory texts applied to the lids of foundation boxes were conceived of as being analogous to lapidary inscriptions.

Building with Square Bricks

The use of square bricks in post-Akkad Lagash created a special set of difficulties for the planners and bricklayers who worked on the New Eninnu, and they had to solve problems that were quite different from those faced by earlier Sumerian builders. As is well known, the shape of the standard brick that was used by Early Dynastic builders before the Akkad interval was rectangular and planoconvex: its corners were approximately right-angled, and its base and sides were flat, while the top was slightly convex. Why Early Dynastic builders preferred a curved top is not clear, but they presumably felt that it somehow helped the bricks to stick together, using a principle that is the inverse of the one used on many modern bricks, where the top of the brick is formed into a cavity that fills up with mortar when the brick is laid. Perhaps the Early Dynastic builders calculated that the dried or baked bricks were more stable than the clay mortar that was used to stick them together and that it was therefore best to try to maximise the structural load carried by the bricks themselves. The ideal ratio of the brick rectangle's short to long sides is about 1:2, which means a wall made of two rows can be knitted together by placing a single brick perpendicularly over two bricks laid side by side. This points to the clear advantage of rectangular bricks in general: they very easily form bonding patterns, and that is doubtless why the rectangular brick remains the usual unitary building block to the present day. To bind a corner formed of two walls made of single rows of rectangular bricks is simply a matter of turning the last brick perpendicularly with respect to the wall that has just been built, and the resulting thickness (of approximately half a brick in the ideal case) produces overlaps in both directions—a procedure that is evident on almost any modern brick wall. As in all periods of Sumerian history, the Early Dynastic builders sometimes favoured extremely thick walls, which complicate matters considerably, but the principle remains comparable, as was observed at an early stage of the excavations on Tell K by Sarzec. Heuzey's two drawings (1900, p. 9 (Heuzey's Fig. 4), not reproduced here) show one example of how the bricklayers on Tell K laid rectangular planoconvex bricks on the multi-row corners of the Ur-Nanshe Building by elaborating on the basic principle to create binding patterns.

There is an often-stated and long-standing assumption that Early Dynastic builders preferred to lay planoconvex bricks in a herringbone pattern, forming the zigzag shape by placing bricks vertically on their narrow sides, and alternating one or more of these layers with courses of bricks laid flat to provide stability. It may be that this practice was common elsewhere in ancient Sumer, but in Girsu it was seemingly rare. The principal structures on Tell K, for example, including the Lower Construction, as well as the fired-brick walls of the Ur-Nanshe Building and the Enmetena Block, were all built with planoconvex bricks laid flat, as can be seen in the various photos discussed in Chapter 9 above. The same

is true of the smaller installations on Tell K, including the many cisterns (often wholly or partly coated with bitumen), which were also built with bricks laid flat and bonded with more conventional patterns. The notable exception is the shaft of the Well of Eanatum, where the bricks were indeed beautifully laid in a herringbone pattern, with single courses of vertically placed angled bricks alternating with courses of bricks laid flat. According to Sarzec and Heuzey, the walls of the inner sanctum of the Ur-Nanshe Building were constructed of facings of fired bricks laid flat that contained thick cores of mud-bricks laid in a herringbone pattern (see Chapter 5). Unfortunately, the mud-brick cores are not marked on Sarzec's Plan C (1), and the French reports provide no record of whether the herringbone courses were laid flat, vertically or in alternating series.

To lay the square bricks that became standard in Girsu after the Akkad interval presents a much more intricate problem than laying rectangular bricks that readily form repeatable bonding patterns. One distinct manufacturing advantage of the Lagash II bricks used by Ur-Bau and Gudea, however, is that they were flat on both sides. All ancient Sumerian bricks were almost certainly moulded in square or rectangular frames with open tops and bottoms. In order to make a flat brick, the narrow-sided frame would have been laid on the drying ground and filled with wet clay (actually clay mixed with inclusions of straw), which was levelled to the height of the frame with a skimming implement. The excess material could then be returned to the pile of mix, while the frame was lifted up and removed from around the brick, which stayed where it was on the drying ground, presumably separated from the bricks around it by two frame widths: one for the newly made brick and one for each of its neighbours. As mentioned above, the removal of the frame caused the slight ridges on the perimeters of the preserved examples of fired rectangular Gudea bricks, showing that they were deliberately moulded. In due course the finished brick would then have been stamped or otherwise marked and left to dry (for about two weeks for an unbaked brick) before being either taken directly to the building site or fired. Double frames could have made the process quicker, and it is easy to imagine that a small team of three brickmakers (one to prepare the clay mix, one to transport the mix to the manufacturing and drying ground, and one to mould the bricks) could have comfortably made as many as 1,000 bricks a day (120 bricks an hour over eight hours). If this assumption is even broadly correct, it would imply a time span of about four and a half years for one team to make the approximately 1.45 million bricks that were needed for the New Eninnu (as shown in Table 9). Since it is reasonable to assume that several teams were employed, however, the process of producing the necessary bricks can be accounted for. The manufacture of planoconvex bricks was a little more time-consuming because instead of simply skimming off the excess clay, the top of the brick was shaped by hand into a shallow convex curve before eventually being inscribed.

The difficulty that has to be solved when building with square bricks is that they do not easily form bonding patterns because the ratio of their sides is 1:1, so a brick cannot be turned to create a corner or a bond in the way that a rectangular brick can. Take the example of a simple wall of square bricks that is one brick wide and (say) five bricks long (Fig. 229.1). The first course of five bricks and mortar is laid on the prepared ground, one next to another. As any Lego builder knows, the bricks cannot then just be piled on top of each other because the result will be five unstable towers. Instead, the builder must begin the second row with half a brick then lay four full bricks before completing the course with a second half-brick. The third course is then made of five whole bricks, the fourth of a half-brick plus four wholes followed by another half, the fifth of five whole bricks and so on. In this way the vertical joins between the bricks on one course are covered with the middles of whole bricks laid on top to form a binding pattern. In reality, both for symbolic reasons and also because the bonding patterns were an inalienable part of the mode of construction, the bricklayers would probably have preferred to begin the entire process with a rectangular brick, even if they were building just an isolated stretch of wall.

As indicated by the laying of the first brick in the ceremony detailed above, the corners were, of course, the foundational elements of the New Eninnu, and for every one of them the builders had to apply the bonding principle from the very outset, beginning each and every course with a half-brick and continuing with wholes (as on the second and fourth courses of the simple wall described in the previous paragraph). Conversely, if an untrained builder tried to start a corner with a whole brick, they would almost immediately realise that the square bricks in the first two courses of one of the perpendicular façades would not bond. The lack of a bonding pattern would then alternately affect dual courses

of square bricks in each of the two façades, causing instability. To envisage the way the corners were actually formed, consider a building that is to be constructed with its corners facing the cardinal points so that its four outer façades will face north-east, south-east, south-west and north-west, respectively. Beginning with the NW façade, for example, the builder lays a half-brick at the N corner, with one of its angles pointing north and its outer short side facing north-west (Fig. 229.2). The bricklayer then uses whole bricks to extend the NW wall towards the south-west, eventually finishing it at the W corner with another half-brick, the short outer side of which also faces north-west. The SW wall can then be extended from the W corner towards the S corner, where the final brick to be laid, with one of its corners pointing southwards and its outer short side facing south-east, is a half-brick. The SE façade can then be laid using square bricks, again finishing with a half-brick that has one corner pointing towards the east. Finally square bricks are used to complete the NE wall, finishing at the first rectangular brick that was laid in the N corner. The N corner is then built up by beginning the second course of the NW façade with a half-brick that is laid so that its corner points north and its outer short side faces north-east (Fig. 229.3). This establishes the bonding pattern for the façades as in the simple wall outlined above, with the middles of the whole bricks in the second course covering the vertical joins between the bricks below. Successive courses can then begin at the N corner, with half-bricks whose short outer sides face successively north-west and north-east (Fig. 229.4). Since every course that is begun with a half-brick must also finish with one, the other corners will automatically be formed of alternating half-bricks. In practice, it means that in each course only two parallel walls will begin and end with half-bricks, which, in the example given, means: the NW and SE façades in the first course, the NE and SW in the second, the NW and SE in the third, the NE and SW in the fourth and so on.

Irrespective of whether they were built with rectangular or square bricks, ancient Sumerian walls on prestige buildings were often extremely thick for the clear reason that they did not have buried foundations, but were built on the ground surface and were therefore stabilised solely by their own weight and thickness. The walls forming the Temple of Ningirsu in Gudea's New Eninnu, for example, were made up of approximately seven rows, though the use of foundation footings meant that the bases of the walls were in many

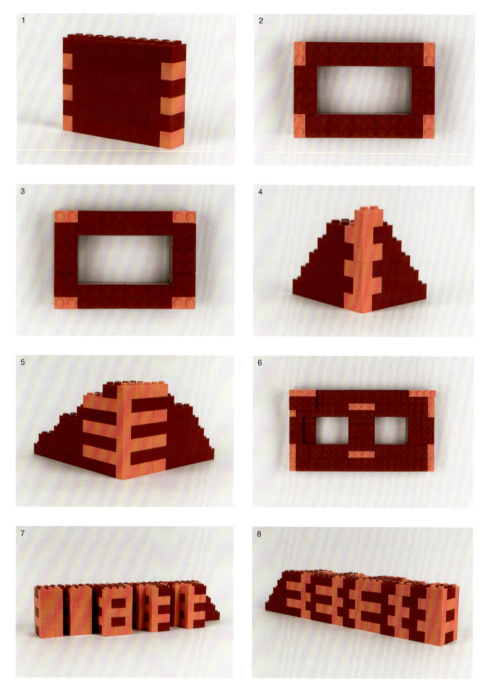

FIGURE 229. Models of structures built with square bricks (red) and rectangular half-bricks (pink): 1. Bonding pattern for a self-standing wall built with a single row of square bricks; 2. The first course of a simple rectangular structure, showing the half-bricks in the corners; 3. The second course of the same rectangular structure, showing the opposed half-bricks in the corners; 4. Bonding pattern at the corner of a structure built with a single row of square bricks; 5. Bonding pattern at the corner of a structure built with three rows of square bricks; 6. Bonding pattern for a partition wall keyed into two main walls, where every other course of the partition begins and ends with half-bricks, such that the course of the partition above the one shown in the model would be finished with whole bricks; 7. Possible bonding pattern used to build the Gate of Gudea, showing the intricate combinations of square bricks and rectangular half-bricks; 8. The Gate of Gudea reconstruction seen from behind.

cases thicker than their upper sections. The corners of such substantial walls were built in exactly the same way as the simple façades just described, except that the parallel walls in successive courses (NW and SE then NE and SW in the example just given) all began and finished with the same number of half-bricks as were used to make up the thickness of the wall—as in Fig. 229.5, which shows a representative corner formed of two walls, each with a thickness of three bricks. One consequence of this is that the builders needed a great many half-bricks: approximately 560 for each of the corners of the Gudea's innermost Ningirsu temple (assuming the walls were seven bricks thick and 8 m high and that each metre of height was made up of approximately eleven or twelve courses of bricks, including mortar). As noted above, the rectangular half-bricks, in particular the fired ones, were almost certainly specially moulded, but in case of shortfalls it would also have been possible for the bricklayers to cut whole bricks into two halves (perhaps by first scoring them with a blade of some kind and then simply snapping them). It would clearly have been undesirable for the bricklayers to cut inscribed bricks, but only the fired bricks contained texts, and not all of them were actually inscribed or stamped. If the bricklayers did indeed sometimes cut unmarked square bricks as and when they were needed, that might also help to explain the relative infrequency of rectangular bricks with texts. Unfortunately, as noted previously, it is impossible to be sure whether or not the unbaked half-bricks were moulded because the mud-brickwork inevitably becomes compacted over time, making it extremely difficult to judge the profile of individual bricks.

A further issue that arises is whether the builders bonded the adjacent rows of thick walls, and the answer seems to be that they generally did not. It would have been possible to create a bond by systematically or sporadically interspersing sets of half-bricks along the length of the wall, away from the corners. It should also be remembered that half-bricks used in this way (even if they were used on entire courses) would not be distinguishable from full bricks on the walls' outer and inner faces, so the only way for an archaeologist to know precisely how a wall was constructed would be to take it apart (not forgetting that the state of preservation, particularly of mud-brick walls, inevitably creates uncertainty). The short sides of the half-bricks used at the corners would be visible when seen on unplastered walls from outside the building, but otherwise there would be no detectable difference between the kinds of bricks used in the lengths of the façades. The evidence of the two-row Ur-Bau wall uncovered on Tell A (Fig. 121), where whole bricks can be seen side by side, is that the adjacent rows of bricks that made up thicker walls were probably not bonded, which also seems to be demonstrated by the British Museum team's plans and photos of the brickwork in and around Gudea's Ningirsu temple (see Fig. 139). In any event, the bricks and mortar, which were made of almost exactly the same materials, tended to settle into a homogeneous mass over time, and further stability could be added by plastering (and periodically replastering) the walls, usually with mud plaster, but sometimes with lime cement or bitumen.

The Ur-Bau remains are also interesting for the insight they give into the construction of buttress-like protrusions and partition walls. Sarzec's photo (Fig. 121) shows the interior of the base of the Ur-Bau platform on Tell A, which was formed of a fired-brick shell that was filled with mud-bricks. Two anchoring structures can be seen: one in the foreground and one further away in the background. These almost certainly did not extend across the entire width of the fired-brick casing, but rather acted as relatively compact supports. Nonetheless, they were built into the side walls, using the same method as for the simple wall described above, with half-bricks alternating with full bricks at the ends of successive courses to create the bonding pattern. As can be seen in the photo, it seems that the buttress was begun with half-bricks laid on alternate courses of the innermost row of bricks in the main walls to create a key pattern in which every other course of the inner buttress was built into the perpendicular outer wall. A partition or dividing wall would have been constructed in exactly the same way, by extending the keyed-in wall across the width of the building and bonding it into the inside of the facing wall by finishing every other course with half-bricks in the usual way (Fig. 229.6). As can be imagined in the case of the Ur-Bau wall, which is just two bricks thick, it would have been possible to start a partition wall or buttress with a half-brick laid on the outermost row of the building's façade, so that the partition was effectively built through (or knitted into) the entire thickness of the wall, but since that was not done in this very simple case, it seems reasonable to suppose that it was probably not the usual procedure for extremely thick walls. The assumption is probably also supported by the British Museum team's plan of the partition walls in Gudea's Ningirsu temple (Fig. 139).

640   The Mound of the Palace

TABLE 8. The approximate number of Gudea square bricks used in the sections of walls excavated during the British Museum Team's soundings.
The calculations, which are performed for square bricks, do not deal separately with the many rectangular bricks that were used, so the absolute numbers of manufactured units, including squares and rectangles, would have been greater than those given below and in Table 9. Wall context numbers refer to Fig. 139. Wall measurements in the central column are approximate. The number of square bricks in each section of wall is shown in the column on the right. The usual measurements of Gudea square bricks are 0.32 m × 0.32 m × 0.07 m (t), but an additional 17 mm has been factored into the dimensions to account for the mortar bondings (as explained in Chapter 39).

The Temple of Ningirsu: The Façades and Partition Walls		
Built Structures	**Dimensions**	**No. of Bricks**
The NE Façade		
Wall 2008	5.2 m (l) × 2.2 m (w) × 0.52 m (h)	602
Wall 2017	3.45 m (l, including foundation footing) × 2.7 m (w) × 0.3 m (max. h)	283
Wall 2048	3.72 m (l, including large foundation footing) × 2.98 m (w) × 0.15 m (max. h)	168
Wall 2140	Lower section with foundation footing: 5.5 m (l) × 2.75 m (w) × 0.5 m (h)	2,046
	Upper section: 5.5 m (l) × 2.3 m (w) × 1 m (approx. h)	
The SE Façade		
Wall 2139	Lower section with foundation footing: 12.64 m (l) × 2.9 m (w) × 0.5 m (h)	4,797
	Upper section: 12.64 m (l) × 2.3 m (w) × 1 m (max. h)	
The SW Façade		
Wall 2068	Lower section with foundation footing: 12.08 m (l) × 3.05 m (w) × 0.5 m (h)	3,251
	Upper section: 12.08 m (l) × 2.35 m (w) × 0.35 m (h)	
Wall 2159	10.3 m (l) × 2.3 m (w) × 1 m (max. h)	2,398
The NW Façade		
Wall 2003	4.8 m (l) × 2.3 m (w) × 0.65 m (max. h)	726
Wall 3011	5.57 m (l) × 2.33 m (w) × 0.77 m (max. h)	1,011
The NW Partition Wall between the Cella and the Antecella		
Wall 3026	13.3 m (l, including foundation footing) × 3.5 m (w) × 0.46 m (avg. h)	2,167
The SE Partition Wall between the Antecella and the Stairwell		
Wall 2160	8.5 m (l, including foundation footing) × 2.75 m (w) × 0.6 m (max. h)	1,419
Wall 2162	Lower Section: 1.6 m (l) × 2.75 m (max. w) × 0.5 m (h)	558
	Upper Section: 1.6 m (l) × 2.3 m (w) × 0.9 m (h)	
Passageway Threshold	1.15 m (l) × 2.75 m (w) × 0.5 m (h)	160
Installations in the Temple's Inner Rooms		
Offering platform 3039	3.55 m (l) × 2.95 m (w) × 0.36 m (h)	382
Podium 2073	2.09 m (l) × 1.66 m (w) × 0.65 (h)	228
Display platform 2035	6.89 m (l) × 2.30 m (w) × 0.6 m (approx. h)	962
The NW Inner Wall and the Inner Gate		
Wall 2001	4.8 m (l) × 2.3 m (w) × 0.26 m (h)	291
Wall 3006	9.7 m (l) × 2.3 m (w) × 1.13 m (max. h)	2,552
The SW Inner Enveloping Wall		
Wall 3049 and 2032	5.75 m (l) × 2.3 m (w) × 0.7 m (h)	937
Wall 2031	20 m (l) × 2.3 m (w) × 0.4 m (h)	1,862

TABLE 8. (*continued*)

The Temple of Ningirsu: The Façades and Partition Walls		
Built Structures	**Dimensions**	**No. of Bricks**
The L-Shaped Complex: The Temenos Gates and Walls		
SW Wall 2058 and 2031	35 m (l) × 4 m (w) × 0.5 m (h)	7,085
SE Wall 2137	5.51 m (l) × 4 m (w) × 0.97 m (h)	2,164
Passageway Threshold in the SW Gate 2057	4 m (l) × 1.15 m (w) × 0.5 m (h)	233
Tower 3060	6.9 m (l) × 5.53 m (w) × 0.3 (h)	1,159
Tower 2105	7.35 m (l) × 5.51 m (w) × 0.3 (h)	1,230
NE Wall 5002 and 5237	11.8 m (l) × 4 m (w) × 0.4 m (h)	2,455
Tower 5245	6.3 m (l) × 5.5 m (w) × 0.7 m (h)	1,911

TABLE 9. The estimated number of Gudea square bricks used in the New Eninnu in its entirety. These calculations, which are extrapolated from the figures given in Table 8 above, do not include the bricks used to build display platforms, offering tables and other internal features. Nor do they take into account the astronomical number of additional bricks that were used to establish the upper and lower foundational terrace platforms on which the New Eninnu was built.

The New Eninnu		
Built Structures	**Dimensions**	**No. of Bricks**
The Temenos Walls	282 m (l) × 4 m (w) × 6 m (h)	684,985
Thirteen Towers (each measuring)	4 m (l) × 4 m (w) × 8 m (h)	168,415
Twelve Buttresses (each measuring)	4 m (l) × 3 m (w) × 6 m (h)	87,444
The Inner Walls	65 m (l) × 2.3 m (w) × 6 m (h)	90,785
The Ningirsu Temple Walls (incl. 26 m of partition walls)	111 m (l) × 2.3 m (w) × 8 m (h)	206,710
The Bau Temple and Annexes (estimated total as for the Temple of Ningirsu)	111 m (l) × 2.3 m (w) × 8 m (h)	206,710
Total		**1,445,049**

The same method as was used to create the Ur-Bau internal buttresses and any partition walls, namely by beginning alternating courses with half-bricks, would also have been used to form the protruding towers and stepped recesses that are characteristic of the structures built by Gudea. The square or rectangular towers were built with very simple patterns, but the more elaborate sets of deeper and shallower buttress-like stepped recesses were much more complicated, though the intricacies are perhaps not apparent in the photos of the surviving façades (for example, Sarzec's Pl. 50 (1 and 2); Figs. 118 and 119) because, as noted above, from the outside it is difficult to tell the difference between the whole and half-bricks that were used to create stable bonded structures (see Fig. 229.7 and 229.8). If the assumption is correct that the adjacent rows that make up thick walls were not usually bonded internally then it may be that the towers and buttresses on the temenos walls, which seem to have been principally aesthetic features of the Gudea complex, were originally thought of in order to add extra stability to the mass of mud-bricks of which the main façades of buildings were formed. It should also be borne in mind that they were placed on the outer surfaces of walls that (in the case of the New Eninnu's temenos) had a total thickness of about 4 m. That said, however, the very elaborate brickwork that formed the ceremonial Gate of Gudea, reconstructed in Fig. 229.7 and 229.8, does appear to have been bonded all the way through the thickness of the structure. This can be seen in the interesting photo taken by Cros (Fig. 130), which seems to show the finished end of one of the stretches of buttressed wall that made up the monumental partition wall that separated the Ningirsu temple from the rest of the New Eninnu.

Finally, any display podiums, including the one for the statue of the god in the cella in the Ningirsu temple, that were bonded to the inner sides of the façades would have been keyed into their respective back walls using the same principle, so that alternate courses were started and finished with half-bricks. The slight exception to this was for any structures (notably including some of the self-contained foundation boxes that were not keyed into other walls) that might have had one or more sides whose lengths were formed of a number of square bricks plus a half-brick. In these cases, for obvious reasons, the half-bricks were used either at the beginning or at the end of every course, and not at the beginnings and ends of alternate courses, as in the previous example.

CHAPTER 43

The Inscribed Clay Nails of the New Eninnu

A TOTAL OF TWENTY-EIGHT INSCRIBED TERRACOTTA cones, or clay nails as they should more properly be called, were found *in situ* in the brickwork of the New Eninnu during the excavations carried out by the British Museum team between 2016 and 2021 (Fig. 230). The number of examples, together with the fact that they were found in what is reasonably presumed to be their intended locations, increases their significance considerably because this is the largest cache of deposited Sumerian cones that has been discovered in recent times. As is considered further below, comparable objects were found *in situ* during older excavations, notably the ones found by Sir Leonard Woolley in Ur, but the recovery of the cones deposited in the walls of the New Eninnu provides an opportunity to reconsider the placement and function of such objects in exceptional detail.

Apart from a single cone (TG1602) that was found in the NE wall of the roofed passage in the SW gate, the other twenty-seven found by the British Museum team were all placed in the walls of the open-air ambulatories that encircled the Ningirsu temple at the heart of the sacred complex. Seven were placed in the temple's exterior façades (two in the SE wall (TG3539 and TG3540), three in the SW wall (TG1603, TG2635 and TG2636) and two in the NW wall (TG372 and TG373)); four were found in the inner (temple-side) face of the NW wall (3006) that ran across the complex from the south-west to the north-east, forming the NW side of the ambulatory around the Ningirsu temple and separating the most sacred structure from the rest of the complex (TG374, TG375, TG376 and TG378); twelve were found in the inner NE face of the SW envelope wall that was built inside the SW

façade of the L-shaped enclosure, where it followed the line of Ur-Bau's precursor temenos and formed the outer SW side of the SW ambulatory around Gudea's Ningirsu temple—ten in contexts 3049 and 2032 (TG984, TG2640, TG2639, TG985, TG986, TG982, TG987, TG2676, TG3533 and TG3532), and two in 2031 (TG979 and TG2637); and lastly, four were found in the NE wall (2059) associated with the inner porch of the SW gate—a wall that formed part of the NE façade of the SW ambulatory (TG980, TG1604, TG983 and TG981).

Some potentially significant information about the cones can be derived even from this unelaborated summary of their placements. None were found inside the Ningirsu temple itself, in the interior walls (including the partition walls) of the cella, antecella and stairway. Instead, they were uncovered in the brickwork that formed the ambulatory space around the sanctum sanctorum, except for the additional one that was in the SW gate passage, but this covered walkway gave access to the encircling corridors and might therefore have been conceptually associated with them. The recovered clay nails were therefore overwhelmingly situated in open-air settings, and they seem to have formed a type of symbolic crown or cordon around the holiest rooms.

It is also noteworthy that no clay nails were found in the external façades of the L-shaped complex. Nails placed in the temenos walls would, of course, have been vulnerable at all periods on many counts: they might have been accidentally damaged or lost, and they could easily have been removed, perhaps by thieves, for instance. Any deposited clay nails might additionally have been broken or gone missing during the extensive rebuilding that was carried out in the Isin-Larsa

643

FIGURE 230. A clay nail inscribed in the name of Gudea, seen *in situ* in the inner envelope wall (2031).

period, followed much later by the Hellenistic levelling that was overseen by Adadnadinakhe. Similarly, the trenches dug by Sarzec and his successors could have caused further losses, especially from the SW and NE enclosure walls, which, as a result of the French excavations, were preserved to lower heights than some of the other walls investigated by the British Museum team. Nonetheless, in view of the emphatic use of the artefacts in the ambulatory corridors, in spaces around the sanctum sanctorum, the lack of nails in the sanctuary's external walls should in all likelihood be taken as a sign of the greater sanctity of the inner walls. Furthermore, when assessing the relative sacredness of the inner walls, it should be recalled that, on at least three sides, the temple was definitively separated from the temenos: on the SW side it was protected by the interposed envelope wall; on its NW side, where it faced the main courtyard and the extended NW end of the complex, it was also screened by a double layer of walls; and on the NE side it was again not directly adjacent to the temenos, but was instead fronted by the plaza containing the old Ur-Bau shrine, except in the NE corner of the ambulatory corridor, but there the wall was doubled such that the innermost spaces were again isolated from the inside face of the temenos. The exception was the temple's SE side, but this end of the structure was occupied by the stairway passage that led up to the roof—effectively a kind of hallowed service area—and this ensured there was a distance of about 9 m (including the width of the SE ambulatory) between the SE wall of the antecella and the inside face of the SE temenos wall.

The heights at which the clay nails were installed adds further information that should be understood in the context of the ground level of the New Eninnu, which was found at a narrow range of topographical heights of between 15 m and 15.1 m—the recorded height of the newly raised upper surface of the mound on which Gudea's walls were directly built. On top of that were the subfloor packings (with a thickness of about 0.5 m) that raised the Gudea floor horizon to a height of about 15.5 m, while the cones were found in the preserved sections of the Gudea walls at a range of heights between 15.7 m and 16.49 m. Importantly, therefore, with the floor horizon at about 15.5 m, and since no cone deposits were found below the height of 15.7 m, it can be concluded with some confidence that clay nails were not inserted in the foundation sections of the walls, and none were buried under the floors.

In terms of their placement in the brickwork, twelve nails were unequivocally fitted into the bedding joints of the mud-brick courses, either in the flat layers of mortar between the courses or in the vertical joints (the perpends) between adjacent bricks; four cones were clearly inserted in the corners of the bricks themselves (not in the mortar between bricks); while the positioning of the other twelve cones with respect to the bricks and mortar could not be positively determined. The four cones that were found in the corners of bricks (not in the mortar) must unquestionably have been installed after the walls were built, and this seems to have been the case for all the recovered cones. The conclusion is further confirmed by the example that was uncovered in the inner passage of the SW gate, where mud plaster was used to fix the single retrieved cone into a hole that was evidently carved or drilled into the wall for that express purpose, after which the wall must then have been refinished. This is also consistent with the evidence provided by cone TG373 (found in the external face of the temple's NW wall), which left an imprint of its inscription in the mud plaster that was used to secure it in the prepared hole. The implication is not that it was installed while the walls were being built, but rather that it was inserted into the completed wall and secured with mud mortar, leaving an impression of its cuneiform text. The twelve cones that were found in the mortar bedding joints do not contradict the assumed sequence; they only show that it was more convenient to make or drill the cavity in which the nail was inserted in the softer parts of the brickwork, namely in the mud mortar that was laid between the bricks, rather than in the bricks themselves.

A seemingly inexplicable puzzle is why four cones were discovered with their pointed ends deliberately cut off, such that none of the detached tips were found inside the cavities. The fact that the tips were not in the holes confirms that the breaks did not happen accidentally, when the cones were *in situ*, while the breaks on at least three of the four were extremely clean, again suggesting that they were broken on purpose. One possibility is that the clay nails could have been removed and refitted during a refurbishment project, but why were they deliberately broken? Perhaps the removal process caused them all to break in similar ways, but this is speculative and unlikely. In two other instances, where the tip of a broken cone was found inside its designated hole, the intact cones might have been snapped because they were forced into cavities that had not been drilled or cut deep enough to accommodate them. Although it is difficult to see an alternative explanation, it is also hard to imagine

that such sacred objects would have been treated with insufficient care, though the vagaries of human actions, especially in the context of an operation such as this one, which was carried out countless times, cannot be ruled out. Five nails were found with their flat heads missing, but these are far less problematic, since the breaks can readily be explained as a consequence of the various renovations that were carried out, as enlarged upon below.

A further important question is whether the cones were fitted at all heights in the faces of the walls or just in the relatively low sections where they were found. The answer is almost certainly that they were placed at a wide variety of heights above the ones recovered. For one thing, the simple reason why the cones were found only in the bottom parts of the walls is because these low sections were the only parts that survived. Significantly, even within those truncated expanses, cones were found at all heights, and not exclusively within a defined horizon. This in itself might not be conclusive, but the remains of a partially collapsed wall were also identified (a section of the inner face of the NW wall that separated the temple from the NW end of the complex) that probably dated back to a time before the Isin-Larsa renovations. The collapsed brickwork, which presumably represented the full height of the original wall (or much of it), yielded twenty-one cones—a number that is not consistent with the idea that they were only inserted in limited shallow sections towards the walls' bases.

Especially with regard to the symbolism of the cones—a subject that is closely examined later in this chapter—it is vital to consider when exactly the clay nails were fixed in position. The conclusion that emerges from the observations just outlined is that they were probably inserted into the brickwork after the walls were erected. The further question that then arises is whether they were positioned before or after the deposition of the subfloor packings that abutted onto the bottommost courses of the walls. As noted above, no *in situ* nails were found below the flooring horizon of 15.5 m; indeed the lowest two of the *in situ* nails recovered by the British Museum team were positioned at a height of 15.7 m—therefore approximately 0.2 m above the floor. More generally, only four contexts that can be associated with the original Gudea subfloor packings were identified, and these contained fragments of four cones, only one of which was marked with Gudea's Standard Inscription, while the texts on the others were illegible, making it impossible to know whether they were deposited by Gudea. Compared to the *in situ* cones, it is difficult to draw unambiguous conclusions from these rare pieces, but their presence might suggest that cones were inserted into the constructed brickwork of the walls before the floors were established and paved, in which case some remains of cones that could potentially have snapped while being drilled into the walls might have been discarded in the subfloor packings by Gudea's workers. How likely is this, however, in view of the fact that the cones were not in any sense mere building materials, but rather, by their very nature, sacred objects that performed a special function within the fabric of the consecrated structure? Like the buried foundation pegs and boxes, for example, they could well have been fitted in association with particular rituals, and this in turn makes it unlikely that some of them were carelessly or accidentally broken and then thrown away by a bricklayer. Furthermore, the contexts in which the fragments were found had been disturbed during the later renovations that were undertaken in the Ur III and Isin-Larsa periods, and also by Hellenistic pits—all of which increased the likelihood that the isolated pieces of cone were in fact strays that were randomly deposited at one or more periods after the New Eninnu was finished in the reign of Gudea. Taking all these points into account, it can therefore reasonably be assumed that the cones were fitted after the walls were erected and the floors laid.

A potentially thornier problem is whether the nails were inserted into the brickwork before or after the walls were plastered. This is a multi-faceted issue that also raises the question of whether or not the circular convex heads of the cones were visible in the finished façades. The British Museum team found traces of some of Gudea's original mud plaster in limited areas in a few portions of the walls, and in these instances it is evident that the plaster did not cover the tops of the cones, but left their protruding heads visible and standing proud of the plastered surface. One caveat is that all that remained of the Gudea plaster in these cases was a thin coat that had been scraped off entirely on other parts of the walls during the course of later renovations, and even where some of the plaster survived it might have been sanded down (or cut back in some way) as part of the refurbishment process. Consequently, the original Gudea plaster might have been thicker than that found in the preserved areas. That said, the fact that no cones were seemingly placed in the hidden sections of the walls' bases might indicate that they were

intended to be visible (as is considered further below). This is speculative to a degree, but the idea is perhaps confirmed by the way the clay nails were formed. Why would their makers have been instructed to include the convex heads of the nails (and indeed to take pains to give the heads their characteristic rounded shape) if their symbolic form was not intended to be manifest? Had that been the case, it would have been sufficient to make actual cones—headless nails, so to speak—that could have been placed underneath the plaster, flush with the face of the brickwork, in a way that would also have facilitated the plastering of the walls because the plasterers would not have had to work around the convex protrusions. As this suggests, the well-shaped convex heads were probably included to affirm that the so-called cones were indeed meant to represent nails, with pointed shafts and rounded heads, expressly because they were installed in order to fasten two (or more) things together—not physical objects, but symbolic features of the sacred space. What those conceptual entities might have been is discussed below, but the function of the clay nails as sacred fixing agents was something that users of the temple must presumably have been aware of because it represented the binding together of hallowed components that were parts of the building's divine (or cosmic) fabric. The symbolism of the clay nails hammered into the walls of the shrine to hold one or more figurative things in place therefore had a graphic aspect to it that was expressed in the objects' form, and this might also tend to confirm that their convex stud-like heads were visible on the surface of the walls.

Another point that should be taken into consideration is that most of the clay nails were inserted into the mortar between the bricks. For mathematical reasons, the exteriors of the sides of the bricks made up a higher proportion of the surface area of the walls as a whole than the thinner layers of mortar that bonded them. Statistically speaking, that is, if the walls were covered in plaster before the nails were installed then more of them should have been placed in the bricks than in the mortar—the opposite of what was found. Similarly, three of the four nails that were definitely inserted into bricks per se were placed in the corners of the bricks. This is another highly unlikely outcome if the people who made the holes that accommodated the nails could not see the bricks while they were working. Again, it does not demonstrate that the inserted cones were hidden from view, however, because it was possible to plaster round the heads, as is probably confirmed by the Gudea examples mentioned at the beginning of this part of the discussion.

The New Eninnu was incontrovertibly renovated on a large scale during the Isin-Larsa period, when sections of the original Gudea walls were rebuilt and replastered, and the associated floors were raised. As a result, thick layers of Isin-Larsa mud plaster were found covering at least three cones. Additionally, a mud-brick structure was built against the original Gudea wall in the inner porch of the SW gate, and the cone that was recovered from Gudea's passageway wall was found behind the added Isin-Larsa brickwork. This suggests either that the Isin-Larsa renovators did not know the cones were there because they were hidden behind plaster that was applied by Gudea (or in Ur III times), or that they did not consider it important to ensure that the cones remained visible, perhaps because the shrine was to be rededicated or because the beliefs with which the cones of the New Eninnu were invested when they were fitted by Gudea had been superseded. The covering of the cones in Isin-Larsa times therefore provides no conclusive proof as to whether or not they were visible under Gudea and in the Ur III period. What is nevertheless clear is that the original Gudea façades were cleaned up and reworked during the Isin-Larsa renovations, and this might explain why some of the cones were found without their convex heads, which were probably damaged when the walls were being prepared for replastering. Some might feasibly have become detached and removed during the course of the repairs, but if—as seems to have been the case—the Isin-Larsa workmen were not instructed to take great care over the cones, that was perhaps because their sacred significance was either no longer understood (which is improbable because Isin-Larsa rulers installed cones of their own in other temples, as noted below) or no longer considered to be relevant.

Another clear finding is that the heads of the clay nails were not painted. Though this might tend to indicate that they were hidden behind the plaster, it is again far from conclusive because the walls themselves were lavishly painted, as is discussed below with reference to the Cylinder Inscriptions (A27). There is also a strong argument that the fired earth of which the objects were made was important in and of itself as an aspect of their symbolism (also detailed below) so that the contrast between the terracotta nail heads and the background of applied colour might have been inherently desirable.

The further issue that arises in this context is the ordering principle: were the clay nails placed randomly or systematically? If they were not installed according to a given design then there might have been no intrinsic reason why they should necessarily have been visible, but if they did express a particular pattern, it would presumably have made sense if the pattern could be seen. As noted above, the spatial distribution of the *in situ* examples recovered by the British Museum team suggests that they were fitted primarily in the open-air corridors around the Ningirsu temple (including in the temple's outer façades, which formed the inner wall of the ambulatory on all four sides) and in some of the passageways that gave access to the walkways. The evidence also shows that they were not placed inside the main two rooms of the Ningirsu temple, or in the brickwork associated with the stairway that led to the temple's roof. Finally, they were not incorporated into the base sections of the walls, below the level of the floor paving; nor were any found in the external façades of the L-shaped temenos. As suggested at the outset, therefore, it seems that they were deliberately placed in corridor walls inside the shrine that were open to the sky, or in one instance (the SW gate passage) in a transitional space that brought visitors from outside the complex directly into the temple's open-air ambulatory. Since the SW and SE gates were the only two portals that led directly into what must have been the shrine's most sacred walkway around the Ningirsu temple's walls, it might be inferred that cones were also fitted in the SE gate passage, but that area fell outside the scope of the British Museum team's excavations so no data was collected. Furthermore, they were installed in areas of wall that were never completely shrouded in darkness, as a closed room must sometimes have been, and at heights that meant they were not automatically hidden by fixed features of the building's structural fabric, specifically the floors. Another conscious choice was in all likelihood expressed by the positioning of the four cones that were deliberately drilled or otherwise inserted into the hard mud-brickwork rather than into the softer mud mortar (where twelve of the other cones were placed). The fact that three of the four were found in the corners of the bricks further adds to the impression that they might have been fitted according to a pre-established pattern.

It would hardly be surprising to find that such important sacred artefacts, which were conceivably the focus of special rituals, were systematically placed. The problem is that no pattern or principle can be discerned in their positioning. The recovered clay nails do not demarcate a geometric figure or figures; nor are they placed in straight lines or along clearly marked out curves, for example. The cones were all inserted at different angles from their neighbours, and the distances between them were not consistent. These facts in themselves might add substance to the idea that they were not randomly situated, however, since cognitive studies consistently show that the human mind tends to apply recurrent patterns whenever a human subject is asked to place or draw any number of objects or things without being given further explicit instructions about how the items should be positioned. In other words, if the cones were not installed according to a preconceived plan, their placement would probably have evinced an apparently greater level of coherence than they in fact do. The further difficulty here is that it is a circular argument—the presence and absence of a design both indicating a pattern.

One small clue about a possible pattern might tentatively be derived from the orientation of the inscription on the *in situ* cones. The text on all the cones is the same Gudea Standard Inscription (RIME 3.1.1.7.37) that is found on countless Gudea bricks as well as on other artefacts: 'For Ningirsu, mighty warrior of Enlil, Gudea, ruler of Lagash, made everything function as it should. He built for him his Eninnu, the White Thunderbird, and restored it to its (proper) place.' As applied to the surface of each nail, the cuneiform signs read laterally from just below the base of the head (which is left blank) to the pointed tip, and they are arranged in ten lines plus a blank space that wrap around the nail's conical spike in two rows or strips: a longer one closest to the head of the nail and a shorter one next to that—below or to the right of it, depending on whether the nail is viewed vertically or laterally (Fig. 231). Placed around the fatter part of the spike next to the head, the first row of text (see Table 10 below), contains the bulk of the inscription, which is divided into eight lines (the seventh being subdivided into two parts to reflect the indent in the second part of the cuneiform phrase): 'For Ningirsu, mighty warrior of Enlil, Gudea, ruler of Lagash, made everything function as it should . . . his Eninnu, the White Thunderbird . . .' The space that is left blank and the parts of the text that are missing from the first row (indicated by ellipses in the preceding quote) are placed at the pointed end of the spike: 'He built for him . . .', which comes next to (or below) 'his Eninnu' (line 8); as well as '. . . and restored it to its (proper) place', which is next to

(or below) 'For Ningirsu' (line 1). In passing, it can be noted that the division of the text is interesting in and of itself because the designers of the nails seem deliberately to have relegated the actions that relate to Gudea's actual building work to the pointed end of the spike, the remainder of which was invariably filled with the blank space. As an alternative, they could presumably have divided the text more evenly between the first (fatter) part of the spike and the second strip that includes the blank, and the fact that they did not might therefore provide an indication of the relative importance of the respective words and phrases: the words in the first strip being noun phrases that refer to Ningirsu, Gudea and the temple, with the exception of the verbal formation that says Gudea 'made everything function as it should'. If its placement is anything to go by (and as mentioned in Chapter 42), the latter phrase might consequently be taken to have a universal significance relating to the proper regulation or functioning of the state ('everything'), with the temple as its sacred centre, rather than referring just to the construction work.

Table 10 shows how frequently each line of text in the first strip (closest to the head of the clay nail) was found facing upwards. The name and epithet of the god ('Ningirsu, mighty warrior') was placed upwards eight times; the ruler and his epithet ('Gudea, ruler of Lagash') faced upwards eleven times; and the next most frequent upward-facing word was 'Eninnu', the temple's name, which was found facing upwards three times. Admittedly, this is an extremely small sample, but it does seem to show that there was a preferential orientation that favoured the names and epithets of Gudea and Ningirsu, which together represent nineteen out of the total of twenty-eight *in situ* cones that were uncovered by the British Museum team, a figure that equates to sixty-eight per cent. It is impossible accurately to gauge the aggregate number of cones that were installed in the walls (though further estimates are given below), but approximately 1,600 were published before the British Museum team's excavations began. In addition, lots more are in small and private collections, and many hundreds more were found by the British Museum team, including the twenty-eight that were discovered *in situ*. It should also be stressed again that the text was inscribed on the spikes of the cones, which were inserted into holes in the brickwork, so that the signs were categorically out of sight once the cones were in place. This might imply that a general, but perhaps not over-rigorously enforced priority

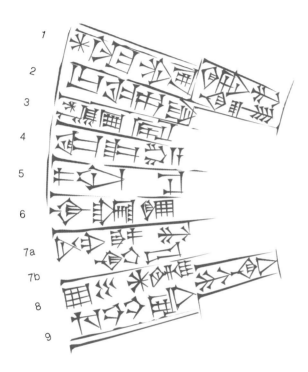

FIGURE 231. Diagrams showing the placement of Gudea's Standard Inscription on a clay nail.

was accorded to the names of Ningirsu and Gudea when the nails were fitted, and if the figure of sixty-eight per cent is representative, that would mean that more than 1,000 of the 1,600 published cones (to focus just on them) shared that orientation.

Although the paucity of the data makes this an unprovable hypothesis, it is in accord with examples of *in situ* clay nails recorded at other sites, in particular a small cache from the Isin-Larsa period that were found in Ur by Sir Leonard Woolley, who discovered thirty-six *in situ* cones that were deposited by Urnamma in Ur III times, together with several more inscribed in the names of two kings of Larsa—Warad-Sin and his younger brother, Rim-Sin. The preferred orientation of the texts on the cones was not noted at the time, and in the majority of cases the information is now sadly irretrievable, but recent analysis of the glass negatives of the excellent photos that were taken on site (Woolley 1939, Pls. 15a, 29a and 31b) reveals that eight cones deposited by Warad-Sin were meticulously placed to reflect the reading order of the cuneiform words (Taylor 2021, pp. 45–6). Interestingly, the clay nails excavated by Woolley, including the thirty-six Ur III deposits, were all fitted so that their rounded heads protruded above the plastered surfaces of the walls, and the Ur III cones made up a grid pattern.

Even if the total number of clay nails installed in the walls of the New Eninnu cannot finally be known, some further extrapolations from the data can be added to the figures given above (1,600 published cones, plus many more owned by collectors and smaller institutions, plus the numerous examples (450) found by the British Museum team between

TABLE 10. The comparative orientation of the lines of the first strips of text (closest to the heads of the clay nails) on the spikes of the *in situ* cones.
The first and second columns in the table show the line numbers and the line-by-line translation of the text; the third column shows the number of times the corresponding line was placed face up; the fourth column (TG) contains the British Museum team's index numbers of the respective cones.

Line	Text	Upward-facing	TG number
1	For Ningirsu,	5	374, 375, 979, 982, 983
		1	3539
2	mighty warrior	3	378, 2637, 2640
3	of Enlil,	1	1602
4	Gudea,	6	372, 373, 980, 986, 1604, 2635
		1	376
5	ruler	2	987, 2676
		1	2639
6	of Lagash,	3	984, 3533, 3532
7a	made everything function	0	
7b	as it should.	1	2636
8	his Eninnu,	3	3540, 985, 981
9	the White Thunderbird,		
10	[Blank space in the second strip of text.]	1	1603

2016 and 2021). Table 11 shows how many *in situ* cones were found per square metre of wall. As can clearly be seen, the cones were well spaced, ranging from a maximum of 2.5 cones per square metre in the entire excavated surface of wall 2059 (where cones were found only on one side of the gateway by which the wall was pierced) down to just half a cone in the SW section of wall 2159 (indicating that only one cone was found in an area measuring 2.06 m^2). Depending on how the cones found in context 2059 are counted (namely, whether or not the coneless section on the NW side of the gateway passage is included), the average number of cones per square metre of wall works out at 1.5 (for the maximum possible area of 16.76 m^2) or 1.6 (for the slightly reduced area of 15.86 m^2), which also means that each cone, on average, was placed in an expanse of wall measuring between 0.67 m^2 and 0.63 m^2 (though in reality some were placed closer together and further apart than is suggested by the mean distance). The calculations can be extended to the walls of the open-air corridors immediately around the temple, including: the temple's four external façades; the inner face of the interior NW wall that separated the temple from the NW side of the complex; the NE addition to the interior NW wall that extended towards the Ur-Bau plaza; the inner face of the SE temenos, opposite the temple's SE façade; and the SW envelope wall. If the height of the walls is taken to be 8 m, this gives a total surface area of roughly 1,360 m^2 for the original walls of the ambulatory, and this in turn would give an average total number of cones for the ambulatory walls of 2,040 or 2,176 (at 1.5 cones and 1.6 cones per m^2, respectively).

The sum totals for the original ambulatory walls are only indicative approximations, and the real number of cones in the walls around the temple could have been much greater, depending on how many were placed in the SW and SE gateway passages, and whether cones were also inserted into the inside faces of the temenos walls that surrounded the Ur-Bau plaza, or indeed into the exterior face of the SW wall of the old Ur-Bau shrine. In addition, cones might have been installed at higher frequencies in more prominent areas of the walls— in the middles, for example. Nonetheless, a figure somewhere in excess of 2,000 is also indicated by the Gudea clay nails that are known to exist, and it might therefore be very tentatively assumed that at least 2,000 were installed in the walls of the ambulatory. That being the case, and if the cones were not placed randomly, what possible design principle could have been applied to make sense of that many objects, each of which was situated in an average space measuring about 0.67 m^2 or 0.63 m^2 (naturally, with some closer together and others further apart)? Huge numbers of clay nails had to be accommodated, but they also had to occupy a very large overall surface area, and if they were visible on the surface

TABLE 11. Calculations of the number and density of *in situ* cones per square metre of excavated wall.

Context No.	Excavated surface area (in m^2)	No. of *in situ* cones	Cones per square metre
2059 (total)	1.6102	4	2.5
2059 (NE section in which cones were found)	0.9354	4	4.3
2032 and 3049	4.3528	10	2.3
2031	0.66487	1	1.5
3006	4.3717	5	1.1
2139	1.785	2	1.1
2159 (NW section)	1.9172	2	1.0
2159 (SW section)	2.0645	1	0.5

of the plastered walls then they would have been manifest as numerous individually distinct clay circles with diameters of about 50 mm (or generally a little less). Any resulting pattern would have looked nothing like the coloured mosaic surfaces made of tightly arranged cones (actual cones, not clay nail heads) that are attested on the surfaces of walls elsewhere in ancient Sumer. Nor does any kind of straightforward representational design make sense—a tree with branches and leaves, for example. Any ordering system, which must have been relatively abstract in appearance, but which cannot be interpreted as a series of geometrical figures, might perhaps have looked something like a modern scatter graph, with a mix of isolated instances, clusters of points and blank spaces. With this in mind, there was one very familiar and significant model that could have been used to help guide the designers of any pattern: the night sky, with its circling constellations and myriad points of light. The Yale Bright Star Catalogue contains a total of 9,110 stars that are judged to be visible on the celestial sphere without optical aids, meaning that around half of them, namely about 4,500 stars, can potentially be seen from any given location on the earth's surface. In practice, the number must be halved again to account for atmospheric disturbances, in particular horizon haze, which leaves a final tally of some 2,250 stars that fill the canopy of the night sky. Although the surprisingly close correlation between the visible stars and the retrieved number of clay nails might add credence to the idea, the conclusion can by no means be drawn categorically. Nonetheless, further support might be derived from the potent association between the New Eninnu and An, the sky god, that is invoked in the Cylinder Inscriptions (discussed below), where the narrative arguably suggests that the connection between the shrine and the sky was activated by the clay nails.

A Typology of the Inscribed Cones from Girsu

A typical Lagash II cone, which measures between 10 cm and 14 cm in length and has a maximum diameter of between 3.5 cm and 5 cm, is made of solid clay, with a roughly mushroom-shaped cap on its thicker end (Fig. 232). The preserved corpus displays both consistency and variation, such that the size and shape of sets of cones varies at different dates and with respect to the particular buildings that the cones were made to commemorate. Indeed, the physical characteristics of particular cones can often provide enough information for a researcher to determine the ruler who commissioned them, without the need to read a word of the inscribed text. Within the more restricted corpus of Lagash II and Ur III cones found in Girsu, the distinctions are more subtle, but it is still possible to distinguish cones with a relatively high degree of accuracy solely on the basis of their appearance. The differences cannot just be accounted for as expected incremental changes over time or the inevitable variations that affect such handmade objects. On the contrary, they indicate that the cones' shapes and sizes were a matter of deliberate choice, and it seems reasonable to assume that such decisions were made following discussions between respective rulers and their experts. The same sorts of procedures must presumably have been followed when the wording of the inscriptions was chosen. Consequently, sets of cones have distinctive characteristics, meaning that the variants produced for Gudea's New Eninnu, for example, are easily distinguishable, even from cones that were made to commemorate other constructions that Gudea commissioned, including the closely related EPA.

Compared to the ones made for the EPA, which have shaft diameters of between 48 mm and 49 mm, Gudea's New

FIGURE 232. Close-up views of the Standard Inscription on the stem of a single clay nail.

Eninnu cones are slightly narrower, with diameters typically ranging between 35 mm and 40 mm, though the Standard Inscription for the New Eninnu (used on Gudea's cones) is occasionally found on a cone of the EPA type. The cones commissioned by Ur-Bau to commemorate his earlier Eninnu are typically thicker, with diameters ranging between 40 mm and 50 mm, while some examples are even larger. The cones' lengths also fall within a narrow range. Too few examples of Gudea's EPA or Ur-Bau's Eninnu cones have been preserved to form a reliable data set, but Gudea's New Eninnu cones are typically between 110 mm and 120 mm long.

The sizes and shapes of the cones' heads (their mushroom-shaped caps) are also subject to clear variations (Fig. 233). The heads of Gudea's New Eninnu cones are usually between 43 mm and 56 mm in diameter, though a significant minority of cones with much larger heads are similar in appearance to the Gudea cones commemorating the shrines of Igalim and Shulshaga. In terms of profile, the heads can be sloped, domed or rimmed, and the profile can be applied just to one side or to both sides. Of the 450 Lagash II cones that were retrieved during the British Museum team's excavations, it is striking that the heads of cones commissioned by Ur-Bau for his earlier Eninnu were mostly type B (68%, or fifteen excavated examples). More variation is found on the heads of Gudea's cones, but they do seem to fall into three main categories: type B (23%, or eighty-six excavated examples), type F (16%, or sixty excavated examples) and type G (25%, or ninety-six excavated examples).

The inscriptions on the cones also differ in interesting ways. The individual texts, which are very consistent, contain remarkably few errors, but there are variations in the handwriting and the ways in which the cuneiform characters are arranged on the clay surface. Probably reflecting the chosen diameter of the cone type, Gudea's Standard Inscription almost always occupies two columns, and the division is always in the same place. By contrast, on the handful of

The Inscribed Clay Nails of the New Eninnu   653

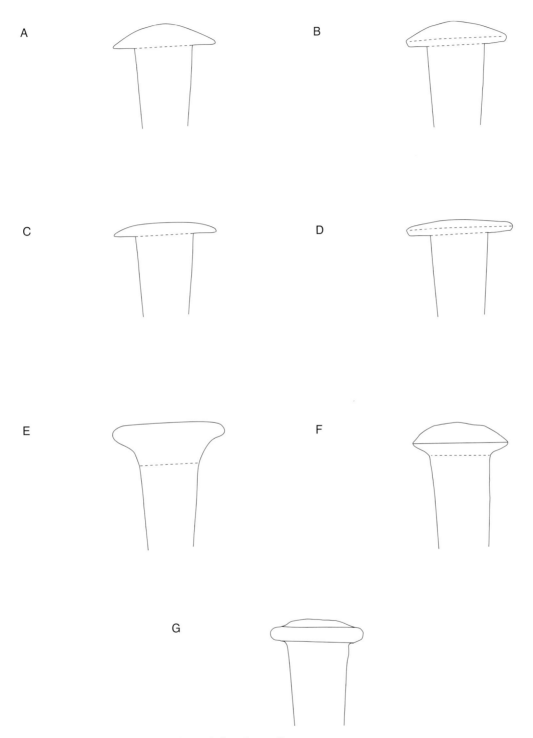

FIGURE 233. A typology of the clay nails found on Tell A.

examples of thicker New Eninnu cones, the entire text is laid out in a single column. Ur-Bau's inscription for his earlier Eninnu (on which Gudea's text was extremely closely based) is also arranged in two columns. As with Gudea's cones, the break between columns always comes at the same point in the text, but the dividing line (so to speak) differs on Ur-Bau's cones and on Gudea's, and this makes it possible to distinguish between cones inscribed for Ur-Bau's old Eninnu and those produced for Gudea's New Eninnu, even on very badly broken specimens. The distinction, which was seemingly deliberate, was perhaps intended to communicate the identities of the two rulers to later renovators of their respective temples.

The Meaning of the Clay Nails

The objects' shape, which was presumably related to both tradition and their symbolic function, was clearly meaningful, and though (as just noted) there are slight dissimilarities between the examples created by individual rulers at different historical periods, and even by one ruler for distinct projects during the same reign, their overall form is clear: they are clay nails. As such, they must have been intended—not physically, but symbolically—to hold two or more things together. That is why, though it remains convenient to refer to them as cones, the modern terminology (at least in English) is weak and inaccurate. It says something about the artefacts' conic spikes but nothing whatsoever about their convex heads and their figurative use. One of the most remarkable facts about the Gudea inscribed clay nails is that they are seemingly not mentioned once in the Cylinder Inscriptions, even though almost every other feature of the complex is described or alluded to in reverential detail. It is also somewhat surprising to discover that the word 'nail' is found only once in the text, but it occurs in a fascinating section of the narrative in which epic comparisons are drawn between various parts of the finished complex and aspects of the natural world and fabulous beasts (A26): 'The shining roof-beam nails hammered into the house are dragons gripping a victim'. The fixing ability of the nails, which is not conceived of as a mere function of physical forces, is instead pictured as an action that is performed by the objects: they actively grasp the roof beams that they are intended to secure. The nails themselves are accordingly endowed with agency, and this is perhaps indicative

of the symbolic power that was ascribed to the Gudea clay nails. They were doubtless installed to bind elements of the sacred structure together, or maybe even more importantly to secure the complex within the cosmos, just as the buried foundation pegs fixed it to the earth.

The foregoing discussion of the condition and find locations of the *in situ* nails indicates that they were part of the temple's infrastructure. Though this seems incontrovertible, it is worth pausing to consider the alternative, which is that they might have been installed after Ningirsu had taken up residence in the building. No textual evidence exists to support the idea, and it is also contradicted by the key aspect of the objects' presumed function as symbolic securing devices. What part of the structure's sacred fabric could they possibly have been intended to fix in place at that late stage, after the temple was deemed suitable for its divine inhabitant, and after Ningirsu had actually moved in. They cannot possibly have been inserted in order somehow to tie the god to his residence—that must be ruled out because it would imply that humans were capable of restricting the god's freedom of movement. The nails could in principle have secured or consolidated the sanctity of the space, but that is done earlier in the narrative under the auspices of An, as is discussed further below, and at the end of the text it says explicitly that An has made the temple 'appropriate' (B12)—a condition of holiness that is clearly consummated when Ningirsu enters it. Nor were they deterrents (perhaps by analogy with the dragons' claws quoted above) because the images of terrifying creatures who might be placed as guards around the shrine are installed immediately after the building is completed (in A25–6, for example, where the Slain Heroes are associated with the god's weapons). Finally, even on a purely practical level, it is extremely improbable that 2,000 clay nails would have been inserted into the brickwork after the walls were meticulously finished and painted.

As the British Museum team's findings confirm, therefore, they must have been installed in an earlier construction phase, in which case they might conceivably have been referred to in the text on Cylinder A, which details the actual building work, in a word or passage that has either not survived or is extremely obscure. It is by no means certain that reference was ever made to them, but if it was then the clay nails would presumably have been mentioned somewhere in the long section (A20–5) that narrates the stages of construction of the complex from the laying of the first brick to its final completion. This is the part of the narrative in which Gudea finishes marking out the ground plan of the complex, raises its walls, adds the roof, buries symbolic foundation deposits, commissions and installs the statues and steles, fits the door sockets and doors, and lastly furnishes the god's dining hall and bedchamber, at which point the structure is said to be ready: 'He finished with the building, which made the hearts of the gods overflow with joy'. Perhaps the most likely moment in this construction sequence at which the cones might have been inserted is when quantities of an enigmatic claylike substance (or a plurality of objects made from it) are liberally added to the walls. The brief passage, which describes an event of considerable sacred importance, contains some compelling difficulties (A21–2):

> The mud-wall of the house was covered with the abundance (?) of the abzu and they tied its ... to it. The shrine of Eninnu was thus placed in the ... hand of An.

To begin with, the brickwork of the temple is smeared or adorned with hi.nun.abzu (A22), a compound term in which hi-nun means 'abundance' or 'plenty', and the inclusion of the word abzu indicates that the plentiful product is derived from or associated with the underground sweetwater sea that was the domain of Enki. Since it makes little sense to 'smear' or 'adorn' the walls with water in this context (or perhaps in any other), the product from the abzu that is applied to the walls must presumably be earth or clay that has perhaps been worked with fresh (possibly sanctified) water, so the words seem to describe the application of an earthen substance to the mud-brick walls. This could in principle imply that the brickwork surfaces were at least partially coated with mud plaster at this moment in the construction sequence. And yet, though that meaning cannot be entirely ruled out, the words do not relate to the general plastering of the complex because that is mentioned subsequently, in a passage that is discussed further below, where it clearly states that the plaster of the Eninnu was mixed with 'clay taken from the Edin canal' (A27), and not therefore from the abzu. Accordingly, the enigmatic term hi.nun.abzu has a presumed significance that goes beyond mere plastering—an idea that might be confirmed in the words that follow, which introduce an intricate doctrinal frame of reference. The end of the hi.nun.abzu line is connected with the one that follows via the protean word A.GAR that can be used as a noun in several

ways (including as a fluid for removing hair from hides), but as a verb it invokes ideas of tying, hanging and binding one thing to another. In this instance, where the word connotes an action, the overall sense seems to be that a number of unspecified agents (x) 'fixed' or 'bound' some feature of the temple (y) to some other unknown thing (z): 'they tied its ... to it' (A22). The context of the latter action is further defined in the following line, where the binding together of the two unknown things (y and z) by the unnamed agents (x) has a momentous theological consequence: the Eninnu was placed in the 'hand' (SHU) of An, the sky god. The word for hand (SHU) is modified by an unclear sign that might be É×BAD, with BAD possibly introducing an idea of 'opening' and É meaning 'house', and for this reason the phrase has on occasion been translated as the 'outstretched hand of An' (Edzard 1997, p. 83)—making the sky god the willing recipient of the thing that is vouchsafed to him—but the precise meaning of É×BAD is by no means certain.

Despite the various problems associated with the narrative, it yields an intelligible symbolic meaning. First, a product made with mud that is brought from the abzu is used to adorn the walls, and some plural fixing agents (the subject of the verb is unclear) actively knit or tie the various elements together ('they tied its ... to it'). The broader sense of the action is revealed in the subsequent sentence, when, as a direct consequence of the fixing process, the brickwork of the shrine (connoting the constructed complex in its entirety) is then ('thus') placed in the hands of An, who takes it into his safekeeping. Since the subterranean abzu was the province of Enki, the last stage of the process must represent a transformative operation. Following the application of the abzu clay product, the mud-brick complex in its entirety is symbolically connected with or translated onto the celestial plane that was the realm of the sky god, An, the shadowy primordial figure who was considered to be supreme among all the gods and the prime mover of the cosmos, not in the metaphysical way that the term might now suggest, but because he was the god who was responsible for regulating the movements of celestial bodies. Consequently, in terms of a sacred action that expresses the temple's location in the Sumerian layered cosmos, the passage seems to mean that, by placing the shrine in the hands of An, the unspecified agents (x) bind or fix the Eninnu (y) to the sky (z).

The remarkable linking of the mud that is brought from the abzu with An instead of Enki is indirectly reaffirmed in the lines that follow (A22), where the deposits that are buried in the ground are said to be placed so deep that the ritual foundation pegs, which are 'shaped like praying wizards', are able to commune with Enki in his underground residence (here called the Eengura):

> The ruler built the house, he made it high, high as a great mountain. Its abzu foundation pegs, big mooring stakes, he drove into the ground so deep they could take counsel with Enki in the Eengura. He had heavenly foundation pegs surround the house like warriors, so that each one was drinking water at the libation place of the gods. He fixed the Eninnu, the mooring stake, he drove in its pegs shaped like praying wizards.

The foundation deposits or 'mooring stakes' associated with Enki are considered to secure the temple like a massive ship at harbour, in which context it should be recalled that the earth was conceived of as floating on the underground sea of sweet water—the abzu—that was Enki's realm. In this context, the anchoring of the temple was also a way of symbolically securing the inherently mobile earth in its proper place in the universal order (as is perhaps implied towards the end of the passage, where the Eninnu itself seems to be described as a another 'mooring stake'). Significantly, the ceremony of the interment of the symbolic foundation pegs that stabilise the temple is placed in apposition to the previous sentence, where the application of mud products from the abzu to the mud-brick walls is associated with the binding of the earthen temple by unknown agents to the sky, the domain of An. This unites the two gods as twin guarantors of the temple's stability with respect to the heavens above (An's realm) and the depths of the earth below (associated with Enki).

The closeness of An's connection with the temple is re-emphasised several times in the Cylinder Inscriptions, perhaps most importantly for the present argument in one of the passages of rejoicing that come immediately after the building work is completed (A27):

> The house! It is founded by An on refined silver, it is painted with kohl, and comes out as the moonlight with heavenly splendour. The house! Its front is a great mountain firmly grounded, its inside resounds with incantations and harmonious hymns, its exterior is the sky . . .

An's founding of the shrine on 'refined silver' is at first glance difficult to interpret, but it might conceivably relate to the way the temple was positioned with respect to the stars that glimmer in the sky with a sheen that is like that of the polished precious metal. The allusion is developed in the following lines, where the structure is slightly confusingly said to be painted with kohl, though it nonetheless shines like moonlight—invoking another connection between the temple and the night sky. Then, when the temple is compared to a 'great mountain firmly grounded' that is filled with music, its 'exterior' is said actually to be the 'sky'. A further addition at the very end of the section, in the course of which the complex is called the 'bright mountain', adds a final flourish: 'Eninnu's clay plaster, harmoniously blended clay taken from the Edin canal, has been chosen by its master Lord Ningirsu with his holy heart, and was painted by Gudea with the splendours of heaven as if kohl were being poured all over it'. Here is an important variation on the doctrinal association between clay products applied to the walls and the sky that is broached earlier in the text (A21). It occurs in this passage in the context of the walls having been plastered with a mix taken from the Edin canal and then lavishly painted. Unlike in the earlier construction phase, where the enigmatic 'abundance' of the abzu is arguably applied in order to fix the earth to the sky, at this later stage the finished painted temple is said to picture the 'splendours' of the sky. The implication might be that this is an ornamental elaboration of the earlier action: in the first case the complex was attached to the sky, or pinned into the cosmic framework (just as it was anchored to the earth with foundation pegs); in the second one the structural relationship between the building and the sky is expressed in the way the walls are decorated to represent the sky—to the extent that its 'exterior' is even said to be the sky. The repeated mention of kohl should not, of course, be taken to mean that the complex was painted black—which is surely out of the question—but rather to invoke the blackness of the night sky and the process (but again not the colour) by which pigments were applied to the walls, which were painted 'as if' with kohl (A27). One possible meaning would seem to be that, against the darkness of the celestial backdrop, the temple gives material form to the 'splendours' of the night sky—a vivid metaphor that adds the image of brilliant stars to that of the 'moonlight' introduced earlier. In both cases the temple shines against the ambient darkness like a heavenly body or bodies—like the moon or like the vast canopy of stars.

However the various lines are finally interpreted, the connection with An is elaborately and repeatedly made, and towards the end of the entire text (as noted above) An's primary importance is further stressed, when the contributions of other chief gods are also celebrated (B12): 'Holy An made the location appropriate'. The suitability of the sacred residence, as conferred upon it by An, might logically imply a cosmic connection between the completed earthen structure and the sky. As described above, this was a divine occurrence of the first order, in which the mud-brick structure was symbolically translated onto a celestial plane by being placed in the protective hands of An. In a Sumerian religious context, an event of such fundamental import must unquestionably have been the focus of a ritual, and that is conceivably what is actually being referred to in the slightly opaque narrative contained in the relevant lines (A22), namely a ceremony in which the suitability of the shrine as the residence of Ningirsu is enhanced, and An becomes another of its divine protectors, alongside Enki—and also, incidentally, Enlil, whose founding patronage of the entire project represents the starting point of the narrative of the Cylinder Inscriptions on Cylinder A.

It cannot finally be known with certitude whether or not the inscribed clay nails, perhaps made especially with mud that was in some sense supposedly or symbolically brought from the abzu, are the unknown agents that cause the temple to be attached to the sky. The connection with An, the sky god, seems clear, however, in terms of both the cosmic framework that was integral to the belief system that was an inalienable part of the way the temple was planned and built, and later to the way the building was decorated. The passage in which the doctrinal action of tethering the complex to the sky is described (albeit briefly) is analogous to the one that comes immediately after it in which the building is moored to the depths of the earth with foundation pegs. The only thing apparently missing from the sky passage are the sacred artefacts that must presumably have been the equivalent of the pegs. Could these be the inscribed clay nails? The answer could well be yes, in which case the 'abundance of the abzu' might refer to the plentiful clay products that adorned the walls, which were plastered and washed with paint, turning the massive surface area into an image of the sky, studded with stars in the form of the rounded convex heads of the clay nails. The nail heads themselves were not painted, as is clear from the recovered examples, but since they were made not of ordinary clay plaster, but of earth that was taken from the abzu—whatever that meant in practice—there is a strong argument that the very material of which they were manufactured was itself a sign of their preciousness. In addition, they appear to have undergone a transubstantiating procedure by which their earthen nature was translated onto a heavenly plane. Though none of this can be proved categorically, the argument would appear to provide a convincing interpretation of the objects' form and symbolic function.

CHAPTER 44

The Foundation Deposits of the New Eninnu

THE FOUNDATION DEPOSITS DEDICATED IN GUDEA'S name were made up of two elements: an inscribed symbolic foundation peg in the form of a copper figurine that was manufactured using the direct method of lost wax casting, together with a rectangular stone tablet bearing the same text as that found on the pegs (Figs. 234–6). Two different types of Gudea foundation pegs have been unearthed in contexts associated with the New Eninnu, but it should be stressed at the outset that the data relating to many of the Tell A deposits was very poorly recorded by the French excavators, so much of it is subject to significant uncertainty. The overwhelming majority of the copper statuettes, comprising perhaps twenty or more documented examples, were fashioned as kneeling male figures holding a large inscribed peg or post in their hands and between their knees. All the recovered examples are more or less identical except for some differences in size, but the inscriptions on a small number of them diverge from Gudea's usual formula for foundation offerings because, as is explained below, they were dedicated to gods other than Ningirsu. The second type takes the form of a standing male figure that is usually identified as a portrait of Gudea (an idea that is reassessed below), carrying a basket on his head. Just two specimens of this sort have emerged that can be associated with the New Eninnu, but only one comes with a well-reported find location.

The kneeling male figures, which were seemingly the standard type of New Eninnu foundation figurine, present noticeably upright torsos, necks and heads. They each grasp a proportionally oversized inscribed peg between their hands (above) and knees (below), such that the tops of the pegs are approximately level with the figures' upper chests or chins, and the pegs' pointed tips descend beneath what might be referred to as ground level, which is defined by the positioning of the kneeling right knee and the two feet. In all cases the right knee and the ball of the bent right foot are placed on the notional ground, while the left leg is bent at the knee so that the flat left foot also rests on the ground. Since the figures are kneeling on just one knee, the position might most aptly be described as a genuflection, but the terminology is fluid. On average, the recorded figures are about 19.6 cm in height by about 5 cm wide (viewed face on), and when the ratios of the various parts of the objects are considered with respect to their overall heights, it appears that the proportions were fairly carefully worked out. The heights of the genuflecting figures from head to toe are very similar to the heights of their adjoining pegs from top to tip (1:1), and though several of the tips are damaged, the length of the end of the pegs that is below ground (so to speak) seems comparable to the length of the figures' heads, including the headdresses, above the top of the peg (again roughly 1:1, though some of the tips seem to be a little shorter). Finally, the ratio of the heights of the figures (or the pegs that they are holding) to the below-ground lengths of the points of the pegs and to the heights of the heads of the figure above the tops of the pegs is about 3:1. The figures, who all have long beards that fall from their chins and shaven upper lips, are endowed with headdresses composed of four tiers of horns that are considered to be attributes of divinity. Their torsos and arms are bare, but they are shown wearing belted skirts that cover their lower bodies from the waists down. The fronts of the New Eninnu pegs

658

FIGURE 234. The inscribed stone tablet (TG1501) found *in situ* in its foundation box (2092) by the British Museum team.

are inscribed with the most common variant of Gudea's Standard Inscription, though some slight adjustments in wording have also been noted (RIME 3.1.1.7.41 and 42).

The use of kneeling figures of this type for this special sacred purpose was instigated by Ur-Bau, who was responsible for reviving the Sumerian tradition of burying foundation deposits composed of pegs and tablets after the period of the Akkad ascendancy. Indeed, the kneeling copper foundation figure seems only to have been used in Girsu, where the tradition of interring figurative pegs under temples was vigorous throughout Early Dynastic times. It should be mentioned in passing that a stone sculpture (SB6 in the Louvre), which was discovered in Susa, includes an image of a kneeling deity holding a post that is remarkably similar in appearance to the figures introduced by Ur-Bau. It has been dated to the reign of Puzur-Inshushinak, who was possibly a contemporary of the last Akkad rulers of Girsu, but the chronology is so problematic that he might alternatively have lived after the time of Ur-Bau. In any event, it is not known whether the Susa sculpture relates somehow to the Ur-Bau and Gudea figures. With respect to Tello, just one Ur-Bau copper foundation peg of the kneeling figure type has been recovered from Tell A, and like the Gudea examples it was also cast using the lost wax technique. A second figure found on Tell B has often been attributed to Ur-Bau, but this cannot be confirmed categorically because the brickwork with which it was associated could well have been constructed with salvaged Ur-Bau bricks at a later date. The form of the deposit instituted by Ur-Bau diverges significantly from the traditional Early Dynastic pegs that were found in large numbers on Tell K—a subject that is considered below. In this respect, as in many others, however, Gudea seems to have consciously followed his father-in-law's lead when planning some of the important symbolic or theologically expressive features of the New Eninnu. As is explained in Chapter 33, the details of the Ur-Bau deposit were unfortunately incorrectly recorded and interpreted by Sarzec, so it is not known whether Ur-Bau's deposits were placed in specially constructed brick boxes, but it would not be surprising if that was the case. This modification of the Early Dynastic practice of burying deposits directly in the mud-brick mound was adopted by Gudea, whose offerings seem without exception to have been installed in rectangular or square boxes built of baked bricks. The interior faces of the brick containers were sometimes coated with bitumen, and it seems that they were all originally sealed with two enlarged capping bricks that were held in place with a bitumen and reed-mat fixative.

The surviving rectangular stone tablets inscribed in Gudea's name that accompanied the copper pegs are all shaped like miniature planoconvex bricks, with flat fronts and slightly convex backs. On average, the markedly rectangular ones measure a little less than 10 cm × 7 cm, while the squarer one found by the British Museum team has dimensions of 9.4 cm × 8.5 cm. All have an average thickness of a little less than 2 cm. The squarish example found by the British Museum team is inscribed only on the obverse, while the cuneiform text on the others fills the fronts of the tablets and continues onto their convex backs. The reverse sides of all the tablets were stuck to the bottoms of the brickwork boxes with a bitumen and reed-mat adhesive. The planoconvex brick was a distinctly archaic form by the time of Gudea, who (like Ur-Bau) built with flat square bricks and flat rectangular half-bricks (as considered in Chapter 42), so the introduction of the planoconvex shape in these important foundational contexts was presumably a way of paying tribute to longstanding Sumerian traditions, thereby invoking ancestral sanction for a contemporary project. The Ur-Bau tablet (inscribed in his name with a dedication to Ningirsu and other gods) that was deposited to accompany his kneeling figure peg is rectangular

FIGURE 235. Inscribed stone tablet from the reign of Gudea, showing the front (left) and back (right). British Museum 91008.

and slightly planoconvex, as is the large fragment of a second Ur-Bau tablet (TG168) that was found by the British Museum team on Tell A in the backfill of Genouillac's Central Trench (detailed in Chapter 28 above). Notwithstanding the meagre attestation, Ur-Bau's use of the planoconvex shape was presumably another detail that he bequeathed to Gudea.

Gudea's kneeling figurines were in certain instances (and conceivably always) wrapped in cloth, as is confirmed by the textile impressions recorded on some of the Gudea Tell A foundation pegs. Sarzec and Genouillac both found signs of a wrapping, while analysis of one example (AO76) has identified markings left by a textile made of stem fibres—presumably linen (Thomas 2012, p. 153; and Garcia-Ventura 2012, p. 246). The figures were conceivably placed on their sides next to the stone tablets, and not upright, as is often stated—a likelihood that is discussed further below. After the objects had been deposited, the opening of each box was covered with reed matting, which was then coated with a layer of bitumen and capped with two oversized bricks featuring a dedicatory inscription on their lower (inside) faces (for which see Chapter 34).

There is no evidence to suggest that the pegs shaped as standing men with baskets on their heads were also wrapped, and unlike the kneeling figures they were manufactured in a form that is evidently a development of the older kind of figurative foundation peg that was used in Early Dynastic times (a subject that is also considered further below). The inscribed basket-carrying pegs, which were also placed in fired-brick foundation boxes and accompanied by inscribed tablets, are shaped as bare-chested males with shaven heads. The figures' rounded faces are evenly proportioned, with a high forehead, large eyes and marked brows, a prominent rounded nose, distinctly formed ears, a compact mouth with pursed lips and a rounded chin. Their two arms are raised to support a wide, shallow basket that rests on their heads. The hypothesis that the figures represent Gudea (Parrot 1948, p. 204; and Ellis 1968, pp. 20–3) is regularly repeated in the literature, where comparisons are made with the ceremony of the moulding of the first brick that is described in the Cylinder Inscriptions (see Chapters 38 and 42) and the images of Ur-Nanshe on his Plaques A and D (closely examined in Chapter 16). Both of these parallels have met with general acceptance, but they hardly bear close scrutiny. No support for the idea that the peg might incorporate an image of Gudea is provided by the peg figures' rather anonymous facial features, which Heuzey, for example, suggested were expressly intended to portray a labourer. It is not viable to point to any kind of convincing resemblance with the preserved faces of Gudea on other statues, partly because of the differences in

FIGURE 236. Four views of a copper foundation peg inscribed in the name of Gudea. British Museum 96566.

media (cast copper vs hard stone) and partly because of the damage caused to the metal surface of the pegs by oxidation. More important questions are provoked by the raising of the two arms to support the basket, which was seemingly a sculptural response to the traditional form of the Girsu foundation peg. The earlier pegs are shaped essentially like nails, with wide tops formed by the figurative parts of the objects that resolve into long, thin spikes below. The positioning of the arms on the Gudea pegs adds a comparable sort of symmetry and overall profile to the basket carriers. The device works very well as an expression of the objects' symbolic function as nail-like pins, but much less so in terms of royal and sacred iconography.

In this respect, it is instructive to look more closely at the contrast between the portrait of Ur-Nanshe on Plaque A and Gudea's basket-carrying foundation nails. Carrying his basket as a crown-like emblem, Ur-Nanshe supports the object by lightly touching the side of it with the fingertips and thumb tip of his right hand, while his left forearm is positioned across his torso in a gesture of prayer or worship that is echoed by the other figures on the relief, whether with one hand or two. The carrying of the basket and the placement of the hands are appropriate to the sacred ceremony in which the ruler plays the leading role—probably the investiture of the crown prince, though perhaps combined with the motif of the laying of the first brick—and the same pose exactly is adopted in the replay of the event on Plaque D. The pose differs markedly from the depiction of the hands on Gudea's copper statuettes, where the figures cup the upper parts of the basket in the palms of their hands, and their long fingers stretch out across the top of the container. By contrast with Ur-Nanshe, that is, the Gudea figurines are shown actively holding the object with both hands, and although this might be perfectly apt if the figures are conceived of as divine labourers who are symbolically involved in the construction of the temple, it contradicts the iconography of kingship as evidenced by the figure of Ur-Nanshe on the royal plaques, and also by the portrayal of Gudea (and Ur-Bau for that matter) on all of the Tell A diorite statues, where, without exception, the ruler's hands are clasped together in front of his body in a pose of piety. It is also revealing to look at the basket carriers on the obverse of Fragment B on the Stele of the Vultures. As argued in Chapter 18, they are conceivably depicted in the act of carrying earth to create the tumulus that will contain the Lagash dead, and they are also shown supporting their baskets with just one hand. The receptacles on their heads must, in representational terms, be thought of as filled with heavy clay, but the ritual character of the sacred act in which they are presumably engaged—the burial of the heroic dead—outweighs considerations of realism, and the containers are supported in the same way as Ur-Nanshe wears his 'holy crown' (the term used in the Cylinder Inscriptions to describe the same object when it is carried by Gudea). For these reasons, it is probably incorrect to suggest that Gudea might have had himself portrayed supporting the weight of the object with both hands because it would have contradicted the conventional Sumerian imagery of the king or sacerdotal ruler taking part in a religious rite.

The further suggestion that the basket-carrying pegs from the reign of Gudea were designed to represent the ceremony of the moulding or laying of the first brick is similarly unconvincing, precisely because those events were two of the holiest moments in the entire history of the construction of the New Eninnu (as explained above). A sculpted image that was meant to invoke Gudea's role in them would therefore surely have prioritised the consummate sacred character of the occasion, and the ruler's pose would have been modelled accordingly, as Ur-Nanshe's is on Plaques A and D, for example. With respect to the Tell A figurines, a link between the brick-moulding ceremony and the basket carriers might more plausibly derive from the fact that, as is explained in Chapter 42, the first brick was rectangular in shape. Thereafter, in order to establish the necessary bonding pattern, all the bricks used to build the corners of every wall in the New Eninnu must, in principle, have also been rectangular, and the corners were, of course, the points that were marked out on the ground with real surveyors' pegs and usually solemnised with inscribed tablets and emblematic copper figures. The shape of the sanctified first brick is thereby inevitably invoked by the basket carriers, but since (at the very least) many tens of thousands of rectangular bricks were needed to construct the corners of the complex it is problematic to suggest that the copper figures were designed to symbolise a connection between the labour of transporting and laying them and the vitally important rituals that were celebrated by the ruler in the New Eninnu's preconstruction phase. An additional complication is that neither of the examples of basket-carrying figures that were recovered in Tell A contexts were positively associated with corners.

As a result, it is perhaps more likely that the characters shown on the basket-carrying foundation nails from the reign of Gudea personify divine auxiliaries—spirits or minor deities—like the supernatural beings that form the top sections of their Early Dynastic counterparts. Sculpturally, the Gudea foundation pegs nevertheless display some fascinating differences from the older shapes, and indeed from the superficially similar objects that were commissioned by later rulers. Wearing a belted garment that descends from the waist to just above the knees, the figures' legs are well sculpted, as are the feet, which stand upon a clearly defined base or floor below which the object tapers to a point to indicate the tip of a peg, and the inscriptions on the pegs are placed on the figures' skirts. Whereas the bottom parts of earlier and later

figurative foundation pegs from Girsu, including the ones made in the reign of Shulgi, resolve into spikes, the sculpted lower bodies of the Gudea figurines are differentiated from the points of the pegs. The composition as a whole shows a figure standing on an imaginary ground, with the truncated tip of a nail below, and this complicates the intended relationship between the objects' symbolic function and their representational content. Furthermore, as is evident on AO258, for instance, the left foot and left lower leg of each figure is placed slightly ahead of the right foot, almost certainly to intimate the idea of walking. Along with the separation of the figure from the tip of the peg, this surprisingly naturalistic detail has some significant symbolic connotations that are discussed further below.

As is detailed previously in Chapter 23, Sarzec, Cros and Genouillac all unearthed foundation deposits dating from the reign of Gudea in the vicinity of Tell A, but they are sketchily described in the published sources. Sarzec also uncovered some Gudea foundation boxes on Tell K, including one that was associated with the inferred memorial shrine that Gudea erected when he built the New Eninnu and extensively refashioned the religious landscape of Girsu. That box, which was found close to wall O on Sarzec's Plan C (1 and 2), contained a figurine in the form of a kneeling deity, and it is worth noting that a box that was excavated nearby included a Shulgi peg that was shaped as a basket carrier (see Chapter 5). Sarzec's rarest find was a basket-carrying figure (AO258) and an accompanying inscribed tablet that were dedicated by Gudea to commemorate the construction of the New Eninnu. The discovery is quite closely analysed by Heuzey (Sarzec and Heuzey 1912, p. 245), but it is nevertheless hard to know exactly where it was located. One possibility that derives from Sarzec's more systematic description of the excavations (Sarzec and Heuzey 1912, pp. 71–2) is that it might have been uncovered in Sarzec's area S, which is unfortunately not marked on his Plan B, but it seems to have been on the SE side of Tell A. At least four foundation boxes were excavated in this location, of which three still contained their deposits, though it is practically impossible to correlate the finds with the published accounts. Sarzec refers to this particular statue as a female basket carrier—a judgement that was accepted by Heuzey, who attributes it to Shulgi. The gender assumption, which was based on the contours of the objects in their freshly excavated states (cf. Sarzec and Heuzey 1912, Pl. 28 (1)) was mistaken, since restored figures of this type are unquestionably male, as is attested by numerous examples in the Louvre (mostly, it should be said, from Susa). Despite that, it can still be stated with some confidence that the find made by Sarzec in area S was probably a Shulgi figure because Heuzey was acutely aware of the difference between the Gudea pegs, with their sculpted feet standing on a defined base and a truncated spike tip below, and the later ones commissioned by Shulgi that lacked these refinements. He even discusses the distinguishing features of the two types, concluding that the Shulgi style is 'poor and lacking in character' (Sarzec and Heuzey 1912, p. 246). His assessment that the find made in area S was a Shulgi peg was therefore almost certainly not based solely on the erroneous idea that the figure was female, but on a combination of factors. That being the case, the original location of AO258, the New Eninnu Gudea basket carrier that was found by Sarzec, is unknown.

Additionally, in 1877 or 1878, Sarzec discovered four Gudea foundation boxes on monticule R, as it is referred to (see Chapter 27). Marked on Sarzec's Plan B, this was a low rise on the SW side of the shaded rectangular area that is labelled on the plan as the 'Palace' (*Palais*). The contents had been removed from one of the boxes, but the deposits in the other three, which were complete, included the typical Gudea foundation pegs in the form of kneeling copper figurines, together with stone tablets inscribed in his name. The inscriptions on the monticule R deposits, which differ from the standard Gudea texts used on his foundation offerings, record that they were installed to commemorate constructions dedicated to Igalim and Shulshaga, two of Ningirsu's divine sons. Heuzey also mentions another kneeling figure dedicated to Igalim and a basket carrier dedicated to Shulshaga 'for his temple', either of which might conceivably have come from the empty box, but this cannot be confirmed (Sarzec and Heuzey 1912, p. 244). The sacred structures, which are referred to respectively as Emehushgalanki and Ekitushakkilli, probably formed a dual shrine to the two brothers, but no conclusive corroborating evidence has survived. Similarly, it is disappointing that the exact find locations of the boxes were not more precisely reported by Sarzec because that information might have helped to clarify the relationship between the structure (or structures) for which the boxes were installed and the New Eninnu. As drawn on Sarzec's Plan B, monticule R was very close to the SW side of the Palace, which is rather impressionistically marked as a rectangular block. This is probably misleading,

however, because the Igalim and Shulshaga shrines were presumably placed adjacent to Tell A, around the base or stairways of the mud-brick platform (faced with fired bricks) that Gudea enlarged, raised and reinforced prior to building the complex. That being the case, the Igalim and Shulshaga monuments and foundation deposits were in all probability associated with the dedication of the New Eninnu's substructural platform.

This was also the case for at least two of the three foundation boxes that were discovered by Cros in the area of the Mound of the Steles between Tells A and B (for which see Chapter 23). The assemblage of structures included a stone stairway leading to the upper levels of Tell A that was built into the side of the mud-brick mass that formed the mound's lower tier. Facing the stone ascent were a brick base that supported a monument and the remains of a two-room shrine that was fitted with some external pedestals. Two foundation boxes were excavated next to the stairway— one on each side—and both contained a copper foundation peg in the form of a kneeling figure, together with an inscribed stone tablet. They were installed above the local ground level in the substructural mud-brick platform, and marked with the Standard Inscription recording Gudea's construction and dedication of the New Eninnu. Inside the nearby shrine, under the floor of room F, as it is labelled on Cros's Plan H (Fig. 113), which records the layout of the excavated structures, was another Gudea foundation box made of fired bricks that contained a stone tablet and a second example of one of the Gudea copper foundation pegs shaped as a basket carrier (EŞEM6506). The fact that this peg was reasonably well documented provides firm proof that such objects were used by Gudea in structures associated with the New Eninnu, though perhaps exclusively in outlying areas. As noted above, however, the find location of the only other specimen of this kind of peg that was inscribed with a New Eninnu text was not recorded by Sarzec so no final conclusion can be drawn about their general placement.

Lastly with regard to the work carried out by the French excavators, Genouillac (1936, p. 10) discovered three foundation boxes close to the SE side of the Gate of Gudea, all of which contained stone tablets and kneeling figures holding pegs. Though he correctly attributes the deposits to Gudea, he unfortunately provides very little further information about them. Thankfully, one of the boxes was recorded in two photos (Figs. 133 and 134), the first of which shows the rather large inscribed tablet face up and conceivably still stuck to the brickwork base (a subject considered further below), with the wrapped or encrusted copper figurine upright next to it. Several courses of bricks had undoubtedly been removed from the walls of the box before the photo was taken, while the statuette had almost certainly been displaced from its original position on its side inside the cavity, and propped up so it could be seen more clearly. The stone tablet was seemingly still *in situ*. The second image appears to show the same box after it had been investigated further—upper courses of bricks having been removed. The contents of the box can be seen on the ground between the slender spade handle on the right and the man with a cap on the left (whom Genouillac calls his clerk or secretary). The stone tablet must have been repositioned by the time the photo was shot because its bright rectangular form is visible, standing upright (leaning slightly leftwards) above the side of the cavity, close to the clerk's shadow, and the figurine can be seen propped up on its side against the low remains of the inside front wall of the box.

It is disappointing that Genouillac does not confirm how many courses of bricks he removed from the sides of the boxes (or box) before the pictures were taken, and that he does not give any dimensions. Nonetheless, a comparison of the inferred sizes of the boxes found by Cros with the example seen in Genouillac's first photo (Fig. 134) would suggest that the Genouillac cavities measured 0.32 m (l) × 0.16 m (w). This is confirmed by the square brick (presumably one of the Gudea standard bricks with sides of 0.32 m that were used to build walls of the box) in the photo's bottom right-hand corner, which is the same length as the long side of the cavity. When the measurements of the sides of the cavities are set against the sizes of the deposited objects it is clear that the figures could comfortably be laid lengthways on their sides next to the tablets. Accordingly, a stone tablet with an average width of less than 7 cm was placed across the cavity at one end, and a figurine with an average height of about 20 cm was probably positioned lengthways on its side next to it. No depth measurements are given by Genouillac (or Cros for that matter), but the preserved section of the inside of the box in Fig. 134 appears to be about 0.16 m deep, or about half the size of a Gudea square brick, and this would also correlate well with the average sizes of the objects in proportion to the depths of the cavities in Genouillac's photos.

In his report Genouillac states that the three sets of deposits were found under the Hellenistic brick paving of the 'great room' that was accessed via the Gate of Gudea (entirely rebuilt in Hellenistic times), though the portal itself had been almost completely dismantled before he started work. This would indicate that they were concealed some 1.2 m under the Hellenistic floor of Court A (on Sarzec's Plan A; Fig. 111), and this in turn would support the conclusion that the deposits were all found inside the L-shaped temenos, probably in the unidentified mud-brick mass that constituted the core of the upper terrace platform (H on Sarzec's Plan A) that was associated with the gateway that led from Gudea's NW courtyard up to the Ningirsu temple that was elevated on the SE side of the complex. Genouillac mentions that the bricks were 'turned over' (*renversées*). The description is very vague, but he is probably referring to the Gudea capping bricks used to seal the tops of the boxes, which were conventionally laid with their texts face down. As stated previously, one of the figurines found by Genouillac was marked with the texture of the linen cloth that had been used to wrap it (the middle one of the three reproduced on his Pl. 87). Accordingly, he refers to the copper peg seen in Fig. 134 as being 'wrapped' (*enveloppée*), but whether the rather formless outlines of the statuette as it appears in the photo were in fact due only to the thickness of the wrapping (which had surely rotted away) or to a combination of the wrapping and nearly four millennia of oxidation was not noted. Furthermore, since there is no way that the soft textile could have produced an imprint directly on the much harder metal statue, the marks must have been created while the patina was being formed during the long period when the object lay undisturbed in its foundation box—a point also made by Heuzey (Sarzec and Heuzey 1912, p. 242). Finally, if the stated find location of the boxes is broadly accurate then the great significance of Genouillac's discoveries is that they are the only finds that definitely confirm the presence of foundation deposits with kneeling figures within the confines of the New Eninnu, and not only in its peripheral features and probably also its temenos walls.

The British Museum team's discovery of four foundation boxes, as well as clear signs of several others that had been completely removed, adds considerably to the evidence recorded by the French pioneers. The detailed excavation report can be consulted in Chapter 34, but boxes were found in the NE and SW gates, where they were built into the corners of thick mud-brick walls forming structures that were part of the complex's temenos. The most complete box (2092) was uncovered in the E corner of tower 2105, associated with the SW gate. It was rectangular, like the ones found by Genouillac and Cros, and its long and short sides were aligned so that they followed the lines of the New Eninnu's walls. This is in accord with Sarzec's observation that the boxes he found were positioned with their corners facing the cardinal points (Sarzec and Heuzey 1912, p. 71). Box 2092, which was made of slightly oversized square bricks with sides of 0.35 m, was three bricks long and two and a half bricks wide, with a central void that was one brick long and half a brick wide. If the slight metrological deviation from the usual Gudea square brick (with sides of 0.32 m) is set aside, the cavity had the same unitary lateral dimensions as the ones recorded by Cros and Genouillac. Box 2092 was seemingly built with rather high sides. Including the base, its walls were eight bricks high, which would equate to somewhere between about 0.56 m and 0.64 m, depending on the thickness of the mortar, indicating a depth of around 0.48 m or 0.56 m for the cavity (taking the base to be one course thick), but whether this was the usual height for boxes of this type in all areas of the New Eninnu cannot be confirmed, as mentioned above. As also noted previously, though the copper figurine was unfortunately missing from box 2092, the accompanying inscribed stone tablet (TG1501) was found *in situ*, and it was placed with its text pointing directly towards the cult podium in the cella of the Ningirsu temple. Since box 2092 was clearly in line with the New Eninnu's walls (as all the boxes appear to have been), and the tablet was deliberately stuck to the brickwork base in its slightly offset position, it is logical to suppose that this might have been the conventional way of placing the inscribed tablets inside the foundation boxes, namely ensuring that their inscriptions pointed towards the statue of the god at the sacred heart of the complex.

Interpreting the Gudea Foundation Pegs

The method and broader significance of using pegs and ropes to lay out the ground plans of sacred buildings are explained in great detail in Chapter 14. The process, which was much more than a branch of metrology (as narrowly defined), was associated with fundamental aspects of Sumerian cosmology, including beliefs about how the world was ordered, as well as its maintenance and ongoing functioning under the protective authority of the gods. As also noted in Chapter 14, particularly with regard to the probable meaning of the ideogram of the temple, the system of defining areas with pegs and ropes was used in secular settings for measuring and demarcating plots of land. The inevitable slippages between interconnected earthly and cosmic matters, and between human and divine spheres of activity, are reflected in the complex connotations of Sumerian words relating to foundations that are discussed below. It should be re-emphasised at the outset, however, that overlapping meanings are inherent in the Sumerian understanding of real and symbolic pegs, and in the Sumerian approach to pegging out areas of land for sacred and secular purposes, because the objects and procedures both raised issues that went to the heart of their theology.

The laying out of the New Eninnu with pegs and ropes is clearly described in the Cylinder Inscriptions in a fascinating passage that is also discussed in Chapters 14 and 38. The copper artefacts that were deposited in the ground by Gudea were intended to be symbols of the real surveying pegs (perhaps made of wood) that were used for practical purposes on the construction site. This was also true of the copper pegs deposited in Early Dynastic times, with the significant difference that the earlier ceremonial foundation pegs, which were stuck directly in the mud-brick mound, more closely approximated the shapes of objects that could actually have been used to lay out the ground plans of buildings. The figurative pegs from Tell K from the period of the Lower Construction and from the reigns of Ur-Nanshe and Enmetena, for instance, are all shaped as male deities with their arms crossed in front of their chests. In every preserved example, the body below the elbows ceases to be representational, and is instead formed into an elongated spike so that the silhouette of the object in its entirety is comparable with that of a nail, with a wide head above and a long, narrow point below. The similarity is further stressed by the ratio of the full length of the pegs to their pointed ends beneath the upper bodies of the figures. By way of illustration, an Enmetena peg in the Louvre (AO2353) has a total height of about 240 mm, of which the spike below the elbows forms around 170 mm, which is just a little less than three-quarters of the whole. The spikes on some other Enmetena pegs were considerably longer (for example, EŞM1521 in Istanbul, which has a total length of 350 mm—most of the extra length being added to the spike).

The two kinds of Gudea pegs associated with the New Eninnu (Fig. 237) were rather differently formed because in both cases the figures and spikes are treated as sculpturally distinct elements, and the ground is made into another represented component of the composition. These deceptively simple changes invoke some sophisticated meanings that were far less developed in their Early Dynastic counterparts. The basket-carrying and kneeling figurines might almost be described as copper tableau. They respectively suggest miniature histories of making bricks or more probably the building of walls, and the insertion of pegs or posts into the ground. The meanings are highlighted by the portrayed actions of the figures, who either hold a basket or grasp a peg or spike, and by the clear separation of the tips of the foundation nails from the ground level that is occupied by the figures. The distinction is more accentuated with the basket carriers, whose relationship with the point of the spike is purely formal and thematic because, unlike the kneeling deities, they do not directly use or touch the pegs, and their depicted role in the building of the temple is at one remove from the pegging out process. They bring bricks to build the walls whose corners and extents have previously been marked out on the earth, as confirmed by the motifs of the below-ground spikes. This also generally reflects the order of events described in the Cylinder Inscriptions, and it tends to confirm that (as previously argued) the composition shows the figures performing the labour of bringing bricks to be laid in the marked-out temple walls, perhaps specifically at the corners, and not carrying clay for moulding. The basic fact that they are engaged in a particular labour is further stressed by the way the feet are positioned to introduce an idea of walking.

Despite the additional symbolism, in terms of their overall nail-like outline it is clear that the basket-carrying pegs are a sculptural elaboration of the Early Dynastic form, but this cannot be said of the kneeling figures, which diverge much more significantly from the older varieties of figurative pegs that were used in Girsu for many centuries. Most obviously, when looked at in the round, they are not shaped like foundation nails. Instead, the peg or post is incorporated into an elaborate composition that shows the kneeling deity holding

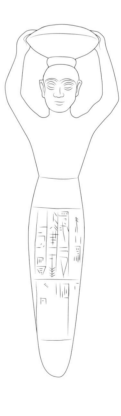

FIGURE 237. Three copper foundation pegs from Girsu: a kneeling deity with an oversized peg (left) and a figure carrying a basket of bricks (centre) from the reign of Gudea; a basket carrier (right) from the reign of Shulgi.

0   50mm

a peg-like or post-like object that might be conceived of in two ways. On the one hand, it can be thought of as a representation of a surveying peg that is being held firmly in the ground by the supernatural agent. On the other hand, it seems evidently to illustrate something much bigger and more substantial than a peg, and the placement of the figure next to the spike inevitably invites a comparison of their comparative sizes. If it is therefore correlated with the average height of a man at that period (say 1.6 m), the spike or post would be around 1.2 m tall and perhaps 0.4 m wide. The applicability of the calculation might be corroborated by the basket that is carried by the Gudea figurine, which is sized in proportion to the dimensions of a human body. This characteristic of the kneeling figurines was remarked upon by Heuzey, who described the object held by the Ur-Bau figure from Tell A (the most important surviving prototype for the Gudea deposits) as 'a conical stake, a sort of boundary post or piling' (Sarzec and Heuzey 1912, p. 241). Though the kneeling figures are usually described as straightforward foundation pegs, therefore, in terms of their formal attributes and expressed function that is probably an oversimplification, as is considered further below.

One of the sacred functions of the figurative pegs used as foundation deposits was to act as temple guardians, thereby joining certain other defenders of the god's household, which were openly displayed in the complex in the form of statues. Useful parallels can again be drawn with some of the Early Dynastic pegs that were found on Tell K. The Enmetena pegs, like those of his Early Dynastic forebears, represent wide-eyed figures in attentive attitudes of prayer, and despite some important differences of emphasis, an observant air is also discoverable in the faces of the two kinds of Gudea figures on the statuettes associated with Tell A, both of which have large, open eyes. The anomaly is that some (if not all) of the Gudea kneeling statues were wrapped in linen cloth, and they were all probably laid down on their sides in their respective boxes, as the basket carriers might also have been. The most obvious reason why this was probably the conventional placement for the figures is that the bases of the foundation boxes were made of fired bricks. Whereas Early Dynastic pegs could be stuck directly into the mud-brick substructure of the sacred mound, therefore, Gudea's Lagash II pegs were inside sealed boxes that cut them off from the ground below. This correlates neatly with the fact that the below-ground points of the spikes on the two types of Gudea deposits associated with

the New Eninnu were extremely small in proportion to the overall sizes of the statues, thus indicating their mainly symbolic function, and that the kneeling figures were wrapped in cloth so the points would almost certainly have been covered. The generally proposed idea that the figurines might have been positioned upright (see, for example, Ellis 1968, p. 62) is largely based on the way they appear in Genouillac's photos, which do not provide a reliable guide because the figure (and in one instance also the tablet) were undoubtedly rearranged, perhaps primarily to make them easier to photograph. The conclusion that the statues were found lying on their sides is inevitably circumstantial, and it is unfortunate that no precise information was recorded by Sarzec, Cros or Genouillac about the exact placement of the two types of figures inside their respective boxes, but the wrapping of the Gudea kneeling figures in cloth adds a further strand of meaning that is unique to them. The peg bearers were apparently swaddled and positioned as though they were sleeping. The significance of this is a speculative matter, but it seems that they were laid out in sarcophagus-like repositories in a state of dormancy or suspended animation. If the objects were thought to perform stabilising functions, the pose was perhaps intended somehow to preserve their divine strength; if they were thought of as temple defenders, it might possibly have signified that their divine powers were held in abeyance, in a state of perpetual readiness. No definitive judgement can be made.

A number of themes and motifs that add substantially to the discussion are developed in the fascinating lines in the Cylinder Inscriptions (A22) that are discussed in detail above in the discussion of Gudea's clay nails, but which bear repetition in this context. As noted previously, the passage is difficult to understand, but the treatment of the foundation pegs in particular, along with the Sumerian terms that are used to express their apparent functions, arguably reflect the sophisticated theological beliefs with which the foundation deposits were invested:

> The ruler built the house, he made it high, high as a great mountain. Its abzu foundation pegs, big mooring stakes, he drove into the ground so deep they could take counsel with Enki in the Eengura. He had heavenly foundation pegs surround the house like warriors, so that each one was drinking water at the libation place of the gods. He fixed the Eninnu, the mooring stake, he drove in its pegs shaped like praying wizards.

To begin with, the objects that are 'shaped like praying wizards' (abgal₂.bi) would seem to allude to, or reflect the appearance of, Gudea's kneeling peg bearers, whose genuflecting stance might be taken to indicate that they are at prayer, or petitioning the greater gods. The word 'wizard' is a poor way to capture the divine quality of the depicted figures, who might more aptly be referred to as 'sages' or 'magi', though even these terms do not adequately express the idea of a minor divinity as opposed to an exalted human. Nonetheless, the magi (to adopt that word) are associated with the idea of the 'mooring stake' that is an evocative translation of the Sumerian word dim (connoting some type of bonding that can equally be a rope holding a boat or a column supporting a floor) that occurs earlier in the passage in connection with the abzu: temen abzu.bi dim. This introduces the adaptable word temen, which has several nuances associated with foundations as the literal or figurative base on which a temple was built, together with the objects and texts that were manufactured and installed when the foundations for the sacred building were laid down: a foundation inscription, the object on which an inscription was written, a foundation installation or even the substructural platform itself (see Dunham 1986). As concluded in connection with the New Eninnu's clay nails, the fixing device or 'mooring stake' (dim) is associated with the abzu as the underground domain of Enki (the Eengura), and the bond is framed in terms of a foundation. A link is therefore established between the deeply buried genuflecting pegs, the foundations of the temple and the abzu as the subterranean home of Enki—factors that combine to secure the temple to the earth, not merely as a matter of structural engineering, but within the fabric of the layered Sumerian cosmos.

The frame of reference recalls the lines discussed earlier in connection with the clay nails in which the temple is entrusted to the sky god, An. It invokes an interchange between cosmic levels—the abzu, the surface of the earth and the heavens—that is couched in words relating to foundations. The term temen an.na, meaning something like 'sky foundations', is introduced in apposition to the preceding phrase, temen abzu.bi dim, presumably to create a heuristic contrast between the fixing of the temple to the respective realms of An and Enki. How exactly the sky bond is effected in this case is not clear because temen might connote any of the ideas to do with foundations that are noted above. The most plausible explanation, however, is that in this instance,

as in more prosaic texts that record the areas of plots of land, temen refers principally to the ground plan of the temple, which was established with respect to observations of the sky and marked out with pegs. That being the case, the protean word temen would embrace the celestially determined plan, together with the action of laying out the plan, as well as the real or symbolic pegs. Though it cannot be conclusively demonstrated, this would also re-emphasise the theological thinking that defined the various strata of which the world was formed as the provinces of particular gods. In any event, the 'sky foundation' (temen an.na) is said to surround the temple or house like 'heroes' or 'warriors', and if the association of the Sumerian term with the temple's ground plan and its foundation pegs can be relied upon, it seems plausible to identify the guarding 'warriors' with some of the figurative pegs.

It should again be stressed that these arguments cannot finally be confirmed, but they seem to synthesise some key tenets about the securing of the temple with stakes driven deep into the earth and a related set of beliefs about its star-aligned ground plan—the dual binding of the temple to the subterranean abzu and the overarching heavens that evidently formed a composite cornerstone of Sumerian doctrine. In that inferred context, the passage from the Cylinder Inscriptions might suggest that foundation deposits were—emblematically or in reality—installed at two different levels: the 'warriors' that surround the walls and the 'magi' that were buried in the earth. This might further point to the idea of two different kinds of deposits: the warrior-like foundation pegs at the intersections of the walls that define the 'sky foundation', and the interred magi that hold the mooring posts that secure the temple in the depths of the earth. This does not correlate with the archaeological evidence, however. Two kinds of objects carrying Gudea's New Eninnu inscription were installed as foundation deposits—the basket carriers and the kneeling figures—but the scant evidence indicates that the basket carriers were used only in limited and specific contexts, probably on the periphery of the complex, while the kneeling figures were the standard form of the pegs that were installed in areas directly associated with the New Eninnu. Admittedly, the proofs are largely conjectural, but only two basket-carrying figures were uncovered, one of which has no identified find location, while the other was unearthed by Cros in the shrine next to the stone stairway at the base of the mound in the monumental area between Tells A and B. Conversely, more than twenty examples of the kneeling figure pegs are known to exist, and though their original locations are mostly uncertain, at least three (the ones found by Genouillac) were certainly deposited inside the space defined by the temenos walls of the New Eninnu, and there is no reason to suspect that the majority of the other New Eninnu examples found on Tell A originated anywhere else. The idea gains further support from the specimen found by Sarzec on Tell K, in association with wall O, which probably belonged to the shrine that was built by Gudea in honour of the Ningirsu temple's immemorial home. Also containing Gudea's Standard Inscription, the kneeling figure was probably deposited on Tell K to create an emblematic bond between the old and the new shrines.

Nor is there any evidence that distinctions were made between kneeling figures that were buried at different levels. Some were certainly deposited around the base of the mound, while others were in mud-brick layers within the compound, but all—probably including the ones that were almost certainly contained in the foundation boxes found by the British Museum team in the temenos walls—were at or above the localised level of the ground where they were inserted, not forgetting that the entire mound was structured as a series of terrace-like platforms. It is to be expected that undiscovered deposits were buried at key points beneath the Ningirsu temple walls, especially under the four main corners. This was the practice on Tell K, and it is difficult to conceive of a reason why it would not have continued under Ur-Bau and Gudea. These underlying levels were not reached by the French, and the British Museum team did not dismantle the surviving walls of the temple in the areas that were investigated, so their existence cannot be ruled out. Low-lying foundation deposits could therefore, in principle, have been buried at very low altitudes, but in practice that is perhaps unlikely because it would have necessitated piercing the New Eninnu's substrata, which were made up of ritually sealed older platforms. In any case, such extremely low levels could not in any realistic sense have been linked with the abzu because deposits buried in the New Eninnu's mud-brick platforms would still have been placed in the artificially elevated substructure of Tell A, and not deep in the earth itself. Symbolically, that is, they would have occupied levels analogous to those in which Cros's deposits were found. It would therefore not be surprising to discover that any deposits that were symbolically placed below the walls of the sanctum

sanctorum were either in the bottoms of the walls, comparable to the foundation boxes in the temenos, or just below the floors, comparable to the box found by Cros in room F of the shrine between Tells A and B. Unfortunately, there is no evidence to confirm this hypothesis.

For these reasons, the images in the Cylinder Inscriptions that invoke the depths of the earth, where the praying magi with their mooring posts are in close contact with Enki, should perhaps be regarded as metaphors. By the same token, the kneeling figures appear to have performed two functions: they acted as updated variants of traditional Girsu foundation pegs, in which sense they were placed like 'warriors' or 'heroes' at the intersections of walls to safeguard the New Eninnu's ground plan or 'sky foundation', but they were also conceived of as the magi who helped to stabilise the mooring stakes that secured the complex in the subterranean cosmic depths that were closely connected with the abzu. The interwoven strands of text from the Cylinder Inscriptions and the recovered pieces of archaeological evidence are hard to disentangle, but together they seem to attest to a theological framework that accommodated the inception of the New Eninnu, followed by its laying out along lines that were generated according to an initial celestial observation, and its ongoing cosmic stability with respect to the sky and the abzu. Several of these meanings are implied by the Early Dynastic foundation deposits, as is especially noteworthy when the placement of distinct groups of figurines under the Lower Construction is taken into account. After moving the sacred complex from Tell K to Tell A, Ur-Bau seemingly introduced a novel kind of kneeling foundation figurine that combined the symbolism of pegging out the ground plan with that of anchoring a sacred building in the earth and securing it to the heavens. The innovative sacred artefacts (probably also including the specific way in which the clay nails were treated, as is discussed in Chapter 43) were used by Ur-Bau to express an extremely refined and developed theological outlook. Modifying and giving new impetus to a thousand-year-old tradition, these were clearly not trivial reforms, and that inferred fact might help to explain why Gudea so readily adopted Ur-Bau's new practices. In the case of the kneeling figures, Gudea did not merely copy a novel aesthetic form, but rather accepted a revised or clarified set of theological principles that were expressed in a new kind of sculptural ensemble.

PART 4 The Ningirsu Temple
in the Hellenistic Era

CHAPTER 45

The Renaissance of the Eninnu

The Enigma of Adadnadinakhe

In the Hellenistic period, after an interval of approximately 1,500 years, new construction work was undertaken in the Sumerian sacred city of Girsu, which had been abandoned since about 1750 BCE. The large building, which was erected in the central part of Tell A, was discovered by Sarzec soon after he arrived at the site in 1877. As detailed in Chapter 23, Sarzec apparently began excavating around the SE end of the NE façade (on Sarzec's Plan A; Fig. 111), and he soon discovered the blind passageway or external niche (N on Plan A) that contained the bottom section of the Gudea Colossus (Statue D). Having subsequently cleared the entire NE façade and its accompanying fired-brick paving, he established the length of the building's long axis. Thereafter, in later campaigns, he removed materials that he considered to be spoil and overburden. It should be re-emphasised that, during these early seasons, Sarzec believed that he had discovered the remains of a Sumerian structure—the so-called Palace—that was built by Gudea. Lacking the secure chronology that would nowadays be established through pottery analysis, he thought that the countless cuneiform signs on a wealth of unearthed materials all dated back to the reign of Gudea. One thing gave him pause for thought, however. Among the fired bricks that made up the dismantled façades he found some bricks that were marked solely with cuneiform script, while others were stamped with Greek and Aramaic characters. In material terms, the stamped bricks were all about the same size, and they were made with similar materials. The main differences between them were the length and sharpness of the cuneiform inscriptions, compared with the stamps that used Greek and Aramaic characters, and the fact that the cuneiform texts were divided into registers. Sarzec began to suspect that the two types of bricks represented earlier and later building phases, but at that stage he had no conception of the unimaginable expanse of time that separated them.

During the many subsequent seasons of work that were carried out by Sarzec and his French successors (all detailed in Chapters 23–5), the archaeological picture was slowly brought into some kind of focus. With regard to the bricks stamped with Greek and Aramaic letters, the structures that Sarzec had initially unearthed were dated to the Hellenistic period. Below them lay a much earlier Sumerian building that was constructed during the reign of Gudea. The later bricks, it was realised, were marked in the name of a certain Adadnadinakhe, whose Babylonian name (invoking the god Adad, as the 'giver of brothers'), was transliterated into the Greek and Aramaic alphabets (Fig. 238). Incidentally, the rather simple stamps on Adadnadinakhe's bricks were all the same, and the only other examples of Aramaic that have been found on the site were two small sherds with inked texts and a piece of a stamped vessel that were unearthed by the British Museum team (detailed below). The understanding of the Hellenistic remains was slowly and gradually further refined. The Hellenistic building, which was still thought of as a Palace, had been built in three phases. As marked on Sarzec's Plan A and Heuzey's New Plan (Fig. 114), the first works were centred around Court A, when wall OP was built as the principal NW façade, including the monumental

673

entranceway that was referred to as the Gate of Gudea, together with its associated Platform H. In a second major phase, the building was enlarged to the north-west, and a new set of rooms was built around two additional courtyards (B and C). At the same time, a new NW façade wall was erected, while the original NE façade was rebuilt, and both walls were decorated with intricately laid brickwork, including half-columns and stepped recesses that doubtless created changing effects of chiaroscuro, depending on the season and the time of day. Some sherds of beautiful turquoise glazed tiles unearthed by the British Museum team indicate that some of the walls were even more elaborately finished than has previously been supposed (Fig. 239). Sometime later, when the shrine was renovated, Gate M was blocked, and structures O, O' and O" were added. Finally, at the end of its life, the Hellenistic building was destroyed by fire.

Though the time frame of the Hellenistic construction was not entirely clear to the French researchers, some widely accepted theories were formed about its enigmatic instigator, Adadnadinakhe. The discovery of the base of the broken Gudea Colossus in niche N and then of seven other damaged and decapitated Gudea Statues in Court A confirmed a hypothesis that was implicit in the discovery of Sumerian and Hellenistic bricks side by side in the Hellenistic walls. More than two thousand years before Sarzec came to Girsu, Adadnadinakhe had excavated the Sumerian remains, salvaging its bricks and other useful or valuable materials, and installing the Gudea Statues in what was considered to be a newly built palatial residence, which was thought by the French pioneers to date from the mid-second century BCE. The dating of the Hellenistic building, and the accompanying assumption that it was a palatial residence or administrative centre for a local governor or official, were based on a hoard of 732 coins that were supposedly found buried under the floor of room 27 (on Plan A). Including a complete sequence of bronze issues from the reign of the important ruler Hyspaosines (who died in 124 BCE; mentioned again below) to that of Attambelus VII (who reigned from about 113 CE), the coins almost certainly had no historical connection with either Adadnadinakhe or the later Hellenistic builders of the Palace. The cache must have been buried after 116 CE (the date of the most recent coin), long after the site was abandoned, and it is actually much more likely that the coins, which were not directly associated with Girsu, came from the large Partho-Sasanian site of Medain, a short distance away. In any case,

FIGURE 238. A Hellenistic brick stamped in the name of Adadnadinakhe, found *in situ* by the British Museum team on Tell A.

as is detailed below, the British Museum team's work has rendered these arguments redundant because the Hellenistic construction was built about two centuries earlier than was assumed by the French.

With their inaccurate time frame established, the French investigators worked up a more complete portrait of Adadnadinakhe, who was considered to be a local Aramaic-speaking dignitary. Typically, Heuzey's view was the most nuanced. Looking at Sarzec's excavation reports, he was unsure whether the building was a palace or a temple, though he and Sarzec both stressed the presence of architectural features and ritual deposits that were known to be typical of religious sanctuaries. The more cautious interpretation was later abandoned, however. According to Genouillac (1936, p. 9), Adadnadinakhe was a *prince araméen*, who set himself up in style on the former Sumerian site, but the fullest and most

FIGURE 239. Sherd of a Hellenistic glazed tile found by the British Museum team on Tell A.

influential view of Adadnadinakhe was advanced by Parrot (1948, pp. 309–14), who imaginatively described him as a second-century *araméen de culture grecque*. Picturing Adadnadinakhe as a regional ruler who attempted to establish a new dynasty in the political vacuum that arose following the collapse of the Seleucids, Parrot argued that the building was a palatial residence with two distinct areas: a public space for ceremonial events, centred around Court A on the SE side of the structure, and a large suite of private rooms on the NW side, including a selamlik for male gatherings (Court B) and a harem (Court C). The epoch-making discovery of the praying Gudea Statues in a Hellenistic context in Court A—Parrot's ceremonial courtyard—led the recently appointed head of the Department of Oriental Antiquities at the Louvre to envisage the building not just as a palatial residence and a centre of local government, but also as a magnificent museum. Perhaps backprojecting his own role as the archaeologist and curator who was responsible for looking after and displaying the Gudea Statues in the Louvre, Parrot seems to have conceived of Adadnadinakhe as a ruler-cum-curator, or an archaeologist prince—an interpretation that has been largely accepted by subsequent scholars.

The British Museum team's findings, which necessitate a comprehensive reconsideration of the Hellenistic strata in Girsu, mean that these outdated theories can finally be discarded. The results of the excavations, together with the associated arguments and interpretations, are laid out below. In summary, Adadnadinakhe was a contemporary of Alexander the Great, and the original Hellenistic structure was almost certainly built shortly after 331 BCE, when Alexander took control of Babylonia. The extension was added probably around 250 BCE, while the Hellenistic-era construction was eventually destroyed in the latter part of the second century BCE, in the tumultuous decades that followed the rise of the Parthians, when Hyspaosines of Characene repeatedly attempted to extend his area of influence across the region. The large number of varied Hellenistic votives and the Hellenistic foundation deposits that were excavated by the British Museum team strongly suggest that the building was indeed founded as a shrine, but one that could accommodate the Gudea Statues alongside a range of other imagery—all of which must have had special associations for the many visitors who travelled to Girsu, and indeed for the authorities who commissioned it and oversaw its construction from the time of Adadnadinakhe onwards. In order to understand the history of the building, it is essential to present a broad chronology of events from the mid-sixth century to the late second century BCE.

The Rise and Fall of Regional Powers in Mesopotamia from 539 BCE to 125 BCE

The overarching sense of continuity that ran through the rise and fall of successive ancient Mesopotamian states and regional powers was ruptured in 539 BCE, when the Persian Cyrus the Great took control of Babylon. The territories that were ruled by Babylon, including the old Sumerian regions of southern Mesopotamia, were absorbed into Cyrus's Achaemenid empire, which became the major power in the region for the next two centuries. Persian rule in Mesopotamia was subsequently brought to an end by the stunning victories achieved by Alexander III of Macedon, later known as Alexander the Great, over Darius III, the last Persian king of kings. Alexander reached Babylon in 331 BCE, where, according to one of his early biographers, he was met outside the gates by the surrendering Persian governor, together with the state treasurer, who is said to have carpeted the road with flowers and perfumed it with incense burnt at silver altars (Curtius 5:17–27). Presented with an array of gifts, including lions and caged leopards, Alexander entered

Babylon in his chariot, accompanied by his army and a procession of citizens. He remained in the city for more than a month—the longest sojourn in his entire campaign—before continuing eastwards and extending his empire as far as the Indian subcontinent, before eventually returning to Babylon, where he died prematurely in 323 BCE.

A period of turmoil followed, during which the territories conquered by Alexander were partitioned, and a series of leading figures vied for control. The situation in Mesopotamia was resolved in the spring of 311 BCE, when Seleucus I Nicator, at that time one of Alexander's less prominent Macedonian generals, consolidated his hold on Babylon and founded the eponymous Seleucid empire, which controlled territories stretching from the Mediterranean to India. Accordingly, the year 311 BCE was taken as the beginning of the Seleucid era in the new calendar that was retained for centuries after the end of Seleucid rule in the region. From 305 BCE to his assassination in 281 BCE, Seleucus spent very little time in Babylon, but around 307 BCE he founded the new Greek city of Seleucia on the Tigris (about 30 km south of modern Baghdad) as the capital of his eastern empire. Comparable in size and influence to Alexandria in Egypt, it quickly became a flourishing centre for the dissemination of Hellenistic culture in Mesopotamia. At the time of his death at the ripe old age of seventy-seven, Seleucus was the last surviving general to have served under Alexander, and he was arguably enjoying the crowning moments of his career. He had enlarged his empire to its greatest extent and initiated its expansion into western Asia Minor, Thrace and Macedonia.

Despite the violent circumstances of Seleucus's demise, the kingship passed smoothly to his son Antiochus I Soter, who ruled for the next twenty years, but by the mid-third century BCE the empire was in decline. A series of internecine struggles was followed by the loss of Babylonia to the Egyptian Ptolemy III, who took the city of Babylon in 246 or early 245 BCE. It was quickly regained (in July 245 BCE) by Seleucus II, but Seleucid authority was further weakened by the loss of Parthia in north-eastern Iran, Bactria in Central Asia and a huge portion of the western empire that was effectively seized by Seleucus II's brother. More upheavals ensued, including the loss of western Asia Minor in 238 BCE, and episodes of unrest were recorded in Babylonia. Fifteen years later the young king Seleucus III, who was murdered in 223 BCE, was succeeded by his brother Antiochus III, whose

reign was immediately disrupted by a revolt led by Molon, the governor or satrap of Media. Having seized Babylon, Seleucia on the Tigris and the city of Susa to the east, Molon was defeated by Antiochus in 220 BCE, but that did not mean that Antiochus's troubles were at an end. His uncle Achaeus, the governor of Asia Minor, led another rebellion that was not quelled until 213 BCE. Thereafter, Antiochus spent seven years (from 212 to about 205 BCE) travelling the length and breadth of the empire, engaged in a superficially successful attempt to cement his authority. This brought a degree of stability to Babylonia, as is confirmed by increased Seleucid activity (probably under Antiochus III and Antiochus IV) in the important trade routes that crossed the Persian Gulf.

In 188 BCE, however, with the signing of the Treaty of Apamea, the Seleucids suffered a seismic blow, when they were forced to cede control of most of their western territories to the Romans. Though this drastically reduced the size of the empire, which by then included Syria, Mesopotamia and western Iran, it magnified a constantly repeated trend in the Seleucid era by further enhancing the role of Babylonia in what remained of the empire, as both a stabilising force and a source of prosperity. The remaining decades of Seleucid authority in the region were undermined by internal dynastic struggles and a failure to deal with the growing threat presented by the Parthians of western Iran, while further complications were caused by a clause in the humiliating Treaty of Apamea, which dictated that the heir to the Seleucid throne had to remain in Rome as a hostage. A series of revolts and failed policies continued to weaken the regime over succeeding decades until, shortly after 148 BCE, the Parthians conquered Media (in north-west Iran). By 141 BCE they were established in Babylon, and they might also have had control of some southern territories, including Girsu. The next two decades saw ongoing conflicts in Babylonia between the Parthians, the Seleucids and other pretenders to the crown of Babylon, notably the Elymaeans and the Characeneans (rulers of an area to the south of Mesopotamia that included parts of the Euphrates, the Tigris and the Shatt al-Arab waterway that discharges into the Persian Gulf). Parthian control of Babylon was boosted by their defeat of the Seleucid Antiochus VII Sidetes at a battle in Media in 129 BCE, but they were thwarted in their efforts to secure their supremacy by Hyspaosines of Characene, whose repeated incursions led to his being recognised as the king of Babylon in about

127 BCE. Hyspaosines continued to frustrate the Parthians until 125 BCE, when he was forced to accept Mithridates II of Parthia as his overlord and to return to Characene. This is the turbulent and violent backdrop to the final destruction and abandonment of the Hellenistic building in Girsu, and the continued period of unrest might have deterred subsequent efforts to reoccupy the site.

Mesopotamian Culture in the Hellenistic Era

The ascent of the Achaemenids, led by Cyrus, did nothing to diminish the intellectual vigour and cultural pride of the inhabitants of Babylonia. On the contrary, a series of breakthroughs, particularly in astronomy and astrology, testify to the continuing vitality of regional scholarship in the Achaemenid era. Learned culture was subsequently preserved and even enhanced under the incoming Macedonians. As Curtius (5:24) remarks, when Alexander and his men entered Babylon, it was 'the city itself, with its beauty and antiquity, that commanded the attention not only of the king, but of all the Macedonians', and Alexander is reputed to have ordered the restoration of some previously damaged shrines. Though the point should not be overstressed, it is hardly an exaggeration to say that Mesopotamian art, craft and literacy enjoyed a resurgence in the wake of Alexander's conquest and the consolidation of Seleucid rule, particularly with regard to sacred art and ritual performance.

A wealth of epigraphic material from important scholarly libraries and temple archives has been found in Hellenistic Babylon and Uruk. The texts include chronicles, king lists, astronomical diaries, literary, mathematical and scientific writings, instructions for the performance of rituals, hymns, prayers, prophecies, legal documents and the texts of formal public pronouncements. In addition, a large corpus of Greek inscriptions has emerged. In terms of architecture, excavations at sites in Seleucid Borsippa, Uruk, Babylon and Larsa have all yielded the spectacular ruins of renovated temples that were dedicated to the ancient gods, including the Ezida of the god Nabu, the Eanna and Irigal shrines of Inanna (Babylonian Ishtar), the Esagila of Marduk and the Ebabbar of the sun god, Shamash. New religious complexes were also founded, notably the Bit Resh temple of An (or Anu) and his consort Antum, and the Eshgal of the goddess Nanaya.

The proliferation of cultural activities was fostered by the period of relative stability that the region enjoyed under Seleucus and during the reigns of his son Antiochus I Soter (who died in 261 BCE) and his grandson Antiochus II Theos (who died suddenly in 246 BCE). With their base in Babylonia, which was the administrative centre of the empire, the Seleucid kings increasingly took it upon themselves to govern in an atmosphere of pomp and splendour that was worthy of the traditional Babylonian potentates. Cuneiform inscriptions record that Seleucus and Antiochus I repaired temples and ziggurats, and that they sacrificed to some of the Mesopotamian gods. Even down to the time of Antiochus III, who ruled from 222 BCE to 187 BCE, Seleucid leaders performed many of the rites associated with Babylonian kingship, including the celebration of the important New Year festival. Outside the capital, high officials and Greek dignitaries took part in local cults.

Conversely, though the degree to which Babylonia was Hellenised under the Seleucids is a matter of scholarly debate, it is clear that the Mesopotamians adopted some distinctive aspects of Hellenistic material culture. They notably began to organise their cities in ways that can be compared to the Greek city states (poleis); they introduced marketplaces (agoras) and Greek-style coinage; they wore apotropaic Greek amulets (bullae) and made seals in the Greek style; and they began to organise theatrical performances after the manner of Greek drama. In many instances, as the archaeological evidence shows, to greater and lesser degrees the customs of the Greeks and the Babylonians appear inevitably to have fused to create syncretic forms. This was especially the case with regard to religious and ritual practices, the taking of meals (household commensality) and craftsmanship. The British Museum team's finds further confirm the use of Greek pottery forms and the introduction of terracotta figurines that were manufactured using techniques and styles that were brought from the Aegean, while Greek iconography was adapted for the depiction of local deities, and characteristic Graeco-Babylonian styles of artwork were developed.

With more specific reference to Mesopotamian attitudes to history, the deep interest that the people of Mesopotamia took in their own culture and ancestry is noteworthy at all periods. It is exemplified by the immemorial custom of excavating the foundations of earlier temples so that, when they came to renew or restore them, later rulers could add their own foundation deposits to those left by their predecessors. The practice was developed to an unprecedented extent by the bookish Nabonidus, the last independent ruler of Babylon, who left detailed cuneiform records of his activities and findings, including carefully worked out estimates of the dates of his ancient forebears. Such traditions were perpetuated down to Seleucid times, and the post-Alexander era has sometimes been regarded as a pioneering epoch of antiquarianism that was marked by an intense interest in the past. Following in the footsteps of their ancestors since the fall of the last Neo-Sumerian dynasty of Ur, Mesopotamian scribes in Seleucid Babylonia reverently preserved Sumero-Akkadian literacy and knowledge by producing annotated copies of archaic hymns and myths, as well as many other texts, on fired-clay memorial tablets. Like Nabonidus, many Neo-Babylonian monarchs regarded restoration work, including the retrieval of ancient artworks and the revival of old rituals, as a pious obligation, and they nurtured well-established conventions surrounding the renewal and refurbishment of shrines.

Clearly, these are important contexts for the work that was carried out in Girsu, and Adadnadinakhe himself has regularly been viewed as a key exemplum in support of the idea that late first-millennium BCE Mesopotamia was populated by learned proto-archaeologists. A note of caution must be sounded, however, because the British Museum team's findings allow for a more detailed interpretation of Adadnadinakhe's activities than has previously been possible. Whereas, formerly, the discovery of the Gudea Statues seemed to define the Hellenistic building in Girsu as a kind of memorial dedicated to the architect of the long-abandoned Eninnu, the new findings strongly suggest that the Hellenistic-era shrine incorporated a special fusion of Mesopotamian and Hellenistic elements. In order to gain an insight into the meaning of the syncretism and the character of the Girsu institution in which it flourished, it is therefore vital to set aside previous assumptions about Adadnadinakhe as an early archaeologist or an antiquarian curator and to try to reassess the evidence that relates to his revival of the Sumerian on its own merits, as indicative of its Babylonian–Hellenistic setting.

Adadnadinakhe and his Hellenistic Successors

Adadnadinakhe's restoration project has no exact parallels in the later history of the great shrines of ancient Mesopotamia because, with some exceptionally ambitious aims in mind, he dramatically transformed procedures that had previously been followed elsewhere. On the one hand, he expressed what might be termed a typical Mesopotamian mentality by employing a tried and tested methodology that had precedents, for example in the actions carried out by Nabonidus in Ur in the mid-sixth century BCE. In general terms, later rulers sometimes carefully located and exposed foundation deposits in order to place their own named and dated artefacts alongside those of their cultural and architectural forebears. This was a delicate business, however, and malefactors risked incurring the wrath of the gods. On at least one such important occasion—namely, Naram-Sin's reconstruction of the Egal in Nippur—it was widely held that the gods had wreaked their destructive vengeance on the Akkad empire. Adadnadinakhe acted differently. Instead of merely adding his credentials to those of his ancestors, he salvaged and reused the ancient artefacts that he excavated, taking them from their foundational positions and painstakingly repositioning them in his new building.

His task was both complicated and facilitated by the passage of time—some fourteen centuries, during which Gudea's meticulously decommissioned New Eninnu lay in a state of neglect. Although it was at least partly interred when it was finally closed, the complex was nevertheless affected during the long interval by episodes of severe erosion and collapse. Consequently, as it presented itself to Adadnadinakhe's workers and priestly agents, Tell A must have seemed a battered and misshapen distortion of its former glory. The British Museum team's excavations revealed the preparatory and initial phases of Adadnadinakhe's project, which, broadly speaking, were executed in three stages. First, the builders retrieved artefacts dating to the third millennium BCE, apparently paying special attention to those deriving from the reign of Gudea (and to a much lesser extent from the time of Gudea's father-in-law, Ur-Bau). Secondly, they recovered enough of Gudea's walls to enable them to follow the general outlines of the ancient ground plan and to reference Sumerian architectural features in their contemporary design. Thirdly, in accordance with age-old Mesopotamian practices, it was necessary actually to incorporate at least some key parts of the old building within the newly constructed walls.

The most renowned objects retrieved by Adadnadinakhe were the magnificent Gudea Statues that were later re-excavated by Sarzec. They were found in Hellenistic contexts, mainly in Court A (on Sarzec's Plan A; Fig. 111), though it should be stressed that, when Sarzec unearthed them, they were not in the display locations intended for them by Adadnadinakhe. On the contrary, the statues had been deliberately removed from the niches in which they were placed in the Hellenistic-era building and brought to Court A to be desecrated and decapitated when Girsu was overrun by invaders in the mid-second century BCE. As this implies, the statues were clearly a principal focus in the Hellenistic construction, though the British Museum team's findings would suggest that they were probably part of a more comprehensive cross-cultural display. It has been suggested (Kosmin 2018, p. 200) that Statue B, the representation of Gudea with the blueprint of the temenos of the New Eninnu inscribed on the tablet in his lap, might have provided inspiration for Adadnadinakhe when he was planning his own shrine. There is some merit in the idea, though it is also problematic, in particular because it assumes that Adadnadinakhe's focus was fundamentally local, even Sumerian, but this was not necessarily the case. Most importantly, with the possible exception of the positions of the entranceways and perhaps some external niches, the ground plan of the Hellenistic building that was recorded by Sarzec on his Plan A represents a structure that differed very considerably indeed from the Eninnu as it is shown on Statue B—a fact that would not be affected by the possible shortcomings of Sarzec's neatly unified diagram, which synthesises different construction phases. With respect to Plan A, it should be stressed from the outset that the building shown on that diagram is not Adadnadinakhe's original shrine, but the later Hellenistic complex, after it was rebuilt and extended in the mid-third century BCE.

In place of Gudea's L-shaped design, the structure shown on Sarzec's Plan A is generally oblong. Like Gudea's Eninnu, its corners face the cardinal points, and its long walls are on the NE and SW sides of the building, while its principal façade was seemingly either on the north-east or (more plausibly, as is discussed below) the north-west, though the main approaches to the structure might have changed over time. Most significantly, the NE and SW walls of the later building swell out at points close to their middles (though not from points directly opposite each other) to create two oblique façades that project out from corners whose angles are slightly greater than ninety degrees. The obtuse angles on the corners of the NE façade appear to have been slightly larger than those on the SW side because the diagonals of the NE façade are a little more pronounced than those on the opposite wall. Sarzec's plan is not precise enough to allow for proper measurements, but the difference might have been as little as one degree. In any event, it was sufficient to differentiate the two sides of the building. The reasons for this unusual irregularity are unclear, and it is important again to emphasise that Sarzec's plan, with its two graded long walls, does not represent Adadnadinakhe's initial design, which, as is detailed in the British Museum team's results below, was focused on Court A and mainly comprised those areas immediately around and on the SE side of the Hellenistic courtyard. The NW part of the building on Sarzec's Plan A, including Courts B and C, together with the rooms around them, formed a later extension that was added more than half a century after the time of Adadnadinakhe, though early variants of the outer walls in the NW area were probably used in the first iteration of the shrine to create an open-air communal space (also described below). Adadnadinakhe's main structure was therefore built above the SE part of Gudea's New Eninnu, in particular over the space that was occupied by Gudea's Ningirsu temple, with the important walls that are together known as the Gate of Gudea situated on the NW side of the Hellenistic-era shrine. The Ur-Bau plaza to the north-east of the temple area (in the horizontal bar of Gudea's L-shaped complex) was cut off by Adadnadinakhe, as can be seen by the position of the Ur-Bau corner on Sarzec's Plan A (assuming this is broadly accurate). Accordingly, the need to redefine the lines of the ancient walls that ran from the area of the NE gate in the middle of the NE façade, or the Battle Gate (see Chapter 40; the gates are referred to by the names marked on Fig. 219) in Gudea's New Eninnu to a point on the NW side of the Sunrise Gate (on Gudea's SE façade) might partly explain the overall angled effect of the NE façade on the NE side of Court A. Similarly, on the SW side, the angle might have been introduced to connect a locus defined by the protruding towers of Gudea's City Gate to points determined by the lines of Gudea's main temenos walls on this side of the new building.

The ground plan decided upon by Adadnadinakhe was nonetheless unusual, and even if his architects were responding to what they perceived to be the lines of some of Gudea's Sumerian walls, they must also have had in mind a sense of the aesthetics that were thus implied. If it is assumed that the lines of the outer walls on the NW side of the complex were

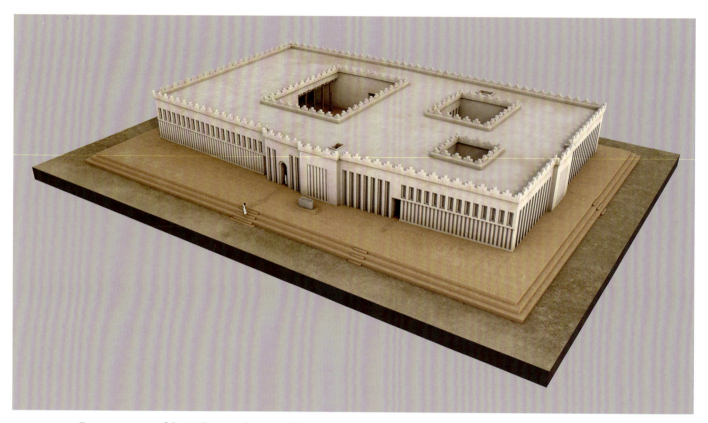

FIGURE 240. Reconstruction of the Hellenistic shrine on Tell A after it was enlarged around 250 BCE, showing the N corner and the articulated NE façade. Inside the building are the three internal courtyards (from left to right): Court A, the largest on the SE side, and Courts B and C to the north-west.

already established by Adadnadinakhe, the later architects who rebuilt this area to create the NW extension retained the angled effects in the continuations of the NE and SW façades (Figs. 240 and 241). Consequently, on both sides of the complex the walls presumably followed lines that connected the bulges on the NE and SW sides of Adadnadinakhe's building with points defined by the positioning of Gudea's original temenos walls, which were narrowest on the NW side of the Ningirsu temple (where they formed the vertical bar of the L in Gudea's L-shaped design). It would unquestionably have been structurally simpler for both Adadnadinakhe and his successors to build (or rebuild) façades that followed parallel lines and had right-angled corners, and the resulting inner spaces would have been functionally much easier to deal with. Similarly, conventional brick walls that strictly followed parallel and perpendicular lines would have been intrinsically slightly more stable because they could be more securely bonded using the square and rectangular bricks that Adadnadinakhe found in such profusion on the site. The resulting walls would also have more easily accommodated any necessary structural features, including doorways and stairways. Thereafter, the rectangular or square spaces created inside the parallel and perpendicular façades would have facilitated the addition of non-structural fittings such as storage areas and platforms for offerings and statues. As has been seen repeatedly in this study, and as is confirmed by numerous examples from all around the region, cultic architecture in Mesopotamia had long emphasised regularity of design in order to create a harmonious whole that reflected the religious principles on which the buildings were based. That aesthetic had conceivably been reinforced by the architectural cosmopolitanism of the Achaemenids, followed by the Hellenistic influences that were disseminated in the wake of Alexander the Great and under the Seleucids.

Apart from the need to deal with the practical problems of how to derive a new ground plan from the preserved traces

FIGURE 241. Close-up of the reconstruction of the Hellenistic shrine's NE façade, showing entrance M (right) and the niche containing Statue D, the Gudea Colossus (left).

of Gudea's temenos, the departures from regular square and rectangular walls might be explained in a number of ways. Structural clues found on the outer façades, as well as inside individual rooms and in the courtyards, together with the overall layout of the building, all indicate that Sarzec's Plan A uncritically amalgamates at least two construction phases. The roughly barrel-shaped outline that it shows might not have been an especially noteworthy characteristic of Adadnadinakhe's main design, which might have looked like a slightly irregular squarish diamond, or a trapezium (above the old Ningirsu temple area). Ground plans of this general type existed in Babylon—the Emah (the 'exalted house', or Temple of Ninmah) and the Temple of Ninurta (a cognomen of Ningirsu), for example. Instead, Sarzec's plan reflects the final shape of the building as it appeared between around 250 BCE and 150 BCE, after the NW extension was completed. Despite that, the lines of the outer façades on the NW side were probably defined during the earlier phase, when

the areas occupied by Courts B and C on Sarzec's Plan A might have formed a large, open courtyard. This would have provided the complex with a walled open-air congregational area that it appears to have lacked in its latest manifestation, and this could have been the site of the principal altar, which was outside the main walls in the two sacred complexes in Babylon mentioned above, as it also was generally in Hellenistic temples. This was, of course, a dramatic change of emphasis from the Sumerian approach. The British Museum team's investigations would confirm that the dimensions of the building recorded by Sarzec on Plan A probably do generally relate to the footprint of the outer walls as they were established during the first construction phase, including a NW courtyard. Subsequently, however, the NW area was considerably remodelled. Notably, the NW and NE façades were comprehensively rebuilt and embellished with ornamental stepped recesses and half-columns, while the large, open courtyard to the north-west was infilled and raised to provide a base for Courts B and C, together with associated suites of rooms.

If it is assumed that the shape of the building as it appears on Sarzec's Plan A was implicit from its inception then the compromises that were needed in order to make rational sense of the inner spaces shed further light on the manner of construction. The fact that the walls to the north-west and the south-east were parallel to each other probably provided the builders with baselines that helped them to position the interior partition walls. This would help to explain why the internal walls with NE–SW orientations (parallel to the shorter end walls) appear to follow more regular lines than those placed on the long NW–SE axis. Particularly in the early stages of construction, which was concentrated around Court A, it would presumably have been most convenient to define the walls by marking out lines that were parallel to the SE façade and then to work from the centre outwards. In this way the irregularities of the angled NE and SW façades could have been accommodated into a rational scheme, albeit as unconventional elements, though this was not especially uncommon, as can be seen by comparing the ground plans of the Emah and the Temple of Ninurta in Babylon, for example. Conversely, if the builders had worked from out to in, from the inner sides of the NE and SW walls towards the centre of the space that was defined by Court A, then the angles of the façades would inevitably have created difficulties.

Furthermore, if the general footprint of the building as it is represented on Sarzec's Plan A was initiated at the outset, it is important to suggest a possible historical context for the expressed architectural and aesthetic choices. The ground plan in its entirety has no exact parallel in Mesopotamian architecture, though the two overall trapezium-like shapes of which it is formed (the Adadnadinakhe stage to the southeast and the later extension to the north-west) seem clearly to reflect Neo-Babylonian traditions of sacred architecture. This is also true of the courtyard arrangements in the first and second phases of the shrine. Nonetheless, some eclecticism might be observed in the way the various elements and features were combined. The building's decorative brickwork was made using ancient fired bricks that were salvaged from the segmented column bases that were found in Gudea's New Eninnu. It included the Mesopotamian stepped buttresses that were found on the NW and NE external façades and on the SE side of Court B (inside the Hellenistic complex). Furthermore, the two ends of the NE façade and the middle

of the NW façade all featured circular engaged columnar buttresses (made of Gudea-era bricks) that recall kinds of brickwork that were used elsewhere in southern Mesopotamia from relatively early times, though perhaps not in combination with stepped recesses. Examples of both the stepped and the columnar brick buttresses have also been excavated in Uruk, which was well known as the major centre of later Hellenistic–Mesopotamian culture in southern Mesopotamia. Elsewhere, they were used in buildings from both the Achaemenid and the almost contemporary Parthian periods (Ghirshman 1954, Figs. 50 and 80). The implied eclecticism might also be evidenced in the overall form of the building, with its eventual incorporation of three contiguous courtyards—a feature of Neo-Babylonian temples (Downey 1988, pp. 38–42). Accordingly, the Hellenistic-era building on Tell A could have been designed in response to styles of late Mesopotamian decorative eclecticism that were widely used in the region, even in Achaemenid buildings from as far away as Persepolis. A second possibility is that the varied (and, to the modern eye, possibly rather incoherent) mixture of elements was used to invoke notions of antiquity. This would not define Adadnadinakhe as an antiquarian in the modern sense invoked by Parrot, however, since the new building was seemingly a kind of creative restoration—a temple built in a contemporary style that was intended to revive the ancient shrine, without trying slavishly to imitate Sumerian architectural structures. In that context the decorative elements used on the Hellenistic façades might be seen as contemporary recreations—much reduced and decidedly ornamental in intention—of the buttresses and other structural features that might have been observed among the remains of Gudea's original walls. Lastly, as Heuzey pointed out, the overall shape of the Hellenistic structure in its final form seems curiously reminiscent of a later foundation cylinder (Sarzec and Heuzey 1912, p. 15), and that effect might conceivably have been intentional. If that was indeed the case then the entire Hellenistic complex could have been conceived of as an oversized foundation deposit that was intended to assert a distinctive Babylonian political identity in a framework that was perhaps defined by Greek and Seleucid imperial rule.

Compared with the actions of previous high-ranking builders from the Sumerian era down to the time of Nabonidus, for example, the evidence indicates subtle but important differences in the way Adadnadinakhe used the objects that he recovered. In almost all earlier archaeologically documented cases from Sumerian times onwards, the ruler or high priest typically sought out foundation deposits that were often contained inside fired-brick boxes. Having accessed the original cavities, they would then replace one of the original inscribed objects with new artefacts that were marked with their own name and credentials. In accordance with the testimony of Sarzec and Parrot, the British Museum team's observations suggest that, having located ancient foundation deposits, Adadnadinakhe proceeded to remove them from their original positions and then to transfer them to his own building, either putting them on display (as was the case for the Gudea statues) or embedding them in the fabric of his construction. The Hellenistic walls, for example, were made of Gudea-era fired bricks that were laid side by side with Hellenistic bricks, juxtaposing past and present. Only one instance of a Hellenistic feature resembling a foundation deposit was found inside a brick box (see below), but the objects that were perhaps ceremonially interred differed markedly from superficially similar examples found elsewhere. Instead of the accumulation of old and new objects (inscriptions on stone tablets, clay or stone cylinders, or votive anthropomorphic foundation pegs, for example), Adadnadinakhe's box contained a stack of four fired bricks inscribed in Gudea's name, with the inscriptions placed upwards and carefully oriented, as described below. This suggests a break with traditional practices in terms of the objects that were buried, but perhaps a degree of continuity in the privileging of inscriptions.

In some respects, the emphasis on inscribed objects did not necessarily extend to the inscribed clay votive nails that were originally embedded in high numbers in the walls surrounding the sanctuary of Ningirsu, quantities of which were found randomly discarded in a wide range of contexts. The texts on the votive nails were inscribed individually, with densely spaced cuneiform signs that were characteristic of handwriting from the third millennium BCE, while the bricks were uniformly and distinctly marked with a stamp, but there is little or no doubt that the educated architects of the shrine—almost certainly Babylonian intellectuals, as outlined below—could recognise and read the script, so this would probably not account for the somewhat different treatments of the bricks and the clay nails. One obvious reason for the distinction might be that, while the bricks could be reused, the nails served no structural purpose. This would further imply that the Hellenistic-era builders were not reverently trying to preserve every detail of the old religion,

but were rather incorporating salient signs of it into a new structure that was intended to be a fusion of past and present traditions. Similarly, though they could surely read the texts on the clay nails, it is highly unlikely that they would have found much relevance in the hyper-sophisticated Lagash II theology (probably stemming from Ur-Bau) that was represented by the clay nails (see Chapter 43). That said, one particular group of clay nails was—almost beyond doubt—deliberately put together as a representative selection that related to the range of building works carried out mainly by Gudea, but also by Ur-Bau, and interred as a composite foundation deposit when the original shrine was expanded in the mid-third century BCE. This cache of cones (context 5439 in the British Museum team's Area B10, as further detailed below) would confirm that the Hellenistic-era builders were indeed aware of the objects' significance, but that, for whatever reason, the planners of the shrine only used them in an extremely limited way as foundation deposits.

A Babylonian–Hellenistic Revival of a Sumerian Shrine

The evidence unearthed by the British Museum team (detailed in Chapter 46) unequivocally confirms that the original shrine built by Adadnadinakhe soon after 331 BCE was of considerable interest to Hellenistic pilgrims, worshippers and visitors, and that its popularity and relevance grew markedly and steadily over the succeeding decades. Accordingly, more inner spaces were soon added, presumably around 250 BCE, and new decorative features were applied, especially to the façades. If Adadnadinakhe's outer walls stretched from the SE façade as it is shown on Sarzec's Plan A to a NE–SW line defined by wall OP (on Heuzey's New Plan; Fig. 114), together with the Gate of Gudea (which was seemingly rebuilt by Adadnadinakhe, such that the axis of the Sumerian entranceway was retained), then the extension increased the size of the main building by about fifty per cent. In addition, an altar was located on a new extended terrace, which was established at a slightly lower level than that of the main building, in front of the extension's new NW façade. This communal space would have enlarged the complex still further (Fig. 242). The discovery of the later altar would possibly imply that a NW altar was also a feature of Adadnadinakhe's earlier building, where it was perhaps

684   The Ningirsu Temple in the Hellenistic Era

placed in what is assumed to have been an open courtyard (enclosed with mud-brick walls and also at a lower level than the main building) on the NW side of the shrine. No sign of an earlier offering platform was found by the British Museum team, but that is not surprising, since the area in which it would presumably have been sited was levelled and elevated in the second wave of Hellenistic-era activity in order to create a stable foundation for the extension.

One piece of circumstantial evidence that would tend to confirm the deduction about the earlier altar is the relatively clear axis that leads through the two NW entrances (G and F on Heuzey's Plan A) to a point on the SE side of Court A. In comparable Neo-Babylonian sacred buildings an axis of this general type often led to the temple's principal cella, as can be seen on the ground plan of the Emah, which was probably built during the long reign of Nebuchadnezzar

FIGURE 242. Plan of the British Museum team's Area B12, a little to the north-west of Tell A, beyond the spoil heaps that surround the central part of the mound.

(605–562 BCE). The altar was positioned outside the Emah's NW façade, and the podium for the cult statue lay at the SE end of the building, on the other side of an open courtyard. Whether the similar orientation of the Emah and the first Hellenistic shrine in Girsu was purely coincidental is impossible to say, but the overall open arrangement, including the introduction of the courtyard, was conceivably the same. In Girsu, it meant that an inferred cult statue might have been visible almost from the temple's entrance, unless it was shielded behind inner walls, and a fairly uninterrupted line of sight probably extended from the vicinity of the cult podium to the external altar. This might well have given the surmised statue an immediate impact for visitors entering the temple, but it also implied that the activities taking place on and around the altar could, in principle, be observed by the deity. Variations on the layout were also possible, and the Babylonian Temple of Ninurta, for example, had three entrances, with the altar in front of the NE façade facing one of three open cellas that were lined up next to each other on the inside of the opposite SW wall (see Downey 1988, pp. 39–42). Generally, the cellas were open and visible from approaches that led through the buildings. Similarly, both of the cited Babylonian temples were organised around one or more courtyards, as were Adadnadinakhe's first temple, which was centred on Court A, and the later enlargement, which added Courts B and C. No traces of a cella were recorded at the SE end of the Hellenistic shrine in Girsu, but as can be seen on Sarzec's Plan A the area in which it was probably positioned was severely damaged before Sarzec started work, so it is impossible to judge the original arrangement. In addition, the many other open rooms (often referred to as niches) that completed the layout of the earlier and enlarged shrines were doubtless intended to house other relevant images, almost certainly including the diorite statues of Gudea.

Embedded in this brief summary are a host of tricky questions and a central paradox, which perhaps goes to the heart of the matter: if the revived Girsu shrine was indeed built in a familiar Babylonian style, and if it was in some important sense a genuine successor to Gudea's New Eninnu, as would be suggested by the inclusion of the Statues of Gudea, why did it appeal so strongly to a Hellenistic audience? It should also be stressed that, though the signs of ongoing Greek interest that were found by the British Museum team understandably relate mainly to the shrine in its extended form, important objects were also retrieved that date to the last decades of the fourth century BCE. Itemised below, they would suggest that (as indicated above) Adadnadinakhe's temple was built soon after the arrival in Babylon in 331 BCE of the Hellenistic forces led by Alexander the Great, and that the enlargement was carried out a little more than half a century later, under the Seleucids. The probable narrative deriving from this bare-bones chronology is laid out in Chapter 47, but it is important to say immediately that the Greeks who held power in the region and controlled the purse strings of the state must have been committed to the revival of the shrine from the outset and that their commitment did not wane over time. The construction of a renewed Eninnu on an abandoned site more than 200 km from Babylon (the region's capital under Alexander and for a time under the Seleucids) required a substantial investment of money and expertise that cannot be explained away by the discredited idea that Adadnadinakhe was a kind of regional Croesus who built a fanciful palace, presumably at his own expense. Similarly, it is hardly conceivable that ancient Girsu was attractive to the Greeks purely on account of Gudea's legendary renown. The inference must therefore be that the history of the Eninnu—the Temple of Ningirsu, together with Gudea, its Sumerian architect—could somehow be tied in with the mythology surrounding one or more Greek deities, and that this made it especially attractive to the Greek authorities, as well as to the many visitors who made the journey to Girsu. The basic hypothesis is confirmed by the numerous Hellenistic terracottas (probably votives) that were discovered by the British Museum team and are itemised in Chapter 46.

The further points of extreme interest are the style of the original building and the fact that the style was retained and enhanced when the shrine was enlarged. The possible open approach to the surmised cella would perhaps have appeared somewhat recognisable to Hellenistic visitors, but the internal layout of rooms and courtyards was very different to that of a Greek temple. By the same token, however, the Adadnadinakhe shrine and its enlargement bore little or no resemblance to a typical Sumerian sacred complex. In Gudea's New Eninnu, to take the most relevant comparison, the cella housing the cult podium was installed at the end of a labyrinthine series of turns at the very heart of the huge complex (see Chapter 40). The statue was dramatically—even theatrically, if that term can be introduced—hidden from public view, but profoundly connected to the outside world by the complicated set of theological meanings that were built into the shrine's orientation and layout (including its corners, walls and entrances) and expressed in foundation deposits (pegs that secured it to the earth and clay nails that attached it to the sky), together with steles, statues and inscriptions that gave form to the many associated mythological and religious narratives. Adadnadinakhe and his advisors seem unquestionably to have known exactly where the New Eninnu was located, and they might well have derived a pretty good idea of its Sumerian footprint from the plan on Statue B, but they did not try to recreate it in its original shape. As suggested above, the general outlines were probably based on perceptible remains that were identified on the higher parts of Tell A, notably the gateways and towers of the Battle Gate and City Gate on the NE and SW façades (Nos. 1 and 2 on Fig. 219), and those de facto apexes were joined to points on, or very close to, lines determined by the positions of Gudea's temenos walls. Apart from that, some of the entrances and external niches in the Hellenistic-era shrine seem to refer to the ones marked on Gudea's plan, and the later foundation deposits were no doubt also intended to reference those installed by Gudea, though a difference is also implied by the special way in which Adadnadinakhe treated them. Not content merely to add his name to a roll-call of predecessors in the time-honoured manner, Adadnadinakhe resited Gudea's deposits next to his own in a way that suggests both continuity and a break with the past. The ancient shrine was not simply being refurbished in honour of Ningirsu. Rather, it was being refounded in the revised context of fourth-century BCE religious practices and beliefs. It would be particularly interesting to know whether Adadnadinakhe's bricks were placed in a significant way with respect to those left by Gudea (whether their stamps were intended to be a kind of supplement to the Gudea texts, for example), but Sarzec unfortunately recorded no details of the exact relationship between them. Beyond that, in a Mesopotamian context, the

later Hellenistic deposits might in some ways appear rather anomalous, but the context was not, by definition, a purely Mesopotamian one.

Most significantly, the Hellenistic-era plan of the Adadnadinakhe shrine and its enlargement seem evidently to have been based on the court plans that were characteristic of Babylonian temples. The examples adduced for comparison above were built some two centuries before work began on the revived Girsu shrine at the end of the fourth century BCE, so the style might well have appeared both traditional and even rather archaic, especially to the eyes of the Greeks. Such traits would presumably have been considered appropriate for the reconstruction of a temple that was known to be extremely old (though it is perhaps unlikely that the Hellenistic-era builders had an accurate idea of its real age). As this suggests, the Babylonian design was conceived and implemented in an extremely sophisticated way, and the preparatory works (detailed below) were undertaken with great care, practical know-how and intellectual understanding, presumably under the supervision of Babylonian high priests or scribes (architects, historians, astrologers and scholars). The fascinating conclusion (developed in Chapter 47) is that the reconstruction, which was probably authorised and financed by the Greeks, was carried out by Babylonian designers, who introduced some Hellenistic elements, including Greek-style foundation deposits. The project was presumably represented as the restoration of an ancient shrine that could be said to have both Mesopotamian and Hellenistic associations, but in reality the planners built a new temple, possibly in a slightly archaic Babylonian style (perhaps in keeping with the surmised historical narrative), on a Sumerian site, incorporating some clear references to the original Sumerian building and embedding some Hellenistic ritual features, notably the foundation deposits.

CHAPTER 46

The Stratigraphy of the Hellenistic Shrine

EVIDENCE OF THE HELLENISTIC-ERA DIGGING WAS unfortunately obscured by the French re-excavations. Indeed, most of the Hellenistic cuts and subsequent backfills for the construction of Adadnadinakhe's shrine and its later extension were recut by the French pioneers, as is indicated by a detailed examination of the French work (see Chapter 28). In addition, the British Museum team's ability to identify Hellenistic pits was impeded by the individually smaller, but cumulatively severe truncations that were caused by modern looting, which was distributed unevenly across the site (see Chapter 29). The various truncations are described above, but it is worth restating them here. Most of the Hellenistic buildings and deposits from Tell A were removed almost entirely in modern times, in the late nineteenth century and the early part of the twentieth century. This destructive work left behind only very small parts of the SW and NW façades. All of the most important elements of the complex, including its external walls, its internal partition walls and the three courtyards, were dismantled. Mud-brick remains were largely overlooked, but the fired bricks that could be salvaged were transported to the southern part of the site (the city of Girsu rather than just Tell A in particular), where they were used to build a series of dig houses.

The Hellenistic-era shrine was therefore almost entirely obliterated, with only a few small parts of the complex surviving above the cella in Gudea's Temple of Ningirsu on the SE side of the mound. Miraculously, however, the previous excavators inflicted only localised damage in this area. Although the Hellenistic levels were eliminated, and trenches were excavated in the SE and SW parts of the old cella, as well

as on the NW side of Gudea's antecella, enough survived to enable the team to identify discrete pits that were dug in the early Hellenistic period. Despite extensive truncation and erosion, some Hellenistic pits, together with parts of the outer NE mud-brick terrace wall (presumably from the first phase that was overseen by Adadnadinakhe), survived in Areas B6 and B9 (Fig. 139). More substantial parts of the Hellenistic foundations and some signs of the effects of Hellenistic disturbance on foundation deposits survived in Areas B4, B5 and B8 on the SW side of the Hellenistic shrine. Fortunately, more extensive remains were preserved in Areas B10 and B12 (Figs. 139 and 242), to the north-west of the temple complex, where the team was able to unearth a stratigraphic sequence related to the NW extension of the shrine in the post-Adadnadinakhe phase. Even here, however, a deep sounding in the SE corner of the excavation in Area B10 had led to severe localised erosion that was caused by water channels that had cut through the original Hellenistic precinct wall.

Preparing the Ground

The first stage of Adadnadinakhe's project left traces that were investigated by the British Museum team (Fig. 243). When the initial phase of the building work began, the fourth-century BCE architects must have been confronted with the badly deformed mound that was all that remained of Sumerian Tell A. Rather low and uneven, the tell must have been cut and damaged on its edges by erosion gullies, and further worn away due to the more regular effects of weathering. The

FIGURE 243. Excavated section of the SW façade of the original Hellenistic shrine, constructed shortly after 331 BCE, viewed from the south-west, with the Hellenistic foundation box visible on the right.

prevailing weather patterns would indicate that the north-western parts of the tell were more severely affected than other areas of the mound. The highest parts of the tell were almost certainly located above the walls of Gudea's Eninnu, which had been repaired and refurbished during the first half of the early second millennium BCE. Thereafter it had been neglected, and the summit of the mound was doubtless poorly defined as a consequence of the gradual collapse of the Sumerian precinct during the intervening centuries (from around 1750 BCE to sometime shortly after 331 BCE). The height differential between the more elevated Ningirsu temple on the south-east side of Gudea's complex and the lower-lying Bau temple to the north-west was probably signalled by distinct humps. The Bau shrine was presumably less prominent, partly due to its inherently lower elevation, but also to its location on the north-west side of the mound, where it was more vulnerable to the prevailing patterns of weathering and erosion. Any remains of the Ur-Bau plaza to the north-east were also presumably at a lower level, reflecting its original elevation by comparison with that of Gudea's Ningirsu temple.

Four further sources of information might conceivably have been available to the Hellenistic prospectors when they started work. First, it has been speculated that Statue B (showing Gudea with the plan of the New Eninnu) might have been discovered at an early stage of the project and used as a guide to help define the general limits and configuration of the exterior of the Eninnu. This is a tempting idea, and it works well with the conception of Adadnadinakhe as a self-styled successor to Gudea (a theory that is re-evaluated in Chapter 47), but it would not explain why the L-shaped complex was so dramatically reduced to the irregular rectangle that became the Hellenistic-era variant of the Sumerian shrine. If, from the outset, the builders knew that Gudea's shrine included the Ur-Bau plaza, for example, and if (perhaps for reverential reasons) they wished to follow the Sumerian design as closely as possible, it would presumably have made sense for them to try to recreate a variant of the outline of Gudea's actual walls as they were recorded on the plan. One feature that the Hellenistic-era builders seemingly did derive, either from the plan on Statue B and (or) from observation of the remains, was the positioning of the gates, which are closely correlated with the locations of the gates in Gudea's temenos. Indeed, this is a feature of the Hellenistic shrine that differs markedly from the possible Babylonian analogues noted above that had very few entrances (one in the Emah and two in the Ninurta temple, respectively), which were clearly designed to stress principal axes through the building. This was also probably the case for one axis in the Hellenistic shrine in Girsu (as is discussed below), but the entrances marked on Sarzec's Plan A seem to have been expressly added to reference the original Sumerian ground plan of Gudea's New Eninnu. That being the case, it is also important to re-emphasise that Sarzec's plan relates to the expanded shrine that was completed around 250 BCE, thereby raising the possibility that it was the later Hellenistic builders in particular who might have paid special attention to Gudea's ground plan on Statue B. Indeed, the fact that they rebuilt some façade walls makes it extremely difficult to determine the extents to which the earlier and later planners of the Hellenistic-era structure might have made use of Gudea's plan.

Secondly, a great number of inscribed clay cones in varying states of preservation could potentially have been found on or close to the surface of the tell and in the mud-brick masses of the collapsed walls. Recording the names of specific subshrines that made up the complex as a whole, and therefore possibly preserved in clusters relating to particular parts of the New Eninnu, they might have provided guidance as to the internal layout of the complex. Thirdly, most of the Sumerian complex was built with fired bricks inscribed in the name of Gudea, but considerable quantities in the name of Ur-Bau must also have survived. In particular, sections of Ur-Bau's old Ningirsu temple, which was retained in its entirety by Gudea in the Ur-Bau plaza (facing north-east at the SE end of the complex), were preserved largely intact until they were rediscovered by Sarzec in the 1880s. It is not clear whether the Hellenistic builders were aware of this area of the complex, but their knowledge of it could have been confirmed by the plan on Statue B. Nonetheless, they appear to have simply cut across the Ur-Bau plaza, without taking it into account in any significant way when they built the outer wall of the new precinct in this area. Though it is still conceivable that the underlying Ur-Bau remains provided some kind of guide for the marking out of the new walls, therefore, it is apparent that they did not contribute substantially to the executed ground plan. Fourthly, and perhaps most importantly, some vestiges of the higher and most substantial parts of the Sumerian complex, and indeed of its facings on the fronts of its massive terraces, might have left visible impressions on the surface of the ground, perhaps especially the mammoth gate towers

and buttresses and the outer fired-brick facings of the terrace platforms. Some of these especially thick structures, particularly the ones at higher elevations in the area of the Ningirsu temple might have been preserved at relatively shallow levels below the mound's surface. Any remains would undoubtedly have been in a poor and collapsed state, but they might conceivably have acted as practical markers.

The second stage of the Hellenistic preconstruction phase involved digging pits into the body of the tell. Several were discovered during the British Museum team's investigations, and it became clear that they were executed systematically, targeting specific locations and features. The exact positions in which they were dug would seem to indicate that the Hellenistic-era workers had a reasonably good knowledge of the probable layout of the Sumerian shrine, and the exploratory soundings were apparently opened using techniques designed to cause as little damage to the fabric of the original structure as possible. Apart from a desire to respect the ancient building and the rituals surrounding its closure, the degree of care might have stemmed from a wish to reference the Sumerian structure in particular ways in the layout of the new complex, as noted with regard to the gateways. The initial Hellenistic soundings can be broadly divided into two kinds: pits that were dug to investigate special features, and those that were opened in search of deliberately buried artefacts and deposits, including the favissas that were created when the Sumerian shrine was finally closed. In all cases the intention was to exhume objects that could be reused in one way or another in the later structure (as detailed below), but the locations that were sought out most intensively were those in and around the gateways, together with other points in the Sumerian complex where the Hellenistic-era planners might have expected to find foundation boxes. Signs of the initial excavations were identified in the new trenches cut by the British Museum team, and all were placed either in the vicinity of Gudea's Ningirsu temple at the SE end of the complex or in the temenos gates that gave access to the interior of the Eninnu. By contrast with the indiscriminate excavations carried out by the French pioneers, the evidence suggests that the Hellenistic-era builders had a good idea where to dig and how to avoid causing unnecessary damage to the underlying remains.

In eight instances the team found signs that the third-millennium foundation boxes had been disturbed in the Hellenistic period, though the degree of certainty varied slightly, depending on the locations. The first six instances, relating to the two temenos gateways that were exposed on the NE and SW sides of the complex, respectively (discussed in Chapter 36 above), provided clear examples of the retrieval of foundation deposits. The other two were associated with strategic positions around the Ningirsu shrine itself, namely the passageway in the partition wall that separated the cella and the antecella, and the Ningirsu temple's N corner.

Two disturbances were identified in Area B9, in the NE gateway in the middle of the NE façade of the temenos (Gudea's Battle Gate; No. 1 on Fig. 219). Both had been slightly damaged by erosion that occurred relatively recently, as a consequence of the deep nineteenth-century excavations that Sarzec carried out just to the south of the main cavities. The first was an oval pit (5211), which, as confirmed by its position, probably signalled the removal of a foundation box. The cavity was partially sealed by mud-brick coursing (5222), which was a component of the Hellenistic terrace platform that extended out around the rebuilt sacred precinct, and the pit was dug into Gudea's Lagash II temenos wall (5245). Measuring 2.05 m (north-west to south-east) × 1.4 m (north-east to south-west) × 0.5 m (deep), it contained a single backfill (5210) that was made up of a sandy silt deposit with inclusions of fired brick and bitumen, together with possible remnants of a foundation box and one Lagash II cone (TG1867) commemorating Gudea's rebuilding of Bau's shrine, referred to as the Eurukug.

Oval pit 5211 was associated with a linear cut (5236), but the relationship between the two was difficult to clarify, partly because of the damage that was directly caused by the earlier excavations carried out by Sarzec, and partly due to subsequent water erosion. Cut 5236, which measured 11 m × 6 m (north-west to south-east and north-east to south-west, respectively), was judged to be an exploratory trench that was dug by the Hellenistic-era investigators, and if this interpretation is correct, it would indicate that the linear cut was excavated before the more precisely located oval pit (5211). Cut 5236 contained a backfilled deposit (5201). More interestingly, however, it had also been used as a foundation trench for the Hellenistic terrace wall (5222), suggesting that its original exploratory purpose was later changed, when the trench was subsequently used to provide space for the workers who cut back the face of the tell, and eventually turned into a foundation trench for the Hellenistic terrace wall. Noteworthy finds in deposit 5201 included a Thunderbird

brick (TG1685), a fragment of Sumerian terracotta (TG1668) and a piece of Hellenistic figurative terracotta (TG1670) in the form of a Macedonian rider wearing a wide-brimmed flat hat, known as a *kausia*.

Pit 5209, which was found in the temenos wall on the SE side of the central NE gateway (the Battle Gate), was subcircular in shape, with measurements of 1.68 m × 1.3 m and a maximum depth of 0.4 m. It had been obliquely truncated by French excavation clearance work that was carried out sometime between the late nineteenth century and the early part of the twentieth century, and it contained a single backfill (5208) that showed very frequent inclusions of mud-brick fragments, with fewer fragments of fired bricks that possibly originated from a foundation box. The fill yielded a single Lagash II cone (TG1908) that was marked with Gudea's Standard Inscription. Also on the SE side of the gateway, and originally built into the tower on the NE side of the temenos, was foundation box 5203, which had been almost totally dismantled, leaving behind just its floor and one course of its fired-brick walls. Curiously, immediately to the south-west, a Lagash II stamped fired brick (5220) was found installed on bed at the same level as the floor of the box. Lacking any associated walls, it was unlikely to have formed part of another box, and was perhaps deposited in the course of a refoundation ritual, though this is conjectural. To the north-east, the counterpart of box 5203 had been entirely destroyed by destroyed by pit 5211 (mentioned above).

In Areas B4, B5 and B8, around the SW temenos gateway (the City Gate), two similar pits were identified that also seemed to have targeted Lagash II foundation boxes. Irregular pit 2130, with measurements of 1.4 m × 1.1 m × 0.89 m (deep), was found on the NW side of the monumental entrance tower (3060), and it seemed to have formed a pair with its counterpart (2101), which was unearthed to the south-east, namely in the SE tower on the other side of the gateway passage. No objects were retrieved from pit 2130. Subrectangular pit 2101, which measured 1.59 m × 1.34 m × 1.07 m (deep), contained a single fill (2093) of compacted mud-brick fragments and mud mortar. Sealed by Hellenistic platform 3062, it also yielded no finds. On the SE side of the City Gate's SE tower, foundation box 2123 appeared at first sight to have been truncated by robbers' pits, but on closer inspection it became evident that they were probably dug to locate the box, which was carefully dismantled so that its contents could be removed. Indeed, parts of its NE and SW sides were intact, and as in other areas, destruction and disturbance appeared to have been minimised in sections adjacent to the foundation boxes themselves.

Three more pits (2020, 2027 and 2046) were found in Areas B2 and B4, in structures closely connected to the Ningirsu shrine. Pit 2020 was located in the middle of the gateway (the King's Gate) that led from the main courtyard in the centre of the New Eninnu into the walkway that encircled the Ningirsu temple at the SE end of the complex. Shaped as a subcircular cut that was initially thought to have been made by the French pioneers, pit 2020 contained two fills (2009 and 2010), the lower of which (2010) was composed almost exclusively of fired-brick rubble that probably derived from dismantled foundation boxes. With overall measurements of 4.75 m × 3.8 m × 0.85 m (deep), the pit yielded nine small finds, notably including five Lagash II cones and fragments of cones, three of which were marked with Gudea's Standard Inscription, while the other two were indeterminate. Somewhat larger than pit 2020, but also subcircular in shape, pit 2027 measured 6.4 m × 3.3 m (north-west to south-east and north-east to south-west, respectively), and it also contained two fills (2002 and 2007). The lower of them (2007) contained a great number of fired-brick inclusions and one Lagash II cone (TG219) that was marked with Gudea's Standard Inscription. Some uncertainty about the classification of pit 2027 should be noted because its upper fill (2002) appeared to be made up of laminated deposits of naturally infilled material. Fills of this kind, which were most commonly found in old excavation trenches, including those dug by the French, differed markedly from the materials found in Hellenistic cuts, which seemed to have been carefully backfilled almost immediately after they were excavated. Nonetheless, the location of the pit in the brickwork that formed the N corner of the Ningirsu temple—a highly charged point in the construction—suggested that it might well have been another targeted cut from the Hellenistic period. It yielded no noteworthy finds. Inside the cella, on the E side of the divine podium, was an irregular oval pit (2046) measuring 4.14 m × 1.99 m × 0.3 m (deep) that was filled with a single deposit (2047) of lenses of ash mixed with fragments of mud-bricks. It contained no significant finds. Finally, a third group of four pits (2031, 2038, 2042 and 2040), which were tentatively attributed to the opening of favissas that probably contained some of the Gudea statues, are discussed in detail in Chapter 36.

The Construction Sequence of the Adadnadinakhe Shrine

Although the French pioneers systematically removed and dismantled a great many Hellenistic structures, quite substantial remains of Adadnadinakhe's original shrine were found in Areas B4, B5 and B8 (on the SW side of Tell A), in Areas B6 and B9 (to the north-east), and in Areas B10 and B12 on the NW side of the mound (Figs. 139 and 242). Preserved Hellenistic features were centred around Court A, with Adadnadinakhe's buttressed wall (OP on Heuzey's New Plan; Fig. 114) serving as the new shrine's NW façade. To the north-west of wall OP was a large, open courtyard that was demarcated by the remains of a wide mud-brick precinct wall.

Excavations in Areas B4, B5 and B8 uncovered parts of the SW façade of Adadnadinakhe's original building. The remains of the façade included a length of fired-brick wall (3057) that was found at a maximum topographical height of 17.59 m, together with an associated foundation box (3064), at a maximum height of 17.32 m, adjoining the outside of the wall. Both features were built on top of a mud-brick terrace that took the form of a three-step platform or podium of typically Greek construction (3062), known as a crepidoma, which was found at a maximum height of 17.21 m. The Greek podium was associated with a stairway (3074) that reached a maximum topographical height of 16.6 m. The evidence suggested the following construction sequence. First, before the bricklayers started work on the walls, the area occupied by the Sumerian Eninnu was levelled, horizontally truncated and comprehensively infilled in order to create the massive new terrace platform that provided the solid foundation layer for the Hellenistic complex, as initially envisaged by Adadnadinakhe. In addition to its structural function, and in accordance with time-honoured Mesopotamian practice, the platform surrounded and protected the earlier shrine. Secondly, once the terrace was established, the foundations for the walls (represented by 3057) were built of fired bricks at a topographical height of 16.64 m. Thirdly, it seems that the higher mud-brick platform (3062)—the Greek crepidoma—was then built around the fired-brick foundations, as was indicated by the fact that no traces of construction cuts were found running through any of the mud-brick courses that made up the platform. The Hellenistic mud-bricks were distinguished from Sumerian examples by their mid-brownish grey colour and slightly more friable consistency, which was caused largely by greater inclusions of sand in the later clay matrix. Although it was at first difficult to differentiate the Hellenistic platform from its third-millennium BCE predecessor, the Greek three-step platform seemed to be approximately five or six courses thick, and it included the substantial stairway (3074, mentioned above), which was 2.8 m wide and formed of half a dozen steps built with reused brick fragments from the reign of Gudea. A noteworthy find on the edge of the terrace platform was a half-brick stamped in the name of Adadnadinakhe, with an upward-facing inscription. With regard to the exterior of the Hellenistic building, the events just outlined represent a well-planned and well-executed series of consecutive procedures that were part of a coherent operation that included the levelling and consolidation of the ancient structures, the construction of a lower platform, the building of a fired-brick external wall marked with a foundation box, and lastly the erection of a higher terrace platform around the external wall

Traces of a similar construction were found in Areas B6 (5044) and B9 (5222) to the north-east, on the N side of the Hellenistic complex, at a maximum height of 16.2 m, though the Hellenistic mud-brickwork in Area B6 was severely damaged by French excavation trenches and consequent erosion. The better preserved section to the north-east (5222) clearly sealed an oval pit that contained Hellenistic pottery. This enabled a secure dating of the structures, which could also be correlated with other areas of well-preserved masonry to the south-west. The Hellenistic mud-brickwork in this part of the site was found in a parallel construction trench (5236) that had been used to cut back the eroded face of the tell in areas where it had been damaged after the sacred precinct was taken out of service in the Old Babylonian period. Trench 5236 was also used to help the builders find a solid earlier foundation on which to build the Hellenistic terrace platform and its accompanying precinct wall. The extensive erosion that had occurred in a range of periods, together with the severe disturbance and truncation that was caused by the French excavators, made it difficult to judge whether the type of trenching operations represented by 5236 extended all the way around the circumference of the Sumerian mound, or whether they were carried out only where the eroded topography made them necessary.

The SW façade wall of Adadnadinakhe's shrine (3057, mentioned above), which was aligned north-east to south-west,

was found preserved in Area B4 over a length of 8.7 m, to a width of 1.2 m and to a maximum height of 0.9 m. It represented one of the very rare sections of Hellenistic brickwork that had survived the wholesale demolition that was carried out by the French in the late nineteenth and early twentieth centuries. The façade wall was pierced by a narrow doorway, with a width of just 1.1 m, making it similar in size to other entrances into the Hellenistic building that were recorded by Sarzec. Although signs of slight collapse were found on the inner face of the SW façade, enough of the brickwork survived to indicate that the inner doorway on this side of the shrine was decorated with an ornamental engaged half-column that was constructed using spolia from some of the Sumerian segmented column bases that were recovered from the third-millennium BCE building. When the entrance was compared with the finds made by Sarzec, it was identified as door K on Sarzec's Plan A (Fig. 111).

A small sondage was opened on the SW side of the façade to reveal the brickwork and to investigate the relationship between the wall's foundations and the surrounding mud-brick terrace platform. This showed that the foundations of the wall were built first, with the platform that was subsequently constructed around it acting as an additional support. It also reconfirmed that the foundation was placed on a fired-brick plinth (with a thickness of between one and two courses) that projected out from beneath the wall's external face. Interestingly, of the bricks that made up the wall and its foundation, none of the examples that could be examined bore stamped inscriptions in the name of either Gudea or Adadnadinakhe. This could have been an accidental consequence of the construction materials that happened to be available when the wall was built, or it might have been a characteristic of just those bricks that were visible to the team during the excavations, but it might also suggest that epigraphic bricks were reserved for other parts of the building. The majority of the bricks used in the wall and its foundation, together with the segmented column bases and other architectural elements, were salvaged from the third-millennium temple complex.

One of the uses for epigraphic bricks was vividly illustrated by the fired-brick Hellenistic-era foundation box (3064) found adjacent to wall 3057, directly associated with the doorway that pierced the wall. The box was probably deliberately placed by the entranceway, possibly to serve an apotropaic function. Measuring 0.8 m × 0.7 m (north-west–south-east and north-east–south-west, respectively), it contained four fired bricks marked with Gudea's name that were purposefully stacked in a single column with their inscriptions facing upwards. The reading order on inscriptions of this type is subject to some uncertainty because there was seemingly a change in orientation towards the end of the third millennium BCE, when texts were read from left to right in horizontal rows rather than from top to bottom in vertical columns, as they had been previously. The guiding assumption was that these texts were placed in accordance with the later practice, which persisted into the Hellenistic period. That being the case, the topmost Gudea brick was placed with its inscription facing south-west, along the external axis of the adjacent doorway; the texts on the two below faced north-west, along the axis of the wall; and the brick at the bottom of the stack faced in the opposite direction (south-east).

The pitting found in Area B11 was so intensive that it proved impossible to differentiate between pits belonging to the Hellenistic period and those from more recent times. In some cases the later pits were identified by the objects that were found in their fills (glass bottles repurposed as lamps, for example) and by the loose compaction of the material with which they had been backfilled. The severe and extensive truncation in this area, much of it probably carried out very recently, meant that very little survived of the earlier structures, and only a few badly preserved features were considered to date from Hellenistic times. In particular, a partly circular fragmentary fired-brick structure (2149), which was found at a topographical height of 16.51 m, was judged to have been established at a level above that of the preserved temple walls. Located in the E corner of the shrine, it survived to a height of just four courses.

The earliest Hellenistic layer found in Area B10 was a dark greyish-brown deposit of sand (5477) that was found at a topographical height of 14.77 m, with a thickness of between 0.1 m and 0.25 m. This type of sand was encountered only in this trench, and the fact that it had been completely eradicated on its SE side by French excavation trenches meant that its original extent and its relationship with the first Hellenistic complex could not be determined. Deposit 5477 contained twenty-one finds, notable among which were eight Lagash II cones and fragments of cones, four of which contained Gudea's Standard Inscription, while two commemorated his construction of the EPA; the other two were indeterminate. Other rare objects included a Hellenistic

potsherd with an inscription in Aramaic (TG4554), eleven fragments of Sumerian and Hellenistic terracottas (TG4508, TG4516, TG4519, TG4520, TG4521, TG4522, TG4524, TG4528, TG4539, TG4541 and TG4555) and a fragment of a stone vessel (TG4512).

Five small features were noted on the surface (5510) of the sand deposit, a few centimetres above and below the topographical height of 14.8 m: four small burnt patches (5511, 5512, 5513 and 5514) and an uninscribed square brick from the reign of Gudea (5515) with sides of 0.3 m and a thickness of 90 mm. Embedded in the surface of the sand (5477), the brick might have acted as a marker when the Hellenistic shrine was built, probably to define the extent of the precinct on this side of the mound. Burnt patch 5511, which measured 0.46 m × 0.4 m (east–west and north–south, respectively), was 0.15 m thick. Two fired-brick fragments were found set into the upper surface of 5511, perhaps to act as a makeshift support. Patch 5512, which was subrectangular in plan, measured 0.48 m × 0.24 m (north-west–south-east and north-east–south-west, respectively), and it was 0.1 m thick. Oval in shape, patch 5513, which measured 0.24 m × 0.16 m (east–west and north–south, respectively), was 50 mm thick, while patch 5514, which was also oval, was slightly smaller, measuring 0.18 m × 0.16 m (north-west–south-east and north-east–south-west, respectively) × 50 mm (t). The patches seemed to have resulted from localised short-lived episodes of burning and charring that perhaps occurred during the preparatory stages of the construction of the Adadnadinakhe temple, or possibly when the foundations were being built.

The most prominent feature running across Area B10 was the thick mud-brick precinct wall (represented by deposits 5441, 5478, 5479 and 5518), on a SW–NE alignment, that was found at a maximum topographical height of 16.14 m (Fig. 244). The wall had been severely disturbed by the French excavations (especially on its S side, where a deep trench extended towards the south-east) and by erosion channels that cut into the older trenches left by Sarzec and Genouillac, descending from higher strata of undisturbed archaeology to the north-west (see Chapter 28). Despite the damage, the precinct wall was exposed over a length of 17 m along a NW–SE axis, and enough of it was preserved to indicate its probable place in the overall scheme of the Hellenistic complex. The wall was made of dark greenish-grey sandy clay square bricks with average measurements of 0.31 m × 0.31 m × 0.11 m (t) that differed noticeably from the

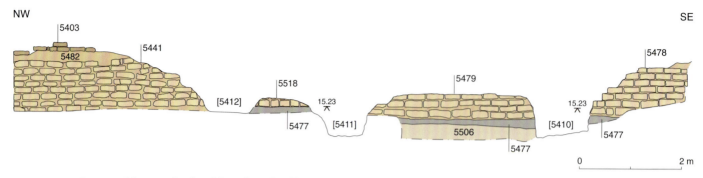

FIGURE 244. Section of the NW façade of the enlarged Hellenistic shrine, showing the underlying mud-brick temenos of Adadnadinakhe, founded on dumped deposits. Above left are the scant remains of the later wall of fired bricks, dating from around 250 BCE.

dimensions of bricks from the third and early second millennia BCE. Laid on bed in staggered courses, and bonded using a mid-brownish-grey clayey silt mud mortar, the bricks formed a wall that was originally 2.9 m thick, as was confirmed by the intact section at the wall's NE end, where it was undisturbed by the French excavation trenches. The structure was preserved to a maximum height of 0.8 m, but this did not represent its original elevation, since it had been partly demolished in order to provide a foundation for the subsequent building phase that is described in the following section.

The Enlargement of the Shrine

The second phase of the Hellenistic construction, which was identified most clearly in Areas B10 and B12, involved the extension of the building on the NW side of Adadnadinakhe's shrine to create Courts B and C, together with surrounding suites of rooms (on Sarzec's Plan A). In addition, a new NW façade wall was constructed of fired bricks on top of Adadnadinakhe's mud-brick walls, which had previously defined the NW area, and a broad terrace was raised on the NW side of the new NW façade (Figs. 245 and 246). The NE façade (which was completely dismantled by the French pioneers) was also rebuilt as part of the extension, though no remaining traces of the later Hellenistic wall were identified in the British Museum team's excavation areas.

Parts of the poorly preserved NW façade wall that was erected during the Hellenistic extension phase (5403) were found at a maximum height of 16.48 m, above the levelled older temenos or enclosure wall (5441) built by Adadnadinakhe. The fired bricks used to build the new façade were a mixture of freshly made uninscribed bricks, together with reused bricks stamped in Adadnadinakhe's name (doubtless fired bricks that were parts of his earlier NW façade), and salvaged bricks marked in the name of Gudea. Since most of the new NW façade was removed by the French excavators, the fragment of the wall that remained (5403) measured just 4 m × 2.5 m (north-east to south-west and north-west to south-east, respectively), and only three foundation courses were preserved. The remains were made using the mix of bricks just mentioned, but most of them were in a fragmentary condition—the more complete examples presumably having been reserved for the upper parts of the new wall that were dismantled by Sarzec and his successors.

Examination of ceramic materials from around the wall appeared to confirm that it was built sometime after Adadnadinakhe's initial shrine, while its position with respect to the rest of the complex further indicated that it was probably part of the later Hellenistic façade, forming a section close to entrance G on Sarzec's Plan A, though no traces of the gateway were found. The low stub of fired-brick masonry could have been part of the foundations for the mud-brick platform shown to the north-west of gate G on Sarzec's plan (marked *Brique Crue*), but this was still less certain. No evidence of the dense buttressing that seems to have been a feature of the later NW façade was found during the excavations, probably because the only part of the wall that survived belonged to its foundation layer. Similarly, limited excavations carried out adjacent to the wall failed to discover any clear signs of parallel foundation trenches that might have been dug to the north-west or to the south-east, but their absence might again have been due to the extreme disruption caused by the

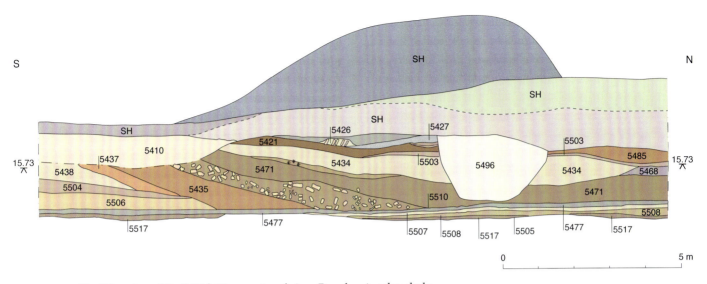

FIGURE 245. The W section of the British Museum team's Area B10, showing the whole sequence of remains from the Lagash II period to Hellenistic times, together with the French pits and spoil heaps.

French excavators. Nonetheless, the NW side of the low section of foundation wall was found largely undisturbed.

The rebuilding of the NW façade wall was accompanied by three associated episodes of dumping that elevated the ground to the north-west in order to create a raised terrace that was found to extend beyond the confines of B10. The first of the three episodes probably represented the dumping of materials that were removed when the ground to the north-west of Adadnadinakhe's building was cleared and levelled to facilitate the creation of Courts B and C on Sarzec's Plan A. The extension presumably occupied the area that was formerly an open-air gathering space, which lay at a lower topographical height than the floor of Adadnadinakhe's shrine. Secondly, the mud-bricks forming the older Hellenistic precinct wall were probably used to establish a solid foundation for the fired-brick façade. Thirdly, the ground surface beyond the line of the new wall, on the lower side of the mound, was raised and levelled to create a flat terrace. Cumulatively, these episodes raised the ground level by about 1.1 m to the north-west of the original Hellenistic mud-brick precinct wall.

The first phase of dumping was made up of a series of deposits (5438, 5489, 5490, 5491, 5492, 5435, 5506, 5504 and 5437). Deposit 5438, which lensed out to the north-west and had a maximum thickness of 0.5 m, was thickest immediately adjacent to the mud-brick wall. It comprised a compact light reddish-brown sandy silt, with moderate inclusions of mud-brick fragments and occasional pebbles, that compared closely to deposit 5504 in the SW corner of B10, from which it was separated by an erosion channel. The latter (5504), which was a compact light brownish-grey clayey silt with occasional charcoal and pebble inclusions, measured 4.25 m × 1.9 m (east–west and north–south, respectively) and it was 0.35m thick. Deposit 5438 was sealed by another layer (5489) that had a maximum thickness of 0.4 m. Neither compact nor loose, it consisted of a light greyish-brown sandy silt deposit with occasional shell and fired-brick fragments and frequent pieces of mud-bricks. Deposit 5490, which varied in thickness between 0.1 m and 0.3 m, was a compact light greyish-brown sandy silt deposit with occasional inclusions of fired bricks, together with mud-brick and bitumen fragments. Above that was a compact dump of dark greyish-brown clayey silt mud-brick rubble (5491) with a thickness of 0.25 m. Deposit 5492, which was laid down after 5491 and ranged in thickness between 0.25 m and 0.4 m, was made up of compact light brownish-grey silty clay that also represented mud-brick rubble. The final deposit of the first phase of dumping (5435), which had a maximum thickness of 0.8 m, consisted of a compact light whitish-grey clayey silt layer with frequent mud-brick fragments, along with occasional traces of bitumen and pebbles. The laying down of these initial layers created a surface that abutted onto the original Hellenistic precinct wall, from where it sloped downwards to the north-west. The

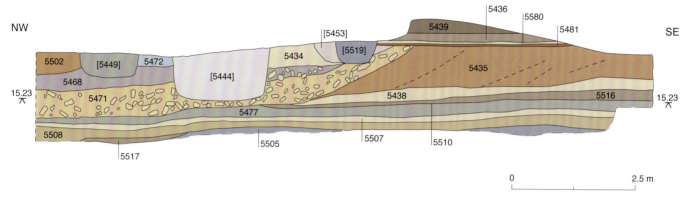

FIGURE 246. The E section of Area B10, showing the sequence of remains from the Lagash II period to Hellenistic times.

operation probably served two purposes. First, it created a reinforcing protective barrier at the base of the original precinct wall so that it could act as a foundation. Secondly, when the upper parts of the mud-brick wall were demolished, its mud-bricks were used to provide a stable base for the raised ground of the NW extension, including the new façade.

A total of 114 finds were derived from these initial dumping deposits, including thirty-five Lagash II cones and fragments of cones, three of which were marked in the name of Ur-Bau to commemorate his reconstruction of Ningirsu's Eninnu. Fifteen cones contained Gudea's Standard Inscription, and one was inscribed with Gudea's usual variant text. A further two cones commemorated Gudea's construction of the EPA, while one was inscribed in Gudea's name to celebrate the Eurukug shrine of Gatumdug; another was dedicated to Inanna and her Eanna shrine in Girsu, and two commemorated the Egirsu shrine of Dumuziabzu. The dedications on the other nine could not be determined. Other notable finds included an Akkad leaf-shaped arrowhead (TG4499), four fragments of stone vessels (TG4450, TG4483, TG4497 and TG4525) and, most remarkably, approximately fifty fragments of terracotta figurines, most if not all of which were Hellenistic (discussed further below).

The second stage of the dumping operation, which involved the partial demolition of the first Hellenistic mud-brick precinct wall, was represented by a pair of very compact layers (5468 and 5471). This limited dismantling was carried out in order to create a relatively low, solid foundation on which the much more elaborate fired-brick precinct wall could be built. Both layers derived directly from the demolition of the mud-brick wall. The first layer (5471), which resulted from a major dumping episode, was a light yellowish-grey silty clay deposit of mud-brick rubble with a maximum thickness of 1 m. On top of this was the second layer (5468), with a maximum thickness of 0.35 m, consisting of a dark brownish-yellow silty clay deposit with very frequent pieces of mud-brick and occasional charcoal and ash lenses.

Twenty-three finds were derived from the two layers, including nine Lagash II cones and fragments of cones, one of which was marked in the name of Ur-Bau (TG4406). Six cones contained Gudea's Standard Inscription, while one was inscribed with Gudea's name, but the names of the commemorated god and temple had not survived; one cone contained no preserved signs. Other notable finds included four Hellenistic terracotta figurines (TG4368, TG4373, TG4370 and TG4379) and a carved stone slab (TG4427) that possibly came from a Lagash II stairway in Gudea's New Eninnu.

The third dumping phase, which was represented by layers 5433, 5434, 5472, 5503, 5485, 5486 and 5487, created a level working surface that formed the base for the later clay terrace that is marked on Sarzec's Plan A. Deposit 5433, which was between 0.1 m and 0.4 m thick, was made up of a compact layer of light yellowish-brown clayey silt with occasional inclusions of fired bricks and pebbles. Deposit 5434 was formed of compact light yellowish-grey sandy silt, including moderate mud-brick inclusions; it had a maximum thickness of 0.7 m. Above that, layer 5472 was formed of a compact light greyish-brown clayey silt (0.4 m thick), while layer 5485, which ranged in thickness between 0.45 m and 0.95 m, was composed of a compact dark greyish-brown clayey silt. With a maximum thickness of 0.15 m, deposit 5503 was a compact light brownish-grey silty clay with occasional charcoal flecks;

it was traced over a length of 12.35 m from east to west. Finally, two less substantial layers, 5486 and 5487, represented the last events in the third episode of dumping. The former, 5486, which was just 0.28 m long, with a thickness of 60 mm, was a layer of sandy silt that was neither compact nor loose. Concluding the sequence, deposit 5487, which was 1.1 m long and 0.1 m thick, comprised a clayey silt deposit that was again neither compact nor loose.

These deposits yielded ninety-seven finds, including twenty-one Lagash II cones and fragments of cones, fifteen of which were marked with Gudea's Standard Inscription. A further two cones commemorated the same ruler's construction of the EPA, while one was inscribed in Gudea's name to celebrate the Ekitushakkilli shrine of the god Shulshaga. Another cone contained Gudea's name, but the names of the god and the temple were not preserved, while the dedication on another one was indeterminate. Exceptionally, one cone contained a previously unknown Lagash II inscription (TG4298). The cone was sadly broken and the name of the ruler had not survived, but it appeared clearly to date to the Lagash II period; the deity's name was also lost, but the name of the construction was partially preserved. The deciphered text reads: 'made everything function as it should. He built for him(?) his … chosen by the heart, and restored it to its (proper) place'. Among other notable finds were: a Lagash II inscribed door plaque (TG3721; Fig. 193), on which the preserved text might possibly have been the end of Gudea's Standard Inscription; a Lagash II stone mace head (TG4144; Fig. 193), which presumably bore a dedication that probably ended with the words 'Gudea, the one who built Ningirsu's Eninnu'; a Middle Uruk stamp seal carved in the shape of a wild boar (TG3283); and thirteen fragments of Sumerian and Hellenistic terracottas (TG3247, TG3279, TG3281, TG3389, TG3689, TG3390, TG3391, TG3392, TG3723, TG3725, TG4041, TG4122 and TG4313).

Seven Hellenistic pits (5444, 5449, 5446, 5499, 5457, 5453 and 5119) were subsequently dug into the upper surface of the dumped materials. Most of them (5444, 5449, 5446 and 5499) appeared to be filled with quite carefully deposited sequences, including ash and other backfills, while two (5453 and 5119), which were possibly cesspits, seemed to contain greenish fills associated with latrines. Finally, deposit 5457, which contained a very complex series of fills that yielded abundant large fragments of pottery, might have been a favissa. These four pits, which probably resulted from the

FIGURE 247. Sumerian stone demon amulets, one of which (TG3419, on the left) was unearthed in a Hellenistic pit associated with the enlarged shrine.

activities of the Hellenistic workers, were presumably dug when the new façade wall (5403) was being constructed. Of the other three, pit 5444, which was circular (with a diameter of 1.65 m and a depth of 1 m), contained four fills: 5465, 5450, 5454 and 5455. Fill 5465 was a compact light greyish-brown clayey silt with moderate ash lenses and occasional charcoal, bitumen, fired-brick and mud-brick fragments. Fill 5450 was a light brownish-grey silty sand deposit with very frequent ash lenses and occasional pieces of charcoal and fired bricks. Fill 5454 comprised a light pinkish-brown sandy silt deposit with moderate inclusions of charcoal, fired bricks and ash lenses. The base of pit 5444 was filled with a light greenish-grey silty sand with frequent ash lenses and pieces of charcoal, together with occasional mud-brick fragments and pebbles (5455). Pit 5444 yielded ten finds, notably including two Lagash II fragments of cones (one bearing Gudea's Standard Inscription, while the other was indeterminate) and a Sumerian stone demon amulet (TG3419; Fig. 247).

Pit 5444 was cut by pit 5499, which measured 2.25 m × 1.5 m × 0.9 m (deep), and contained two fills (5498 and 5500). The upper fill (5498) was a compact light beige brown clayey silt backfill with moderate inclusions of mud-brick fragments and occasional pieces of charcoal and pebbles. Context 5500 consisted of a loose light pinkish-grey sandy silt fill, with frequent ash lenses and pieces of charcoal, together with moderate burnt clay fragments. Seventeen finds were retrieved from pit 5499, among which were three Lagash II fragments of cones, two of which were marked with Gudea's Standard Inscription, while the other one contained Gudea's name, but the names of the god and the temple were not preserved. Also found was a fragment of a stone vessel (TG3757).

Pit 5449, which was subrectangular to oval in shape and 1 m deep, contained four fills (5451, 5448, 5466 and 5467). Fill 5451, which was neither compact nor loose, was a light reddish-beige clayey silt with frequent mud-brick inclusions. Fill 5448 was a compact light whitish-grey silt material with frequent ash lenses and moderate amounts of charcoal. Fill 5466 consisted of a loose light greyish-brown silt with frequent ash lenses and occasional inclusions of fired-clay fragments (probably pieces of a tannoor—a bread oven dug into the ground) and charcoal. Finally, fill 5467 was a very loose deposit of light grey silt with frequent fired-clay tannoor fragments and ash lenses, and occasional pieces of charcoal. Among the few noteworthy finds in pit 5449 was a Seleucid loom weight. Pit 5446, which was circular (with a diameter of 1.2 m and a depth of 0.6 m), contained two fills (5445 and 5488). Fill 5445, which was neither compact nor loose, was a deposit of light brownish-grey clay silt with frequent ashy lenses, moderate inclusions of pieces of fired bricks and occasional fragments of bitumen. Fill 5488, which was again neither compact nor loose, consisted of a dark brownish-grey clay silt deposit.

Pit 5453, which appeared to have been a cesspit, was circular with a diameter of 1.15 m and a depth of 0.55 m. It contained a single fill (5452), which was a deposit of light yellowish-green clayey silt (neither compact nor loose) with occasional fired-brick fragments. The pit yielded no finds. Pit 5119, which was probably another cesspit, was circular in plan, with a diameter of 1 m and a depth of just 0.3 m. It contained a single fill (5447), which was a deposit of loose light greenish-grey sandy silt with frequent light greenish-grey ash lenses, moderate inclusions of charcoal and occasional burnt clay lenses. Among the notable objects found in pit 5119 was a Lagash II cone (TG3339) commemorating Gudea's construction of the EPA.

Lastly, pit 5457 was also circular in plan, but with more moderately sloping sides than the other pits, and it was also larger than the others, with a diameter of 2 m, though it was relatively shallow, with a depth of 0.8 m. It contained five fills (5461, 5462, 5463, 5464 and 5456). Fill 5461 was a compact deposit of light brownish-grey clayey silt with occasional pieces of charcoal and fired-brick fragments. Fill 5462 consisted of very loose light grey powdery ash, together with silt and charcoal, and a high frequency of more concentrated lenses of ash and charcoal. Fill 5463 was a loose light grey silt, together with an ash and charcoal backfill. Fill 5464 was a

deposit of compact light brownish-grey clayey silt with moderate ash lenses and pieces of charcoal. Finally, at the bottom of the pit, was layer 5456, which was formed of compact light greyish-brown clayey silt with occasional fired-brick and bitumen fragments and frequent charcoal and ash lenses. Pit 5457 contained seven finds, notably including one Lagash II fragment of a cone (TG4034) celebrating Gudea's construction of the Egirsu (a shrine for Meslamtaea) and a fragmentary astragalus (TG4145). Several examples of astragaluses (animal bones used for ritual purposes) were found in the course of the excavations. All detailed below, such deposits were almost certainly a feature of foundation rituals especially associated with Hellenistic practices.

Perhaps on account of the cesspits that were dug in this area, three capping layers and surfaces were laid down, probably in order to seal off the pits. Capping layer 5442, with a length of 3.45 m (north-west to south-east) was 0.25 m thick. It was made up of a compact dump of light pinkish-grey silty clay with occasional inclusions of fired brick, ash lenses and charcoal. Surface 5480, which was 60 mm thick, was traced for 2.15 m on a NW–SE orientation. It comprised a compact deposit of light greyish-brown silty clay with moderate charcoal inclusions. The last surface to be laid down (5481), which was between 40 mm and 70 mm thick, and traced over a length of 3.3 m, was formed of light brownish-grey clayey silt (neither compact nor loose), with moderate charcoal inclusions. Noteworthy finds in these layers included a Hellenistic terracotta figurine (TG3334) and a stone vessel fragment (TG3496).

Above these layers the sequence became slightly unclear because the upper strata had been heavily disturbed by the French excavators, as well as by erosion on the N side of the original surface of the tell (as it was encountered by Sarzec and his successors), before the raising of the French spoil heaps in this area. A possible Hellenistic mud-brick surface (5421) was tentatively identified over a thinner bedding layer (5422) made up of a light brownish-grey silty clay with occasional pieces of fired brick. Surface 5421 comprised a compact dark brownish-grey silty clay with frequent fired-brick fragments, moderate bitumen and charcoal fragments and occasional ash lenses. The surface was traced in plan over a length of approximately 4 m (north-east–south-west) and 3.5 m (north-west–south-east), with a maximum thickness of 0.15 m, and it was constructed of roughly shaped pieces of mud-bricks with maximum dimensions of 170 m × 150 mm ×

80 mm (t). The compaction of layer 5421 suggested that it was probably an exterior surface that might have been part of an entrance leading into the later Hellenistic complex through a gateway that was not preserved (conceivably because it was dismantled by the French excavators). It should be stressed, however, that it was not possible to make a definitive judgement because the surface was greatly disturbed. Surface 5421 yielded one fired brick with five perforations (TG3534), but no objects were retrieved from deposit 5422.

The surface layers were partly or wholly sealed by two foundation layers (5436 and 5439), which formed subfloor packings that were exposed over a length of 7.75 m (north-west to south-east). The first packing (5436), which was 0.15 m thick, comprised a layer of compact dark brownish-grey silty clay with moderate inclusions of fired bricks and occasional pebbles, together with pieces of bitumen and charcoal. The main part of this foundation was formed by layer 5439 (0.25 m thick), which was a deliberately compacted dark brownish-grey silty clay deposit, again with moderate inclusions of mud-bricks and occasional pieces of charcoal.

Layer 5436 contained ten finds, notably including one Lagash II cone (TG3288) marked with Gudea's Standard Inscription and one Lagash II stone vessel (TG3436; Fig. 193) inscribed with a text in the name of Ur-Ningirsu II, the son of Gudea. This was of interest because only a few inscriptions have survived from his reign, though in this case only his name and titles were preserved, together with some illegible traces of signs. Also found was a fragment of a Hellenistic terracotta figurine depicting a Macedonian rider (TG3350). Foundation layer 5439 yielded 109 finds, including ten Lagash II cones and fragments of cones, three of which celebrated Ur-Bau's rebuilding of the Eninnu for Ningirsu, while another commemorated the same ruler's reconstruction of Bau's shrine, the Eurukug. Two cones contained Gudea's Standard Inscription, while another two commemorated his construction of the EPA, and one was inscribed in his name to celebrate the Ekitushakkilli shrine of Shulshaga. Finally, another Gudea cone recorded the construction of the Esirara for Nanshe.

Among other noteworthy finds from the same layer (5439) were a fragmentary inscribed Lagash II object made of obsidian (TG3783; Fig. 193) that was marked with a text closely resembling the inscriptions on some of Gudea's statues: 'Within it, [he planted] his beloved giguna'. Also recovered was a cuneiform tablet (TG3817) dating to the Lagash II

or Ur III period, with traces of cuneiform signs that appeared to be the ends of personal names. The tablet presumably recorded a list of supplies that were distributed to named individuals. Other rare finds included two cylinder seals, one from the Early Dynastic period (TG3827) and one dating to Lagash II times (TG3897). The latter (Fig. 142) presents an unusual image of Ningirsu in his guise as the warrior god: holding a mace decorated with two lions' heads, he faces the goddess Bau, who is enthroned. The following finds were also of considerable interest: a rare impression of a Jemdet Nasr or Early Dynastic I seal on a potsherd (TG4143) featuring a flock of sheep belonging to Inanna's temple; a Middle Uruk stamp seal in the shape of a wild boar (TG3969); three ritual astragaluses (TG3876, TG3906 and TG3965); a unique Sumerian handmade terracotta figurine (TG3842) in the shape of a nude horned goddess; two fragments of Hellenistic terracotta figurines, one showing the god Apollo playing a lute (TG3838), and the other depicting a god wearing a tall cap (TG3958); a further three Hellenistic terracottas (TG3866, TG4069 and TG3792); and one fragment of a stone vessel (TG4007).

Deposit 5439 acted as the foundation for an area of paving (5404) that was found at a topographical height of 17.08 m. Constructed of complete and fragmentary fired bricks that were laid on bed directly on top of 5439, the pavement's preserved remains measured 1.35 m × 0.65 m (north-east to south-west and north-west to south-east, respectively), and it was 0.15 m thick, including its clay bedding layer. Paving 5404 was bounded on its NW and SW sides by a sequence of three rectilinear gullies (5476, 5474 and 5432, listed chronologically, from the earliest to the latest) that enclosed an area measuring approximately 10 m × 4.75 m (north-east to south-west and north-west to south-east, respectively). Gully 5476, which was 0.2 m wide, ranged in depth between 0.11 m and 0.3 m; gully 5474, which was 0.25 m wide, ranged in depth between 0.25 m and 0.3 m; and gully 5432, which was 0.3 m wide, had a depth of between 0.11 m and 0.38 m. All three were filled with loose silty material, with occasional inclusions of fired bricks, and they had all been cut into the surface of 5439. Given the effort that must have been needed to cut through the carefully prepared surface, the gullies might not have formed part of the original design in this area. No objects were retrieved from gullies 5476, 5474 and 5432.

Clear evidence of important ritual activities associated with the enlargement of Adadnadinakhe's shrine were found in Area B12, in front of the Hellenistic terrace complex along the NW slope of Tell A. In a first phase of work erosion channels that lay on top of outlying eroded and weathered Lagash II structures (25024 and 25025) and an Early Dynastic structure (25021) were infilled with a series of deposits (25008, 25010 and 25018). The infillings might have been slightly affected by subsequent water erosion, but the fresh condition of the pottery found in them suggested that any such damage was limited. Deposit 25022 was also grouped with this first phase, even though its precise character could not be finally determined. Preserved in the form of a mound on the NW periphery of B12, with a height of 0.7 m, its date, colour and composition all compared closely to the three Hellenistic deposits just mentioned. Its slightly anomalous make-up was probably due to its location in the NW area, where it was especially exposed to prevailing patterns of erosion.

Seventy finds were retrieved from the four deposits, notably: fifteen Lagash II cones and fragments of cones, five of which were inscribed in the name of Ur-Bau to celebrate his construction of Ningirsu's Eninnu, while seven were marked with Gudea's Standard Inscription; a further two commemorated Gudea's construction of the EPA, and one was inscribed in Gudea's name to celebrate the shrine of Nindara. Also from the Lagash II period was a fragment of an inscribed stone vessel (TG4776) that appeared to have been marked with Gudea's Standard Inscription. Other noteworthy finds included a large piece of a Hellenistic turquoise glazed basin or vat made of a coarse material that was coloured on the outside with a bluish-greenish glaze, while the inside was coated with plaster (TG4778). The vessel was decorated with a seven-branched palm tree whose trunk was marked with crescent-shaped segments; next to the tree was a partly preserved impressed rectangular frame that seemed to represent a recessed niche. Also found were a fragment of a beautiful Hellenistic glazed oil lamp (TG4787) with multiple wicks (possibly as many as twenty), another ritual astragalus (TG4763), nine fragments of stone vessels and thirteen fragments of Hellenistic terracottas.

The infilling of the erosion channels was carried out in conjunction with the deposition of a rammed clay levelling surface to form a terrace platform that was found in the centre of Area B12. The clay levelling deposit, which was approximately 0.3 m thick, lay at a topographical elevation of approximately 13.67 m. On top of it was built a small mud-brick platform or sacrificial

altar (25019), with its upper surface at a height of 13.85 m, and overall dimensions of 1.65 m × 1.2 m (north-east to south-west and north-west to south-east, respectively). It survived to a height of 0.26 m, represented by two courses of square bricks that measured (on average) 310 mm × 310 mm × 110 mm (t). A silver drachm (TG4649) that was minted in Babylon under the authority of Alexander the Great and dated to between 331 BCE and 325 BCE was found directly to the south-west of the altar's SW corner. Placed precisely on the prepared surface on which the altar was built, it shows the beardless head of a youthful Heracles wearing the skin and head of the Nemean lion on one side, while the other side presents a seated Zeus with an eagle perched on his right hand and a staff or sceptre in the other (Fig. 269). Traces of a standard monogram (probably the Greek letter phi) were found under Zeus's throne, and traces of another (probably the Greek letter mu) were observed in the left field (discussed further in Chapter 47). Alexander's name would almost certainly have originally been stamped vertically in Greek to the right of Zeus's staff, but the lettering had not survived. The altar was precisely oriented so that it followed the line of the new NW façade wall of the enlarged shrine in Area B10, and it was carefully aligned with the entrance that led through the façade into the shrine. This was typical of the position of altars in Babylonian shrines of the period (as in the temples of Ninmah and Ninurta mentioned above), but also of Hellenistic shrines. They were placed outside the walls of their respective temples, in front of the doorway that led directly along a straight internal axis towards the cella.

The small platform or altar (25019) seemed to have been deliberately buried at a later stage, when the terrace was again raised by approximately 0.3 m, as represented by deposit 25004. The subsequent raising was associated with the construction of what was presumed to be a semi-underground storage annexe, which was probably a late addition to the Hellenistic extension. Deposit 25004 yielded twelve finds that notably included: two Lagash II cones marked with Gudea's Standard inscription; one fragment of a Hellenistic glazed oil lamp (TG4634); one fragment of a Lagash II pot (TG4632) that appeared to have been marked with the sign sila$_3$ (translated as 'litre'); and three fragments of Sumerian and Hellenistic terracottas (TG4610, TG4622 and TG4635).

The semi-subterranean annexe (made up of walls 25027, 25028, 25029 and 25030) was exposed in the SE part of B12, where its foundation trench was formed by the cutting back of the SE edge of the old Lagash II foundation terrace (25013). The annexe appeared to have been originally built mostly of mud-bricks, with very occasional reused fired bricks. The walls, which were 0.35 m thick, were preserved to a maximum height of 0.5 m, made up of four courses of rectangular bricks laid alternately as headers and stretchers; the tops of the walls were preserved to topographical heights of between 13.42 m and 13.8 m. The rectangular mud-bricks, which were predominantly of a dark brownish-grey colour, measured 350 mm × 150 mm × 100 mm (t). Differing in size, shape and colour from the square mud-bricks used to build the altar (25019), they added cogency to the suggestion that the annexe was built during a second post-Adadnadinakhe phase of construction in this NW area, after the main extension was added.

One underground room was exposed to its full width of 2.45 m (north-east to south-west) within the excavation trench, though it extended beyond the limits of the trench to the north-west, where it was excavated over a length of 7.75 m. Slight traces of a mud-brick wall that probably formed the NW side of the room suggested that almost all of the room was uncovered in Area B12. Parts of two additional rooms were exposed over a length of 1.75 m to the south-east, where they extended beyond the limits of the trench. Three installations were discovered in the largest and most complete room. First, a bench was found in the W corner, abutting onto walls 25027 and 25029. Built almost exclusively of mud-bricks, it measured 1.65 m × 0.75 m (north-west to south-east and north-east to south-west, respectively) × 0.15 m (h). A second low bench or platform was located in the centre of the room, aligned with the room's long NE–SW axis, that measured 1.15 m × 0.3 m (north-east to south-west and north-west to south-east, respectively) × 0.15 m (h). Lastly, a possibly later installation (25026), which was found in the SE part of the room, was built of a mixture of fragmentary and complete salvaged fired bricks from the Lagash II and Isin-Larsa periods, including some complete Lagash II square bricks and some Lagash II and Isin-Larsa rectangular half-bricks. Overall, the third feature, which measured 1.66 m (north-west to south-east), with a height of 0.43 m, was built on top of wall 25028 (which was made mostly of mud-bricks). Projecting out by 0.91 m in a NE–SW direction from the room's internal wall, its NW–SE length was 0.7 m. The feature was first thought to be a foundation box, but its overall dimensions indicated that it was more likely to have formed part of a stairway that led down into the cellar from the south-east.

The probable stairway corroborated the idea that the annexe was a semi-subterranean store room for the extended shrine. Remains of two superimposed surfaces or floors were found inside the sunken room: 25015 (the earlier of the two) and 25014.

Pottery from the Hellenistic Strata

The Hellenistic pottery assemblage that was retrieved during the British Museum team's excavations was made up of six types: glazed and eggshell ceramics, fine pots and utilitarian, storage and cooking wares. Since only a modest number of cooking vessels were found, the functional component of the assemblage was generally formed of utilitarian, glazed and storage wares. Eggshell and fine ceramics were very well attested, however. Indeed, there was a clear preponderance of high-status wares (glazed, eggshell and fine types) over more functional ceramics (the utilitarian, storage and cooking varieties)—a mix that reflected the building's purpose as a shrine rather than a domestic structure. The types of pottery recovered were therefore typical of a religious building, though their ultimate provenances indicated an institution that was fully integrated into the wider Hellenistic world, despite its relative geographic isolation.

Hellenistic pottery, which was mostly recovered from Areas B9, B10 and B12, came from a range of contexts, mostly from layers associated with clearance, ground-raising and consolidation operations (B10 and B12), but also from pits (B9 and B10). Occupation deposits were encountered in Areas B10 and B12, but they yielded very little material. In general, the recovered items closely reflect the wider Hellenistic pottery tradition, primarily in the appearance of fish plates (named on account of their characteristic shape) and bowls with incurved rims, but forms that were inherited from the earlier Achaemenid period were also frequently found. The latter include eggshell bowls, shallow bowls with external ledge rims and large and medium-size jars with rolled rims. Also of late Achaemenid derivation (synonymous, in this case, with the early Hellenistic period), and probably originating from manufacturing sites located in Iran, are examples of zoomorphic handles portraying *capra ibex* (goat antelopes). The recovered pottery shapes express the liveliness of regional traditions during the Hellenistic period. Carinated bowls, for instance, are frequently found in pottery assemblages from sites in central and southern Iraq, while the more strictly local forms from the south of Iraq that were found in Girsu include jars with short vertical necks and applied bosses.

Comparisons with other sites (detailed below) confirm two broad chronological phases for the Girsu building. The first phase, associated with Adadnadinakhe's original shrine, represents the early Hellenistic period, namely the late fourth century BCE through to the first half of the third century BCE; secondly, linked with the Girsu shrine's subsequent enlargement, the later phase reflects the Hellenistic presence in the region from around the second half of the third century BCE through to the middle and later part of the second century BCE. New pottery shapes were introduced during the extension phase, notably jars with short vertical necks and applied bosses. More generally, a striking resemblance can be observed between the assemblage derived from the extension phase in Girsu and pottery from the same period that has been retrieved from other important sites in the region, especially Larsa and Uruk (in particular the Bit Resh and the Irigal temple).

The earlier phase initiated by Adadnadinakhe was represented by a few hundred retrieved fragments. Open forms originating in the earlier period include fish plates and various types of bowls. Fish plates, which were widely used in Mesopotamia during the period, were common among the finds made in Girsu. The Girsu types exhibit some variations in the morphology of the rims, and they have disc-shaped or concave bases. The decorations on the vessels are mostly glazed, though a few plainer examples were also found, and they generally have an overhanging rim (Fig. 248.1). Most of the retrieved bowls belong to one of two categories: carinated bowls and echinus bowls with inverted rims. The carinated types can be further subdivided into more conventional carinated bowls (Fig. 248.3) and low carinated bowls with a shallow profile and an everted rim (Fig. 248.4). These are mainly glazed, while the echinus bowls (Fig. 248.5 and 248.6) are almost exclusively plain. Bowls with rounded profiles and thinned and rounded rims were less commonly encountered (Fig. 248.2), but eggshell bowls were frequently found (Fig. 248.7). Deep bowls, which were excavated in extremely limited numbers, include an example with a triangular rim (Fig. 248.9). Lastly, fine wares are represented by examples of bowls with sinuous profiles and flared plain rims (Fig. 248.8). The range of closed shapes is more limited

than the variety of open shapes. Most common among the closed shapes are the well-defined group of pilgrim flasks (Fig. 248.10 and 248.11), with a number of examples being found in strata belonging to the Adadnadinakhe phase. The recovered jars are mostly of two types: tall-necked jars with an external thickened band rim (Fig. 248.12 and 248.13) and shoulders decorated with horizontal combed lines; and jars with rolled or external rounded rims (Fig. 249.1 and 249.2) that are further distinguished by a rib just below the rim. Other types of closed shapes that were encountered include small jars with a plain vertical rim (Fig. 249.3), some of which include a closely spaced series of horizontal combed lines on the shoulder, and jars with a short neck and an external rounded rim (Fig. 249.4).

Finds from the extended shrine exhibit patterns of continuity with those deriving from the original building, most notably in the persistence of fish plates (Fig. 249.5–7) and carinated bowls (Fig. 249.8 and 249.9). As in the earlier phase, most examples of these types were glazed. Other examples of open shapes that were found in large quantities in strata from the original and extended shrine are bowls with inturned rims (Fig. 250.4). Glazed types that persisted into the later period include low carinated bowls with everted rims and ring bases (Fig. 249.11), while bowls with rounded profiles and a thinned everted rim (Fig. 249.10) were also commonly found. Eggshell bowls, which continued to be conspicuous, exhibit characteristics similar to those deriving from the original shrine (Fig. 249.12 and 249.13). A similar continuity was observed with respect to fine wares, which exhibit the same morphologies as bowls from Adadnadinakhe's original building (Fig. 250.1 and 250.2), though shallow bowls with external ledge rims displaying a slight internal incline (Fig. 250.3) were found more rarely in the later period. Finally, deep bowls with triangular rims (Fig. 250.5), which form a well-defined group in the assemblage deriving from the extended shrine, are also attested in a variant with thickened external rims. Among the closed shapes, the numerous flasks and small jars from the later period merit particular attention because of the wide range of variant forms that were found (Fig. 250.6–8). They include a rare example of a jug with a narrow neck, a stepped interior profile and an exterior angular flared rim, placed above a pronounced rib, below which is a loop formed of two twisted rod handles (Fig. 250.11). No precise comparisons for this fragment are attested in the ceramics production of central and southern Iraq from the period. Another type of plainware jug has a long neck and a flared profile with a band rim immediately above a loop attachment (Fig. 250.9).

Among the most common medium-size and large jars are types with vertical necks and loops located below their rims (Fig. 251.1 and 251.2), together with those exhibiting ovoid profiles and external rolled or thickened rims (Fig. 252.2 and 252.3). One type of large jar has a short vertical neck with at least four applied vertical cables or bosses of clay on the exterior of the rim. Two of the bosses were found to be pierced, but only one had a regularly applied suspension hole that ran all the way through the boss. This type of jar (Figs. 251.5 and 252.1) was found exclusively in strata associated with the enlarged shrine. With regard to storage jars, numerous specimens were found to have biconical bodies, long necks and band rims (Fig. 252.4 and 252.5), but the most distinctive shape encountered from the later period was a large three-handled amphora, distinguished by a wide shoulder surmounted by a narrow flared neck, that was finished with an everted band rim (Fig. 251.3 and 251.4). Two examples of zoomorphic handles in the form of rampant mountain goats (*capra ibex*) were also found among the closed forms. One, which was excavated in a primary context (Fig. 250.12), is preserved almost intact (having only lost part of its forelegs); by contrast, the second specimen, which was found out of context, shows only the head (Fig. 250.13). In both cases the handles were modelled by hand before being attached to their respective vessels. The head of the more complete example, which has a tapered body, is placed on a high, thin neck and has applied eyes, while the ears, which are partially preserved, were formed with a pinch of clay to create a conical shape with a deeply incised central line along the centre. The head is crowned with long ridged horns (divided from each other by a deep incision) that curve backwards, while the arched spine ends in a short, upturned tail.

Some specimens that were found out of context also belong to the ceramic corpus associated with the Hellenistic strata of Tell A. Three particularly important fragments from this group bear inscriptions. In two instances the texts were added with black paint or ink to the exteriors of closed shapes: a small rimless jar with an ovoid profile (Fig. 253.5; TG740) and a body sherd from a medium-size jar (Fig. 255; TG4554). The third inscription was found on a body sherd of a storage jar or amphora lined with bitumen (Fig. 255; TG3865). The text is an almost complete, rectangular stamped impression (missing only the upper right

corner of part of a letter) in a frame with rounded corners. The probable meanings of the texts are considered separately below.

Two other sherds that were excavated out of context derive from a krater and the shoulder of a large jar, respectively, and both were have found to have elaborate external decorations. The former (Fig. 253.4) has five bands of repeated stamped impressions from four different dies—the bands being separated by raised shallow cordons decorated with regular vertical nicked incisions. The top band displays triangular impressions with short lines radiating around their exteriors; the one below that was made with an upright leaf-shaped die, articulated with a raised central rib and short radiating lines. The third band down from the top is decorated with circular impressions in the form of a ten-pointed star surrounding a hollow circle. The two lower two bands, which were both made using a square die with rounded corners, display three concentric raised squares with short lines radiating around the exterior of the outermost square. Below the carination is an incised zigzag line, while the rim is ornamented with cables marked with nicked incisions, and the top of the rim is pierced with equidistant deep circular holes (1.3 cm apart). Very few comparisons for the high-quality krater can be cited from pottery assemblages recovered from other sites in the region, though one probable analogue, which comes from Uruk, was found in the Gareus temple. Although it is rimless, the Uruk example has the same profile, with a low carination and a similar decorative pattern of stamped and incised geometrical motifs arranged in three bands (Finkbeiner 1992, p. 571). The second non-contextualised Hellenistic fragment from Girsu, which was part of a rimless jar (Fig. 253.6), was judged to be a section of the vessel's shoulder and body, and the junction of the two parts was found to be accentuated with a raised cable. Otherwise, the decoration (limited to the shoulder) displays a pattern made up of an applied standing human figure, of which just the legs are preserved, together with rows of triangular incisions, along with two stamped concentric circles with short radiating lines and four impressed circles.

In summary, the Hellenistic pottery assemblage from Girsu exhibits an interesting range of open and closed shapes, including forms that spread westwards from Greece and those associated with local traditions. Among the most common open shapes are fish plates (Fig. 248.1 from the original shrine; Fig. 249.5–7 from the later period), exhibiting a variety of rims, together with generally flat or concave bases, and very rarely an interior central shallow depressed circle. All the examples are coated with glazes ranging in colour from various shades of green to a more yellowish hue, and they are occasionally marked on their interiors with engraved signs interpreted as potters' marks (Fig. 249.6). Fish plates of this type are widely attested in the pottery assemblages from sites in southern Iraq and neighbouring areas, notably Babylon, Uruk and Larsa in Iraq, Susa in Iran and the island of Failaka in the Persian Gulf (see Cellerino 2004; Hannestad 1983 and 1984; Lecomte 1983 and 1989; De Miroschedji 1987; and Finkbeiner 1991 and 1992). This ceramic form was produced from the fourth century BCE to the second century BCE, and it continued to be manufactured in the Parthian period.

Another of the well-attested pottery shapes from Girsu is the high carinated bowl with a sharp angular profile (Fig. 248.3 from the original shrine; Fig. 249.8 and 249.9 from the later period). Examples of the same kind (mostly glazed, especially with green, yellow and whitish colours; less commonly unglazed) have been unearthed in Babylon, Failaka, Nippur, Larsa, Susa and Uruk. The type was excavated in layers associated with Adadnadinakhe's shrine and with the extension phase.

Among other bowls are specimens of low carinated bowls with everted rims and ring bases (Fig. 248.4 from the original shrine; Fig. 249.11 from the later period), and most are coated with a deep green glaze. The best comparisons, which come from Larsa, are dated to the middle of the Hellenistic period (Lecomte 1983, Pls. 2.1 and 29.1), while examples from Uruk show a less prominent carination and have a more rounded profile (see Finkbeiner 1991 for specimens from the Irigal temple (188); and Finkbeiner 1992 for examples from the Gareus temple (428–30 and 885)). The type has also been found at Failaka (Hannestad 1983, Pls. 2.24–9 and 3.30–4; and Hannestad 1984, Fig. 6).

The manufacture of eggshell ware, which is characterised by extremely thin walls (generally about 2 mm thick), required high technical proficiency on the part of the potters. The fragments of this kind found on Tell A make up 4.8% of the total collected, and they derived exclusively from open forms, including bowls with hemispherical or bell-shaped profiles and plain or flared everted rims (Fig. 248.7 from the original shrine; Fig. 249.12 and 249.13 from the later period). No full profiles were recovered, but the fragments suggested that these bowls had rounded bases. The type was found in

strata associated with the original shrine and the later extension, and it is more generally attested in Iraq from at least the Achaemenid period (Fleming 1989). Parallels for the examples from Girsu have been found widely in Babylon, Failaka, Larsa, Nippur, Susa and Uruk. The retrieved specimens of hemispherical, conical or bell-shaped eggshell bowls are examples of an older type of deep bowl than the type with a shallower profile that is attested from the second century BCE (Lecomte 1987, p. 232). Other excavation sequences from southern Iraq suggest that the older type that was found in Girsu dates from between the late fourth century BCE and the very early second century BCE. Particular comparisons include the earliest Hellenistic strata in Larsa and levels 3D and 3B of the Ville Royale II in Susa. Examples of deep bowls found in Susa, deriving from phases 3E and 3D, have been dated to between 320 BCE and 150 BC (Cellerino 2004, p. 101).

Fine ware, which is generally characterised by the high quality of its fabric, is dominated in the Girsu assemblage by open shapes, notably bowls with sinuous or (more rarely) angular profiles and a smooth flared rim. This type makes up about 4.5% of the total pottery repertoire retrieved from the extended shrine. Other specimens were recovered from strata associated with the original shrine (Fig. 248.8) and the extension phase (Fig. 250.1 and 250.2). Some were found to have engraved or impressed decorations on their exteriors, mostly in the form of a single row of vertical lines, although items with a rocker decoration were also recorded on bowls that were found out of context (Fig. 253.1 and 253.2). This type of bowl has parallels in the ceramic assemblages from a number of sites, including Babylon, Failaka, Larsa, Nippur and Uruk.

Utilitarian ware is represented in the Girsu repertoire by numerous bowl shapes, including a type with an inverted curved rim (known as echinus bowls) that are very typical of the Hellenistic period (Fig. 248.5 and 248.6 from the original shrine; Fig. 250.4 from the later period). Vessels of this kind, which have been found in ceramic repertoires of the Seleucid period dating from the fourth century BCE (at sites in Babylon, Failaka, Larsa, Nippur, Susa and Uruk) were widely used in the following two centuries.

Shallow bowls with external ledge rims that curve slightly inwards were also commonly encountered in Girsu (Fig. 250.3). This type is well attested from the Achaemenid period in Susa (De Miroschedji 1987, p. 23), but it does not appear in Larsa between the second half of the second century BCE and the first century BCE. Although the type was common in Babylon (Cellerino 2004, Fig. 10.64) and Failaka (Hannestad 1983, Pl. 5.58), it appears only sporadically in Uruk in the Gareus temple (Finkbeiner 1992, p. 402). With regard to the Girsu examples, the comparisons would suggest a date ranging from the early Hellenistic period through to the end of the third century BCE or the first half of the second century BCE.

The deep bowls that were also frequently found in Girsu are all utilitarian wares, and most are later examples that came from the enlarged shrine. Displaying external square, triangular or thickened rims and a more or less sinuous profile (Fig. 250.5), some of these vessels bear a stamped decoration that is always limited to the upper part of the exterior, as exemplified by a sherd that was found out of context (Fig. 253.3). Another exceptional specimen (Fig. 253.7), which was also found out of context and might be a sherd deriving from a deep krater, is decorated with the applied head of Alexander the Great (described above) that was made in a single mould but showed signs of extraneous clay. Elsewhere in the Greek world kraters similar to this one were decorated with mythological figures and used as mixing bowls at banquets, but this particular example, which appears to be unique among the repertoires of the southern part of central Iraq, seems clearly to depict Alexander.

With regard to closed shapes, the most common vessels found in the Hellenistic strata are flasks with ovoid or globular bodies, and handles mounted on the shoulder or the neck. The necks of such flasks are generally well defined and vertical (though occasional flared examples were also found); their rims are thickened on the outsides (Fig. 248.10 and 248.11 from the original shrine; Fig. 250.6 and 250.7 from the later period). Small jars were also frequently encountered (Fig. 250.8). The latter, which was not a standardised product, is known in numerous variant forms, with comparisons coming from sites including Babylon, Failaka, Larsa and Uruk.

Long-necked jugs with a flared profile, band rims and handles appearing just below the rim were also found. There are few known parallels for this form, the closest being a glazed example from Phases 5E and 5D of the Apadana Est at Susa (Boucharlat 1987, Fig. 63.12), which has been dated to the middle of the Hellenistic period.

Among medium-size jars, a type with a vertical neck and a thickened or squared outer rim is well attested in Girsu (Fig. 251.1 and 251.2). Parallels for this type of vase are known from Failaka (Hannestad 1983, Pl. 23.2–6; and Hannestad 1984, Fig. 11) and Larsa (Lecomte 1983, Pls. 8.1 and 21.10; and Lecomte 1987, Pl. 15.32 and 15.36). The medium-size and large jars (Figs. 248.12, 248.13, 249.1, 249.2 and 249.4 from the original shrine; Fig. 251.2 and 251.3 from the later period) were commonly excavated in Girsu. They are distinguished by their narrow necks and rolled rims, which are generally rounded towards the outside, though more rarely the rims display a triangular or pointed external profile. These were widespread in the region, as corroborated by parallels from Babylon, Failaka, Larsa, Susa and Uruk. Jars of this type, which were first manufactured in the Achaemenid era, remained in use in the Hellenistic period, especially in early Hellenistic times, as seemed to be the case in Girsu, where such jars were well established in layers associated with Adadnadinakhe's original shrine. Indeed, they constituted the main types of medium-size jars from the early Hellenistic strata in Girsu, but became less common in strata associated with the enlarged shrine. Also among the closed forms were the two zoomorphic handles (Fig. 250.12 and 250.13) portraying a rampant *capra ibex* mentioned above.

Finally, numerous fragments of storage jars and amphoras were found (Fig. 254). One type of large jar (Figs. 251.5 and 252.1) has a short vertical neck and rims featuring two applied bosses, both aligned on the same axis, but one has a bored hole running all the way through it, while the other features a closed hole. Examples of this type of jar from the middle of the Hellenistic period have been found in Larsa; the pierced bosses on the rims were probably used to seal lids onto the mouths of the jars (Lecomte 1989). The hypothesis is probably confirmed by the internal stepped form of the jars' rims. Parallels for this type have been found in sites in southern Iraq, in particular in Larsa, but occasional examples have also been found in Uruk. Long-necked jars with band rims (Fig. 252.4 and 252.5) were also quite commonly encountered in the Hellenistic layers in Girsu, where they were often lined with a coat of bitumen, and their shape would suggest that they were used for the transport and storage of liquids. Parallels for this type are attested from Babylon, Susa and Larsa, and the data from other sites indicates that such jars remained in use throughout the Hellenistic period, as shown especially in Larsa, where two items with the same rim shape were found in contexts that date, respectively, to the early and middle parts of the Hellenistic period. Large amphoras with three handles (Fig. 251.3 and 251.4), which were

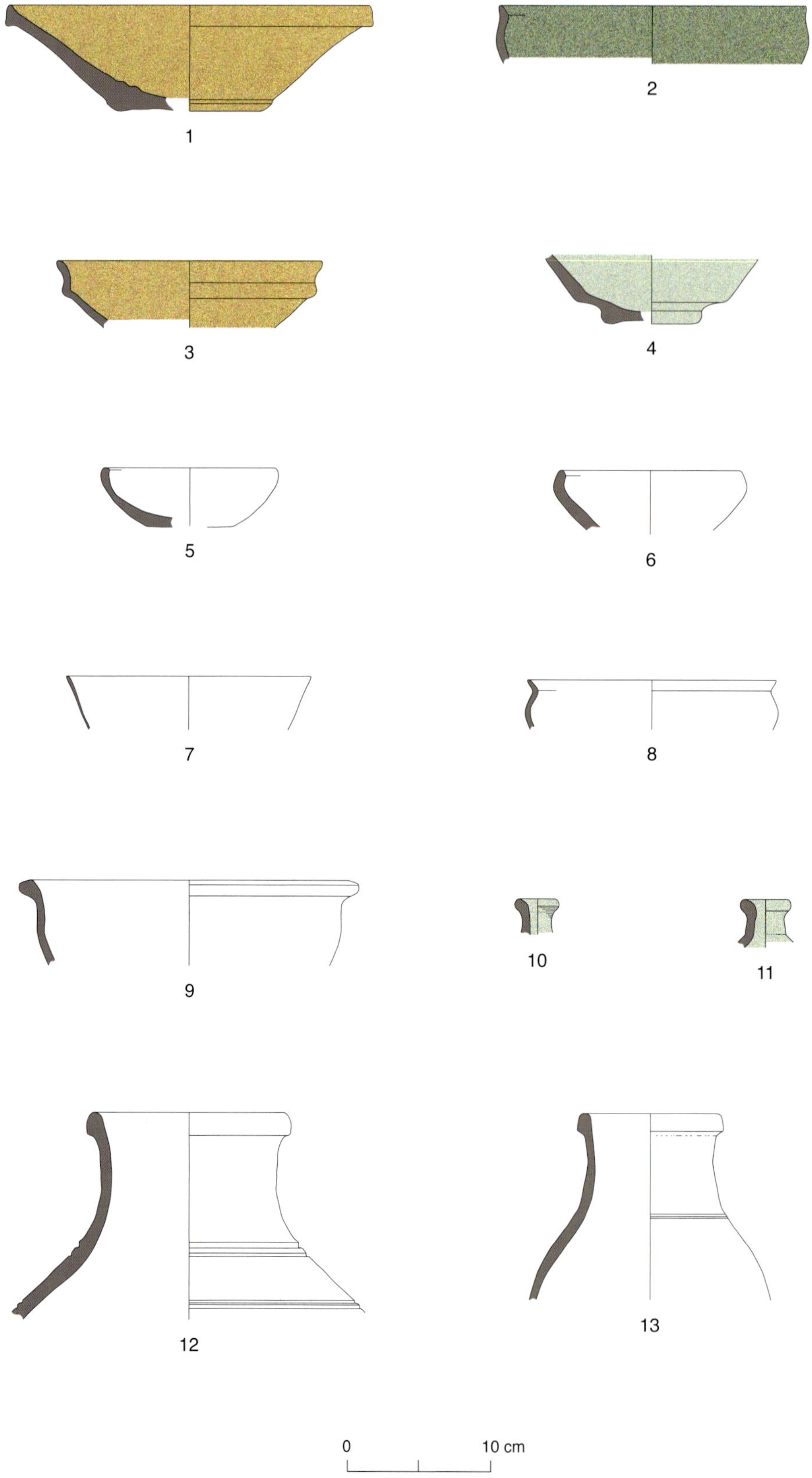

706   The Ningirsu Temple in the Hellenistic Era

FIGURE 248.   Pottery from the Hellenistic shrine I.

The Stratigraphy of the Hellenistic Shrine 707

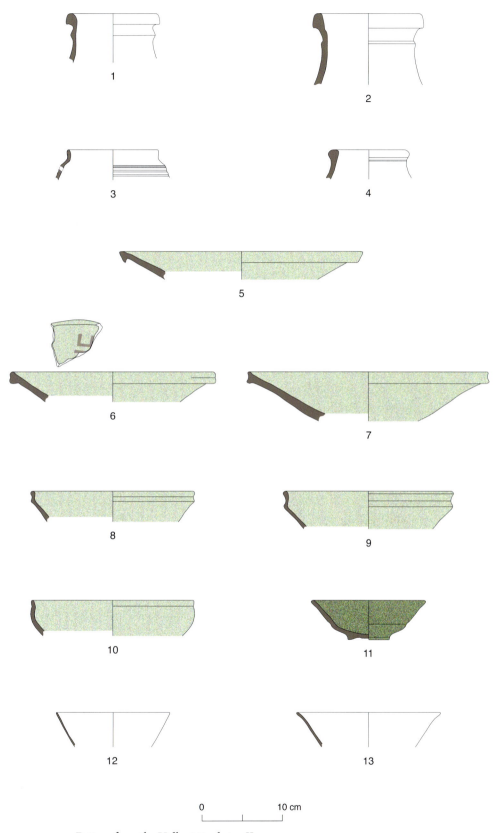

FIGURE 249. Pottery from the Hellenistic shrine II.

708 The Ningirsu Temple in the Hellenistic Era

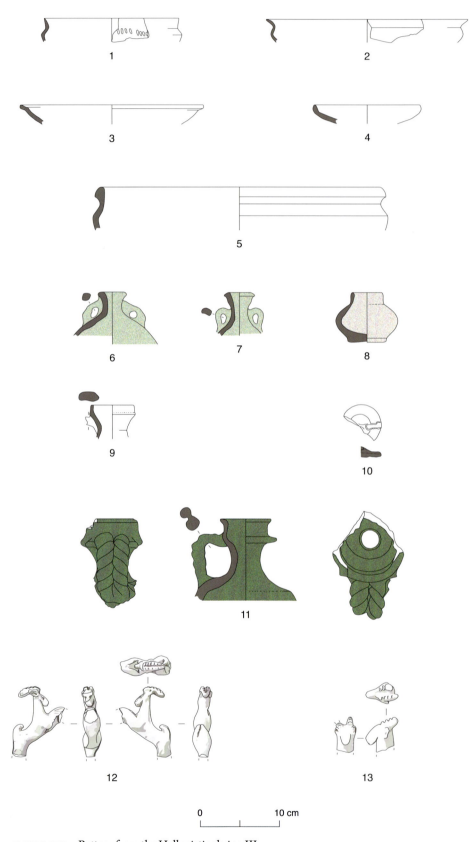

FIGURE 250. Pottery from the Hellenistic shrine III.

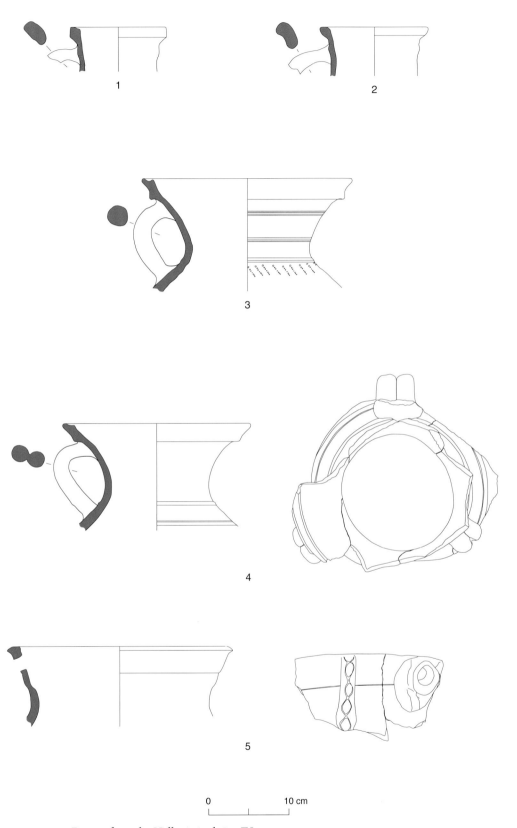

FIGURE 251. Pottery from the Hellenistic shrine IV.

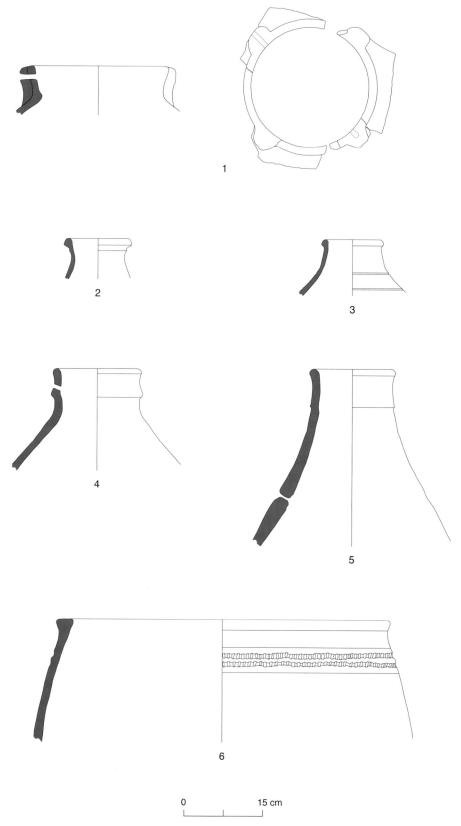

FIGURE 252. Pottery from the Hellenistic shrine V.

The Stratigraphy of the Hellenistic Shrine 711

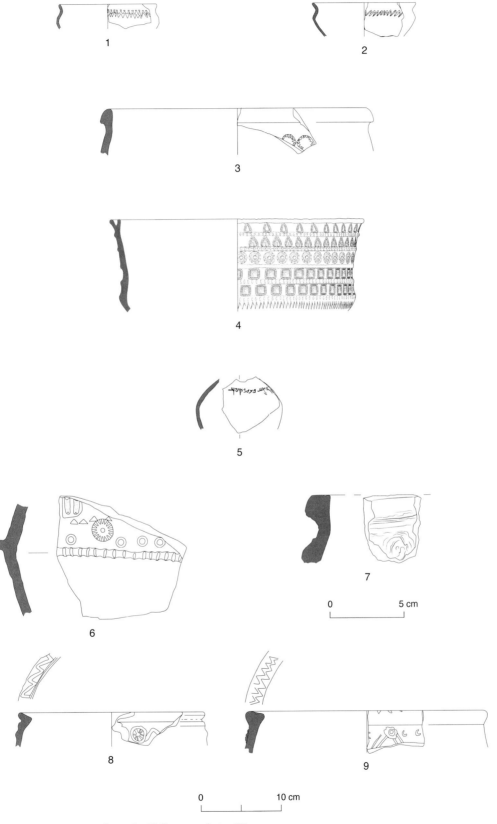

FIGURE 253. Pottery from the Hellenistic shrine VI.

FIGURE 254. Hellenistic storage jar with a vertical neck and a band rim, dating from the late fourth century or early third century BCE.

typically found in strata associated with the enlarged shrine in Girsu, are generally decorated with simple combed lines or engraved geometric motifs at the bases of their high necks. Few parallels exist for this type, though a close comparison dating to the second half of the third century BCE comes from the Bit Resh in Uruk (Finkbeiner 1991, p. 60).

Three Aramaic Inscriptions

Very few Mesopotamian Aramaic inscriptions are preserved from the Hellenistic period, partly because the texts were typically recorded on perishable materials, and partly because they were often written in ink or paint, which tends not to survive, even when it is applied to more durable substrates. In consequence, very few parallels exist to aid the understanding of particular inscribed objects. The individual letters are also difficult to interpret, and the problem is further compounded by the fact that most of the surviving inscriptions are incomplete. Associated cuneiform texts can sometimes be of assistance, but cuneiform script was used for an increasingly limited range of documents by this date, and there is no cuneiform context for the three Girsu inscriptions unearthed by the British Museum team. The three texts are therefore important, but frustratingly difficult to interpret unless and until more evidence becomes available.

The inscription on the medium-size vase TG4554 (Fig. 255), which is the most problematic of the three, appears to include five letters, two of which are ambiguous, followed by a space and a sixth letter: *g t d/r k d/r* <space> *b*. The first five characters might well form part of a non-Semitic personal name, though no clear candidate can be found in the relevant Akkadian, Greek and Iranian onomastic handbooks. Nonetheless, if the first inferred word is indeed a name then

The Stratigraphy of the Hellenistic Shrine 713

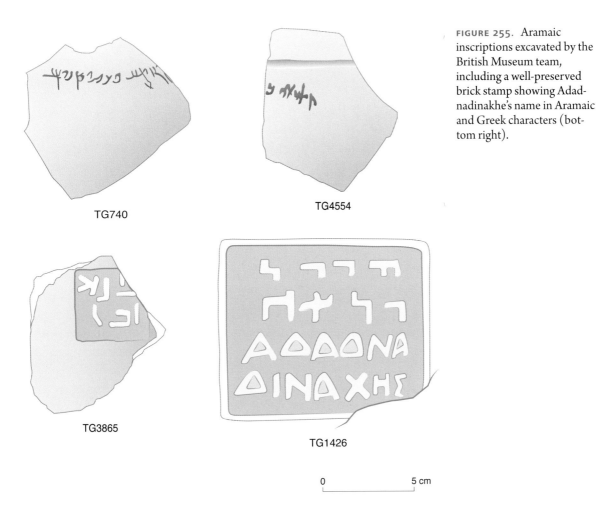

FIGURE 255. Aramaic inscriptions excavated by the British Museum team, including a well-preserved brick stamp showing Adad-nadinakhe's name in Aramaic and Greek characters (bottom right).

the letter *b* after the space presumably belongs to a filiation introduced by the expression *br*, meaning 'son of'. This is cursive writing, however, and it is impossible to say whether the faint traces of an expected ligature can be made out after the *b*. Conversely, the opening three characters, when read as *gtr*, might be connected with the masculine noun *geṭrā* (in the emphatic state), meaning 'dregs' or 'sediment' in Syriac. Together with the inferred following word *kd* (if that is correct), the first five letters would therefore connote the 'dregs at the bottom of a jar', with the *b* after the space perhaps being the preposition 'in' or 'with'. This is ostensibly persuasive, but the idea is fraught with problems, not least that the key noun, *geṭrā*, which is attested only in Syriac as a loan word from Arabic, might not have existed in Aramaic (see Brockelmann 1928, p. 137). The likeliest conclusion is probably that the text derives from a votive vase that was marked with the donor's name and deposited in the shrine.

The first three letters of the stamped text on TG3865 (Fig. 255), a large storage jar for liquids, do not correspond with any known shapes in ordinary Aramaic writing, which reads and was written from right to left, but Babylonian brick impressions, especially from earlier periods, feature many instances of individual characters and combinations of characters being written from left to right because they were added by illiterate labourers (see Sass and Marzahn 2010, pp. 159–60). Starting with the rightmost character, therefore, the following options might result for the first three letters: *p* (written right to left) or *ṭ* (left to right); *l* (left to right); *k* (right to left) or *ʾ* (left to right; *ʾ* being the transliteration of Aramaic alif). Taking into account the possible defective formations, the word could therefore be interpreted as *plʾ*, a form of the personal name *Pīlā*, meaning 'elephant' or 'ivory', as attested in Aramaic inscriptions from Palmyra (see Stark 1971, pp. 47 and 108). Conversely, since the root meaning of *plʾ* ('to be wondrous') is vestigial in Aramaic, the entire word, including the individual characters, could be read from left to right as ʾlp, which can be readily translated as 'thousand'. A further possibility is that all three characters might be written left to right to give the reading ṭlʾ, which is an attested Aramaic personal name related to the common noun ṭall, meaning 'dew' (see Gzella 2021, p. 47). There are other viable options for this combination of letters, but the most intriguing possibility—perhaps no more than a tempting coincidence—is that ṭlʾ might be connected with the Arabic place name Tello, etymologically meaning a 'mound' (tell in Arabic) and possibly associated with 'tablets' (lawḥ in Arabic)—though the derivation is unconfirmed. The difficulty is that the modern Arabic form of Tello starts with a t instead of the ṭ that would connect it with the equivalent Aramaic letter, and it is difficult to see a reason why that significant shift from t to ṭ might have occurred.

The second line of TG3865 is fortunately less problematic. Reading from right to left, the straight vertical downstroke for the letter z has exact parallels in other regional Aramaic scripts from the post-Achaemenid period, notably in Hatra, Assur and their surroundings, while the open-headed middle letter can be identified as a b. The shape of the third letter strongly suggests an n, with a downstroke bending to the right, which differs from the usual form in the Greek and Aramaic brick stamps from Seleucid Girsu, but has parallels elsewhere, for example on Aramaic boundary stones from Armenia (notably from the early second century BCE). The second line thus reads zbn, which derives in all likelihood from the root zbn, meaning 'to buy' in the basic stem and 'to sell' in the factitive stem. Interpreted as a verb in agreement with a personal name (plʾ or ṭlʾ) in the first line, it could be parsed as a third-person masculine singular perfect, meaning 'he bought' or 'he sold' (depending on the stem, but both are written identically in Aramaic). Alternatively, the passive participle Zabīn ('sold' or 'redeemed'), written as zbn in defective spelling, is well attested as a personal name. Nonetheless, if the first line is assumed to have been mangled by an illiterate worker, and the whole text was clearly not checked for accuracy by an educated scribal overseer, then it seems conceivable (particularly when the analogy with the defectively written brick texts is taken into consideration) that the text was a mark or label indicating the manufacturer and supplier of the bitumen-lined storage jar on which it was inscribed. The stamped text would therefore have been added to the jar when it was made. The fact that the stamp was not corrected before being applied, possibly to numerous vessels, is fascinating in and of itself. It is also interesting to consider that the miswritten characters seemingly did not impede an understanding of the text, which might therefore have been viewed almost like a logo by the jar's users.

Lastly, the inscription on TG740 (Fig. 255), a small votive jar, probably includes at least one other personal name, seemingly that of the vessel's owner or donor. The fragmentary text contains a sequence of four or five letters, followed by a space, after which is another word (or possibly two) made up of eight letters. Reading from right to left, the remnants of the first letter in the first word could be part of an r, while the most likely option for the second character, which is written below the imaginary line on which the text sits (possibly due the convex shape of the jar), seems to be a w, though that is not certain. Since the last two, t and ʾ, are reasonably clear, however, it can perhaps be assumed that the middle one of the five is an ḥ. The tentative reading would therefore be ⌈r⌉wḥtʾ, a complete word that might be parsed as an emphatic state of the feminine singular noun rawḥā (or rawḥtā), meaning 'free space', 'spaciousness' or 'relief' (see Brockelman 1928, p. 719). It is attested in cuneiform as part of a theophoric name (a particular god being a person's 'relief' or comfort; see Beyer 2004, pp. 50 and 481), and that could well be its function here.

The second word, which is made up of eight letters, also ends with the combination t and ʾ, both of which are clear. The preceding three letters appear to be, from right to left: y, t and n (the y and the t are somewhat conjectural). The word appears to begin with a p, possibly followed by a ʾ (a cautious reading), but the third letter is indeterminate, especially as the ink or paint seems to have been smudged. If the faint remaining traces perhaps derive from an m or an s, however, the second word might then be read as pʾ⌈m⌉ytntʾ or pʾ⌈s⌉ytntʾ, both of which would appear at first glance to be personal names, beginning with pʾ⌈m⌉y or pʾ⌈s⌉y, though no convincing parallels for these formations can be cited. The second letter, ʾ (alif), might alternatively be read as ʿ (ayn), to give a personal name beginning with PʿMY, though this is again difficult to corroborate. The following string of letters, tntʾ, which is also puzzling, might represent TTN, a conceivable Aramaic equivalent of the widespread Akkadian name Tattannu. The reading strains credulity for a variety of technical reasons, but the popularity of Akkadian Tattannu in the region in the fifth and fourth centuries BCE increases its likelihood. Finally, it is difficult to say whether *p'my* and *tnt'* (whatever the true readings may be) were separated by a tiny space, which would mark them as two different names, or whether they were written together as two elements of a double name that was further combined with the preceding theophoric. In any case, the entire sequence would appear to confirm the idea that, as with the inscription on TG4554, the text was the name of the donor (or donors) of a votive vessel that was deposited in the shrine.

The Terracotta Figurines

Although they share some common features with examples from other sites, the large number of Hellenistic fired-clay figurines that the British Museum team retrieved from Tell A exhibit some interesting differences from Hellenistic figurative terracottas that were made around the same time elsewhere in Mesopotamia. First, the Girsu figurines were mostly manufactured in traditional, even old-fashioned ways that can be dated back to Sumerian times (the Lagash II, Ur III and Old Babylonian periods; Fig. 256). Some were pressed into open moulds and finished with plain flat backs, while the rest, which were modelled by hand, were also made with figurative fronts and plain backs. Unlike in Babylon and Seleucia on the Tigris, to cite two of the most important centres for the production and use of such objects, none of the Girsu terracottas were made in the innovative two-part moulds that transformed local terracottas from old-style low reliefs into small three-dimensional sculptures that could be viewed in the round. The latter form, which was imported by the Greeks, represented a new direction in Mesopotamian figurine manufacture, and the notable absence of such three-dimensional figurines in Girsu shows both that the new techniques were not adopted universally, but also that visitors to the Girsu institution found the low-relief figures perfectly serviceable.

Another feature of the Girsu figurines differentiates them from the standard Hellenistic types: they lack the coating of white gypsum slip that was applied to conceal the baked clay on figures made in Babylon and Seleucia on the Tigris, for example (Karvonen-Kannas 1995; and Menegazzi 2012, pp. 157–67). The comparable absence of the slip coating on figures found at other sites outside the main Hellenistic centres (including Uruk, Charax Spasinou and Failaka, and a few examples from northern Iraq) would suggest that the Girsu examples were possibly made at one or more as yet unidentified workshops in the region. A further characteristic of the Girsu figurines that would tend to confirm that they were not produced in manufacturing bases close to the shrine is that they were made of a remarkably diverse variety of clay fabrics—a finding that is in agreement with the analysis of the varied pottery fabrics used to make artefacts uncovered by the British Museum team (discussed in the previous section). In particular, the numerous fabrics used to make the terracotta figurines found in Girsu feature a range of different mineral insertions. Combined with the fact that no Hellenistic-era terracotta slags or waste heaps were found on the site, the variety of clay types would tend to confirm that the figurines were indeed made elsewhere.

The team found three main types of figurines in Girsu: horses and riders, nude goddesses and a range of individuals, including possible historical figures and a small number of deities that could be identified with a reasonable degree of confidence. Horses and riders are generally the most distinctive type of Hellenistic figurative terracotta that have been excavated in the region more widely, and numerous finds have been recovered from Hellenistic deposits in Seleucia on the Tigris (Menegazzi 2009, pp. 67–81). In many documented instances only parts of the horses are preserved, but they often have attachment scars on their backs or at the bases of their manes—evidence that the rider was secured to the animal at the wet stage of modelling, with the complete figurine then being fired as a single object. Conversely, where no attachment marks are found, the horses and riders were manufactured and fired separately. Though the riders on horseback are a generic type of figurine, the makers adjusted the riders' clothing and headgear to express their affiliations.

The horses and riders found in Girsu were mostly modelled as two separate pieces, after which the riders were luted onto the backs and lower manes of their horses at the wet stage of manufacture (Fig. 257). This was confirmed on the retrieved examples by the presence of distinctive scars that were made when the two parts of the figurines were later severed. The riders from Girsu are shown wearing either a conical cap (see TG2448 and TG1829), sometimes with a long diadem cloth wrapped around their heads and

716 The Ningirsu Temple in the Hellenistic Era

FIGURE 256. Sumerian terracotta figurines found by the British Museum team.

trailing down behind (TG2084), or a wide-brimmed flat hat (TG1670), which probably represents the kind of Macedonian headwear known as a *kausia*. Introduced into the Near East and south-west Central Asia by Alexander the Great, this characteristic type of hat was worn by the elite during his lifetime and after his death (Kingsley 1991). The riders' garments are not described in detail in the modelling, but the folds of clay that were used to lute the riders onto their horses' manes indicate that the horsemen were shown wearing long robes.

The second type of Girsu figurine (Fig. 258), which was also very common in Hellenistic Babylonia, is the familiar

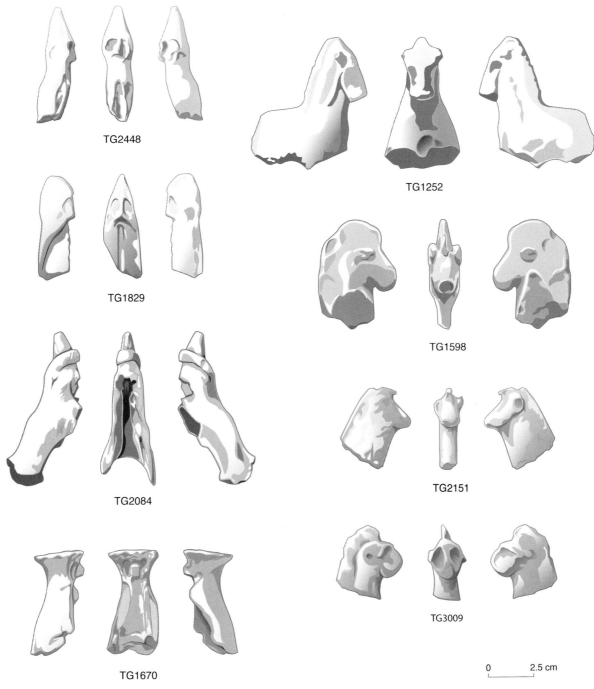

FIGURE 257. Terracotta figurines of riders on horseback from the Hellenistic shrine.

nude female that is generally identified as a mother or fertility goddess (though the significance of these figures might be even more general, as is argued in Chapter 47). Shown either holding or supporting their breasts (TG1850, TG3558 and TG4179), or with their arms hanging down by their sides (TG3542, TG4204 and TG4293), all the examples found in Girsu have strongly frontal postures, elaborated genitalia and marked navels, while their legs are invariably positioned close together (TG3541, TG4373 and TG4462). Female figurines of the same kind have been recovered from the Seleucid heroon in Seleucia on the Tigris (Menegazzi 2014, p. 71), and it is also worth noting that the type made in the Hellenistic

718　The Ningirsu Temple in the Hellenistic Era

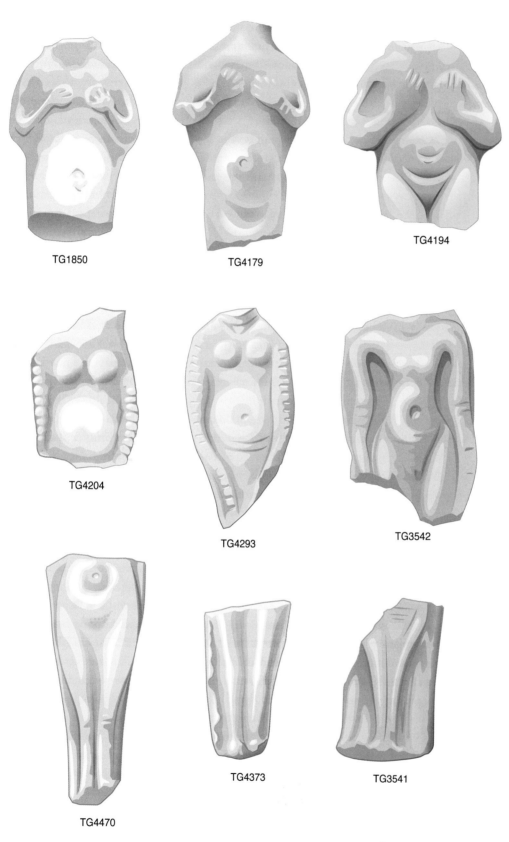

FIGURE 258. Nude female terracotta figurines from the Hellenistic shrine.

The Stratigraphy of the Hellenistic Shrine 719

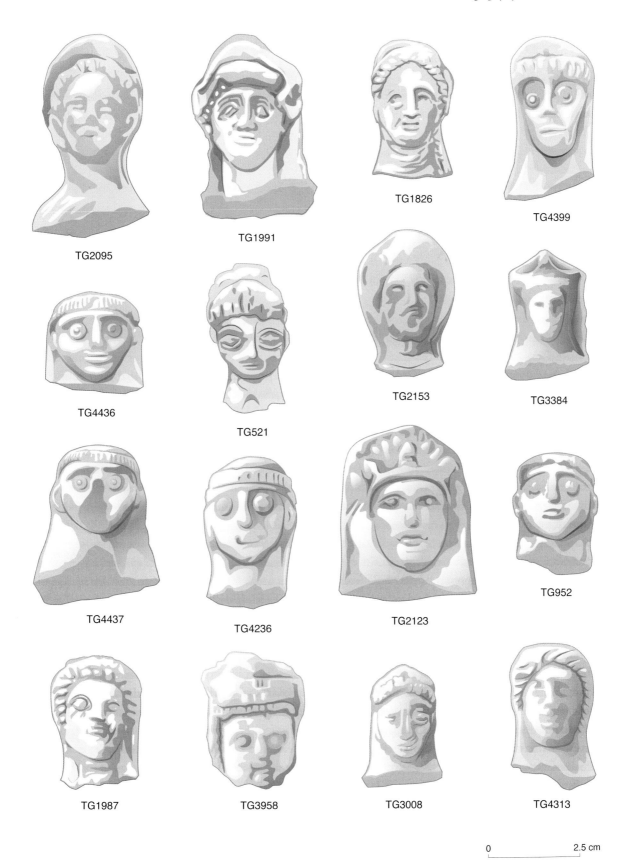

FIGURE 259. Terracotta heads of deities and presumed royal figures from the Hellenistic shrine.

era has much in common with terracotta figures that were prevalent in Sumerian times.

Lastly, a number of bas-relief terracotta figurines were found depicting female and male characters in classical Hellenistic styles (Fig. 259). The females are often shown wearing veils or scarves that cover their hair, which is worn on the tops of their heads; other figures wear diadems or horned headdresses. With a great deal of caution, some might be associated with Greek gods and goddesses, including Aphrodite, Heracles and Apollo, while others perhaps represent historical figures, as discussed in Chapter 47.

One find of special interest and significance was the cache of broken terracottas that the British Museum team unearthed in Area B10. The items were clearly not just dumped, but rather placed in a favissa that held discarded objects from Adadnadinakhe's original shrine. Deposited when the shrine was extended and refurbished in the mid-third century BCE, the objects uncovered in the favissa provide a wealth of insights into the material sacred contents of the first Hellenistic temple and potentially also into the ritual activities that were carried out there. In addition, the manner in which they were discarded during the rebuilding phase reveals possible new information about the way such cult artefacts might have been ritually cancelled when they were no longer considered to be serviceable, or perhaps about the ways in which they were used by worshippers. The favissa (contexts 5438, 5489, 5490, 5491, 5492, 5435, 5506, 5504 and 5437) yielded a total of approximately fifty Hellenistic terracotta figurines, all of which appeared to have been deliberately broken, as is discussed further below. The inventory of the fragmentary sherds, none of which could be matched or joined to other retrieved pieces, is illuminating. It includes eleven fragments of nude goddesses—three torsos (TG4179, TG4204 and TG4293) and eight lower bodies or legs (TG4213, TG4234, TG4434, TG4441, TG4442, TG4462, TG4470 and TG4500), but no heads. A number of riders on horseback were found, among which are the head of a Macedonian rider (TG4492), six bodies or torsos of horses (TG4209, TG4464, TG4475, TG4479, TG4487 and TG4509), two horses' heads (TG4182 and TG4206) and about twenty equine legs. In addition, four more heads (TG4436, TG4437, TG4236 and TG4399) were cautiously judged to belong to historical figures. Finally, among the rare terracottas are at least one fragmentary plaque or bas-relief, possibly of a warrior (TG4235), and one of a lion-hunting

hero (TG4526) that most probably depicts Heracles with the pelt of the Nemean lion.

Three of the British Museum team's heads (TG4436, TG4437 and TG4236), which are noticeably rather round in shape, have distinctive circular eyes with very well-defined pupils. The mouth of TG4436 turns upwards at the sides, possibly with the hint of a smile, and that might also be the case for TG4236, though it is impossible to be definitive. Unlike heads TG4436 and TG4437, which are upright, however, TG4236 is inclined to the left (as we look). Furthermore, TG4436, TG4437 and TG4236 all appear to be wearing narrow diadems with vertical bands, though the band might be part of another kind of headwear. The eyes of TG4399, which are formed with applied strips of clay, similar to the ones just discussed, have marked pupils, but they are almond shaped (quite unlike the other three) and obliquely positioned so that they point down and outwards from either side of the bridge of the broad nose. Other characteristics of TG4399 differentiate it from TG4436, TG4437 and TG4236: the shape of the head is not round, but elongated and hollow cheeked, while the mouth is rather horizontal, with perhaps the suggestion of a downward turn at its sides. Nor does TG4399 have a diadem. Instead, it appears either that the hair is piled rather high on top of the head, though with a notably concave horizontal band running across it at the top, or (probably more likely) that the figure is shown wearing some kind of head covering. Similarly, TG4399, which seems to represent a male figure, is very slightly inclined to the left (as we look), perhaps by about nine or ten degrees, but by no means as much as TG4236, which might be inclined by as much as fourteen or fifteen degrees. The possible identities of these archaic-looking heads, which might relate to historical figures, are elucidated further in Chapter 47.

Another of the many fascinating pieces unearthed by the British Museum team was an extremely unusual terracotta (TG2767; Fig. 260), which was found in the Hellenistic levels of Area B10, at the NW end of Adadnadinakhe's original complex, close to the original Hellenistic temenos wall. Measuring 7.3 cm (h) × 6 cm (w) × 3.8 cm (t), and made of a very fine fabric, the fragment represents the upper part of moulded fired-clay plaque (with an arched top and rounded and flattened edges) that shows a seated female figure wearing a mural crown (the walls being expressed by three towers on a plain base). Perhaps originally depicting an enthroned goddess (or less likely a queen), the very well-preserved figure, which was carefully modelled with deep lines, is placed in a

FIGURE 260. Terracotta plaque showing a goddess wearing a mural crown.

rectangular frame formed of a thin impressed outline, against a smooth blank background. The locks of hair, which puff out into round bunches on either side of the face, are indicated with vertical regular lines (at intervals of about 0.1 cm). The coiffure is possibly finished with a thin band that wraps around the head, above the forehead. The woman's arch-shaped brows are marked with diagonal strokes, and her eyelids are thick; her nose is large and flattened, and her full lips create a stern or serious impression. Her chin is dimpled, and she wears a necklace with four bands above a flounced robe with a wide neckline. Her hands are clasped together in an attitude of prayer or solemnity that compares closely with the hands on the Gudea Statues. The exact archaeological provenance of the piece could not be determined, but it was recovered from erosion deposits that were associated with the French excavations, at a topographical height of 15.7 m, all of which strongly suggested that it had been transported from its Hellenistic context by processes of erosion. The find location was also 1 m to the north-west of an eroded fragment of Hellenistic precinct wall (5479), the top of which was preserved to a topographical height of 15.45 m. A comparison of the level at which the plaque was found with the heights of nearby deposits left some uncertainty about the exact context in which the piece might have originated, but it seemed likely that it derived from the deposits that were laid down in order to raise the ground when the Hellenistic shrine was expanded in the mid-third century BCE. This would mean that it was deposited at about the same time as most of the figurines and plaques discussed above, namely before the demolition of Adadnadinakhe's precinct wall. Based on some of these inferences, the object's Hellenistic history can be tentatively outlined: it was probably displayed as a sacred artefact in Adadnadinakhe's temple, before being subsequently removed and redeposited as part of the clearance operations that were carried out during the preconstruction phase of the extended shrine (further strengthening the idea that a cache of terracottas was deliberately placed in a favissa); it then arrived at its find location as a consequence of the erosion that resulted from the French excavations. As with the four archaic heads, its age and broader significance are considered in Chapter 47, but it is worth mentioning here that it was almost certainly a Sumerian terracotta that was recovered by Adadnadinakhe's workers and then incorporated into the original Hellenistic building.

Without exception, all the Hellenistic-era figurines that were found in the favissa were broken. As for the many

FIGURE 261. Close-up of the point of impact on a Hellenistic-era terracotta fertility goddess (TG4293) that was possibly broken intentionally.

Sumerian objects that have been subjected to forensic examination in the course of this study, including the Ur-Nanshe Plaques and the Gudea Statues, it is important to consider whether these later terracottas might have been damaged deliberately—are the perceived breaks signs of accidental damage, or do they evince patterns of intention? As is the case for those previous discussions, it should again be stressed that it is extremely difficult to give a categorical assessment of the types of damage found on such artefacts, and any conclusions must be advanced with the utmost caution because, even when they are observed under a microscope, many of the break marks on the recovered Hellenistic figurines cannot be explained conclusively. It is simply not possible to say with certainty that particular edges or fractures exhibit points of impact that resulted from the use of tools, for example, or whether the artefact was randomly or accidentally broken, leaving irregular or uneven surfaces and fractures. Additionally, the edges of many of the sherds were subsequently eroded over time, and in such instances it is usually impossible to judge what happened when they were damaged in antiquity. Another factor that has to be noted is the type of clay that the object was made from and the exact circumstances of its manufacture. The consistency and quality of the clay fabric must have played a role in any patterns of breakage, as must the precise ways in which the objects were made, perhaps especially their firing.

With these caveats stated, when examined microscopically a significant number of the figurines found in Girsu appear to have been deliberately damaged. Several sherds from nude goddesses show similar angles of fracture, especially where the lower bodies have been separated from the torsos. Distinct oblique angles can be observed running from left to right, from right to left and from front to back, perhaps indicating that the figures were all broken in the same way, possibly by being struck or snapped against a sharp or hard surface. Furthermore, the break edges in these cases appear to be consistently flat, exhibiting a clean snap that would suggest the same method of fracture. Objects would usually break first at the weakest points—at the necks and limbs, or at places where different parts of the figure were joined together. Conversely, the fractured areas on the majority of nude goddess sherds were found at thicker, structurally stronger points. This might suggest the use of more directed force, providing possible evidence of intentional breakage. Similarly, other nude goddesses perhaps show signs of having been deliberately decapitated. This is again suggested by the consistently repeated angles of the breaks, which run from right to left, with the left edge being generally higher. On one

FIGURE 262. Second close-up of the lower edge of the break on the same terracotta fertility goddess (TG4293).

FIGURE 263. Terracotta of a figure wearing a diadem (TG4436), showing possible intentional damage or decapitation. The angle of the flat, clean break suggests an impact from behind, when the figure was conceivably fractured against a hard surface.

of the nude figures (TG4293), for example, the fracture is defined by probable points of impact at its upper and lower edges (Figs. 261 and 262).

With respect to the riders on horseback and the individual heads, though it is equally difficult to be sure, some clues might also provide signs of deliberate damage. The nature and number of the sherds—including heads, the torsos of animals and riders, and the legs of horses and humans—would confirm that very few bodies or torsos belonging to the individual heads were retrieved. Statistically, this might suggest a pattern of deliberate damage. Furthermore, some of the heads, particularly those that have been tentatively described as archaic in style, seem more clearly to have been deliberately decapitated. TG4436, for example, exhibits a relatively clean oblique fracture that extends slightly upwards from back to front, suggesting that the object was possibly struck or snapped against a hard or sharp surface (Fig. 263).

The reasons why the figurines might have been damaged in such a manner remain enigmatic, though several possible explanations can be provisionally advanced. The analysed artefacts were found discarded in the favissa that was placed against the decommissioned temenos wall of the original Adadnadinakhe complex in Area B10 (as noted above). It is therefore unclear whether the terracottas were intact when they were removed from the shrine in the preconstruction phase of the extension work, in which case they might have been deliberately broken by attendant priests in a variant of the cancellation rituals that were common in the history of Mesopotamia all the way back to Sumerian times, as corroborated by several instances discussed previously in this study. Alternatively, if the figurines were taken inside the shrine by pilgrims, they might have been deliberately broken while the visitors were praying or worshipping, or before they exited the sacred space. That being the case, it is conceivable that worshippers took parts of the figurines away with them, after the artefacts had been blessed or sanctified, leaving other parts behind in the shrine as ongoing signs of their piety, for example. These are conjectural matters, but the fact that most, if not all, of the retrieved Hellenistic figurines were fragmentary—including those found in the favissa and those retrieved elsewhere in the course of the team's excavations—would appear to suggest that the terracottas were indeed ritually broken by pilgrims during acts of worship.

CHAPTER 47

The Meaning and Purpose of the Hellenistic Eninnu

THE NATURE AND VARIETY OF THE OBJECTS AND deposits excavated by the British Museum team provide unequivocal proof of a number of previously unknown, misunderstood or neglected facts about the revived Eninnu. First and foremost, it was constructed in two phases. An original Hellenistic-era shrine was built by Adadnadinakhe sometime shortly after the arrival in Babylon in 331 BCE of Alexander the Great. As detailed above, that initial building was made up principally of the area centred around Court A (Fig. 264) on the SE side of the structure shown on Sarzec's Plan A (Fig. 111), and it had an open-air courtyard, walled with mud-bricks, on the NW side of the Gate of Gudea façade, which partly cuts through the building on Sarzec's Plan A on a NE–SW axis. Subsequently, around 250 BCE (but perhaps a little earlier, as is explained below), more than half a century after Adadnadinakhe's shrine was established, an extension was added on the NW side of the building (to the north-west of the Gate of the Gudea façade) that included Courts B and C. Various other refurbishments were carried out in this phase (as described previously), including the renewal of several outer walls, though the full extent of the changes made to Adadnadinakhe's building is difficult to gauge. Importantly, however, there was an altar outside the NW façade of the enlarged construction, in front of the NW entrance, on an axis that led more or less directly from the NW façade through the Hellenistic-era Gate of Gudea and Court A to a presumed cella on the SE side of the complex. This key sacred locus probably occupied an equivalent spot in front of the NW façade of Adadnadinakhe's original shrine, but this cannot be confirmed.

Furthermore, like other Babylonian shrines, but generally unlike a typical Greek temple, the first and later complexes both included a number of niches or cellas in which a variety of sacred imagery could be displayed, and the range of votives found by the British Museum team would seem clearly to confirm that offerings to more than one deity were made in the Hellenistic shrine at all periods of its active life. The historical reasons why Babylonian temples developed in this way are beyond the scope of this study, but it should be noted that the trend was already present in Sumerian times. In Gudea's New Eninnu, for example, the shrines of Ningirsu and Bau were situated together in a single walled complex, where they were separated by a courtyard, while smaller installations were set up in the vicinity to other deities—Ningirsu's sons, Igalim and Shulshaga, for example. In addition, several other monuments were displayed in Gudea's Eninnu, including the images of Ningirsu's legendary foes, the Slain Heroes, while certain artefacts had associations with other deities. The sun standard placed at the SE gate, for example, was linked with Utu, though it should be recalled that he and Ningirsu were partly assimilated. More distinctly, Enlil, An and Enki, who are key figures in the narrative of the Cylinder Inscriptions, were honoured in one form or another, notably on the Gudea Steles and in the foundation deposits and clay nails. The development from the Sumerian complex to a shrine with multiple cellas, niches or podiums was therefore almost certainly an organic one. Finally, the Gudea Statues were also exhibited in the Hellenistic shrine, doubtless from the time of Adadnadinakhe onwards (Figs. 265 and 266). They were found by Sarzec in Court A, but this was where they were discarded

724

The Meaning and Purpose of the Hellenistic Eninnu 725

FIGURE 264. Reconstruction of Court A inside the Hellenistic shrine, showing the probable colonnades to the north-east (left) and south-west, and some of the niches in which sacred monuments and the Gudea Statues were displayed. The principal cult podiums were probably beyond the courtyard, behind the inferred wall in the reconstruction, around the building's SE corner.

when the shrine was destroyed, after they had been decapitated. Very little information has survived to confirm where precisely they were situated in the working temple, or what their role might have been, but they are by far the most significant Sumerian relics to emerge from the Hellenistic shrine. One important piece of data relates to the location of Statue D (the Gudea Colossus), which was almost certainly kept in the external niche (N on Sarzec's Plan A). It therefore seems reasonable to presume that the others were displayed inside the shrine in some of its many smaller internal spaces, and one was placed in the second external niche (T) on the SW façade (considered further below).

Several conclusions can be drawn about the nature and purpose of the revived shrine from this brief synopsis. Despite the presence of the Gudea Statues, the building could not have been simply a memorial to the Sumerian ancestors of the native inhabitants of Babylonia. This idea, of course, stems ultimately from the incorrect assumption made by Parrot that its founder, Adadnadinakhe, was operating in a kind of historical vacuum, almost in the manner of a modern museum curator, but the Hellenistic character of most of the sacred objects found in the shrine clearly indicates that—irrespective of any beliefs that local people or Hellenistic arrivals might have had about Gudea and Girsu's Sumerian heritage—the revived temple had strong and enduring Greek religious associations. Indeed, it is reasonable to presume that it was the site's markedly Hellenistic connections that enabled it to flourish between the time of its refoundation by Adadnadinakhe and approximately 250 BCE, when it was enlarged and extravagantly refitted under the Seleucids. The finds made by the British Museum team indicate that the first phase dated from around the time of Alexander, but it is perhaps possible to be even more precise about the time frame. Alexander, who took control of

FIGURE 265. Close-up of the reconstruction of Court A, showing the area inside the NE façade, with an opening leading into more enclosed spaces and a deep niche.

Babylon in 331 BCE, stayed in the city for a little more than a month before continuing his march eastwards towards India (as is described further below). He returned to Babylon eight years later, in 323 BCE, when he died in June of that year, apparently in the palace of Nebuchadnezzar II. The circumstances of his untimely demise at the age of just thirty-two have long aroused suspicion, and it seems that he might have been poisoned. Be that as it may, his death led to a lengthy period of significant disruption, when several contenders to the throne strove to install themselves as his successor. The situation was finally resolved eighteen years after Alexander's death, with the accession of Seleucus in 305 BCE. Since it is extremely difficult to imagine that Adadnadinakhe's revived shrine could have been conceived of and executed in the tumultuous years between 323 BCE and 305 BCE, it must presumably have been commissioned between 331 BCE and 323 BCE, while Alexander was still alive, or at least while his stabilising influence was still in the ascendancy.

With respect to the shrine's re-establishment, it is interesting that no dependable evidence whatsoever has emerged to suggest that Tell A was occupied in the long interval between its abandonment in the Old Babylonian period (probably around 1750 BCE) and the building work that was carried out by Adadnadinakhe soon after 331 BCE. One possibility is that Girsu might have been a kind of lost city, almost a legendary place. Another conjecture is that the site was genuinely forgotten and only rediscovered when a fragment of Sumerian cuneiform was found (on a sherd of a statue, for example) and taken to Uruk or Babylon, where learned scribes were able to read it. Conceivably, they might then have associated it with the epic Lugale, which includes the story of the Gudea Statues, and a great rediscovery might have ensued—all of which is, in essence, a backprojection of the narrative of Girsu's recovery by Sarzec in the nineteenth century. A piece of evidence that would contradict both of these ideas is that the Hellenistic shrine was placed not just generally on the ruins of the expansive ancient site, but precisely on the mound that was occupied by Gudea's New Eninnu. Similarly, the relative precision with which the first Hellenistic soundings were executed would tend further to confirm that the location of

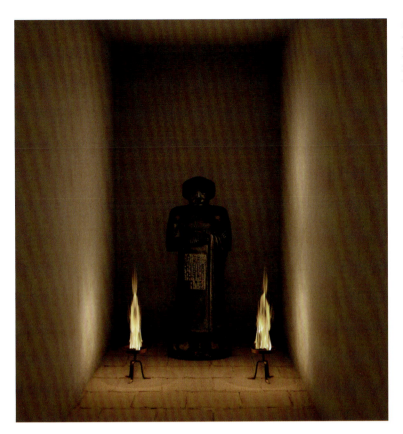

FIGURE 266. Reconstruction of a niche inside the Hellenistic shrine, containing Statue A, a standing portrait of Gudea.

the Sumerian temple was known to the people who commissioned and built the revived shrine. At that time the site must have looked roughly as it does today (minus the reshaping effects of the destructive French excavations), with huge mounds entombing a buried sacred urban centre that the architects and planners were able to survey and map out in the requisite amount of detail. The exact circumstances of Girsu's reclamation remain hypothetical, but the latter narrative would appear to be the likeliest.

Having been established between 331 BCE and 323 BCE, the Hellenistic heyday of the revived Eninnu coincided with the decades of relative calm that followed the ascent to power of Seleucus in 305 BCE. As noted above, this continued after Seleucus's death in 281 BCE, through the reigns of his son Antiochus I Soter (who ruled from 281 BCE to 261 BCE), and his grandson Antiochus II Theos (who ruled from 261 BCE to 246 BCE). Greatly increased instability affected the empire from 246 BCE onwards, though the Seleucids managed to retain control of large parts of Mesopotamia until the mid-second century BCE. It is nevertheless clear that the Hellenisation of the region was most marked under Alexander and his immediate Seleucid successors—the time when the first temple was constructed by Adadnadinakhe and expanded under the authority of the first Seleucids. As this strongly implies, and as the British Museum team's finds confirm, the shrine was an active centre of worship that appealed forcefully to Greek or Hellenistic religious worshippers and pilgrims, as well as to Mesopotamians. With this framework in mind, it is also possible to be slightly more exact about the date of the shrine's expansion, which was probably carried out in the peaceful decades that preceded 246 BCE, and therefore perhaps a little earlier than 250 BCE, at a time when the long-term outlook still appeared to be relatively stable. It must be stressed that the date cannot currently be pinpointed with greater accuracy.

The British Museum team's finds from the earlier and later phases of the Hellenistic building provide some extremely good insights into its function, but it is important to note that the team's groundbreaking discoveries could, to some extent, have been anticipated on the basis of many objects that were

FIGURE 267. Artist's impression of the bronze statue of Heracles (AO2890) found on Tell A by Sarzec.

discovered by the French explorers between the times of Sarzec and Genouillac. The Louvre website lists numerous terracottas (catalogued in Barrelet 1968), vases, lamps and other objects (including some bronzes) that derive from Hellenistic occupation strata, but they played little or no part in the early seminal discussions of the shrine that defined subsequent scholarly perceptions of it. It might be invidious to suggest that the neglect took hold because the wealth of Hellenistic materials simply did not fit the thesis that Adadnadinakhe was almost exclusively interested in the Sumerian past, but it is difficult to think of another reason. The test case is perhaps the bronze statue of Heracles (AO2890; Fig. 267) that was found by Sarzec during his first seasons, presumably before 1881. Sarzec, who initially believed that the Hellenistic remains dated from the time of Gudea, seemingly did not know what to make of this apparently anomalous find, and it is relatively easy to see why it might have escaped the focused attention of Heuzey, who was dealing with the recovery of the lost civilisation of Sumer on a grand scale. Nonetheless, it is astonishing to realise that no mention of it whatsoever is made in *Découvertes en Chaldée*, and the figure was basically lost from sight until the Louvre recently released its searchable database. This was by no means the only Hellenistic object that Sarzec found, however, and many more were unearthed by Genouillac. All of this data was available to Parrot, but its implications have never been properly addressed. Among the numerous other Hellenistic artefacts in the Louvre that might be mentioned is a small bronze lioness (AO96), found by Sarzec and accessioned in 1881, when the finds from his early seasons were returned to Paris and catalogued. The little statue is illustrated in Sarzec and Heuzey (1912, Pl. 45 (4)), but it is shown without comment on a page that contains a number of much older artefacts—the unstated implication being that it might have been Sumerian.

Fortunately, the Hellenistic context of the revived Eninnu can now be more cogently assessed. As detailed above, the British Museum team found rich pottery assemblages from the shrine's earlier and later phases. They include artefacts of exceptional quality and diversity that clearly derive from a temple setting. Just as importantly, both the objects and the materials of which they are made represent a variety of locations in Mesopotamia and further afield in the Hellenistic world, meaning that they were brought to Girsu by visitors who came from far and wide to visit the shrine and deposit luxury vases, offering vessels, figurines and other votives. Among the extremely rare pieces (listed previously) is the sherd of a vessel that contains a partly preserved portrait of Alexander (Fig. 268) and a silver coin that was struck in Babylon under Alexander's authority (Fig. 269). The latter was almost certainly reused as a foundation deposit when the later altar, which was probably the successor of an original one established on the same axis by Adadnadinakhe, was consecrated in front of the enlarged shrine's NW façade. As noted previously, it shows Heracles (in a youthful, clean-shaven portrait that strongly recalls conventional representations of Alexander) on one side, with Zeus on the other. Heracles was an extremely popular figure in Greek myth, but he was of special importance for Alexander, as indicated by the numismatic iconography and for reasons that are discussed in greater detail below. Additionally, with respect to the construction of the original and expanded Hellenistic temples, the British Museum team found several buried astragaluses—the knuckle bones of animals that were commonly used as foundation deposits in the Hellenistic world.

The team also unearthed a particularly informative layer that was clearly associated with the enlargement of the shrine in the mid-third century BCE. Layer 5439 in Area B10, which is detailed above, was a foundation layer for the exterior paving that was added on the NW side of the later temple. Its contents differed greatly from those found in other reliably contextualised Hellenistic strata—for example, those contained in the favissa, which is also described above. The objects found in layer 5439 included an extremely interesting group of ten Lagash II inscribed clay nails that cover almost the whole range of the building activities carried out by Gudea, but they also include inscriptions relating to the old Eninnu of Ur-Bau. Among this carefully selected—even curated—collection were cones celebrating all the major structures associated with the New Eninnu: three in the name of Ur-Bau recording the construction of Ningirsu's Eninnu, and one in Ur-Bau's name for the temple of Bau; two Gudea cones with his Standard Inscription commemorating the building of the New Eninnu; two for Gudea's construction of the EPA; and one in honour of the Gudea shrine of Shulshaga. There were two exceptions—the absence of Gudea cones for the construction of the shrines of Bau and Igalim—and one seeming anomaly in the form of a cone commemorating Gudea's construction of a shrine for Nanshe, which was not on Tell A. Otherwise, it is clear that the entire set of cones was purposefully buried as a coherent assemblage of foundation deposits that recorded and venerated the Sumerian buildings that lay beneath the Hellenistic shrine. Furthermore, the cones were found juxtaposed with other objects (also listed previously) that add significantly to an understanding of the Hellenistic shrine's sacred framework. The latter included a piece of an obsidian object (TG3783) inscribed with a Gudea text commemorating the giguna, another part of the New Eninnu (see Chapter 23). There was also a Lagash II or possibly Ur III cuneiform tablet (TG3817) recording distributions made to listed individuals, which was doubtless deliberately placed by the later Hellenistic-era builders. Perhaps most important, at least with regard to the principal god or gods to whom the Hellenistic temple was sacred, were two exceptionally rare cylinder seals—one badly worn example from the Early Dynastic period and one dating to Lagash II times (described previously) displaying an unusual image of Ningirsu holding a double lion-headed mace and facing the goddess Bau (TG3897). The mace with its lions' heads evokes Ningirsu in his role as the warrior god and promotes a link with his Hellenistic counterpart, Heracles (further elucidated below), while the presence of Bau introduces several aspects of female divinity that were well represented in the

FIGURE 268. Sherd of a ceramic vessel decorated with a portrait of Alexander the Great.

shrine by Hellenistic deities. Noteworthy in this context is the interesting Sumerian terracotta found by the British Museum team that seems to portray a horned nude goddess (TG3842; Fig. 270). Other foundation deposits in the same layer were identified as having more particular Hellenistic associations. They include three ritually interred astragaluses and two fragments of Hellenistic terracotta figurines, notably one that shows the god Apollo playing a lute (TG3838). The richly evocative inventory of deposits detailed in Chapter 46 deserves fuller consideration than can be attempted here, but it should be pointed out that the figure of Apollo (often partly syncretised) unquestionably had special meaning for the Seleucids, under whose authority the enlargement of the shrine was commissioned and executed, and the importance of the god perhaps increased during and after the reign of Antiochus I, as is mentioned further below. Indeed, the entire assemblage seems unequivocally to confirm a syncretising impulse that infused every aspect of both stages of the Hellenistic-era temple, perhaps gaining in momentum as the third century BCE wore on.

The great number of terracotta figurines that the British Museum team found provide a still more detailed context for some of the cultic activities that took place inside the shrine. Like the pottery assemblages, the recovered figurines, which originated in a range of places in the Hellenistic world, must in many instances have been carried to the temple by visitors. Had they been manufactured in Girsu, they would generally have been made of a similar clay fabric, but this was by no

FIGURE 269. A silver coin struck in Babylon shortly after the arrival of Alexander the Great in 331 BCE. The obverse (left) contains a youthful image of Heracles, wearing the pelt of the Nemean lion, that closely resembles traditional portraits of Alexander; the reverse shows Zeus enthroned with an eagle and a lightning bolt.

means the case (as mentioned above). On the contrary, the artefacts were made with many different clay compositions. This does not categorically prove that no terracotta figurines or vessels whatsoever were produced in the environs of Girsu, but it does show that clay artefacts were usually transported to the site from other locations. As previously noted, the varied corpus, which is detailed in Chapter 46 and elucidated further below, can be broken down into three or four main categories. First, there are the Macedonian riders on horseback, which have strong associations with Alexander, but would also confirm a cult of warlike heroism. Secondly, there are a great many nude female figurines, all of the same overall type, suggesting the cult of a goddess who might be linked with fertility, love or other aspects of Mesopotamian and Greek worship. Thirdly, there are statues of a small number of other male and female deities that can be fairly securely identified: Apollo playing the lyre, for example, and a terracotta statuette of Heracles. With regard to this group, it is probable that pilgrims brought statues of their own personal or household deities to the shrine, and there is every reason to suppose that some of the many cellas or niches that the temple contained were specially devoted to the small core group of gods and goddesses represented among the finds. Lastly, as argued below, several of the terracotta heads that do not have clear divine attributes conceivably represent historical figures, almost certainly including some of the Seleucid kings and queens under whom the temple remained vibrant during the third century BCE. In addition to the divinities to whom the shrine was sacred, historical rulers played a significant role in the institution's meaning and organisation from the very outset, not least through the recovery and display of the Gudea Statues.

The monumental Gudea Statues, which were doubtless exhibited at various points in and around the temple, must without question have been the most important Sumerian objects in the building, but they were by no means the only Sumerian artefacts that were incorporated into the shrine. Along with the several smaller Sumerian votives that were seemingly buried in the foundation layers, there was the large limestone basin (2.5 m × 0.6 m × 0.7 m (h)) that was found by Sarzec in front of gate M (on Sarzec's Plan A) in the NE façade, where it was prominently displayed on a stepped pedestal (see Chapter 23 for this and the associated finds). Inscribed in Gudea's name and dedicated to Ningirsu, it was carved in relief with deities or priestesses holding overflowing vases (Fig. 108). Also closely connected with gate M were the two large diorite door sockets that Sarzec excavated in the gateway. With diameters measuring between 0.5 m and 0.6 m, one was marked with a Gudea inscription, while the other was probably inscribed in the name of Ur-Bau. Similarly, two fragments of another limestone basin (AO73; Fig. 271), including a very well-preserved corner (measuring 0.42 m × 0.32 m × 0.15 m (h)) were found by Sarzec in entrance passage F in the NW Gate of Gudea façade. Decorated with an extremely well-carved lion's head (probably the head of a Thunderbird), it was also inscribed in the name of Gudea

(RIME 3.1.7.59), and it appears to have been placed in the passageway connecting the original SE side of the shrine with the area to the north-west of the Hellenistic-era Gate of Gudea. Furthermore, many of the small figures, especially the terracottas of divinities, had dual associations reflecting the syncretising trend that was a general feature of the Hellenistic expansion and occupation under Alexander and increasingly under his Seleucid successors, when local gods and goddesses were identified with members of the Greek pantheon. The inclusive approach to the religions of conquered regions had clear advantages for the Hellenistic authorities, but it was not an alien concept in Mesopotamia, where Sumerian deities were co-opted into later Assyrian and Babylonian worship. Sometimes, as with Inanna (later Ishtar), this was basically just a matter of changing one name for another, since the goddess' functions and mythology remained largely continuous, but there was also a tendency for later gods to consolidate some of the roles and attributes of several of their forebears, as was notably the case for Marduk, who eventually acquired fifty names that covered almost the whole spectrum of Mesopotamian male divinity. This trend is significant with respect to the later history of the shrine because worship appears to have been concentrated on a small number of key divinities. Some theories about the syncretic identities of a few of the figurines found in Girsu are advanced below, but there is one god who towers above the rest in importance, and whose identity must in some sense contribute a defining meaning to the shrine: Ningirsu. As a counterbalance to earlier interpretations of the revived Eninnu, it is crucial to stress that the site must have been a thriving centre for Hellenistic worship, but that must be further nuanced in the broader context of the temple's Sumerian origins and historical character. The Hellenistic-era planners and builders knew very well that Ningirsu was the principal deity to whom the ancient temple was devoted. His name was proclaimed on nearly every inscription in the name of Gudea—on bricks, statues, foundation deposits, clay cones and numerous other artefacts. Similarly, to invoke just one other Sumerian figure, the goddess Bau must unquestionably have been a very familiar figure, since she was also richly commemorated in many texts from Gudea's reign. What, then, was the attitude of the fourth-century BCE builders and their successors to the chief Sumerian deity and the rest of the Girsu pantheon?

One way of approaching this problem is to consider what might have been known about Gudea, the founder of the

FIGURE 270. Sumerian terracotta figurine of a horned nude goddess (TG3842), retrieved by the British Museum team from the Hellenistic strata of Tell A.

legendary New Eninnu. Narratives about the famous ancient ruler must have existed, and it was conceivably acknowledged, at least in scribal and sacerdotal circles, that he had been posthumously deified—an event that occurred in the Ur III period, when the image of the worshipping Gudea acquired cult status. Later documents preface his name with the determinative (dingir) to signal his acquired divinity: $^{d}Gu_3.de_2.a$. Similarly, many cuneiform tablets record the ritual offerings that were made to his statues, while cylinder seals were dedicated to him in his deified guise. The Gudea Statues themselves do not attribute divinity to him (as discussed in Chapter 35), but their inscribed texts nonetheless threaten that the gods will mete out the direst punishments to anyone who might dare to interfere with them or interrupt their scheduled offerings. It was doubtless also known that the statues were ritually animated, thereby promoting them to a liminal region that was symbolically closer to the realm of the gods than it was to the world occupied by mere mortals. These are matters that the clergies of Ur, Uruk, Larsa and Babylon in the fourth and third centuries BCE must have been aware of to a greater or lesser degree.

Also available to the Hellenistic-era planners of the revived shrine were the cuneiform writings on the Gudea Statues, which gave details of the actual construction of the New Eninnu, including the sourcing of some of the rare and precious materials that were brought from abroad. Absent from

FIGURE 271. Corner of a limestone basin with a lion's head (part of a Thunderbird motif), inscribed in the name of Gudea, found by Sarzec in the Hellenistic shrine. Musée du Louvre AO73.

the statue texts and foundation inscriptions are the expansive mythological narratives about Ningirsu that would have been very well known to Sumerian worshippers, and which therefore did not need to be stated because they were an inherent part of the New Eninnu's raison d'être. Many of them were nonetheless recorded for Sumerian audiences in the Cylinder Inscriptions and expressed in other monuments, notably the Gudea Steles and the images of the Slain Heroes. A wide-ranging source of relevant mythology that was still fairly widely known as late as the Hellenistic period was Lugale, the Sumerian epic poem that recounts some of the deeds of Ningirsu (referred to in the poem as Ninurta). Indeed, at least one bilingual (Sumerian and Akkadian) manuscript of the work was in circulation in the Seleucid period (see Frazer 2017). At the beginning of Lugale, Ningirsu/Ninurta is shown feasting with his wife (Bau), his father (the supreme god, Enlil) and other members of the Mesopotamian pantheon in the Ekur (Enlil's temple in Nippur). Warned by his divine weapon (Sharur) that the monstrous Asag (the child of heaven and earth) has sired a fearsome band of stone warriors in the mountains at the ends of the earth, Ningirsu journeys to the inhospitable wilderness and eventually destroys the stone army, killing each of the named Slain Heroes. With the cosmic order restored, Ningirsu returns to his father, appearing from the east like Utu, the sun god. Most importantly for the present purpose, the Eninnu in Girsu is mentioned by Ningirsu when he addresses each of the stone warriors in turn. Speaking to Esi (diorite), and looking ahead into the future, he expressly mentions the statues that a noteworthy ruler will one day erect in the god's temple, the Eninnu (ETCSL, 466–78):

Esi, your army in battle changed sides separately (?). You spread before me like thick smoke. You did not raise your hand. You did not attack me. Since you said, 'It is false. The Lord is alone the Hero. Who can vie with Ninurta, son of Enlil?'—they shall extract you from the highland countries. They shall bring (?) you from the land of Magan. You shall shape (?) Strong Copper like leather and then you shall be perfectly adapted for my heroic arm, for me, the Lord. When a king who is establishing his renown for perpetuity has had its statues sculpted for all time, you shall be placed in the place of libations—and it shall suit you well—in my temple Eninnu, the house full of grace.

The 'king' who eventually celebrates his eternal renown by commissioning a number of indestructible diorite statues is Gudea, and the Eninnu to which the god refers is none other than the New Eninnu of Girsu.

When Adadnadinakhe and his associates decided to build an updated version of the Eninnu, therefore, they must surely have known that they were reviving a sacred locus that represented a point of intersection between Sumerian–Mesopotamian mythology and historical reality. It was, in a sense, the architectural site that corroborated the truth of a time-honoured religious story. In addition, there is every reason to suppose that the shrine had (or could be shown to have, which is perhaps the vital point) richly symbolic meanings for the Hellenistic administrators under whose overarching authority it was refounded. This is because, as a number of recent scholars have maintained, Ningirsu is generally acknowledged as a key Mesopotamian source for the tales of the labours of Heracles (see Van Dijk 1983, vol. 1, pp. 17–18; Penglase 1994, p. 70; and West 1997, pp. 467–9). The most essential and specific associations are represented by the marked affinities between the monstrous creatures that were overcome by Heracles and the Slain Heroes of Ningirsu that appear in Lugale and were commemorated in the monuments that were erected by Gudea at sacred points in the New Eninnu (as described in the Cylinder Inscriptions (A25–6); see Chapter 40). There are some differences, notably the fact that the Sumerian sources list only ten or eleven Slain Heroes by contrast with Heracles's twelve, though this can be accounted for by the fact that the legends developed over millennia. The respective narrative frames of reference also evince some cultural diversity. Ningirsu's battles with the Slain Heroes, for example, have cosmogenic significance because the god is, so to speak, performing some running repairs on the system of the world by repressing the forces of chaos that threaten the cosmic order that he established when he gave shape to the universe. By contrast, the labours of Heracles are carried out at the behest of Apollo in order to make amends for the hero's murder of his wife and child (acts that were committed when the demigod was driven temporarily insane by Hera, who hated him because he was the illegitimate son of her husband, Zeus). But the change from the cosmogenic to the potentially tragic fate of an individual illustrates a general shift of emphasis that distinguishes the Mesopotamian and Greek outlooks—a wide-ranging subject that can only be mentioned here. In other respects, the differences between the two narratives are far outweighed by the similarities, including the fact that, like Heracles, Ningirsu was the son of the foremost deity. More parallels between Ningirsu and Heracles are discussed below, but it could doubtless have been argued by those who wished to revive Gudea's Eninnu under the authority of the incoming Hellenistic governors that the half-forgotten shrine was a site of the highest importance for the ancient history and mythology of Heracles, whose character and deeds were prefigured by his Mesopotamian avatar, Ningirsu. In the case of both gods it is difficult to say how Babylonian and Hellenistic intellectuals of the fourth century BCE might have explained the relationships between history and myth, but it is not hard to imagine that the material existence of a place that was so intimately associated with a pivotal Mesopotamian god who vividly prefigured and predated Heracles must have been a source of considerable interest, excitement and possibly even some bewilderment to the Hellenistic incomers.

The bringing together of Ningirsu and Heracles probably therefore provided the bedrock syncretism on which the Babylonian–Hellenistic shrine was founded. Archaeological signs of the Hellenistic side of the equation include the small bronze Heracles (AO2890) who is holding his club and the skin of the Nemean lion. Incidentally, the curvature of the figure's pose adds a characteristically Hellenistic air of life-likeness, while the piercing in the back of the torso is a vent hole to allow for smoother moulding and for gases to escape during the production process. In addition, the sherd of the terracotta figurine found by the British Museum team contains a portrait of Heracles with the head of the Nemean lion, as does the Alexander foundation coin, which also inescapably introduces some interesting connections with Ningirsu's chief emblem, the Thunderbird (further explicated below).

Other gods and goddesses are clearly represented among the Hellenistic finds made in Girsu. Nor was Ningirsu the only Sumerian deity who was honoured on the Gudea Statues, which might well have been the principal point of reference for the priests, scholars and historians who advised on the Hellenistic shrine's contents and potential divine dedicatees. Gudea's Statues B and D (the Colossus), together with Statue G, were dedicated to Ningirsu for the construction of his Eninnu, as was the statue of Gudea's predecessor, Ur-Bau, which was also found by Sarzec in the Hellenistic strata of Tell A. Statues E and H were dedicated to Ningirsu's wife, Bau, in her Tarsirsir house (which must refer to the NW area of the New Eninnu, close to the Tarsirsir Gate, on either the NW or NE façades; see Fig. 219). In addition, Statue C was dedicated to Inanna in her Eanna temple in Girsu, while Statue A was dedicated to Ninhursag in her House of the City of Girsu, and Statue F was carved in honour of Gatumdug in her House of the Shining City. At first glance, therefore, it appears that the names of five separate deities, all mentioned in the inscriptions on the Gudea Statues, were introduced into the shrine: Ningirsu, Bau, Inanna, Ninhursag and Gatumdug. And yet, in Sumerian times Bau was already synthesised with Gatumdug, especially in the reign of Gudea (as noted in Chapter 11), perhaps particularly in respect of Gatumdug's function as the protectress of the city—hence the name of her shrine. Furthermore, Bau might also have developed characteristics that blended her with Ninhursag, the archetypal mother goddess, since she appears to have played a vitally important role in the regulating of mensual and seasonal cycles, and therefore in guaranteeing the harvest (as discussed further below). Consequently, the total list of archetypal divine figures deriving from the names on the Gudea Statues might initially be reduced to just four: Ningirsu, Bau/Gatumdug, Bau/Ninhursag and Inanna. But the fertility and generative aspects of Bau/Ninhursag clearly overlap with the some of the characteristics of Inanna, as the goddess of carnal love (and also warfare, though that feature was seemingly covered by Ningirsu in this case), potentially bringing the number down to three. If it is further assumed that three Sumerian divine figures with multiple aspects might have been correlated with a group of Hellenistic deities, as is considered further below, then many of the artefacts retrieved from the revived Eninnu are brought more sharply into focus. First and foremost, the last shreds of the outdated idea that the temple was established as a memorial shrine to Gudea can finally be jettisoned because the inscriptions on the Gudea Statues connect them with the principal gods and goddesses to whom the revived temple was devoted. Gudea himself might accordingly be regarded as a kind of intercessor—the ancient ruler who provided a historical and human point of contact between a core group of Mesopotamian deities and their Greek counterparts, who were the main interest for fourth- and third-century BCE Hellenistic

worshippers. From a more markedly Mesopotamian point of view, Gudea's presence, and especially the commemorative texts on his statues, connected the small group of local deities who were venerated in the shrine with the ancient pantheon from which they derived, dramatically providing continuity and perhaps validating the evolving religious practices.

These matters are necessarily speculative, but affiliations between Greek and Mesopotamian deities can tentatively be suggested for some of the recovered terracotta figurines. The starting point for a discussion of the naked goddesses, which were evidently an extremely popular type from the earliest times down to the Hellenistic period represented in Girsu, is that they might represent Inanna (later Ishtar), who is often said to be a prototype for Aphrodite and later Venus—thereby incorporating the association with the planet. Nude figures of Aphrodite became extremely popular in the Hellenistic period, though the form favoured by the Greeks, which was modelled on the celebrated Aphrodite of Knidos by Praxiteles, presented the goddess in a rather modest, lifelike pose that is quite unlike that of the Girsu terracottas. Generally showing the figure face on, with closed legs, a plump belly, broad hips and simplified outlines (such that the goddess's arms are either by her sides or raised so that she covers her breasts), the nude goddesses found in Girsu relinquish the allure associated with Greek Aphrodite in favour of far more elemental ideas of fertility. The theme of carnal love was not necessarily discarded, but the shift to reproductive fecundity is important for the Mesopotamian side of the syncretism because Bau, the wife of Ningirsu, had a fertility aspect. Setting aside the complications of ancient calendars, her chief annual festival in Sumerian times apparently fell in the seventh month, coinciding with the autumn equinox and therefore with the harvest (see Cohen 1993, pp. 53 and 66–9). Consequently, Bau was a goddess of the harvest—a figure who represented seasonal renewal and the cyclical power of natural productiveness. Her regenerative aspect was probably also expressed through her connection with the Bison, one of the Slain Heroes commemorated in monuments erected in Gudea's New Eninnu, and a symbolic figure that appears in Lugale, where the mythological creature (closely allied with a bull) is killed in battle by Ningirsu. In Sumerian times the mythical Bison was presumably also linked with the waning and waxing crescent moon (as discussed in Chapter 40). Against this background, the Bison standard erected by Bau's shrine (her 'inner room'), on the north-west side of the New

Eninnu, might have honoured Bau as the mother goddess who ensured the monthly rebirth of the crescent moon, after its brief disappearance into darkness. The nude goddesses from Girsu were therefore perhaps intended to interweave threads of meaning formerly associated with Inanna and Bau to suggest a blended Mesopotamian precursor of Aphrodite. The missing link from the Hellenistic side would seem to be the agricultural functions that were expressed through the presence of Bau, but which, in Greek religion, were the province not of Aphrodite, but of Demeter and her daughter Persephone, whose defining connection with the underworld seems also to have been partly anticipated by Bau in Sumerian times (see Cohen 1993, p. 54). Two things should be stressed, however: first, the nude goddesses, which appear to have been archetypal syntheses of several immemorial themes, were inherently open-ended in meaning; and secondly, small distinctions might have been discerned in forms that now appear to be practically identical—in which regard it should again be noted that not a single head belonging to any of the preserved torsos has been found (either by the British Museum team or by the French explorers), so there is currently no way of knowing exactly what any of the complete statues originally looked like.

Bau was also known as the tutelary goddess of the city walls of Girsu (as mentioned in Chapter 32), and her protective role invokes possible connections with the British Museum team's recently unearthed terracotta showing a female figure wearing a mural crown (TG2767). As described above, the plaque shows a relief image of a female figure, seen face on, with her hands clasped in the familiar Sumerian gesture of prayer. Two irregular objects (generally oval, but with notable disruptions) appear to be placed on top of her hands. It is not clear what they are intended to be or what their relationship is with the hands—are they shown with stems placed between the hands and the body, for example, or are they simply sitting on the tops of the hands? The way the woman is portrayed is overwhelmingly Sumerian, but the fact that the plaque was found in excellent condition in an unmistakably Hellenistic context gives slight pause for thought. Could it have been made by a fourth-century BCE coroplast in imitation of a terracotta from the third millennium BCE, for example? Divine figures shown in traditional styles, notably wearing garments made up of rows of pleats, were current in Uruk and Babylon, so it is not entirely implausible. Nonetheless (as suggested above), TG2767 almost certainly

dates back to Sumerian times. It can be compared with several Sumerian terracotta relief plaques from Tello that depict female figures, some wearing diadems that are like the crown worn by the woman in the British Museum team's plaque (see, for example, AO28904 and AO12244; and Barrelet 1968, nos. 273, 274, 278, 315, 320 and 368). Also comparable are the seated pose (though the bottom half of TG2767 is lost) and the position of the hands under the breasts. Furthermore, some Sumerian figures are shown carrying offerings—a possible precedent for the unidentified objects that rest on the hands of the woman in TG2767. Similarly, portrayals of women dating back to Sumerian times often depict their subjects dressed in the same kinds of pleated robes, with corresponding neck ornaments and the same hairstyle. Looking more closely at the way Sumerian terracottas were formed, details in the modelling of the ancient examples recall that of TG2767, especially the facial features and the distinctive heavy lower eyelids.

The image of the protectress of a city wearing a mural crown had a very long Mesopotamian pedigree. The goddess's role as the defender of the city walls of Girsu is probably expressed in the plaque by the placing of the figure in the simple linear frame that might suggest a gate, for example, in which context the mural crown would confirm that the goddess is enthroned as the guardian of the city. Gatumdug, whose temple is named the House of the Shining City on Statue F (as noted above), also played a protective role as a city guardian. In the absence of more specific information, the image on the plaque might therefore most plausibly be viewed as a portrayal that could relate equally to her and Bau. With regard to the mural crown, at least three figurines from Sumerian Girsu are shown wearing crowns with very similar verticals: AO15114 and AO12059 from the Ur III period; and AO15085, probably from Isin-Larsa times. Interestingly, the two Ur III artefacts portray smiling, rather joyful-looking figures, while the Isin-Larsa portrayal, which integrates attributes of the nude goddess, shows a musician playing a tambourine. The rather stern face of TG2767 is by no means unprecedented at a range of periods, however, as can be seen in some of the physiognomies on fragments from the Gudea Steles (EŞEM1533, for example) and on the statue of a goddess (probably Bau) that was found in Ur and probably dates from about 1800 BCE (now in the Iraq Museum in Baghdad). From a much later time, the seminal example of a woman wearing a mural crown is surely that of Ashursharrat, the wife

FIGURE 272. A selection of the Hellenistic spindle whorls unearthed by the British Museum team on Tell A.

of Ashurbanipal, who is shown wearing the characteristic headgear in a superb relief on the Stele of Ashursharrat (dating from the seventh-century BCE) from the city of Ashur.

From a Hellenistic point of view, the goddess wearing a mural crown carries unmistakably associations with Tyche, the Greek goddess of chance, who also presided over a city's fortunes. Tyche was a well-loved deity in Seleucid times, when she appeared in Babylonia on coins and private seals, and her image is one of the most popular motifs on seals found in public and private archives in Uruk and Seleucia on the Tigris. With reference to Girsu in particular, the British Museum team excavated a bronze coin bearing her image. Poorly preserved and found out of context, the coin certainly dates from the Hellenistic period and it seems clear that the stamped figure represents Tyche. The character of the goddess in Greek culture was quite different from that communicated by the facial features of TG2767, though not necessarily from the temperaments conveyed by the Ur III and Isin-Larsa figures mentioned in the previous paragraph. As the goddess of fortune (Fortuna in Roman times), she was by definition a capricious force, inseparable from uncertainty and risk. By contrast, the serious face of the Sumerian woman in TG2767 proclaims dependability—a staunch defender of urban stability rather than a tempting conduit for chancy unreliability. And yet, as with other correlations between Mesopotamian and Hellenistic divinities, the differences can be largely set aside because there can be little or no doubt that the goddess shown on TG2767 must have appeared to Hellenistic eyes as a counterpart of Tyche. Accordingly, supplementary to the provenance of the piece outlined in Chapter 46, it was probably retrieved from the New Eninnu, together with other Sumerian artefacts, during the initial Hellenistic soundings and displayed in the Adadnadinakhe shrine. Subsequently removed during the enlargement phase, it was seemingly interred as a foundation deposit in the Hellenistic layers that were laid down at the NW end of Adadnadinakhe's complex, close to the first Hellenistic temenos wall—the location being especially appropriate for a goddess believed to be the defender of a city or its walls.

Another Greek god associated with the Hellenistic Eninnu is Apollo, who was increasingly venerated by successive Seleucid rulers. He is a vitally important figure in the legend of Heracles because he is the instigator of the labours that the demigod must carry out in order to atone for his crimes. Apollo was also the Greek sun god, however, and this indicates a parallel with Utu, the Sumerian sun god, who

FIGURE 273. Some of the Hellenistic loom weights unearthed by the British Museum team on Tell A.

appears numerous times in narratives associated with Ningirsu. Utu's standard was raised by Gudea at the SE gate of the New Eninnu (the Sunrise Gate; No. 4 on Fig. 219), where it was linked with the iconography of the Bison—the Slain Hero—in his Sumerian aspect, probably as a symbol of the crescent moon (drawing on an analogy between the animal's horns and the points of the crescent). In Lugale, when the triumphant Ningirsu returns to the heavenly abode of the gods, he does so in the guise of Utu (as mentioned above)—signalling the close affinity between the warrior god and the sun god. This could potentially be important because, if it was the case that a gradual shift took place in the divine affiliations of the Seleucids, then it is conceivable that the primary importance of Heracles in the Hellenistic shrine was eventually somewhat reduced by the presence of Apollo—a potential transition that might have been smoothed by the age-old association between Ningirsu and Utu. This is nevertheless a highly speculative matter, which, as with so many aspects of this history, indicates the need for a systematic reconsideration of the preserved artefacts. A coin (TG51) that possibly shows Apollo was found out of context on Tell A by the British Museum team. Probably dating from the first reign of Demetrius II Nicator (146–138 BCE), and therefore a little before the destruction of Hellenistic shrine, the obverse contains the damaged image of either Apollo or the king himself, while the reverse shows a standing Zeus (or perhaps Poseidon) with a restored inscription that reads Basileus Demetrius ('King Demetrius').

Finally, reference should be made to the unexpected cache of seventy-six spindle whorls and thirty-one loom weights (Figs. 272 and 273) that the British Museum team unearthed in Area B8 (context 2078). All made of unbaked clay and typical of the Hellenistic period, the disc-shaped whorls had average measurements of 29.79 mm (h) × 40.34 mm (diameter), while the pyramidal loom weights, which typically weighed 46.31 g, had average dimensions of 52.07 mm (h) × 27.74 mm (l) × 30.4 mm (w); the diameter of the hole in the top of each weight was 5.5 mm. They were found by the British Museum team in a spoil heap, where they had been discarded by the French pioneers, having no doubt been excavated in the adjacent Hellenistic layers of Tell A in the area occupied by the Adadnadinakhe shrine and its enlargement. The evident lack of care with which they were treated by the French had caused some minor damage, but the objects were otherwise in very good condition and showed no signs of wear. This would tend to imply that they were not actually used for spinning and weaving—an idea that would be further corroborated by the absence of any sign of a Hellenistic-era weaving house or similar installation on the site, and no indication that the manufacture of textiles might have taken place close to Tell A at that period. It was common to weave sacred cloths in Greek temple complexes, but the fact that the Girsu examples were seemingly unused would suggest that was not the reason for their presence in this instance. Loom weights—and spindle whorls to a lesser degree—were also quite regularly deposited in temples as votives in the Hellenistic world, so that probably explains their presence in the Girsu shrine.

Unlike many votive loom weights found in other Hellenistic settings, the Girsu objects, which are not decorated or inscribed, bear no indicators of the god or goddess to whom they were devoted. Athena was the principal Greek deity of weaving, and perhaps the most famous sacred cloth in the whole of the Greek world was the Peplos that was woven on the Acropolis in her honour to celebrate the Great Panathenaia, which took place in Athens every four years. No Athena terracottas have emerged in Girsu, though other goddesses, notably Demeter, Persephone, Aphrodite and Artemis, were also commemorated with votive loom weights in different parts of the Hellenistic world (Gleba 2008, p. 181). Perhaps surprisingly, though, Heracles was considered to be a patron deity of textile crafts. He was commemorated on votive loom weights and sometimes depicted with a spindle and a distaff (Gleba 2008, pp. 181–2). The iconography derives in part from his role as a god of pastoral farming, together with the seasonal movement of grazing animals to different pastures and the production of wool. But the spindle almost certainly invoked another association that is found in the story of his relationship with Omphale, the queen of Lydia in Asia Minor, to whom he was temporarily enslaved. This occurred after the completion of his twelve labours, and after he had accidentally killed his friend Iphitus. To atone for Iphitus's death Heracles was sold into slavery and bought by Omphale, who eventually took him as her lover. In a twist of identities, he was ordered by the queen to wear women's clothes and do their accustomed work, including spinning. In many representations from a very wide range of periods, Heracles is shown dressed as a woman and carrying a spindle, while Omphale is pictured with his familiar attributes, often including his club and the skin of the Nemean lion. The myth is capable of expressing many meanings, but one that would

perhaps be most relevant in this context is as a cautionary tale—warning the Greeks that they should take care not to become enfeebled (or emasculated) by succumbing to the dangerous pleasures of the orient (a term used advisedly), as Alexander's army famously did, when they arrived in Babylon in 331 BCE (discussed further below).

A Hellenistic Shrine to Ningirsu–Heracles: Alexandrian and Seleucid Contexts

In summary, the Sumerian Eninnu was almost certainly refounded between 331 BCE and 323 BCE, during the lifetime of Alexander, when it was infused with dual Mesopotamian and Hellenistic connotations, principally based on a connection between Heracles and Ningirsu, but radiating outwards to incorporate other syncretised deities. The Sumerian aspect of the temple was incarnated most forcefully through the Gudea Statues, which were on display, presumably in large part because of Gudea's role as both an intercessor and perhaps a kind of historical mediator between ancient and modern divinities. Iconography relating to Alexander himself has also been recovered, notably the foundation coin, but also the sherd of a vase adorned with Alexander's portrait that was found by the British Museum team. Alexander links are also expressed in the many terracotta Macedonian riders on horseback that have been unearthed, while the theme of the all-conquering warrior is an essential component in the myths of Ningirsu and Heracles, respectively. Furthermore, as proclaimed on the Girsu coin, Alexander personally identified himself extremely closely with Heracles. Combined with the clear signs of an Alexandrian presence in the shrine, this raises the intriguing possibility that Alexander was directly and actively instrumental in its re-establishment, and (or) that it came to include a memorial to the departed Macedonian after his early death. In order to understand how such connections might have worked in practice it is necessary very briefly to retrace Alexander's route from Asia Minor to Mesopotamia and to say a word about his affiliations with some key figures in Greek mythology. First and foremost, however, it must be stressed that the thesis, which builds on the conception that the shrine was a living Hellenistic temple in a Mesopotamian sacred context, is unavoidably conjectural and is here presented with the utmost caution.

Alexander claimed Achilles and Heracles as his ancestors, while his family relationship with Heracles in particular was universally regarded as a matter of historical fact—accepted 'without any question', as Plutarch remarks in his life of Alexander (II:1). Upon arriving in Asia Minor, Alexander immediately set up altars to Zeus, Athena and Heracles, and he then visited the tomb of Achilles in Troy. When the people of Tyre in Phoenicia refused to allow him access to the shrine of Tyrian Heracles, he besieged the island city and built a causeway to connect it to the mainland, encouraging his men by telling them that he had 'seen in a dream the figure of Heracles extending his right hand to him, and himself entering Tyre as Heracles led him and opened the way' (Curtius 4:2:1). Subsequently, having gained control of Egypt and laid out the ground plan of the city of Alexandria, he undertook the arduous journey across the desert to reach the temple of Ammon, nearly 600 km south-west of Alexandria, in order to consult its famed oracle, who informed him that he was the son of Zeus (later legends explain that Zeus visited Alexander's mother, Olympias, in the guise of a snake). Alexander's trip to the oasis (now known as Siwa), which was partly inspired by his desire to emulate Perseus and Heracles (Arrian 3:3), confirmed to him that—like his legendary forebear and exemplum—he was another of Zeus's sons. Alexander and Heracles could henceforth be regarded as brothers, and the direct inspiration of Heracles was reaffirmed when Alexander travelled eastwards through Mesopotamia and Persia towards India, again believing that he was following in the footsteps of Heracles, who was supposed to have conquered the region (Curtius 9:4:1–33). Furthermore, Alexander had an illegitimate son, named Heracles of Macedon, who almost became his nominated successor (Curtius 10:6:10). As this brief history recalls, Alexander regarded himself as the descendant and half-brother of Heracles, and he was eager to recognise a syncretised avatar of the legendary Greek hero in Lebanon. Tyrian Heracles was a union of the Greek figure with his Phoenician counterpart, Melqart, the son of the chief Phoenician god, Baal. Similarly, Alexander's visit to the Egyptian oracle, who informed him that he was the son of Zeus, was considered to be reliable because the Greek god Ammon was identified with the supreme Greek deity, Zeus.

With regard to his conquest of Babylonia, following his triumph over the Persian leader Darius at the Battle of Gaugamela (near Arbela, now Erbil in northern Iraq, about 80 km to the east of Mosul), Alexander arrived in Babylon in October 331 BCE, where (according to his ancient biographers) he was met with a hero's welcome. The Persian governor of the city, Mazaeus, who had fought alongside Darius at Gaugamela, immediately surrendered and was treated by Alexander with respect, partly (it appears) on account of the Persian's demeanour, but also because it was felt that the surrender of so eminent a person would encourage others to follow his example, as indeed it did (Curtius 5:1:17–23). Mazaeus was subsequently reappointed to the governorship. Greeted with the title of 'king of the world', Alexander showed considerable regard for the ancient culture of Mesopotamia. According to Arrian (3:16), he sacrificed to Belus (Marduk), following the instructions given to him by the 'Chaldaeans', or learned Babylonians, who might also have explained to him that Marduk had assimilated many of the traits and deeds formerly ascribed to the warrior god Ningirsu, the Mesopotamian counterpart of Heracles (Johandi 2018). Thereafter, he gave orders for the shrines that had been destroyed by Xerxes I in the mid-fifth century BCE to be restored, with particular attention being paid to the Etemenanki, the Temple of Marduk. Whether reconstruction work was actually carried out on the Etemenanki under Alexander is uncertain, but it appears that he began to clear the site in preparation for the rebuilding of the famous ziggurat (George 2005, p. 91). He and his soldiers enjoyed an exceptionally long sojourn in Babylon, where they stayed for thirty-four days—long enough for the army to become rather too immersed in the pleasures of the city (Curtius 5:1:36). Having been joined by reinforcements, however, they eventually marched onwards to Susa, 450 km to the east.

It is not known whether Alexander visited Girsu, and in point of fact there would have been nothing for him to see there in 331 BCE, but he might have had the opportunity to go there, either during his stay in Babylon, or by taking a shortish detour on the way to Susa. Significantly, he was able to pay his soldiers after taking Babylon because the city's coffers were surrendered to him (Curtius 5:1:45). This meant that Alexander and his generals had control of the region's wealth, and they presumably used Babylonian silver to mint the many coins that were struck in the city. Given the revived Eninnu's Hellenistic focus, this is a significant fact because it would confirm the need for Hellenistic approval of the project, especially if it was being financed by the state. In terms of the very existence of the shrine and its possible Hellenistic connections, there is no doubt that Alexander and his officials had contact with Babylonian intellectuals (the Chaldeans mentioned by Arrian), who could presumably have alerted them to the Eninnu's location and significance. This might have been especially relevant to Alexander himself, given the closeness of his affiliation with Heracles, the Greek counterpart of Ningirsu.

The silver drachm unearthed by the British Museum team was struck in Babylon between 331 BCE and 325 BCE. As described above, it was found by the SW corner of a mudbrick platform (an offering table or sacrificial altar) that was positioned in front of the NW façade of the enlarged Hellenistic shrine, aligned with the façade, and facing the entrance of the complex. Coins deliberately installed on prepared ground close to the corners of buildings or installations are well-attested components of Hellenistic foundation deposits, particularly of those found in the eastern regions of the Greek world (Hunt 2006, p. 117). That was almost certainly the purpose of the Alexander drachm, which was carefully placed on the terrace platform on which the altar was built. It is reasonable to suppose (though currently impossible to prove) that, having been deposited to consecrate an original altar that probably stood in an equivalent position in front of the Hellenistic Gate of Gudea outside the NW façade of the initial Adadnadinakhe building, the coin was later redeposited during the shrine's expansion phase. Incidentally, the recovered offering platform was also strikingly well aligned with the altar inside the cella in Gudea's New Eninnu, which was preserved below the surface of the ground, and it is by no means impossible that the planners of the original shrine, and perhaps also the later one, were aware of this. The arrangement might perhaps provide a further scrap of circumstantial evidence to support the strong hypothesis that the later Hellenistic altar replaced an original one that stood on the same axis in what was then the open-air courtyard on the NW side of Adadnadinakhe's first temple. The Alexander coin is of special interest for an understanding of the Girsu project (Fig. 274). Bearing a portrait on its obverse of Heracles wearing the head and skin of the Nemean lion (killed as the first of his labours), the reverse shows Zeus seated on a throne, holding an eagle and a long staff-like artefact that seems to be formed of numerous droplet-shaped elements, as though it is not really a solid object. This is particularly apparent towards the bottom of the long quasi-pole, where its compositional elements are distinctly separated. Probably, therefore, the implement Zeus holds in his left hand is not a stick

FIGURE 274. Partly reconstructed drawings of the Alexander coin found on Tell A by the British Museum team.

but a lightning bolt—one of his two cardinal attributes, along with the eagle. Next to the lightning bolt is Alexander's name (Alexandros), which is stamped vertically towards the edge of the coin (the name is worn away on the example found by the British Museum team). Underneath Zeus's throne is the Greek letter phi, a monogram that probably belonged to Philoxones, the master of Alexander's travelling mint at this period, while below the god's right arm (in front of his right shin) is another monogram (partly eroded on the example found by the British Museum team), the Greek letter mu, which could indicate that the coin was part of a batch that was used to pay Alexander's troops—mu standing for the word misthos or misthophoria in Greek.

In general terms, the imagery on the coin inevitably invokes links with the deeds and character of Ningirsu. In particular, the lion's head on the obverse, and the eagle and the lightning bolt on the reverse are motifs that were inextricably associated in Sumerian mythology and cosmology with Imdugud, the White Thunderbird—the titanic lion-headed eagle, with its thunderous roar and a body that flashed lightning. Ningirsu subdued the hybrid creature on the cosmic mountain on the northern edge of the world, the source of the life-giving waters of the Tigris and the Euphrates, but instead of killing it he made it into his avatar, such that the god and the storm bird were fused. The countless artefacts adorned with Thunderbird motifs that the late fourth-century BCE prospectors unearthed from the Sumerian Eninnu, not least the wonderfully carved basin (Fig. 271) that was prominently placed in entrance F (on Sarzec's Plan A) in Adadnadinakhe's revived Gate of Gudea, must therefore have had a profound resonance for Hellenistic visitors. The visual devices were differently deployed in Sumerian and Hellenistic contexts, but the marked overlaps must have been unmistakable.

Much more specifically, however, in the circumstances of the refounding of the Eninnu, the coin's iconography communicates a particular message that is best explained by comparison with another of the important foundation objects that were deposited when the Hellenistic temple was built: the stamped bricks. It is sometimes rather loosely said that the text on the Hellenistic bricks is written in Aramaic and Greek, but that is not quite accurate. As a typical Babylonian theophoric patronym with royal associations, the Neo-Babylonian name Adadnadinakhe, which means 'Adad, the giver of brothers', was clearly chosen as a ceremonial title on account of its archaising tone and symbolic connotations. All the evidence points to the fact that the name was extraordinarily rare. It is not attested in the large corpus of Hellenistic-era cuneiform tablets from Babylon that are currently known, and there are no occurrences of it in the onomastics of contemporary Uruk. A comprehensive list of comparable names that take the generic form (a god who gives a brother or brothers) shows that several deities from the Babylonian pantheon could be called upon or commemorated in this way, but Adadnadinakhe appears only once (Annus 2002, p. 211), and this might further confirm that it was only ever used on the bricks of Girsu. The phrasing of the name draws on the high culture of Akkadian, the Semitic language that was used in learned and formal circles, thereby establishing a strong link with Aramaic, the local demotic, but the name was not written in Aramaic per se on the inscribed bricks. It was not translated, but rather transliterated from a variant of high Akkadian into the Aramaic script, as it also was into the Greek alphabet, thereby invoking three frames of reference: the ceremonial language of the age-old religious traditions of the region, together with Aramaic, which was spoken on a daily basis, and the Greek of Alexander. As with other known dual-script titles, particularly from the slightly later Seleucid period (see Sherwin-White 1987; and Kuhrt 1987), it must therefore have been an officially approved inscription. Sanctioned by the Hellenistic authorities, it deliberately combined the connotations just noted, including Aramaic as the lingua franca, Greek as the language of de facto political authority and traditional Akkadian, and its official character adds convincingly to the idea that the Girsu reconstruction project was dependent on Hellenistic approval.

Although it was not a bilingual name (or even a trilingual one, for that matter), it was very much a syncretising epithet. The very unusual title has generally been thought to have belonged to a regional official or southern Mesopotamian high priest, but this was against an interpretative background in which the temple was thought to have been refounded by a somewhat eccentric local dignitary who wished, for reasons that are difficult to explain, either to revive the worship of Ningirsu in Gudea's Eninnu or to create a shrine to Gudea—his illustrious Sumerian ancestor. Within the limits of his understanding, an individual named Adadnadinakhe supposedly adhered as closely as he could to the foundation rituals that were prescribed in Sumerian (Mesopotamian) religious culture by depositing bricks stamped with his name alongside those of Gudea. Conspicuous by its absence from the Adadnadinakhe inscription when it is read in this strictly localised way, however, is the second part of Gudea's foundation inscriptions: the name of the god to whom the commemorated shrine was sacred.

Conversely, in the context of the creation of a Hellenistic monument to Ningirsu–Heracles, the inscribed name in and of itself exhibits a much more precise significance. Sumerian counterparts for Adad, the later Semitic storm god, include Ishkur and even Ningirsu himself, but such fluidity is dispelled when Adad is considered in a Hellenistic framework, where he can be clearly identified with Zeus, the chief Greek sky god, whose primary symbols are the eagle and—most importantly for the present comparison—the bolt of lightning, both of which are shown on the Alexander drachm described above. Furthermore, when Zeus famously acknowledged Alexander as his son through the agency of the Ammon oracle, he became quite literally the 'giver of brothers' because he affirmed a fraternal bond between Alexander and Heracles. The same message is communicated by the coin, which shows Zeus on the reverse as the link between Alexander, whose name appears next to his lightning bolt, and Heracles on the obverse. The close relationship between Heracles and Alexander is further stressed on the coin by the portrait of Heracles, who is shown—very unusually in terms of his iconography—as a young man, at about the same stage of life as Alexander was in 331 BCE, presumably after the completion of his first labour, when his great career of expiatory labours was still in its infancy. Consequently, as counterparts and divine brothers, the identities of the two young heroes seem intentionally to be merged.

And yet, Alexander's career was dramatically cut short, so if the Hellenistic shrine was commissioned and built under his authority, whether directly or indirectly, and

FIGURE 275. Terracotta showing a crowned head (TG2123).

probably finished before his death in 323 BCE, as would be confirmed by the latest presumed date of the foundation coin (325 BCE), there is every reason to think that it might soon have incorporated a memorial to him. Nor should it be forgotten that Alexander considered himself to have been deified in 324 BCE, a year before his death, and the possibility that the recently deceased leader was venerated in one of the several cellas that made up the shrine might be partly confirmed by the coin, the portrait vase and the other Alexander-related objects mentioned above.

Alexander was unquestionably not the only historical ruler who was honoured in the shrine, however. In addition to the conspicuous example of the Gudea Statues that were displayed in the temple, a number of the terracotta heads unearthed by the British Museum team have quite specific Hellenistic associations. Included in the favissa, for example, were four slightly anomalous heads that appear to have been made in an earlier style than the more readily identifiable Hellenistic figures. One of these (TG4399), which is also mentioned in Chapter 46, is preserved as a small head with a gaunt, beardless face, a slightly downturned mouth and downturned oval eyes that almost evoke the idea of a Greek tragic mask. Probably modelled in an archaic manner, with bossed strips of clay defining the eyes, it can conceivably be dated to the decades following Alexander's arrival in Babylon.

With that in mind, it seems plausible to suggest that TG4399 shows a portrait of Seleucus, whose grim and haggard face is preserved on his coins, but also on the Roman copy of a Hellenistic original from Herculaneum (NAMN5590). Otherwise, the stern-faced, almost tragic representation might conceivably relate to Alexander, though it is also possible that the image of Alexander's untimely death might have had an influence on some of the iconography of kingship associated with his immediate successor. These matters, it must be stressed again, are highly conjectural.

It is extremely difficult to be precise about the possible identities of the other heads that are here provisionally referred to as archaic in style (TG4436, TG4437 and TG4236). They all seemingly show the same person, who is wearing a narrow diadem with vertical bands that was favoured by a number of Hellenistic kings—Macedonians, in particular. That might link with the way Seleucus's son and grandson were portrayed. In particular, Antiochus I Soter, who was coruler with his father from 291 BCE and became sole king for twenty years after his father's death in 281 BCE, might be a candidate. The difficulty is that the rather austere portraits favoured by Macedonian kings in the western part of the Hellenistic world gave way to a more ostentatious manner in the east, where the image of kingship was soon influenced by Babylonian traditions (Shipley 2000, pp. 60–73). The tendency accelerated through the third century BCE, under Antiochus I and Antiochus II. Accordingly, Antiochus I's numismatic portraits show an individual with thick locks of rather long wavy hair that is difficult to correlate with the three archaic-looking heads, though that does not rule out the possibility that the presumed early heads might express a more markedly Macedonian idea of kingship.

Potentially slightly less problematic are some of the other heads that were unearthed by the British Museum team. TG2123 (Fig. 275), for example, shows a king wearing a crown with three radiating upstanding ornaments that surely invokes the iconography of Apollo, the sun god, who became a primary deity for the Seleucids (as previously noted). This was especially the case after the reign of Seleucus (who claimed Apollo as his ancestor, but associated himself with Zeus (Shipley 2000, p. 65)) in the reign of Antiochus I. The historical picture is again further complicated by the syncretising efforts of the Seleucids (including Seleucus and Antiochus), who forged strong links between Greek deities and their Babylonian counterparts as integral aspects of their changing conceptions of kingship—all of which relates to the discussion of the religious character of the shrine presented in the earlier part of this chapter. Other probable images of as yet unidentified Seleucid kings might be TG1991, TG1987 and TG3384, which is heavily eroded but might again show a figure with a sun crown. TG2095, which shows a woman wearing a headscarf, seems to relate very closely to some of the well-known portraits of Seleucid queens, particularly those from a later period. The historical identities of the figures represented on the heads found by the British Museum team must for the time being remain elusive. The overarching conclusion, however, is that the Girsu terracottas should be comprehensively re-evaluated in the light of the new information found by the British Museum team, together with the revised chronology for the life of the Hellenistic shrine detailed above.

CHAPTER 48

The End of the Hellenistic Eninnu

Changing Political Circumstances in the Seleucid Era

The evidence assembled in Chapters 46 and 47 helps to establish the chronology of the Hellenistic-era Eninnu with a fair degree of accuracy. It was founded in the name of Adad-nadinakhe between 331 BCE and 323 BCE, when Alexander the Great was still alive, and it might be further surmised that the platform supporting Adadnadinakhe's original altar (probably on the NW side of the Hellenistic Gate of Gudea) was established in or around 325 BCE—the year in which the British Museum team's Alexander drachm was struck. It is impossible to be categorical about the latter point because it necessarily depends on some unprovable hypotheses, but the overall time frame, which is reliable, is in accord with the pottery finds detailed in Chapter 46. The enlargement and refurbishment, which are less precisely datable, were carried out sometime in the mid-third century BCE, probably towards the end of the reign of Antiochus II Theos (who ruled from 261 BCE to 246 BCE), prior to the period of turbulence that erupted after his death. As is detailed further below, the complex was eventually desecrated and destroyed in the second half of the second century BCE, when the Seleucids gradually lost their grip on the region and the Parthians took control.

The Hellenistic shrine, which was built with the approval of the Alexandrian authorities, therefore prospered under the Seleucids, who doubtless ratified and presumably encouraged its expansion. With respect to the summarised chronology, the temple must have maintained its initial ground plan, based around Court A, with an open-air courtyard that was possibly the site of the original altar in front of the NW Gate of the Gudea façade, for a period of approximately eighty or ninety years, from the mid-320s BCE to sometime around the early or mid-240s BCE. After its enlargement, the complex remained in service for about another century, until the mid-second century BCE. Together with the detailed narrative of the actual history and purpose of the shrine presented above, the time frame indicates that it must have been a salient feature of the religious and political dynamics that were played out, particularly in southern Mesopotamia, while the Hellenistic authorities were in charge. The rituals that accompanied its foundation and enlargement, for example, evince recognised and sanctioned modes of behaviour in Seleucid Babylonia—synthesising age-old indigenous beliefs and traditions with an essentially Greek religious outlook. The procedures are apparent in the juxtaposition of Sumerian and Hellenistic bricks and foundation deposits in the fabric of the building, and they extend to the sacred objects that were displayed in the temple, as well as to the gods who were the focus of worship. On the one hand, the Sumerian deities appear to have been viewed less as the individual personalities that they once were and rather more as inclusive divine powers or force fields, while on the other hand a certain amount of flexibility was seemingly injected into the Hellenistic pantheon. This promoted the creation of a broad-based syncretic sacred space that seems to have allowed Mesopotamians and people with a Greek outlook to worship in the same temple. The detailed arguments are made above, but it is worth recapping some of its main points here. Ningirsu and Heracles were almost certainly extremely

744

closely associated from the outset, and it may be (though less clearly) that Apollo was later added to the mix, or he may have been an independent presence. Bau, who seems to have consolidated the fertility, regulatory and protective functions that were the province of more than one Sumerian goddess, was consequently closely associated with Aphrodite and probably Tyche, and (though again much less obviously) perhaps also Demeter and Persephone. The Gudea Statues on which the Sumerian deities were named were a kind of portal to the distant past, with Gudea himself acting as a real historical presence, but also as an intercessor. His role in the temple's iconographic programme was seemingly balanced by the introduction of historical figures from the Hellenistic period, including Alexander and one or more Seleucid kings. It must also be recalled that, for Alexander and his Seleucid successors, Heracles and Apollo (to mention the two seminal examples) were not only mythical figures, they were also historical actors—which is why Alexander could claim Heracles as his ancestor and Seleucus could claim Apollo as his. The lineages were not regarded as fictions, but as attested facts. This must inevitably have invoked a further parallel between the Hellenistic leaders and Gudea, who was extremely closely connected to Ningirsu, and was named in his inscriptions as the son of Gatumdug (later integrated with Bau). Probably also relevant in this regard is the fact that Alexander and Gudea were both famously given pivotally important instructions in dreams by Heracles and Ningirsu, respectively.

When details such as these are mined for their significance, it becomes ever clearer that the general pattern of the Hellenistic modus operandi in Babylonia was worked out in a specific way in Girsu, where the Greek outlook flexibly responded to the regional heritage. Another instance of the same tendency is represented by the style of the Hellenistic-era terracotta figures that were found in the revived shrine. Unlike some of the elaborate three-dimensional miniature sculptures that were made in Babylon, for example, many of which were fashioned in an overtly Hellenistic manner, the terracotta images from Girsu retain the traditional form of relatively simple relief plaques, while the figures are distinguished with only rather rudimentary attributes. Since the terracottas, which were manufactured outside Girsu, were brought there by visitors, it is by no means impossible that more elaborate figures were also displayed in the shrine, but it is surely significant that no evidence of that has been found. It might have been a simple matter of logistics or availability, but the more intriguing possibility is that the contrast between the high Hellenism of Babylon and Seleucia on the Tigris with the simpler styles of Girsu deliberately reflected the circumstances and ethos that prevailed in the south of Mesopotamia compared with those in the Mesopotamian centres of power.

It is clear that, from the moment of their arrival in Babylonia, Alexander and the Macedonians were fascinated by the ancient culture that they encountered. Accordingly, as discussed in Chapter 47, when founding the Hellenistic shrine, Adadnadinakhe might well have been operating under the aegis of Alexander and his advisers, while his highly unusual—possibly unique—ceremonial name conceivably contains a tribute to the Macedonian conqueror—recognising him as the brother of Heracles. Established in the last third of the fourth century BCE, almost immediately after the arrival of the Greeks, the Girsu shrine must have been one of the very earliest instances of a practice that became prevalent during the next century. Acting as an Alexandrian agent, Adadnadinakhe might conceivably have inaugurated a pattern that later increasingly gained currency. By the second half of the third century BCE, shortly after the shrine was enlarged, evidence exists of a number of ancient sites in Babylonian regional centres that were similarly revived, with local elites sponsoring traditional sacred spaces, architecture and statuary. These commissions were part of a wider phenomenon in the Hellenistic world, where sites and forms of material culture that could be seen as potent symbols of ancient heritage were patronised and promoted. The aim was to harness the power of autochthonous cultures and immemorial belief systems as useful and significant mechanisms within the dynamics of contemporary political frameworks (see Kosmin 2018).

The most notable of these activities in Seleucid Babylonia was the monumental programme of regenerative building in Uruk, which was organised over a period of approximately twenty years by two renowned local leaders: Anu-uballit Nikarkhos and the later Anu-uballit Kephalon. These men, who were active in the mid-220s BCE and the late 200s BCE, respectively, held important posts in the city. Nikarkhos was shaknu ('governor'), while Kephalon fulfilled a role that combined civic and sacred authority. Both were given their Greek names (Nikarkhos and Kephalon) by the contemporary Seleucid kings, Antiochus II and presumably Antiochus III, respectively (Stevens 2019, pp. 226–7). In 224 BCE,

Anu-uballit Nikarkhos dedicated Uruk's new Bit Resh (the 'great house', which was the sanctuary of Anu) 'for the life of the kings' Antiochus II and Seleucus III, and in 204 BCE, in the reign of Antiochus III, Anu-uballit Kephalon dedicated the city's new Anu-Antum temple in the Bit Resh complex, together with the Irigal (the sanctuary of Ishtar and Nanaya, also known as the Eshgal) 'for the sake of the life of Antiochus'. Incidentally, a possible sign of Antiochus III's association with the shrine in Girsu was unearthed by the British Museum team in the form of a bronze coin (TG2253), dating from about 210 BCE and depicting a war elephant, that came from a military mint associated with Ecbatana in western Iran (Fig. 276).

Despite being members of the priestly elite of Babylonia, with deep roots in the ancient socio-religious soil of Uruk, the two men ostensibly undertook these important construction works on behalf of the reigning Seleucid kings. For their part, by lending their names to the projects, the Seleucid rulers acted in the capacity of *in absentia* temple builders—fulfilling a traditional obligation of Babylonian and Mesopotamian rulers, while at the same time aggrandising, and creating headroom for their local supporters and quasi-representatives in the priesthood. Consequently, in so far as they increased the prestige and political influence of Nikarkhos and Kephalon, the conspicuous projects tended to consolidate the interdependency of the kings and the mediators of their regional support (Monerie 2012, p. 351). In a context in which the health of religious observance was regarded as a reflection of the well-being of society at large, high-standing local agents, especially priests, were pivotal in affirming the ongoing legitimacy and piety that the Seleucid rulers demonstrated through their sponsorship of the revival of ancient sacred sites (Stevens 2016, p. 71). This was a vital part of a more general Seleucid strategy of arm's-length rule, whereby they allowed traditional positions of authority to be filled by members of the local elite (Kosmin 2018), and it sometimes led to situations in which high-ranking members of the priesthood became the de facto arbiters of royal legitimacy (Ristvet 2014). Furthermore, the Uruk works were carried out at a momentous epoch in the fluctuating fortunes of the Seleucid rulers of Babylonia—after the potentially conclusive Ptolemaic invasion and the loss of Parthia and Bactria (detailed in Chapter 45). The backdrop of political and military upheavals must have added extra significance to the formulaic wording of the dedications of the renovated ancient

FIGURE 276. Partly reconstructed drawings of the coin from the reign of Antiochus III found on Tell A by the British Museum team. The obverse (left) shows Antiochus; the reverse shows a war elephant.

sanctuaries in Uruk, giving real force to the phrase 'for the life of the kings'.

The enlargement of the shrine in Girsu, which perhaps predated the work in Uruk by about twenty years, was seemingly again representative of a trend that subsequently accelerated and evolved. If it is correct to say that the temple was expanded during a period of relative calm before the onset of a coming political storm then it perhaps also represents an older mode of Seleucid involvement in local affairs, exemplified by Antiochus I, who took a close interest in the construction and renewal of Mesopotamian shrines—one that might have gone beyond hard-headed political expediency. As a literary composition, for example, the text on his famous Cylinder of Borsippa compares remarkably well with standard Neo-Babylonian royal inscriptions. It was created to celebrate Antiochus's restoration work on the Ezida Temple of Nabu, together with his reconstruction of the Esagila of Marduk in Babylon, which was probably damaged after the death of Alexander, during the long conflict that ensued between Seleucus I and the other contenders for the crown. Mesopotamia lay at the heart of the Seleucid empire, which was more integrated than is sometimes supposed, and the strength of the ethos that underpinned Seleucid authority was the willingness of the Hellenistic rulers to incorporate local influences, beliefs and traditions. With his building work and near-authentic Babylonian text, Antiochus I was therefore following in the footsteps of his father, Seleucus, who symbolically aligned the dating system of the new Seleucid Era with the start of the Babylonian religious calendar year in 311 BCE (1 SE), when he returned to Babylon in triumph after a period of exile. Against this backdrop, it might be inferred that the enlargement of the Girsu shrine was carried out in the same spirit of enlightened mutual self-interest as the foundation of the original Hellenistic Eninnu in the late fourth century. The salient fact that, unlike in Uruk, no named local leader left inscriptions or signed foundation deposits to signal his mediating presence in the project might be taken to indicate a high degree of continuity and cooperation, such that the enlargement was considered to be a reaffirmation of the synergistic principles that were embedded in the Hellenistic renewal from the outset. These speculative matters require further study, but there is a potential contrast to be explored between the implied circumstances in Girsu and the influence wielded in Uruk by Anu-uballit Nikarkhos and Anu-uballit Kephalon, who were operating at a time when the vulnerability of the Seleucid kings made the forging of political allegiances with powerful local partners—regional actors who could become arbiters of their fate—into an urgent strategic necessity.

The Destruction of the Shrine

Almost as soon as he began excavating on Tell A, Sarzec found evidence that led him and Heuzey to postulate that the Hellenistic shrine had been violently and deliberately destroyed by fire (see Chapter 23 above; and Sarzec and Heuzey 1912, p. 53)—a hypothesis that is corroborated by the British Museum team's findings relating to this later period (presented below). Uncovering the inner rooms of the complex, Sarzec discovered calcination on the fired-brick floors and more fire damage on some of the stone thresholds. Significantly, and as the British Museum team's findings confirm, the damage seems to have been localised, mostly affecting the area around Court A. Sarzec's Plan A (Fig. 111) further corroborates the hypothesis because it shows that the walls in the NW part of the shrine (the enlargement) were generally intact, and must, at the very least, have presented a complete ground plan when Sarzec excavated them. Conversely, some of the walls close to the temple's S corner were destroyed, including a significant section of the SW façade and part of the adjacent NE–SW inner partition wall. More damage is evident a little to the north-east in the broken NW–SE wall that protrudes into Court A, while signs of yet more destruction can be seen in one or two stubs of walls on the NW and SW sides of Court A. Additionally, however, the large, open irregular space on the SW side of Court A (in front of entrance K) was surely not a planned part of the original design—at least in the form in which it is shown on Plan A. As noted above (Chapter 24), it might have contained one or two wooden colonnades on its NW and SE sides, and this might help to account for its shape on the plan. An arrangement containing further walls or columns, possibly defining niches relating to a rectangular inner courtyard, would have been generally in accord with the ground plans of the Babylonian temples that are cited as comparisons in Chapter 45. Similarly, all the walls that Sarzec recorded in the Hellenistic shrine were made of fired bricks, but any wooden elements would, of course, have been destroyed and presumably overlooked. Also worth noting is the fact that the courtyards in the extension on the NW side of the shrine do not appear to have been formed as completely regular rectilinear shapes. Instead, partition walls break the lines of the courtyard façades, particularly in their entranceway and passageway areas, for example on the NW and SW sides of Court B and on the SW side of Court C, and signs of similar irregularities can be seen on the NE side of Court A. The design of both phases apparently eschewed regularity in favour of an almost baroque interplay of overlapping walls that must have created a slightly disorientating effect for visitors as they explored the temple's many niches, particularly after it was enlarged.

The stabilising anchor for that intricacy was the NW–SE axis that ran directly through the building. It is clear in the enlarged temple on Plan A, where it runs from the entrance (G) in the NW façade through the Hellenistic Gate of Gudea and along the SW side of Court A towards the most damaged part of the shrine on the SE side. The extension presumably maintained and responded to an already existing design feature, with the NW façade containing the Hellenistic iteration of the Gate of Gudea as a defining point, such that the NW–SE line was an integral part of the ground plan from the outset. As discussed in detail above, it is therefore probable that the first altar established by Adadnadinakhe lay on that axis in front of the original NW temenos wall (the Gate of Gudea façade), parallel to the later offering platform found by the British Museum team, and the corollary to that is that there was probably a cella in the SE area, presumably close to the S corner, where parts of the walls are damaged and missing. Though it cannot be proven categorically, the circumstantial evidence indicates this must have been the main focus of attention when the complex was deliberately destroyed and presumably set ablaze. The comparisons with the ground plans of temples in Babylon discussed in Chapter 45 would suggest that the Girsu shrine in both its original and later forms perhaps had more than one cella, and that a range of sacred (and perhaps also historical) imagery was displayed in them. The numerous niches, which perhaps functioned like side chapels or secondary cellas, must have contained interesting and relevant artefacts. Speculative though it may be, the overall impression is of a richly evocative array of objects, displayed in an elaborate arrangement of inner spaces, that were ancillary to a small number of principal cult platforms, and that whichever one of the main cellas was situated close to the S corner was a priority for the marauders who overran Girsu and destroyed the shrine.

The British Museum team found further evidence of the temple's destruction in Area B10, in the vicinity of the NW façade on Sarzec's Plan A, where deposits of fragmentary fired-brick remains (5414 and 5426) were encountered towards the top of the recorded archaeological sequence. The two very similar deposits of fired-brick rubble and sandy silt had collapsed directly onto a level surface that represented the final phase of Hellenistic occupation. In particular, deposit 5426 had collapsed from the south-east towards the north-west in reasonably well-defined brickwork courses, but it appeared to have fallen directly onto the mud-brick ground surface (5412). Six finds were retrieved from the rubble of collapsed wall 5414, most notably a Lagash II cone (TG2951) containing Gudea's Standard Inscription, while another six finds came from the remains of collapsed wall 5426, the most important of which were two Lagash II cones (TG3427 and TG3428), both marked with Gudea's Standard Inscription, and a large fragment of a decorated Seleucid pythos (TG3255).

Of the many mostly fragmentary objects that Sarzec found in the building, by far the most remarkable were the Gudea Statues—some of the most compelling Sumerian artefacts from anywhere in Mesopotamia. They were found in Court A, where they were separated into two groups, such that the standing portrayals were distinguished from the seated ones. The first group, which was found in the SE corner of Court A, included Statue E (dedicated to Bau in her Etarsirsir shrine), Statue C (for Inanna in her Eanna shrine in Girsu) and Statue G (for Ningirsu in his Eninnu). They were piled up, one on top of the other, while standing Statue A (for Ninhursag in her House of the City of Girsu) was lying nearby. The group of seated statues, including Statue B (dedicated

to Ningirsu in his Eninnu and showing Gudea with the plan of the temenos), Statue F (for Gatumdug in her House of the Shining City) and Statue H (for Bau in her Etarsirsir), were found in the centre of the courtyard, and they too were heaped up. In addition, and set slightly apart, were a fourth fragmentary seated statue dating from the Early Dynastic III period, together with a life-size shaven head of a Lagash II ruler—possibly Gudea. Clearly, the four portrayals devoted to Ningirsu and Bau (Statues G, B, E and H) must have originated in the New Eninnu complex, where the temples of the two principal deities were situated, but the same is almost certainly true of Statue F (for Gatumdug) because, as repeatedly noted, she and Bau were syncretised during the reign of Gudea. Similarly, the fundamental importance of Ninhursag as the mother goddess, together with the fertility and agricultural associations that could well have linked her with Bau, make it reasonable to presume that Statue A was also displayed in the New Eninnu, or in a nearby ancillary shrine (like the ones to Igalim and Shulshaga detailed in Chapters 27 and 44). These six statues were doubtless unearthed by Adadnadinakhe's late fourth-century BCE prospectors in favissas (comparable to the ones found by the British Museum team in the walls of the Ningirsu temple) on Tell A, in the area occupied by the New Eninnu. The slight anomaly in the group of seven found in Court A is Statue C (dedicated to Inanna in her Eanna temple in Girsu), which was probably sited elsewhere by Gudea, perhaps in the extended sacred precinct, but conceivably beyond its enclosing walls. Unfortunately, there is simply no way of knowing when Statue C was brought to Tell A—whether in Sumerian times, before the New Eninnu was finally decommissioned, or in the Hellenistic era. On the one hand, it would appear unlikely that Adadnadinakhe launched large-scale excavations that extended over vast tracts of the ancient city of Girsu, while on the other, it seems equally implausible to suggest that the Hellenistic-era planners had sufficiently detailed information at their disposal to enable them to uncover a single statue in a self-contained temple that was not sited on Tell A. By the same token, however, it is speculative to think that the statue was brought to Tell A at an unknown point in the centuries immediately after the New Eninnu was completed by Gudea. If those difficulties can be set aside, it nevertheless appears overwhelmingly likely that all seven of the mutilated statues found in Court A (including the one dedicated to Inanna) were enshrined in niches and small rooms in the SE part of the Hellenistic complex, in the first temple that was planned and built by Adadnadinakhe. Furthermore, the very fact that they were found in Court A, at the heart of Adadnadinakhe's shrine, would tend to confirm that they remained in their foundational spots until they were removed by marauders in the mid-second century BCE.

Apart from the main set of seven, four more important Lagash II carvings were found by Sarzec: Statues D, K and W (all from the reign of Gudea), and the earlier portrait of Ur-Bau. Statues K and W were found close to each other in front of entrance L in the NE façade (on Plan A), while the statue of Ur-Bau was found inside the enlarged complex, in front of the Gate of Gudea façade in the passageway leading to a niche (16 on Plan A) that also contained a large vessel made of bronze or copper. Statue D (the Colossus, dedicated in Gudea's name to Ningirsu in his Eninnu) was uncovered partially *in situ* in niche N in the NE façade on Sarzec's Plan A (see Chapters 2 and 37). It seems reasonable to presume that one of the Gudea statues might have been placed in the second external niche (T) in the SW façade, but this cannot be confirmed. It should be stressed, however, that both external niches (N and T on Plan A) were in sections of the façades that were established by Adadnadinakhe, even though those walls were rebuilt or refaced in the enlargement phase. Statue K was extremely badly damaged, but probably also dedicated by Gudea to Ningirsu, and Statue W was again dedicated by Gudea to Ningirsu in his Eninnu. The statue of Ur-Bau was similarly devoted to Ningirsu in his Eninnu, but in this case the inscription (RIME 3.1.1.6.4) refers to the old temple that was built by Ur-Bau, the founder of the second dynasty of Lagash, prior to the construction of the later New Eninnu by Gudea. Ur-Bau's old temple was, of course, retained intact within the walls of Gudea's shrine, in the NE protrusion at the SE end of the L-shaped complex, but the find location of the Ur-Bau statue on the NW side of the Gate of Gudea façade would seem not to reference that historical structure.

Forensic analysis confirms that the statues were all, without exception, systematically defaced and decapitated (as discussed in Chapter 37), and it appears that the main groups found in Court A were then purposefully heaped up in two small mounds, almost like the tumuli of vanquished foes seen on ancient Mesopotamian steles. It cannot be determined whether the two groups were formed simply on account of the contrasting seated vs standing attitudes of the figures, or whether they resulted from the arrangement of the statues

in the Hellenistic shrine, where the two modes of portrayal might have led to the two groups being shown in different ways or places. With this in mind, it is worth noting that there might have been a theological underpinning to the groupings because there are close correlations between the deities to whom the three standing and three seated portrayals of Gudea were respectively devoted. Both sets included a statue in honour of the state's tutelary god, Ningirsu (standing Statue G and seated Statue B, showing Gudea with the plan of the New Eninnu), and both sets included one that was directly devoted to Bau: standing Statue E and seated Statue H. Beyond that, each group was completed with carvings in honour of two distinct goddesses: standing Statue C (dedicated to Inanna) in the first group, and seated Statue F (sacred to Gatumdug, and showing Gudea with a blank tablet and measuring rod in his lap) in the second. As argued in Chapter 47, in the Hellenistic context of the revived shrine, Inanna and Gatumdug could loosely be taken to relate to Aphrodite and probably Tyche, respectively, but in those capacities they could both also be closely linked with Bau, as could Ninhursag, the dedicatee of standing Statue A, which was found on the ground close to the other three standing portrayals. The way the two sets of carvings were differentiated, together with the parallels between the venerated deities in the two groups, might further confirm that the Hellenistic shrine was focused on a core cluster of Sumerian gods, who were conceived of as having fluid identities. They could therefore take on the roles formerly ascribed to other Sumerian divinities, while being flexibly associated with some specially significant members of the Hellenistic pantheon.

The circumstances in which the two groups were found would indicate that they were not damaged as a result of mindless iconoclasm, but were rather gathered in the courtyard to be defaced and beheaded in an act of *damnatio memoriae* (see Chapter 37). Supine on the floor of Court A, the statues might have been subjected to a politically symbolic quasi-execution, for example, before being heaped up in death mounds. The heads, which were detached from all of the bodies—including the four statues that were not found in Court A—with controlled strokes, have never been recovered. It is therefore probably safe to say that they were taken away as trophies, or perhaps as material proof that the executions (so to speak) had indeed been carried out.

Finally, the question remains: who was responsible for destroying the Hellenistic shrine and carrying out the acts of *damnatio memoriae* just described? The identity of the marauders must remain speculative, but the second half of the second century BCE, especially after the conquest of Babylonia by Mithridates I of Parthia in 141 BCE, was a period of ongoing military action and geopolitical turmoil in the region. The decades that marked the transition from Seleucid to Parthian rule witnessed the decline and depopulation of Babylon and Uruk, and the conflagration of some of the great temples in Uruk, including the Bit Resh and the Irigal (though the Bit Resh complex, which was actually rebuilt in the Parthian period, was still in service under Mithridates II, who reigned from 124 to 91 BCE). It is possible that the large-scale destruction of these famous temples was perpetrated by vanguards of the invading Parthians, or by raiding parties that pillaged the countryside, and that the Hellenistic shrine in Girsu fell victim to the same forces. And yet, the systematic and carefully orchestrated damage that was inflicted on the Gudea Statues, for example, gives pause for thought, suggesting that the shrine was perhaps attacked by someone with very specific aims—a local warlord, for instance, who wished to obliterate the cultural weight of the past in order to attempt to establish his own dynasty on a fresh footing.

The difficulty that hangs over this discussion is to try to understand what the targets of the action in Girsu actually were. Without question, the most legible evidence derives from the Gudea Statues, which were very specifically treated, but it is dangerous to take that as an unequivocal sign that the marauders were exclusively concerned with the Sumerian historical presence represented by the ancient treasures displayed in the shrine. As is discussed at length above, Sumerian sacred and political imagery (with the Gudea Statues spanning both categories) was decisively recontextualised in the Hellenistic temple. Sumerian deities were associated with later Greek counterparts, and there was also seemingly an emphasis on historical figures from ancient and modern times, notably Gudea, Ur-Bau, Alexander and members of the Seleucid ruling dynasty, including one or more Seleucid queens. In that setting, the acts of *damnatio memoriae* carried out on the Gudea Statues, which seem to have adopted a pattern that is familiar in Mesopotamia and elsewhere, might not have been aimed at Gudea per se, but rather designed to erase more recent bad memories. To give one example, the intention could have been to cancel Gudea's reputation because of his de facto association with the Hellenistic authorities who built and maintained the temple. The antagonism in that case

would not have been directed towards Gudea as the historical ruler of Lagash and builder of the New Eninnu in the late third millennium BCE, but towards his imagery as appropriated, interpreted and harnessed by a series of Hellenistic rulers (probably acting through their local agents), culminating under the late Seleucids in the third and second centuries BCE.

Two more types of evidence that provide insight into the destruction of the shrine have to be considered against that background: the less clearly legible and the purely circumstantial. As outlined above, for nearly two centuries the Hellenistic shrine was a working temple that was visited by pilgrims, many of whom deposited votives, and throughout that time it was almost certainly dedicated to the worship of a small roster of closely connected deities, most saliently Ningirsu and Heracles. That being the case, it would be bizarre to argue that no significant cult images were displayed there. Some small but tangible signs of that are the bronze Heracles and the terracottas found by Sarzec, Genouillac and the British Museum team, all of which deserve to be re-evaluated in the light of the revised chronology presented above. A further indicator is probably the focused nature of the damage done to the fabric of the building. It was concentrated on the SE end of the temple, as established by Adadnadinakhe, and in particular it was aimed at the rooms and spaces on the SW side of the original shrine, towards the S corner, on the SE and SW side of Court A, in an area that probably housed a principal cella. As with the Gudea Statues, any iconographical programme that had a Sumerian (or generally Mesopotamian) character must have been viewed through the prism of the Greek-oriented temple culture that was maintained after the Eninnu's revival during two centuries of Hellenistic ascendancy. It is impossible to speculate about the form any Hellenistic-era cult images might have taken, but their (or its) possible disappearance would not be unusual. On the contrary, cult statues have rarely, if ever, been retrieved from any temples anywhere in Mesopotamia (or classical Greece, for that matter). The uncommon fact is the preservation of the damaged Gudea Statues, but that might well be a reflection of Gudea's exceptional prescience—he very consciously made them from a material that was almost impossible to smash, too heavy to remove and too hard to salvage.

This nuanced approach to the end of the Hellenistic Eninnu necessarily leads to some rather provisional conclusions. The marauders' compelling interest might have been in erasing the Hellenistic presence per se, in which case the Gudea Statues (to take the pivotal example) could have been viewed as mere instruments of Seleucid control, with little or no regard being paid to their intrinsic meaning. Alternatively, for forces with more knowledge of the local political and historical situation, the statues might have additionally been considered to be corrupted by their absorption into a Hellenistic frame of reference, such that they were a symbol of Hellenistic dominance, but also signs of the debasing effect of the Hellenistic presence on traditional Mesopotamian values and culture. The first scenario would probably point towards the incoming Parthians, whose primary concern was with replacing the Seleucids, in which case the temple would presumably have been regarded—perhaps almost exclusively—as a Seleucid institution. The systematic damage done to the statues would again suggest the need for caution, however, and one historical figure who might have had more reason to demonstrate his regional cultural credentials

was Hyspaosines (209–124 BCE), the former Seleucid governor, or satrap, of the Erythrean Sea, who led his army north from Charax to claim the kingship in Babylon in the wake of the collapse of Hellenistic rule. Though he did manage to establish a dynasty, his territory of Characene was soon incorporated as a vassal state into the Parthian empire. In the context of the now revised interpretation and chronology of the Hellenistic shrine, the potential role of Hyspaosines as the central actor in the destruction of the temple in Girsu requires further study. Nonetheless, if he did indeed wish to target the legitimising presence of the Gudea Statues as symbols of Seleucid control, it is conceivable that the renewed fieldwork that is being carried out in many places in southern Iraq—spearheaded by the British Museum team's work in Girsu—might one day unearth a favissa containing the heads of the Gudea Statues in Charax Spasinou, the capital of Hyspaosines's state of Characene.

ACKNOWLEDGEMENTS

The Temple of Ningirsu would never have seen the light of day without the backing of a great many important stakeholders, colleagues and friends. Indeed, the list of people and organisations to thank is so long that it is unfortunately impossible to mention them all. Nonetheless, I must start with the generous commitment of the J. Paul Getty Trust, which has made this immense task possible. Nor should I fail to record my deep appreciation for the unstinting support of the British Museum, in particular from the Director, Hartwig Fischer; the Keeper of Middle East, Paul Collins; and the former Keeper, Jonathan Tubb. In addition, I am especially grateful to Timothy Potts, the Director of the Getty Museum, for his unfailing guidance. Heartfelt thanks also go to the British Museum's Friends of the Middle East for their assistance, and to the UK Government's Department for Digital, Culture, Media and Sport for its funding of the British Museum's first series of excavations at Girsu.

The Girsu Project is a collaborative venture with the State Board of Antiquities and Heritage in Iraq. I would like to express my deep gratitude to the board's Director General, Laith Majeed Hussein, as well as to his predecessors, Qais Hussein Rashid and the late Abdulameer al-Hamdani. I extend my appreciation to the many SBAH officials in Baghdad who have provided much help and support, including the Director of Excavations, Ali Obeid Shalgham, and his predecessors. In London, I owe an enormous debt of gratitude to the Ambassador of Iraq, His Excellency Mohammad Jaafar Al-Sadr, for facilitating the progress of the Girsu Project in numerous ways, supported by the helpful staff at the Iraq Embassy. Nor would the work in Iraq have been possible without the help and support of people on the ground: the archaeological police force in Dhi Qar Governorate and their commanding officers, who ensured the team's security

and well-being; and the directors and archaeologists of the SBAH office in Nasiriya, including the inspectors who were present during successive seasons in Girsu. The contributions of the guards and the hundreds of friends and colleagues from Nasr and the area around Tello who have worked at the site have been vital. At the very heart of the whole enterprise are the Iraqi colleagues and students who took part in the field training. It has been an immense privilege to work with these talented and dedicated individuals whose experiences and insights have been an inspiration.

The work at Girsu could not have been carried out without the determined leadership of the project's assistant director, Fatma Yassir Husain; the drive and skill of the project's manager, Uxue Rambla Eguílaz; and the guidance of the project's heritage manager, Ebru Torun. I owe an incalculable debt to the members of the Girsu excavation team, who worked for long periods, often under difficult conditions, sharing their special skills and expertise in a spirit of international cooperation. *The Temple of Ningirsu* reflects this holistic outlook, and though I take final responsibility for any errors, the book could not have been brought into being without the essential input of an outstanding group of contributors: Angelo Di Michele, who established the pottery repertoires that are fundamental for stratigraphic dating; Elisa Girotto, who did invaluable work on the statues, steles and many newly excavated objects; Holger Gzella, who read the unearthed Aramaic inscriptions; Ashley Pooley, who led the excavations on Tell A; Jon Taylor, who read the Sumerian inscriptions and provided valuable feedback on the manuscript of the book; and Paul Williamson, who rewrote the entire text and to whom I am indebted for innumerable ideas about sacred art and architecture, not least the groundbreaking concept of the Sumerian tessellated earth.

Also vital to the book are materials and information supplied by Eleanor Atkins, Dita Auzina, Stefka Bargazova, Gareth Brereton, Julien Chanteau, John and Vesta Curtis, Guido Della Lena Guidiccioni, Amelia Dowler, Ella Egberts, Charlotte Faiers, Irving Finkel, James Fraser, Andrew Ginns, Sandra Grabowski, Tina Greenfield, Nancy Highcock, Luke Jarvis, John MacGinnis, Gianni Marchesi, Julian Reade, Simone Rotella, Lleonard Rubio y Degrassi, St John Simpson, Joanna Skwiercz, Dani Tagen, Mathilde Touillon-Ricci, Göze Üner, Faith Vardy, Christopher Walker, Rachel Wood and Gábor Zólyomi. In addition, I am most grateful to Holly Pittman for her encouragement and support.

For their expertise in producing *The Temple of Ningirsu* I would like to express my appreciation to the talented staff at Penn State University Press; warmest thanks go to the Director of Penn State University Press, Patrick Alexander, and to the Eisenbrauns Acquisitions Editor, Maria Metzler.

Finally, on a personal note, it is difficult to express what it means to have had the opportunity to excavate the ancient site of Girsu in search of the Temple of Ningirsu. Before the commencement of the British Museum team's work, archaeologists had given up on the site. A hundred years ago it was already deemed to be 'exhausted', a 'lost cause', a 'colossal wreck'. Yet I always regarded these views as unnecessarily pessimistic and cherished the belief that all traces of the sanctuary of the White Thunderbird had not in reality been obliterated. It is true that the return to Tello sometimes felt like a challenge worthy of Ningirsu or his mythical successor Heracles, who combatted the many-headed dragon or Hydra, but I took inspiration from the mesmerising mantra endlessly repeated by Gudea when he was constructing the New Eninnu, that things should be made to 'function as they should'. With the publication of this study, the hope now is that the collaborative effort of all involved will—to borrow another phrase from Gudea—help to restore the Temple of Ningirsu to its 'proper place' as a foundational component of our collective memory.

Sébastien Rey
Curator for Ancient Mesopotamia
Director of the Girsu Project
The British Museum
London, May 2023

TABLE OF CORRESPONDENCES

This table shows correspondences between the British Museum team's registration numbers of finds (TG) cited in the book and accession numbers in the Iraq Museum in Baghdad (IM). Some finds do not have IM numbers because they are listed in a separate inventory for batch study; some small sets of related finds have been grouped together under the same IM number.

TG Number	IM Number		TG Number	IM Number		TG Number	IM Number
39	—		606	12708		1252	233844
41	233239		699	—		1278	—
51	12707		740	—		1299	233846
77	233242		743	233578		1305	233847
103	—		777	227837		1326	—
136	227737		836	233596		1368	233850
168	227752		839	233598		1370	—
192	—		844	—		1478	—
193	—		851	233601		1479	—
218	233249		855	233602		1501	227863
219	—		870	227841		1534	—
222	—		879	233603		1591	—
241	—		892	—		1596	227889
244	—		915	233608		1602	227891
248	—		936	—		1603	227892
299	233246		947	—		1604	—
300	233247		951	—		1605	233869
301	—		974	227846		1606	233870
318	233248		979	227848		1624	236705
319	233249		980	227849		1639	—
331	—		981	—		1645	236560
356	—		982	227850		1647	—
366	227764		983	—		1659	—
372	227765		984	—		1668	—
373	227766		985	227851		1670	—
374	227767		986	227852		1676	236561
375	227768		987	227853		1685	—
376	227769		988	227854		1735	236567
378	—		991	233615		1737	236705
381	—		1011	—		1739	236568
382	233259		1015	—		1746	236706
383	233360		1046	—		1771	236705
418	233559		1198	—		1773	—
521	233567		1202	233840		1781	236573
585	233570		1251	233843		1800	236706

Table of Correspondences

TG Number	IM Number
1816	236574
1817	—
1826	236576
1829	—
1843	—
1848	—
1850	236578
1851	—
1853	236579
1862	236580
1867	236718
1869	236706
1871	236643
1908	236719
1987	236587
1991	236588
1993	236648
1994	236589
1999	236590
2009	236592
2020	—
2021	—
2023	236705
2058	236705
2059	236705
2069	—
2072	236599
2084	236600
2093	236602
2095	236603
2102	—
2114	236705
2117	236705
2123	236604
2127	236605
2132	236723
2133	236682
2134	236683
2145	236606
2150	236607
2151	—
2153	236608
2162	236705
2163	236705
2166	236705
2167	236705
2168	236705
2169	236705
2170	236705
2171	236611
2172	236705
2179	236705
2184	236612
2189	236705
2190	236705

TG Number	IM Number
2195	236705
2222	236705
2225	236705
2248	236705
2253	12774
2255	236705
2265	—
2266	—
2273	236707
2350	236695
2351	236696
2353	—
2435	236697
2436	236698
2448	236626
2449	236685
2470	236699
2476	—
2481	236687
2482	236688
2483	236689
2520	—
2573	236639
2574	236690
2609	236705
2610	236705
2611	—
2635	236691
2636	236692
2637	—
2639	—
2640	—
2666	241167
2676	—
2680	—
2767	241182
2868	—
2871	241302
2951	241310
2965	241206
2981	—
2982	—
2991	241310
2992	241207
2995	241286
3001	241285
3005	241208
3044	241302
3067	241215
3126	241294
3160	241294
3162	241294
3165	241294
3166	241294
3167	241230

TG Number	IM Number
3169	241294
3170	241294
3176	241294
3177	241232
3223	241303
3224	241303
3225	241303
3226	241303
3239	241241
3247	241243
3254	241244
3255	241303
3279	—
3281	241283
3283	241248
3288	241310
3319	241253
3323	241310
3326	241254
3334	241302
3339	241310
3350	241286
3384	241258
3389	—
3390	—
3391	241284
3392	—
3393	241260
3395	241294
3412	241310
3414	241310
3415	241308
3419	241263
3427	241310
3428	—
3436	241265
3496	241299
3504	—
3532	241275
3533	241310
3534	—
3536	241276
3539	241277
3540	241278
3541	241702
3542	241593
3545	241596
3558	241703
3567	241603
3584	241724
3589	—
3598	—
3689	241701
3721	241630
3723	—

TG Number	IM Number
3725	241701
3757	—
3783	241642
3792	—
3817	241645
3827	241646
3838	—
3842	241647
3865	241648
3866	241708
3876	241720
3897	241651
3906	241720
3958	241656
3965	241720
3969	241657
4007	—
4034	241729
4041	241705
4069	—
4081	241728
4122	—
4143	241667
4144	241668
4145	241720
4179	241669
4182	—
4204	241703
4206	—

TG Number	IM Number
4209	241708
4213	241702
4234	241702
4235	—
4236	241704
4293	241703
4298	241729
4313	241681
4368	241702
4370	—
4373	241702
4379	—
4399	241688
4406	241729
4427	—
4434	241702
4436	241704
4437	241704
4441	241702
4442	241702
4450	—
4462	241702
4464	—
4470	241702
4475	241708
4479	—
4483	—
4487	241708
4492	241708

TG Number	IM Number
4497	—
4499	241717
4500	241702
4508	241705
4509	241708
4512	—
4516	—
4519	—
4520	241702
4521	—
4522	—
4524	—
4525	—
4526	—
4528	—
4539	—
4541	—
4554	241695
4555	241707
4610	243457
4622	243457
4632	—
4634	—
4635	243457
4649	12947
4763	243450
4776	243452
4778	243453
4787	—

REFERENCES

Adams, R. McC. (1981) *Heartland of Cities, Surveys of Ancient Settlement and Land Use on the Central Floodplain of the Euphrates*. Chicago, IL; London: University of Chicago Press.

Adams, R. McC. and Nissen, H. J. (1972) *The Uruk Countryside: The Natural Setting of Urban Societies*. Chicago, IL; London: University of Chicago Press.

Alster, B. (2003–4) 'Images and Text on the "Stele of the Vultures"', *Archiv für Orientforschung*, 50, pp. 1–10.

Amiaud, A. (1887) 'L'inscription H de Goudéa', *Zeitschrift für Assyriologie und Vorderasiatische Archäologie* 2, pp. 287–98.

André-Salvini, B. (2003) 'Tello (Ancient Girsu)', in Aruz, J. and Wallenfels, R. (eds.) *The Art of the First Cities: The Third Millennium BC from the Mediterranean to the Indus*. New York, NY: The Metropolitan Museum of Art, pp. 68–9.

Annus, A. (2002) *The God Ninurta in the Mythology and Royal Ideology of Ancient Mesopotamia*. Helsinki: University of Helsinki.

Armstrong, J. A. and Gasche, H. (eds.) (2014) *Mesopotamian Pottery: A Guide to the Babylonian Tradition in the Second Millennium B.C.* Gent: University of Ghent.

Arnaud, D. et al. (1981) 'Textes divers concernant le royaume de Larsa', *Syria*, 58(1; 2), pp. 70–100.

Arrian (1884) *The Anabasis of Alexander: The History of the Wars and Conquests of Alexander the Great*. Translated by E. J. Chinnock. London: Hodder and Stoughton.

Aruz, J. and Wallenfels, R. (eds.) (2003) *The Art of the First Cities: The Third Millennium BC from the Mediterranean to the Indus*. New York, NY: The Metropolitan Museum of Art.

Barrelet, M.-T. (1968) *Figurines et reliefs en terre cuite de la Mésopotamie antique, vol. I: Poiers, termes de métier, procédés de fabrication et production*. Paris: Paul Geuthner.

Barrelet, M.-T. (1970) 'Études de glyptique akkadienne: l'imagination figurative et le cycle d'Ea', *Orientalia*, NS 39(2), pp. 213–51.

Beyer, K. (2004) *Die aramäischen Texte vom Toten Meer*, vol. 2. Göttingen: Vandenhoeck and Ruprecht.

Biggs, R. D. (1974) *Inscriptions from Tell Abū Ṣalābīkh*. Chicago, IL: University of Chicago Press.

Boese, J. (1971) *Altmesopotamische Weihplatten. Ein sumerische Denkmalsgattung des 3. Jahrtausends V. Chr.* Berlin: De Gruyter.

Bottéro, J. and Kramer, S. N. (1989) *Lorsque les dieux faisaient l'homme: mythologie mésopotamienne*. Paris: Gallimard.

Boucharlat, R. (1987) 'Les niveaux post-achéménides à Suse, secteur nord', *Cahiers de la Délégation Archéologique Française en Iran*, 15, pp. 145–311.

Braun-Holzinger, E. A. (1991) *Mesopotamische Weihgaben der frühdynastischen bis altbabylonischen Zeit*. Heidelberg: Heidelberger Orientverlag.

Braun-Holzinger, E. A. (2007) *Das Herrscherbild in Mesopotamien und Elam: spätes 4. bis frühes 2. Jt. v. Chr.* Münster: Ugarit-Verlag.

Britton, J. and Walker, C. (1996) 'Astronomy and Astrology in Mesopotamia', in Walker, C. (ed.) *Astronomy before the Telescope*. London: The British Museum Press, pp. 42–67.

Brockelmann, C. (1928) *Lexicon Syriacum*. 2nd ed. Halle: Sumptibus M. Niemeyer.

Cavigneaux, A. (2016) 'L'énigme du gigunû', in Quenet, P. (ed.) *Ana Ziqquratim. Sur la piste de Babel*. Strasbourg: Presses Universitaires de Strasbourg, p. 74.

Cellerino, A. (2004) 'La ceramica dal sondaggio di Shu-Anna a Babilonia', *Mesopotamia*, 39, pp. 93–168.

Chanteau, J. (2017) *La divine machinerie: l'invention du temple au Moyen-Orient ancien*. Paris: Paul Geuthner.

Cohen, M. E. (1993) *The Cultic Calendars of the Ancient Near East*. Bethesda, MD: CDL Press.

Cole, S. W. (2014) 'Chronology Revisited', in Armstrong, J. A. and Gasche, H. (eds.) *Mesopotamian Pottery: A Guide to the Babylonian Tradition in the Second Millennium B.C.* Ghent: University of Ghent, pp. 3–6.

Cooper, J. S. (1983) *Reconstructing History from Ancient Inscriptions: The Lagash-Umma Border Conflict*. Malibu, CA: Undena Publications.

Crawford, H. (1987) 'The *Construction Inférieure* at Tello: A Reassessment', *Iraq*, 49, pp. 71–6.

Cros, G. (*avec le concours de L. Heuzey et de F. Thureau-Dangin*) (1910) *Nouvelles fouilles de Tello*. Paris: Ernest Leroux.

Curtius Rufus, Quintus (2004 [1984]) *The History of Alexander*. Translated by J. Yardley. London: Penguin Books.

Delougaz, P. (1952) *Pottery from the Diyala Region*. Chicago, IL: University of Chicago Press, 1952.

Diakonoff, I. M. (1974 [1959]) *Structures of Society and State in Early Dynastic Sumer*. Malibu, CA: Undena Publications.

Dolce, R. (1997) 'Aux origins de la royauté à Tello', *Akkadica*, 103, pp. 1–5.

Downey, S. B. (1988) *Mesopotamian Religious Architecture: Alexander through the Parthians*. Princeton, NJ: Princeton University Press.

Eliade, M. (1959) *The Sacred and the Profane: The Nature of Religion*. Translated by W. R. Trask. New York, NY: Harcourt, Brace and Company.

Edzard, D. O. (1983) 'Königlisten und Chroniken: A. Sumerisch', in Edzard, D. O. (ed.) (1980–3) *Reallexikon der Assyriologie und Vorderasiatischen Archäologie*, Band 6. Berlin: De Gruyter, pp. 77–86.

Edzard, D. O. (1997) *Royal Inscriptions of Mesopotamia Early Periods, vol. 3/1: Gudea and His Dynasty*. Toronto: University of Toronto Press.

Ellis, R. S. (1968) *Foundation Deposits in Ancient Mesopotamia*. New Haven, CT: Yale University Press.

Emelianov, V. (2016) 'The Identity of Gudea as a Cultural and Historical Problem', in Kämmerer, T. R., Kõiv, M. and Sazonov, V. (eds.) *Kings, Gods and People: Establishing Monarchies in the Ancient World*. Münster: Ugarit-Verlag, pp. 63–76.

Englund, R. K. (1998) 'Texts from the Late Uruk Period', in Bauer, J., Englund, R. K. and Krebernik, M. *Mesopotamien: Späturuk-Zeit und Frühdynastische Zeit*. Freiburg, CH: Universitätsverlag; Gottingen: Vandenhoeck und Ruprecht, pp. 15–217.

Evans, J. M. (2007) 'The Square Temple at Tell Asmar and the Construction of Early Dynastic Mesopotamia, ca. 2900–2350 B.C.E.', *American Journal of Archaeology*, 111(4), pp. 599–632.

Falkenstein, A (1966) *Die Inschriften Gudeas von Lagaš, I. Einleitung*. Rome: Pontificium Institutum Biblicum.

Finkbeiner, U. (1991) 'Die Keramik der seleukidischen und parthischen Zeit aus den Ausgrabungen in Uruk-Warka I', *Baghdader Mitteilungen*, 22, pp. 537–637.

Finkbeiner, U. (1992) 'Die Keramik der seleukidischen und parthischen Zeit aus den Ausgrabungen in Uruk-Warka. II', *Baghdader Mitteilungen*, 23, pp. 473–580.

Finkbeiner, U. and Röllig, W. (eds.) (1986) *Ǧamdat Naṣr, Period or Regional Style? Papers Given at a Symposium Held in Tübingen, November 1983*. Wiesbaden: Reichert Verlag.

Fischer, C. (1996) 'Gudea zwischen Tradition und Moderne', *Baghdader Mitteilungen*, 27, pp. 215–28.

Fleming, D. (1989) 'Eggshell Ware Pottery in Achaemenid Mesopotamia', *Iraq*, 51, pp. 165–85.

Forest, J.-D. (1999) *Les premiers temples de Mésopotamie: 4e et 3e millénaires*. Oxford: Archaeopress.

Fossey, C. (1926) *Manuel d'Assyriologie 2: Evolution des cunéiformes*. Paris: Louis Conard.

Foster, B. R. (1985) 'The Sargonic Victory Stele from Telloh', *Iraq*, 47, pp. 15–30.

Frayne, D. (2008) *Royal Inscriptions of Mesopotamia Early Periods, vol. 1: Presargonic Period (2700–2350 BC)*. Toronto: University of Toronto Press.

Frankfort, H. (1936) *Progress of the Work of the Oriental Institute in Iraq, 1934/35: Fifth Preliminary Report of the Iraq Expedition*. Chicago, IL: University of Chicago Press.

Frankfort, H. (1954) *The Art and Architecture of the Ancient Orient*. Harmondsworth: Penguin Books.

Frazer, M. (2017) 'Commentary on Lugale (*CCP* 1.2)', *Cuneiform Commentaries Project*, 2013–23. https://ccp.yale.edu/P461247; doi: 10079/h44j1bm.

Gabbay, U. (2014) 'The Balaǵ Instrument and Its Role in the Cult of Ancient Mesopotamia', in Westenholz, J. G., Maurey, Y. and Seroussi, E. (eds.) *Music in Antiquity: The Near East and the Mediterranean*. Berlin; Boston, MA: De Gruyter; Jerusalem: Hebrew University Magnes Press.

Garcia-Ventura, A. (2012) 'The Emperor's New Clothes: Textiles, Gender and Mesopotamian Foundation Figurines', *Altorientalische Forschungen*, 39(2), pp. 235–53.

Gelb, I. J. (1982) 'Terms for Slaves in Ancient Mesopotamia', in *Societies and languages of the Ancient Near East. Studies in Honour of Igor Michailovitch Diakonoff*. Warminster; Atlantic Highlands, NJ: Aris and Phillips, pp. 81–98.

Gelb, I. J., Steinkeller, P. and Whiting Jr., R. M. (1989–91) *Earliest Land Tenure Systems in the Near East: Ancient Kudurrus*. Chicago, IL: Oriental Institute of the University of Chicago.

Genouillac, H. de (1934) *Fouilles de Telloh I: Époques Présargoniques*. Paris: Paul Geuthner.

Genouillac, H. de (1936) *Fouilles de Telloh II: Époques d'Ur IIIe Dynastie et de Larsa*. Paris: Paul Geuthner.

George, A. R. (1993) *House Most High: The Temples of Ancient Mesopotamia*, Winona Lake, IN: Eisenbrauns.

George, A. R. (2005) 'The Tower of Babel: Archaeology, History and Cuneiform Texts', *Archiv für Orientforschung*, 51, pp. 75–95.

Ghirshman, R. (1954) *Iran: From the Earliest Times to the Islamic Conquest*. Harmondsworth: Penguin Books.

Gibson, M. (1982) 'A Re-Evaluation of the Akkad Period in the Diyala Region on the Basis of Recent Excavations at Nippur and in the Hamrin', *American Journal of Archaeology*, 86(4), pp. 531–8.

Gibson, M. (2011) 'The Diyala Sequence: Flawed at Birth', in Miglus, P. A. and Mühl, S. (eds.) *Between The Cultures: The Central Tigris Region from the 3rd to the 1st Millennium BC*. Heidelberg: Heidelberger Orientverlag, pp. 59–84.

Gibson, M. and McMahon, A. (1995) 'Investigation of the Early Dynastic-Akkadian Transition: Report of the 18th and 19th Seasons of Excavation in Area WF, Nippur', *Iraq*, 57, pp. 1–39.

Gibson, M. and McMahon, A. (1997) 'The Early Dynastic-Akkadian Transition Part II: The Authors' Response', *Iraq*, 59, pp. 9–14.

Glassner, J.-J. (2000) 'Les petits États mésopotamiens à la fin du 4e et au cours du 3e millénaire', in Hansen M. H. (ed.) *A Comparative Study of Thirty City-State Cultures*. Copenhagen: C. A. Reitzels Forlag, pp. 35–53.

Glassner, J.-J. (2004) 'Du bon usage du concept de cité-État?', *Journal des Africanistes*, 74(1; 2), pp. 35–45.

Gleba, M. (2008) *Textile Production in Pre-Roman Italy*. Oxford: Oxbow Books.

Grayson, A. K. and Sollberger, E. (1976) 'L'insurrection générale contre Naram-Suen', *Revue d'Assyriologie et d'archéologie orientale*, 70(2), pp. 103–28.

Gruber, M. (2015) '". . . somewhat smaller and shallower": The Development of Conical Bowls in Third Millennium Mesopotamia', in Dittmann, R. and Selz, G. J. (eds.) *It's a Long Way to a Historiography of the Early Dynastic Period(s)*. Münster: Ugarit-Verlag, pp. 129–68.

Hannestad, L. (1983) *Ikaros—The Hellenistic Settlements, vol. 2: The Hellenistic Pottery*. Aarhus: Jutland Archaeological Society Publications.

Hannestad, L. (1984) 'The Pottery from the Hellenistic Settlements of Failaka', in Boucharlat, R. and Salles, J.-F. (eds.) *Arabie orientale, Mésopotamie et Iran méridional*. Paris: Éditions Recherche sur les civilisations, pp. 67–83.

Hansen, D. P. (1992) 'Royal Building Activity at Sumerian Lagash in the Early Dynastic Period', *The Biblical Archaeologist*, 55(4), pp. 206–11.

Hartman, L. F. and Oppenheim, A. L. (1950) 'On Beer and Brewing Techniques in Ancient Mesopotamia According to the XXIIIrd Tablet of the Series ḪAR.r a = ḫubullu', Supplement to the *Journal of the American Oriental Society*, 10.

Heimpel, W. (1981) 'The Nanshe Hymn', *Journal of Cuneiform Studies*, 33(2), pp. 65–139.

Heimpel, W. (1996) 'The Gates of the Eninnu', *Journal of Cuneiform Studies*, 48(1), pp. 17–29.

Heinrich, E. and Seidl, U. (1982) *Die Tempel und Heiligtümer im alten Mesopotamien: Typologie, Morphologie und Geschichte*. Berlin: De Gruyter.

Heuzey, L. (1900) *Une villa royale chaldéenne vers l'an 4000 avant notre ère, d'après les levés et les notes de M. de Sarzec*. Paris: Ernest Leroux.

Heuzey, L. (1902) *Musée national du Louvre. Catalogue des antiquités chaldéennes: sculpture et gravure à la pointe*. Paris: Librairies-imprimeries réunies.

Hilprecht, H. V. (1903) *Explorations in Bible Lands During the 19th Century*. Philadelphia, PA: A. J. Holman and Company.

Huh, S. K. (2008) *Studien zur Region Lagaš: Von der Ubaid- bis zur Altbabylonischen Zeit*. Münster: Ugarit-Verlag.

Hunt, G. R. (2006) *Foundation Rituals and the Culture of Building in Ancient Greece*, PhD thesis. Chapel Hill, NC: University of North Carolina.

Jacobsen, T. (1976) *The Treasures of Darkness: A History of Mesopotamian Religion*. New Haven, CT; London: Yale University Press.

Jacobsen, T. (1987) *The Harps That Once...: Sumerian Poetry in Translation*. New Haven, CT; London: Yale University Press.

Jagersma, B. (2007) 'The Calendar of the Funerary Cult in Ancient Lagash', *Bibliotheca Orientalis*, 64(3; 4), pp. 289–307.

Jagersma, B. (2010) *A Descriptive Grammar of Sumerian*, PhD thesis. Leiden: Leiden University.

James, P. and Sluijs, M. A. van der (2008) 'Ziggurats, Colours and Planets: Rawlinson Revisited', *Journal of Cuneiform Studies*, 60(1), pp. 57–79.

Karvonen-Kannas, K. (1995) *The Seleucid and Parthian Terracotta Figurines from Babylon: In the Iraq Museum, the British Museum and the Louvre*. Firenze: Le Lettere.

Kingsley, B. (1991) 'Alexander's "Kausia" and Macedonian Tradition', *Classical Antiquity*, 10(1), pp. 59–76.

Kosmin, P. J. (2018) *Time and Its Adversaries in the Seleucid Empire*. Cambridge, MA; London: Harvard University Press.

Kuhrt, A. (1987) 'Berossus' *Babyloniaka* and Seleucid Rule in Babylonia', in Kuhrt, A and Sherwin-White, S. (eds.) *Hellenism in the East: The Interaction of Greek and Non-Greek Civilizations from Syria to Central Asia after Alexander*. Berkeley and Los Angeles, CA: University of California Press, pp. 32–56.

Kuhrt, A. (2002) 'Greek Contact with the Levant and Mesopotamia in the First Half of the First Millennium BC: A View from the East', in Tstetskhladze, G. R. and Snodgrass, A. M. (eds.) *Greek Settlement in the Eastern Mediterranean and the Black Sea*. Oxford: Archaeopress, pp. 17–25.

Labat, R. and Malbran-Labat, F. (1995) *Manuel d'épigraphie akkadienne: Signes, Syllabaire, Idéogrammes*. Paris: Paul Geuthner.

Lecomte, O. (1983) 'La céramique du niveau séleuco-parthe de Larsa (1981)', in Huot, J.-L. (ed.) *Larsa et 'Oueili: Travaux de 1978–1981*. Paris: Éditions Recherche sur les civilisations, pp. 305–52.

Lecomte, O. (1987) 'Un problème d'interprétation: l'E.babbar de Larsa aux époques hellénistique et séleuco-parthe, approche archéologique, économique et culturelle', in Huot, J.-L. and Anselm, G. (eds.) *Larsa, 10e campagne, 1983 et 'Oueili, 4e campagne, 1983*. Paris: Éditions Recherche sur les civilisations, pp. 225-46.

Lecomte, O. (1989) 'Fouilles du sommet de l'E.babbar'; 'Un dispositif de fermeture des vases à l'époque hellénistique', in Huot, J.-L. (ed.) *Larsa, Travaux de 1985*. Paris: Éditions Recherche sur les civilisations, pp. 83–150.

Lecompte, C. (2009) *Listes lexicales et représentations spatiales des époques archaïques à la période paléo-babylonienne*, PhD thesis. Versailles: Université de Versailles Saint-Quentin-en-Yvelines.

Lecompte, C. (2020) 'A propos de deux monuments figurés du début du 3e millénaire: observations sur la *Figure aux Plumes* et la *Prisoner Plaque*', in Arkhipov, I., Kogan, L. and Koslova, N. (eds.) *The Third Millennium: Studies in Early Mesopotamia and Syria in Honor of Walter Sommerfeld and Manfred Krebernik*. Leiden; Boston, MA: Brill, pp. 417–46.

Maeda, T. (1988) 'Two Rulers by the Name of Ur-Ningirsu in Pre-Ur III Lagash', *Acta Sumerologica*, 10, pp. 19–35.

Maiocchi, M. and Visicato, G. (2020) *Administration at Girsu in Gudea's Time*. Venice: Edizioni Ca' Foscari—Digital Publishing.

Marchesi, G. (2015) 'Toward a Chronology of Early Dynastic Rulers in Mesopotamia', in Sallaberger, W. and Schrakamp, I. (eds.) *History & Philology*. Turnhout: Brepols, pp. 139–56.

Marchesi, G. and Marchetti, N. (2011) *The Royal Statuary of Early Dynastic Mesopotamia*. Winona Lake, IN: Eisenbrauns.

Margueron, J.-C. (2004) *Mari: Métropole de l'Euphrate au IIIe et au début du IIe millénaire av. J.-C*. Paris: Editions Picard.

Martin, H. P. (1988) *Fara: A Reconstruction of the Ancient Mesopotamian City of Shuruppak*. Birmingham: Chris Martin and Associates.

Matthews, D. M. (1997) 'The Early Dynastic-Akkadian Transition, Part 1: When Did the Akkadian Period Begin?', *Iraq*, 59, pp. 1–7.

Matthews, R. J. (1993) *Cities, Seals and Writing: Archaic Seal Impressions from Jemdet Nasr and Ur*. Berlin: Gebr. Mann Verlag.

McMahon, A. (2006) *Nippur V. The Early Dynastic to Akkadian Transition: The Area WF Sounding at Nippur*. Chicago, IL: Oriental Institute of the University of Chicago.

Menegazzi, R. (2009) 'Seleucia al Tigri. Il saggio sul versante meridionale della piazza degli archivi (1972–1976)', *Mesopotamia*, XLIV, pp. 147–76.

Menegazzi, R. (2012) 'Creating a New Language: The Terracotta Figurines from Seleucia on the Tigris', in Matthews, R. and Curtis, J. *Proceedings of the 7th International Conference on the Archaeology of the Ancient Near East, 12–16 April 2010*, vol. 1. Wiesbaden: Harrassowitz Verlag, pp. 157–67.

Menegazzi, R. (2014) 'Seleucid, Parthian Mesopotamia, and Iran, Archaeology of', in Smith C. (ed.) *Encyclopedia of Global Archaeology*, New York, NY: Springer, pp. 6554–64.

Michalowski, P. (1989) *The Lamentation over the Destruction of Sumer and Ur*. Winona Lake, IN: Eisenbrauns.

Michalowski, P. (1993) *Letters from Early Mesopotamia*. Atlanta, GA: Scholars Press.

Michalowski, P. (2011) *The Correspondence of the Kings of Ur: An Epistolary History of an Ancient Mesopotamian Kingdom*. Winona Lake, IN: Eisenbrauns.

Miroschedji, P. de (1987) 'Fouilles du chantier Ville Royale II à Suse 1975–77: II. Niveaux d'époques achéménide, parthe et islamique', *Cahiers de la Délégation Archéologique Française en Iran*, 15, pp. 11–114.

Monerie, J. (2012) 'Les communautés grecques en Babylonie (VIIe–IIIe s. av. J.-C.)', *Pallas*, 89, pp. 345–65.

Moon, J. (1982) 'The Distribution of Upright-Handled Jars and Stemmed Dishes in the Early Dynastic Period', *Iraq*, 44, pp. 39–70.

Moon, J. (1987) *Abu Salabikh Excavations, vol. 3: Catalogue of Early Dynastic Pottery*. London: British School of Archaeology in Iraq.

Nigro, L. (2001–3) 'La stele di Rimush da Tello e l'indicazione del rango dei vinti nel rilievo reale accadico', *Scienze dell'antichità*, 11, pp. 71–93.

Nissen, H. J. (2015) 'Die ältere Frühdynastische Zeit als Forschungs-problem', in Dittmann, R. and Selz, G. J. (eds.) *It's a Long Way to a Historiography of the Early Dynastic Period(s)*. Münster: Ugarit-Verlag, pp. 1–31.

Oliver, G. (ed.) (2012) *The Oxford Companion to Beer*. Oxford; New York, NY: Oxford University Press.

Oppert, J. (1882) 'Les inscriptions de Gudéa', *Comptes rendus des scéances de l'Académie des Inscriptions et Belles-Lettres*, 26(1; 2), pp. 28–40; 123–6.

Otto, R. (1923 [1917]) *The Idea of the Holy*. Translated by John W. Harvey. London: Oxford University Press.

Parrot, A. (1948) *Tello: Vingt campagnes de fouilles (1877–1933)*. Paris: Editions Albin Michel.

Paulette, T. (2020) 'Archaeological Perspectives on Beer in Mesopo-tamia: Brewing Ingredients', in Borrelli, N. and Scazzosi, G. (eds.) *After the Harvest: Storage Practices and Food Processing in Bronze Age Mesopotamia*. Turnhout: Brepols, pp. 65–89.

Penglase, C. (1994) *Greek Myths and Mesopotamia: Parallels and Influence in the Homeric Hymns and Hesiod*. London; New York, NY: Routledge.

Perlov, B. (1980) 'The Families of the ensi's Urbau and Gudea and Their Funerary Cult', in Bendt, A. (ed.) *Death in Mesopotamia: Papers read at the XXVIe rencontre assyriologique internationale*. Copenhagen: Akademisk Forlag, pp. 77–81.

Pillet, M. (1958) 'Ernest de Sarzec, explorateur de Tello (1832–1901)', *Comptes rendus des scéances de l'Académie des Inscriptions et Belles-Lettres*, 102(1) pp. 52–66.

Plutarch (1919) *Lives, vol. VII: Demosthenes and Cicero. Alexander and Caesar*. Translated by Bernadotte Perrin. Cambridge, MA: Harvard University Press.

Pongratz-Leisten, B. (1988) 'Keramik der frühdynastischen Zeit aus den Grabungen in Uruk-Warka', *Baghdader Mitteilungen*, 19, pp. 177–319.

Rassam, H. (1897) *Asshur and the Land of Nimrod*. Cincinnati, OH: Curts and Jennings; New York, NY: Eaton and Mains.

Reade, J. (2002) 'Early Monuments in Gulf Stone at the British Museum, with Observations on some Gudea Statues and the Location of Agade', *Zeitschrift für Assyriologie und vorderasiatische Archäologie*, 92, pp. 258–95.

Ristvet, L. (2014) *Ritual, Performance, and Politics in the Ancient Near East*. Cambridge: Cambridge University Press.

Roaf, M. (2001) 'Doubts about the Two-Lobed Burial and the Survival of Early Dynastic to Akkadian Transitional Building Levels in Area WF at Nippur', *Iraq*, 63, pp. 55–66.

Robson, E. (2007) 'Mesopotamian Mathematics', in Katz, V. J. (ed.) *The Mathematics of Egypt, Mesopotamia, China, India and Islam: A Sourcebook*. Princeton, NJ: Princeton University Press, pp. 57–186.

Rochberg, F. (2007) 'Marduk in Heaven', *Wiener Zeitschrift für die Kunde des Morgenlandes*, 97, pp. 433–42.

Rogers, J. H. (1998) 'Origins of the Ancient Constellations: I. The Mestopotamian Traditions', *Journal of the British Astronomical Association*, 108(1), pp. 9–28.

Romano, L. (2008) 'La corona del dio. Nota sull'iconografia divina nel Protodinastico', *Vicino Oriente* XIV, pp. 41–57.

Romano, L. (2014) 'Urnanshe's Family and the Evolution of its Inside Relationships as shown by Images', in Marti, L. (ed.) *La famille dans le Proche-Orient ancient: réalités, symbolismes, et images. Proceedings of the 55th Rencontre Assyriologique Interna-tionale at Paris, 6–9 July 2009*. Winona Lake, IN: Eisenbrauns, pp. 183–92.

Rosengarten, Y. (1960) *Le concept sumérien de consommation dans la vie économique et religieuse: Étude linguistique et sociale d'après les textes présargoniques de Lagaš*. Paris: Editions de Boccard.

Sallaberger, W. (1993) *Der kultische Kalender der Ur III-Zeit*. Berlin; New York, NY: De Gruyter.

Sallaberger, W. (2018) 'Festival provisions in Early Bronze Age Meso-potamia', *Kaskal*, 15, pp. 171–200.

Sallaberger, W. and Schrakamp, I. (eds.) (2015) *Associated Regional Chronologies for the Ancient Near East and the Eastern Mediterra-nean, vol. 3: History and Philology*. Turnhout: Brepols.

Sallaberger, W. and Westenholz, A. (1999) *Mesopotamien: Akkade-Zeit und Ur III-Zeit*. Freiburg, CH: Universitätsverlag; Gottingen: Vandenhoeck und Ruprecht.

Sarzec, E. de and Heuzey, L. (*avec le concours de A. Amiaud et de F. Thureau-Dangin*) (1912 [1884–1912]) *Découvertes en Chaldée*, Paris: Ernest Leroux.

Sass, B. and Marzahn, J. (2010) *Aramaic and Figural Stamp Impres-sions on Bricks of the Sixth Century B.C. from Babylon*. Wiesbaden: Harrassowitz Verlag.

Schaudig, H. (2012) 'Death of Statues and Rebirth of Gods', in May, N. N. (ed.) *Iconoclasm and Text Destruction in the Ancient Near East and Beyond*. Chicago, IL: Oriental Institute of the University of Chicago, pp. 123–49.

Selz, G. J. (1990) 'Studies in Early Syncretism: The Development of the Pantheon in Lagaš; Examples for Inner-Sumerian Syncretism', *Acta Sumerologica*, 12, pp.111–42.

Selz, G. J. (1995) *Untersuchungen zur Götterwelt des altsumerischen Stadtstaates von Lagaš*. Philadelphia, PA: University of Pennsylvania Museum.

Selz, G. J. (1997) '"The Holy Drum, the Spear, and the Harp": Towards an Understanding of the Problems of Deification in Third Millennium Mesopotamia', in Finkel, I. L. and Geller, M. J. (eds.) *Sumerian Gods and their Representations*. Groningen: STYX Publications, pp. 167–209.

Selz, G. J. (with Daniela Niedermayer) (2015) 'The Burials After the Battle: Combining Textual and Visual Evidence', in Dittmann, R. and Selz, G. J. (eds.) *It's a Long Way to a Historiography of the Early Dynastic Period(s)*. Münster: Ugarit-Verlag, pp. 387–404.

Sherwin-White, S. (1987) 'Seleucid Babylonia: A Case Study for the Installation and Development of Greek Rule', in Kuhrt, A. and

Sherwin-White, S. (eds.) *Hellenism in the East: The Interaction of Greek and Non-Greek Civilizations from Syria to Central Asia after Alexander*. Berkeley and Los Angeles, CA: University of California Press, pp. 1–31.

Shipley, G. (2000) *The Greek World after Alexander: 323–30 BC*. London; New York, NY: Routledge.

Sigrist, M. (1992) *Drehem*. Bethesda, MD: CDL Press.

Sollberger, E. (1967) 'The Rulers of Lagaš', *Journal of Cuneiform Studies*, 21, pp. 279–291.

Sollberger, E. (1980) 'Ibbi-Suen', *Reallexikon der Assyriologie 5*, pp. 1–8.

Sommerfeld, W. (2006) 'Der Beginn des offiziellen Richteramtes im Alten Orient', in Hengstl, J. and Sick, U. (eds.) *Recht Gestern und Heute: Festschrift zum 85. Geburtstag von Richard Haase*. Wiesbaden: Harrassowitz Verlag, pp. 3–20.

Stark, J. K. (1971) *Personal Names in Palmyrene Inscriptions*. Oxford: Clarendon Press.

Steinkeller, P. (2002) 'Archaic City Seals and the Question of Early Babylonian Unity', in Abusch, T. (ed.) *Riches Hidden in Secret Places: Ancient Near Eastern Studies in Memory of Thorkild Jacobsen*. Winona Lake, IN: Eisenbrauns, pp. 249–58.

Steinkeller, P. (2003) 'An Ur III Manuscript of the Sumerian King List', in Sallaberger, W., Volk, K. and Zgoll, A. (eds.) *Literatur, Politik und Recht in Mesopotamien: Festschrift für Claus Wilcke*. Wiesbaden: Harrassowitz Verlag, pp. 267–92.

Steinkeller, P. (2017) *History, Texts and Art in Early Babylonia: Three Essays*. Berlin; Boston, MA: De Gruyter.

Stevens, K. (2016) 'Empire Begins at Home', in Lavan, M., Payne, R. E. and Weisweiler, J. (eds.) *Cosmopolitanism and Empire: Universal Rulers, Local Elites, and Cultural Integration in the Ancient Near East and Mediterranean*. New York, NY: Oxford University Press, pp. 65–88.

Stevens, K. (2019) *Between Greece and Babylonia: Hellenistic Intellectual History in Cross-Cultural Perspective*. Cambridge: Cambridge University Press.

Stoddart, W. (ed.) (2003) *The Essential Titus Burckhardt: Reflections on Sacred Art, Faiths, and Civilization*. Bloomington, IN: World Wisdom.

Such-Gutiérrez, M. (2005–6) 'Untersuchungen zum Pantheon von Adab im 3. Jt', *Archiv für Orientforschung*, 51, pp. 1–44.

Sürenhagen, D. (1999) *Untersuchungen zur Relativen Chronologie Babyloniens und Angrenzender Gebiete der Ausgehenden 'Ubaidzeit bis zum Beginn der Frühdynastisch-II-Zeit*. Heidelberg: Heidelberger Orientverlag.

Suter, C. E. (2000) *Gudea's Temple Building: The Representation of an Early Mesopotamian Ruler in Text and Image*. Groningen: STYX Publications.

Suter, C. E. (2012) 'Gudea of Lagash: Iconoclasm or Tooth of Time', in May, N. N. (ed.) *Iconoclasm and Text Destruction in the Ancient Near East and Beyond*. Chicago, IL: Oriental Institute of the University of Chicago, pp. 57–87.

Szarzyńska, K. (1992) 'Names of Temples in the Archaic Texts from Uruk, *Acta Sumerologica*, 14, pp. 269–85.

Szarzyńska, K. (1993) 'Offerings for the Goddess Inana in Archaic Uruk', *Revue d'assyriologie et d'archéologie orientale*, 87(1), pp. 7–28.

Taylor, J. (2021) 'Sîn-City: New Light from Old Excavations at Ur', in Frame, G., Jeffers, J. and Pittman, H. (eds.) *Ur in the*

Twenty-First Century CE: Proceedings of the 62nd Rencontre Assyriologique Internationale at Philadelphia, July 11–15, 2016*. University Park, PA: Penn State University Press, pp. 35–48.

Thalmann, J.-P. (2003) 'Le bâtiment B33', in Huot, J.-L. (ed.) *Larsa: Travaux de 1987 et 1989*. Beirut: Institut français d'archéologie du Proche-Orient, pp. 35–139.

Thomas, A. (2012) 'Restes textiles sur un clou de fondation de Gudea: Étude préliminaire', *Paléorient*, 38(1–2), pp. 149–57.

Thureau-Dangin, F. (1903) *Recueil de tablettes chaldéennes*. Paris: Ernest Leroux.

Thureau-Dangin, F. (1905) *Les cylindres de Goudéa: Transcription, traduction, commentaire, grammaire et lexique*. Paris: Ernest Leroux.

Thureau-Dangin, F. (1910) *Lettres et contrats de l'époque de la première dynastie babylonienne*. Paris: Paul Geuthner.

Tunca, Ö. (1984) *L'architecture religieuse protodynastique en Mésopotamie*. Leuven: Peeters.

Tünca Ö. (2004) 'A propos d'une figure de la plaque perforée d'Ur-Nanše (Urn. 20): fille/femme, fils ou devin?', *Nouvelles Assyriologiques Brèves et Utilitaires*, pp. 22–3.

Van Dijk, J. (1983) *Lugal ud me-lám-bi nir-gál: Le récit épique et didactique des Travaux de Ninurta, du Déluge et de la Nouvelle Création*. Leiden: Brill.

Van Dijk, R. M. (2013) 'Mesopotamian Early Dynastic Bull-Lyres', in *XIV Jornadas Interescuelas / Departamentos de Historia, 2 al 5 de octubre de 2013*. Mendoza: Universidad Nacional de Cuyo, pp. 1–18.

Van Dijk-Coombes, R. M. (2017) 'Lions and Winged Things: A Proposed Reconstruction of the Object on the Right of the Lower Register of the Mythological Side of Eannatum's Stele of the Vultures', *Die Welt des Orients*, 47(2), pp. 198–215.

Veldhuis, N. (2004) *Religion, Literature, and Scholarship: The Sumerian Composition 'Nanše and the Birds'. With a Catalogue of Sumerian Bird Names*. Leiden; Boston, MA: Brill.

Volk, K. (1992) 'Puzur-Mama und die Reise des Königs', *Zeitschrift für Assyriologie und Vorderasiatische Archäologie*, 82, pp. 22–9.

West, M. L. (1997) *The East Face of Helicon: West Asiatic Elements in Greek Poetry and Myth*. Oxford: Clarendon Press.

Westenholz, A. (2002) 'The Sumerian City-State', in Hansen, M. H. (ed.) *A Comparative Study of Six City-State Cultures*. Copenhagen: C. A. Reitzels Forlag, pp. 23–42.

Westenholz, J. G. (2012) '*Damnatio memoriae*: The Old Akkadian Evidence for Destruction of Name and Destruction of Person', in May N. N. (ed.) *Iconoclasm and Text Destruction in the Ancient Near East and Beyond*. Chicago, IL: Oriental Institute of the University of Chicago, pp. 89–122.

Wilcke, C. (1995) 'Die Inschrift der "Figure aux Plumes": ein frühes Werk sumerischer Dichtkunst', in Finkbeiner, U., Dittmann, R. and Hauptmann, H. (eds.) *Beiträge zur Kulturgeschichte Vorderasiens: Festschrift für Rainer Michael Boehmer*, Mainz: Verlag Philipp von Zabern, pp. 669–74.

Wilcke, C. (2011) 'Eine Weihinschrift Gudeas von Lagaš mit altbabylonischer Übersetzung', in George, A. R. (ed.) *Cuneiform Royal Inscriptions and Related Texts in the Schøyen Collection*. Bethesda, MD: CDL Press, pp. 29–48.

Wilson, K. (2012) *Bismaya: Recovering the Lost City of Adab*. Chicago, IL: Oriental Institute of the University of Chicago.

Winter, I. J. (1985) 'After the Battle is Over: The *Stele of the Vultures* and the Beginning of Historical Narrative in the Art of the Ancient Near East', in Kessler, H. L. and Simpson, M. S. (eds.) *Pictorial Narrative in Antiquity and the Middle Ages.* Washington, DC: National Gallery of Art, pp. 11–32.

Winter, I. J. (1989) 'The Body of the Able Ruler: Toward an Understanding of the Statues of Gudea', in Behrens, H. et al. (eds.) *Dumu-É-dub-ba-a: Studies in Honor of Åke W. Sjöberg.* Philadelphia, PA: The University Museum, pp. 573–83.

Winter I. J. (1992) 'Idols of the King: Royal Images as Recipients of Ritual Action in Ancient Mesopotamia, *Journal of Ritual Studies,* 6(1), pp. 13–42.

Winter, I. J. (2000) 'Opening the Eyes and Opening the Mouth: The Utility of Comparing Images in Worship in India and the Ancient Near East', in Meister, M. W. (ed.) *Ethnography and Personhood: Notes from the Field.* Jaipur; New Delhi: Rawat Publications, pp. 129–62.

Wittfogel, K. (1957) *Oriental Despotism: A Comparative Study of Total Power.* New Haven, CT; London: Yale University Press.

Woolley, C. L. (1939) *Ur Excavations V: The Ziggurat and its Surroundings.* Oxford: Oxford University Press.

Zettler, R. L. (1989) 'Pottery Profiles Reconstructed from Jar Sealings in the Lower Seal Impression Strata (SIS 8-4) at Ur: New Evidence for Dating', in Leonard, A. and Williams, B. B. (eds.) *Essays on Ancient Civilization Presented to Helen J. Kantor.* Chicago, IL: Oriental Institute of the University of Chicago, pp. 369–93.

Zólyomi, G. (2014) *Copular Clauses and Focus Marking in Sumerian.* Warsaw; Berlin: De Gruyter Open.

ILLUSTRATION CREDITS

Fig. 1 — Photo © Trustees of the British Museum.

Fig. 2 — Map drawn by Sébastien Rey © The Girsu Project.

Fig. 3 — Photo by Dani Tagen © The Girsu Project.

Fig. 4 — Digital model by Sandra Grabowski © The Girsu Project and artefacts-berlin.de.

Fig. 5 — Illustration by Simone Rotella © The Girsu Project.

Fig. 6 — Photo © RMN-Grand Palais (Musée du Louvre) / Raphaël Chipault and Benjamin Soligny.

Fig. 7 — Photo © RMN-Grand Palais (Musée du Louvre) / Mathieu Rabeau.

Fig. 8 — Photo © RMN-Grand Palais (Musée du Louvre) / Raphaël Chipault.

Fig. 9 — Photo © RMN-Grand Palais (Musée du Louvre) / Raphaël Chipault and Benjamin Soligny.

Fig. 10 — Reproduced from Sarzec and Heuzey 1912, Pl. 18.

Fig. 11 — Digital model by Sandra Grabowski © The Girsu Project and artefacts-berlin.de.

Fig. 12 — Photo by Sébastien Rey © The Girsu Project.

Figs. 13 and 14 — Photos by Dani Tagen © The Girsu Project.

Fig. 15 — Plan digitised by Elisa Girotto and Sébastien Rey © The Girsu Project.

Fig. 16 — Plan by Sébastien Rey © The Girsu Project.

Figs. 17 and 18 — Photos by Dani Tagen from Sarzec and Heuzey 1912, Pl. 63 (2).

Fig. 19 — Reproduced from Sarzec and Heuzey 1912, Pl. 9.

Figs. 20 and 21 — Photos © Trustees of the British Museum.

Fig. 22 — Photo © RMN-Grand Palais (Musée du Louvre) / Philippe Fuzeau.

Fig. 23 — Photo © RMN-Grand Palais (Musée du Louvre) / Thierry Ollivier.

Fig. 24 — Photo by Dani Tagen from Cros's unpublished album © The Girsu Project.

Fig. 25 — Photo by Dani Tagen from Genouillac 1934, Pl. 1 (2).

Fig. 26 — Photo by Dani Tagen © The Girsu Project.

Figs. 27 and 28 — Illustrations by Faith Vardy © The Girsu Project.

Fig. 29 — Photo © RMN-Grand Palais (Musée du Louvre) / Franck Raux.

Figs. 30–2 — Illustrations by Angelo Di Michele, based on Genouillac 1934, Pls. II–XIII © The Girsu Project.

Figs. 33 and 34 — Photos by Dani Tagen from Sarzec and Heuzey 1912.

Figs. 35–8 — Photos by Dani Tagen from Cros 1910.

Figs. 39–52 — Photos by Dani Tagen from Sarzec and Heuzey 1912, with coloured overlays by Dani Tagen and annotations by Sébastien Rey.

Fig. 53 — Diagram by Paul Williamson, digitised by Sébastien Rey © The Girsu Project.

Fig. 54 — Photo by Dani Tagen from Sarzec and Heuzey 1912, with coloured overlays by Dani Tagen and annotations by Sébastien Rey.

Figs. 55 and 56 — Photos by Dani Tagen from Cros 1910, with coloured overlays by Dani Tagen and annotations by Sébastien Rey.

Figs. 57 and 58 — Photos by Dani Tagen from Genouillac 1934, with coloured overlays by Dani Tagen and annotations by Sébastien Rey.

Figs. 59–61 — Plans and table prepared by Sébastien Rey © The Girsu Project.

Fig. 62 — Photo © RMN-Grand Palais (Musée du Louvre) / Thierry Ollivier.

Fig. 63 — Photo © RMN-Grand Palais (Musée du Louvre) / Mathieu Rabeau.

Illustration Credits

Figs. 64 and 65 — Photos by Dani Tagen © The Girsu Project.

Figs. 66 and 67 — Digital models by Sandra Grabowski © The Girsu Project and artefacts-berlin.de.

Figs. 68 and 69 — Photos by Dani Tagen © The Girsu Project.

Fig. 70 — Digital model by Sandra Grabowski © The Girsu Project and artefacts-berlin.de.

Fig. 71 — Illustration by Elisa Girotto © The Girsu Project.

Fig. 72 — Digital model by Sandra Grabowski © The Girsu Project and artefacts-berlin.de.

Figs. 73 and 74 — Illustrations by Elisa Girotto © The Girsu Project.

Figs. 75–7 — Reconstructions by Elisa Girotto © The Girsu Project.

Figs. 78 and 79 — Illustrations by Elisa Girotto © The Girsu Project.

Fig. 80 — Photo © Trustees of the British Museum.

Fig. 81 — Diagrams by Paul Williamson, digitised by Sébastien Rey © The Girsu Project.

Fig. 82 — Digitised by Elisa Girotto from Labat and Malbran-Labat 1995, p. 148 © The Girsu Project.

Fig. 83 — Illustrations by Sébastien Rey © The Girsu Project.

Figs. 84 and 85 — Digital models by Sandra Grabowski © The Girsu Project and artefacts-berlin.de.

Fig. 86 — Photos by Dani Tagen © The Girsu Project.

Fig. 87 — Photo © RMN-Grand Palais (Musée du Louvre) / Franck Raux.

Fig. 88 — Digital models by Sandra Grabowski © The Girsu Project and artefacts-berlin.de.

Fig. 89 — Illustrations by Faith Vardy © The Girsu Project.

Fig. 90 — Digital model by Sandra Grabowski © The Girsu Project and artefacts-berlin.de.

Fig. 91 — Photo by Dani Tagen © The Girsu Project.

Figs. 92–4 — Reconstructions by Elisa Girotto © The Girsu Project.

Figs. 95 and 96 — Digital models by Sandra Grabowski © The Girsu Project and artefacts-berlin.de.

Fig. 97 — Photo © RMN-Grand Palais (Musée du Louvre) / Philippe Fuzeau.

Figs. 98–100 — Digital models by Sandra Grabowski © The Girsu Project and artefacts-berlin.de.

Fig. 101 — Reconstruction by Faith Vardy © The Girsu Project.

Fig. 102 — Photo © Trustees of the British Museum.

Fig. 103 — Illustration by Faith Vardy © The Girsu Project.

Fig. 104 — Photo © RMN-Grand Palais (Musée du Louvre) / Raphaël Chipault.

Fig. 105 — Photo by Dani Tagen © The Girsu Project.

Fig. 106 — Photo © RMN-Grand Palais (Musée du Louvre) / Thierry Ollivier.

Fig. 107 — Reconstructions by Elisa Girotto © The Girsu Project.

Fig. 108 — Illustrations by Faith Vardy © The Girsu Project.

Figs. 109 and 110 — Illustrations by Faith Vardy © The Girsu Project.

Fig. 111 — Photo by Dani Tagen from Sarzec and Heuzey 1912.

Fig. 112 — Photo © RMN-Grand Palais (Musée du Louvre) / Philippe Fuzeau.

Fig. 113 — Photo by Dani Tagen from Cros 1910.

Fig. 114 — Photo by Dani Tagen from Sarzec and Heuzey 1912.

Fig. 115 — Photo by Dani Tagen from Genouillac 1936.

Figs. 116–28 — Photos by Dani Tagen from Sarzec and Heuzey 1912, with coloured overlays by Dani Tagen and annotations by Sébastien Rey.

Figs. 129 and 130 — Photos by Dani Tagen from Cros's unpublished album © The Girsu Project.

Figs. 131 and 132 — Photos by Dani Tagen from Cros 1910, with coloured overlays by Dani Tagen and annotations by Sébastien Rey.

Figs. 133–5 — Photos by Dani Tagen from Genouillac 1936, with coloured overlays by Dani Tagen and annotations by Sébastien Rey.

Fig. 136 — Superimposition by Sébastien Rey © The Girsu Project.

Fig. 137 — Photo by Sébastien Rey © The Girsu Project.

Fig. 138 — Plan drawn by Sébastien Rey and Dita Auzina © The Girsu Project.

Fig. 139 — Plan digitised by Elisa Girotto and Sébastien Rey © The Girsu Project.

Fig. 140 — Photo by Sébastien Rey © The Girsu Project.

Fig. 141 — Photo by Dani Tagen © The Girsu Project.

Fig. 142 — Illustrations by Elisa Girotto © The Girsu Project.

Fig. 143 — Photo by Sébastien Rey © The Girsu Project.

Figs. 144–6 — Photos by Dani Tagen © The Girsu Project.

Fig. 147 — Plan compiled by Elisa Girotto and Sébastien Rey © The Girsu Project.

Fig. 148 — Photo by Dani Tagen © The Girsu Project.

Illustration Credits

Fig. 149 — Sections drawn by Luke Jarvis and Elisa Girotto © The Girsu Project.

Figs. 150–3 — Photos by Dani Tagen © The Girsu Project.

Figs. 154–64 — Illustrations by Angelo Di Michele © The Girsu Project.

Fig. 165 — Photo © RMN-Grand Palais (Musée du Louvre) / Philippe Fuzeau.

Fig. 166 — Photo by Dani Tagen © The Girsu Project.

Fig. 167 — Plan by Sébastien Rey © The Girsu Project.

Fig. 168 — Reproduced from Sarzec and Heuzey 1912, Pl. 7.

Fig. 169 — Photo © RMN-Grand Palais (Musée du Louvre) / Raphaël Chipault and Benjamin Soligny.

Figs. 170–2 — Digital models by Sandra Grabowski © The Girsu Project and artefacts-berlin.de.

Fig. 173 — Photo by Dani Tagen © The Girsu Project.

Figs. 174 and 175 — Sections drawn by Andrew Ginns and Elisa Girotto © The Girsu Project.

Fig. 176 — Illustrations by Faith Vardy © The Girsu Project and the British Museum.

Figs. 177 and 178 — Illustrations by Simone Rotella © The Girsu Project.

Fig. 179 — Photo by Eleanor Atkins © The Girsu Project.

Figs. 180 and 181 — Photos by Dani Tagen © The Girsu Project.

Fig. 182 — Section drawn by Andrew Ginns, Ashley Pooley and Elisa Girotto © The Girsu Project.

Fig. 183 — Section drawn by Andrew Ginns and Elisa Girotto © The Girsu Project.

Figs. 184 and 185 — Digital models by Sandra Grabowski © The Girsu Project and artefacts-berlin.de.

Fig. 186 — Illustration by Simone Rotella © The Girsu Project.

Fig. 187 — Section drawn by Andrew Ginns and Elisa Girotto © The Girsu Project.

Figs. 188 and 189 — Photos by Dani Tagen © The Girsu Project.

Figs. 190–2 — Reconstructions by Elisa Girotto © The Girsu Project.

Fig. 193 — Illustrations by Faith Vardy © The Girsu Project.

Fig. 194 — Table compiled by Sébastien Rey © The Girsu Project.

Figs. 195 and 196 — Sections drawn by Andrew Ginns and Elisa Girotto © The Girsu Project.

Figs. 197 and 198 — Photos by Dani Tagen © The Girsu Project.

Figs. 199–206 — Illustrations by Angelo Di Michele © The Girsu Project.

Figs. 207 and 208 — Illustrations by Faith Vardy © The Girsu Project.

Figs. 209 and 210 — Illustrations by Elisa Girotto © The Girsu Project.

Figs. 211 and 212 — Reproduced from Sarzec and Heuzey 1912, Pls. 14 and 15.

Fig. 213 — Superimposition by Sébastien Rey © The Girsu Project.

Fig. 214 — Illustration by Elisa Girotto © The Girsu Project.

Fig. 215 — Extrapolation by Lleonard Rubio y Degrassi © The Girsu Project.

Fig. 216 — Overlay and labels by Sébastien Rey © The Girsu Project.

Fig. 217 — Diagrams by Lleonard Rubio y Degrassi, digitised by Sébastien Rey © The Girsu Project.

Figs. 218 and 219 — Diagrams by Paul Williamson, digitised by Sébastien Rey, based on the software generously made available by Dr Andrew J. Marsh (andrewmarsh.com/apps/releases/sunpath2d.html © 2014) © The Girsu Project.

Figs. 220–7 — Reconstructions by Elisa Girotto © The Girsu Project.

Fig. 228 — Illustrations by Faith Vardy © The Girsu Project.

Fig. 229 — Lego models by Paul Williamson; photos by Artshots, London © The Girsu Project.

Fig. 230 — Photo by Dani Tagen © The Girsu Project.

Fig. 231 — Illustrations by Faith Vardy © The Girsu Project.

Fig. 232 — Photos by Dani Tagen © The Girsu Project.

Fig. 233 — Typology by Angelo Di Michele © The Girsu Project.

Figs. 234–6 — Photos by Dani Tagen © The Girsu Project.

Fig. 237 — Illustrations by Julia Jarrett and Faith Vardy © The Girsu Project.

Fig. 238 — Photo by Dani Tagen © The Girsu Project.

Fig. 239 — Photo by Eleanor Atkins © The Girsu Project.

Figs. 240 and 241 — Digital models by Sandra Grabowski © The Girsu Project and artefacts-berlin.de.

Fig. 242 — Plan drawn by Ashley Pooley and Elisa Girotto © The Girsu Project.

Fig. 243 — Photo by Dani Tagen © The Girsu Project.

Figs. 244–6 — Sections drawn by Ashley Pooley and Elisa Girotto © The Girsu Project.

Fig. 247 — Illustrations by Faith Vardy © The Girsu Project.

Figs. 248–53 — Illustrations by Angelo Di Michele © The Girsu Project.

768   *Illustration Credits*

Fig. 254	Photo by Dani Tagen © The Girsu Project.
Figs. 255–9	Illustrations by Faith Vardy © The Girsu Project.
Figs. 260–3	Photos by Dani Tagen © The Girsu Project.
Figs. 264–6	Digital models by Sandra Grabowski © The Girsu Project and artefacts-berlin.de.
Fig. 267	Reconstruction by Faith Vardy © The Girsu Project.
Fig. 268	Photo by Dani Tagen © The Girsu Project.
Fig. 269	Photo by Eleanor Atkins © The Girsu Project.
Fig. 270	Photo by Dani Tagen © The Girsu Project.
Fig. 271	Photo © RMN-Grand Palais (Musée du Louvre) / Mathieu Rabeau.
Figs. 272 and 273	Photos by Dani Tagen © The Girsu Project.
Fig. 274	Reconstructions by Faith Vardy © The Girsu Project.
Fig. 275	Photo by Dani Tagen © The Girsu Project.
Fig. 276	Reconstruction by Faith Vardy © The Girsu Project.

INDEX

Page references in *italics* indicate an illustration; page references in **bold** indicate a table.

Adab (Sumerian city), 7, 88, 150, 299, 308, 577
Adad (Babylonian god), 20, 673, 741
Adadnadinakhe (builder of the Hellenistic Eninnu)
　Adadnadinakhe's temple building, 678–86, 687–701, 724–43
　bricks stamped in the name of, 20, 23, 331, 333, 339, 686, 673, 674, 692, 713
　enigma of, 673–5
　meaning of the name, 740–1
Akkad (historical period)
　chronology of, 42–5
　Tell A in the, 419, 429, 435–43
　Tell K in the, 307–17
Akkad Stele, 57, 310–17, *311*, *312*, 460
Akshak (Mesopotamian city), 7, 154
Akurgal (ruler of Lagash I)
　Akurgal's temple building in the Gu'edena, 237
　chronology of, 46–7, **46**
　on the plaques of Ur-Nanshe, *36*, *152*, 229, 230–6, *231*, 276–9
Alexander the Great (Alexander III, king of Macedon)
　affiliation with Heracles, 728, 738–41, 745
　conquest of Babylon, 657–6
　divine origins of, 738–9, 741
　krater depicting, 705, 728, 729
　reign of, 675–6, 725–6
　silver drachm (coin) of, 700, 728, *730*, 733, 738, *740*, 741, 742
Amar-Sin (king of Ur III), 507, 511
An (Sumerian god), 6, 10, 655, 656, 657, 677, 678
Antiochus I Soter (Seleucid king), 328, 676, 677, 727, 729, 742, 743, 746

Antiochus II Theos (Seleucid king), 677, 727, 742, 744, 745, 746
Antiochus III (Seleucid king), 398, 676, 677, 745, 746
Anu-uballit Kephalon (governor of Uruk), 745, 746, 747
Anu-uballit Nikarkhos (governor of Uruk), 745, 746, 747
Anzu. *See* Thunderbird
Aphrodite (Greek goddess), 720, 734, 735, 738, 745, 749
Apollo (Greek god), 699, 720, 729, 730, 733, 736, 737, 743, 745
Arad-Nanna (governor of Lagash), 507, 511, 567, 568
Aramaic inscriptions, 396, 712–15, *713*
Area of the Gudea Steles (Girsu)
　Cros's excavations of the, 326, 335–8, 374–6, *374*, 380, 386, 387, 476, 505
　plan of the (Plan H), 349–51, *349*
Area R (Area of the Red Bricks, Girsu), 26, 30, 450
Area S (Area of the Three Boxes, Girsu), 26, 30, 450, 662, 663
Area T (Area of the Graves, Girsu), 26, 30, 450
Athena (Greek goddess), 64, 738, 739

Babylon (Mesopotamian and Hellenistic-era city), 6, 7, 19, 44–5, 513–15, 581, 675–8, 681–2, 685, 700, 704–5, 715, 724–6, 728, 730–1, *730*, 735, 738–42, 745–6, 748, 750–1
Badtibira (Sumerian city), 154, 259, 451, **453**
Barakisumun (legate of Enanatum I), 176, 242
Bau (Sumerian goddess, wife of Ningirsu)
　dedicatory inscriptions to, 210, 444–7, *446*
　fragmentary relief depicting, *445*
　guardian of the city walls, 735

role of, 5, 16–17, 444–7
stele devoted to Gatumdug and, 620–3, 622
stele devoted to Ningirsu and, 618–20, *621*
syncretised with Gatumdug, 146, 155, 415, 557, 581, 634, 734
temple of, 23, 25, 38, 151, 274, 286–7, 293, 444–57, *450*, **452**, **454**, **456**, 458–61, 464–5, 471–8, 494, 603
bronze coin of Antiochus III, 398, *746*

Carved Basin of Gudea, 328–30, *330*, 345, 346, 348, 730
Circular Bas-Relief, *62*, *63*, 147, *149*, 150, 162, 185–92, *186*, 207, 208, 210, 217, 250
City Seal Impressions, 146–7
clay nails (inscribed cones)
　belonging to Gudea, 413–15, *414*, 643–57
　belonging to Shulgi, 395, 396, 398, *414*, 415
　belonging to Ur-Bau, 395, 396, 398, 400, 403, *414*, 415, 463, 524, 529, 696, 700, 729
　meaning of, 654–7
　typology of, 651–4, *653*
Colossal Spear Head, 61, *62*, 209–10, 229
cones (inscribed). *See* clay nails
Copper Blade with Lions, *62*, *63*, 209–10
Copper Heads of Bulls, 59, 61, 279–81, *280*, 284
Copper Ring Post (associated with the Ur-Nanshe Building), 61, 115–16, *115*, 171–2, 229, 279, 283–4
Cros (Gaston Cros, second director of the French excavations in Girsu)
　excavations in the area of the Gudea Steles, 335–8
　excavations on Tell A, 334–41
　excavations on Tell K, 71–9
　role of, 36–9
cylinder seals, *155*, *167*, *188*, *249*, 313, 314, 333, 334, 395, *397*, 398, 399, 400, 404, 411, *503*, *508*, *533*, 699, 729, 731

769

770 Index

Cylinders of Gudea, 3, 7, 16, *17*, 32, 34, 162,
   195, *197*, *199*, 317, 319–21, 325, 473, 502

Demeter (Greek goddess), 735, 738, 745
door sockets
   belonging to Arad-Nanna, 511, 567
   belonging to Enanatum II, 70, 290, 291
   belonging to Enmetena, 60, 68, 260, 261,
      269, 293, 297, 298
   belonging to Gudea, 32, 56, 143, 317, 329,
      333, 400, *481*, *482*, *484*, *485*, 522, 526, 730
   belonging to Nammahni, 505
   belonging to Ur-Nanshe, 58, *59*, *218*, 222,
      226, 227, 228, 279, 284
   belonging to Urukagina, 292
Dudu (high priest of Ningirsu)
   Plaque of, 293, 294, 296–7, 298
   role of, 67, 262, 448
Dumuziabzu (Sumerian god), 258, 395, 399,
   456, 459, 463, 507, 553, 572, 696

Eanatum (ruler of Lagash I)
   chronology of, 46–7, **46**
   Eanatum's temple building, 237–40, **452–3**
   stele of (Stele of the Vultures), 35, 58, 70,
      175–6, 179, 185, 188, 208, 221, 225, 229,
      233, 237–8, 240, 241, 242, 243–58, 244,
      245, 247, 252, 253, 275–6, 285, 291, 295,
      301, 302–5, 306, 310, 314, 333, 413, 445,
      446, 548, 550, 552, 565, 615, 616, 661
   Stone Monument of, 58, *59*, 276, 305–6
Early Dynastic I (historical period)
   chronology of, 42–3, 45
   Tell A in, 416–22, 426–9
   Tell K in, 10–16, 53–5, 61–5, 71–5, 80–90,
      91, 94–7, 102–4, 113–14, 135–44, 145–51,
      157–73, 174–92, 203–11
Enanatum I (ruler of Lagash I)
   chronology of, 46–7, **46**
   Enanatum I's temple building, 240–2,
      452–3
   Mortar of, 58, *59*, 242, 276, 305
Enanatum II (ruler of Lagash I)
   chronology of, 46–7, **46**
   Enanatum II's temple building, 290–1,
      454
   inscribed door sockets of, 70, 290, 291
   Plaque of, *47*
Enentarzi (ruler of Lagash I), 46–7, **46**, 151,
   291, 448, 515
Enki (Sumerian god), 6, 8, 9, 10, 15, 88, 155,
   173, 196, 199, 255, 258, 261, 268, 301, 303,
   453, **456**, 459, 463, 503, 511, 512, 553, 570,
   571, 572, 573, 612, 616, *617*, *618*, 655, 656,
   657, 667, 668, 669, 724
Enlil (Sumerian god), 6, 8, 10, 14, 16, 146, 150,
   151, 155, 180, 188, 199, 216, 238, 248, 255,

258, 259, 262, 268, 292, 293, 294, 301, 303,
   305, 318, 329, 335, **453**, **455**, 456, 463, 503,
   505, 509, 512, 516, 517, 518, 534, 555, 571,
   572, 574, 576, 577, 598, 611, 612, 614, 631,
   633, 634, 635, 648, **650**, 657, 724, 732
Enmetena (ruler of Lagash I)
   chronology of, 46–7, **46**
   Enmetena's temple building, 228–9, 259–
      76, **452–3**
   foundation pegs of, *59*, 267, *268*, 269
   inscribed door sockets of, 60, 68, 260, 261,
      269, 293, 297, 298
   silver Vase of, 35, *37*, 67, 262, 293–6, 298
   statue of, 259, 458, 551
Eridu (Sumerian city), 5–7, *7*, 155, 268, 299,
   301, 514, 577

Feathered Figure (archaic stone plaque), *12*,
   14, 61, *62*, 147–8, 164, 174–81, 183–4, 195,
   199, 201–2, 217, 279–80, 284–6, 296
First brick (ritual of the), 3, 5, 196, 216, 232,
   337, 474, 570, 573, 579, 595, 617, 630, 631,
   632, 633, 637, 654, 660, 661, 662
First Dynasty of Lagash. *See* Lagash I
foundation boxes, 40, 56, 70, 76, 94, 96, 98,
   99, 101, 118, *119*, 121, 171, 308, 317, 326, 337,
   341–2, 349, 350, 356, 375, *376–7*, 387, 388,
   499, *500*, 501, 530, 633, 635, 642, 660,
   662–5, 667, 669, 689, 690–2
foundation pegs
   from the Early Dynastic I period, *62*, 160–
      2, *160*, *161*, 168–9
   from the Early Dynastic III period, *59*, 153,
      215–18, *216*, 267–9, *268*, 665, 667
   from the Lagash II period, *21*, 462–3, *462*,
      658–69, *661*, 666
   from the Ur III period, 662–3, 666

Gatumdug (Sumerian goddess), 146, 150,
   155, 196, 212, 217, 218, 268, 301, 331, 395,
   396, 398, 399, 400, 413, 415, **452**, 467,
   468, 469, 517, 554, 555, 557, 565, 571, 572,
   581, 611, 620, 622, 623, 634, 696, 734, 735,
   745, 748, 749. *See also* Bau
Genouillac (Henri de Genouillac, third
   director of the French excavations in
   Girsu)
   excavations on Tell A, 341–2
   excavations on Tell K, 40, 80–1, *132*
   role of, 39–41
Geshtinanna (Sumerian goddess), **456**, 459,
   460, 553
Gilgamesh (Sumerian hero), 31, 88, 145, 238,
   468, 517
Girsu (Sumerian city)
   abandonment of, 25, 146, 532–4, 726
   contextualised chronology of, 42–5

emergence of, 146–51
   Girsu–Lagash alliance, 147, 150, 152, 155,
      217
   periodisation for the archaeology of, 45–6
   rediscovery of, 7, 28–41
   significance of, 3–23, 145–6, 502–18,
      738–43
Girsu Land Stele, *62*, 63, 147, 148, 150, 181–4,
   182, 185, 192, 207, 208, 210, 217
Gisha. *See* Umma
Gudea (ruler of Lagash II)
   carved basin of, 328–30, 345, 346, 348, 730
   chronology of, 47–9, **48**, **49**
   clay nails of, 413–15, *414*, 643–57
   cylinder seal of, *503*
   Cylinders of, 3, 7, 16, *17*, 32, 34, 162, 195, *197*,
      199, 317, 319–21, 325, 473, 502
   deification and posthumous influence of,
      506–9, *508*
   dream of, 3–5, 12, 18, 195, 197, 471, 502, 564,
      570, 572–4, 578, 579, 612, 618, 630, 631,
      745. *See also* Gudea, Cylinders of
   foundation pegs of, *21*, 376–7, 658–69, *661*,
      666
   Gudea's temple building (the New
      Eninnu), 16–19, 467–501, 519–34. *See
      also* Tell A (Gudea's New Eninnu)
   inscribed door sockets of, 32, 56, 143, 317,
      329, 333, 400, *481*, *482*, *484*, *485*, 522, 526,
      730
   paradox of, 467–71
   Pillar of, 57, 76, 99, 101, 102–5, 107, 118–21,
      123–9, *124*, *125*, *126*, *128*, 198, 214, 219–20,
      230, 239, 242, 310, 317–21, 495, 582
   Standard Inscription of, 328, 394, 633, 634,
      635, *649*, 652
   statues of, 4, 5, 16, 17, *18*, 20, 21, 23, 25, 29, 31,
      32, 33, 34, 38, 39, 319, 320, 547–69, *549*,
      560, *561*, 570–80, *571*, 581–90. *See also*
      Gudea Statues
   steles of, *336*, 608–29, **613**, *617*, *619*, *621*,
      622, *624*, *625*, *627*, *628*. *See also* Gudea
      Steles
Gudea Statues
   condition of, 559–69, *560*, *561*
   origins and meaning of, 547–59, *549*
   ritual pits for the burial of, 537, 546
Gudea Statue A, *549*, 553, 554, 556, 557, *560*,
   565, 566, 727, 734, 748, 749
Gudea Statue B (Architect with a Plan)
   incised temenos plan on, 572–80, *573*
   metrology of, 581–90, *586*, *589*
   significance of, 16–18, *18*, 570–2, *571*
Gudea Statue C, *549*, 554, 557, *560*, 562, 565,
   611, 734, 748, 749
Gudea Statue D (Gudea Colossus), 29, *31*,
   32, *33*, 325, 329, 446, *549*, 553, 554, 555,

556, 557, 559, *560*, *561*, 564, 565, 566, 567, 602, 673, *681*, 725, 749

Gudea Statue E, 473, 549, 555, *560*, 563, 565, 634, 748, 749

Gudea Statue F, 549, 553, 554, 555, 556, 557, 558, *560*, 563, 565, 573, 574, 581, 584, 634, 734, 735, 748, 749

Gudea Statue G, 553, 555, 557, *560*, *561*, 564, 565, 566, 567, 733, 748, 749

Gudea Statue H, *560*, 565, 600, 601, 748, 749

Gudea Statue I, 563, 564, 567, 568, 569

Gudea Statue K, 331, 553, 555, 556, 558, *561*, 563, 564, 565, 566, 749

Gudea Statue R, 507, 555

Gudea Statue W, 331, 749

Gudea Steles
  fragments found by Cros, *336*
  installation and associations with the Slain Heroes, 611–15, **613**
  the music stele, 626–9, *628*
  reconstructed, 608–29
  the relief of abundance, 623–6, *625*
  with the seven-headed mace, 620, *621*
  stele devoted to Bau and Gatumdug, 620–3, *622*
  stele devoted to Enki, 616–18, *617*
  stele devoted to Ningirsu and Bau, 618–20, *621*
  the sunrise relief, 623, *624*
  two-sided stele, 626, *627*

Hammurabi (king of Babylon I), 45, 292, 513, 514–15

Hellenistic (historical period)
  historical context, 675–8
  Tell A in the, 673–5, 678–86, 687–723, 724–43, 744–51

Heracles (Greek god)
  bronze statue of, *728*, 733, 750
  Hellenistic Temple of Ningirsu and, 673–5, 678–86, 687–701, 724–43
  role of, 733, 738–9
  silver drachm of Alexander the Great depicting, 700, *728*, *730*, 733, 738, *740*, 741, 742
  syncretised with Ningirsu, 604, 729, 733, 738, 739, *740*, 741, 744, 745, 750

Heuzey (Léon Heuzey, curator at the Louvre Museum), 5, 34, 38, 39, 41, 53–5, 325–7

Hexapolis (the Kiengir League), 150, 151, 153, 154, 192, 217

House of the Fruits (Ur-Nanshe Building). *See* Tell K (Ur-Nanshe Building)

Hymn to the Reeds, *15*, 173, 261

Hyspaosines (Seleucid governor and king of Characene), 674, 675, 676–7, 751

Ibbi-Sin (king of Ur III), 511, 512, 513

Igalim (Sumerian god), 293, 387, 388, 395, 396, 415, **454**, 465, 519, 555, 571, 572, 577, 652, 663, 724, 729, 748

Imdugud. *See* Thunderbird

Inanna (Sumerian goddess), 6, 43, 88, 145–6, 151, 155, 166, *167*, 238, 241, 254, 255, 258, 259, 267, 301, 331, **452**, **453**, 459, 463, 469, 506, 509, 553, 554, 557, 565, 572, 577, 618, 626, 677, 696, 699, 731, 734, 735, 748, 749

Ishme-Dagan (king of Isin), 513–14, 517

Isin (Sumerian city), 7, 151, 308, 513, 514, 516, 517

Isin-Larsa (historical period)
  chronology of, 42–6
  Tell A in, 512–14, 519–46

Kiengir League. *See* Hexapolis

Kish (Mesopotamian city), 12, 61, 150, 151, 153, 154, 176, 191, 192, 209, 210, 212, 217, 237, 238, 249, 255, 258, 259, 285, 302, 308

Lagash (Sumerian city and city-state)
  city of, 5, 7, 22, 299, 300, 464
  city-state of, 5, 6, 7, 14, 21, 22, 146, 147, 150, 153, 154, 156, 162, 180, 183, 212, 237, 238, 243, 259, 295, 298, 299, 300, 309, 316, 449, 451, 460, 464, 472, 473, 504, 513, 518
  Lamentation over the Destruction of, 38–9, 220, 299–302, *300*
  union of Lagash and Girsu. *See* Girsu, Girsu–Lagash alliance

Lagash I (historical period including Early Dynastic IIIb, Presargonic era)
  chronology of the rulers of, 46–7
  Tell A in, 416–19, 422–6, 426–8, 429–35, 436–43, 444–57
  Tell K in, 10–16, 53–5, 56–61, 65–70, 71–9, 80–90, 91–106, 107–23, 129–34, 135–44, 151–6, 203–11, 212–30, 237–42, 259–76, 283–6, 287–9, 290–1, 298–302, 305–6

Lagash II (historical period)
  chronology of the rulers of, 47–9
  Tell A in, 458–66, 467–501, 502–6, 519–46, 570–80
  Tell K in, 307–8, 317–21

Lamentation over the Destruction of Lagash, 38–9, 220, 299–302, *300*

Larsa (Sumerian and Hellenistic-era city), 6, 7, 89, 146, 147, 154, 299, 513, 514, 515, 516, 649, 677, 702, 704, 705, 731

List of the Rulers of Lagash, 467, 515, 516

Lugalanda (ruler of Lagash I), 46–7, **46**, **454**

Lugale (Sumerian epic poem), 6, 261, 297, 508, 509, 516, 553, 726, 732–3, 734, 737

Lugalshaengur (ruler of Lagash), 12, 61, 150, 209

Lugalzagesi (king of Umma and Uruk), 12, 21, 39, 43, 44, 151, 154, 219, 220, 221, 229, 238, 285, 288, 291, 293, 298, 299, 300, 301, 306, 307, 308, 309, 314, 444, 451, **452**, **453**, **455**, 460

Lugirizal (governor of Lagash), 56, 509, 511, 512

Mace of Mesilim, *13*, 61, 62, 175, 176, 191, 209–10, 282

Manishtusu (king of Akkad), 307, 308, 548, *550*, 551, 553

Mesilim (king of Kish)
  Mace of, *13*, 61, 62, 175, 176, 191, 209–10, 282
  role of, 150, 151, 191, 210, 212, 237, 238, 259, 302

Mortar of Enanatum I, 58, 59, 242, 276, 305

Mound of the House of the Fruits. *See* Tell K

Mound of the Palace. *See* Tell A

Nabonidus (king of Babylon), 678, 682

Nammahni (ruler and governor of Lagash II)
  chronology of, 47–9, **48**, **49**
  inscribed brick pillar of, 318
  Nammahni's temple building, 504–5
  reign and governorship of, 459, 468, 504–6, 509

Nanna (Sumerian god), 6, 146, 459, 514

Nanshe (Sumerian goddess)
  role of, 3, 16, 217
  temples and shrines of, 3, 40, 235, 301, 407, **452**, **453**, **455**, 503, 568

Naram-Sin (king of Akkad), 185, 307, 308, 310, 311, 313, 314, 315, 316, 460, 506, *550*, 552, 553, 678

Nigin (Sumerian city), 14, 31, 146–7, 150, 152–3, 155–6, 212, 217, 287, 449, 451, **453**, **455**, 464, 517, 577, 579, 634

Ninagala (Sumerian goddess), 458, 459, 463, 465, 467, 468, 553, 634

Ningirsu (Sumerian god, chief god of Girsu)
  Feathered Figure depicting, 12, 14, 61, 62, 147–8, 164, 174–81, 183–4, 195, 199, 201–2, 217, 279–80, 284–6, 296
  role of, 6–8
  shell plaque depicting, 179, *180*
  stele devoted to, 618–20, *621*
  Stele of the Vultures depicting, 35, 58, 70, 175–6, 179, 185, 188, 208, 221, 225, 229, 233, 237–8, 240, *241*, 242, 243–58, 244, 245, 247, 252, 253, 275–6, 285, 291, 295, 301, 302–5, 306, 310, 314, 333, 413, 445, 446, 548, 550, 552, 565, 615, 616, 661
  syncretised with Heracles, 604, 729, 733, 738, 739, *740*, 741, 744, 745, 750
  temple of, 3–6, 10–27, 135–44, 146–56, 157–73, 203–7, 212–30, 237–42, 259–76, 290–1,

772 Index

Ningirsu (*continued*)
298–302, 307–10, **452**, **454**, **456**, 458–64, 467–501, 519–34, 570–90, 591–607
Ningishzida (Sumerian god), 3, 39, 40, 332, 460, 464, 468, 469, 474, 503, 507, 552, 555, 568, 572, 610, 618, 620, 626, 629.
Ninhedu (queen of Lagash II), 459, 504, 505, 507, 512
Ninhursag (Sumerian goddess), 175, 176, 238, 243, 244, 246, 247, 248, 249, 252, 254, 255, 256, 258, 268, 303, 304, 305, 331, 403, 411, **453**, **455**, **456**, 459, 469, 550, 553, 554, 557, 565, 572, 734, 748, 749
Nippur (Sumerian city), 5, 6, 7, 35, 43, 44, 88, 89, 146, 147, 150, 151, 152, 154, 155, 188, 291, 299, 301, 308, 337, 437, 514, 515, 516, 537, 678, 704, 732
Nisaba (Sumerian goddess), 3, 18, 196, 301, 515, 570, 573, 579, 618

Old Babylonian (historical period)
chronology of, 42–6
Tell A in the, 514–18, 519–46
Onyx Lion of Ur-Nanshe, 293, 297–8

Parrot (André Parrot, fourth director of the French excavations in Girsu)
characterisation of Adadnadinakhe, 674–5
excavations on Tell K, 80–1, 132
role of, 41
Persephone (Greek goddess), 735, 738, 745
Pirigme (ruler of Lagash II), 47–9, **48**, **49**, 458, 459
Plaque of Dudu, 293, 294, 296–7, 298
Plaques of Ur-Nanshe, 36, 152, 229, 230–6, 231, 276–9
pottery repertoires
from the Early Dynastic and Akkad temple on Tell A, 425, 436–7, 438–43
from the Early Dynastic layers on Tell K, 81–90, 83–5, 83
from the Early Dynastic temple platforms on Tell A, 425, 426–9, 430–4
from the Hellenistic strata on Tell A, 701–5, 706–11, 712
from Lagash II to the Old Babylonian era on Tell A, 534–7, 538–45
Puzurmama (ruler of Lagash II), 48, 317, 470–71, 515

Rim-Sin (king of Larsa), 513, 514, 516, 649
Rimush (king of Akkad), 307, 308, 309, 310, 460, 461

Samsuiluna (king of Babylon I), 46, 513, 515
Sargon (king of Akkad), 21, 43, 44, 299, 307, 314, 315, 458, 470, 471

Sargonic period. *See* Akkad (historical period)
Sarzec (Ernest de Sarzec, first director of the French excavations in Girsu)
excavations on Tell A, 328–34, 338–41
excavations on Tell K, 56–70
impact of, 28–36
Second Dynasty of Lagash. *See* Lagash II
Seleucid period. *See* Hellenistic (historical period)
Seleucus I Nicator (Seleucid king), 676, 677, 726, 727, 742, 743, 745, 746
Sharkalisharri (king of Akkad), 307, 308, 317
Shulgi (king of Ur III)
chronology of, 509
clay nails of, 395, 396, 398, 414, 415
foundation pegs of, 662, 663, 666
Shulgi's temple building in Girsu, 25, 56, 69, 138, **140–1**, 142, 308, 321, 511, 512, 522, 526, 528, 662
Shulshaga (Sumerian god), 216, 217, 293, 387, 388, 395, 396, 403, 415, **454**, 504, 555, 572, 652, 663, 697, 699, 724, 729, 748
Shuruppak (Sumerian city), 7, 88, 89, 150, 151, 308
Shu-Sin (king of Ur III), 507, 508, 511, 567
silver drachm (coin) of Alexander the Great, 700, 728, 730, 733, 738, 740, 741, 742
silver Vase of Enmetena, 35, 37, 67, 262, 293–6, 298
Slain Heroes (Sumerian mythological beings)
Dragon and Date palm, 597, 598, 599, 608
Fish-man and Copper, 597, 608, 609
Lion (terror of the gods), 597, 602, 604, 608
Magilum boat and Bison, 598, 600, 601, 608, 613, 623
Seven-headed serpent, 597, 603, 604, 608
Six-headed wild ram, 597, 602, 608
Standard of Utu and Bison head, 597, 598, 608, 627
Standard of Ur, 185, 189, 190, 243, 246, 249, 251, 280, 281, 282, 311, 627
Stele of the Captives (fragment discarded by Sarzec), 114, 147, 149, 150, 184–5, 184, 192, 203, 207, 208, 210, 217, 285
Stele of the Vultures, 35, 58, 70, 175–6, 179, 185, 188, 208, 221, 225, 229, 233, 237–8, 240, 241, 242, 243–58, 244, 245, 247, 252, 253, 275–6, 285, 291, 295, 301, 302–5, 306, 310, 314, 333, 413, 445, 446, 548, 550, 552, 565, 615, 616, 661
Stele of the Vultures (interpretations)
historical reverse, 248–51
mythological obverse, 246–8
patterns of effacement, 302–5
royal inscription, 251–8

Stone Basin with Thunderbird motifs, 331, 332, 730–2, 732, 740
Stone Heads of Lions, 59, 60, 279, 281–3, 284
Stone Monument of Eanatum, 58, 59, 276, 305–6
Sumerian King List, 48, 145, 151, 154, 307, 515–16
Susa (city in ancient Iran), 7, 255, 3, 470, 550, 659, 663, 676, 704, 705, 739
syncretism (concept), 25, 155, 557, 581, 620, 634, 677, 678, 724, 729, 731, 733, 734, 738, 739, 741, 743, 744, 748

Tablet of Destinies (supernatural object), 6, 7, 8
Tell A (British Museum team's results)
archaeological mounds and spoil heaps, 386–9, 387, **390**, 395
central depression, 385–6
Early Dynastic and Akkad sequence, 419–20, 420
enigmatic platform and temple building (Early Dynastic and Akkad), 429, 435
French deep, narrow trenches, 401, 403
French deep soundings, 404–6
French pits, 402–3
French ramped trenches, 401, 402
French spoil heaps, 394–9, 396
grey platform (Early Dynastic IIIb and Akkad), 426, 429
Hellenistic Eninnu (destruction), 744–51
Hellenistic Eninnu (Heracles–Ningirsu temple), 673–5, 674, 675, 678–86
Hellenistic Eninnu (purpose), 724–43
Hellenistic Eninnu (stratigraphy), 687–701, 688, 694, 695, 696
modern looting, 408–11, 409, 410
plan of the British Museum team's excavations, 24, 392
red platform (Early Dynastic I–IIIa), 418, 420–3, 421
topsoil and wash, 399–401
trenches and spoils (overview), 385
Ur-Bau's Ningirsu temple platform (the Old Eninnu), 461–4
Ur-Bau's sacred enclosure, 465–6
Ur-Bau's Temple of Bau, 464–5
wadis and natural gullies, 406–7
white platform (Early Dynastic IIIb), 418, 421, 423–6, 423
Tell A (French results, 1877–1930)
Adadnadinakhe wall (OP), 365–8, 366, 367
cistern, 368–72, 369, 370, 371
exedra, 368
foundation box, 376–7, 376, 377
Gate of Gudea, 359–62, 359, 361, 363–7, 365, 366, 372–4, 372, 373, 376–7, 376

Genouillac's plan and elevation of, 353–4, *353*

Heuzey's New Plan of, 351–3, *351*

NE façade of the Hellenistic building, 356–8, *357, 358*

overview of French results, 325–7

Sarzec's plan of (Plan A), 344–7, *345*

Sarzec's plaster maquette of, 347–9, *348*

Ur-Bau's temple platform, 362, *363, 364*, 369–72, *370, 371*, 461–4

wells, 378–9, *378*

Tell A (Gudea's New Eninnu, British Museum team's results)

  ambulatory walkways, transitional walls, entrances, 490–4, *491, 493, 494*

  central courtyard, 494–5

  deconsecration and closure, 532–4

  Ningirsu temple antecella, 486–9, *489, 490*

  Ningirsu temple cella, 486

  Ningirsu temple design, 478–80

  Ningirsu temple NE façade, 480–2

  Ningirsu temple NW façade, 483–4

  Ningirsu temple NW partition wall, 484–5

  Ningirsu temple SE façade, *482*

  Ningirsu temple SE partition wall, 485–6

  Ningirsu temple stairwell chamber, 489–90

  Ningirsu temple SW façade, 482–3, *483*

  origins of, 471–6

  preparatory work for, 476–8

  stratigraphy (Lagash II to Old Babylonian times), 519–46, **520–1**, *525, 528, 533*

  temenos gates and walls, 495–501, *498, 528*

Tell A (Gudea's New Eninnu, features and history)

  basket-carrying foundation figurines, 666–7, *666*

  bent-axis approaches to the Ningirsu temple, 604–7

  brickwork, 630–42, *632, 638*, **640, 641**

  design of the temenos, 572–80, *573, 575*

  display locations of the Gudea Steles, 611–15, *613*

  the first brick, 630–3, *632*

  foundation deposits (tablets and figures), 658–65, *659, 660, 661*

  kneeling foundation figurines, 667–9

  metrology and Gudea's standard unit, 581–90, *582, 584, 586, 589*

  monuments to the Slain Heroes, 597–604

  orientation with respect to solar and lunar cycles, 591–7, *593*,

  placement of the clay nails, 643–51, *644, 649*, **650, 651**

  positioning of the gates, 597–604, *596, 613*

quantities of bricks used in its construction, 640–2, **640, 641**

renown in Sumer and Babylonia, 502–18, *503, 508, 510*,

theology of the clay nails, 654–7

theology of the foundation figurines, 668–9

typology of the clay nails, 651–4, *652, 653*

Tell B (Mound of the Large Bricks), 26, *30*, 39, 326, 335, *450*, **452**, 659

Tell G (Mound of the Four Thresholds), 26, *30, 450*

Tell H (Mound of the Necropolis), *30*, 39, 563, 610

Tell I (Mound of the Pillars), 26, *30*, 35, 39, 57, 70, *103*, 318, *450*

Tell I' (Mound of the Turning Path), 16, 26, *30, 32*, 319, 325, *450*

Tell J (Mound of the Sword), 26, *30*, 70, *138*, 219, 243, 264, 290–1, 301

Tell K (Lower Construction)

  bitumen-coated cavities of, 169–73

  French excavations of, 61–5

  orientation of, 166–9

  outer block (P'Q'R'S') of, 203–7

  pavement V, 162–6

  photos of, 113–14, *113*

  reinterpretation of, 157–73

  Sarzec's plan and elevation of (Plan C (2)), 93, 94–7

  semi-subterranean design of, 158–60, *158, 159, 162, 163, 164, 165, 166, 171, 172, 177*

  two-room core (PQRS) of, 157–62

Tell K (Mound of the House of the Fruits)

  Akkad layers on, 308–10

  Akkad wall *Mur* on, 16, 221, 225, 308–9, 317

  brewhouse and beer-making on, *214, 260*, 269–74, *270, 271, 272*, 290, *292, 293*

  chambered gateway in the enclosing wall of, *213, 214*, 230, 264

  end of the Early Dynastic IIIb period on, 298–302, 305–6

  introduction to the French excavations on, 53–5

  Lagash II structures on, 317–19

  oval enclosing wall on, 219–20

  Plan A (Cros's plan of the principal areas), 99–101, *100*

  Plan B (Cros's plan of the central area), 101–2, *102*

  Plan D (Sarzec and Heuzey's general plan), 97–9, *97*

  rectangular construction, 78–9, *105*

  Sarzec gap in the stratigraphic record of, 57, 220–1, 225, 228, 229, 243, 299, 308

  Sarzec heights for the recording of finds (definition of), 54, *93, 103*

Sarzec's rectangular blocks of earth, 76

sections (general), 102–4, *103*

stairways, 77–8, 104–6, *105*, 129–32

three-step platform on, 213–19

Trench 5, 75

Trench 6, 76–7, *130, 131*

Trench 7, 76–7, *130, 131*

Trench 8, 73

Trench 9, 73–5

Trench 10, 73–5

Trench by the Well, 72–3

Ur III remains on, 321

water supply network, 78, 104–5, *105*

Tell K (temple annexes)

  channels M and N, 66

  cistern blocks (IJ, KL), 65–6

  double cistern (G), 65

  Enmetena Block, 67, 110–11, *110*, 262–6

  Enmetena Esplanade, 67–8, 239–40, 266–74

  oval reservoir, 68–9, 111–13, *112. See also* Tell K, brewhouse and beer-making

  stairways of Tell K, 70, 118–21, *119, 120*

  structures north and east of the oval reservoir, 69–70

  Well of Eanatum, 66–7, 116–17, *116*, 113–14, *133*, 239, 261

Tell K (Ur-Nanshe Building, House of the Fruits)

  covered gallery and peripheral corridor of, 223

  destruction of, 223–7

  Enmetena restoration of, 274–6

  French excavations of, 56–61

  photos of, 107–10, *108, 109*

  positioning with respect to the annual solar cycle, 594–5, *593*

  reinterpretation of, 212–20

  Sarzec's plan of (Plan C (1)), 92–4, *93*

  stratigraphic problems of, 220–1

  walls of, 221–2

Tell L (Mound of the Temple of Nanshe), *30*, 86, 415, **452**, 456

Tell N (Mound of the Bull), 26, *30, 450*, 464

Tell O (Mound of the Bituminated Cistern), 26, *30, 450*

Tell P (Mound of the Devil's Gate), 26, *30*, 39, 86, 87, *450*.

Tell V (Tablet Hill), *30*, 35, 36, 38, 39, 40, 211, 326, 448, 563, 564, 567

temple (concept)

  meaning of, 8–10

  ideogram (Sumerian sign) for, 199–202, *200, 201*

terracotta figurines

  heads of deities and royal figures, *719, 723, 742*

774   Index

terracotta figurines (*continued*)
    from the Hellenistic period, 396, 399, 407,
      677, 696, 698, 699, 715–23, 729, 730, 733,
      734
    Hellenistic riders on horseback, *717*
    from Lagash II to the Old Babylonian
      period, 396, 399, 400, 407, 699, *716,
      720–1, 721, 731*
    nude female deities, *718, 722, 723*
tessellated earth (concept), 167, 168, 181, 193–
    9, *194*, 200, 201, 215, 449, 591
Third Dynasty of Ur. *See* Ur III
Thunderbird (supernatural lion-headed
    eagle)
    avatar of Ningirsu, 8, 14, 176, 295, 465
    bricks stamped with the, 631, 632, 633, 690
    Mace Head depicting the, *8, 176, 242*
    Mace of Mesilim depicting the, *13*, 61, 62,
      175, 176, 191, 209–10, 282
    myth of the, 6–8
    Plaque of Dudu depicting the, 293, *294,
      296–7*, 298
    silver Vase depicting the, 35, *37*, 67, 262,
      293–6, 298
    Stele of the Vultures depicting the, 35, 58,
      70, 175–6, 179, 185, 188, 208, 221, 225, 229,
      233, 237–8, 240, *241, 242*, 243–58, *244,
      245, 247, 252, 253*, 275–6, 285, 291, 295,
      301, 302–5, 306, 310, 314, 333, 413, 445,
      446, 548, 550, 552, 565, 615, 616, 661
    Stone Basin depicting the, 331, 332, 730–2,
      732, 740
Thunderbird bricks, 631, 632, 633, 690
Thunderbird Mace Head, *8, 176, 242*
Tyche (Greek goddess), 456, 736, 745, 749

Umma (Sumerian city, also known as
    Gisha), 6, 7, 12, 43, 48, 150–1, 154, 195,
    212, 220–1, 229, 237–8, 240–3, 248–50,
    254–8, 259, 299, 300–6, 308–9, 451, 473,
    576

Ur (Sumerian city), 5, 6, 7, 146, 151, 154, 259,
    299, 301
Ur III (historical period)
    chronology of, 42–5
    Tell A in, 506, 519–46
    Tell K in, 307–8, 317–19, 321
Ur-Bau (ruler of Lagash II)
    chronology of, 47–9, **48**, **49**
    clay nails of, 395, 396, 398, 400, 403, *414,
      415*, 463, 524, 529, 696, 700, 729
    foundation deposit (peg and tablet) of,
      462–3, *462*
    relocation of the sacred complex, 19–22,
      317, 418. *See also* Ur-Bau's temple
      building
    statue of, 331, *459*, 463, 552, 533, 562, 749
    Ur-Bau's temple building (the Old
      Eninnu), 19–22, 458–66, **456**. *See also*
      Tell A (the British Museum team's
      results)
Urabba (ruler of Lagash II), 47–9, **48**, **49**,
    459, 504
UrGAR (ruler of Lagash II), 47–9, **48**, **49**,
    459, 504, 505
Urmama (ruler of Lagash II), 47–9, **48**, **49**,
    459, 504
Urnamma (king of Ur III), **49**, 292, 504, 505,
    506, 509, 649
Ur-Nanshe (ruler of Lagash I)
    chronology of, 46–7, **46**
    foundation pegs of, *153*, 215, 216, 218
    genealogical plaques of, *36*, 152, 229, 230–
      6, *231*, 276–9
    influence of, 151–6
    inscribed door sockets of, 58, *59*, *218*, 222,
      226, 227, 228, 279, 284
    Onyx Lion of, 293, 297–8
    Ur-Nanshe's temple building, 212–23,
      229–30, **452–3**
Ur-Nanshe Building (House of the Fruits).
    See Tell K (Ur-Nanshe Building)

Ur-Ningirsu (ruler of Lagash II), 47–9, **48**,
    49, 458, 467, 515
Ur-Ningirsu II (ruler of Lagash II)
    chronology of, 47–9, **48**, **49**
    reign of, 459, 468, 503–4
    statue of, 39, 313
    Ur-Ningirsu II's temple building, 503–5
Ur-Ningirsu III (governor and possible
    ruler of Lagash III), 512–13
Uruk (Sumerian and Hellenistic-era city),
    5–6, 7, 12, 145–7, 149–50, 154–5, 158, 160,
    162, 164, 169, 209, 220, 237–8, 259, 280,
    299, 301, 308, 577, 603, 677, 682, 702–5,
    712, 715, 726, 731, 735–6, 741, 745–7, 750
Urukagina (ruler of Lagash I)
    chronology of, 46–7, **46**
    foundation tablet of, 67, 292, 293, 298
    lament of, 38–9, 220, 299–302, *300*. *See also*
      Lamentation over the Destruction of
      Lagash
    reign of, 291–3
    Urukagina's temple building, 298–302,
      454–5, *456*
Uruk List of Cities, 146
Uruk Vase, 172, 243, 311
Urukug (sacred precinct of Girsu), *20*, 25, 26,
    290, 319, 386, 415, 447, 448, 449, 450,
    451, **452**, **454**, **456**, 457, 460, 461, 464,
    472, 473, 474, 478, 495, 511, 517, 518, 557,
    579, 609
Utu (Sumerian god), 6, 146, 254, 255, 258,
    453, **455**, 473, 514, 572, 597, 598, 600,
    608, 623, 626, 724, 732, 736, 737

Warad-Sin (king of Larsa), 514, 649

Zeus (Greek god), 700, 728, 730, 733, 737,
    739, 740, 741, 743